Lecture Notes in Computer Science 12562

More information about this subseries at http://www.springer.com/series/7408

Maurizio Morisio · Marco Torchiano ·
Andreas Jedlitschka (Eds.)

Product-Focused Software Process Improvement

21st International Conference, PROFES 2020
Turin, Italy, November 25–27, 2020
Proceedings

 Springer

Editors
Maurizio Morisio ⓘ
Politecnico di Torino
Turin, Torino, Italy

Marco Torchiano ⓘ
Polytechnic University of Turin
Turin, Torino, Italy

Andreas Jedlitschka ⓘ
Fraunhofer Institute for Experimental
Software Engineering
Kaiserslautern, Rheinland-Pfalz, Germany

ISSN 0302-9743   ISSN 1611-3349   (electronic)
Lecture Notes in Computer Science
ISBN 978-3-030-64147-4   ISBN 978-3-030-64148-1   (eBook)
https://doi.org/10.1007/978-3-030-64148-1

LNCS Sublibrary: SL2 – Programming and Software Engineering

This Springer imprint is published by the registered company Springer Nature Switzerland AG
The registered company address is: Gewerbestrasse 11, 6330 Cham, Switzerland

Preface

On behalf of the PROFES Organizing Committee, we are proud to present the proceedings of the 21st International Conference on Product-Focused Software Process Improvement (PROFES 2020). The conference, due to the COVID-19 outbreak, was held in a fully online format, during November 25–27, 2020. Since 1999, PROFES has established itself as one of the top recognized international process improvement conferences. In the spirit of the PROFES conference series, the main theme of PROFES 2020 was professional software process improvement (SPI) motivated by product, process, and service quality needs.

PROFES 2020 is a premier forum for practitioners, researchers, and educators to present and discuss experiences, ideas, innovations, as well as concerns related to professional software development and process improvement driven by product and service quality needs. PROFES especially welcomes contributions emerging from applied research to foster industry-academia collaborations of leading industries and research institutions.

The technical program of PROFES 2020 was selected by a committee of leading experts in software process improvement, software process modeling, and empirical software engineering. This year, 50 full research papers were submitted. After thorough evaluation that involved at least three independent experts per paper, 19 technical full papers were finally selected (38% acceptance rate). In addition, we had a record number of industry paper submissions, 10, of which we accepted 6 for the final program.

Furthermore, we received 8 short paper submissions. Each submission was reviewed by three members from the PROFES Program Committee. Based on the reviews and overall assessments, 3 short papers were accepted for presentation at the conference and for inclusion in the proceedings (37.5% acceptance ratio).

The technical program consisted of the following tracks: Agile Methodologies, Data Science, Software Testing and Evolution, Social and Human Aspects, and Software Development.

Continuing the open science policy adopted since PROFES 2017, we encouraged and supported all authors of accepted submissions to make their papers and research publicly available.

We are thankful for the opportunity to have served as chairs for this conference. The Program Committee members and reviewers provided excellent support in reviewing the papers. We are also grateful to all authors of submitted manuscripts, presenters, keynote speakers, and session chairs, for their time and effort in making PROFES 2020 a success. We would also like to thank the PROFES Steering Committee members for the guidance and support in the organization process.

October 2020   Andreas Jedlitschka
                                                             Maurizio Morisio
                                                             Marco Torchiano

Organization

Organizing Committee

General Chair

Maurizio Morisio   Politecnico di Torino, Italy

Program Co-chairs

Andreas Jedlitschka   Fraunhofer IESE, Germany
Marco Torchiano   Politecnico di Torino, Italy

Short Paper Co-chairs

Luca Ardito   Politecnico di Torino, Italy
Michael Kläs   Fraunhofer IESE, Germany

Industry Papers Co-chairs

Liliana Guzmán   DSA, Germany
Federico Tomassetti   Strumenta, Italy

Proceedings Co-chairs

Anna Maria Vollmer   Fraunhofer IESE, Germany
Riccardo Coppola   Politecnico di Torino, Italy

Journal First Chair

Antonio Vetrò   Politecnico di Torino, Italy

Local Arrangement Co-chairs

Mariachiara Mecati   Politecnico di Torino, Italy
Isabeau Oliveri   Politecnico di Torino, Italy

Web Co-chairs

Simone Leonardi   Politecnico di Torino, Italy
Diego Monti   Politecnico di Torino, Italy

PC Members, Full Research Papers, and Short Papers

Sousuke Amasaki	Okayama Prefectural University, Japan
Stefan Biffl	Vienna University of Technology, Austria
Andreas Birk	SWPM, Germany
Luigi Buglione	ETS, Canada
Danilo Caivano	University of Bari Aldo Moro, Italy
Marcus Ciolkowski	QAware GmbH, Germany
Maya Daneva	University of Twente, The Netherlands
Bruno da Silva	California Polytechnic State University, USA
Torgeir Dingsøyr	Norwegian University of Science and Technology, Norway
Michal Dolezel	Prague University of Economics and Business, Czech Republic
Anh Nguyen Duc	University College of Southeast Norway, Norway
Christof Ebert	Vector Consulting Services GmbH, Germany
Davide Falessi	California Polytechnic State University, USA
Michael Felderer	University of Innsbruck, Austria
Lina Garcés	ICMC, USP, Brazil
Carmine Gravino	University of Salerno, Italy
Noriko Hanakawa	Hannan University, Japan
Jens Heidrich	Fraunhofer IESE, Germany
Martin Höst	Lund University, Sweden
Frank Houdek	Daimler AG, Germany
Andrea Janes	Free University of Bozen-Bolzano, Italy
Petri Kettunen	University of Helsinki, Finland
Jil Klünder	Leibniz Universität Hannover, Germany
Jingyue Li	Norwegian University of Science and Technology, Norway
Oscar Pastor Lopez	Universitat Politècnica de València, Spain
Stephen MacDonell	University of Otago, New Zealand
Tomi Männistö	University of Helsinki, Finland
Silverio Martínez-Fernández	Universitat Politècnica de Catalunya, Spain
Kenichi Matsumoto	Nara Institute of Science and Technology (NAIST), Japan
Juergen Muench	Reutlingen University, Germany
Edson Oliveirajr	State University of Maringá, Brazil
Paolo Panaroni	Intecs Solutions, Italy
Dietmar Pfahl	University of Tartu, Estonia
Rudolf Ramler	Software Competence Center, Austria
Daniel Rodriguez	University of Alcalá, Spain
Bruno Rossi	Masaryk University, Czech Republic
Barbara Russo	Free University of Bozen-Bolzano, Italy
Gleison Santos	UNIRIO, Brazil
Giuseppe Scanniello	University of Basilicata, Italy

Contents

Data Science

Test and Evolution

Social and Human Aspects

Software Development

Agile Software Development

A Systematic Literature Review on Agile Coaching and the Role of the Agile Coach

Viktoria Stray[1,2]([envelope]) [ID], Bakhtawar Memon[1], and Lucas Paruch[1] [ID]

[1] Department of Informatics, University of Oslo, Oslo, Norway
{stray,bakhtawm,lucasp}@ifi.uio.no
[2] SINTEF, Trondheim, Norway

Abstract. There has been a recent increase in the use of agile coaches in organizations. Although the use of the job title is popular, empirical knowledge about the tasks, responsibilities and skills of an agile coach is lacking. In this paper, we present a systematic literature review on agile coaching and the role of the agile coach. The initial search resulted in a total of 209 studies identified on the topic. Based on our inclusion and exclusion criteria, a total of 67 studies were selected as primary studies. Our findings suggest that agile coaching facilitates the adoption and sustainability of agile methods and deals with agile adoption challenges. Agile coaches help in training and developing software development teams and all the stakeholders involved in the agile adoption process. The primary skills of an agile coach identified herein are leadership qualities, project management skills, technical skills, and expertise in agile methods. Based on the findings, it can be argued that agile coaches play a significant role in addressing challenges in an agile transformation such as resistance to change. Coaches focus on removing barriers to team autonomy in agile teams and making agile meetings more valuable.

Keywords: Agile coaching · Skills · Tasks · Systematic literature review · Agile transformation · Software development practices

1 Introduction

Agile software development is a popular software development methodology, due to its focus on quick response to change and improved interactions with customers. However, adoption of agile methodology is not straight-forward. Agile started out with software teams, but today, whole organizations seek to adopt agile to be able to create, react to, embrace, and learn from change while enhancing customer value in a digital transformation [8]. Such an agile transformation requires changes throughout the entire organization, involving changes to roles, practices, tools and people's behaviors, mindsets, and responsibilities [15,25,59]. The adoption is usually slow and gradual, and it can take up to several years to complete [30]. Agile transformation is especially challenging in larger organizations, because of complex infrastructures, numerous legacy systems, mature organizational culture, and an increase in the number of inter-dependencies between actors, tasks, and goals [35,60].

© Springer Nature Switzerland AG 2020
M. Morisio et al. (Eds.): PROFES 2020, LNCS 12562, pp. 3–19, 2020.
https://doi.org/10.1007/978-3-030-64148-1_1

Coaching has been found to be one of the most important success factors in an agile transformation [10,36]. To help companies adopt agile methods smoothly, a new role has emerged; *an agile coach* has been introduced, and having an agile coach to help with agile transformations is constantly gaining in popularity [27,40,51]. An agile coach is an individual who coaches and facilitates agile teams and managers in adopting and implementing agile practices, processes, and values in software development [49]. It is a valuable role for organizational change [40,51]. However, there are a number of challenges in agile adoption, the majority of which are human-related and include resistance to change [7,31], lack of effective communication [26], lack of customer collaboration [34] and insufficient experience and knowledge of agile methods and practices [13,34]. The organizational adoption challenges include cultural issues or cultural mismatch to agile methods due to managers being unwilling to change from commanders to team facilitators, lack of management support, and lack of capacity to change the organizational culture [29]. Furthermore, many agile coaches are confused about their role and responsibilities [24].

The motivation to conduct this literature review was to explore what academic literature says about what agile coaching is and how agile coaches can help address and overcome the above mentioned challenges to help in the adoption of agile methodologies in software development organizations and help agile coaches better understand their role.

The remainder of this paper is organized as follows. Section 2 describes background on agile coaching. Section 3 details the review method and presents the research questions and the search strategy. Section 4 presents the results. Section 5 discusses the main ndings and our study limitations. Section 6 concludes the paper and proposes future work.

2   Agile Coaching and the Role of an Agile Coach

Agile coaching is considered a sub-field of coaching [40], which focuses on helping teams or individuals adopt and improve agile methods and rethink and change the way they develop software. Agile coaching is used to mitigate problems during agile adoption and it makes the transition easier and more effective [45]. Agile coaching involves advocating agile methods and their introduction into daily routines of teams in an organization. Nowadays, many organizations considers agile coaching as a dedicated full-time employment [51].

There are several practitioner's guides and books available (e.g., [3,9]). According to one of the first books on agile coaching, the role of the agile coach is to grow a productive agile team [9]. Moreover, the tasks of the coach are to educate, facilitate, support, notice and give feedback to the teams and one of the main skill sets that coaches must have is listening skills [9]. In addition, there are also certifications for agile coaches. For example, the International Consortium for Agile, lists learning outcomes of agile coaching education as individuals who are knowledgeable in agile practices, have fundamental skills in facilitation, and the self-leadership to coach a team [1]. Scrum Alliance lists expectations for their certified coaches as individuals who have humility, are creative, resourceful, and able to solve their own challenges [2].

The academic literature has reported some studies in which an agile coach is hired to help companies adopt agile methods smoothly [4,19,25,57]. If the transition is happening on a larger scale, such as an entire IT division or an entire company, several coaches are needed for sustained agile usage [12,19,57]. These coaches can be external consultants or internal to the company. Often, companies hire external coaches to provide initial training and kick-start agile development. At the same time, they help train and develop internal coaches who take over the main coaching role later on [25,45].

Agile coaches mentor projects and organizations seeking to adopt agile [62]. Agile coaches can help the teams resolve process related problems by ensuring that the teams follow the process correctly [48]. According to Fraser [14], "Coaches help team members become a cohesive unit, understand the'rules-of-the-game', facilitate interaction, optimize skills, and build motivation towards common goals". An agile coach's job is to help introduce and guide one or more teams in how to use agile methodologies such as Scrum and Kanban. One of the tasks of an agile coach is to facilitate and support the organization during their agile transformation [49,50]. The coaches work on changing the mentality of managers [18]. Essential traits for agile coaches is being emphatic, people-oriented, able to listen, diplomatic, and persistent [61]. An agile coach brings numerous benefits to an organization; the benefits have been found to exceed the financial cost of employing an agile coach [40].

3   Review Method

The following section describes the method used to conduct this systematic literature review (SLR). The review procedure is based on guidelines for performing SLR in software engineering by Kitchenham et al. The review's objective was to better understand what agile coaching is, what agile coaches do, and how they can help in the adoption of agile methodologies in software development organizations. In particular, the paper aims to do this by answering the following research questions [28].

RQ1: What are the tasks and responsibilities of an agile coach?
RQ2: What are the skills required of an agile coach?

3.1   Search Strategy

The search query was developed iteratively (Fig. 1). We began the search process by identifying relevant search keywords. Based on reading both academic and practitioner literature regarding the area, the two commonly emergent keywords were agile coach and agile coaching. We identified several more keywords and developed an appropriate search query for the review.

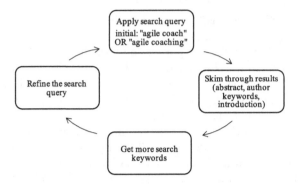

Fig. 1. Process of developing search query

We conducted a trial search with ("agile coach" OR "agile coaching") in the Scopus database, intending to skim through the first 30 relevant publications and get an understanding of the appropriate search keywords, to continually refine our search query. This action was repeated several times with database Scopus, Web of Science, and Google Scholar until we felt all relevant keywords were identified.

Table 1 shows the final search query and keywords. We decided to apply the final query to Scopus only, as Google Scholar usually gives too many results from non-journal sources and unpublished materials [33]. Web of Science gave us too few, and did not display new articles that were not already found on Scopus. Second, we used Scopus because it also subsumes results from both SpringerLink and Wiley Inter-Science Journal. As an additional benefit, we found that Scopus provides a user-friendly interface and advanced filters that simplified the search process.

3.2 Study Search

The final search query was applied to Scopus in March 2020, in which 209 results were returned. We exported metadata of each of the results, such as authors, title, year, publication source, abstract, author, and document type into a spreadsheet. We also performed a manual verification process to ensure that the information was correctly entered into the Excel file. For example, we checked the publication sources by searching for the paper. Mistakes were found regarding this aspect, as information exported from Scopus did not correctly reflect the publication sources of the studies. These were manually corrected.

3.3 Study Selection

Study selection was carried out by an extensive inspection of the studies' abstracts and author keywords, and simultaneously applying the inclusion and exclusion criteria. The inclusion and exclusion criteria that have been used in

Table 1. Search strategy

Search keywords	Agile coach, Scrum coach, XP coach, Kanban coach, Lean coach, DevOps coach, Agility coach, Internal coach, Agile coaching, Team coaching, Scrum coaching, XP coaching, Kanban coaching, Lean coaching, DevOps coaching
Final search query	"agile coach" OR "agility coach" OR "Scrum coach" OR "Lean coach" OR "Kanban coach" OR "XP coach". OR "DevOps coach" OR "agile coaching" OR "Scrum coaching" OR "Lean coaching" OR "Kanban coaching" OR "XP coaching" OR "DevOps coaching" OR ("internal coach" AND (agile OR scrum OR Lean OR Kanban OR XP OR DevOps)) OR ("team coaching" AND (agile OR Scrum OR Lean OR Kanban OR XP OR DevOps))
Target for search query	Full document
Data sources	Scopus

this review are listed in Table 2. Each inclusion (IC) and exclusion (EC) criterion is given an ID, so that during study selection each study is assigned an ID based on the criteria it matches.

Both inclusion criteria include publications in journals and conference proceedings, as well as relevant book chapters. We identified these studies by evaluating the abstract's relevancy to the agile coach topic. Studies that did not qualify for the inclusion criteria above were excluded, as well as workshop proposals that were limited to one page and only had a descriptive content of the process happened at the workshop. Other systematic reviews or mapping studies were not included as primary studies, but we treated them as a checklist in order to compare their process against ours. We did not include studies for which full-text were not available, and we only focused on studies utilizing agile processes within the area of software development. Last, we excluded studies on students learning agile methods, and non-English contributions. These criteria were developed iteratively, while performing study selection. The spreadsheet containing the Scopus search results, together with inclusion and exclusion decisions is available online (https://doi.org/10.6084/m9.figshare.13014893.v1).

Out of 209 studies, 46 studies met the inclusion criteria IC1, three studies met the inclusion criteria IC2 and 18 studies met IC3, see Fig. 2. The remaining 143 studies met one or more of the exclusion criteria, and were thus excluded. Most of the excluded studies (73) did not have abstracts related to the research topic (EC1). Many studies (27) focused on software engineering education in undergraduate courses (EC7). Some studies (15) were workshops, tutorials, and books (EC3). A few (EC4) related to usage of agile methods other than in the software development domain, and were therefore also excluded.

Table 2. Inclusion criteria (IC) and exclusion criteria (EC)

ID	Criterion
IC1	Relevant publications published in conference proceedings
IC2	Book chapters relevant to the research topic
IC3	Relevant publications published in journals
EC1	Publications published in journals and in conference proceedings where abstract and keywords revealed that the paper was not related to the topic of agile coaching
EC2	Duplicate studies were not included as primary studies
EC3	Workshop proposals, panels and tutorials were excluded
EC4	Systematic reviews or mapping studies
EC5	Study full text was not available
EC6	Studies based on the use of agile processes, practices and methods in settings other than the software development domain (for example car or cement manufacturing industry, military, and healthcare)
EC7	Based or focused on student learning of the agile methods such as Scrum, Kanban in university or undergraduate courses
EC8	Articles not in English
EC9	Books were excluded

Table 3. Data collection form

Collected Information	Purpose
Author	General information
Title	
Year	Data analysis and synthesis
Venue	
Research method	
Tasks or responsibilities of an agile coach	RQ1
Skills required for an agile coach	RQ2

3.4   Data Extraction and Synthesis

During this step, a thorough reading of each of the 67 included studies was performed to extract relevant information. A data collection form was designed (Table 3) to record the full details of the study, from general information to specific information. General information of studies included: author, title, year and venue. Specific information included data from each study that could assist in answering the research questions.

Let us exemplify a study that mentions the tasks an agile coach does: A detailed reading was performed to note the specific tasks. The identified information was copied as is from the study and pasted in the data collection form, maintained in an Excel file. The parts of the study where particular information was found were highlighted for future reference.

Once data extraction was complete, the extracted data related to the research questions were closely analyzed to identify common themes. We used thematic

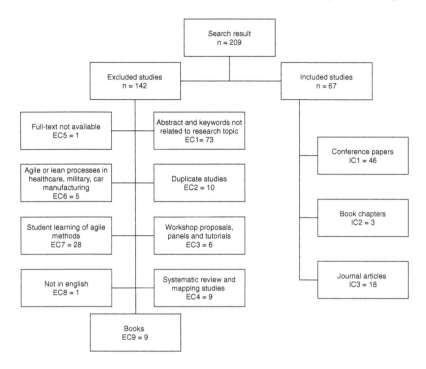

Fig. 2. The study selection process

analysis [6] and all authors were involved in the coding of the papers. Next, we present the results of the data analysis and synthesis.

4   Results

Figure 3 shows the number of papers published on agile coaching and agile coaches between 2003 and 2020. It can be argued that the publication volume during the years 2017 to 2019 is an indicator of researchers growing interest in agile coaching. More than half of the studies are from the last five years which shows that agile coaching and issues surrounding it are gaining research interest and being more actively studied. A multitude of research methods have been reported in these studies. The most common are case study (19 studies) and grounded theory research (14 studies). The majority of the studies included in the review are published as conference papers. Out of the 67 studies included in the review, 46 are conference papers, 18 are journal articles and the remaining 3 are book chapters.

Based on the papers' findings and synthesis, we first present the eight most common tasks and responsibilities (see Table 4) in Sect. 4.1. Then, in Sect. 4.2, we present our findings of the skills (Table 5) required by agile coaches that emerged from our systematic literature review.

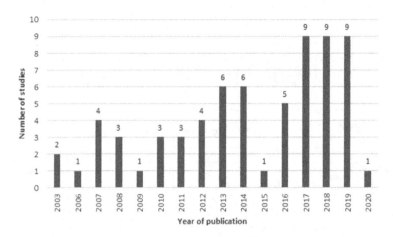

Fig. 3. Distribution of studies by publication year

4.1   Tasks and Responsibilities of an Agile Coach

Table 4. Themes in reviewed studies addressing RQ1

Theme	Frequency	Reporting studies
Develop and train the teams	12	[12, 14, 17, 18, 23, 24, 43, 46, 50, 51, 54, 58]
Support stakeholders and managers to understand and apply agile methods	8	[4, 5, 17, 18, 18, 20, 25, 49, 53]
Facilitate and monitor effective implementation of agile	8	[20, 24, 25, 40, 49, 54–56]
Understand context and metrics to adapt agile implementation to the organization	5	[4, 21, 38, 47, 52]
Help in creating guidelines and setting goals and roadmaps	4	[41, 42, 45, 56]
Build trust among team members	3	[4, 11, 14]
Remove bottlenecks that hinder successful teamwork	3	[22, 24, 44]
Select a pilot project	2	[16, 51]

Develop and Train the Teams. The primary role or duty of an agile coach, is building teams by providing realistic support during implementation of agile processes [50], leading the team toward self-organization [23]. Also, to help the team explore their potential and to foster self-organization, they teach techniques such as Open Space and Brainwriting [54]. Additional agile coaching duties include teaching agile methods, techniques and related tools [46], and guiding by conducting workshops and training on agile methods [12, 18, 51]. By supporting team members in acquisition of the entrepreneurial and agile mindset [58], coaches can help design the steps to the targets, and support the teams in implementing the agile practices [43]. Citing Fraser, *"Coaches help team members become a cohesive unit, understand the rules-of-the-game, facilitate interaction, optimize skills, and build motivation towards common goals"* [14].

Support Stakeholders and Managers to Understand and Apply Agile Methods. The tasks of an agile coach are not limited to the team level. A good coach communicates and collaborates with all the stakeholders involved in the agile transition process such as top management [18], and directly coach the people involved in the transition by teaching them what they need to know to be familiar with their new roles and responsibilities [49]. Additional duties of an agile coach include supporting Scrum Masters and distributed Scrum teams [20,53], and supporting product owners [5]. Agile coaches were typically based within a team and working with several teams within the organization while also supporting it as a whole in collaboration with other coaches and leaders [4]. Some coaches worked on shifting the managers' focus, from "what" the teams were doing to "why" they were doing what they did, and training them to have an agile mindset, for example not to dictate a date and budget without involving the teams [18].

Facilitate and Monitor Effective Implementation of Agile. The agile coach facilitates and monitors effective implementation of Scrum practices [20,55], identifies and discusses issues, potential suggestions and innovations [25], and presents solutions to teams to help them think about what to do next and to make them take responsibility for their actions [54]. An agile coach facilitates the adaptation of agile methods and practices by proposing the required adjustments and helps all the practitioners to overcome their problems during the transition process and facilitate the change process [49]. They also teach how to apply agile to legacy code and how to track the progress of an agile project [40].

Understand the Context to Adapt Agile Implementation to the Organization. Successful agile adoption depends on context. An important task of an agile coach is to understand the context of agile projects. Understanding the context will help agile coaches to adapt development processes to fit their project's contexts [21]. Coaches also increase the context-sensitivity of others. According to Ng [38], "Our experiences taught us that context evolves as agile coaches interact with development organization and teams. The context description evolves and converges to the team's desired way of working after the agile coach leaves the scene". Some coaches also use metrics such as cycle time, flow efficiency and throughput to facilitate agile implementation and team improvements [47].

Help in Creating Guidelines and Setting Goals and Roadmaps. Agile coaches and management work together to define common values for an organization, creating a road-map of where they want to see their organization in coming years and how they will work to achieve those goals [45]. Furthermore, they create agendas and instructions for software teams [41] and develop guidelines for full-scale agile roll-out [42].

Build Trust Among Team Members. Another important task of an agile coach is to build trust with the team he or she is coaching and to improve trust among individuals on the team by frequent and open communication [4]. Additionally, exposing team members' expertise, particularly through knowledge sharing activities, has been effective to build trust across different sites [11].

Remove Bottlenecks that Hinder Successful Teamwork. Agile coaches focus on understanding how to help teams be productive and successful. When they see people or other impediments that slow teams down, they do what they can to help fix the situation. For example, they contact senior management to remove people from teams [22] and facilitate inter-team retrospectives [44].

Collect Data on the Activities Carried Out by the Team. To perform effective agile coaching, it is necessary to collect data in the form of metrics on the activities carried out by the team to let it know the way it works using different tools such as Actionable agile [47].

Select a Pilot Project for Agile Transformation. Another important task of an agile coach is to select a pilot project during the agile transformation process [16,51]. A pilot project plays a critical role in the agile transformation process, as it acts as a training and evaluation project for a company that aims to adapt to agile methods or practices. Conducting a pilot project may help to predict future challenges, and organizations will need to critically consider the duration, size and required resources while selecting them [16].

4.2   Skills Required by an Agile Coach

As shown in Table 5, there are four main types of skills that seem essential for agile coaches: leadership skills, project management skills, expertise in agile methods and technical skills.

First, the most important set of skills an agile coach must possess is leadership qualities and skills. A coach needs to have good communication skills [45,57], an understanding of teamwork and team dynamics [40], conflict management and team building [18]. An agile coach needs strong social skills to facilitate learning [54]. Furthermore, they should have a range of traits supporting these skills such as positivity, persistence and patience [17,40].

Table 5. Themes in reviewed studies addressing RQ2

Theme	Frequency	Reporting studies
Leadership skills	7	[14, 17, 18, 40, 43, 54, 57]
Project management skills	4	[17, 37, 40, 51]
Expertise in agile methods and practices	4	[40, 50, 55, 57]
Technical skills	3	[24, 40, 46]
Other	2	[18, 24]

Second, an agile coach must have some project management skills to achieve goals and meet success criteria at specified times such as skills in change management [40], expertise to facilitate identification and management of risks in the system [37], knowledge management skills [51] and the ability to help teams make more realistic estimates [17].

Third, an agile coach needs to have knowledge and expertise in agile methods and processes [40, 55, 57]. An agile coach has a significant influence on the sustained use of agile methods [55]. However, it should be noted that there are different views on whether certifications are critical [57] or not [40].

Fourth, an agile coach needs to have technical skills, including diversity in IT skills [40], as well as software design and development skills [46]. For example, a coach often translates between the business terms used by customer representatives and technical language used by agile teams, and may also question proposed technical solutions [24].

Finally, other skills are also necessary. For example, being able to understand group psychology and behavioral software engineering aspects [18]. One study also found that agile coaches are often confused about their role on an agile team, and what is expected of them [24]. A coach must therefore be able to tackle confusing and unclear requirements about what their role entails.

5   Discussion

Most of the studies reviewed used case study or grounded theory research approaches. Both are well-established research methodologies from social sciences that emphasize investigating a phenomenon in its real-world setting [32]. This highlights that researchers have acknowledged that agile methods, their adoption in software development organizations, and agile coaching are social processes that need to be investigated and understood within their real-life settings.

The majority of the studies that ended up being reviewed after passing the inclusion criteria belong to various conferences (69%) and a smaller number of studies are journal articles (27%) and book chapters (4%). This is because a larger number of journal articles were excluded (due to one or more exclusion criteria) from the search query's initial Scopus results, which consisted of ≈51%

conference publications and $\approx$29% journal articles. However, both before and after exclusion, the proportion of conference publications in the search results was greater which is not surprising due to a larger number of conference venues and publication frequency.

In general, an agile coach facilitates agile adoption or agile transformation in software development organizations [25,49]. Agile adoption is a complex process requiring socio-technical changes in the organization [36]. The studies reviewed here reveal several important tasks that may fall upon the shoulders of an agile coach. These range from teaching and mentoring to helping the teams understand the agile methods, empowering them to ask relevant questions, discovering the knowledge already hidden in the team, resolving conflicts, and facilitating the overcoming human impediments in overall process improvement. Some of these tasks are often Scrum Master activities in Scrum projects, for example process facilitation, ceremony facilitation and impediment removal [24,39]. Many of these tasks are also discussed in practitioner literature [1–3,9].

An agile coach needs to have numerous skills to effectively manage the agile adoption process. The studies reviewed reveal that the skills of an agile coach can be wide ranging, such as leadership skills to guide and motivate teams and organizations, technical skills to help individuals and teams design and develop software, systematically dealing with the transition or transformation of an organization's goals, processes, or technologies, and identifying risks, knowledge management skills, and expertise in multiple agile methods and processes.

Over half of the studies are from the last five years (and 59 out of 67 studies are from the last 10 years), which is a strong indication that the topic of agile coaching and issues directly or implicitly related to it are being actively studied. A study conducted by Kettunen et al. revealed that 17% of the respondents working as agile coaches have this as their primary role in the organization [27], which somewhats supports our claim that agile coaching and the role of agile coach in agile adoption are currently evolving and gaining popularity in the research community.

5.1   Limitations

Ideally, a systematic literature review should include studies from several sources [28]. In this review, the final search query was applied only to Scopus. However, the preliminary search queries were also applied to Google Scholar and Web of Science, but were not included in the final result selection. Even though many results from these two sources were also available on Scopus, there may have been some primary studies that were not indexed by Scopus and have therefore not been considered (for example, relevant practitioner literature). Furthermore, the possibility of imprecision in data collection and data analysis is always prevalent in SLRs. We acknowledge that other researchers may have formed other clustering and combinations of the raw findings. However, we have minimized our own bias and formation of themes by continually refining the search-string (including performing prior test-runs) as well as having all authors examine the papers and cross-check and discuss the themes at hand.

6 Conclusion and Future Work

This systematic literature review was conducted to understand the role of the agile coach, as there is a lack of understanding of what agile coaching is, what agile coaches do, and how agile coaches can help in agile transformations.

The thematic analysis of 67 papers provided insights into the tasks, responsibilities, and skills required of agile coaches. Agile coaches help overcome challenges in large-scale agile adoption, such as resistance to change and difficulty in understanding and implementing agile methods at scale. They also play a role in removing barriers to team autonomy and help managers and stakeholders in understanding the agile journey. The skills required by agile coaches are leadership, project management, and technical skills. Additionally, they need to have expertise in agile methods and team coaching.

Future work can involve investigating the inherent challenges of agile coaching itself. This may include issues and problems hindering effective agile coaching, and countermeasures that coaches enact to overcome these challenges and make their work more effective. It would also be interesting to investigate tools and techniques used by agile coaches to support them in their work. Additionally, as our paper is a secondary study, other researchers may perform case studies with interviews and observation of agile coaches, and relate their findings with ours.

Acknowledgments. This research was supported by Scrum Alliance, Comparative Agility and the Research Council of Norway (grant 267704).

References

1. International consortium for agile, icagile learning roadmap agile coachingtrack (2018). https://www.icagile.com/Portals/0/LO%20PDFs/Agile%20Coaching%20Learning%20Outcomes.pdf. Accessed 28 Sept 2020
2. Scrum alliance, summary of expectations for certified enterprise coach (2020). https://www.scrumalliance.org/Media/Coaches/CEC_summary-of-expectations.pdf. Accessed 28 Sept 2020
3. Adkins, L.: Coaching Agile Teams: A Companion for ScrumMasters, Agile Coaches, and Project Managers in Transition. Pearson Education India (2010)
4. Bäcklander, G.: Doing complexity leadership theory: how agile coaches at spotify practise enabling leadership. Creat. Innov. Manag. **28**(1), 42–60 (2019)
5. Bass, J.M.: Agile method tailoring in distributed enterprises: product owner teams. In: 2013 IEEE 8th International Conference on Global Software Engineering, pp. 154–163. IEEE (2013)
6. Braun, V., Clarke, V.: Thematic analysis (2012)
7. Cockburn, A., Highsmith, J.: Agile software development, the people factor. Computer **34**(11), 131–133 (2001)
8. Conboy, K.: Agility from first principles: reconstructing the concept of agility in information systems development. Inf. Syst. Res. **20**(3), 329–354 (2009)
9. Davies, R., Sedley, L.: Agile Coaching. Pragmatic Bookshelf, London (2009)
10. Dikert, K., Paasivaara, M., Lassenius, C.: Challenges and success factors for large-scale agile transformations: a systematic literature review. J. Syst. Softw. **119**, 87–108 (2016)

11. Dorairaj, S., Noble, J.: Agile software development with distributed teams: agility, distribution and trust. In: 2013 Agile Conference, pp. 1–10. IEEE (2013)
12. Drummond, B.S., Francis, J., et al.: Yahoo! Distributed agile: notes from the world over. In: Agile 2008 Conference, pp. 315–321. IEEE (2008)
13. Eloranta, V.P., Koskimies, K., Mikkonen, T., Vuorinen, J.: Scrum anti-patterns-an empirical study. In: 2013 20th Asia-Pacific Software Engineering Conference (APSEC), vol. 1, pp. 503–510. IEEE (2013)
14. Fraser, S., Reinitz, R., Eckstein, J., Kerievsky, J., Mee, R., Poppendieck, M.: Xtreme programming and agile coaching. In: Companion of the 18th Annual ACM SIGPLAN Conference on Object-Oriented Programming, Systems, Languages, and Applications, pp. 265–267 (2003)
15. Gandomani, T.J., Nafchi, M.Z.: Agile transition and adoption human-related challenges and issues: a grounded theory approach. Comput. Hum. Behav. **62**, 257–266 (2016)
16. Javdani Gandomani, T., Zulzalil, H., Abd Ghani, A.A., Md. Sultan, A.B., Sharif, K.Y.: Exploring key factors of pilot projects in agile transformation process using a grounded theory study. In: Skersys, T., Butleris, R., Butkiene, R. (eds.) ICIST 2013. CCIS, vol. 403, pp. 146–158. Springer, Heidelberg (2013). https://doi.org/10.1007/978-3-642-41947-8_14
17. Ganesh, N., Thangasamy, S.: Lessons learned in transforming from traditional to agile development. J. Comput. Sci. **8**(3), 389–392 (2012)
18. Gren, L., Torkar, R., Feldt, R.: Group development and group maturity when building agile teams: a qualitative and quantitative investigation at eight large companies. J. Syst. Softw. **124**, 104–119 (2017)
19. Hanly, S., Wai, L., Meadows, L., Leaton, R.: Agile coaching in British telecom: making strawberry jam. In: AGILE 2006 (AGILE 2006), pp. 9-pp. IEEE (2006)
20. Hobbs, B., Petit, Y.: Agile methods on large projects in large organizations. Proj. Manag. J. **48**(3), 3–19 (2017)
21. Hoda, R., Kruchten, P., Noble, J., Marshall, S.: Agility in context. In: Proceedings of the ACM International Conference on Object Oriented Programming Systems Languages and Applications, pp. 74–88 (2010)
22. Hoda, R., Noble, J., Marshall, S.: Balancing acts: walking the agile tightrope. In: Proceedings of the 2010 ICSE Workshop on Cooperative and Human Aspects of Software Engineering, pp. 5–12 (2010)
23. Hoda, R., Noble, J., Marshall, S.: Developing a grounded theory to explain the practices of self-organizing agile teams. Empir. Softw. Eng. **17**(6), 609–639 (2012)
24. Hoda, R., Noble, J., Marshall, S.: Self-organizing roles on agile software development teams. IEEE Trans. Softw. Eng. **39**(3), 422–444 (2012)
25. Jovanović, M., Mas, A., Mesquida, A.L., Lalić, B.: Transition of organizational roles in agile transformation process: a grounded theory approach. J. Syst. Softw. **133**, 174–194 (2017)
26. van Kelle, E., Visser, J., Plaat, A., van der Wijst, P.: An empirical study into social success factors for agile software development. In: 2015 IEEE/ACM 8th International Workshop on Cooperative and Human Aspects of Software Engineering, pp. 77–80 (2015)
27. Kettunen, P., Laanti, M., Fagerholm, F., Mikkonen, T.: Agile in the era of digitalization: a finnish survey study. In: Franch, X., Männistö, T., Martínez-Fernández, S. (eds.) PROFES 2019. LNCS, vol. 11915, pp. 383–398. Springer, Cham (2019). https://doi.org/10.1007/978-3-030-35333-9_28
28. Kitchenham, B., Charters, S.: Guidelines for performing systematic literature reviews in software engineering (2007)

29. Kompella, L.: Agile methods, organizational culture and agility: some insights. In: Proceedings of the 7th International Workshop on Cooperative and Human Aspects of Software Engineering, pp. 40–47 (2014)
30. Korhonen, K.: Evaluating the impact of an agile transformation: a longitudinal case study in a distributed context. Softw. Qual. J. **21**(4), 599–624 (2013)
31. Lalsing, V., Kishnah, S., Pudaruth, S.: People factors in agile software development and project management. Int. J. Softw. Eng. Appl. **3**(1), 117 (2012)
32. Laws, K., McLeod, R.: Case study and grounded theory: sharing some alternative qualitative research methodologies with systems professionals. In: Proceedings of the 22nd International Conference of the Systems Dynamics Society, vol. 78, pp. 1–25 (2004)
33. Martín-Martín, A., Orduna-Malea, E., Thelwall, M., López-Cózar, E.D.: Google scholar, web of science, and scopus: a systematic comparison of citations in 252 subject categories. J. Inf. **12**(4), 1160–1177 (2018)
34. Melo, C.d.O., et al.: The evolution of agile software development in brazil. J. Braz. Comput. Soc. **19**(4), 523–552 (2013)
35. Mikalsen, M., Moe, N.B., Stray, V., Nyrud, H.: Agile digital transformation: a case study of interdependencies. In: International Conference on Information Systems 2018, ICIS 2018 (2018)
36. Misra, S.C., Kumar, V., Kumar, U.: Identifying some important success factors in adopting agile software development practices. J. Syst. Softw. **82**(11), 1869–1890 (2009)
37. Muntés-Mulero, V., et al.: Agile risk management for multi-cloud software development. IET Softw. **13**(3), 172–181 (2018)
38. Ng, P.W.: A canvas for capturing context of agile adoption. In: Emerging Innovations in Agile Software Development, pp. 37–50. IGI Global (2016)
39. Noll, J., Razzak, M.A., Bass, J.M., Beecham, S.: A study of the scrum master's role. In: Felderer, M., Méndez Fernández, D., Turhan, B., Kalinowski, M., Sarro, F., Winkler, D. (eds.) PROFES 2017. LNCS, vol. 10611, pp. 307–323. Springer, Cham (2017). https://doi.org/10.1007/978-3-319-69926-4_22
40. O'Connor, R.V., Duchonova, N.: Assessing the value of an agile coach in agile method adoption. In: Barafort, B., O'Connor, R.V., Poth, A., Messnarz, R. (eds.) EuroSPI 2014. CCIS, vol. 425, pp. 135–146. Springer, Heidelberg (2014). https://doi.org/10.1007/978-3-662-43896-1_12
41. Paasivaara, M.: Adopting safe to scale agile in a globally distributed organization. In: 2017 IEEE 12th International Conference on Global Software Engineering (ICGSE), pp. 36–40. IEEE (2017)
42. Paasivaara, M., Behm, B., Lassenius, C., Hallikainen, M.: Large-scale agile transformation at Ericsson. Empir. Softw. Eng. **23**(5), 2550–2596 (2018)
43. Paasivaara, M., Lassenius, C.: Agile coaching for global software development. J. Softw. Evol. Process **26**(4), 404–418 (2014)
44. Paasivaara, M., Lassenius, C.: Scaling scrum in a large globally distributed organization: a case study. In: 2016 IEEE 11th International Conference on Global Software Engineering (ICGSE), pp. 74–83. IEEE (2016)
45. Paasivaara, M., Väättänen, O., Hallikainen, M., Lassenius, C.: Supporting a large-scale lean and agile transformation by defining common values. In: Dingsøyr, T., Moe, N.B., Tonelli, R., Counsell, S., Gencel, C., Petersen, K. (eds.) XP 2014. LNBIP, vol. 199, pp. 73–82. Springer, Cham (2014). https://doi.org/10.1007/978-3-319-14358-3_7

46. Pacheco, M., Mesquida, A.-L., Mas, A.: Being agile while coaching teams using their own data. In: Larrucea, X., Santamaria, I., O'Connor, R.V., Messnarz, R. (eds.) EuroSPI 2018. CCIS, vol. 896, pp. 426–436. Springer, Cham (2018). https://doi.org/10.1007/978-3-319-97925-0_36
47. Pacheco, M., Mesquida, A.-L., Mas, A.: Image based diagnosis for agile coaching. In: Walker, A., O'Connor, R.V., Messnarz, R. (eds.) EuroSPI 2019. CCIS, vol. 1060, pp. 481–494. Springer, Cham (2019). https://doi.org/10.1007/978-3-030-28005-5_37
48. Padula, A.: Organically growing internal coaches. In: 2009 Agile Conference, pp. 237–242. IEEE (2009)
49. Parizi, R.M., Gandomani, T.J., Nafchi, M.Z.: Hidden facilitators of agile transition: agile coaches and agile champions. In: 2014 8th Malaysian Software Engineering Conference (MySEC), pp. 246–250. IEEE (2014)
50. Paterek, P.: Agile transformation in project organization: knowledge management aspects and challenges. In: 18th European Conference on Knowledge Management (ECKM 2017), Spain, Barcelona, pp. 1170–1179 (2017)
51. Pavlič, L., Heričko, M.: Agile coaching: the knowledge management perspective. In: Uden, L., Hadzima, B., Ting, I.-H. (eds.) KMO 2018. CCIS, vol. 877, pp. 60–70. Springer, Cham (2018). https://doi.org/10.1007/978-3-319-95204-8_6
52. Qumer, A., Henderson-Sellers, B.: Empirical evaluation of the agile process lifecycle management framework. In: 2010 Fourth International Conference on Research Challenges in Information Science (RCIS), pp. 213–222. IEEE (2010)
53. Raith, F., Richter, I., Lindermeier, R.: How project-management-tools are used in agile practice: benefits, drawbacks and potentials. In: Proceedings of the 21st International Database Engineering & Applications Symposium, pp. 30–39 (2017)
54. Santos, V., Goldman, A., Roriz Filho, H.: The influence of practices adopted by agile coaching and training to foster interaction and knowledge sharing in organizational practices. In: 2013 46th Hawaii International Conference on System Sciences, pp. 4852–4861. IEEE (2013)
55. Senapathi, M., Srinivasan, A.: An empirical investigation of the factors affecting agile usage. In: Proceedings of the 18th International Conference on Evaluation and Assessment in Software Engineering, pp. 1–10 (2014)
56. Shamshurin, I., Saltz, J.S.: Using a coach to improve team performance when the team uses a Kanban process methodology. Gov. Gov. Proj. Perform. Role Sover. 7(2), 61–77 (2019)
57. Silva, K., Doss, C.: The growth of an agile coach community at a fortune 200 company. In: Agile 2007 (AGILE 2007), pp. 225–228. IEEE (2007)
58. Stettina, C.J., Offerman, T., De Mooij, B., Sidhu, I.: Gaming for agility: using serious games to enable agile project & portfolio management capabilities in practice. In: 2018 IEEE International Conference on Engineering, Technology and Innovation (ICE/ITMC), pp. 1–9. IEEE (2018)
59. Stray, V., Moe, N.B.: Understanding coordination in global software engineering: a mixed-methods study on the use of meetings and slack. J. Syst. Softw. 170, 110717 (2020)
60. Stray, V., Moe, N.B., Aasheim, A.: Dependency management in large-scale agile: a case study of DevOps teams. In: Proceedings of the 52nd Hawaii International Conference on System Sciences (2019)

61. Stray, V., Tkalich, A., Moe, N.B.: The agile coach role: coaching for agile performance impact. In: Proceedings of the 54th Hawaii International Conference on System Sciences (2021, in Press)
62. Tengshe, A., Noble, S.: Establishing the agile PMO: managing variability across projects and portfolios. In: Agile 2007 (AGILE 2007), pp. 188–193. IEEE (2007)

Agile Leadership and Agile Management on Organizational Level - A Systematic Literature Review

Sven Theobald[1]([⊠]), Nils Prenner[2], Alexander Krieg[3], and Kurt Schneider[2]

[1] Fraunhofer IESE, Kaiserslautern, Germany
sven.theobald@iese.fraunhofer.de
[2] Software Engineering Group, Leibniz Universität Hannover, Hannover, Germany
{nils.prenner,kurt.schneider}@inf.uni-hannover.de
[3] borisgloger Consulting GmbH, Frankfurt am Main, Germany
alexander.krieg@sidelooks.de

Abstract. *Context:* Organizations start understanding the need to become an agile organization in order to fully benefit from agility and be competitive on quickly changing markets. Leaders at every level, not just top managers, need to buy into agility as an organizational value. Since the mid 1990s, many software development teams have very successfully adopted agile methods and proved that they can deal with continuous change. However, it is not clear how agility looks like outside the software development department on the organizational level. *Objectives:* The aim of this work is to create a better understanding on what leadership and management can look like in the context of an agile organization. We focused our work on scientific papers to build a scientific overview as starting point for future research. *Method:* We conducted a systematic literature review to identify the existing scientific literature on leadership and management approaches in the context of agile on the organizational level. *Results:* We provide an overview of existing work on this topic. The analysis of the identified papers focused on the definition of and motivation for agile leadership and agile management. *Conclusion:* Practitioners can use the results for improvement, while researchers can build on the results to help companies with their agile transformation.

Keywords: Agile leadership · Agile management · Agile organization · Motivation · Systematic literature review

1 Introduction

Leaders at every level, not just top managers, need to buy into agility as an organizational value. Thus, a culture of change must be pervasive at every level. The world is complex and specialized knowledge is an appropriate response [32]. A major downside of specialization is that one views the world from a specialized lens and becomes overly focused on a narrow task area. An agile organization

© Springer Nature Switzerland AG 2020
M. Morisio et al. (Eds.): PROFES 2020, LNCS 12562, pp. 20–36, 2020.
https://doi.org/10.1007/978-3-030-64148-1_2

unites organizational processes and people with advanced technology to meet customer demands for customized high quality products and services within a relatively short time frame [18]. This can only happen when agility is considered a systemic organizational value and a strategy championed by leadership.

People drive companies as a complex and dynamic system with culture, leadership, and applications as key factors affecting organizational success in a rapidly changing environment. The critical factor in adapting to change is how to design organizations to maximize the tacit knowledge base within them. Suitable tools are necessary to identify underlying strengths and weaknesses to allow initiating targeted discussions and provide a baseline for measurement. Both researchers and practitioners have observed that the rate of change caused by this explosion of technology, globalization, and complexity has been increasing for decades [40]. Leaders are faced with continuously changing environments, where fast adjustments are necessary to handle threats and opportunities.

Many organizations are unable to make the adjustments needed to quickly adapt to changes. On the contrary, typical organizational designs are not invented to deal with those changes, having rigid leadership hierarchies, organizational structures, and information systems that are not aligned with current needs, and corporate cultures that resist new ideas or processes [16,41,42]. Many companies struggle with implementing successful change in terms of increased flexibility, customer centricity, reduced bureaucracy and blocking processes [37]. Executives who recognize that speed is a critical factor to prosper in the twenty-first century often must find a way towards agility, fighting with traditional leadership, systems, and culture [14,16]. Centralized control and classical hierarchical structures are not suited to operate in fast-paced environments [15]. Centralized control may yield increased efficiency in predictable and stable business climates. However, in the complex volatile business world of the twenty-first century, corporate responsiveness is more critical to success than efficiency. Many researchers have concluded that organizations designed using traditional hierarchies with strong command and control structures are inherently anti-change [15,41,42]. A typical problem in many organizations is that senior management at the top of the hierarchy takes too long to make decisions [38]. Agility therefore relies on implicit leadership that enables knowledge sharing, seeks consensus, trusts people, delegates more, and provides an environment for people to improve inherent tacit knowledge [38]. Traditional management that operates from outside the team and controls the team with the help of metrics is no longer appropriate [4]. This does not mean that there is no need for managers in the future. However, agile teams are more efficient and faster taking decisions on their own, aligned with the goals and strategies set by management.

Haneberg [13] defined agility as the efficiency with which organizations respond to continuous change by consistently adapting. In today's business environment, companies must be agile and adaptable to respond in small increments of any kind of products and services they deliver that ultimately change the leadership, systems, and culture allowing the firm to survive and prosper in a different environment [33].

Companies should start their agile transformation by analyzing their products and services and reorganize them in value streams. Vertical organizational structures and functional departments have to be transformed towards a focus on the value streams and services. This transformation of the organizational design needs to be implemented by leadership and has to involve management on all levels of all areas [25]. The need for intense interactions to rapidly address an increasingly fast-paced and complex business environment became more and more apparent. This observation coincided with the fact that an increasing number of employees are hired for their knowledge and not for their physical contributions to work. The trend toward knowledge workers and knowledge economy has been documented by many researchers and authors for decades [10, 12, 34]. Feedback by leaders from the top and middle management suggested that this changing demographic called for a different leadership style requiring more involvement and engagement throughout their organizations. Creating and maintaining an environment enabling knowledge workers to maximize unique and valuable abilities required focus of attention and constant energy to maintain.

In summary, leadership concepts need to adapt in order to enable agility throughout the organization. There is a lack of understanding how agile leadership and agile management can look like outside of software engineering. In order to shed light into this topic, we want to get an overview of agile management and leadership concepts on the organizational level, with the help of a systematic literature review. Our analysis focuses on how agile leadership and agile management are defined, and what reasons the identified sources mention for changing to agile leadership and agile management.

The remainder of this paper is organized as follows: Sect. 2 discusses related work and clarifies the background regarding our topic. Section 3 presents the study design, including the research questions and the research procedure. Section 4 provides insights into the findings concerning our research questions. Finally, Sect. 5 provides the conclusion and suggestions for future work.

2 Related Work and Background

According to previous studies such as Status Quo Agile [20], Agile Swiss Study [27], the ChaosReports of the Standish Group and the survey by VersionOne [44], many agile initiatives start at the level of clearly defined projects, mostly with a great tendency towards IT or software development projects. The studies mentioned focus on technical areas and not on the agile development of an entire organization [26]. For some years now, the agile trend has been moving more and more in the direction of non-technical areas and thus increasingly leads to the areas of agile organizational development as well as management and management levels [31]. Basically, agile initiatives that are started within an organization can be understood as agile change management. Krieg [24] discussed agile leadership, planning, risk management, QA, budgeting, documentation and contracts. In 2016, a "Maturity Level Model for Agile Corporate Development" [23] was developed and published. The aim of the model is to provide orientation and an overview of what it means if a company wants to develop in a holistic, agile manner. The model shows that, similar to a company balance sheet, all areas have to be considered and evaluated. Theobald and Diebold [43] collected problems at the interface between agile and traditional approaches and classified these problems based on a categorization into interfaces (e.g., to traditional organizational units such as HR department or Sales) and problem areas (such as planning, reporting or budgeting). So that agile culture is not neglected, an approach to transformation must be chosen that takes into account both technical and cultural agility [11]. Furthermore, 50 factors were identified that influence the development of an agile culture [28]. Yet, there is no clear definition of management and leadership outside of agile development teams. This knowledge would be important to facilitate organization-wide change to support an organization's agile transformation.

2.1 Management vs. Leadership

The distinction between management and leadership is often blurred. Kotter [22] coined the term leadership and explored its differences to management. According to Kotter, management's main task is to maintain order and stability, whereas leadership creates change and movement in the organization.

Kotter [22] defines three core processes each for leadership and management. The core processes for management are: *planning* and *budget allocation*; *organizational tasks* and *human resources tasks*; and *controlling* and *resolving of problems*. Accordingly, managers are there to control the processes, review plans and results, coordinate employees, and resolve problems of all kinds. Managers are therefore responsible for the daily business and for friction-less processes.

The core processes for leadership are: *providing goals and vision*; *aligning employees with these goals*; and *motivating and inspiring the employees*. The need for leadership in organizations was also accompanied by the insight that the market situation of companies often changes rapidly and that organizations have to adapt to new situations in order to remain competitive. Therefore, it is the task of leadership to explore new options and directions to stay ahead.

2.2 Traditional Management

Parker et al. [39] explored the characteristics of traditional management in the context of a literature review. In traditional management, strict control procedures are used to cope with change and uncertainties. Hierarchies and vertical organizational structures are established to create order. Rigid hierarchy is seen as a necessity for stability and planning. The assumption is that an increase in control also increases the structure of processes and order and reduces risk. Employees are considered as a resource and are seen as interchangeable. Work is processed by being broken down into tasks and then allocated to an accountable person. Managers deal with risks through extensive up-front planning.

In summary, traditional management is characterized by a command and control structure and strict compliance with processes and plans.

2.3   Agile Organization

An agile organization unites organizational processes and people with advanced technology to meet customer demands for customized high quality products and services within a relatively short time frame [18]. This can only happen when agility is considered a systemic organizational value and a strategy championed by leadership. To implement agility as a systematic organizational value means to implement the key values of agility, e.g., customer-centricity, continuous delivery of products, and reacting quickly to market changes, and align those values from the top management down to the teams level.

3   Research Design

As the concepts of agile leadership and agile management are not clearly defined, we performed a systematic literature review to gain an overview over scientific literature, focusing on what constitutes agile leadership and why companies should change from a traditional leadership approach to an agile one. In the following, we will describe our research procedure, first presenting the research goal and the research questions. Then we will describe our research method, including the selection of the search database, the definition of the search strings, as well as the definition of inclusion and exclusion criteria. Next, we will present our selection, including the sequential steps, remaining papers, and inter rater agreement. Finally, we will explain how the literature was analyzed and what threats to validity exist.

3.1   Research Questions

The goal of our systematic literature review was to get an overview over the scientific literature on agile management and agile leadership on organizational level. Therefore, we formulated the following two research questions:

RQ1: How is agile leadership and agile management on organizational level defined in scientific literature?
With this first research question we want to understand how agile leadership and agile management is defined in the scientific literature. There is already a lot of work that deals with the management of the development team. But it is widely recognized that companies need to embrace agility on all organizational levels and in all departments of the company so that the whole company is able to react to market changes. Therefore, we are interested in agile leadership and agile management on the organizational level of companies.

RQ2: What motivation for agile leadership and agile management on organizational level is provided by scientific literature?
A lot of companies want to be more agile and change their way of working, but they only transform the software development department and leave the rest of the company untouched. This means that these companies are still traditionally managed on a high level. With this second

research question, we want to show the need for companies to change to an agile leadership and agile management approach on all levels in order to completely embrace agility. We will do this by analyzing the benefits of agile leadership and agile management, as well as the drawbacks of traditional approaches.

3.2 Research Method

In order to answer the research questions, we conducted a Systematic Literature Review (SLR). For the process of an SLR, it is important to systematically choose the right databases, to accurately specify the keywords, respectively the keyword string(s), and to clearly define the inclusion and exclusion criteria [19]. In the following, we will describe each of these aspects in more detail.

Search Database. Scopus contains 57 million articles, primarily in the fields of engineering and computer science. For this SLR, Scopus was selected because it covers many important software development and project management conferences, such as ICSSP, ICSE, PROFES, and XP. At these conferences, a lot of scientists and practitioners present and discuss the most important und newest topics and results in software engineering and agility.

Definition of the Search String. After selecting the databases for our SLR, we started to collect the keywords that best represent our research topic. Initially, we made the assumption that there is not much research yet on this topic. For this reason, we chose keywords at a high level of abstraction. The keywords and the search strings were tested with several pilot searches on Scopus and were iteratively improved based on an analysis of the results. Although all authors have a practical and research background in agile methods, practices and culture, another agile expert from the Fraunhofer Institute for Experimental Software Engineering was consulted to assess the completeness and suitability of the keywords with an independent view from outside the research team. This helped us ensure that the final set of keywords was suitable to identify relevant literature. We constructed two search strings to (1) cover management concepts in agile organizations and (2) agile leadership concepts. The first search string deals with management concepts.

(agile OR agility) AND (organization OR enterprise OR company) AND ("modern management" OR "management 3.0" OR "management 4.0" OR "management cybernetics" OR "viable systems model")

We were interested in publications dealing with management concepts in agile organizations. Therefore, we added *agile* and *organization* to our search string. In order to reach publications that do not use these terms, we added synonyms for both term, e.g., agility and enterprise. The term management was too generic to be used efficiently. New management concepts are often described by using the terms *management 3.0* or *management 4.0*. In order to get a more focused result, we decided to use these expressions and also added synonyms.

> (agile OR agility) AND (organization OR enterprise OR company) AND leadership

We used the second search string to collect publications dealing with agile leadership concepts. Therefore, we added the term *leadership* to our search string. The other expressions were similar to our first search string.

Definition of Inclusion and Exclusion Criteria. In order to have guidelines during the selection process of the literature review, we formulated detailed inclusion and exclusion criteria. The concrete criteria are shown in Table 1. As our focus was on analyzing the state of the art of management and leadership at the organizational level, we excluded papers where management concepts are only described at the level of a single team. Since our paper has a practical background, we excluded papers with a teaching background. Our focus was also on the underlying concepts of management and leadership, so we excluded papers where only technical solutions for these concepts are discussed.

Table 1. Inclusion and exclusion criteria

	Criteria	Description
Inclusion	IC1	The paper describes agile leadership and agile managment concepts, practices, etc. on the organizational level.
	IC2	The paper describes agile leadership and agile management concepts for large-scale development environments.
	IC3	The paper describes the benefits of agile leadership and agile management.
Exclusion	EC1	The paper is not written in English or German.
	EC2	The paper is not a peer-reviewed contribution to a conference or journal.
	EC3	The paper describes management and leadership at the development team level, e.g., in Scrum or Kanban.
	EC4	The paper describes knowledge management, e.g., teaching methods.
	EC5	The paper deals with technical solutions of existing concepts, e.g., tools, algorithms, or AI.

3.3 Selection Method

The search was conducted on the 19th of June 2019. The search string for "leadership" led to 329 papers, while the search string for "management" led to 12 papers. Overall, 341 papers were identified. The first selection of the papers was done by the first and second author. In this process, the inclusion and exclusion criteria were first applied to the titles of the identified publications. Five publications were selected for the "management" search string, while 89 publications were selected for the "leadership" search string for further investigation. The selection of the publications by title was performed together by the first and second author. Both authors rated the titles resulting from the "management" search string. The titles resulting from the "leadership" search string were mainly rated by the first author. The second author also rated one third of the papers to evaluate the filtering process. For that, we calculated *Cohen's Kappa Statistic*, which calculates the agreement between two raters [7]. We reached a value of 0.76 which indicates *substantial* agreement [29].

In the second step, we read the abstracts of all selected papers. The abstracts of the publications resulting from the "management" search string were all rated by the first and second author. In this filtering step, two papers remained. The abstracts resulting from the "leadership" search string were mainly rated by the second author. For the evaluation of the abstract selection process, the first author read one third of the abstracts. We again calculated *Cohen's Kappa statistic* and reached a value of 0.51, which indicates *moderate* agreement [29]. After this step, 38 papers remained for the "leadership" search string.

In the next step, we had to exclude some of the publications because they were not available or were not peer-reviewed contributions to a conference or journal. After this step, two papers remained for the "management" search string and 19 papers remained for the "leadership" search string.

In the last step, the first three authors thoroughly read the whole papers and analyzed their content. In this process, both papers for the "management" search string were excluded. From the "leadership" search string, 14 papers remained. In cases of uncertainties, the inclusion and exclusion of papers was discussed among the first three authors. Figure 1 shows the process of paper selection.

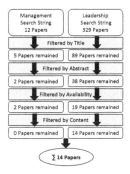

Fig. 1. Representation of the search and filtering process

3.4   Data Analysis

For the qualitative analysis process of the identified publications we used an extraction sheet. This was a MS Excel sheet containing the research questions including certain concrete aspects we wanted to analyze. The extraction sheet was used to collect text phrases from the publications that were directly assigned to the respective research question. Finally, each of the first three authors who extracted information from the final set of papers put the relevant information about their respective papers from the extraction sheet into the corresponding section of an online word processing file. Afterwards, text parts that describe similar aspects were grouped together and discussed by the authors in multiple video conference sessions.

3.5   Threats to Validity

Our literature review is subject to some threats to validity. According to Wohlin et al. [45], we will discuss construct, internal, conclusion, and external validity.

Construct Validity. Construct validity concerns the creation of the search string and the selection of the database. In order to mitigate the threat caused by the creation of the search string, we tested different search strings before we started our database search. In this way, we avoided choosing the wrong keywords. To cover further publications we added synonyms for different keywords, e.g., agility or enterprise.

Internal Validity. The literature review was performed by the first three authors in order to decrease mono researcher bias. The decision about the inclusion and exclusion of a publication is subjective. In order to mitigate this threat, we established a comprehensible decision process and formulated concrete inclusion and exclusion criteria. To evaluate our research process, we calculated *Cohen's Kappa statistic* [7]. The results show that agreement was at least *moderate* throughout the whole selection process [29]. In situations where the inclusion or exclusion of a publication was unclear, the paper was peer-evaluated by at least one of the other authors.

Conclusion Validity. Conclusion validity depends on the papers we selected. We mitigated this threat by using the Scopus database in order to get high-quality publications and excluded publications that are not peer-reviewed.

External Validity. We can not guarantee that we found all relevant papers. We wanted to get an overview of the state of the art of agile leadership and agile management concepts. Therefore, we intentionally focused our search string on modern organizational management methods and left the generic *management* term out. This narrow focus may be a threat, but also shows that there are not many publications on modern agile management methods.

4   Results

Table 2 shows the list of papers that were selected during the SLR. In the following sections, we answer both our research questions.

4.1   RQ1: Definition of Agile Leadership and Agile Management

This section discusses agile leadership and agile management, especially what typical responsibilities and traits of agile leaders and managers are.

Table 2. Selected publications

Paper	Title	Author	Year	Reference
P01	Doing complexity leadership theory: How agile coaches at Spotify practise enabling leadership	Bäcklander	2019	[6]
P02	Business disruption is here to stay – What should leaders do?	Lang and Rumsey	2018	[30]
P03	Organizational Evolution - How Digital Disruption Enforces Organizational Agility	Jesse	2018	[17]
P04	Asymmetric leadership: Supporting a CEO's response to turbulence	Boxer and Eigen	2018	[5]
P05	Agile Organisation und Führung 4.0: Entscheidungshilfe für unternehmensspezifische Weichenstellungen	Korge	2017	[21]
P06	The challenges of organizational agility: part 1	Appelbaum et al.	2017	[1]
P07	The challenges of organizational agility: part 2	Appelbaum et al.	2017	[2]
P08	The performance triangle: a model for corporate agility	Nold and Michel	2016	[37]
P09	A model to guide organizational adaptation	Cross	2015	[9]
P10	Influence of large-scale organization structures on leadership behaviors	Moore	2009	[35]
P11	Agile principles as a leadership value system: How agile memes survive and thrive in a corporate IT culture	Baker and Thomas	2007	[3]
P12	Managing a large "Agile" software engineering organization	Beavers	2007	[4]
P13	New leadership strategies for the enterprise of the future	Murray and Greenes	2006	[36]
P14	The human side of organizational agility	Crocitto and Youssef	2003	[8]

From Economies of Scale to Economies of Scope. Leadership is a key enabler for good relationships between employees and their suppliers or customers. Agility is dependent upon leadership's ability to define an agility vision and mission, supported with organizational rewards for adapting to change [8, P14]. Leaders need to promote a learning organization and acceptance of change. Manufacturers may experience an IT challenge as we move to an e-economy. IT allows manufacturers to develop new supply chains that are quicker and reach further than existing chains. However, some manufacturers may be so accustomed to existing IT or manufacturing technology that they may choose not to change, potentially losing competitiveness. Changes in IT and other organizational subsystems have a long and wide reaching impact on organizational processes and relationships and can only happen with the support of top management. Therefore, management must recognize the relationship between such innovations and learning [8, P14]. Implicit in all the theories described is the strategic role of leadership as change agents. In order for an organization to become agile, managers need to promote a strategic paradigm shift. The role of leadership in this process is not really delineated in the literature.

Effective leadership is defined as effective communication and interaction with people at all levels throughout the organization [37, P08]. Nold and Michel [37, P08] report that although studies investigated leadership behaviors and traits, successful leadership depends on organization and context. A leadership style that is successful in one organization in a specific situation may not necessarily be effective if applied in a different organization or situation. However, Nold and Michel [37, P08] identified the need for communication and interaction with followers as recurring research themes. Those communication and interaction skills need to be natural and unique to the leader and organization.

Leaders should seek to create meaning for persons, organization, or society to stimulate innovation to achieve shared value [30, P02]. Lang and Rumsey [30, P02] names four attributes that make the difference to traditional leaders: "humble, adaptable, visionary, engaged". Leaders are responsible to create a vision, communicate meaning and purpose, and "kill and hide bureaucracy". Good leaders are curious and willing to fail fast. They are good listeners, fast at executing, and continuous learners that accept unpredictability of change [30, P02].

While leaders in stable environments take decisions for their teams, a new style of leadership becomes important where leaders acknowledge that they do not know everything in order to enable collaborative discovery and increased productivity [5, P04].

Organizational Structures vs. Agile Leadership. Moore [35, P10] showed that organizational structure is not as important as having leaders that live and exemplify a set of behaviors, among them the ability to lead the team instead of managing the team. This is done by setting directions and visions, aligning team members as well as mentor and motivate them with the help of one-on-one and team communication. These leaders understand the needs and goals of individuals and consider them when setting up a team. The organizational structures that aligned leaders with their teams (hierarchical and matrix structures with multiple sub-team leaders) tended to influence more managing versus leading as their role was more narrowly focused on these teams and their members. Moore [35, P10] reported that leaders used all capacity beyond fulfilling the normal tasks like resource management or addressing team obstacles was used for deeper engagement with the team, often leading to micro management. Also, when being approached by team members with concerns, the tendency was to try to solve the issue instead of facilitating and enabling the team to find a suitable solution themselves [35, P10].

Productivity vs. Flexibility. The leader has to become a coach and enabler for his team or employees. He has to create the optimal environment and purpose to his employees, and trust them that they will take over personal initiative and responsibility. Traditional concepts enable productivity, but limit flexibility and motivation [21, P05]. Influential leaders have to establish shared values and mobilize their followers to adopt those values [1, P06]. Transformational leadership is comfortable with experimentation, uses decentralized decision making and is able to align people from a diverse network towards a common purpose [2, P07]. A collaborative community is seen as the opposite of command and control leadership. Leaders need to create opportunities for workers to be both responsible and accountable for their processes [2, P07].

Agile Leadership vs. Agile Management. A manager achieves his or her goals through planning and budgeting, organizing and staffing, and controlling and problem solving. In contrast, a leader sets a direction, aligns people, and motivates and inspires to achieve the goals [17, P03] [9, P09] [3, P11]. With a "leader" who focuses on management instead of leadership, team empowerment is reduced due to external control being applied" [35, P10] [17, P03]. Bäcklander [6, P01] argues that leadership roles that do not have managerial authority are common in agile. Managers should function as facilitator, become creators of conditions favourable for performance, or become enablers of informal network dynamics in complex adaptive systems. Direction, alignment and commitment are needed for self-organizing teams, and support can be provided by a Scrum Master or agile coach as an alternative leadership role [6, P01]. They also state that leadership roles without managerial authority are common in entrepreneurial firms that practice agile software development.

Agile management is about the empowerment of the development team to trust their abilities. The duty of management is to provide teams with the necessary requirements and prioritization and let them organize themselves [4, P12].

4.2   RQ2: Motivation for Agile Leadership and Agile Management

In this section, we present the results concerning our second research question by discussing what motivations for agile leadership and agile management could be found in the identified sources. We will first present arguments for why traditional leadership and management concepts do not work anymore and must be changed. Afterwards, we will show the benefits of and reasons for agile leadership and agile management.

Contra Traditional Leadership and Management. The literature mentions two reasons why traditional leadership and management concepts have to be replaced. First, traditional top-down command and control management is no longer appropriate. Second, new drivers change the way organizations can operate and demand other ways of working.

Top-Down Command and Control Is No Longer Appropriate. Whereas for a long time, productivity was the primary goal, nowadays human factors such as employee motivation also play an important role. An increase in knowledge work and in the complexity of the products to be developed has led to decentralization, autonomy, and self-organization [21, P05]. Traditional management operates from outside the team using metrics to control the work of the team and putting increased pressure on the team when deviations in the plan can be seen. However, management has to be integrated into the team in the form of self-organization [4, P12]. Leadership can no longer be executed from a single position at the top of the hierarchy, but has to take place at the level of contact with the customer [5, P04]. Traditional managerial control is now both less possible and less useful [6, P01] in a setting where teams organize their work in a decentralized manner. Top-down and disciplinarian-style leadership is no longer appropriate and prevents collaboration and innovation [2, P07]. Thus, most traditional management approaches rather interfere with people's ability to perform instead of improving performance [37, P08]. Rigid command and control structures need to be removed in order to move quickly in the future [36, P13].

Traditional Organizations Cannot Cope with New Demands. Traditional organizations aim at increasing productivity and stability, e.g., by centralizing decisions, specialization and functional silos, or by using experts to plan the work for other workers who blindly follow instructions. These organizational and leadership concepts have proven their success over the last decades [21, P05].

However, drivers like changing markets and increasing expectations on the part of employees pose new requirements that traditional concepts can only address to a certain degree. External influences like digitalization, globalization, demographic change, and trends towards individualization increase complexity and pose new challenges to organizations [21, P05]. Traditional leadership approaches must change in order to be competitive in this environment [36, P13]. Therefore, it is necessary to replace slow, hierarchically-structured organizations with a more fluid and adaptable organizational design like social networks [36, P13]. Network structures allow for flexible use of valuable resources, capabilities and information in order to be competitive on rapidly changing markets [1, P06].

Pro Agile Leadership and Agile Management. The literature mentions three reasons why agile leadership and agile management concepts have to be adopted. First, innovative and agile leadership approaches are needed to handle new market demands. Second, enabling leadership is needed to empower teams in order to allow for fast decision making and innovation. Finally, agile leaders function as change agents to drive cultural change in the organization.

Agile Leadership Needed to Cope with New Demands. It has been proven that innovative organizations and leadership address the following three future demands [21, P05]: increase the agility of the organization; design good working conditions that foster employee motivation and health; and master complexity. Situational management of complex tasks and unexpected changes will replace upfront planning due to the requirements of VUCA (volatility, uncertainty, complexity and ambiguity) [21, P05]. The goals of "innovative" organizations and leadership are flexibility, adaptability, and innovation. Autonomy and decentralization push responsibility to where the actual work takes place. A self-organizing team is then enabled to take decisions. Only then can decisions be made timely and using the expertise of the right people [21, P05]. Thus, asymmetric leadership is required to react fast to customer needs [5, P04].

Enabling Leadership. Adaptive organizations need enabling leadership [6, P01]. It is up to leaders to build organizations that are dedicated to fulfilling the needs and values of their employees, so that people can reach their full potential and creativity [37, P08]. Interactive leadership is an important tool for creating a work environment where people feel comfortable and satisfied with themselves and their work [37, P08].

Agile Leaders as Change Agents. Business disruption is only possible with the help of agile leaders [30, P02]. Management plays an important role in moving to an agile culture [8, P14]. For a successful adoption of organizational change, leaders have to describe the mission, vision, and values of an organization so that people share the goal and believe in the higher purpose [37, P08].

5   Conclusion and Future Work

Leadership and management throughout the whole organization play an important role as key enablers for an agile transformation. Many companies did already make experiences with agility, using ideas and experiences from the area of software engineering. However, to run the whole organization in an agile way, some questions in the area of organizational structures, modern management and leadership are still not answered. In volatile and unstable times, traditional leadership and management approaches might no longer be the right choice for economical success, as more and more markets are driven by constant changes, and companies need flexibility and the ability for quick change. The structures and managing models from the economies of scale appear unhelpful and even blocking. Modern leadership has to take over to navigate teams and companies with flat structures, empowered and self-managed teams through an unstable industrial times with continuously unexpected changes in many branches.

However, it is not clear what leadership and management should look like in order to support agility throughout the whole organization. We therefore investigated the body of research on agile leadership and agile management applied at the organizational level with the help of a systematic literature review. The 14 identified sources provide an overview of the research field. In this work, we focused on the definition of agile leadership and agile management at the organizational level, and also analyzed the motivation for the usage of agile leadership and agile management at the organizational level. This study was a first step towards understanding agility at the organizational level. Practitioners can use the insights to improve their agile transformation, and researchers can build on the results to conduct further investigations into the topic of organizational agility.

In future work, we want to extend and detail our analysis of the identified papers from this literature review. A possible next step could be to consult non-scientific publications on agile leadership, and to speak with agile experts about the results of this study in order to identify the gap between research and practice. Based on the knowledge about agile leadership and agile management concepts, we also plan to conduct an analysis of the state of the practice with the help of interviews and survey research. Further, a definition of the terms agile leadership and agile management can be proposed using the study results and experiences from practice, taking into consideration established definitions of leadership and management.

Acknowledgments. Part of this research is funded by the German Ministry of Education and Research (BMBF) as part of a Software Campus project (01IS17047). We would like to thank Sonnhild Namingha for proofreading.

References

1. Appelbaum, S., Calla, R., Desautels, D., Hasan, L.: The challenges of organizational agility: Part 1. Ind. Commer. Train. **49**, 6–14 (2017)
2. Appelbaum, S., Calla, R., Desautels, D., Hasan, L.: The challenges of organizational agility: Part 2. Ind. Commer. Train. **49**, 69–74 (2017)
3. Baker, S.W., Thomas, J.C.: Agile principles as a leadership value system: how agile memes survive and thrive in a corporate IT culture. In: Agile 2007 (AGILE 2007), pp. 415–420 (2007)
4. Beavers, P.A.: Managing a large "agile" software engineering organization. In: Agile 2007 (AGILE 2007), pp. 296–303 (2007)
5. Boxer, P., Eigen, C.: Asymmetric Leadership: supporting a CEO's response to turbulence, January 2008
6. Bäcklander, G.: Doing complexity leadership theory: how agile coaches at Spotify practise enabling leadership. Creat. Innov. Manag. **28**(1), 42–60 (2019)
7. Cohen, J.: Weighted kappa: nominal scale agreement provision for scaled disagreement or partial credit. Psychol. Bull. **70**(4), 213 (1968)
8. Crocitto, M., Youssef, M.: The human side of organizational agility. Ind. Manag. Data Syst. **103**, 388–397 (2003)
9. Cross, S.E.: A model to guide organizational adaptation. In: 2013 International Conference on Engineering, Technology and Innovation (ICE) & IEEE International Technology Management Conference, pp. 1–11. IEEE (2013)
10. Davenport, T.H., Prusak, L., et al.: Working Knowledge: How Organizations Manage What They Know. Harvard Business Press, Brighton (1998)
11. Diebold, P., Küpper, S., Zehler, T.: Nachhaltige agile transition: symbiose von technischer und kultureller Agilität. Projektmanagement und Vorgehensmodelle **2015** (2015)
12. Drucker, P.F.: Landmarks of Tomorrow: A Report on The New. Harper & Row, New York (1957)
13. Haneberg, L.: Training for agility: building the skills employees need to zig and zag. Hum. Resour. Manag. Int. Dig. **20**(2), 50–58 (2011)
14. Hopkins, W.E., Mallette, P., Hopkins, S.A.: Proposed factors influencing strategic inertia/strategic renewal in organizations. Acad. Strat. Manag. J. **12**(2), 77 (2013)

15. Hugos, M.H.: Business Agility: Sustainable Prosperity in a Relentlessly Competitive World, vol. 12. Wiley, Hoboken Hoboken (2009)
16. de Jager, P.: Who me, change? Com. L. Bull. **19**, 16 (2004)
17. Jesse, N.: Organizational evolution-how digital disruption enforces organizational agility. IFAC-PapersOnLine **51**(30), 486–491 (2018)
18. Kidd, P.T.: Agile Manufacturing: Forging New Frontiers. Addison-Wesley Longman Publishing Co., Inc., London (1995)
19. Kitchenham, B., Charters, S.: Guidelines for performing systematic literature reviews in software engineering. Technical report EBSE 2007-001, Keele University and Durham University Joint Report (2007)
20. Komus, A., Kuberg, M.: Abschlussbericht: Status quo agile 2016/2017. Studie über Erfolg und Anwendungsformen von agilen Methoden (2017)
21. Korge, A.: Agile Organisation und Führung 4.0: Entscheidungshilfe für unternehmensspezifische Weichenstellungen. ZWF Zeitschrift für wirtschaftlichen Fabrikbetrieb **112**, 289–292 (2017)
22. Kotter, J.P.: A Force for Change: How Leadership Differs from Management. The Free Press, New York (1990)
23. Krieg, A.: Reifegradmodell zur Messung agiler Unternehmensentwicklung. Lecture Notes in Informatics, Gesellschaft für Informatik, Bonn, S, pp. 162–169 (2016)
24. Krieg, A.: Agiler Projektleiter-Vermittler und Moderator im hybriden Projektumfeld. Projektmanagement und Vorgehensmodelle 2017-Die Spannung zwischen dem Prozess und den Mensch im Projekt (2017)
25. Krieg, A.: Agile Organisationsentwicklung und agiles Change-Management. In: Gesellschaft für Informatik eV (GI), p. 253 (2019)
26. Krieg, A., Theobald, S., Küpper, S.: Erfolgreiche agile Projekte benötigen ein agiles Umfeld. Projektmanagement und Vorgehensmodelle - Der Einfluss der Digitalisierung auf Projektmanagementmethoden und Entwicklungsprozesse (2018)
27. Kropp, M., Meier, A.: Swiss agile study 2014. Agile Software-Entwicklung in der Schweiz. Zürcher Hochschule für Angewandte Wissenschaften (2014)
28. Küpper, S., Kuhrmann, M., Wiatrok, M., Andelfinger, U., Rausch, A.: Is there a blueprint for building an agile culture? Projektmanagement und Vorgehensmodelle - Die Spannung zwischen dem Prozess und den Mensch im Projekt (2017)
29. Landis, J.R., Koch, G.G.: The measurement of observer agreement for categorical data. Biometrics (1977)
30. Lang, D., Rumsey, C.: Business disruption is here to stay - what should leaders do? Qual. Access Success **19**, 35–40 (2018)
31. Larman, C., Vodde, B.: Large-Scale Scrum: More with LeSS. Addison-Wesley Professional, Boston (2016)
32. Lawrence, P.R., Lorsch, J.W.: Organization and Environment: Managing Differentiation and Integration. Harvard Business School Press, Brighton (1967)
33. Michel, L.: The Performance Triangle: Diagnostic Mentoring to Manage Organizations and People for Superior Performance in Turbulent Times, vol. 12. LID Publishing, London (2013)
34. Mládková, L.: Knowledge management for knowledge workers. In: Proceedings of the European Conference on Intellectual Capital, pp. 260–267 (2011)
35. Moore, E.: Influence of large-scale organization structures on leadership behaviors. In: 2009 Agile Conference, pp. 309–313 (2009)
36. Murray, A., Greenes, K.: New leadership strategies for the enterprise of the future. VINE **36**, 358–370 (2006)
37. Nold, H., Michel, L.: The performance triangle: a model for corporate agility. Lead. Organ. Dev. J. **37**, 341–356 (2016)

38. Nold, H.A.: Linking knowledge processes with firm performance: organizational culture. J. Intellect. Cap. **13**(1), 16–38 (2012). https://doi.org/10.1108/14691931211196196
39. Parker, D., Holesgrove, M., Pathak, R.: Improving productivity with self-organised teams and agile leadership. Int. J. Prod. Perform. Manag. **64**, 112–128 (2015)
40. Salmador, M., Bueno, E.: Knowledge creation in strategy-making: implications for theory and practice. Eur. J. Innov. Manag. **10**, 367–390 (2007)
41. Scott, W.R.: Developments in organization theory, 1960–1980. Am. Behav. Sci. **24**(3), 407–422 (1981)
42. Scott, W.R., Davis, G.F.: Organizations and Organizing: Rational, Natural and Open Systems Perspectives. Routledge, Abingdon (2015)
43. Theobald, S., Diebold, P.: Interface problems of agile in a non-agile environment. In: Garbajosa, J., Wang, X., Aguiar, A. (eds.) XP 2018. LNBIP, vol. 314, pp. 123–130. Springer, Cham (2018). https://doi.org/10.1007/978-3-319-91602-6_8
44. VersionOne: The 11th Annual State of Agile Report (2017)
45. Wohlin, C., Runeson, P., Höst, M., Ohlsson, M.C., Regnell, B., Wesslén, A.: Experimentation in Software Engineering: An Introduction. Kluwer Academic Publishers, Norwell (2000)

A Study of the Agile Coach's Role

Kadri Daljajev, Ezequiel Scott[✉] [iD], Fredrik Milani, and Dietmar Pfahl [iD]

Institute of Computer Science, University of Tartu, Tartu, Estonia
kadri.daljajev@gmail.com, {ezequiel.scott,fredrik.milani,
dietmar.pfahl}@ut.ee

Abstract. While Agile Software Development has recently received much attention in industry, the implementation of agile methods and practices is not straightforward, partly because the approach focuses on people and their interactions. To
facilitate the adoption of agile methods and the further development of agile teams,
the role of an agile coach has been introduced. However, this role has not been
sufficiently explored from the perspective of those whose perform that role. To
address this gap, we conducted a case study where we interviewed agile coaches
with experiences from multiple companies. We identified the main objectives of
agile coaches, the methods they use to achieve those objectives, the challenges
they frequently face, the skills required by the role, and the value they provide
to organizations and teams. Our findings contribute to a better understanding of
the role and the construction of a professional identity. In addition, we offer a
characterization that can be useful for professionals that are new in the role.

Keywords: Agile software development · Agile coach · Agile adoption

1 Introduction

Many organizations have either adopted agile software development methods or are
in the process of doing so. Those who have implemented an agile approach, follow a
specific method such as Scrum [1] or Kanban [2] while others combine different methods
[3]. Meanwhile, some companies are actively working to replace traditional plan-driven
methods, such as Waterfall, with agile methods.

Maintaining effective teams or transitioning to Agile is not straightforward. One
reason is that agile methods are human-centric, i.e., people and their interactions, both
within teams and with customers, take precedence over rigid processes, tools, and contract negotiations [4]. Thus, building functional teams, improving team performance,
and aiding companies to implement agile methods, require adopting and developing an
agile mindset [5]. Agile coaches aid organizations and teams in such activities.

The main role of an agile coach is to facilitate team discussions in pursuit of improved
team performance [6]. In executing this role, agile coaches have the responsibilities of
facilitation, problem-solving, coaching, teaching, and mentoring [1, 6–8]. Agile coaches
also help teams to identify how they can improve their work to achieve better performance
[9]. Furthermore, agile coaches also aid companies who are transitioning into employing
agile methods [10]. Agile coaches, therefore, contribute with a better understanding

© Springer Nature Switzerland AG 2020
M. Morisio et al. (Eds.): PROFES 2020, LNCS 12562, pp. 37–52, 2020.
https://doi.org/10.1007/978-3-030-64148-1_3

of agile methods and practices [11], enhance teamwork [12], raise productivity [13], improve product quality and reduce cost [14], create better solutions, and contribute to successful projects conclusions [15].

Despite the importance of agile coaches [16], little research has been conducted about this role. Most studies focus on exploring the role of agile coaches from the perspective of scrum masters. For instance, Adkins [6] compare the role of an agile coach to that of scrum masters and project managers. Noll et al. [17] conducted a systematic literature review and a case study to identify the role of scrum master and its intersection with other roles, such as project manager. However, agile coaches are not confined to Scrum only. Rather, they can aid companies following other agile methods and those transitioning from sequential plan-driven methods to agile methodologies. Furthermore, several studies [11, 15, 18] have explored the role and function of agile coaches from a company perspective. For instance, how agile coaching is structured at British Telecom [11] or how agile coaching is conducted at Spotify [18]. Thus, existing work focuses on agile coaching as a variant of scrum master or from an organizational perspective, but not from the perspective of those who are performing the role, i.e., agile coaches. We seek to address this gap.

This paper aims to explore different aspects of the agile coach role from the perspective of those who work as agile coaches. We explore what the objectives of agile coaches are, the methods they use, the challenges they face, the skills required, and finally, the value they add. In our attempt to explore these topics, we use the case study research method where we conduct in-depth interviews with agile coaches [25]. Our study contributes to the field of Agile Software Development by adding to the existing knowledge empirical data that leads to a better understanding of the role and the construction of a professional identity. Thus, our contribution is particularly relevant for agile coaches and organizations considering enlisting the help of agile coaches.

The remainder of the paper is structured as follows. In the next section, we present the background related to the agile coach role. Next, in Sect. 3, we present our research method. Following that, in Sect. 4, we present our results. Section 5 discusses our results. Section 6 summarizes the limitations, and Sect. 7 concludes the paper.

2   Related Work

The study of the role of the agile coach involves two fundamental concepts that must be clarified, *role* and *coach*. A *role* can be understood as an institutionalized behavior pattern, defined in terms of their rights and obligations [19]. In this regard, the IEEE Professional & Educational Activities Board (PEAB)[1] propose a model of IT professional role. This model includes the definition of the job role as a type of position in an organization that is characterized by the responsibilities for the performance of activities assigned to a position. The board also recommends that job roles should be clearly defined in terms of responsibilities and the competencies required.

On the other hand, the concept of *coach* has been originally linked to instruction and training, where *coaching* referred to a process used to transport people from where

---

[1] PEAB Web site – https://www.computer.org/volunteering/boards-and-committees/professional-educational-activities.

they are to where they want to be. The development of *coaching* has been influenced by many fields, such as in education, sports, leadership studies, and various subfields of psychology [20, 21]. In the context of Agile Software Development, the concept of *coaching* has been applied to *agile coach*.

Several authors have aimed to discuss the role of agile coaches. For example, agile coaches have been related to well-defined roles, such as the scrum master. According to Adkins [6], an agile coach is "a scrum master who takes teams beyond getting agile practices up and running into their deliberate and joyful pursuit of high performance". Adkins understands agile coach as a role different from that of the scrum master, but the author also remarks that some responsibilities can overlap depending on the goals.

According to the Scrum Guide [1], a scrum master is mainly responsible for helping the scrum team in removing impediments and maximizing the value the team creates. The responsibilities include the achievement of the goals, determining the scope, the team's understanding of the product domain, and finding techniques to manage the product backlog in the most effective way. Interestingly, the scrum guide also indicates that scrum masters should *coach* the team in self-organization and cross-functionality, which points to the fact that both, scrum masters and agile coaches, have coaching responsibilities in common [1, 6].

A practitioner playing a scrum master's role can also play other roles at the same time. In fact, Noll et al. [17] found that the scrum master performs several activities in addition to the traditional ones, such as process facilitation, ceremony facilitation, and impediment removal. Among these additional activities, project management is commonly performed by scrum masters, which leads to a conflict of interest that can compromise the balance between the interests of external stakeholders and the scrum team.

To better understand the job of an agile coach, several authors have described the responsibilities that the role involves. For example, Santos et al. [22] point out that an agile coach has to facilitate the team to consider different alternatives on how to improve their processes, help the team to see what to do next, and also guide them on how to take responsibility for their doings. Similarly, Adkins [6] describe the agile coach as a teacher, facilitator, coach-mentor, conflict navigator, collaboration conductor, and problem solver whose main goal is to help the team to adopt and improve their use of agile methodologies.

O'Connor and Duchonova [10] contextualized the agile coach's role depending on the stage of adoption of agile methods, that is, if the teams are in the process of adopting agile methods or are already working with agile practices. In both cases, teams need help to either resolve an issue or to improve efficiency, and the agile coach can introduce benefits to companies that exceed the financial costs of using an agile coach. It is also possible to distinguish between external agile coaches (temporarily hired as consultants) and in-house coaches, and sometimes a combination of them [15]. Another way to differentiate the coaches is according to whether they use a directive or non-directive approach. In the directive approach, the coach is an expert whereas the goal of his work is to help the team to learn and solve not just a specific problem in hands but also problems in future [23].

Althoff [24] describes the role of the agile coach as the composition of other roles such as a planner, motivator, reflector, and process supervisor. The Agile Coaching Institute[2] suggests eight competencies that are needed for performing the agile coach role: Professional Coaching, Facilitating, Domain Mastery (Transformation Mastery, Business Mastery, Technical Mastery), Mentoring, Teaching and Agile-Lean Practitioner [7]. Table 1 summarizes the roles and the activities that have been related to the role of agile coach.

Table 1. Summary of the roles and activities performed by agile coaches.

Roles and activities	Adkins [6]	Scrum guide [1]	Bass [8]	Noll et al. [17]	Althoff [24]	Spayd and Adkins [7]
Facilitator	X	X	X	X		X
Problem solver	X	X	X	X		
Coach	X	X			X	X
Teacher	X	X				X
Mentor	X		X			X
Leader		X	X			X
Process anchor			X	X	X	
Collaboration conductor	X	X				
Change management agent		X				X
Sprint planner			X	X		
Integration anchor			X	X		
Conflict Navigator	X					
Sprint reviewer				X		
Planner					X	
Motivator					X	
Life coach	X					
Agile-Lean practitioner	X					
Prioritization				X		
Estimation				X		
Travelling				X		
Project management				X		

3 Method

The case study research method employs qualitative methods to investigate a particular reality within its real-life context [25], in particular when the boundaries distinguishing the object of study and its context are not clear [26]. Case studies can be used for

[2] Agile Coach Institute Website – https://www.agilecoachinginstitute.com.

confirming a hypothesis [25, 27], evaluate a method [28], and for exploratory purposes [25, 27]. For our research, the case study method is suitable as it enables an in-depth exploration of the role of agile coaches in its real-life setting. Yin [26] argues for the necessity of defining a research question when designing a case study. We use the case study method to explore the following research questions:

RQ1 - *What are the objectives of an agile coach?*
RQ2 - *What methods do agile coaches use to achieve their objectives?*
RQ3 - *What challenges do agile coaches encounter in their work?*
RQ4 - *What skills do agile coaches require and use?*
RQ5 - *What value do agile coaches perceive themselves to add?*

These research questions are relevant given that the agile coach role is relatively new, little research has been conducted so far, and, thus, there is a need to empirically explore this role further.

3.1 Case Study Design and Execution

The design of our case study is shown in Fig. 1. It consists of three main steps, i.e., preparation (first step), data collection (second step), and analyzing the collected data (third step). In the following, we describe the steps in more detail.

Fig. 1. The design of our case study.

The first step of the case study was preparation. As part of the preparation, we identified the method to gather data, prepared for the data collection, and defined and selected sources for data collection. We used interviews for data collection. According to Merriam [29], the interview method is particularly suitable for eliciting information about something that is difficult to observe. We employed semi-structured interviews with open-ended questions. We used open-ended questions as they provide more in-depth responses than closed questions. The interview questions were derived from our research questions. The questions focused on the personal experience of the participants as agile coaches in general rather than on the specific experience in one company. The interview questions are available as supplementary material.

As interviewees, we sought people who actively work as agile coaches. In order to identify candidates, we approached a network created and run by professional agile coaches in northern Europe. Before selecting, we ensured that they had working experience as agile coaches and were willing to be interviewed. The interviewees varied in their working experience as agile coaches and/or scrum masters (years of experience), experience with multiple companies (concurrent engagements), and number of teams they concurrently work with on average (concurrent reams) as can be seen in Table 2. In total, we selected eight interviewees. All interviewees insisted on full anonymity; thus, we do not disclose full demographical information.

Table 2. Characteristics of the interviewees who participated in the study.

Participant	Experience (years)	Multiple engagements[a]	Teams[a]
P1	>5	Yes	1
P2	>5	Yes	1
P3	2–5	Yes	>5
P4	<2	No	2–5
P5	<2	No	2–5
P6	>5	Yes	1
P7	>5	No	2–5
P8	2–5	Yes	2–5

[a]Concurrent

In the second step of our case study, we collected data by conducting interviews. The interviews were conducted face-to-face and online by the first author. The interviews were recorded, either by using the online tool used or with a voice recorder. The average length of the interviews was about one hour. Initially, 6 interviews were planned. Having conducted these interviews, we noted data saturations i.e., no new information is being provided by additional interviews. We, however, sought and conducted two more interviews to ensure we had enough interviews [30].

In the third step, we analyzed the collected data. All interviews were transcribed and encoded. The coding process was conducted according to the guidelines proposed by Braun and Clarke [31], i.e., familiarizing with data, generating and searching for initial themes, reviewing themes, and finally, defining and naming themes. Therefore, we first familiarized ourselves with the data by compiling all the transcripts into one document. Then we carefully read them and added notes. Next, we generated a set of initial themes. The themes corresponded to a research question. Each theme was further refined into codes, each of which relates to a specific aspect of the theme (research question). For instance, the theme named *Objectives* correspond to the first research question. Within this theme, we identified four codes, *Educating*, *Aiding*, *Creating Spaces*, and *Improvements*. Following this, the second and third authors reviewed the themes and codes through discussion. The final set of themes and codes, together with their frequency, are listed in Table 3.

Table 3. Finalized themes and sub-themes of the analysis.

Theme	Codes	Frequency
Objectives	Educating	7
	Aiding	6
	Creating spaces	4
	Improvements	2
Methods	Coaching	10
	Teaching/Mentoring	7
	Observation	5
	Facilitation	5
	Calming down	1
Challenges	Preserving authority	6
	Problem understanding	6
	Mindset	3
	Aligning plans	1
	Team changes	1
Skills	Agile knowledge	15
	People skills	12
	Coaching	4
	Teaching skills	3
	Facilitation skills	3
Value	Development of teams	7
	Influence	6
	Contextual	4
	Knowhow	2
	Measures	2

4   Results

In this section, we present the results of our case study following the order of our research questions. We first present the results regarding the objectives of agile coaches (RQ 1). Then, we examine what methods they use (RQ 2) and what challenges they encounter in their work to achieve the objectives (RQ 3). Next, we investigate what skills are required and used by agile coaches (RQ 4) and, finally, we probe what value agile coaches perceive they provide (RQ 5).

4.1   The Objectives of Agile Coaches

The first research question refers to the objectives of agile coaches. The results presented are from the perspective of those interviewed. We noted that the role of an agile coach is difficult to define. As one participant noted, *"this is a very big role"* and, as another stated, *"Agile coach is more like this umbrella term"*. Thus, the practitioners found it challenging to define their role. We, therefore, approach the role of an agile coach by exploring the objectives of an agile coach. Objectives, in this context, refer to what companies expect agile coaches to achieve. The objectives identified relate to training teams, aid teams in performing better, create and maintain spaces for knowledge sharing and discussions, identifying improvement opportunities, and helping individual team members.

We note that the most often mentioned objective is that of educating different stakeholders about agile methods. One participant noted that, as agile coaches, they work with *"a portfolio of trainings, which we do for the organization"*. The second most common objective relates to aiding teams. Several practitioners explained that their objective is to help teams perform better. For instance, one interviewee noted that their objective is partly to *"help the team to be together, to be in contact with each other, ... to help them to continuously focus on the goals"*. Part of this objective is to work with teams to foster better cooperation. One practitioner noted that *"...but also, more like human topics, like cooperation and what are the agreements between team members and how things are done"*.

Several practitioners also noted that, as part of their objective, they create and maintain different forms of communities (forums) that enable and foster knowledge sharing and discussions. One practitioner stated that *"I have done these gatherings knowledge exchanges for Scrum Masters and for product owners. ... I will talk about their role, what are their challenges..."*. Another objective we noted is that of identifying opportunities for improvement. Spaces dedicated to knowledge sharing and discussions can provide input for identifying improvement opportunities. As one practitioner stated, one of the objectives is that of trying to *"...identify things that we can work together, me and that person, to improve their way of working and for that I use this one on one Coaching"*. The scope of agile coaches is not restricted to teams only. Rather, agile coaches work with individual team members when needed. One of the agile coaches noted that they also work with *"solving personal development related problems"*.

4.2   The Methods Used by Agile Coaches

The second research question concerns what agile coaches do, i.e., how they achieve their objectives. Agile coaches adopt a cautious approach when working with teams. To achieve their objectives, agile coaches *"try not to help people, who do not ask for our help. ...If we see that something doesn't work, we are not the unit who will come and say hello guys, you are wrong. This is not our approach. We are helping only those who are willing to get our help. Because only in this case, there will be some results"*. Naturally, the method is, to some extent, dependent on the context. Practitioners might *"choose an approach according to the situation"*. However, some methods were mentioned more frequently.

The most frequently mentioned method was observation. Most interviewees mentioned that the first step is to observe. Agile coaches need to observe the team so to understand the current situation. One practitioner stated that *"...when I'm going to a new team, it starts with observation"*. Observation is used throughout the work agile coaches do. It is important for agile coaches to observe, for instance, the daily interactions and problem-solving methods of the teams they coach. Such observations are shared with the team as basis for discussion. For instance, one agile coach expressed that *"I will discuss my observations with the teams... and see what we are gone do about that."*.

It is worth to note that the COVID-19 pandemic developed at the time when the interviews were being conducted, and the Nordic countries went into lockdown. Therefore, companies changed their modality to the use of remote working. This introduced new challenges for conducting observations. The interviewees stressed the importance of physical presence during the observation and the limitations of online tools. One participant expressed: *"... if I'm used to observe peoples' body language, conversations, then this is lost [now], and of course, it makes it more difficult for me ..."*. The coaches also noted differences according to the experience of the teams, and particularly noticeable for new teams: *"When there is one new team, with them it's very hard, we have to create a vision and decide where we want to get with the team. Usually it's like this, that we come together with a team in one room ... and will not exit before we have a concept. Today it's very hard to do"*.

As expected, the activity of *coaching* was also mentioned. One participant expressed that *"... I try coaching as a discussion between me and the team"*. In addition to coaching, mentoring and teaching were mentioned as well. For instance, as one participant stated, *"...we have meetings and we discuss their situations and I talk about what's in the book and what other teams are doing and share the knowledge"*. Likewise, agile coaches teach the team about certain aspects of agile methodologies. For instance, shared that it is common to do *"...teaching, e.g. how to write user stories"*.

Facilitation is another method used by agile coaches. As one participant stated, *"I facilitate and put together different kind of workshops that are needed in order to improve the teamwork or the process, because for example there are teams, were roles are quite mixed up"*. Facilitation is not restricted to workshops, but also used for different ceremonies and *"the other thing is then retrospectives..."*.

Agile coaches interviewed have *"one-on-one talks"* with *"open questions"*. At times, when emotions run high, agile coaches employ methods for calming down, such as, *"...breathe deeply and be calm..."*

4.3 The Challenges that Agile Coaches Face

Agile coaches, when working with achieving their objectives, encounter challenges. Here, we explore the third research question of what challenges agile coaches encounter in their work. The most frequent challenge mentioned was about persevering authority. Agile coaches do not have authority to decide and enforce decisions. Often, the agile coach has the right experience and knowledge to know what will work and what will not. However, they work with educating and influencing the teams. As one participant expressed, *"Coaching itself, well mentoring is easy, but those situations, where you are like ... you are doing it wrong, I would so much like to tell you that, I have done it for years, this will work. This is the most painful thing"*. At the same time, they need to maintain a certain degree of authority so to be taken seriously, listened to, and their advice heeded. Thus, as one of the practitioners said, it is a challenge to *"preserving authority and being friend to the team at the same time"*.

Agile coaches need to understand the real problem that is to be solved. This is a challenge. To identify the real problem, both experience and time with the teams are required. Junior agile coaches have not yet accumulated enough experience to confidently identify the real problem. Experienced agile coaches who work with several projects, find it difficult to dedicate enough time to each engagement to identify the real problem. As one agile coach stated, *"there is a lot of running around and talking to people. ... I can say that, when working with many teams simultaneously, the Coaching quality or teaching quality ... drops, compared to the case when I would have the time to focus and physically be near to this one team, see their problems and understand how to help"*. Meanwhile, the expectations on agile coaches to find the problem and solve it is, at times, high or even unrealistic. As a practitioner expressed it, *"sometimes these expectations to the coach are that, he will come and fixes everything quickly and solves all the problems. But usually the problems are somewhere very deep in the organization, inside the culture of the organization ..."*.

Another challenge noted refers to working with the mindset of mangers and team members. As one of the interviewees expressed it, *"... people have previous mentality of waterfall and they are not used to this way of working that is maybe very dynamic for them or too dynamic in their opinion. They are used to think about the problem ... every detail of everything and then start to implement it..."* This challenge is not confined to only mangers, but also team members. In particular, when agile coaches work with guiding and aiding organizations to adopt agile practices. Furthermore, this challenge arises when companies implement an agile method as a plug in. For instance, one agile coach stated that *"many problems that I see, come from that, that people kind of take the model of Scrum, implement it in their organization and then say, it didn't work. ...it assumes, that you actually make structural changes in your company"*.

The interviewees also mentioned that confirming and aligning plans with stakeholders, is challenging. One participant stated that *"aligning with everyone, meaning the team, the key account manager, also POs would actually be happy and it would fit to everyone's plans. This is a challenge"*. Another challenge mentioned was that of dealing with changes, i.e., *"in my experience ... I have not had the luxury of having so stable teams ..., that I shouldn't make any changes, or the team should not make any changes or that there are no new members joining or leaving the team"*.

4.4   The Skills of Agile Coaches

Agile coaches, as noted above, perform their role as an "umbrella" when achieving one or several objectives. Thus, it is expected that the skills required by agile coaches varies. Furthermore, agile coaches are different and, thereby, require different skills. One agile coach noted that *"there might be different competencies, some people know more about products and are stronger in product management area. Every agile coach ...have their own handwriting, so quite often we are different and work differently ..."*. Nevertheless, we noted that the main skills required are either related to abilities to interact with others and knowledge about agile methods.

The most frequent skill mentioned related to knowledge about agile methods. Several in interviewees stressed that it is important to have knowledge about several agile methods and frameworks. As one participant said, *"first, there has to be like a strong knowledge of Agile Frameworks, not just Scrum, but preferably others as well ...;"*. It is not sufficient to know about the method, but one has to understand the process as well. One practitioner expressed that it is important to grasp *"process management ... kind of like an engineer, but not software engineer, but process engineer ... who understands systems and how they work ..."*. Furthermore, another practitioner emphasized, in addition to understanding of agile methods, the importance to believe in agile values: *"...he ... needs to believe in agile values ... he needs to understand why agile is important and how to implement it in a Software company ..."*.

Another frequently mentioned skill is "people skills" which was quite expected. As one practitioner expressed it: *"they need to be able to understand people and work with people"*. Closely related to people skills, are coaching, mentoring, facilitation, and teaching skills. For instance, one interviewee said *"Aaa, coaching, obviously..."* while another said, when discussing about skills, that *"... and others are like mentoring, so you mentor... in your teams"*. Given that agile coaches work with teams and train teams, it is also expected that they have facilitation and teaching skills.

Although this knowledge can be gained with experience, it is still necessary to have it as an agile coach. One of the participants explained that: *"... you can also start working as a Scrum Master very young, sort to say after school and I have seen some very good young people, who work as Scrum Masters, but let's say, for one to be good in their job, this is a thing, that comes with time ... it is not possible to learn to job of a Scrum Master so that I attend a course, read two books and start doing it ... yes, you have to know and understand the framework and have to have heard about the mindset, but addition to that comes the dimension of experience"*.

4.5   The Value Delivered by Agile Coaches

The fourth research question concern the value agile coaches deliver, as perceived by themselves. The value an agile coach can contribute with is dependent on the coach. As one practitioner said, *"it depends a lot on that, ... on what level you are ... with your maturity"*. Furthermore, the value agile coaches contribute with, is often not easily discernable. For instance, as one participant stated, *"...it's a lot of work behind the scenes. So, no one will ever congratulate the Scrum Master or the Agile Coach for some big success in the project, but they are holding the team together, holding the process there, making sure that everyone is doing the right thing at the right time"*.

Nevertheless, agile coaches add value to those being coached, such as team members, specific roles, teams, departments, or an organization, to become better in what they do. As one agile coach expressed it, an *"... agile coach is the person who helps organization to become their best the same way like usual coach, like life coach helps coachee to decide what to do with their life and to get the most out of this. Agile coaches help the organization but within some boundaries ... so agile coaches know quite a lot about ... agile ways of working, having expertise in this area, while there quite a lot of competencies for agile coaches, this is competence why agile coaches are hired and needed*". The value of agile coaches is not confined to making teams better in terms of agile practices. Agile coaches also add value by addressing aspects that help teams to be happy. One of the agile coaches interviewed expressed that an "Agile *coach keeps the mood up, by letting the people feel and understand, that they are always more important than the processes*". In addition, agile coaches deliver value with their knowhow born of their experience and knowledge. As explained by one of the agile coaches, "*one is relaying on his or her experience, and because of that, can actually give practical advice on the matters of agile software development*".

The value added by agile coaches is difficult to directly measure. None of the interviewed agile coaches reported their contribution having been measured quantitatively with, for instance, a Key Performance Indicators (KPI). The work of the coach is very dependent on the willingness and motivation of the team to work with the agile coach. Therefore, measuring the value should be a mutual responsibility. One practitioner expressed this idea that there has to be "*mutual responsibility. Because I cannot as an agile coach, we are not supposed to make the change, we are supposed to help the people to make change. And if we agree on something and counterparty is not doing this, then we cannot do anything with this.*".

However, when asked about how such value could be measured, their suggestions considered using indicatory measures, i.e., measuring aspects that could be used as indicators of value added. For instance, one participant proposed the 360 degrees feedback method from those who the agile coach worked with. As one participant formulated it, the "*only KPI that I can say right now, is 360 feedback. In case you get positive feedback, it shows that you have been doing something right*". Such a measure would indicate degree of satisfaction with the work of the agile coach i.e., "*when we are receiving this customer satisfaction surveys, they are positive, they mention for example our efficacy, our value ..., or how things are going in general*". These measures would indicate the value of an agile coach as perceived by team members. However, the value can also be considered from the perspective of the team. This could be measured, as proposed by the practitioners, clarity of the process and its implementation in the daily work. One participant expressed it as "*...what they need to do every day is clear for them and why do they do the things they do every day, how they translate it in to the bigger plan or the bigger vision, see why is it important, you see people motivated at work*". The idea of measuring the motivation, in particular, its expression in the mood of the team, was also stated. For instance, one agile coach expressed that an indicator is when teams "*... want to do things by themselves and not waiting for someone to give them work to do, they are proactive, if ... yeah it's basically the measurements ... but the biggest indicator is the mood in the room and how people take work*". Another way to measure the value, is to measure the performance of the teams. For instance, one agile coach thought it would be possible to use scrum charts, "*like measuring velocity, the burndown charts*".

5   Discussion

Defining the role of an agile coach can be a challenging task even for practitioners with several years of experience. The literature on the topic has related the role of an agile coach to other well-defined roles such as to that of the scrum master [1, 6]. From the interviews, we observed that both roles have several goals in common: to help teams with the implementation of agile practices, the achievement of their goals, and to facilitate the whole software development process. However, the interviewees stressed that they also have an educational goal (teaching) both teams and various stakeholders about agile methods and practices. Although coaches work with the team to mainly improve productivity, they emphasize the cooperation and communication of the team as a proxy to achieve the improvement. This is in line with the idea that human factors determine the performance of the team and the process [32].

Agile coaches use a variety of methods and strategies that are aligned to their objectives. Organizing group meetings and workshops are common when the agile coach has the goal of helping the team to identify improvement opportunities or solve a problem. When the coaches aim to educate, they use different strategies ranging from just explaining how to conduct specific practices (i.e., teaching/mentoring) to applying discussion-based meetings where theory and practice are contrasted. Moreover, observation is mentioned as the most frequent method since it is crucial to understand how teams currently work, the needs they have, and the problem they face. In this sense, observation *in situ* becomes a complementary and important method used to understand the context. In this line, Paasivaara and Lassenius [15] indicate that face-to-face communication is very important during coaching.

There seems to be an agreement that there are no silver bullet methods in software development, i.e., practices that work regardless of the context in which they are applied to [33, 34]. This stresses the need of empirical evidence supporting the effectiveness of agile practices in given contexts and ease the selection of agile practices [35]. We found that agile coaches rely on their experience combined with observations to identify the current problems and decide what practices are the best suited for the team. Understanding the problems of a team or organization is a very challenging task and frequently pointed out by the interviewees. The variety of methods used, and the challenges addressed by agile coaches affects what skills are required. An agile coach requires a blend of people skills and a solid understanding of agile practices and methods.

There are additional challenges that agile coaches must deal with. Preserving authority is important since agile coaches cannot decide or enforce decisions. They usually try to influence the team to go in the direction they consider to be the better one. Agile coaches also want to keep friendly relationships since they work daily with the team. However, some interviewees expressed that being friendly can sometimes compromise their authority. The most important challenge that agile coaches pointed out is related to the mindset of team members or managers. Previous experience with plan-driven projects can lead individuals to have a rigid position on how things should be done and create conflicts with agile dynamics. Interestingly, the mindset-problem has been seen often in organizations that embark on an agile transformation journey. In line with existing studies, this supports the fact that agile transformation requires an organization-wide agile mindset [4, 5, 36].

Regarding the value delivered, agile coaches perceive it differently. Some agile coaches express that their results are difficult to measure since they work with the teams to make them better. In this sense, considering the feedback reported by the team that received the coaching can be a meaningful measure. On the other hand, agile coaches understand that if the team works better, it should be reflected in their performance; thus, using Key Performance Indicators could be a way to indirectly assess their contribution to the team or organization.

6 Limitations

When using the case study methodology, there are threats to validity that should be considered, particularly regarding external validity and reliability [25]. External validity concerns the extent to which the findings can be applied beyond the setting of the study. Our case study represents the perception of eight agile coaches. Thus, these findings do not necessarily extend to cover the role of agile coaches. Although the objective of our study was explorative, further studies are required to confirm our findings. Thus, in line with the inherent limitation of the case study methodology, our results are limited in the extent they can be generalized. Reliability refers to the level of dependency between the results and the researcher, i.e. would the same results be produced if another researcher conducted the study. This threat was to some extent tackled by documenting the case study protocol, following a structured method for encoding, and applying several iterations for data analysis. Another reliability threat refers to the limitation to the coach own perspective. To address this limitation, further studies should include other important stakeholders of this role such as the people/teams being coached, and the sponsors/managers willing to pay for agile coaches in order to achieve a certain effect, impact, return, or value. To facilitate the replication of this study, we provide the interview guideline as supplementary material[3].

7 Conclusion

In this study, we explored the role of the agile coach by using a case study research method. We conducted interviews with several coaches and performed a qualitative analysis. We answered research questions regarding what objectives agile coaches have, what methods they use, what challenges they face, what skills are required by the role, and what value agile coaches perceive themselves to provide.

We found that the role mainly aims to educate and aid teams and stakeholders involved in the organization. To achieve these goals, coaches use different strategies such as observing the behavior of the teams *in situ*. Among the main challenges, coaches face issues to preserve authority and work with organizations or individuals without an agile mindset. The agile coach role requires a blend of people skills and a solid understanding of agile practices and methods, and their value is perceived by mainly improving team dynamics. We believe that our findings contribute to a better understanding of the agile coach role, the development of a professional identity, and offers a characterization that can be useful for practitioners that are new in the role.

---

[3] Interview guideline: https://doi.org/10.5281/zenodo.4074965.

Acknowledgement. This work was supported by the Estonian Center of Excellence in ICT research (EXCITE), ERF project TK148 IT, and by the team grant PRG 887 of the Estonian Research Council.

References

1. Schwaber, K., Sutherland, J.: The scrum guide. In: Software in 30 Days, pp. 133–152. Wiley, Hoboken (2015)
2. Huang, C.C., Kusiak, A.: Overview of kanban systems. Int. J. Comput. Integr. Manuf. **9**, 169–189 (1996)
3. Sampietro, M.: The adoption and evolution of agile practices. PM World J. Adopt. Evol. Agil. Pract. **V**, 1–16 (2016)
4. Conboy, K., Coyle, S., Wang, X., Pikkarainen, M.: People over process: key challenges in agile development. IEEE Softw. **28**, 48–57 (2011)
5. van Manen, H., van Vliet, H.: Organization-wide agile expansion requires an organization-wide agile mindset. In: Jedlitschka, A., Kuvaja, P., Kuhrmann, M., Männistö, T., Münch, J., Raatikainen, M. (eds.) PROFES 2014. LNCS, vol. 8892, pp. 48–62. Springer, Cham (2014). https://doi.org/10.1007/978-3-319-13835-0_4
6. Adkins, L.: Coaching Agile Teams: A Companion for ScrumMaster, Agile Coaches, and Project Managers in Transition. Pearson Education, Boston (2010)
7. Spayd, M.K., Adkins, L.: Developing great agile coaches towards a framework of agile coaching competency (2011)
8. Bass, J.M.: Scrum master activities: process tailoring in large enterprise projects. In: Proceedings of the 2014 IEEE 9th International Conference on Global Software Engineering, ICGSE 2014, pp. 6–15 (2014)
9. Davies, R., Sedley, L.: Agile Coaching. J. Chem. Inf. Model. **53**, 1–221 (2009)
10. O'Connor, R.V., Duchonova, N.: Assessing the value of an agile coach in agile method adoption. Commun. Comput. Inf. Sci. **425**, 135–146 (2014)
11. Hanly, S., Waite, L., Meadows, L., Leaton, R.: Agile coaching in British telecom: making strawberry jam. In: Proceedings of the Agile Conference 2006, pp. 194–202 (2006)
12. Victor, B., Jacobson, N.: We didn't quite get it. In: Proceedings of the Agile Conference 2009, pp. 271–274 (2009)
13. Cardozo, E.S.F., Araújo Neto, J.B.F., Barza, A., França, A.C.C., da Silva, F.Q.B.: SCRUM and productivity in software projects: a systematic literature review (2010)
14. Ebert, C., Hernandez Parro, C., Suttels, R., Kolarczyk, H.: Better validation in a world-wide development environment. In: Proceedings Seventh International Software Metrics Symposium, pp. 298–305 (2001)
15. Paasivaara, M., Lassenius, C.: How does an agile coaching team work? A case study. In: Proceedings of the 2011 International Conference on Software and Systems Process, pp. 101–109 (2011)
16. Pavlič, L., Heričko, M.: Agile coaching: the knowledge management perspective. Commun. Comput. Inf. Sci. **877**, 60–70 (2018)
17. Noll, J., Razzak, M.A., Bass, Julian M., Beecham, S.: A study of the scrum master's role. In: Felderer, M., Méndez Fernández, D., Turhan, B., Kalinowski, M., Sarro, F., Winkler, D. (eds.) PROFES 2017. LNCS, vol. 10611, pp. 307–323. Springer, Cham (2017). https://doi.org/10.1007/978-3-319-69926-4_22
18. Bäcklander, G.: Doing complexity leadership theory: how agile coaches at Spotify practise enabling leadership. Creat. Innov. Manag. **28**, 42–60 (2019)

19. Biddle, B.J.: Role Theory: Expectations, Identities, and Behaviors. Academic Press, Cambridge (2013)
20. Cox, E., Bachkirova, T., Clutterbuck, D.: The Complete Handbook of Coaching. Sage Publications, London (2018)
21. Wildflower, L.: The Hidden History of Coaching. Coaching in Practice Series. Open University Press, Maidenhead (2013)
22. Santos, V., Goldman, A., Filho, H.R.: The influence of practices adopted by agile coaching and training to foster interaction and knowledge sharing in organizational practices. In: Proceedings of the Annual Hawaii International Conference on System Sciences, pp. 4852–4861 (2013)
23. Kelly, A.: Changing Software Development: Learning to be Agile. Wiley, Hoboken (2008)
24. Althoff, S.: Qualitative interview-based research: an exploratory study on the role of the agile coach and how the coach influences the development of agile teams. Bachelor's thesis, Univ. Twente. (2019)
25. Runeson, P., Höst, M.: Guidelines for conducting and reporting case study research in software engineering. Empir. Softw. Eng. **14**, 131–164 (2009)
26. Yin, R.K.: Case Study Research: Design and Methods. SAGE Publications, Thousand Oaks (2017)
27. Flyvbjerg, B.: Five misunderstandings about case-study research. Qual. Inq. **12**, 219–245 (2006)
28. Kitchenham, B., Pickard, L., Pfleeger, S.L.: Case studies for method and tool evaluation. IEEE Softw. **12**, 52–62 (1995)
29. Merriam, S.B.: Qualitative Research: A Guide to Design and Implementation. Wiley, Hoboken (2009)
30. Johnson, L., Guest, G., Bunce, A.: How many interviews are enough? Field Methods **18**, 59–82 (2006)
31. Braun, V., Clarke, V.: Using thematic analysis in psychology. Qual. Res. Psychol. **3** 77–101 (2006)
32. Boehm, B., Turner, R.: People factors in software management: lessons from comparing agile and plan-driven methods. CrossTalk J. Def. Softw. Eng. **16**, 4–8 (2003)
33. Smith, P.G.: Balancing agility and discipline: a guide for the perplexed. J. Prod. Innov. Manag. **22**, 216–218 (2005)
34. Clarke, P., O'Connor, R.V.: The situational factors that affect the software development process: towards a comprehensive reference framework. Inf. Softw. Technol. **54**, 433–447 (2011)
35. Dybå, T., Dingsøyr, T.: Empirical studies of agile software development: a systematic review. Inf. Softw. Technol. **50**, 833–859 (2008)
36. Kilu, E., Milani, F., Scott, E., Pfahl, D.: Agile software process improvement by learning from financial and fintech companies: LHV bank case study. In: Winkler, D., Biffl, S., Bergsmann, J. (eds.) SWQD 2019. LNBIP, vol. 338, pp. 57–69. Springer, Cham (2019). https://doi.org/10.1007/978-3-030-05767-1_5

Impediment Management of Agile Software Development Teams

Pascal Guckenbiehl and Sven Theobald[✉]

Fraunhofer IESE, Fraunhofer-Platz 1, 67663 Kaiserslautern, Germany
{pascal.guckenbiehl,sven.theobald}@iese.fraunhofer.de

Abstract. *Context:* Many agile software development teams deal with blockers that prevent them from working efficiently and achieving their (sprint) goals. There is few guidance concerning impediment management, only that you have to collect impediments and specify them in the impediments backlog. Therefore, many teams developed individual solutions to approach impediments. *Objective:* This paper should help to understand how agile teams identify, document and solve impediments in practice. *Method:* Seven semi-structured qualitative interviews were conducted with agile practitioners from German companies. *Results:* An overview of different ways teams might handle their impediments is provided. Based on the results, an initial model of the impediment management process is proposed. *Conclusion:* The results of this study support practitioners when defining or improving the way they deal with impediments.

Keywords: Agile · Impediments · Impediment management · Impediment identification · Impediment documentation · Impediment resolution · Interview study

1 Introduction

Within the software engineering community, agile development approaches are increasingly used [1]. Agile methods, especially Scrum [2] as the most popular agile method [1], help teams to manage complex products. An important aspect of agile approaches is the continuous improvement of the team, guided by the principle of "inspect & adapt". The Agile Manifesto [3] defined the principle as follows: "At regular intervals, the team reflects on how to become more effective, then tunes and adjusts its behaviour accordingly" [3]. An important factor in this context are so-called impediments, which are literal obstacles that hinder the team in working efficiently and restrict overall productivity, such as poor communication or technical debt. Agile methods use mechanisms like daily synchronization meetings or regular retrospectives in order to identify these impediments. In general, impediments may originate from within the team or can be caused by the external environment. These external impediments usually appear when an agile team has dependencies to other teams or organizational parts. Many different problems can arise, especially when the agile team has to collaborate within a traditional environment [4].

© Springer Nature Switzerland AG 2020
M. Morisio et al. (Eds.): PROFES 2020, LNCS 12562, pp. 53–68, 2020.
https://doi.org/10.1007/978-3-030-64148-1_4

Although impediments play a major role in everyday agile work, there is not much guidance by agile methods on how to handle impediments systematically throughout their lifecycle from being identified to finally being resolved. Even Scrum as the most commonly used agile framework does not provide much insight regarding management of impediments. It is only recommended that the Scrum Master should be responsible for removing impediments and that the Daily Scrum helps to identify impediments. Since Scrum is only a framework, the details on how to exactly deal with impediments are intentionally left open. Due to this lack of guidance and the fact that Scrum implementations vary a lot [5], there are potentially many different approaches to handling impediments. Therefore, the primary goal of this paper is the investigation of these different approaches of impediment management in the context of agile software development. This paper is based on an interview study conducted in the context of a master's thesis [6]. Seven semi-structured expert interviews were carried out with practitioners from different companies. The knowledge gained this way is intended to encourage users of agile approaches to experiment and thus serve as the basis for improving individual processes and working methods with regard to impediments. They also provide a basis for in-depth research on this topic, which is not sufficiently represented in scientific literature yet.

The remainder of this paper is as follows: The current state of research based on related work is analysed and the contribution of the study is explained in Sect. 2. The study design, including research goal and questions, interview guideline and execution as well as data analysis, is described in Sect. 3. The interview results regarding the research questions, a proposition of an overall impediment management process and the limitations of this study are presented in Sect. 4. Finally, a conclusion and perspectives for future work are given in Sect. 5.

2   Related Work

For reasons of relevance, mainly recent work dealing explicitly with impediments in the context of agile software development was considered for the current state of research. Due to the strong thematic proximity, this might also include waste in the context of lean software development. Work related to domains other than software development was excluded for the time being. The focus is further on problems occurring in daily development practice. Accordingly, work that examines obstacles to the introduction of and transformation to agile and lean was not investigated. Sources already aggregated by the selected authors were not explicitly delved into explicitly either. Table 1 lists the results of the literature review chronologically.

In general, impediment management appears to be a relatively new research topic. Most of the related work is limited to the 2010s. Wiklund et al. (ID 1, see Table 1) used a case study to investigate which activities in the development process produce the most impediments. Power & Conboy (2) then combined the concepts of impediments and waste in agile software development and reinterpreted them using modern typing. In addition, Power (3) also dealt with techniques for the sensible handling of impediments. Larusdottir, Cajander & Simader (4) examined the constant improvement process through interviews, focusing on activities that either generate or do not generate value. Later Carroll, O'Connor & Edison (5) again aggregated essential related

Table 1. Related work

ID	Year	Author	Title
1	2013	Wiklund et al.	Impediments in Agile Software Development – An Empirical Investigation [7]
2	2014	Power & Conboy	Impediments to Flow – Rethinking the Lean Concept of 'Waste' in Modern Software Development [8]
3	2014	Power	Impediment Impact Diagrams – Understanding the Impact of Impediments in Agile Teams and Organizations [9]
4	2014	Larusdottir, Cajander & Simader	Continuous Improvement in Agile Development Practice – The Case of Value and Non- Value Adding Activities [10]
5	2018	Carroll, O'Connor & Edison	The Identification and Classification of Impediments in Software Flow [11]
6	2019	Alahyari, Gorschek & Svensson	An Exploratory Study of Waste in Software Development Organizations Using Agile or Lean Approaches – A Multiple Case Study at 14 Organizations [12]
7	2019	Power	Improving Flow in Large Software Product Development Organizations – A Sensemaking and Complex Adaptive Systems Perspective [13]

work and thus further deepened the classification of impediments according to Power & Conboy. Alahyari, Gorscheck & Svensson (6) dealt in detail with the adjacent topic of waste, examining understanding, types, and handling in practice. Finally, Power (7) describes further practical studies for the validation of the existing types of impediments in his recently published dissertation and presents a more comprehensive framework for impediment management.

2.1 Wiklund et al. (2013)

For the paper "Impediments in Agile Software Development - An Empirical Investigation" [7] the authors conducted a case study in an organization that was in an early phase of agile transformation (Rational Unified Process). The aim was to find out in which activities of the development process the largest number of impediments occur. The participants were observed, artifacts such as task boards examined, and interviews carried out. The results show, among other things, that most of the impediments were related to the company's centralized infrastructure and project management. In particular, inadequate communication and coordination led to problems both within the development department and across departments overall. In addition, there was a shift in the responsibilities of self-organized teams and the associated need to redefine existing activities and processes. The training that would have been necessary to cope with this was insufficient.

2.2 Power and Conboy (2014)

In the paper "Impediments to Flow - Rethinking the Lean Concept of 'Waste' in Modern Software Development" [8] the authors deal with the eponymous impediments in modern software development. These are interdependencies that arise through the interaction of agents involved in complex, adaptive, and self-organized human systems. Ultimately, they hinder the optimal flow of work and thus the ultimate goal of creating value for the customer. In principle, the previously known types of waste are reinterpreted in the context of modern (agile) software development. The resulting categories are Extra Features, Delays, Handovers, Failure Demand, Work in Progress, Context Switching, Unnecessary Motion, Extra Processes, and Unmet Human Potential. These nine types are intended to support organizations in identifying and eliminating impediments.

2.3 Power (2014)

In the paper "Impediment Impact Diagrams - Understanding the Impact of Impediments in Agile Teams and Organizations" [9] the author presents a technique to support dealing with impediments. In addition to the definition and categorization already described, a possibility is shown to address such obstacles. The approach can be very helpful, especially if impediments exist in large numbers, for example in inexperienced teams. Basically, it makes it easier to prioritize and thus decide in which impediments to invest the limited time available to those affected. In principle, the approach is about visualizing previously collected impediments with regard to the two main criteria "impact" and "influence". The former describes the impact or the benefit that the dissolution brings. The latter relates to the question of whether the team can eliminate the impediment alone or whether outside help is needed. For a more detailed analysis, the individual quadrants can be supplemented by the "Risk" and "Duration" perspectives. In addition, the column for impediments, which can not only be solved by the team itself, can be divided into further columns for the relevant contact persons (e.g., other company areas and hierarchy levels). This makes it easier for the team to assess the existing impediments and decide which of them to address (first). It can be clearly seen how complex the resolution is, what benefits it brings, and which people need to be involved. In addition, the approach supports understanding impediments and their cause and thus forms the basis for sustainable improvements.

2.4 Larusdottir, Cajander and Simader (2014)

The paper "Continuous Improvement in Agile Development Practice - The Case of Value and Non-Value Adding Activities" [10] treats impediments or waste as starting points for improvements. Ten interviews were carried out with users of agile development approaches in different roles. The goal was to research which activities bring real added value and which do not. In addition, processes for continuous improvement and corresponding metrics were examined. The results show that especially involving the customer in the development process offered great added value for the respondents. However, implementation often turned out to be difficult, especially if the customer is not working with agile approaches himself. The majority of the respondents also stated that they did not use a defined process for continuous improvement. The main reason was the inability to effectively implement potential improvement approaches, which in turn demotivated the employees. The targeted measurement of improvements only took place very superficially, if at all. With regard to activities without any added value, the respondents identified partially completed work, delays, and shortcomings as the most important categories. Here, too, problems in dealing effectively with such factors existed. The authors also describe a partial misunderstanding of these types of waste by the respondents.

2.5   Carroll, O'Connor and Edison (2018)

Building on Power & Conboy's "Impediments to Flow", the authors further examined the classification of impediments in their paper "The Identification and Classification of Impediments in Software Flow" [11]. For this purpose, a structured literature search on impediments and waste in software development was carried out. Based on the five resulting papers (published from 2011 to 2017), ten additional types could be identified. These are: Lack of Equipment, Information Overflow, Deferred Verification & Validation, Defects, Outdated Information, Work-related Stress, Lack of Staff, Ineffective Communication, Poor Planning, and Centralized Decision-Making. In addition, both new and old impediment types were combined into overarching categories. These primarily relate to the perspectives of development process, project management, and team dynamics. The paper also provides various insights into the possible causes and potential effects of the impediments.

2.6   Alahyari, Gorscheck and Svensson (2019)

The article "An Exploratory Study of Waste in Software Development Organizations Using Agile or Lean Approaches - A Multiple Case Study at 14 Organizations" [12] addresses waste in (agile) software development. This includes the general understanding as well as the most important categories and how to deal with them. To this end, people responsible for process and requirements in 14 different organizations were interviewed. The results show that the respondents saw the issue primarily as a matter of processes. The respondents' own definitions of different types included, for example, processes that are too long, incorrect requirements, or inadequate customer contact, and thus overlap strongly with the existing literature. With regard to the identification and elimination of waste, the respondents mainly focused on agile and lean methods and practices, such as retrospectives or Kanban boards. However, waste was largely dealt with at the team level and was only given limited attention at higher levels. The respondents therefore expressed a desire to raise general awareness for the issue within their organization. Many also lacked a uniform understanding of waste and the associated concept of value, which makes it even more difficult to deal with it. Finally, possible metrics were examined.

The majority of the respondents did not measure waste. Those who did used parameters such as defects and lead times.

2.7 Power (2019)

The author's dissertation with the title "Improving Flow in Large Software Product Development Organizations - A Sensemaking and Complex Adaptive Systems Perspective" [13] represents the most detailed and up-to-date work on impediments in (agile) software development. It builds on and expands the two previous contributions of the author described above. As part of the study, ten organizations in the field of software development were interviewed on various aspects of the topic, which are briefly listed below.

Categories. In the first part of the thesis, different types of impediments were identified by means of a literature review. The subsequent survey confirmed the results of the research. Additional processes, delays, and partially completed work were most frequently mentioned by the participants. The author also notes that such categories are only to be seen as a reminder. Ultimately, their exact titles only play a subordinate role for the effective handling of impediments, especially since in many cases no clear assignment to a certain category is possible anyway. Rather, it is about recognizing and understanding existing problems (and their causes). Furthermore, factors that favor the occurrence of impediments were examined. The most relevant factors were found to be too much work in progress, failure demands, and large batch sizes (for example with regard to the sprint backlog scope). They can generally be seen as congestion within the system. Finally, this part contains the possible effects of impediments. In particular, the impairment of product quality and employee motivation as well as excessive expenditure of time were mentioned.

Impediment Management Framework. In the second part of the dissertation, the author explains various aspects of a framework for dealing with impediments. The first step is to analyze patterns in the system that may affect the emergence of impediments. This in turn includes the technique of value stream mapping, the use of certain metrics, and the consideration of the organizational culture. The second step involves the concrete identification of impediments. Here, indications for the interpretation of corresponding patterns are given and the occurrence of several impediments is discussed. The importance of permanent monitoring of the system as a means of continuous improvement is also addressed. The third step describes how identified impediments can be better understood. The focus here is particularly on aspects such as their impact on the organization, human influence, and the context of the occurrence. The question of the avoidability of impediments also plays a role. In the fourth step, aspects regarding the resolution of impediments are presented. This is more specifically about their prioritization, general solutions, and the relevance of changes in the system. Finally, the gradual improvement of understanding impediments in the course of the management process is described.

2.8 Conclusion and Contribution

In conclusion, it can be said that the related work is quite diverse. Publications primarily deal with impediments themselves and research is done through practical studies and literature reviews. There is an overall consensus on the similarity and relationship between the concepts of impediments and waste. Otherwise, it is mostly about the categorizations of impediments. Here it becomes clear that these sometimes differ and can be continuously expanded and supplemented. A completely uniform and unambiguous designation of impediment categories seems neither possible nor expedient. Ultimately, however, similar or overlapping problem areas are described. Thus, the various works all make a relevant contribution to understanding the possible forms of impediments. Favorable factors, causes, and effects of such problems also play a role. The authors tend to deal less with the subject of impediment management though. In particular, there still seems to exist only little research regarding a comprehensive process for handling impediments. Basically, the study described in this paper expands the current state of research and aims to further fill this gap. Therefore, the focus lies on impediments in the practice of agile software development, especially the way teams may deal with them. The investigation of the actual impediment management of various companies provides new insights for researchers and suggestions for experimentation and improvements in practice.

3 Study Design

This section provides insights into the design of the underlying study on impediment management. The research goal and the corresponding research questions will be motivated first. Afterwards, the interview guideline will be presented and explained. The chapter concludes with information about the overall execution of the interviews and the data analysis procedure.

3.1 Research Goal and Questions

The goal of this research is to make a first attempt to understand how teams manage impediments in agile software development. The focus of this study is on teams since we expect neither a single person nor the company as a whole to be responsible for handling impediments. Though teams from other domains increasingly work with agile approaches, too, the focus of this particular study was on software development teams only. Agile approaches originated in software development, and many software development teams already have well-established agile processes as well as a corresponding culture. Based on the authors' initial understanding and experiences from work as/with Scrum Masters and Agile Coaches as well as the results of an Open Space session about impediments held at the XPDays Germany 2019, three major aspects of a possible impediment management process were defined: identification, documentation, and resolution of impediments. To take a closer look at these aspects, the following research questions were defined:

RQ1: How do teams identify impediments?
RQ2: How do teams document impediments?
RQ3: How do teams track and resolve impediments?

3.2 Interview Guideline

In order to answer the research questions, a qualitative study using semi-structured interviews was conducted. This study is based on interviews with practitioners that have experienced and dealt with impediments in their software development process. The interview questions were collected in an interview guideline (see Table 2) that contains 15 main questions (and several sub-questions, if needed) divided into three different parts. In the first part, the context of the company and the team is elicited. The second part covers each of the research questions in detail. Finally, the third part contains further questions about the impediment management process and about impediments faced by the participants. It should be mentioned that the questions of parts 1 & 3 were primarily included in order to gain additional insight for future research. Therefore, only the results of part 2, which directly answer the research questions of this paper, will be discussed later on.

The interview guideline was iteratively improved by the authors and finally reviewed by an independent researcher with a background in agile methods. The overall target population of this study were software development practitioners dealing with some form of impediments in their (agile) development process. Although the term "impediment" originated from agile methods, the target population was not intentionally restricted to practitioners of agile methods like Scrum or Kanban, since the ones following more traditional development approaches may deal with impediments as well (though probably referred to differently). For this reason, the term "impediment" was not explicitly defined by the authors during the interviews. Nonetheless, all of the participants were working within an (at least partly) agile environment, using agile methods or incorporating at least some agile practices in their development process.

Part 1 – Context of Company and Team. There are a number of factors that may affect the team, how they work, and what problems they have. The scope of the study does not yet allow quantitative statements and reliable conclusions in this regard, but the information might provide initial insights and ideas. It can further be useful for later in-depth research.

Part 2 – Impediment Management. This deals with how impediments are handled and thus represents the most important and extensive section of the interview. Information on the identification, documentation, and resolution of impediments is gathered through open questions, if necessary supported by more specific sub-questions. This should provide an overview of the most important practices within the participants' impediment management.

Part 3 – Further Questions. Finally, benefits and challenges of the participants' respective impediment management processes are examined. Furthermore, the nature

Table 2. Interview guideline

Part 1 – Context of Company & Team	**1** In which domain does the company operate?
	2 How many employees does the company have?
	3 What is your role within the company/team?
	4 What kind of team are you working with?
	5 How many members does the team have?
	6 How long has the (core) team been in existence?
	7 How long has the team been working agile?
	8 Which external dependencies does the team have?
Part 2 – Impediment Management	**1** How are impediments identified?
	a Where, when and by whom?
	2 How are impediments documented?
	a Is an (explicit) backlog or taskboard used?
	b Are problems or measures documented?
	c Are impediments estimated and planned?
	d Are impediments prioritized?
	3 How are impediments resolved?
	a Who is responsible for tracking progress?
	b Who is responsible for implementing measures?
	c Where are impediments escalated to (if necessary)?
	d How transparent is your impediment management?
Part 3 – Further Questions	**1** Does your impediment management support the continuous improvement of the team?
	2 Which challenges do you see regarding your current impediment management?
	3 Are the causes of your impediments more of internal or external nature?
	a Possible relationship/explanation (context, …)
	4 Which are your most relevant impediments?
	a Frequency, impact and complexity as guidance

of the causes of the impediments encountered by the participants as well as their most relevant impediments (or categories) is addressed. This information can again be used later to understand possible connections to context factors.

3.3 Interview Execution

As already mentioned, expert interviews form the basis of this study. An invitation was sent to 14 contacts from the authors' network. The invitation contained the goal of the study as well as the conditions for participation, such as the time required and the number of questions. Two of these contacts referred the invitation to a colleague they deemed more suitable for participating in the interview. Finally, seven of the contacted experts agreed to participate in this study, leading to a response rate of 50%. The period of interview execution was approximately three months, from November 2019 to January 2020. The interviews were scheduled based on the availability and the suggestions of the participants and then conducted via phone call. Each interview lasted between 30 and 60 min and was based on the open questions of the interview guideline. There were always two interviewers (both authors) involved, one taking over the moderation and one documenting the results and asking for missing aspects or clarification.

After a first introduction to goal and context of the study, the respondents were advised that all information provided by them would be treated anonymously, and that they could terminate the interview at any given time. Furthermore, they were offered the possibility to get the results to allow them to check their answers and, if necessary, correct or censor them. The respondents were asked to share the experiences regarding the impediment management process of their respective team from their own perspective and generally provide their personal perception and opinion. The interviewer always asked the more general main questions for each part of the guide first, only referring to the specific sub-questions if the respondents did not go into further detail. This approach was chosen in order to not guide the participants towards the authors' potentially restricted understanding of an overall impediment management process.

The respondents had the roles of managing director, Scrum Master, agile coach, team leader, and software developer, and were employed in medium-sized and large companies (200–30000 employees), primarily from Germany. These companies can be assigned to the automotive, finance & insurance, (software) product development, and retail sectors. The referenced teams were interdisciplinary software development teams with different specialist foci and dependencies. They comprised 5–10 employees, had existed for between 1 and 5 years, and had worked with agile methods and practices (at least partly) for the majority of that time.

3.4 Data Analysis

All interviews were documented in an Excel file in a predefined template corresponding to the interview guideline. The minutes taken by the moderating interviewer were merged with the more complete minutes taken by the documenting interviewer, and potential discrepancies were discussed and resolved between the two interviewers. As mentioned before, if the respondents requested it, the interview data was sent to them for review and validation purposes. Finally, all information was anonymized so that no conclusions can be drawn about individuals or companies. The data was analyzed qualitatively, summarizing and comparing the different ways the interview partners handled impediments with regard to the research questions. The analysis was carried out by the first author, who discussed the aggregated results with the second author.

4 Study Results

This section first summarizes the interviewees' answers qualitatively according to the research questions of this paper. Afterwards, an overview of the resulting impediment management process proposed by the authors will be given. Both can be utilized as suggestions for experimentation and to raise awareness on what to pay attention to when setting up or improving one's own impediment management process. Finally, possible limitations and threats to validity will be discussed.

4.1 Impediment Management

This section provides an overview of the impediment management of all respondents. A distinction is made between the three research questions (identification, documentation, and resolution). At this point, there is also further differentiation based on the associated sub-questions, which proved to be useful. An assessment of the approaches and practices does not seem to make sense here, since their expression depends heavily on the specific situation of the respective team or company. Accordingly, the following descriptions only represent a section from the state of the practice and therefore suggestions for experimentation.

RQ1: Identification

Impediments are primarily identified in agile meetings, such as the retrospective and the daily stand-up, and, if necessary, in a conversation between the Scrum Master and the team. Accordingly, impediment identification takes place in different time cycles: in retrospectives every 2–4 weeks, in daily stand-ups daily, and in personal conversation practically at any time. The respondents also differentiated between the number and the scope of the respective impediments. Retrospectives primarily address large, long-term problems and those that have grown over time, as well as opportunities for improvement. The daily stand-ups, on the other hand, focus on small, short-term, and acute blockers. Possible impediments can also be discussed or justified to the stakeholders in the Sprint Planning and Review. For teams with a lot of dependencies, an additional status meeting that takes place at greater intervals can help to make dependencies and resulting conflicts transparent.

RQ2: Documentation

Use of Backlogs. For the most part, impediments are documented as soon as they occur, both digitally and analogously. This can be done in a separate column on the team's task board, together with the product or sprint backlog items. It is also possible to use a separate impediment backlog or just a log of the relevant meetings (e.g., retrospective). The latter is particularly useful when minor problems can be resolved very quickly and therefore do not require extensive documentation. This is often the case with experienced and well-rehearsed teams. Which method is chosen further depends on the number and type of impediments and their handling and is probably a matter of preference. This also revolves around the question of whether the solution of impediments and the implementation of improvement measures contribute to overall value or not.

Problems vs. Measures. In general, both the documentation of the actual impediments (problems) and the measures for resolving them are justified. Some of the participants argued that only measures should be documented to promote proactive resolution and improvement. At the same time, however, this is not always possible since one might not be able to find a suitable solution immediately. In the sense of transparency, traceability, and performance review, documentation of the original problems together with the derived (short-, medium-, and long-term) measures appears useful. Impediments can then be treated as epic, for example, and solution approaches as corresponding tasks or items.

Estimation and Planning. As mentioned above, the estimation and planning of impediments or measures depends on the personal perspective of those involved. Some of the respondents estimated measures and planned them for the upcoming sprint, treating them just like Product Backlog Items. Others did not do an estimation, and their resolution was independent of the sprint. However, since time and resources are still used, the team's perceived productivity can be negatively affected in this case. A hybrid approach is also conceivable, depending on the size and complexity of the problem or solution.

Prioritization. In principle, it is possible to prioritize impediments and measures independent of estimates and planning. This can relate to all existing issues or take place after the ownership has been assigned to each responsible person. If impediments and product backlog items are treated equally, the product owner might prioritize them accordingly. However, since this might not be easy to implement, in most cases the team implicitly prioritizes by simply resolving those impediments first that are either hindering them the most or are rather quick to fix. Prioritization does not necessarily have to happen, but if there are more impediments than can be resolved in the course of a sprint or in the foreseeable future, it definitely makes sense.

RQ3: Resolution

Administration/Tracking. The management or tracking of the progress of impediments can be seen as a complementary function to the implementation of measures. The majority of the respondents stated that the Scrum Master (or a comparable role) has this function. If such a role does not exist, a team or project manager can also take on this task; in rare cases even the product owner or the team itself. Tracking includes progress monitoring, for example by addressing current impediments in the daily stand-up. Furthermore, the success of action points is checked at the end of the sprint, for example in the retrospective. It is discussed whether the corresponding problem has been resolved or the desired improvement has been achieved.

Implementation/Solution. In the sense of self-organization, the actual implementation of the measures for resolving existing impediments is in most cases the responsibility of the team itself. For this purpose, about 1–2 people can be appointed to take ownership of one or more impediments. The Scrum Master only takes on an enabling function here, which -depending on the experience and maturity of the team - can result in more or less active participation. In addition, the responsibility for the resolution can or must be passed on to other instances in some cases. Depending on the nature of the impediment and the structure of the company, other business units, leadership and management, as well as the organization itself may also be responsible. If it is not possible to find a solution since the impediment is caused by an unalterable context, an occasional meeting ("complaints round") can help to at least reduce some frustration.

Escalation. As already mentioned, the escalation of impediments describes the transfer of responsibility for their resolution. In general, this happens both professionally and hierarchically. The specific form depends on the company itself or on its size and structure. Some of the respondents escalated directly and spontaneously to the people needed for the resolution. Depending on the maturity of the team, the Scrum Master may act as an intermediary. In other cases, there are detailed escalation routes and dedicated appointments and meetings. In case of doubt, impediments can and must be escalated up to the highest management level. For large organizations and scaling agile frameworks (e.g. SAFe, LeSS or Nexus) [14], a cross-company instance explicitly intended for the escalation of impediments (enterprise level instance or enterprise change backlog) is also possible.

Transparency. The majority of those questioned stated that they strive to deal with impediments transparently. Regardless of how it is identified, documented, and resolved, the relevant information is openly accessible, at least among the team and the stakeholders. In most cases, there is even company-wide insight for anyone interested. This can, for example, accelerate problem solving, make team efforts more visible, and create general synergies. A mutually acceptable exception are sensitive issues, particularly social and interpersonal issues. These should remain within the team and be personally supervised by the Scrum Master in order to create and maintain trust.

4.2 Impediment Management Process

In accordance with the second part of the interview guideline (and research questions), the description of the participants' impediment management is broken down into three parts. These build on one another and in principle form a process for dealing with impediments from their first appearance to their resolution. Figure 1 shows this process and summarizes its parts as well as some relevant aspects for each of them. This should foster the general understanding and awareness of how impediments can be managed and might serve as a guideline for process improvement.

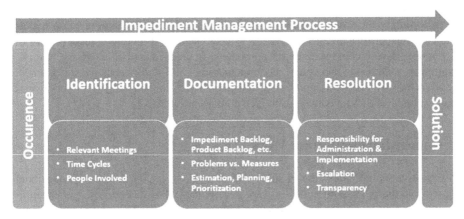

Fig. 1. Impediment management process

Identification. The first part deals with the initial occurrence of impediments and the way in which these are subsequently raised. More specifically, this includes the question of opportunities, e.g., meetings in which problems can be identified, time intervals for doing so, and the people involved.

Documentation. The second part focuses on if and how identified impediments are recorded in the long term. It differentiates between the use of an explicit impediment backlog and the documentation of issues together with the product or sprint backlog items. Furthermore, it matters whether the actual impediments or the measures for resolution derived from them (or possibly both) are recorded. The question then arises as to whether these are estimated and scheduled in the sprint or if the subsequent processing takes place independently. Finally, any possible prioritization plays a role.

Resolution. In the third and final part, the focus is on resolving the impediments. First of all, a distinction is made between who takes responsibility for their administration (general tracking of progress) and the concrete implementation of the (resolution) measures. This further includes the ways of escalation, should the team not be able to find a solution independently. Ultimately, this part also focuses on the question of transparency with regard to handling impediments.

4.3 Limitations

It should be mentioned that the participants' reports and the data collected generally only provide a snippet of reality and are in no way representative of the whole target group. Only seven interviews were conducted, in order to draw a picture of the state of the practice, more data would be necessary. There is also a threat regarding the selection of participants. Most participants were using Scrum, and the ways to handle impediments might be different in teams using other agile methods. Especially with teams using Kanban, the impediment handling might be different in a setting of continuous development instead of iterations.

Accordingly, the results of the study are only suggestions for improvements or opportunities for experimentation. However, in order to achieve a more complete picture of the possible impediment management approaches in practice, and, if necessary, to make quantitative statements and sound recommendations, the study needs to be deepened. Based on the insights of this study, using an adapted questionnaire, an online survey was already conducted in the context of the XP conference 2020.

5 Conclusion and Future Work

This paper essentially describes a study that examined how impediment management can work in the practice of agile software development. For this purpose, seven semi-structured expert interviews were carried out using a previously defined interview guideline. At the beginning, an impediment management process was defined based on three phases. These are the identification, documentation and resolution of impediments, whereby each part is characterized by different aspects. Based on this process, the participants were asked about the specific characteristics of the impediment management in their respective software development team. The various practices were then summarized to draw an initial picture of how an impediments management process might look like. The work thus expands existing research on the subject of impediments. The study offers essential new insights, particularly for the little-researched impediment management as a process and its possible forms.

In future work, the qualitative insights from this study have to be validated and confirmed by a larger number of participants. To this end, in-depth research was conducted in the context of the onsite research track of the XP conference 2020. A survey with users of agile approaches was carried out with the help of a slightly adapted questionnaire. The aim was to validate and, if necessary, supplement the 3-phase process and its specific practices established in this work. With a sufficient number of participants, statements on the dissemination of individual practices can possibly be made and corresponding best practices can be derived.

Finally, the various contextual factors of corresponding teams and companies and their impact on occurring impediments and how to deal with them should be examined in more detail. The variety of such factors could lead to an individuality that complicates clear recommendations. The investigation of this connection would therefore be of great importance for a guide for impediment management that goes beyond the mere mentioning of possibilities.

Acknowledgments. This research is funded by the German Ministry of Education and Research (BMBF) as part of a Software Campus project (01IS17047). We would like to thank all participants of our interview study, and Sonnhild Namingha for proofreading this paper.

References

1. VersionOne & Collabnet: 14th State of Agile Report (2020). https://explore.digital.ai/state-of-agile/14th-annual-state-of-agile-report. Accessed 10 July 2020
2. Sutherland, J., Schwaber, K.: The Scrum Guide. The Definitive Guide to Scrum: The Rules of the GAME. Scrum.org (2013)
3. Manifesto for Agile Software Development (2020). www.agilemanifesto.org. Accessed 10 July 2020
4. Theobald, S., Diebold, P.: Interface problems of agile in a non-agile environment. In: Garbajosa, J., Wang, X., Aguiar, A. (eds.) XP 2018. LNBIP, vol. 314, pp. 123–130. Springer, Cham (2018). https://doi.org/10.1007/978-3-319-91602-6_8
5. Diebold, P., Ostberg, J.-P., Wagner, S., Zendler, U.: What do practitioners vary in using scrum? In: Lassenius, C., Dingsøyr, T., Paasivaara, M. (eds.) XP 2015. LNBIP, vol. 212, pp. 40–51. Springer, Cham (2015). https://doi.org/10.1007/978-3-319-18612-2_4
6. Guckenbiehl, P.: Impediment Management in der Praxis agiler Softwareentwicklung. HS KL, Zweibrücken (2020)
7. Wiklund, K., Sundmark, D., Eldh, S., Lundqvist, K.: Impediments in agile software development: an empirical investigation. In: Heidrich, J., Oivo, M., Jedlitschka, A., Baldassarre, M.T. (eds.) PROFES 2013. LNCS, vol. 7983, pp. 35–49. Springer, Heidelberg (2013). https://doi.org/10.1007/978-3-642-39259-7_6

8. Power, K., Conboy, K.: Impediments to flow: rethinking the lean concept of 'waste' in modern software development. In: Cantone, G., Marchesi, M. (eds.) XP 2014. LNBIP, vol. 179, pp. 203–217. Springer, Cham (2014). https://doi.org/10.1007/978-3-319-06862-6_14

9. Power, K.: Impediment impact diagrams – understanding the impact of impediments in agile teams and organizations. In: Proceedings of the Agile Conference 2014, Kissimmee, pp. 41–51 (2014)

10. Lárusdóttir, M.K., Cajander, Å., Simader, M.: Continuous improvement in agile development practice. In: Sauer, S., Bogdan, C., Forbrig, P., Bernhaupt, R., Winckler, M. (eds.) HCSE 2014. LNCS, vol. 8742, pp. 57–72. Springer, Heidelberg (2014). https://doi.org/10.1007/978-3-662-44811-3_4

11. Carroll, N., O'Connor, M., Edison, H.: The identification and classification of impediments in software flow. In: Proceedings of the AMCIS 2018, New Orleans, pp. 1–10 (2018)

12. Alahyari, H., Gorschek, T., Svensson, R.: An exploratory study of waste in software development organizations using agile or lean approaches – a multiple case study at 14 organizations. Inf. Softw. Technol. **105**, 78–94 (2018)

13. Power, K.: Improving Flow in Large Software Product Development Organizations – A Sensemaking and Complex Adaptive Systems Perspective. NUI Galway, Galway (2019)

14. Theobald, S., Schmitt, A., Diebold, P.: Comparing scaling agile frameworks based on underlying practices. In: Hoda, R. (ed.) XP 2019. LNBIP, vol. 364, pp. 88–96. Springer, Cham (2019). https://doi.org/10.1007/978-3-030-30126-2_11

How to Integrate Security Compliance Requirements with Agile Software Engineering at Scale?

Fabiola Moyón[1]([✉])[iD], Daniel Méndez[2,3][iD], Kristian Beckers[4],
and Sebastian Klepper[5]

[1] Technical University of Munich and Siemens, Munich, Germany
`fabiola.moyon@tum.com`
[2] Blekinge Institute of Technology, Karlskrona, Sweden
`daniel.mendez@bth.se`
[3] fortiss GmbH, Munich, Germany
[4] Social Engineering Academy, Frankfurt am Main, Germany
`kristian.beckers@social-engineering.academy`
[5] Technical University of Munich, Munich, Germany
`sebastian.klepper@tum.de`

Abstract. Integrating security into agile software development is an open issue for research and practice. Especially in strongly regulated industries, complexity increases not only when scaling agile practices but also when aiming for compliance with security standards. To achieve security compliance in a large-scale agile context, we developed S^2C-SAFe: An extension of the Scaled Agile Framework that is compliant to the security standard IEC 62443-4-1 for secure product development.

In this paper, we present the framework and its evaluation by agile and security experts within Siemens' large-scale project ecosystem. We discuss benefits and limitations as well as challenges from a practitioners' perspective. Our results indicate that S^2C-SAFe contributes to successfully integrating security compliance with lean and agile development in regulated environments. We also hope to raise awareness for the importance and challenges of integrating security in the scope of Continuous Software Engineering.

Keywords: Secure software engineering · Scaled Agile Framework · Security standards

1 Introduction

Security compliance is a major concern for several industries [8,18]. Typically, security practitioners (and regulators) hold a holistic view on security affecting people, processes, and technology [8,19,20]. The perspective of practitioners, however, is rather dispersed and security is commonly treated as just another non-functional requirement [17]. Security engineering activities are further too

© Springer Nature Switzerland AG 2020
M. Morisio et al. (Eds.): PROFES 2020, LNCS 12562, pp. 69–87, 2020.
https://doi.org/10.1007/978-3-030-64148-1_5

often applied in an ad-hoc manner to a limited set of security problems, e.g., vulnerability testing or static code analysis [8]. Security concerns are often mixed with software functionality and limited to specific implementations like authentication or encryption [34].

Integrating security into lean and agile processes further intensifies these issues and constitutes a well-known research problem [1,17,35]. This is especially true for large software development projects. One challenge here is to fulfil requirements rigorously to comply with regulations while not limiting the speed and flexibility agile development methodologies promise. However security standards often require a series of processes to define, analyse, and mitigate security vulnerabilities [23] whereas lean and agile methodologies aim at avoiding rigid linear processes. While the agile manifesto states "to value individuals and interactions over processes", "collaboration over contract negotiation", and "responding to change over following a plan" [6], standards explicitly demand documented evidence of responsibilities, agreements, and established development procedures.

Our research shall provide a perspective for resolving this conflict through *Continuous Security Compliance*. In particular, we aim at implementing security standard requirements along with agile development methodologies. To this end, we analysed the issue in a large industrial setting and its currently applied norms: the Scaled Agile Framework (SAFe) as well as the IEC 62443-4-1 standard, later we propose a revised framework dubbed S^2C-SAFe . We chose the IEC 62443-4-1 standard for secure product development, released in 2018 based on previous secure product development standards such as BSIMM [25], ISO27034 [22], or Security by Design with CMMI [33]. Our framework shall maintain SAFe's perspective on development procedures and principles while capturing the essential requirements of security standards. In this paper, we contribute:

1. The proposal of our S^2C-SAFe framework, a security-standard compliant variant of the Scaled Agile Framework.
2. An evaluation of the S^2C-SAFe framework in large-scale software development environments. Given that the introduction of SAFe may take up to 8 years in the chosen organisational context, we conduct our evaluation in a preliminary manner focusing particularly on expert interviews.

We conclude our evaluation with the practitioners' perception of the challenges to achieve security compliance in a continuous manner. By sharing these insights, we particularly hope to raise awareness for the importance, but also challenges of integrating security in large-scale software development organisations following lean and agile principles.

2   Fundamentals and Related Work

Continuous Software Engineering (CSE) utilises lean and agile principles for a rapid and continuous "flow" of activities across business, development, and operations [16].

In their "Continuous *" model of CSE, Fitzgerald et al. [17] describe Continuous Security and Continuous Compliance as related but separate concerns and activities. *Continuous Compliance* (CC) seeks to satisfy regulatory compliance standards on a continuous basis rather than a "big-bang" approach to ensure compliance at release time [18,26]. *Continuous Security* (CS) elevates security from non-functional requirement to key concern by efficiently identifying and addressing security issues throughout all processes [16].

Related work discusses the suitability of agile methods for regulated environments [18] or the extensibility of their use [10]. With regard to security, authors focus on solving security aspects in agile environments, without considering regulations as focus [4,5,9,31]; or deriving security activities from a regulations perspective but lacking attention to lean and agile environments as well as corporate operating procedures, e.g., product life cycle [7,10]. Practical concerns of CS are: adapting the development process to security, better eliciting and tracking security requirements, and incorporating assurance into iterations [5].

Separating CS and CC is illustrated by Fitzgerald et al. [18], concluding that agile methods are suitable for security-critical environments, but not yet adopted in regulated environments.

We aim for *Continuous Security Compliance* (CSC): combining CC and CS through the holistic view of standardisation that spans across people, processes, and technology [20]. Regulatory requirements are utilised to derive security activities and therefore integrating security into a process while also making it standards-compliant [28]. Further work concentrates on security governance best practices [12]. This is complementary to prior work focused on the technology side, integrating security engineering into agile processes [1,3,8,11,13], or on the process side, integrating desirable but not standards-compliant security activities [1,2,32].

S^2C-SAFe is the result of applying this holistic principle to both a security-critical and a regulated domain: industrial and automation control systems. The result is an in-depth analysis of a security standard (IEC 62443-4-1) followed by the integration with lean and agile development practices represented by the Scaled Agile Framework (SAFe).

IEC 62443 constitutes a series of standards for network and system security published by the International Electrotechnical Commission (IEC). The standard focuses on requirements for component providers for industrial automation and control systems (IACS), part 4-1 describes process requirements for secure product development [21]. We reference this part of the standard as "4-1" or "4-1 standard". *SAFe* is a widely used process framework that scales lean and agile development to large organisations with multiple levels. It furthermore defines the corresponding roles, responsibilities, activities, and artefacts [24].

For such IACS environments our contribution aims to bridge the gap between lean and agile development, practical security, and compliance [34].

3   S²C-SAFe Framework in a Nutshell

The overall aim of our work is to improve product development life-cycle by integrating requirements of IEC 62443-4-1 into SAFe, resulting in the "Security Standard Compliant Scaled Agile Framework" (S²C-SAFe). Figure 1 shows how this is achieved by using visual modelling and by merging techniques as presented in our previous work [28]. Essential elements of SAFe and 4-1, such as roles, activities, and artefacts, were captured using Business Process Model and Notation (BPMN), a visual modelling language capable of expressing all of these aspects at once. After refining these models separately with expert practitioners, the process framework model is extended with elements from the security standard model, yielding the S²C-SAFe framework. Previously we found that a visual approach allows for more focused reviews than textual representation.

S²C-SAFe describes how requirements of 4-1 can be implemented within SAFe by showing when to involve roles, execute activities, or generate artefacts. It focuses on SAFe's Continuous Delivery Pipeline (CDP), where the actual product development occurs, and makes it compliant with security requirements (SR), secure implementation (SI), and security verification and validation testing (SVV). These scopes address concerns we captured from practitioners such as frequent vulnerability testing, security requirements traceability, or coding standards review. In addition to a CDP model integrated with SR, SI, and SVV, S²C-SAFe contains detailed models for each practice. Figure 2 shows an overview of the S²C-SAFe CDP. The full framework is available in the online material associated with this paper[1].

3.1   Security Requirements (SR)

SAFe does not specify where and how to elicit security requirements even though (security) requirements elicitation constitutes a major challenge both in practice and research [14], especially when developing a product threat model and deriving requirements to counter threats [5,15]. S²C-SAFe therefore explicitly considers security requirements at program and team level and makes them part of the Backlog, equal to all other requirements in prioritisation and traceability. Security Experts facilitate analysis but are not primarily responsible. Instead, Product Management, Business Owners, and Systems Architects are in charge so they become aware of threats. Similarly, the Product Owner requires adequate training to be able to prioritise and approve security requirements.

---

[1] https://dx.doi.org/10.6084/m9.figshare.7149179.

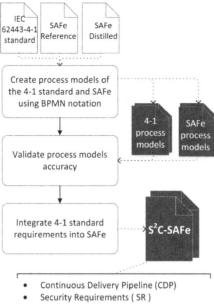

Fig. 1. Creation of S^2C-SAFe by generating and merging visual models of 4-1 and SAFe. Black document symbols designate our contribution. In previous work, we described the integration method [28]. The present contribution presents the S^2C-SAFe framework and its evaluation.

3.2   Secure Implementation (SI)

SI involves following secure coding standards to avoid vulnerabilities. S^2C-SAFe follows a process based on coding analysis as introduced in [2–4]. It defines coding standards early at program level during the PI Planning Event. Security Experts provide guidance so they suit domain and solution. To ensure that coding standards are followed, they are made part of the Definition of Done and agile teams as well as the product owner are trained accordingly.

3.3   Security Verification and Validation Testing (SVV)

SVV focuses on detecting and resolving vulnerabilities. One major concern is independence of testers which is enforced through independence rules during formation of agile teams. S^2C-SAFe also defines how further activities such as security functionality testing, vulnerability testing, or penetration testing apply to features, user stories, or both. It also defines criteria to keep resource allocation efficient and ensure continuous security testing, placing security functionality testing at team level and conducting all testing activities on program level before every System Demo. S^2C-SAFe contains models that shows a 4-1 compliant SAFe System Demo (see System Demo box in Fig. 2). Figure 3 is a more granular

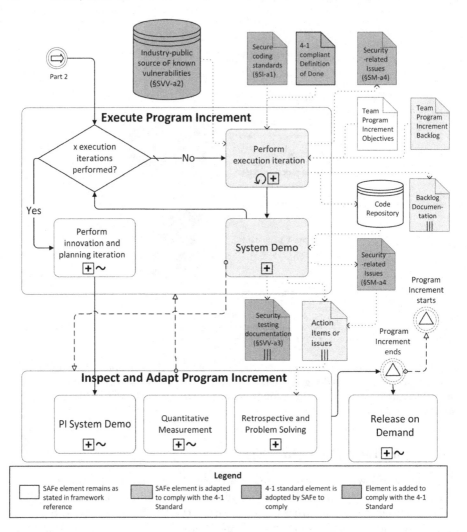

Fig. 2. Excerpt of S²C-SAFe Continuous Delivery Pipeline (CDP). This overview model describes the processes involved to execute and inspect a program increment as described in SAFe plus the artefacts required by the 4-1 standard in the practices of SR, SI, and SVV.

refinement showing testing tasks and artefacts, as referred by the 4-1 practice SVV, and their mapping to SAFe roles. Further models are available in the online material.

4   Study Design

We evaluated S²C-SAFe via expert interviews involving 16 practitioners working at Siemens in security compliance or (agile) software engineering. Among these experts are IEC committee members for 4-1 as well as SAFe core contributors.

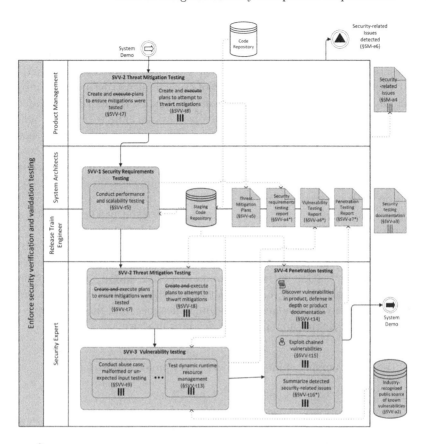

Fig. 3. S^2C-SAFe System Demo refinement model. Process diagram that depicts a new activity for SAFe System Demo to perform security verification and validation testing. A `Security expert` participates for certain types of testing while SAFe Program level actors are also responsible of security testing. Color coding is consistent with Fig. 2.

Our overall goal is to explore the meaningfulness of our approach to the needs in a practical context characterised by security-critical and large-scale agile development of software or software-intensive systems. Our evaluation is guided by the following two research questions:

RQ 1. From the perspective of practitioners, how applicable is S^2C-SAFe in this type of environment?
RQ 2. Which challenges do practitioners see when pursuing security compliance in this type of environment?

Our intention is to explore potential benefits and limitations of the here proposed framework. This shall lay the foundation for a roll-out that is minimally disruptive to the organisation and maximally intuitive for practitioners.

4.1 Subject Selection

In the industrial environment, where S^{2}C-SAFe is meant to be applied, projects are characterised by large-scale agile practices involving security experts on demand. Since industrial systems are part of critical infrastructure, such projects must comply with formal security standards, like the 4-1 standard when referring to product development. Such projects involve various agile teams with six people each. In those settings projects require direct cooperation between security experts and development teams.

We consciously selected from both groups: development teams working in these settings and security experts joining those projects on-demand, e.g., in conjunction with internal audits.

As these are all experienced professionals, we defined profiles to distinguish their level of expertise according to their key role. Table 1 shows each role's background and share of our 16 interviews. We distinguish top experienced subjects who contribute to the 4-1 standard (*Contributor IEC*) or to the SAFe framework and its dissemination within the company (*Contributor SAFe*). We further distinguish *Principle Experts*, having vast knowledge and leading teams, *Senior Experts*, having deep knowledge and guiding colleagues, and finally *Experts* who are responsible for setting up specific topics into practice.

Table 1. Mapping of interviews to subject profile and background.

Profile	Sample size	Interview numbers	Background
Contributor IEC	1	13	IACS software life cycle standardisation
Contributor SAFe	1	12	IACS agile development
Principal Expert	3	4, 5, 8	IACS security standards and processes, security life-cycle, security architecture
Senior Expert	4	1, 2, 6, 9	Cloud security, methods and tools for secure solutions, cyber security coaching, security processes improvement, IT security assessments
Expert	7	3, 7, 10, 11, 14, 15, 16	IACS agile development, quality compliance, development of access control systems, data privacy on smart cities, security design management, DevOps, security tools development, automated security testing, IT security in critical infrastructure

4.2   Survey Instrument

Since our goal is to explore practitioners' opinions about S^2C-SAFe , we identified semi-structured interviews as the most suitable technique [30]. Each interview lasted 1.5 to 2 h and took place in an isolated environment with one interviewee and two interviewers. One interviewer actively followed the questionnaire and the other one documented the answers and controlled attachment to interview protocol, available at our online material.

Each interview was dedicated to one S^2C-SAFe element according to the subject's background: SR, SI, or SVV (c.f. Sect. 3). Subjects were also introduced to the S^2C-SAFe CDP to have an overview of the processes involved the framework as shown in Fig. 4.

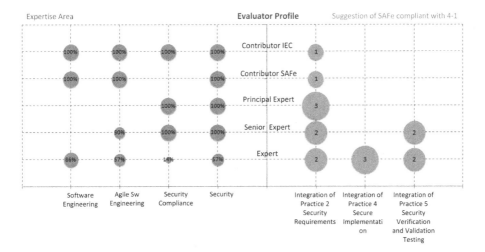

Fig. 4. S^2C-SAFe Suggestions distribution into profile groups. Right side: number of interviewees per suggestion. Left side: percentage of interviewees per expertise area.

Interviewers first briefed individual subjects about the interview flow and the purpose of S^2C-SAFe models as well as their hierarchy (overview model and individual practice models) but did not provide any instruction or training on the actual models. Then they showed a textual excerpt from 4-1 and SAFe, followed by the corresponding individual models and finally merged models from S^2C-SAFe . Subjects rated the perceived usefulness and practical applicability of each representation. Notes from throughout the interview were discussed before the interview's end to complete the picture.

5   Study Results

Evaluation is based on summarising the answers to closed questions and clustering comments and concerns according to commonalities. We further analysed the emphasis of answers to differentiate acceptance vs. conviction, rejection vs. repulsion, and neutrality vs. doubt. Hence, we tabulated answers according to a 9-point Likert scale. In the following, we summarise and interpret our results according to our research questions.

5.1 Subject Knowledge

In total we selected 16 subjects with different levels of knowledge about 4-1 and SAFe. Figure 5 shows that now all of them know 4-1 but all except one are aware of other security and safety standards such as ISO/IEC 27001 or other standards of the IEC 62443 family. Similarly, not all know SAFe but all are familiar with other agile process frameworks such as Scrum.

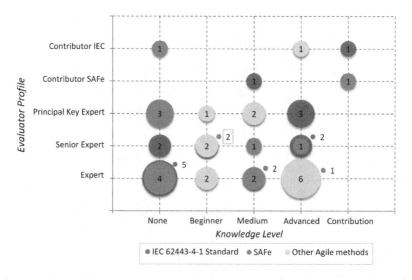

Fig. 5. Subject knowledge of IEC 62443-4-1 and SAFe or comparable process frameworks.

5.2 Applicability of S2C-SAFe (RQ 1)

We consider two aspects: applicability itself and potential implementation problems. Overall, while all interviewees strongly agree on the potential of using the integrated model as a means to foster discussions with their counterparts, they see potential problems in the integration of security aspects.

Applicability
S^{2}C-SAFe demonstrates that SAFe can be compliant with the 4-1 standard. All interviewees deem it usable in their environments and expressed their desire to use it for discussion with other practitioners (see Fig. 6). They particularly stated that it would provide a common language between security and development

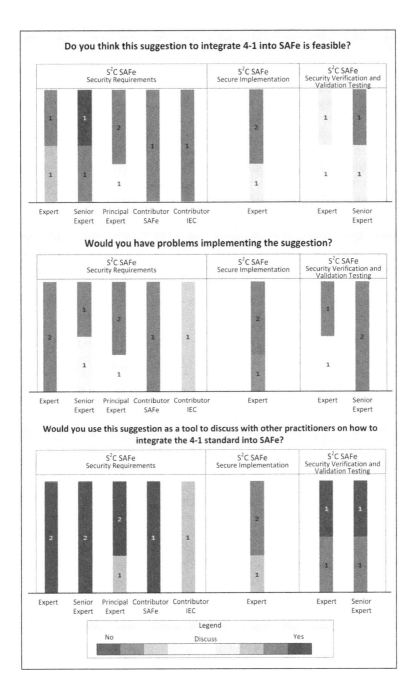

Fig. 6. Summary of opinions about S^2C-SAFe applicability based on suggestions regarding 4-1 practices.

fields; some even saw it as the only such tool they are aware of (see Table 2). The following paragraphs give detailed results for each of the 4-1 practices introduced in Sect. 3.

SR: Subjects strongly agree that this suggestion is feasible. A *principal expert* (#8) did not give a positive answer, but instead argued about the complexity of having security experts within teams in general. Almost all envision problems during implementation, most relate to the lack of security practitioners, team security awareness, or split security requirements. *Contributor SAFe* thinks that proposed security activities overload PI planning while *contributor IEC* sees no problems if models are shown only to people that design processes and not to agile team. However, all subjects plan to use the suggestions as a discussion tool with their respective counterparts.

SI: Subjects strongly agree that this suggestion is feasible. One DevOps *expert* (#7) argues that educating the product owner on security is complex. Instead they propose a "security product owner" who would be capable of extending the definition of done (DoD) with security aspects. In contrast, an *expert* product owner (#14) remarks the adapted DoD as a key to apply. An *expert* security consultant (#11) is confident that problems would exist although they cannot refer to any specific one.

SVV: Although overall positive, opinions on feasibility of this suggestion are not as decided as previously. Two respondents (#11 *expert* scrum master and #1 solutions security *senior expert*) find the suggestion feasible and well integrated. Another security *senior expert* (#6) is concerned about automation support for testing non-functional security aspects and about effort for security practitioners. A security assurance *expert* (#3) argues about the role and interactions of security practitioners throughout the process. Hence, all of them envision problems related to the integration of automatic testing, workload, and expertise of security practitioners.

Additionally, as interviewers we experienced that S^2C-SAFe improves communication among practitioners with different profiles and backgrounds. We actively discussed interviewees' issues on security and agile development. All explanations were based on the models we provided. Subjects with the highest level of knowledge (*Contributor IEC* and *Contributor SAFe*) challenged us with management or operational questions, e.g., how to implement or even potentially bypass certain aspects. We succeeded in explaining our perspective purely by pointing out specific model aspects. Conversations were dynamic, indicating a common understanding between interviewer and interviewee. Table 2 summarises key opinions on S^2C-SAFe while Table 3 lists noteworthy remarks.

Potential Implementation Problems

Our interviewees raised concerns regarding implementation of S^2C-SAFe in their project settings. They are particularly interesting to us as they help steering future adaptations and because some concerns are rather general challenges on

Table 2. Summary of key opinions on S^{2}C-SAFe.

Opinion	Interviews
Facilitates common language to discuss between security experts and agile team	2, 5, 14, 16
Solution is a comprehensible, clear guide	4, 5, 7, 8
Increment effort and workload	5, 6, 9, 12
Concern about roles expertise to accomplish tasks: Product Owner, Product Management	3, 4, 6, 10
Need to increase security awareness	1, 3, 7, 8
Concerns on expertise and profile of security experts	1, 4, 10
To have security practitioners within agile teams is challenging	8, 10
Need to have a deep understanding of own process to implement suggestion	1, 16
It is the only tool available	7, 11
Concerns about fit activities into short cycles	8, 12
Find color-coding is useful	7, 13

Table 3. Interviewees' statements on S^{2}C-SAFe.

Quote	Interviews	Profile	Background
Big advantage, we could speak same language as SAFe experts. This would dramatically reduce problems to adapt SAFe. Yes, I would love to use it as a discussion tool	2	Senior Expert	Security compliance
It makes sense what you did. If it is not possible SAFe is broke	4	Principal Expert	Security research
Sure is feasible, how to measure success I wonder	5	Principal Expert	Head security group
It is a very nice way to reduce complexity to discuss	7	Expert	DevOps
Visibility of security into agile development environment. Transparency of what is being achieved	9	Senior Expert	Security assessments
Sure, there is nothing else. I don't think there is anything	11	Expert	Security consultant/Scrum practitioner
We need to involve a pilot implementation	12	Contributor SAFe	Head development group
I will use it as a basis to communication	14	Expert	Product Owner
I like it. It makes dedicated to think about security	15	Expert	Systems Architect

the integration of security, let alone continuous security engineering. These concerns can be summarised as follows:

Models Should Guide Instead of Comprehending Compulsory Processes
One *senior expert* argued that if a model is too strict, people will not adapt it and bypass compliance efforts (#1). The suggestions seem difficult to implement in iterations or in specific program increments. This seems particularly true for security testing (vulnerability/penetration) prior to or during a *System Demo*. This highlights the need for an incremental prototypical implementation of individual suggestions to shed light on potential adaptation barriers which might differ in dependency to the practices and the roles.

Achievement of Security Expertise and Awareness
During the design phase, we emphasised that S^2C-SAFe cannot compensate for a Product Owner with knowledge of 4-1. Our interviewees confirm that this holds not only for general SAFe roles but also for security practitioners in general. Both security and agile development experts agree that security expertise for each part of the solution requires specialisation. Such specificity on profiles would aggravate the deficit of security professionals. Exemplary statements are "During verification of compliance, people tend to deviate from the standard" (#7) or "Lack of experience on security compliance leads to failed projects" (#3, security *expert*).

Difference Between Agile and Express Development Delivery
Security is generally perceived to be something that slows down agile development processes. Some exploratory questions revealed that agile time constraints are not followed in our settings, e.g., daily meetings last more that 15 min. Our concept of agile therefore seems to relate more to iterative and incremental development than to express delivery and integrating security-related activities will surely expand this gap further. While we understand the need for a trade-off between effort and cost for adapting security (or any other quality facet) this aspect seems particularly hard to achieve and constitutes an open issue.

5.3 Continuous Security Compliance Challenges (RQ 2)

The interviewees were asked to mention priorities among the security activities described in the 4-1 development life cycle. *Security requirements* (SR) seems to be the most challenging practice for our interviewees. Other priorities differ per profile, as shown in the examples for *security management* and *security verification and validation testing*.

The top priority issue is raising awareness for security to achieve continuous security compliance. Second place is taken by an adequate prioritisation of security aspects and common perspectives among management and teams. Challenges for security integration into continuous software engineering seem similar to those with linear development models. Subsequently we summarise our key findings on the challenges raised.

Security Requirements Elicitation: Challenges go beyond elicitation, from prioritisation over allocating them to increments and tracking adequate testing. Respondents extend the concern to overall 4-1 activities into cycles, e.g., threat analysis, testing, or issue management. Some related quotes include "What does the standard says about iterations and when the required process should occur again?" (#15, software architect) or "Problem is to identify what is the most important and which things can be done in parallel" (#12).

Security More Than a Non-Functional Requirement: 4-1 contains an overview of security as described by compliance. Our interviewees state that security is normally addressed via functional requirements while other aspects, such as management-related ones, are too often left behind.

Software Architecture Impact: Software architectures are built incrementally in continuous development. One interviewee argued in particular: "How to have security design or requirements of something we don't know yet, something we create on the go" (#12, *Contributor SAFe*). We argue that security analysis can be done while thinking about the goal and later iteratively extend it to the solution-specific components. However, this needs a certain continuity just like other non-functional properties, which project participants seem to see as difficult to achieve.

Improvement Demand for Security Expertise and Awareness: In development teams the lack of expertise for security seems to be a common theme [5]. Particularly, our group of interviewees seems to have a sound level or security awareness: "I see the need of security" (#15, product owner). They comprehend that challenges also depend on the role and therefore some interviewees even suggest to define new (agile) security-related profiles such as a "secure product owner" or a "secure system architect". Furthermore, respondents argue that security expertise should generally be improved to achieve compliance. This is exemplified in the following quote: "A new secure product owner could do it" (#7). Interestingly, these observations corroborate the need to raise a common awareness for security in the overall agile team: "implementations deviate from standard [and often] lead to fake implementations" (#2, security compliance *senior expert*); "There are guidelines to bypass compliance rules" (#8, security *principal expert*).

Security Compliance as a Common Agreement: Related to our previous observation is that subjects perceive compliance as a complex endeavour. They noticed that management, teams, and even compliance practitioners have different perspectives on compliance. Some see security compliance as a burnout journey, others as a luxury and others again as a worthwhile goal. A common agreement on the need to achieve common security standards is therefore a prerequisite for the success of our undertaking.

Misunderstandings of Agile Engineering Terms: In our interviews we noticed that terms are used often in a cumbersome manner. For instance, subjects with agile development knowledge (e.g., #1, #2, #3) often referred to Scrum only implicitly by mentioning specific elements such sprint, iteration, and product owner; "definition of done" was often used when referring to acceptance criteria; other interviewees had difficulties in capturing the notion of artefacts in context of process models: "the word artefact is not easy" (#10, *expert*). As a matter of fact, such key concepts are still subject to current debates and need further attention in future work generally dealing with software processes [27].

6   Conclusion

In this paper we reported on our work towards integration of security requirements derived from IEC 62443-4-1 into large-scale agile development based on SAFe in order to facilitate CSC. We presented the S²C-SAFe framework and evaluated it based on interviews with 16 industry experts. Evaluation results strengthen confidence that this approach and the resulting models provide a feasibly way for security compliance in large-scale organisations practising lean and agile development.

6.1   Impact and Implications

Results show S²C-SAFe models have a clear impact for practitioners. They show precisely how software engineering and security practitioners have to interact to achieve the goal of security compliance. Furthermore, the models can be understood in a time-effective manner and challenge popular belief that agile processes are a gateway to chaos and therefore not reconcilable with security and compliance concerns. The unanimous response to our work was the exact opposite: Introducing large-scale agile processes demands a culture and mindset change. Even though not our intention, the models helped to convey to sceptical practitioners that both secure and agile development is feasible at scale with reasonable effort.

Our research strongly indicates that models are an excellent way to mediate between agile practitioners and security experts. Particularly visual models allowed them to engage the challenge of continuous security compliance together. Moreover, these models pave the way for analysing various further challenges of the research field: Do models increase the speed of adapting large organisations to secure agile processes at scale? Are models a better way of getting security norms accepted in daily software engineering activities? Can models provide guided and precise support for secure agile security governance? We are confident that our contribution supports researchers to further investigate these questions.

6.2   Relation to Existing Evidence

Our study is in tune with existing trends of empirical studies on secure software engineering [29], but extends the study population in number and profile. To the best of our knowledge, preceding studies involved up to 11 practitioners with mixed background or students as subjects and focused on valuated, yet isolated topics. An integrated view on a security standard compliant agile framework was not in their scope. Our contribution is aimed at this gap and involves 16 experienced professionals, partially with contributing roles to the standards or decision-making roles in the organisation. We focused on the highest ranking experts available. As explained, a SAFe integration may last up to 8 years and the interviewees are high-ranked professionals. Their opinion is the closest to certainty in a timely evaluation.

6.3   Limitations and Threats to Validity

Qualitative studies inherently carry limitations and interview research in particular has threats to validity that need discussion, the most important of which shall be discussed here.

The individual expertise of each participant might influence their attention and interpretation of security requirements as well as agile practices captured in the models. We tried to mitigate this with discussion-intensive preparation procedures, but also by letting subjects interpret the models as they are without any further instruction. We were interested in potential bias towards the subject of security compliance as that reflects on the projects where those models shall be applied.

Similarly, involving experts from each respective field carries the risk of self-selection and confirmation bias. To mitigate this we selected subjects according to typical roles in the target organisation environment instead of their particular interest in the topic. The same is true for which part of S^2C-SAFe they reviewed (requirements, implementation, or testing). We also designed interview plan and questionnaire accordingly and allocated interviewees to models based on previously defined profiles.

Overall, our study already strengthens our confidence in the capability of S^2C-SAFe to integrate security and compliance concerns with lean and agile development. We cordially invite researchers and practitioners to join our endeavour towards facilitating continuous security compliance in large organisations and regulated environments.

Acknowledgements. To the practitioners that evaluate this work and to M. Voggenreiter and F. Angermeir for their accurate review.

References

1. Ahola, J., et al.: Handbook of the Secure Agile Software Development Life Cycle. University of Oulu, Finland (2014)

2. Baca, D., Boldt, M., Carlsson, B., Jacobsson, A.: A novel security-enhanced agile software development process applied in an industrial setting. In: Proceedings of the ARES (2015)
3. Baca, D., Carlsson, B.: Agile development with security engineering activities. In: Proceedings of the ICSSP, pp. 149–158. ACM (2011)
4. Baca, D.: Developing Secure Software -in an Agile Process - Doctoral Dissertation. Blekinge Institute of Technology (2012)
5. Bartsch, S.: Practitioners' perspectives on security in agile development. In: ARES (2011)
6. Beck, K., et al.: Manifesto for agile software development (2001)
7. Beckers, K.: Pattern and Security Requirements - Engineering-Based Establishment of Security Standards. Springer, Cham (2015). https://doi.org/10.1007/978-3-319-16664-3
8. Bell, L., Brunton-Spall, M., Smith, R., Bird, J.: Agile Application Security. Enabling Security in a Continuous Delivery Pipeline. O'Reilly, Sebastopol (2017)
9. Beznosov, K., Kruchten, P.: Towards agile security assurance. In: Proceedings of the NSPW. ACM (2004)
10. Cawley, O., Wang, X., Richardson, I.: Lean/Agile software development methodologies in regulated environments – state of the art. In: Abrahamsson, P., Oza, N. (eds.) LESS 2010. LNBIP, vol. 65, pp. 31–36. Springer, Heidelberg (2010). https://doi.org/10.1007/978-3-642-16416-3_4
11. Chóliz, J., Vilas, J., Moreira, J.: Independent security testing on agile software development: a case study in a software company. In: Proceedings of the ARES (2015)
12. Daennart, S., Moyon, F., Beckers, K.: An assessment model for continuous security compliance in large scale agile environments - exploratory paper. In: CAiSE (2019)
13. Felderer, M., Pekaric, I.: Research challenges in empowering agile teams with security knowledge based on public and private information sources. In: Proceedings of the SecSe (2017)
14. Fernández, D.M., Wagner, S.: Naming the pain in requirements engineering: design of a global family of surveys and first results from Germany. In: Proceedings of the 17th International Conference on Evaluation and Assessment in Software Engineering. ACM (2013)
15. Fernandez, E.B.: Threat modeling in cyber-physical systems. In: Proceedings of the 14th International Conference on Dependable, Autonomic and Secure Computing (2016)
16. Fitzgerald, B., Stol, K.J.: Continuous software engineering: a roadmap and agenda. J. Syst. Softw. 1–14 (2015)
17. Fitzgerald, B., Stol, K.J.: Continuous software engineering: a roadmap and agenda. J. Syst. Softw. **123**, 176–189 (2017)
18. Fitzgerald, B., Stol, K.J., O'Sullivan, R., O'Brien, D.: Scaling agile methods to regulated environments: an industry case study. In: Proceedings of the ICSE. IEEE (2013)
19. Humphreys, E.: How to measure the effectiveness of information security (2017). https://www.iso.org/news/2016/12/Ref2151.html
20. IEC: 62443-1-1 Security for Industrial and Automation Control Systems Part 1–1 Models and Concepts. International Electrotechnical Commission, USA, 2014 (2014)
21. IEC: 62443-4-1 security for industrial automation and control systems Part 4–1 product security development life-cycle requirements (2017)

22. ISO/IEC: 27034 Information technology - Security techniques - Application security (2011)
23. ISO/IEC: 27001 IT - Security techniques - Information security management systems (2013)
24. Leffingwell, D., Yakyma, A., Knaster, R., Jemilo, D., Oren, I.: SAFe Reference Guide. Pearson, London (2017)
25. McGraw, G., Migues, S., Chess, B.: Building security in maturity model. https://www.bsimm.com/about.html
26. McHugh, M., McCaffery, F., Fitzgerald, B., Stol, K.-J., Casey, V., Coady, G.: Balancing agility and discipline in a medical device software organisation. In: Woronowicz, T., Rout, T., O'Connor, R.V., Dorling, A. (eds.) SPICE 2013. CCIS, vol. 349, pp. 199–210. Springer, Heidelberg (2013). https://doi.org/10.1007/978-3-642-38833-0_18
27. Méndez Fernández, D., et al.: Artefacts in software engineering: what are they after all? ArXiv e-prints (2018)
28. Moyón, F., Beckers, K., Klepper, S., Lachberger, P., Bruegge, B.: Towards continuous security compliance in agile software development at scale. In: Proceedings of the RCoSE. ACM (2018)
29. Othmane, L., Jaatun, M., Weippl, E.: Empirical Research for Software Security: Foundations and Experience. CRC (2017)
30. Shull, F., Singer, J., Sjøberg, D.I.: Guide to Advanced Empirical Software Engineering. Springer, London (2007). https://doi.org/10.1007/978-1-84800-044-5
31. Siponen, M., Baskerville, R., Kuivalainen, T.: Integrating security into agile development methods. In: Proceedings of the HICSS (2005)
32. Stephanow, P., Khajehmoogahi, K.: Towards continuous security certification of software-as-a-service applications using web application testing techniques. In: Proceedings of the CAINA (2017)
33. Technology, S.A.C.: Security by Design with CMMI for Development Version 1.3. CMMI Institute (2013)
34. Tøndel, I.A., Jaatun, M.G., Cruzes, D.S., Moe, N.B.: Risk centric activities in secure software development in public organisations. IJSSE 8(4), 1–30 (2017)
35. Turpe, S., Poller, A.: Managing security work in scrum: tensions and challenges. In: Proceedings of the SecSE (2017)

A Portfolio-Driven Development Model and Its Management Method of Agile Product Line Engineering Applied to Automotive Software Development

Kengo Hayashi[1](✉) and Mikio Aoyama[2]

[1] DENSO Corporation, Kariya, Japan
kengo.hayashi.j4d@jp.denso.com
[2] Nanzan University, Nagoya, Japan
mikio.aoyama@nifty.com

Abstract. In recent automotive systems development, realizing both variability and agility is the key competitiveness to meet the diverse requirements in global markets and rapidly increasing intelligent functions. This article proposes a portfolio-driven development method and its management method of APLE (Agile Product Line Engineering). The proposed method is intended to manage agile evolution of multiple product lines while increasing variability of products. To establish a portfolio management of development resources, it is necessary for an organization to manage multiple product lines on APLE in an entire development. We propose a portfolio-driven development method of three layers on APLE and its management method based on a concept of portfolio management life cycle. We applied the proposed management model and method to the multiple product lines of automotive software systems, and demonstrated an improvement of manageability with better predictability of both productivity and development size. This article contributes to provide an entire development management method for APLE, and its practical experience in the automotive multiple product lines.

Keywords: Software product line · Agile software development · Agile product line engineering · Portfolio management · Automotive software development

1 Introduction

The agility and rapid evolution of products is an urgent issue in developing software systems including automotive software systems. ASD (Agile Software Development) has been proposed and practiced for accommodating both agility and rapid evolution of products. ASD enables to evolve products incrementally in a short cycle time.

As an advanced development model of ASD, APLE (Agile Product Line Engineering), which integrates ASD and SPLE (Software Product Line Engineering), has been practiced for accommodating both agility and variability [4, 8, 13]. However, today's automotive software is demanded to even more agile and rapid evolution in the global

© Springer Nature Switzerland AG 2020
M. Morisio et al. (Eds.): PROFES 2020, LNCS 12562, pp. 88–105, 2020.
https://doi.org/10.1007/978-3-030-64148-1_6

market and intelligent functions including autonomous driving [5]. For the competitive advantage, it is necessary to establish a method of optimizing a trade-off triangle consisting of the requirements of the business, the product roadmap realizing its requirements, and the resources of organization [2].

In application engineering of SPLE, the development size of individual software product is relatively small [15]. However, when the delivery dates of a number of products derived from a product line close together, the demanded resources for the product development could pile up within a short development period.

To optimize a trade-off triangle in APLE, conventional management of a single product line is insufficient. It is necessary to extend the trade-off triangle into multiple SPLs, and establish a development model and its management method for agile development of multiple SPLs in an entire development.

Portfolio management has been practiced for decision making in investment and management under limited resources of an organization [14]. A portfolio is a collection of projects, programs and the other operations for achieving the business goals. The authors introduce the concept of portfolio management illustrated in Fig. 1, to manage multiple SPLs development under the constraint of resources in an entire development. The authors introduce the concept of portfolio management illustrated in Fig. 1, to manage multiple SPLs development under the constraint of resources in an entire development.

Fig. 1. View of portfolio [14]

In this article, we aim to optimize the trade-off triangle in an entire development over the multiple SPLs. We set a hypothesis that a resource constraint is the most stringent constraint on the development of multiple SPLs. Based on the hypothesis, we set the following research questions:

RQ1: Is it possible to apply portfolio management to a development model, as a mean of managing multiple SPLs in an entire development?

RQ2: What is a management method of agile development of multiple SPLs in an entire development based on the proposed development model?

RQ3: Is the proposed method effective in an actual development of APLE?

2   Related Work

(1)   APLE (Agile Product Line Engineering)

APLE is an integration of ASD and SPLE for meeting both agility and variability [8, 13]. The theme has been explored for more than a decade [4]. Since the two disciplines deal with significant different aspects of software development, approaches to integrate the two disciplines vary. The two disciplines may have conflicts. Therefore, it is still unclear how to integrate the two disciplines [8]. It is also mentioned that the adoption of ASD into automotive software development is considered difficult due to the stringent quality requirements and long-term practice on the rigid process [5].

In the previous work [6, 7], the authors proposed APLE, an integration of ASD and SPLE for automotive software development. The idea is to allocate fine grain development tasks of variant of SPL based on the delivery date and work load. However, the derivation and allocation of the variants of multiple products were not clearly modeled.

(2) Portfolio Management of SPLE

The portfolio management of SPLE is to govern the entire SPL based on PPA (Product Portfolio Analysis) [15]. By dividing a market segment into four areas with two axes of a market share and growth rate of a product, PPA estimates ROI (Return On Investment) of an SPL for the business strategy [1]. A concrete method of making a product strategy has been proposed. However, there are few works on the management of the portfolio after introducing an SPL [16]. Researches on the models and management in an entire development for individual application engineering are few so far.

(3) Agile Portfolio Management

To govern the agile development, a portfolio management needs to properly coordinate asset and investment management. Krebs defined portfolio as a combination of projects, resources, and assets, and proposed a management method for ASD [9].

To measure, monitor, and control a portfolio, ASD framework, such as Scrum, is applied [3, 11, 12]. The development plan is refined stepwise with statistical estimation using performance statistics for two to three months.

Leffingwell proposed a value-driven approach with a trade-off triangle [11]. The value-driven approach selects requirements with an estimate of the fixed resources and specified delivery date, as illustrated in Fig. 2. Based on the value-driven approach, Leffingwell proposed SAFe (Scaled Agile Framework) as a framework for a large-scale development, which consists of a development model and its management method to operate development resources with three layers of portfolio, program, and team [12].

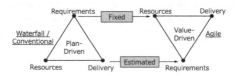

Fig. 2. Trade-off triangle for value-driven

Laanti proposed a management framework for ASD to develop a single product with multiple teams [10]. Turek proposed a management method of multiple projects [17]. However, an effective method is not established yet for products interdependent in an

SPL. A value-driven management framework is difficult to apply when the constraint of resources increases due to the dependency among products. In this article, we extend the method and applicability of this framework by analyzing and controlling the constraint of resources.

3   Approach

(1) Approaches to Research Questions

In this article, we propose the following approaches to the research questions.

RQ1: We propose a development model based on a portfolio-driven approach. We focused on the conflict between shared resources in portfolio management, and its resolution as a mean to manage multiple SPLs.

RQ2: We propose a method to manage multiple SPLs in an entire development with three layers of portfolio, program, and sprint, based on the development model.

RQ3: We apply the proposed method to the development of APLE of automotive software for ultrasonic sensor systems, and demonstrate the effectiveness of the proposed method

In the followings, we explain our portfolio-driven approach based on the discussions on the problems with plan-driven approach and value-driven approach in ASD.

(2) Approach to Problems in the Plan-Driven/Value-Driven Approach in SPLE

It is necessary to allocate the three variables of requirements, delivery date, and resources on a trade-off triangle for elaborating the strategy of development management [2]. As illustrated in Fig. 2, the plan-driven approach and value-driven approach are distinguished by the allocation of variables on a trade-off triangle [11].

In the SPLE, it is common that the products generated from an SPL are interdependent as illustrated in Fig. 3. However, when developing two products concurrently, the products may share and compete for the development resources, even if those are not derived from a single SPL. The dependency between the requirements of multiple products in an SPL may occur due to shared core asset. The core asset developed in a prior product development affects the subsequent product development. For example, if a variation point is generated in a prior product development, it may be necessary to select a new variant of the variation point in the subsequent product, and the requirements of the subsequent products may increase [7].

a) Problems in the plan-driven approach: The dependency between requirements causes problems in the plan-driven approach. If requirements are fixed in the plan-driven approach, the prior product development causes to change, usually increase, the requirements of the subsequent products, and increases the demand for development resources. Thus, it lowers the manageability of development. With the value-driven approach, the manageability can be maintained by trimming the requirements to keep the development resource within the allowable limitation.

b) Problems in the value-driven approach: The dependency between resources causes problems in the value-driven approach. If single product development, fixed release date can be maintained by adjusting the requirements. However, in the concurrent development of multiple products, each product may be set to different release date to different customers, and the development organization alone cannot set the release date. A new approach is necessary to the value-driven approach, which should resolve constraints with variables corresponding to the customer requirements.

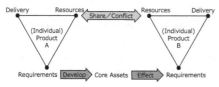

Fig. 3. Interdependence of trade-off triangle for SPL

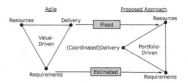

Fig. 4. Concept of portfolio approach: interdependence of trade-off triangle for SPL

(3) A Portfolio-Driven Approach

Figure 4 illustrates the concept of our portfolio-driven approach proposed in this article. In this approach, the resources are fixed, and the requirements are variable, and are selected based on the estimation. After that, the delivery date of the product is determined.

The concept of the proposed method is similar to that of the value-driven approach. However, the delivery date can be coordinated with the customer requirements. Therefore, the delivery date is not decided on the estimated date, but coordinated with the requirements under the constraints of the resources. As illustrated in Fig. 4, the delivery date is located to a middle point between fixed and estimated by inclining the trade-off triangle.

Changing the development resources is not easy due to the needed skills of the development domain. Therefore, we set the highest priority to the development resources of an organization. We call this approach as the portfolio-driven approach by resolving the constraints in an entire development on the requirements and delivery date over multiple products under the constraint of fixed development resources.

4 Portfolio-Driven Development Model

4.1 Overview of the Development Model

Figure 5 illustrates our portfolio-driven development model based on the portfolio-driven approach. Figure 6 illustrates the metamodel of the artifacts and the roles in an organization.

The portfolio-driven development model consists of three layers of management, that is the portfolio level, product, and sprint. By coordinating each layer, the trade-off triangle of requirements, delivery, and resources are optimized in an entire development over the multiple SPLs. We explain the details of each management level below.

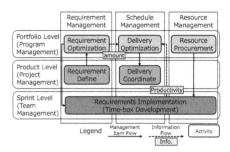

Fig. 5. Overview of portfolio-driven development model

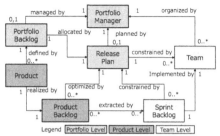

Fig. 6. Metamodel of artifacts and roles in the portfolio-driven development model

In the portfolio-driven development model, a product to be delivered is a component of the portfolio. Each product, is measured by the size of the requirement.

Shared resources for the development are measured by the value gained per unit time for realizing the requirement. We employ story point as the size metric of both requirement and resource to realize the requirement, similar to ASD. Multiple products can be managed in an entire development by unifying the size metric, i.e. story point, for the components and shared resources.

4.2　Portfolio Level (**Program Management**)

At the portfolio level, it is necessary to oversees the entire development for the products of multiple SPLs. Therefore, it is considered as a program management [14].

(1)　Structure of Portfolio

Each product is prioritized based on the trade-off triangle for the portfolio as illustrated in Fig. 4, that is, productivity of the shared resources, requirements for the products, required delivery dates of the products. Since dependency of requirements among products is unavoidable, it is necessary to analyze the dependency, and optimize the requirements and delivery dates based on the analysis.

Each product is registered to the portfolio backlog by the portfolio manager at the time of approval of its plan. The portfolio manager is a role taken by a project manager or PMO (Project Management Office). The role is necessary to make decisions over multiple SPLs.

(2)　Portfolio Management Model

At portfolio management, the portfolio manager is responsible to manage resource procurement, requirements optimization, and delivery optimization. We explain the activities in this section, and the details of the management method in the next chapter.

a)　Resource procurement: For resource procurement, the portfolio manager plans and acquires human resources, and organizes teams based on the business plan of SPL for long term of one to three years. The portfolio manager manages the change of resources needed for the development, and reorganization of the teams in order to meet the estimated resource needed to the development size of the products in the SPL.

b) Requirements optimization: For requirements optimization, the portfolio manager reviews the product backlogs elaborated at the product level, and prioritizes the requirements of the backlog with respect to productivities of the teams and delivery dates of the products as well as the impact to the other products in the same SPL. Requirement optimization aims to minimize the requirements for realizing all the components in the portfolio, and to maximize the requirements fitting in the coordinated delivery dates of each product.

c) Delivery optimization: For delivery optimization, the portfolio manager aims to stabilize resources by reviewing and coordinating the productivities of the teams and size of all the products of the multiple SPLs. The portfolio manager makes release plans of each product, and allocates products to a sprint of each team.

4.3 Product Level (Project Management)

At the product level, the project manager or product owner is responsible to product management.

(1) Structure of Product

Here, a product is a basic component of the portfolio. We measure the size of a product with the story point, a size metric, of requirements.

(2) Project/Product Management Model

At this level, project manager adjusts the project for meeting the requirements and delivery date coordinated at the portfolio level. Therefore, the project manager is responsible to define the requirements and coordinate the delivery date.

For requirement definition, the product owner or project manager defines the product backlog as development items of the product [3, 11, 12]. The product backlog is optimized by a release plan determined at the portfolio level. For delivery coordination, the delivery date of the product is coordinated with the stakeholders by considering the optimized requirements, resources required by the other products, and delivery date of the other products. Therefore, the project manager needs to work with the portfolio manager at the portfolio level.

4.4 Sprint Level (Team Management)

At the sprint level, team manager is responsible to manage the time-box development based on the ASD framework [3, 12]. Each team manager works with the product manager.

(1) Structure of Sprint

A sprint is a unit of the time-box iterated with a fixed cycle-time of one to four weeks. A sprint backlog is a collection of development items for a sprint. A sprint backlog is extracted from multiple product backlogs under the constraint of release plan [6, 17]. To measure the productivity of a team, we employ the size of shared resources.

(2) Team Management Model

The goal of team management at the sprint level is to stabilize the productivity. We introduced some techniques to APLE. For example, in SPLE, an iteration of development process is centered on the variability. Therefore, we employ the process assets concept [6], and structure the incremental development by analyzing the variability [7].

5 Portfolio-Driven Management Method

5.1 Management Life Cycle

Figure 7 illustrates the life cycle model of the management method based on the portfolio-driven development model explained in Sect. 4.

The life cycle model consists of the following six phases:

(1) Establish, (2) Evaluate, (3) Prioritize, (4) Select, (5) Manage, and (6) Feedback.

Five phases from (1) to (5) are based on the life cycle model of project portfolio management proposed by Wysocki [18]. We extended the life cycle model to accommodate multiple SPLs. To accommodate the dependencies between products, each phase is extended to coordinate and control the dependencies in multiple SPLs under the portfolio management.

5.2 Establish

The Establish phase is conducted at the portfolio level. Under the portfolio strategy of an organization, the portfolio manager plans a resource acquisition plan for one to three years based on the estimated size of products of multiple SPLs.

An initial plan of resource procurement includes an estimated number of developers for the teams and estimated resources. In the subsequent phases, the activities are conducted under the resource constraint planned in this phase. However, the plan can be refined at every specific period, e.g. three months, with the actual performance statistics of the productivity and size of delivering products obtained from the Feedback phase.

5.3 Evaluate

The Evaluate phase is conducted with a collaboration between the portfolio level and the product level. At first, the product requirements are estimated at the product level. Next, the estimation is refined by the optimization of the requirements of products of multiple SPLs at the portfolio level.

The Evaluate phase consists of three activities of:

(1) Optimization of the product requirements,

(2) Dealing with core asset evolution, and,
(3) Estimation of the product development size.

Optimization of the Product Requirements. The product requirements are optimized with respect to:

(1) Selection of an SPL for the development, and
(2) Impact caused by the dependency between the products in the SPL.

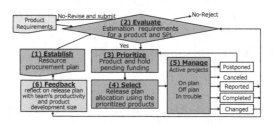

Fig. 7. Portfolio-driven management life cycle

When an organization develops multiple SPLs, the cost of realizing the requirements depends on the selection of an SPL from multiple SPLs. It is desirable to select an SPL, which can realize the highest priority requirements with the minimum cost. Suppose there are two SPLs on different platforms, and some functions are needed to develop on them. If the resources needed for adapting the functions to the platforms exceed that for developing new function after eliminating the difference of the functions between the SPLs, an SPL, which does not need the platform adaptation, should be selected.

If there is a product to be developed in the selected SPL, the product may have dependency to other products through the core asset, as explained in 3 (2). If it needs to change the commonality of the products and/or to add new variation points to the product, the cost to develop the product may increase significantly. Therefore, it is necessary to re-evaluate the development cost of the products. Suppose there is a product A developed already, and a product B to be developed. Since A is developed prior to B, if the requirements needed to B are already implemented in A, the development size of B can be reduced accordingly. If the development of A added new variation points, the development of B needs to configure the variation points. Therefore, the development size of B increases accordingly.

From the selection of an SPL, the requirements are prioritized. If there are requirements of low priority, those requirements are eliminated by the optimization of the product requirements, and optimization of product requirements completes. At this point, the development resource and release date can be set temporarily according to the estimated size of developing the SPL. If the development cost of all requirements included fits into the planned cost, the requirements are not eliminated any more. If the cost of developing all requirements exceeds the planned cost, it is necessary to further eliminate some requirements. The optimization activity helps to avoid resource shortage and contributes to increase ROI of an organization.

Dealing with Core Asset Evolution. If the core asset is required to change significantly, it is unlikely to develop products concurrently. Therefore, products are eliminated from management items. In this case, the development cost of the core asset of an SPL is considered as an investment, and development management is same as to conventional product management.

Estimation of the Product Development Size. From our experience, we found that the development size of the products has smaller difference within an SPL [6]. When the statistics of the actual development size of products in an SPL are collected in the Feedback phase, the development size can be estimated with a high accuracy by referring the statistics of developed products.

5.4 Prioritize

The Prioritize phase is conducted at the portfolio level. It determines the order of development of products based on the priority of the products. Each product has its own delivery plan. The priority is decided for improving the ROI of each delivery while keeping the delivery dates.

5.5 Select

The Select phase is conducted with a collaboration between the portfolio level and the product level. This phase optimizes a delivery plan through the following two activities:

(1) Allocation of the product to the release plan, and,
(2) Coordination of the delivery date.

Allocation of the Product to the Release Plan. A product is allocated to the release plan over the multiple SPLs based on the estimated product development size in the Evaluate phase, and the development priority determined in the Prioritize phase. To allocate the products, we employ the statistics of the productivities of the teams if available. Otherwise, we employ the estimated value.

A release plan is specified with a number of sprints of the fixed period. The story point of the product development of each sprint is allocated backward starting from the product delivery date.

Coordination of the Delivery Dates. The product delivery date needs to be coordinated if there is a sprint has an excess story point for the team when the allocation of the product for the release plan is completed. There are two resolution methods as explained below.

(1) Coordination of Delivery Dates of Individual Product

The delivery date of individual product is coordinated by reallocating the product to either prior or later sprint in order to fit the development size in the resources of each sprint.

(2) Coordination of Incremental Release Plan

The delivery dates of multiple products as the incremental release plan are coordinated through either consolidation of multiple deliveries of the products, or decreasing the development size of the delivery by dividing the delivery into multiple smaller deliveries.

Both coordination methods abovementioned require decision making at the portfolio level because the coordination involves trade-off at the portfolio level. It may cause a delay of value creation by fitting the development size within fixed resources by optimizing the delivery date, or cost overhead by additional releases. Therefore, this process aims to keep the product delivery within the contracted period, even resource shortage and resource conflict occurs. This is essential to sustainability in the organizational SPL development.

5.6 Manage

The Manage phase is conducted at the product level and the sprint level. According to the discipline of the ASD, we conduct time-box development at the sprint level, and project management at the product level.

The Mange phase deals with the products in the development, and the products to be developed. It manages to keep delivery date and scope of requirements. Therefore, if an event arises to detect change of the delivery date and/or scope of requirements, the Manage process transits to another phase. There are following five events triggering phase transition at the portfolio level:

(1) Postponed: When the product development is postponed, the Manage phase transits to the Prioritize phase and the product is set as not yet started.
(2) Changed: When the scope of the product requirements is changed, the Mange phase transits to the Evaluate phase to redo the requirements optimization.
(3) Reported: The Manage phase transits to the Feedback phase temporarily to report the completion of a sprint.
(4) Canceled: When the product development is canceled, the product life-cycle is closed.
(5) Completed: When the product development is completed, the Feedback phase is conducted and the product life-cycle is closed.

5.7 Feedback

The Feedback phase is conducted at the portfolio level. The input to the Feedback phase includes the size statistics of the product development reported from the product level and the productivity statistics of the teams reported from the sprint level. This phase aims to improve the manageability over the multiple SPLs by refining the release plan.

The size statistics of product are used in the estimation of the product development size in the Establish and Evaluate phases. The statistics also used for coordinating the delivery by dividing and consolidating the delivery of products in the Select phase. The statistics are categorized with respect to each SPL, each purpose of releases, and each release phase, which can be determined by domain and organization.

The productivity statistics of teams are used for allocation in the Establish and Select phases. In the case of agile development, the productivity is defined as the moving average of every seven sprints [3, 6]. The productivities of the team changes when developing a product of a new SPL of little knowledge, and when the team members are changed. Therefore, we define a set of nominal productivity.

6 Application to APLE of Automotive Software

6.1 Context of Application

We applied the portfolio-driven development model and its management method to DENSO's automotive system development using ultrasonic sensors. Figure 8 illustrates the development overview of the multiple SPLs of the automotive system on APLE.

Two organizations are involved in the development of the APLE. A core product development team, the core team hereafter, develops core assets for each SPL, and develops several products as the core products. A derivative product development team, the derivative team hereafter, develops derivative products from the core assets. One of the authors participated in the development as the portfolio manager. The effectiveness of the proposed method was evaluated with performance statistics collected from multiple product development projects.

6.2 Application Period and Operation of Teams and SPL

We applied the proposed method for 15 months from October 2016 to February 2018. Each sprint took 2 weeks. The number of SPL was four within the period. We delivered 12 products within the period, and collected the performance statistics.

Two teams, A and B, were organized as the development resources. Team A worked for 52 sprints. The number of developers of Team A changed from 2 to 5 and then to 3. Team B worked for 35 sprints. The number of developers of Team B changed from 2, to 3, to 5 and then to 7.

There was only one portfolio manager at the portfolio level. There were three project managers at the product level.

Fig. 8. Development of multiple SPLs of automotive systems on APLE

7 Evaluation

7.1 Evaluation Method

We evaluated the effectiveness of the proposed method with the following criteria:

(1) Predictability of productivity of resources,
(2) Predictability of development size of products, and,
(3) Controllability of a trade-off triangle.

By (1) and (2), we evaluated the accuracy of the control parameters for an entire development management of the portfolio-driven development model. By (3), we evaluated the validity of the management method.

7.2 Predictability of Productivity of Resources

In the portfolio-driven development model, a resource procurement plan and release plan are elaborated based on the productivity of each team. To apply the portfolio-driven development method with a high manageability, it is necessary that productivity is stable and predictable.

We introduce the metric of productivity volatility to evaluate predictability of productivity [6]. A productivity of a team is measured by the size of development of each sprint as used in the conventional ASD [3]. In this article, the productivity and productivity volatility are respectively defined by Eq. (2) and (3).

$$A\ sprint = 2\ weeks \tag{1}$$

$$Productivity(k) = \sum_{n=k-6}^{k} \frac{(an\ amount\ of\ development\ of\ sprint\ n)}{7}(k > 6) \tag{2}$$

$$Productivity\ volatility(k) = \frac{|productivity(k) - productivity(k-1)|}{productivity(k-1)} \times 100(k > 7) \tag{3}$$

Figure 9 illustrates the change of the size of development, productivity, and productivity volatility of two teams over the development period.

As noted in Sect. 6.2, the number of developers of each team changed during the evaluation period. The color of the bar chart representing the development size changed at the time of the number of developers changed.

Table 1 summarizes the distribution of productivity volatility of two teams.

The number of sprints that the volatility is less than 10% is 63, which accounts 85.1% of all the sprints. Focusing the time when team members changed, we infer that a high volatility of sprints over 10% is caused by the productivity change triggered by the change of members. As a conclusion, the productivity volatility was low, and productivity kept stable, and predictability of productivity was high for the periods when resources kept stable.

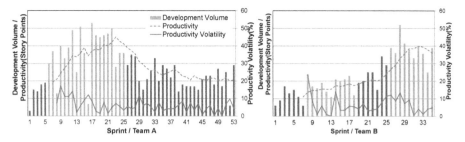

Fig. 9. Productivity and productivity volatility of each sprint

Table 1. Distribution of productivity volatility

Productivity volatility	<10%	<15%	<20%	≥20%	Sum
Number of sprint	63	9	1	1	74
Distribution (%)	85.1	12.2	1.4	1.4	100.0

7.3 Predictability of Development Size of Products

A development size of a product is used for a resource plan in the portfolio-driven development model. The development size is also used for the coordination of delivery date and fitting development volume within allowable resources. Predictability of development size of products is an important measure of project/program management. It is especially important to ensure the manageability of the portfolio-driven management method.

Table 2 illustrates the ratio of actual to estimate of development size of the products. The total number of releases is 48. At each release, the number of products varies, and they may be driven from different SPL. To evaluate the effect of the Feedback phase to predictability in the Evaluate phase, we classify the releases into the following three categories:

(1) No-Feedback: No statistics are used for estimation.
(2) One-Feedback: Statistics are used for estimation only once from the Feedback process.
(3) Multi-Feedback: Statistics are used for estimation twice or more in an iterative way from the Feedback process.

The average of the ratios is lower for one-feedback and multi-feedback than that for no-feedback. This result indicates that the Feedback process contributes higher accuracy of estimation. The standard deviation is also lower, and the volatility is improved by the Feedback process. Feedbacks improved the accuracy and volatility. As the conclusion, the Feedback process contributes to improve the predictability of the development size of the products.

Table 2. Ratio of the actual and estimate of development size

	No-feedback	One-feedback	Multiple-feedback
Number of samples	15	11	22
Average (%)	124.3	118.4	112.7
Standard deviation (%)	53.5	31.5	24.2

7.4 Controllability of a Trade-off Triangle

We evaluated controllability of the three entities of a trade-off triangle: requirements, delivery date, and resources. For the evaluation, we employed CoV (Coefficient of Variation), which is a ratio of the standard deviation from the average. The base metrics used for the evaluation of requirements, delivery dates, and resources are as follows:

(1) Requirements: Development size of 48 product releases.
(2) Time to delivery: Time to delivery by the coordination of delivery date under the condition that the period of one sprint is fixed to 14 days. If no coordination, the time to delivery is 14 days. If it is coordinated to postpone by seven days, it is 21 days. If it is advanced by seven days, it is seven days.
(3) Resources: The variation coefficient of resources within a sprint is zero in principle since the number of developers for each sprint is unchanged. Therefore, for further evaluation, we compare the capability of resources. Here, the capability is defined as the total size of developed products in a sprint while the number of the developers is the same. To evaluate the capability over multiple sprints, we use the average of coefficients of variation of all the sprints.

Table 3 summarizes the CoV of the three entities of the trade-off triangle.

Table 3. Coefficients of variation of the trade-off triangle

Object	Requirements	Delivery dates	Resources	Capability of resources
CoV	0.70	0.38	0.00	0.25

For the reference, we also include the capability of resources. The coefficients of variation are decreasing from requirements, delivery date, capability of resources, and to resources. With the proposed management method, we fix resources and reduce variations of capability of resources, and then optimize the trade-off triangle by changing requirements and delivery date. The statistics proved the validity of the management method in the application.

8 Discussions

8.1 RQ1: A Development Model to Manage Multiple SPLs in an Entire Development

(1) Predictability of Productivity of Resources

As discussed in Sect. 7.2, the proposed development model demonstrated superior stability and predictability of productivity of resources. The statistics proved that the proposed development method for APLE contributed to improve the stability of productivity. We conclude that combining the effects of reusing assets of SPLE and iterative learning disciplined in ASD contributed a high predictability.

(2) Predictability of Development Size of Products

As discussed in Sect. 7.3, the proposed development model demonstrated a high predictability of the size of developed products. Reusability is high in the development on SPLE. The statistics proved that the feedback structure in the management method improved the predictability.

Adopting the story point to measure the development size contributed to improve the predictability since the story point is a robust metric and reduces the variations of the actual size to the estimate [3].

We conclude that combining feedback process with the metric of story points contributes a high predictability and a low variation.

(3) Commonalities and Differences with SAFe

The proposed development model has some commonalities with SAFe, such as the management model consists of three layers based on the disciplines of ASD [12].

SAFe is value-driven, and the release cycles of products is fixed. SAFe is said to be effective in the case that the products evolve independently and linearly.

The proposed development model is portfolio-driven, and coordinates the release timing of products. This model is effective in the case that products have multiple variations which share some commonalities, and the delivery date of the products cannot be determined independently.

8.2 RQ2: A Management Method to Manage Multiple SPLs in an Entire Development

(1) Controllability of a Trade-off Triangle

As discussed in Sect. 7.4, the proposed management method controls the trade-off triangle by changing requirements and delivery dates. As the result, the method enabled to deliver 48 products for 15 months over four SPLs concurrently.

The requirements and delivery dates were optimized by not only coordination with the customers, but also sharing the release plan with the customers. We believe that the proposed management model helps customers to understand the development status and to foster the collaboration by sharing the state of resources, and the state of optimization of the requirements and delivery dates coordinated with other products.

(2) Conditions for Applying the Proposed Management Method

The proposed management method assumes that the requirements and delivery dates are changeable. In the development of automotive software, the requirements were adjusted due to the incremental development, and the manufacturing period of the hardware of the system was used as buffers for delivery dates, which is a unique condition of developing embedded software. If the requirements and delivery dates of the development are not allowed to change, the proposed method might not work properly.

We assume that multiple SPLs have dependencies, and that a development organization is not able to control the requirements and delivery date of the products independently. This is a common condition in the product development of multiple SPLs. However, if products have no dependencies, a simple management method is applicable. For example, the conventional value-driven approach, including SAFe, works properly if an organization can control the requirements and delivery date independently. However, product development of the multiple SPLs is not the case.

We also assume that the developed software has an architecture of a high reusability. On the reusable architecture, variation points are well defined, and development for the variation points is iterated in a similar way. If this is not the case, productivities and development size may not be stable even if the proposed development model is applied.

If the conditions above mentioned are satisfied, the proposed management method can be applied to the development over both SPLE and MPLE.

8.3   RQ3: Effectiveness in APLE

(1) Effectiveness of the Proposed Method in APLE

As discussed in 8.2(1), the proposed development model and management method are proven to be effective in the actual development of APLE. From the delivery statistics, we found that proposed method helps a high commitment to delivery. With the high predictability of the productivity and development size, the proposed method helps to ensure the delivery dates committed to customers even in the complicated development of products over multiple SPLs. Meeting the committed delivery dates helps to build a trust with the customers.

(2) Scalability

In the development, we assumed two teams and up to 10 developers in a team. We believe that the number of teams can be increased as similar to SAFe due to the same structure of management. However, if the number of SPL increases, possible conflicts on the same core assets may increase. If the number of releases increases, the coordination to optimize delivery date becomes complicated. An integrated management tools can relax the burden of management and support for scalability.

9 Conclusions

We proposed a portfolio-driven development method of three layers on APLE and its management method based on a management life-cycle process model. We applied the proposed management model and method to multiple SPLs of automotive software systems, and demonstrated an improvement of manageability with a high predictability of both productivity and development size. And we succeeded to optimize a trade-off triangle by controlling requirements and delivery dates. The proposed model and method are continuously used in the automotive development, and produced more than 100 products.

For future work, we plan to extend the development model to manage domain engineering in an entire development.

References

1. Bekkers, W., van de Weerd, I., Spruit, M., Brinkkemper, S.: A framework for process improvement in software product management. In: Riel, A., O'Connor, R., Tichkiewitch, S., Messnarz, R. (eds.) EuroSPI 2010. CCIS, vol. 99, pp. 1–12. Springer, Heidelberg (2010). https://doi.org/10.1007/978-3-642-15666-3_1
2. Blackman, B., et al.: Managing Agile Open-Source Software Projects with Microsoft Visual Studio Online. Microsoft Press, Redmond (2015)
3. Cohn, M.: Agile Estimating and Planning. Prentice Hall, Upper Saddle River (2005)
4. Díaz, J., et al.: Agile product line engineering-a systematic literature review. Softw. Pract. Exp. **41**(8), 921–941 (2011)
5. Ebert, C., et al.: Automotive software. IEEE Softw. **34**(3), 33–39 (2017)
6. Hayashi, K., et al.: Agile tames product line variability. In: Proceedings of SPLC 2017, September 2017, pp. 180–189. ACM (2017)
7. Hayashi, K., et al.: A multiple product line development method based on variability structure analysis. In: Proceedings of SPLC 2018, September 2018, pp. 160–169. ACM (2018)
8. Hohl, P., et al.: Combining agile development and software product lines in automotive. In: Proceedings of ICE/ITMC 2018, June 2018, pp. 1–9. IEEE (2018)
9. Krebs, J.: Agile Portfolio Management. Microsoft Press, Redmond (2008)
10. Laanti, M.: Is agile portfolio management following the principles of large-scale agile?. In: Proceedings of IEEE Agile 2015, August 2015, pp. 92–96. IEEE (2015)
11. Leffingwell, D.: Agile Software Requirements. Addison-Wesley, Boston (2011)
12. Leffingwell, D.: SAFe® 4.5 Reference Guide. Scaled Agile Inc., Boulder (2018)
13. Mohan, K., et al.: Integrating software product line engineering and agile development. IEEE Softw. **27**(3), 48–55 (2010)
14. PMI: The Standard for Portfolio Management, 4th edn. PMI (2017)
15. Pohl, K., et al.: Software Product Line Engineering. Springer, Heidelberg (2005). https://doi.org/10.1007/3-540-28901-1
16. Savolainen, J., Kuusela, J., Mannion, M., Vehkomäki, T.: Combining different product line models to balance needs of product differentiation and reuse. In: Mei, H. (ed.) ICSR 2008. LNCS, vol. 5030, pp. 116–129. Springer, Heidelberg (2008). https://doi.org/10.1007/978-3-540-68073-4_11
17. Turek, M., Werewka, J.: Multi-project Scrum methodology for projects using software product lines. In: Świątek, J., Borzemski, L., Grzech, A., Wilimowska, Z. (eds.) Information Systems Architecture and Technology: Proceedings of 36th International Conference on Information Systems Architecture and Technology – ISAT 2015 – Part III. AISC, vol. 431, pp. 189–199. Springer, Cham (2016). https://doi.org/10.1007/978-3-319-28564-1_16
18. Wysocki, R.K.: Effective Project Management, 7th edn. Wiley, Hoboken (2013)

Lean R&D: An Agile Research and Development Approach for Digital Transformation

Marcos Kalinowski[1]([email]), Hélio Lopes[1], Alex Furtado Teixeira[2],
Gabriel da Silva Cardoso[2], André Kuramoto[2], Bruno Itagyba[2], Solon Tarso Batista[1],
Juliana Alves Pereira[1], Thuener Silva[1], Jorge Alam Warrak[2], Marcelo da Costa[2],
Marinho Fischer[2], Cristiane Salgado[2], Bianca Teixeira[1], Jacques Chueke[1],
Bruna Ferreira[1], Rodrigo Lima[1], Hugo Villamizar[1], André Brandão[1],
Simone Barbosa[1], Marcus Poggi[1], Carlos Pelizaro[2], Deborah Lemes[2],
Marcus Waltemberg[2], Odnei Lopes[2], and Willer Goulart[2]

[1] Pontifical Catholic University of Rio de Janeiro (PUC-Rio), Rio de Janeiro, Brazil
{kalinowski,lopes,tarso,juliana,thuener,bianca,jacques,bruna,
rodrigolima,hvillamizar,andre,simone,
poggi}@exacta.inf.puc-rio.br
[2] Petrobras, Rio de Janeiro, RJ, Brazil
{alex.teixeira,gscardoso,kuramoto,itagyba,jawk,mceloscosta,
marinhof,cristiance.salgado,carlos.pelizaro,delemes,
marcuswaltemberg,odnei,willer}@petrobras.com.br

Abstract. Petrobras is a large publicly-held company that operates in the oil, gas and energy industry. Recently, they conducted internal dynamics to identify several Digital Transformation (DT) opportunities to leverage their operational excellence. Addressing such opportunities typically requires Research and Development (R&D) uncertainties that could lead traditional R&D cooperation terms to be negotiated in years. However, there are time-to-market constraints for fast-paced deliveries to experiment solution options. With this in mind, they partnered up with PUC-Rio to establish a new DT initiative. The goal of this paper is to present the Lean R&D approach, tailored within this new initiative, and results of two case studies regarding its application in practice. We designed Lean R&D integrating the following building blocks: (i) Lean Inceptions, to allow stakeholders to jointly outline a Minimal Viable Product (MVP); (ii) early parallel technical feasibility assessment and conception phases, allowing to 'fail fast'; (iii) scrum-based development management; and (iv) strategically aligned continuous experimentation to test business hypotheses. In the two reported case studies, Lean R&D enabled addressing research-related uncertainties early and to efficiently deliver valuable MVPs within four months, showing itself suitable for supporting the DT initiative. Key success factors were the business strategy alignment, the defined roles and co-creation philosophy with strong integration between Petrobras and PUC-Rio's teams, and continuous support of a highly qualified research team. Main opportunities for improvement, based on our lessons learned, rely on better adapting Lean Inceptions to the DT context and on scaling the approach to a project portfolio level of abstraction.

© Springer Nature Switzerland AG 2020
M. Morisio et al. (Eds.): PROFES 2020, LNCS 12562, pp. 106–124, 2020.
https://doi.org/10.1007/978-3-030-64148-1_7

Keywords: Digital transformation · Agile methods · Lean · Research and development · Continuous experimentation

1 Introduction

Digital transformation can be seen as a process in which organizations investigate the use of digital technologies to innovate their way of operating, aiming to solve business problems and to achieve strategic goals. The resolution of such problems frequently involves transformations of key business operations that may affect organizational structures, processes, and products [1]. Organizations of almost all industries are conducting digital transformation initiatives to explore digital technologies and exploit their benefits [1].

Petrobras is a large publicly-held Brazilian company operating on an integrated basis and specializing in the oil, natural gas, and energy industry. Internal efforts, including the establishment of a new digital transformation board and initiatives within their main business areas, enabled them to identify several opportunities in which digital transformation could potentially help them to leverage their operational excellence.

Digital transformation and innovating business processes by using digital technologies typically involve Research and Development (R&D) efforts. CENPES is the research center of Petrobras, responsible for coordinating and conducting research initiatives. Such R&D initiatives commonly involve cooperation terms with research institutes and universities. These terms were usually designed in a plan-driven manner, with deliveries that, given research uncertainties, could take up to years. However, in the digital transformation context, there are time-to-market constraints and a need for fast-paced deliveries to experiment solution options.

To address these digital transformation needs, they partnered up with PUC-Rio to establish the ExACTa (Experimentation-based Agile Co-creation initiative for digital Transformation) initiative. With a different mindset from the previously established R&D cooperation terms, ExACTa was created to work with an open scope philosophy, following agile practices for R&D to enable focused and fast deliveries of Minimal Viable Products (MVPs) that can be used to test digital transformation business hypotheses. The ExACTa initiative was launched in September 2019, and the first step involved designing an R&D approach that would allow fast MVP deliveries. The resulting approach was called Lean R&D.

The Lean R&D approach relies on agile and continuous software engineering principles, including establishing a strong link between business and software development (BizDev) and continuous experimentation practices [2]. Based on these principles, we designed Lean R&D integrating the following building blocks: (i) Lean Inceptions [3], to allow stakeholders to jointly outline the vision of Minimal Viable Products (MVPs) that can be used to test business hypotheses; (ii) parallel technical feasibility assessment and conception phases, allowing solution options to 'fail fast'; (iii) scrum-based development management; and (iv) continuous experimentation, to test the business hypotheses in practice, allowing a build-measure-learn feedback cycle [4]. Moreover, the initiative counts on a dedicated research team, specialized in data science and machine learning, to support the development team with parallel investigation activities.

In previous work, reported in a short paper [5], we provided an overview of the first conceptualization of Lean R&D and initial (then, incomplete) experiences. The goal of this full industrial paper is to present Lean R&D in further detail and to report on detailed outcomes of two complete industrial case studies, including closing the feedback cycle with continuous experimentation. Hence, besides providing a more detailed description, we investigate Lean R&D's building blocks in much more detail, discussing the practical experience of applying it, highlighting observed industrial effects.

The herein detailed case studies concern applying Lean R&D in practice to build digital transformation enabling MVPs for two different business areas of Petrobras: industrial and logistics. In both cases, following the approach, valuable MVPs were delivered to stakeholders within a four-month timeframe. Continuous experimentation allowed to test business hypotheses in practice, supporting strategically aligned product increment planning. Throughout these case studies, Lean R&D showed itself suitable for supporting the digital transformation initiative. The business strategy alignment, the defined roles and co-creation philosophy with strong integration between Petrobras and PUC-Rio's teams, and the continuous support of a highly qualified research team, were observed as key success factors. Main opportunities for improvement, based on our lessons learned, rely on better adapting Lean Inceptions to the DT context and on scaling the approach to a project portfolio level of abstraction.

2   Background

Before designing Lean R&D, we tried to find a suitable agile approach that was, simultaneously: (i) digital transformation enabling (e.g., including strategies such as 'fail fast,' focusing on added business value and testing business hypotheses); and (ii) considering joint research and development activities to allow handling complex R&D projects (e.g., investigating and conceiving simulation models). Lean principles have been reported to offer the potential to improve the cost, quality, and speed of the R&D process [6]. However, we found no Lean R&D approach that was tailored for software product based, digital transformation enabling solutions. Lean Startup [7], for instance, inspired us with its business focus but does not consider our specific need to integrate R&D activities within agile methods to allow handling complex and research demanding software projects.

The following two subsections provide the background on continuous software engineering [2] and Lean Inceptions [3]. We used the expected dynamics of the first one to pursue our goal of narrowing the gap between business strategy, development, and experimenting solution options. Lean Inceptions, on the other hand, were used to help to align stakeholders to define digital transformation enabling and business strategy aligned MVPs.

2.1   Continuous Software Engineering

Fitzgerald and Stol [2], in their paper providing a roadmap and research agenda for continuous software engineering, argue that business, development, and operations should

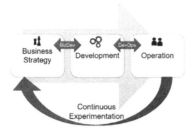

Fig. 1. Relations between business strategy, development, and operation. Adapted from [2].

continuously be aligned with each other. Figure 1 provides an adapted and simplified representation of such alignment.

The authors coin the term *BizDev* as the need to align the business strategy with the development of software [2]. *DevOps* represents the need to align the development of software with the deployment of that software into operation [8]. Finally, continuous experimentation focuses on conducting experiments with stakeholders consisting of repeated Build-Measure-Learn cycles [4, 9].

Reflecting on the implications of these alignments in the context of engineering digital transformation enabling software products, *BizDev* and continuous experimentation play a key role in achieving digital transformation goals. After all, digital transformation commonly involves changes in key business operations that affect business processes and enabling products [1]. A focus on *BizDev* and continuous experimentation helps to enable assuring the development of a business strategy aligned product and to assess the added business value objectively. The importance of continuous experimentation within digital transformation contexts is also highlighted by Fagerholm *et al.* [4]. DevOps, on the other hand, represents a technical competitive advantage to speed up the development process.

2.2 Lean Inception

Lean Inception is defined by its creator as the "combination of Design Thinking and Lean Startup to decide the Minimum Viable Product (MVP)" [3]. It is a collaborative workshop that is intended to help stakeholders to jointly outline the vision of a valuable, feasible, and user-friendly MVP that can be used to test business hypotheses.

The steps involved in a Lean Inception are: defining the product vision; characterizing and scoping the product vision; describing personas; describing user journeys; conducting features brainstorming; conducting a business, technical, and UX review; sequencing of features; and finalizing the MVP canvas.

The final result of a Lean Inception is an MVP canvas, as shown in Fig. 2. Based on such canvas, the business hypotheses to be validated can be stated as "We believe that *(MVP name)* will be able to *(outcome statement)*, we will know that this happened based on *(metrics for business hypotheses validation)*" [3].

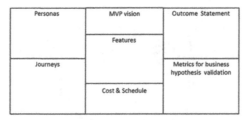

Fig. 2. Lean Inception MVP canvas. Adapted from [3].

3 The Lean R&D Approach

Our goal was to design an R&D approach for digital transformation, based on agile and continuous software engineering principles. CENPES and PUC-Rio's teams jointly brainstormed the following requirements as input for designing our approach.

R1: Maximize business 'value while minimizing 'waste'. A fundamental focus of the lean philosophy is to shorten the time between a customer order and the delivery of that order, in such a way that any activities that do not add 'value' are considered 'waste' and removed [10]. To achieve this goal, there should be a focus on the business strategy and its alignment with development (*BizDev*) [2]. We address this main requirement in our approach by: (i) using Lean Inceptions involving representative stakeholders aiming at precisely defining the MVP that best fits the business strategy and focusing on the essential features to deliver business value; (ii) defining the business hypotheses since the beginning and applying continuous experimentation to validate them; (iii) having dedicated business owner representatives at each customer to help co-creating solutions that maximize business value; and (iii) going for agile and only essential documentation (e.g., agile requirements [11]).

R2: Allow to 'fail fast'. This involves employing the Lean Startup 'fail fast' concept [7], which enables handling opportunities and risks involved in experimenting with digital transformation solution options. The sooner you realize that an idea will not work, the faster you can update it or even replace it with a new idea. This requirement is addressed in our approach mainly by: (i) including 'fail fast' checkpoints; and (ii) including a technical feasibility assessment at the beginning of the process to cope with research-related uncertainties as soon as possible.

R3: Enable addressing complex problems. Digital transformation commonly involves applying cutting-edge digital technology to solve business problems in domains in which they were never applied before. Therefore, our approach considers the co-creation of solutions with domain experts from the customer side and continuous support from a qualified research team with a dedicated research team lead and experts in technologies that are commonly used within digital transformation contexts, such as data science and machine learning techniques.

3.1 Approach Overview

Based on the aforementioned requirements, we decided to design the approach using as building blocks Lean Inception, parallel (early) technical feasibility assessment and conception phases, scrum-based development management, and continuous experimentation. An overview of the designed approach is shown in Fig. 3.

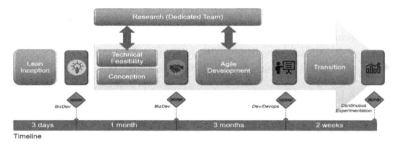

Fig. 3. Lean R&D approach. The timeline is illustrative and specific to our instantiation.

It is possible to observe four checkpoints, a set of activities, and support of a dedicated research team to technical solution related activities. Hereafter we describe the involved roles and activities.

Lean R&D Roles. The following roles are involved in the approach. To ease understanding, we provide examples of how these roles were distributed in the context of the ExACTa initiative.

Steering Committee. The main role of the steering committee is to assess the projects at the depicted checkpoints. This assessment aims at: (i) allowing the 'fail fast' of ideas that would not deliver the expected business value; and (ii) assuring that the approach is being used to address relevant innovation and digital transformation challenges. In our specific case, the steering committee for each project is composed by the coordinators of PUC-Rio's ExACTa initiative and managerial representatives of CENPES and Petrobras' target business area.

Project Manager (Scrum Master). Facilitates the Lean Inceptions and manages the agile research and development teams, assuring that the overall Lean R&D approach is being appropriately followed. In our specific case, we have one manager for four projects in parallel.

Product Owners (POs) and Business Owners (BOs). As in traditional Scrum, POs are responsible for maximizing the business value of the product resulting from the work of the development team. These POs are assisted by additional customer representatives BOs that work with the team to focus on the co-creation of solutions that maximize business value. In our specific setting, we have two POs handling two projects each and at least one BO per project.

Developers. The development teams. Currently, we have twelve full-time developers working in four projects (three per project).

Research Team. The role of the research team is to support the development team in an early technical feasibility assessment and in complex tasks during development (e.g., investigating machine learning techniques to be used, elaborating prediction models). Currently, this team has one research lead supported by four researchers, serving four projects.

UX/UI Design Team. Responsible for designing user interaction mock-ups and high-fidelity prototypes to subsidize the front-end development. Currently, we have one UX/UI team lead and one UX/UI analyst, serving the four projects.

DevOps and Infrastructure Analyst. Responsible for providing the DevOps infrastructure to the development teams. Currently, we have one DevOps analyst serving four projects.

Lean R&D Activities. The approach starts with a *Lean Inception* to allow stakeholders to jointly outline the vision of an MVP that can be used to test business hypotheses. It is important to involve representatives of all relevant stakeholders during this phase. Thereafter, the defined MVP has to be approved by the steering committee (refer to the first checkpoint in Fig. 3). If it gets rejected, a new Lean Inception should be conducted, potentially focusing on a different problem. Referring to the suggestive timeline, the typical duration of a Lean Inception is of five business days [3]. However, in our specific case, we have managed to conduct them within three business days.

In the *Technical Feasibility* phase, the development team, assisted by the research team and the DevOps analyst, starts investigating the technical feasibility of implementing the features identified during the Lean Inception. Following the tracer bullet strategy [12], this phase typically serves as proof that the architecture is compatible and feasible and that there is a way to solve the problem with reasonable effectiveness, as well as providing a working, demo-able skeleton with some initial implementations.

The *Conception* involves the PO detailing the MVP features identified during the Lean Inception by applying product backlog building dynamics with the customer representatives, followed by other typical requirements elicitation techniques (e.g., interviews), to specify user stories. Additionally, aware of severe negative impacts of under-specified agile requirements [13], we complement user stories by specifying Behavior-Driven Development (BDD) scenarios that can later be used as objective acceptance criteria [14]. During the conception phase, the UX/UI team participates by creating low-fidelity prototypes (e.g., mock-ups) for requirements validation and high-fidelity UI prototypes for usability testing.

At the end of the conception, the agile requirements specification (containing user stories, BDD scenarios, and mock-ups) is reviewed and validated with the customer, and usability tests are conducted on the high-fidelity prototypes. It is noteworthy that careful requirements reviews (e.g., inspections) are among software engineering's best practices [15], capturing about 60% of the defects early, when they are cheaper to fix, significantly reducing rework, overall development effort, and delivery schedules [16].

Additionally, defects in requirements have other severe consequences, including customer dissatisfaction and overall project failure [17]. Thus, this phase, concerning the specification of what should be implemented, deserves special attention.

The second checkpoint involves the steering committee analyzing the requirements specification, together with the results of the technical feasibility assessment, requirements review, and usability tests, to decide whether the MVP should be developed.

Thereafter, the *Agile Development* phase involves the development team, with the support of the research team, implementing the MVP. The support of the research team is typically welcome for more complex specific parts (e.g., building machine learning models). Basically, this phase follows standard Scrum-based development with sprint planning, daily meetings, and sprint review cycles. For quality improvement purposes, we recommend using modern code reviews, which enable identifying faults, improving solutions, and sharing knowledge and code ownership [18]. While the sprint duration could be adjusted, in our specific case, we use sprints of two weeks and a custom dashboard that allows monitoring the overall team progress (*cf.* Sect. 5).

Once the MVP is developed, the next checkpoint involves the PO presenting the MVP to the steering committee, so that they can decide upon its transition into production. While this major checkpoint happens at the end of development, the customer representatives (BOs) are also involved in the sprint planning and sprint review activities during the development period, where they can always provide feedback to help co-creating the product that best fits their business needs.

Finally, the *Transition* phase involves the development and infrastructure team preparing the MVP for beta testing in its final environment and assessing the business hypotheses. The last checkpoint concerns analyzing continuous experimentation results, to investigate whether the business hypotheses were achieved and whether it is worth investing in another Lean R&D cycle to further improve the product (in this case the Lean Inception could be replaced by a simplified product increment planning ceremony). The research team is supposed to design the experiment plan, which should outline how to instrument the product to allow gathering the measurements required to test the business hypotheses, and eventually building other assessment instruments (e.g., questionnaires to measure user satisfaction). It is noteworthy that we intend to continuously improve the approach based on causal analysis process improvement practices [19].

4   Case Study Design

The description of our case study design is based on the guidelines for conducting case study research in software engineering by Runeson *et al.* [20].

4.1   Context

Petrobras is the largest company in Brazil and is active in the oil, natural gas, and energy industry. In 2019 they established a new board focusing on digital transformation and identified and prioritized several digital transformation opportunities within different business areas.

Aiming at coping with their digital transformation needs, CENPES partnered up with PUC-Rio's informatics department to establish the ExACTa initiative. Differently from previous experiences, this one should function with an open scope, following agile practices for Research and Development (R&D) to enable focused and fast deliveries of Minimal Viable Products (MVPs) that can be used to test digital transformation business hypotheses. Of course, such a cooperation term relies on strong customer involvement and a previously established relationship of trust between the two parties. The ExACTa initiative was launched in September 2019, and the first step involved designing Lean R&D.

The first two projects started in December 2019, and their first MVPs were delivered within a four-month timeframe. Currently, the ExACTa initiative runs four such projects in parallel. To cope with these demands, the initiative counts on four professors of the informatics department (active in the areas of data science, software engineering, optimization, and human-computer interaction), and hired 21 additional full-time employees (1 scrum master, 1 research team lead, 1 UX/UI team lead, 12 developers, 4 research team members, 1 UX/UI analyst, and 1 DevOps and infrastructure analyst). The case study concerns the first two projects. More details on the case and subject selection are provided in Sect. 4.3.

4.2 Goal and Research Questions

The goal of the case studies can be defined, following the GQM template [21], as follows: "*Analyze* the Lean R&D approach *with the purpose of* characterization *with respect to* its overall outcomes and stakeholder perceptions, and the acceptance of its main building blocks *from the point of view of the* stakeholders and researchers *in the context of* the projects undertaken within the ExACTa co-creation initiative." From this goal, we derived the research questions.

RQ1: What have been the overall outcomes of the Lean R&D approach? To answer this question, we access the data from the agile management system (Microsoft DevOps) and discuss deliverables that have been accepted by the customer.

RQ2: What are the perceptions of the main stakeholders on the Lean R&D approach so far? To answer this question, we asked the main Lean R&D stakeholders from the involved business areas for feedback and analyzed this feedback qualitatively.

RQ3: What is the acceptance of applying Lean R&D's Lean Inceptions to define MVPs? To answer this question, we applied a survey based on the *Technology Acceptance Model (TAM)* [22], which has been commonly used to measure acceptance [23], to all Lean Inception participants.

RQ4: Does Lean R&D's early technical feasibility assessment phase help to address research-related uncertainties? To answer this question, we analyze the tasks and comments within the agile management system and the meeting minutes, to retroactively reflect on each case.

RQ5: Does Lean R&D's agile scrum-based and research-supported development fit well into the digital transformation initiative? To answer this question, we reflect on the dynamics of scrum plannings, reviews, and daily meetings, and data from the agile management system.

RQ6: Does continuous experimentation help to test business hypotheses and provide feedback? To answer this question, we reflect on data regarding the usage of the solutions and on additional evaluation instruments (questionnaire) used to assess the MVP's business hypotheses

4.3 Case and Subject Selection

We selected the first two projects by convenience. Details on each case follow.

Case 1: Intelligent monitoring of gas emissions by oil refineries. This case addresses a need of the industrial business area within Petrobras, and concerns building artificial intelligence models to predict refinery gas emissions, based on operation controls and environmental sensor data. This system should help to improve the capability of environmental monitoring and help to reduce environmental complaints by the community (e.g., regarding bad smells). Besides the ExACTa team, this case had three employees of Petrobras (BOs) working co-located within the ExACTa initiative space at PUC-Rio[1]. All these team members participated in the Lean Inception, as well as the sponsor at CENPES, the sponsor at Petrobras' industrial area, and representatives of employees of the target refineries.

Case 2: Intelligent logistics control of service providing ships, helping to identify and handle off-hire situations. This case addresses a need of the Logistics business area within Petrobras, and concerns building intelligent controls, integrating information from several systems to identify and handle off-hire situations (i.e., situations in which a chartered ship is not available), which should be deducted from payments to the service providers (as well as the fuel used during off-hire periods). Besides the ExACTa team, this case had four employees of Petrobras (BOs) directly involved in co-creating the solutions. While they did not work full time, they participated in all Scrum plannings and reviews and were always available remotely and willing to contribute. All these team members participated in the Lean Inception, as well as the sponsor at CENPES, the sponsor at Petrobras' logistics area, and employees involved in operating ships and administering ship charter contracts.

4.4 Data Collection and Analysis Procedures

The author team includes members of both cases (they participated in discussions regarding the approach and helped to adjust it until reaching the herein described format) and has direct access to all other team members at PUC-Rio and Petrobras. The authors also had representatives in both Lean Inceptions, in the sprint plannings, reviews, and daily meetings, allowing them to precisely observe the approach in its real context. Moreover, they had complete access to the agile management system (Microsoft DevOps) and all project-related artifacts, including meeting minutes.

Additionally, as the Lean Inceptions involved several stakeholders, we conducted a survey based on the TAM questionnaire and open questions, which were analyzed qualitatively and anonymously. Also, for continuous experimentation purposes, we measured

---

[1] Since March 23rd activities moved to home-office due to COVID-19. Following the recommendations in [24] as much as possible and using proper remote tool support (Microsoft Azure DevOps and Teams) allowed us to keep the Lean R&D approach running remotely.

usage data of the provided solutions and applied additional questionnaires. Moreover, we asked the sponsors at Petrobras' involved business areas for additional feedback on their perceptions. This feedback was also qualitatively analyzed to help us further understand the overall acceptance from a managerial perspective.

4.5   Validity Procedures

All the quantitative data was collected from the agile management system and real project artifacts. The agile management system is directly integrated with changes in the source code and any other project artifact. The status of tasks within this system is verified on a daily basis during the daily meetings. Anonymity was employed in all questionnaires, allowing stakeholders to freely express their opinions.

5   Results and Discussion

Hereafter we describe the results of the case studies. We decided to describe them together in a joint analysis and discussion, focusing on answering each research question based on observations from both cases.

RQ1: What have been the overall outcomes of the Lean R&D approach? Regarding the outcomes, both cases recently had their first MVP accepted by the customer and delivered to the end-user within a four-month timeframe. *Case 1* delivered an MVP with 6 features (detailed in 28 user stories), while *Case 2* delivered an MVP with 5 features (detailed in 53 user stories). Figure 4 shows screenshots of functionalities developed for *Case 1* and *Case 2*. MVPs are now available to the end-users for beta testing, evaluating the associated business hypotheses and identifying opportunities for further improvement (e.g., in the format of new MVP versions). The MVP for *Case 1* uses a decision tree model to predict the probability of gas emissions above a certain level and potential causes and enables to register and correlate complaints from the community. The MVP for *Case 2* uses intelligent data crossings to enable effectively detecting and handling off-hire events within ship charter contracts.

Regarding the process outcomes, based on data from the agile management system, it is observable that the development team adjusted to the process and produced the Lean R&D artifacts (process outcomes) as expected. All Lean Inception artifacts were organized in the agile management system's wiki. During the conception phase, features identified in the Lean Inceptions were detailed into user stories with BDD scenarios, mock-ups were built and high-fidelity prototypes designed and validated.

With respect to the technical feasibility and research and development artifacts, in *Case 1*, due to access to confidential data, the team had to use an external Petrobras repository for committing their artifacts (e.g., code, models, and configuration files). Therefore, commits were not directly linked to the tasks in the management system. In *Case 2,* the agile management system's integrated Git repository was used, creating a branch for each task and using modern code reviews to assure code quality during pull-requests.

Regarding the sprint plannings and reviews, meeting minutes were registered for each event (every two weeks) in the agile management system. For *Case 1,* we also

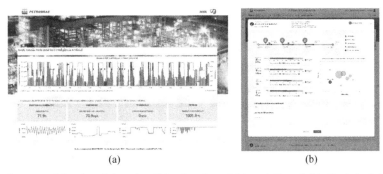

(a)	(b)

Fig. 4. Screens of developed functionalities for *Case 1* (a) and *Case 2* (b). Both had their first MVPs delivered within a four-month timeframe. Figures included for illustrative purposes, the focus of this paper is on the approach, not on the implemented solutions.

conducted weekly managerial status report meetings and registered meeting minutes for them, as critical stakeholders could not promptly adjust their activities to attend our sprint planning and review schedules.

RQ2: What are the perceptions of the main stakeholders on the Lean R&D approach so far? We asked the main stakeholders at Petrobras' industrial (*Case 1*) and logistics (*Case 2*) areas for feedback and analyzed this feedback qualitatively. Therefore, we reached out to them, asking them to write a short open text on their overall perceptions so far. The feedback was extremely positive.

The manager responsible for the industrial business area emphasized the co-creation process, effectiveness in adding business value, speed, and the evolutionary MVP approach: "The integration of the technical process engineering and IT teams of Petrobras with the development teams at PUC-Rio is a main advantage for achieving effective results, adding business value in a fast, collaborative and evolutionary way." It is noteworthy that this area had three Petrobras employees working most of the time collocated (after the pandemic virtually) with the team, offering tremendous help towards achieving the goals and co-creating the solutions.

The representative of the logistics area was in-line with these arguments and emphasized co-creation, agility, and efficiency: "The co-creation partnership with ExACTa has reflected the goals pursued by the logistics area: alignment between planning and accomplishments, agility and efficiency." He also wrote that "The initial impact of the different working method proposal, given the results, soon gave way to confidence. The team demonstrates control over the development, with continuous communication and predictability over the terms and scope of agreed deliveries". This statement highlights the adaptation and acceptance of the new agile method, after a completely understandable initial skepticism, observed from stakeholders of both cases, at the beginning.

RQ3: What is the acceptance of applying Lean R&D's Lean Inceptions to define MVPs? The Lean Inceptions were conducted involving the identified key stakeholders for each case. Figure 5 shows part of both Lean Inception teams in action. It illustrates the dynamics of co-creating a joint vision of an MVP that should add business value, be technically feasible, and user-friendly (Lean Inception includes a specific business, technical, and UX review activity before sequencing identified features into MVPs).

          (a)   (b)

Fig. 5. Kicking off the Lean Inception of *Case 1* (a) and discussing the final feature sequencing with some Lean Inception participants of *Case 2* (b).

To investigate the acceptance, we applied a questionnaire, designed based on the TAM questionnaire [22] adding an open text question asking for suggestions. The questionnaire was applied to all Lean Inception participants, but answering was not mandatory (eleven participants answered in both cases). An excerpt from the results of the TAM questionnaire, regarding the stakeholder perceptions that best help answering RQ3 (speed and precision when defining the MVP, usefulness, ease of use, and intention to adopt) is shown in Table 1 for *Case 1* and Table 2 for *Case 2*. While participants were asked to identify whether they were from Petrobras or PUC, answers were anonymously collected.

To facilitate an overview of the results, we highlighted the cells with the highest value within each line. Based on these highlights, it is possible to observe an overall acceptance of using Lean Inceptions to define the joined vision of the MVP, with mainly neutral to positive perceptions in *Case 1* and mainly positive perceptions in *Case 2*. It may be possible to explain the differences between the cases based on the fact that the Lean Inception conducted in *Case 1* was the overall first one conducted within the ExACTa initiative. Also, based on the feedback collected from the open questions in *Case 1*, we held a contextualization meeting at the customer side before starting the inception of *Case 2*. We also identified some improvement suggestions regarding details of the Lean Inception method within the provided answers.

Based on these results and our overall perception, we believe that the Lean Inceptions helped to understand the overall context, enabling to outline an MVP and a prioritized set of features, which subsidize the next Lean R&D activities (e.g., the conception where features are detailed into user stories and the technical feasibilities, where the *tracer-bullet* strategy is applied to check if it is possible to implement the identified features). Moreover, it also helped to understand the continuous experimentation needs, by identifying the business hypotheses. Among the open text answers the main opportunities for adjustment to the R&D context concern improving the business, technical, and UX review step, as some participants highlighted that this step should not be conducted with the entire group, but properly separating main stakeholders into specific groups for a more precise assessment. I.e., it was observed that developers are typically not able to appropriately judge the business value of features, while business stakeholders have similar difficulties with the technical review on feasibility and effort. Moreover, UX related stakeholders typically found the information gathered during the Lean Inceptions insufficient for subsidizing UX feature assessments. Indeed, in our experiences, the

Table 1. Lean Inception TAM Questionnaire for *Case 1*.

Statement	Comp.	#Answers	SD	D	N	A	SA
High speed	Petro.	5	0%	0%	20%	**80%**	0%
	PUC	6	0%	17%	17%	**33%**	**33%**
High precision	Petro	5	0%	0%	**80%**	20%	0%
	PUC	6	0%	0%	**50%**	**50%**	0%
High usefulness	Petro	5	0%	0%	**40%**	**40%**	20%
	PUC	6	0%	0%	17%	33%	**50%**
Easy to use	Petro.	4	0%	0%	**75%**	0%	25%
	PUC	6	0%	17%	**33%**	**33%**	17%
Intention to adopt	Petro	5	0%	0%	**40%**	**40%**	20%
	PUC	6	0%	17%	17%	**33%**	**33%**

SD: Strongly Disagree, D: Disagree, N: Neutral, A: Agree, SA: Strongly Agree.

Table 2. Lean Inception TAM Questionnaire for *Case 2*.

Statement	Comp.	#Answers	SD	D	N	A	SA
High speed	Petro.	4	0%	0%	0%	**75%**	25%
	PUC	7	0%	14%	0%	29%	**57%**
High precision	Petro	4	0%	0%	25%	**75%**	0%
	PUC	7	0%	0%	29%	29%	**43%**
High usefulness	Petro	4	0%	0%	25%	**50%**	25%
	PUC	7	0%	0%	0%	43%	**57%**
Easy to use	Petro.	4	0%	0%	0%	**75%**	25%
	PUC	7	0%	0%	14%	**57%**	29%
Intention to adopt	Petro	4	0%	0%	0%	**50%**	**50%**
	PUC	7	0%	0%	0%	14%	**86%**

SD: Strongly Disagree, D: Disagree, N: Neutral, A: Agree, SA: Strongly Agree.

assessments had to be reviewed after the product backlog dynamics conducted during the conception phase.

RQ4: Does Lean R&D's early technical feasibility assessment phase help to address research-related uncertainties? We analyzed the tasks and comments within the agile management system, meeting minutes, and the observed experience within the projects. Analyzing the tasks indicated that in both cases, this phase was needed before starting the development sprints, enabling to address research-related uncertainties and infrastructural issues, also with the support from Petrobras' IT teams, as soon as possible.

For *Case 1*, the tasks accomplished within this phase mainly concerned: (a) investigating alternatives for building a prediction model with reasonable accuracy, (b) testing integrations and access to required data, and (c) solving infrastructure-related problems. For *Case 2*, the tasks accomplished within this phase mainly concerned experimenting some architectural solution options and aligning them with Petrobras' standards and investigating the integration and compatibility with Petrobras' legacy systems.

At this point, it is important to highlight the support from the parallel research team and the infrastructure analyst. Of course, this support is also important during development, but in this early technical feasibility assessment phase, it is enabling and crucial. After the delivery of the MVP of *Case 1*, one of the developers mentioned within the team communication channel that "it would not have been possible to properly address this problem within the expected timeframe without the early investigations and support of the research team."

RQ5: Does Lean R&Ds agile scrum-based and research-supported development fit well into the digital transformation initiative? Here we reflect on the dynamics of scrum plannings, reviews, and daily meetings and the transparency provided by the agile management system. Our overall conclusion is that yes, it fits well when using Lean R&D adaptations (e.g., a strong focus on precise, agile specifications, addressing architecture and research uncertainties at the very beginning, and proving continuous research support to the development team).

Sprint planning, review, and daily meetings played a key role in facilitating management and communication and establishing a co-creation team spirit. Transparent and continuous access to all sprint planning and review meeting minutes by all stakeholders helped to provide transparency and building trust. Transparency was also provided by properly configuring tool support for monitoring development progress. We designed a customized dashboard, used within all projects, to show the overall project progress in real-time (i.e., as soon as a developer concludes a task, the dashboard is automatically updated). The dashboards of *Case 1* and *Case 2* can be seen in Fig. 6. We keep these dashboards projected and continuously visible to the whole project team (also always remotely accessible through the Microsoft Azure DevOps system). Nevertheless, considering the initiative as a whole, even organizing information on the different projects with similar dashboards, we noticed shortcomings for managing information at a portfolio level of abstraction.

Initially, we faced some resistance from customers of both cases in following the agile co-working philosophy. As the results started to be delivered, this resistance was replaced by confidence, and a joyful co-creation environment was established. We believe that complete progress transparency also helped in this direction.

RQ6: Does continuous experimentation help to test business hypotheses and provide feedback? The Lean Inceptions helped to identify target business hypotheses for continuous experimentation. We will focus the discussion of this research question on MVP of *Case 1*, mainly due to space constraints and because this one started being used by the end-users earlier (at the beginning of June, while MVP of *Case 2* started being used at the beginning of July). The information we have so far for *Case 2,* is that,

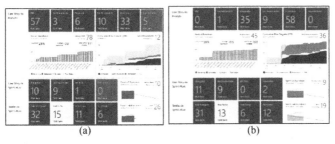

Fig. 6. Standardized and interactive project monitoring dashboards for *Case 1* (a) and *Case 2* (b), showing the progress of the product, the current sprint, and of minor tasks.

according to the representative of the logistics area, "employees involved in operating ships and administrating ship charter contracts [i.e., end users] are satisfied with the delivered MVP and were able to start using it after a very short training period." Indeed, after some days of initial usage, they identified and started handling 16 off-hire events through the system. Nevertheless, this information does not allow us to test the business hypotheses yet (which involve comparing off-hire deductions and handling time).

MVP of *Case 1* was deployed in the cloud, and we could collect usage data directly from the Microsoft Azure cloud platform. We measured the distribution of usage time (proxied by the amount of exchanged data) and the number of users (proxied by the number of active sessions) over time. Figure 7 shows these measures for the period of June 10th to July 10th. It is possible to observe an increase in the usage time and also in the number of users (active sessions). Two refinery operators at Petrobras started using the solution for monitoring gas emissions at least once a week (eventually, there were more than two simultaneous users). It is possible to see that they started spending more time in the system as they were becoming more familiar with it, which provides a preliminary indication of its perceived usefulness.

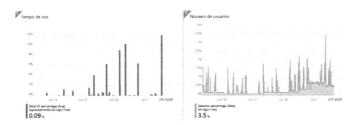

Fig. 7. Microsoft Azure metrics used as proxies for usage time and number of users.

Regarding the evaluation of the business hypotheses, there were two business hypotheses for *Case 1*. *Hypothesis 1*: "We believe that the *MVP for Case 1* will be able to *reduce the number of complaints by the society regarding bad smells related to refinery gas emissions*, we will know that this happened based on *the average number of complaints*"; and *Hypothesis 2*: "We believe that the *MVP for Case 1* will be able to *allow faster diagnosis of the causes*, we will know that this happened based on *the average time spent on the diagnosis.*" In the case of the diagnosis, it was supported by showing the decision tree path that led to the inference of high gas emission, and also letting users consult the whole decision tree.

Unfortunately, while we provided means to monitor the related metrics, the time of deployment would not be sufficient to observe changes in the averages yet. Therefore, we used an additional instrument to preliminarily assess our hypotheses; a questionnaire answered directly by the end-users in the refinery. Both main users answered that they completely agreed that the solution would help to lower the number of complaints and also the cause identification time. Moreover, they provided valuable feedback, with new features to be included in the next product increment (e.g., automatic notification alerts) and also showing to be satisfied with the provided solution. E.g., one of them mentioned that "the interface is well organized and information is properly presented, allowing interactions to filter the period and to understand the decision tree inferences."

6 Concluding Remarks

In this paper, we presented the Lean R&D approach, tailored to meet digital transformation related needs, including the ability to fail fast and agile and fast-paced deliveries of complex solutions. The development of such products commonly involves R&D efforts. However, we found no digital transformation focused approach available that appropriately considers integrating R&D efforts into an agile development philosophy. Lean R&D was designed with this focus, based on the following building blocks: (i) Lean Inceptions, to allow stakeholders to jointly outline a Minimal Viable Product (MVP); (ii) parallel technical feasibility assessment and conception phases; (iii) scrum-based research and development management; and (iv) strategically aligned continuous experimentation to test business hypotheses.

We applied Lean R&D in two case studies. Lean R&D enabled defining a joined MVP vision, addressing research-related uncertainties early, and to efficiently deliver valuable MVPs which were accepted by the end-users. Based on our experience, precisely defining business hypotheses and the focus on continuous experimentation strengthen the *BizDev* integration, helping to guide the overall development efforts since the beginning and avoiding to lose the focus on the main business goals. This business strategy alignment, the defined roles and co-creation philosophy with strong integration between Petrobras and PUC-Rio's teams, and the continuous support of a highly qualified research team, exploring synergies with the university's research program, were observed as key success factors. Main opportunities for improvement, based on our lessons learned, rely on better adapting Lean Inceptions to the DT context and on scaling the approach to a project portfolio level of abstraction.

While we are aware that these case studies were conducted in a specific context, we believe that sharing the approach and our evaluation experiences could help other organizations involved in digital transformation initiatives.

Acknowledgments. The authors would like to thank all ExACTa PUC-Rio and Petrobras employees involved in the projects for their trust and dedication to the new initiative.

References

1. Matt, C., Hess, T., Benlian, A.: Digital transformation strategies. Bus. Inf. Syst. Eng. **57**(5), 339–343 (2015)
2. Fitzgerald, B., Stol, K.J.: Continuous software engineering: a roadmap and agenda. J. Syst. Softw. **123**, 176–189 (2017)
3. Caroli, P.: Lean Inception: how to align people and build the right product. Editora Caroli (2018)
4. Fagerholm, F., Guinea, A.S., Mäenpää, H., Münch, J.: The RIGHT model for continuous experimentation. J. Syst. Softw. **123**, 292–305 (2017)
5. Kalinowski, M., Batista, S.T., Lopes, H. et al.: Towards lean R&D: an agile research and development approach for digital transformation. In: Euromicro Conference on Software Engineering and Advanced Applications (SEAA), Portoroz, Slovenia, 5 p. (2020, in press)
6. Reinertsen, D., Shaeffer, L.: Making R&d lean. Res. Technol. Manage. **48**(4), 51–57 (2015)
7. Ries, E.: The Lean Startup: How Today's Entrepreneurs Use Continuous Innovation To Create Radically Successful Businesses. Crown Business, New York (2011)
8. Debois, P.: Devops: a software revolution in the making. J. Inf. Technol. Manage. **24**(8), 3–39 (2011)
9. Bosch, J.: Building products as innovation experiment systems. In: Cusumano, M.A., Iyer, B., Venkatraman, N. (eds.) ICSOB 2012. LNBIP, vol. 114, pp. 27–39. Springer, Heidelberg (2012). https://doi.org/10.1007/978-3-642-30746-1_3
10. Ohno, T.: Toyota Production System: Beyond Large-Scale Production. CRC Press, Boca Raton (1988)
11. Wagner, S., Mendez, D., Felderer, M., et al.: Status quo in requirements engineering: a theory and a global family of surveys. ACM Trans. Softw. Eng. Methodol. (TOSEM) **28**(2), 1–48 (2019)
12. Thomas, D., Hunt, A.: The Pragmatic Programmer: Your Journey to Mastery, 2nd edn. Addison-Wesley Professional, Boston (2019)
13. Mendes, T.S., de Freitas Farias, M.A., Mendonçam M., et al.: Impacts of agile requirements documentation debt on software projects: a retrospective study. In: Proceedings of the ACM Symposium on Applied Computing (SAC), Pisa, Italy, pp. 1290–1295 (2016)
14. Smart, J.F.: BDD in Action: Behavior-Driven Development for the Whole Software Lifecycle. Manning, Shelter Island (2015)
15. Aurum, A., Petersson, H., Wohlin, C.: State-of-the-art: software inspections after 25 years. Softw. Test. Verif. Reliab. **12**(3), 133–154 (2002)
16. Boehm, B., Basili, V.R.: Software defect reduction top 10 list. IEEE Comput. **34**(1), 135–137 (2001)
17. Mendez, D., Wagner, S., Kalinowski, M., et al.: Naming the pain in requirements engineering – contemporary problems, causes, and effects in practice. Empirical Softw. Eng. **22**(5), 2298–2338 (2017)
18. Bacchelli, A., Bird, C.: Expectations, outcomes, and challenges of modern code review. In: International Conference on Software Engineering, San Francisco, USA, pp. 712–721 (2013)
19. Kalinowski, M., Mendes, E., Card, D. N., Travassos, G. H.: Applying DPPI: a defect causal analysis approach using bayesian networks. In: International Conference on Product Focused Software Process Improvement (PROFES), Oulu, Finland, pp. 92–106 (2010)
20. Runeson, P., Host, M., Rainer, A., Regnell, B.: Case Study Research in Software Engineering: Guidelines and Examples. Wiley, Hoboken (2012)
21. Basili, V.R., Rombach, H.D.: The TAME project: towards improvement-oriented software environments. IEEE Trans. Software Eng. **14**(6), 758–773 (1998)

22. Davis, F.D.: Perceived usefulness, perceived ease of use, and user acceptance of information technology. MIS Q. **13**(3), 319–340 (1989)
23. Turner, M., Kitchenham, B., Brereton, P., Charters, S., Budgen, D.: Does the technology acceptance model predict actual use? A systematic literature review. Inf. Softw. Technol. **52**(5), 463–479 (2010)
24. Ralph, P., Baltes, S., Adisaputri, G., et al.: Pandemic programming: how COVID-19 affects software developers and how their organizations can help. Empirical Softw. Eng. 34 p. (2020, in press)

Success and Failure Factors for Adopting a Combined Approach: A Case Study of Two Software Development Teams

Ingrid Signoretti[1], Maximilian Zorzetti[1(✉)], Larissa Salerno[1],
Cassiano Moralles[1], Eliana Pereira[2], Cássio Trindade[1], Sabrina Marczak[1],
and Ricardo Bastos[1]

[1] MunDDoS Research Group, School of Technology, PUCRS,
Porto Alegre, RS, Brazil
{ingrid.manfrim,maximilian.zorzetti,larissa.salerno,
cassiano.moralles}@acad.pucrs.br
{cassio.trindade,sabrina.marczak,ricardo.bastos}@pucrs.br
[2] Instituto Federal do Rio Grande do Sul (IFRS), Porto Alegre, RS, Brazil
eliana.pereira@restinga.ifrs.edu.br

Abstract. The combination of Agile, User-Centered Design and Lean Startup has emerged as a solution for teams that are struggling with lack of user involvement and delivering products that fulfill stakeholder needs. Adopting such a development approach involves several factors, some of which can assist or hinder the adoption process. Currently, the literature reports on studies on such factors, but only for agile-only methods. Motivated by this knowledge gap, our goal is to map the success and failure factors of a combined approach adoption. We conduct a case study with two software development teams from a large organization transitioning to the combined approach. We used semi-structured interviews and focus group sessions to collect data. Our findings show five success factors categories (e.g., team engagement, technical aspects) and one failure factor category (team autonomy at risk), along with several argumentation points suggested by the teams to argue against a company policy perceived to be a very impactful failure factor. This study contributes to academic literature by reporting on success and failure factors of a combined approach transformation, and could be used as a starting point in defining tools (e.g., maturity models) to aid organizations in transitioning to the combined approach.

Keywords: Agile · User-centered design · Lean startup · Success factors · Failure factors · Agile transformation

1 Introduction

Combining Agile Software Development with User-Centered Design (UCD) and Lean Startup into a novel development approach is a topic that is being widely

© Springer Nature Switzerland AG 2020
M. Morisio et al. (Eds.): PROFES 2020, LNCS 12562, pp. 125–141, 2020.
https://doi.org/10.1007/978-3-030-64148-1_8

explored in literature [7,9,23]. This triad approach helps teams in facing development gaps that agile by itself does not handle (such as stakeholders engagement in the development process) and in exploring and understanding user needs so as to build an assertive product [4]. Due to its many reported benefits in the literature, the combined approach has been the subject of interest in organizations ranging from startups [9] to multinational companies [21]. However, the transformation process to the combined approach implies the same challenges of a transformation to an agile-only approach, possibly even more.

Current literature reports a variety of success and challenge factors faced in an agile-only transformation [17], such as quality, continuous improvement, and waste elimination for success factors [18] and hierarchical issues, cultural aspects, and change resistance for challenge factors [13,17]. As mentioned, these factors were established for agile-only transformations, and therefore might not fully apply to a transformation to the combined approach.

Motivated by this gap in the literature, we conducted a case study with two software development teams that are undergoing a transformation to the combined approach. We observed both teams closely and gathered data to determine the success and challenge factors of the teams' transformation to the combined approach. Our study provides a starting point for teams to improve their continued use of the combined approach; and suggests the need of mechanisms to support and/or accelerate the transformation process, such as maturity models.

The remainder of the paper is organized as follows. Section 2 discourses on the combined approach and transformation processes. Section 3 presents our research method and details the case setting. Section 4 reports the success and failure factors of the teams' transformation. Section 5 discusses our findings. Section 6 wraps up the paper, discusses limitations, and proposes future work.

2   Background

2.1   Combined Approach

The combined use of Agile Software Development, User-Centered Design (UCD), and Lean Startup has been argued as a manner to tackle the limitations of agile, such as lack of customer involvement [1] and proper addressment of stakeholders needs [8]. While its UCD [16] character centers the development on the user, promoting creativity and empathy and helping developers to approach problems using a user-centric view [9], its Lean Startup [19] approach focuses on adding value to business stakeholders by looking for the best solution through experimentation, in which business hypotheses are constantly validated with real data, bringing about the constant pivoting of solutions until a fit resolution is achieved.

Several studies have been made on the combined approach. Fashion retailer Nordstrom report on the very successful case of their innovation team [9], in which they iteratively supplemented their development approach, eventually reaching a combination of Agile, Lean Startup, and Design Thinking. Other studies [4,7,23] propose a process model for the combined approach, while Signoretti et al. discuss the activity and mindset changes that the approach entails [22] and highlight general benefits that the approach brings about [21], along with reporting on the upcoming challenges that teams new to the approach think they will face as the transformation goes on [21].

2.2 Transformation Process

Facing an agile transformation process is an infrastructural project that requires an elaborated and detailed plan from organizations. In such a plan, attention must be paid to the ensuing management, structural, and technical changes while also addressing mindset and cultural issues [17]. Most transformations take place to better align future product development with corporate strategies, so as to better respond to market changes. From a development team perspective, however, motivations to change include a team's lack of engagement or dissatisfaction with the current development method and/or work culture [3].

Julian et al. [11] reports on two transitioning strategies: a "gradual" approach, in which practices are gradually integrated into the organization; or a "big bang" approach, in which all practices are adopted by-the-book. In any case, a transformation has a set of success and failure factors, which are decisive points for organizations to evaluate and scale their transformation strategy. In agile-only transformations, success factors include the use of a pilot transformation team, endorsement of mindset change towards agile values, and promotion of social events [17]; while failure factors include change resistance, intra-organization coordination and communication, and issues with hierarchical and organizational boundaries [3]. As previously stated, however, current literature only encompasses agile-only transformations, and while we assume that a transformation to the combined approach is similar (if not more complicated, given its three-pronged method), there is currently no evidence supporting this.

3 Research Method

In our previous case study [21], we reported on the early benefits (e.g., increased shared knowledge) brought by the combined approach and the current and upcoming challenges (e.g., changing work habits) that the transformation incurs, as perceived by two software development teams that had recently adopted the combined approach. Six months later, we call upon both teams again (now even more entrenched in the combined approach) seeking to understand what pushes the transformation to the combined approach towards success or failure.

3.1 Case Setting

We conducted a case study [20] with two software development teams from ORG (name omitted for confidentiality reasons), a multinational IT company. ORG has software product development sites in the USA (headquarters), India, and Brazil. With over 7,000 employees and responsible for about 1,200 software products. The company started an agile transformation in 2015, but in late 2017 the transformation strategy changed as the CEO understood that the company should improve their user experience by focusing on products. The organization then switched from a project road-map to focus on a product-oriented mindset. This change demanded of teams more in-depth knowledge of their users and business needs. For this reason, the company decided to invest in a combined approach of Agile, UCD, and Lean Startup. The adopted approach was inspired by the Pivotal Labs[1] methodology, which proposes principles and ceremonies based on the three aforementioned approaches. It also suggests the adoption of a cross-functional team composed of three main roles: Product Designer, Product Manager, and Software Engineer. Pivotal Labs' main goal is to help teams to build software products that deliver meaningful value for users and their business. It offers a framework and starting point for any team to discuss its needs and define its own way towards software development. As part of a big bang transformation approach [11], two teams were selected to train daily with consultants from Pivotal Labs. The teams were formed with highly skilled employees that could lead the transformation.

We observed *in-loco* those two teams from the financial area located in Brazil, and both teams develop services for company internal use. The teams are composed of 2 Product Managers, 1 Product Designer, and 4 Software Engineers each. *Team A* is responsible for a software product that manages, calculates, and generates data about company projects related to equipment (e.g, peripherals and computers for personal or server use) and service delivery (e.g., machine installation, support, and replacement). The product manages general project information, such as personnel assignment and time spent on tasks, and also calculates the associated costs of services offered by the products sold by ORG. Team A is tasked with integrating all existing operations of the product into a single application that fulfills user needs and business expectations. *Team B* is responsible for a software product that consumes data from multiple ORG applications (including Team A's) to calculate the average cost of equipment developed in Brazil. The application generates reports for internal accounting, such as inventory reports for tax purposes. Team B had to conduct research to understand current product processes and automate them into the application.

3.2   Data Collection and Methods

To confirm and deepen our previous findings [21], we applied a set of data collection methods that will be explored next. Also, Table 1 shows the profile of the study's participants.

Individual Semi-structured Interviews. We sought to confirm and expand upon our previous findings [21] in regards to the transformation process through individual semi-structured follow-up interviews. We asked the participants to confirm factors collected previously, such as the impact of the combined approach on team engagement, the relationship between team and stakeholders, technical

---

[1] https://pivotal.io/Labs.

Table 1. Participants' profile

ID	Team	Role	IT Exp. (yr.)	ORG Exp. (yr.)
P1	B	Software Engineer	10	4
P2	B	Product Manager	19	0.5
P3	A	Software Engineer	6	1
P4	B	Software Engineer	15	11
P5	A	Product Designer	27	10
P6	A	Software Engineer	21	8
P7	B	Software Engineer	7	7
P8	A	Product Manager	21	6
P9	B	Product Designer	5	4
P10	A	Product Manager	16	7.5
P11	B	Product Manager	23	10.5
P12	A	Software Engineer	5.5	4
P13	A	Software Engineer	20	11
P14	B	Software Engineer	5	5

aspects, team autonomy, and project-centered budget allocation. This led us to new factors such as team and stakeholders trust and communication, and team autonomy at risk. As these interviews unearthed several new impacting factors on the transformation, we decided to conduct a focus group session to discuss them in depth. The interviews were voice recorded and transcribed for analysis, lasting 30 min on average.

Focus Group Session. We conducted a focus group session to discuss the success and failure factors we had mapped from the individual semi-structure interviews. The session was conducted in two time slots of 1.5 h each. First, in two separate rooms, each team freely discussed each of the factors we mapped. To guide their discussion, we organized these factors in the form of a questionnaire in which the team had to indicate its level of agreement to each of the factors. The factors were grouped by the emerged categories. We used a 5-points Likert scale. Table 2 lists these factors by category. We observed their discussions and took note of them. Afterwards, during the 30 min break that we offered to the participants, we briefly analyzed their answers and came up with talking points pertaining to the discrepancies between each team's answers and our notes as a means to prioritize the factors to be first discussed during the second time slot. In the second 1.5 h, we had both teams meet in the same room to discuss their answers. All factors were debated by the teams. The session was also voice recorded and transcribed for analysis.

3.3 Data Analysis

We conducted Krippendorff's [14] content analysis procedure using a qualitative approach to the ethnographic content analysis, where we focused on the narrative description of the situations, settings, and the perspective of the actors

Table 2. Questionnaire

Question	Factors
Q1. How relevant are the following factors to having a team engaged?	Shared knowledge, mutual feedback, co-responsibility for team activities and deliveries, team ownership, shared product vision
Q2. How relevant are the following factors to promoting trust between teams and stakeholders?	Frequent contact with the stakeholders, team empathy, code delivery in production environment, experiments to understand the problem and solution, mutual feedback, stakeholders and teams working together, mutual transparency, stakeholders see teams as problem solvers
Q3. How relevant are the following factors to promoting communication between teams and stakeholders?	Frequent communication, Face-to-face meetings, team empathy, team and stakeholder working together, team understanding about the problem, development considering UCD activities, stakeholders involvement in the whole process, mutual transparency, team proactivity, constant feedback
Q4. How relevant are the following factors regarding the technical aspects?	Behavior-driven development, pair programming, CI/CD pipeline, test-driven development, unit testing, concise stories writing, frequent deliveries
Q5. How relevant are the following factors to promoting team autonomy?	Middle management trust, solution ownership, middle management support, team decision-making autonomy, team autonomy to conduct small releases in production, autonomy to make decisions about the team scope
Q6. How much can the following factors influence and put the team autonomy at risk?	Budget definition, team resistance to change, stakeholders not understanding teams' work, deploys barriers, lack of middle management support, inter-team interlocks, lack of stakeholder support, team being physically close to the organization, excessive control, defined project schedule
Q7. How relevant are the following factors to the investment in the combined approach adoption for the whole organization?	Story cycle time, middle management satisfaction, application downtime, effectiveness in solving problems, return of investment, business satisfaction, user satisfaction, delivery frequency, problem life cycle, Number of defects

involved in the phenomena of our case study. As we use recording/coding units, we organized the analysis into the following steps: organization and pre-analysis, reading and categorization, and recording the results[2]. We first read the dataset, extracted text excerpts, and marked them as codes. These codes were revisited and grouped into larger codes, forming categories. We constantly reviewed our coding scheme with two seniors researchers (the last authors of this paper) aiming to mitigate any limitations or bias in our analysis. Both senior researchers also reviewed the questionnaire and interview scripts.

4 Results

Our results present the success and failure factors for adopting the combined approach, as perceived by both development teams.

4.1 Success Factors

The teams presented a set of success factors. We organized the factors into five major categories that emerged during our analysis: team engagement, team and stakeholder trust, team and stakeholder communication, technical aspects, and team autonomy. Table 3 consolidates all success factors identified per category.

Team Engagement. The teams emphasized the importance of team engagement aspects, such as a shared product vision, shared responsibilities, shared knowledge, team ownership, and feedback between team members.

One of the participants mentioned that a shared product vision promotes greater value for the team, since everyone gets to know the product— *"Everybody has the understanding about the product, not just the Product Designer or the Product Manager. So everybody knows the reason for working on a product and the importance of it."* (P5) Another participant stated the following on shared responsibilities— *"The whole team makes the decisions. Problems are discussed, as well as solutions. The difference is that before the combined approach we had one person deciding things, and now the whole team has this responsibility."* (P10) They also highlight the importance of having shared knowledge— *"When I miss the Daily Stand-up meeting, I start my day feeling out of the loop."* (P5).

Feedback between team members was stated to be an essential factor to promote team engagement— *"We must be free to give and receive feedback. Sometimes we notice that a colleague is distracted and losing track during meetings. We must give them this kind of feedback, seeking to improve team engagement."* (P4) Another factor was team ownership, especially for the Software Engineers— *"Even as the Product Manager and Product Designer are closer to the users and business due to the nature of their work, the software engineers can not lose their sense of ownership. It is essential that they participate in ceremonies with the stakeholders, as a way to promote the feeling of ownership."* (P2)

---

[2] We used the Atlas.TI2 digital tool, available at https://atlasti.com/.

Team and Stakeholder Trust. They state that working in a problem-oriented perspective is great for stakeholder trust— *"The stakeholders see us as problem solvers and not only as requirement developers. They see that we are worried about their real needs and looking to deliver the best solution."* (P2) and that this is made possible due to experiments— *"We produce small things through experiments, and this makes our team more assertive on the understanding of the problem and the possible solution."* (P11) even though they might not be as important to the stakeholders themselves— *"The stakeholders do not know how we get to the product, they only see the final result. They do not understand that what we are doing is an experiment."* (P9)

A Product Designer mentioned that having frequent contact with stakeholders enhances their feelings of trust— *"We gain their trust when we talk with the users and understand their needs."* (P5) As such, the participants identify the importance of having team empathy with the users— *"A user saw that we were engaged to solving his problem, that we worry about his difficulties and are working to improve that. From that moment onward we knew that the user trusted us."* (P5) Mutual feedback was also mentioned as a way to increase stakeholder trust— *"We must consider the users' feedback constantly. Both sides feel more confident when what the stakeholders need is aligned with what the team is producing."* (P9) As a consequence, the team and stakeholders work together closely to guarantee that the product being developed is the right one.

A Product Manager mentioned the fact that code delivery in a production environment is of greater value to the stakeholders, which can then understand the effort and the concerns of the team with their needs— *"The stakeholders observe our efforts to deliver with added value. They are informed about everything."* (P11) Mutual transparency between stakeholders and team was also stated as a contributing success factor— *"We just need to develop this relationship, showing to the stakeholders what we are doing and the results. Always being transparent about delivery dates and the issues that we face during product development"* (P2) although members from team B mention that mutual transparency is more important to user stakeholders, as business stakeholders are more interested in general outcomes than the inner workings of the team.

Team and Stakeholder Communication. Frequent communication was reported as a success factor— *"Meetings are important, promoting stakeholder and team communication, but must be used only when necessary. Decision-making must not happen only in meetings: we communicate with the stakeholders as soon as a decision must be made"* (P2) as well as face-to-face meetings— *"Both team and stakeholders benefit from face-to-face meetings, creating intimacy and improving communication."* (P9) To foster communication, having the stakeholders involved since the product's conception seems to be the way to go— *"The team creates an empathetic view since the beginning, and not just when the delivery is made."* (P5) As a consequence, stakeholders and team work together— *"It is important to share decisions about problem prioritization, about what is the best solution... Have the stakeholder work with us."*

(P5) Given their accounts, the team having a proper problem understanding is of utmost importance.

Team empathy with users was also mentioned as an important aspect in communicating with stakeholders— *"The techniques used to gather user information, such as interviews, help us see the needs of the user and put us at their side, consequently getting us closer to them."* (P2) Team proactivity was mentioned as well— *"We must go and understand the problems that the user has on their application, and not just wait for them to say what we have to do."* (P12) although this might be negatively perceived by other teams— *"We act proactively but other teams do not like our attitude, as they get the idea that we are doing their jobs. We get misunderstood for being proactive."* (P13) Thus, considering UCD activities during development to actively engage users, mostly by the Product Designer, is a great practice— *"The Product Designer helps us on approaching the user. The way that the Product Designer communicates with stakeholders is different and brings benefits to us all."* (P9)

Finally, they mentioned mutual transparency as an important factor related to communication— *"Being clear and transparent with the stakeholders results in a lot of pluses to communication and consequently to our relationship."* (P11) However, this comes with a caveat: team B's current relationship with business people is not ideal— "If we had the same kind of relationship that team A has with their business people it would be great. However, today we do not have that, and having transparency now would reflect negatively on us." (P9)

Technical Aspects. A CI/CD pipeline brings about several benefits— *"A CI/CD pipeline is crucial. It promotes fast feedback and helps us validate stories in the production environment."* (P2) A Software Engineer says that delivering code in such an environment made the software engineers more satisfied with their work— *"If the software engineers see the deliverable going to production, they feel more accomplished, leading to more code quality later"* (P14) even if the pipeline itself does not add value— *"CI/CD helps a lot in improving quality aspects. However, it is not a key aspect in adding value to deliverables."* (P9) Frequent deliveries also helps the developers themselves— *"Having frequent deliveries allows us to be more effective"* (P8) and *"Continuous deliveries are essential for us to confirm if we are delivering the right thing"* (P9).

Regarding code quality (which is a factor in and of itself), the participants mentioned techniques that contribute to it, behavior-driven development (BDD), pair programming, unit testing and test-driven development (TDD)— *"Pair programming, BDD, unit testing, and TDD. Mainly TDD, which made the teams more confident about code quality"* (P6) Concise stories were also mentioned as a success factor— *"We quickly identified the added value to a story when it is written in a concise manner."* (P6)

Team Autonomy. For the teams, having the <u>middle managers' trust and</u> <u>support</u> is essential to their autonomy— *"We must build a relationship of trust*

Table 3. Success factors

Category	Success factor
Team engagement	Shared knowledge
	Shared product vision
	Shared responsibilities
	Feedback between team members
	Team ownership
Team and stakeholder trust	Frequent contact with stakeholders
	Code delivery in production environment
	Mutual transparency
	Working in a problem-Oriented mindset
	Experiments
	Mutual feedback
	Team and stakeholders working together
Team and stakeholder communication	Frequent communication
	Face-to-face meetings
	Team empathy with users
	Team and stakeholders working together
	Team understanding of the problem
	Development considering UCD activities
	Stakeholder involvement since product conception
	Mutual transparency
	Team proactivity
Technical aspects	Pair programming
	Unit testing
	Concise stories
	Test-driven development (TDD)
	CI/CD pipeline
	Behavior-driven development (BDD)
	Frequent deliveries
Team autonomy	Solution ownership
	High management support
	Middle management trust and support
	Team decision-making autonomy
	Small releases in production environment

with middle managers, because we need to have them on our side" (P9) and
"They must help us deliver our best. Their support is really important." (P13)
Higher management support is important as well— *"Higher management support helps middle management understand how they must work with the teams now."* (P6)

Small deliveries in production was considered a factor as it adds value to the product— *"There is a considerable effort on the process of having code delivered to production. However, it is important for autonomy, since only when deliverables are in production that we show the added value to the product. Small deliveries allows us to not break the current deployment, and we need this freedom."* (P5) This implies in having autonomy to make decisions— *"We must have this free pass to make our own decisions. Deciding the solution, what is the best for the user... within reason, of course. The point is that the team is the product owner and this decision is ours."* (P5)

Another aspect that was considered important to team autonomy was having solution ownership— *"The teams must have product ownership, especially the solution itself. It is not just about developing requirements."* (P6)

4.2   Failure Factors

The principal threats to the transformation are barriers to the use of the combined approach itself, or rather any kind of factor that interferes with the teams' autonomy. Table 4 consolidates the identified failure factors.

Team Autonomy at Risk. Teams resented the lack of middle management support— *"The managers are learning how to work with autonomous teams that do not depend much on their job"* (P7) and exemplified that it could cause barriers to the production environment— *"We had our code ready to be in production, but the managers told us to wait for two months because the deployment environment was not stable and had a lot of issues. So we faced these barriers and were not allowed to go to production."* (P2)

The team members are also concerned with the previous *modus operandi* of the organization, especially the practice of project schedules— *"Now we work looking to solve problems, not just 'work on a project'. But the stakeholders do not understand this way of working yet. They still ask for documents and a defined schedule"* (P5) and *"We are worried about this need of a defined schedule because it directly affects our decision-making power."* (P10) Excessive control is also part of old policy— *"We have the challenge of dealing with excessive control on ORG. They have a process to all things, security-level, program-level... and this generates bureaucracy, which impacts our autonomy."* (P9) Budget al.location policy being centered around projects and not for development capacity can put autonomy at risk as well— *"The budget al.location policy is project-based, while we are working in solving problems. The managers are worried about that because they do not know who will give financial support to us."* (P6) Another participant says— *"We highly depend on the business, which*

*provides money to the products. We are worried that they will act as the product
owners and will want to control everything, taking away our autonomy."* (P7)

Table 4. Failure factors

Category	Failure factor
Team autonomy at risk	Lack of middle management support
	Code deployment barriers
	Project schedules
	Excessive control
	Project-centered budget al.location
	Lack of stakeholder support
	Stakeholders not understanding the teams' work
	"Interlocks" with other teams
	Resistance to change
	Team physically close to the organization

Regarding their daily work, they were concerned with <u>lack of stakeholder
support</u> and that <u>stakeholders do not understand how the team works</u>— *"The
stakeholders have a habit to give finished requirements. Now, they are concerned
that we are 'taking' their jobs. We are helping them understand how they must
act now."* (P5) Dependencies with other ORG teams, or <u>interlocks</u> as they call
them, were mentioned as well— *"ORG has a lot of teams, and as such there
are interlocks. We try to remain focused on the problem, but sometimes we can
be looking to accomplish the needs of other teams, stopping the delivery of added
value to our products."* (P12) Another daily factor is <u>resistance to change</u>— *"The
team members must get used to this new way of work. There are some people that
do not accept the change and are resisting it. This takes away some of the team's
autonomy"* (P9) and *"If we have resistance from our manager or someone on
the team, we are sure that it will cause issues to our autonomy."* (P9) It was
also stated that the team not being in an environment cut off from the organization, or rather the <u>team being physically close to the organization</u>, could be
risky— *"I am concerned in how the team will behave when we return to our real
offices. The distance to that site is helping us stay autonomous. We will probably
be pressured to work the old way again."* (P12)

The participants were especially particular about how ORG has their funding
policy set up to be project-based instead of based on pure development capacity,
or on a smaller product-based basis; a practice that causes extreme concerns
to both teams, as the combined approach moves them away from big projects
and into constant problem solving. Unprompted, both teams started to discuss
possible indicators that could be used to argue against this policy, and in favor of
a combined approach-friendly one. Table 5 presents their argumentative points.

Table 5. Points for arguing against the project-centered budget allocation policy.

Failure factor	Argumentative point
Project-centered budget allocation	User satisfaction
	Business satisfaction
	Frequent product deliveries
	Middle management satisfaction
	Product necessity understanding
	Problem understanding
	Solution effectiveness
	Cycle time
	Application downtime
	Number of defects

The teams discussed how to convince the business people that funding the combined approach is worthwhile— *"We have to work to make the business people happy. If we give the business feedback of what and how the team is doing, it could be and an indicator for this funding thing, to justify their investments."* (P12) Factors such as user satisfaction and business satisfaction were considered as good indicators— *"These are related to better communication with stakeholders. If we prove that we are working to solve their problems, they will see us a return of their investment. Consequently, both users and business will be convinced."* (P14)

Having frequent product deliveries was mentioned as well— *"We deliver products with added value. If we deliver sooner, we make the users more happy and engaged. And this could be a factor to change how the business allocates their money."* (P5) A Product Designer also considered middle management satisfaction— *"We must show to our managers that we are adding value to the product, and to the organization as a consequence. Once we have their support, they could tell the same story to higher levels of management."* (P9)

They stated that they can use their increased product necessity understanding to convince the adoption of a product-focused mindset, and that their increased problem understanding is great for arguing for product investments— *"Understanding the problem allows us to discuss it with the stakeholders and explain exactly why we need money to improve our product."* (P5) Overall solution effectiveness was reported as an argument as well— *"We focus on identifying problems and not only on developing pre-defined requirements. This helps our effectiveness, and the users seem to be more confident with this way of working on their needs."* (P7) Story cycle time was also pointed out by a Product Designer— *"One of the things that we can show is the time that a story takes between arriving and going to production. The time spent prioritizing and working on a problem, and making it available to users can be a good indicator."* (P5)

Lastly, they mentioned simple metrics, <u>application downtime</u> and <u>number of defects</u>— *"There are metrics that are easy to prove. These are indicators that help not so technical people understand the gains of using this approach."* (P7)

5   Discussion

The success and failure factors of the transformation are especially useful as they were gathered from a team-level perspective, which is essential to consider when conducting an agile adoption process, since its main focus is on team-level development activities [12].

The success factors promote the encouragement for teams to continue believing in the transition to the combined approach, creating an engaging feeling of teamwork through shared knowledge, shared product vision, shared responsibilities, and team ownership. These factors were all reported as extremely important aspects of the adoption, and that obtaining them requires a strong sense of responsibility and belonging, along with mutual feedback and trust, as corroborated by Mchugh, Conboy, and Lang [15] in their study.

The combined approach also demanded stakeholders to adopt a new perspective and to be more engaged with product development. Having the stakeholders' trust and respect is crucial for agile teams [15], and having them involved with development is also relevant to the combined approach due to its heavy emphasis on UCD and Lean Startup activities [21], which paints an ill omen for team B when analyzing their struggling relationship with the business.

Hoda, Noble, and Marshall [10] state that the lack of customer involvement is a tremendous challenge for agile teams. Without stakeholder engagement and support, teams have a hard time delivering the right product and fulfilling stakeholder needs. Dorairaj and Noble [5] mention that a benefit of having good communication between team and stakeholders is that it forms a strong bond— making both parties very effective when collaborating.

Diebold and Mayer [2] report that the most adopted agile practices originate from XP, even when the adopted agile method is not specifically XP, as is the case with the combined approach. Agile practices such as pair programming, BDD, TDD, and concise user stories were reported as great achievements for the teams. Diebold and Mayer [2] also emphasize that using agile practices reduces project risk and increases team productivity and motivation.

As for team autonomy, the support of higher and middle management were extremely important factors on the transformation in the teams' perspective, seeing as their autonomy is directly impacted by decisions such as project funding. These views are shared by Dikert et al. [3], who state that management support must be ensured during agile adoptions.

Regarding the failure factors, both teams reported that the lack of middle management and stakeholder support is a great challenge for the successful transformation of ORG, corroborating with the work of Dikert et al. [3], which mentions that resistance to change and skepticism towards a new way of working are challenges for transformations.

The project-centered budgeting policy was one of the most interesting factors reported by the teams. Upon reflecting on the transformation by our study's prompt, they seemed enthusiastic to look for solutions to this particular problem, as their way of working seems to be most impacted by it. The current hierarchical structure of ORG (and its decision-making ramifications) is not optimized for the combined approach, but the teams brought up a series of indicators (e.g., story cycle time, business satisfaction, and user satisfaction) that could be used to convince higher staff that the approach is worth investing in.

The study results also highlighted that most of the success and also failure factors are related to human aspects.

As a final consideration, we emphasize how the success and failure factors of the combined approach adoption range from technical-level to hierarchical-level concerns, implying that the development team alone is not the only party that needs adaptation—higher-level staff also need to get involved, which can be difficult due to their lack of knowledge on the workings and needs of the development front. We note how most of the factors are related to human aspects. This is not surprising, given that Agile, UCD, and Lean Startup are people-oriented methodologies. However, it is a surprise that even with several studies on this issue, companies are still struggling with it. Human aspects are crucial issues in an agile-only transformation [6], and just as much in a combined approach one. The difference is in the teams' maturity in understanding that and being able to suggest and make modifications that could decrease these transformational barriers. These issues highlights the need of a tool (e.g., a maturity model) to guide the transformation process—a tool capable of conducting the adoption in a way that facilitates the involvement of teams, stakeholders and higher-level staff, by presenting indicators that such staff could understand, for instance.

6 Conclusions, Limitations, and Future Work

We reported the success and challenge factors of adopting a combined approach of Agile Software Development, UCD and Lean Startup through a case study with two software development teams from a multinational company. Ours findings revealed five major categories of success factors (team engagement, team and stakeholder trust, team and stakeholder communication, technical aspects, and team autonomy), and the ultimate challenge factor type being of risks to team autonomy. We also report possible solutions for the distinct challenge factor of "product-focus instead of project-focus", as teams thought it to be most of utmost importance for the transformation.

The findings contribute to the literature by reporting on success and challenge factors for the transformation to the combined approach, as current literature only comprehends similar studies regarding agile-only methods. Industry practitioners can make use of our findings to understand what types of scenarios they could face when dealing with a similar transformation in large organizations.

As inherent to any empirical study, our study has limitations. To mitigate construct validity concerns, we used multiple data sources to triangulate findings and had senior researchers accompany each step of the study. We also observed teams working in a real setting that were composed of members playing distinct roles, each with unique IT experiences. These actions aimed to mitigate such concerns. In regards to generalization, we can not claim that our results apply to distinct scenarios, since the teams' maturity, organizational vision, and their instance of the combined approach are factors that need to be well-considered during a large-scale adoption.

As future work, we suggest the replication of the study in other organizations of similar configuration, so as to compare findings. The findings could be used as a starting point to building a tool that helps organizations in conducting and scaling up the transformation to the combined approach.

Acknowledgments. We thank the study participants and acknowledge that this research is sponsored by Dell Brazil using incentives of the Brazilian Informatics Law (Law no. 8.2.48, year 1991).

References

1. Bastarrica, M., Espinoza, G., Sánchez, J.: Implementing agile practices: the experience of TSol. In: International Symposium on Empirical Software Engineering and Measurement, pp. 1–10. Oulu, Finland, October 2018
2. Diebold, P., Mayer, U.: On the usage and benefits of agile methods & practices. In: Baumeister, H., Lichter, H., Riebisch, M. (eds.) XP 2017. LNBIP, vol. 283, pp. 243–250. Springer, Cham (2017). https://doi.org/10.1007/978-3-319-57633-6_16
3. Dikert, K., Paasivaara, M., Lassenius, C.: Challenges and success factors for large-scale agile transformations: a systematic literature review. J. Syst. Softw. **119**, 87–108 (2016)
4. Dobrigkeit, F., de Paula, D., et al.: The best of three worlds-the creation of InnoDev a software development approach that integrates design thinking, scrum and lean startup. In: Proceedings of the International Conference on Engineering Design, Vancouver, Canada, pp. 319–328 (2017)
5. Dorairaj, S., Noble, J.: Agile software development with distributed teams: agility, distribution and trust. In: Agile Conference, pp. 1–10 (2013)
6. Gandomani, T.J., Zulzalil, H., Ghani, A., Sultan, A.B.M., Sharif, K.Y.: How human aspects impress agile software development transition and adoption. Int. J. Softw. Eng. Appl. **8**(1), 129–148 (2014)
7. Gothelf, J.: Lean UX: Applying Lean Principles to Improve User Experience. O'Reilly, Newton (2013)
8. Gregory, P., Barroca, L., Sharp, H., Deshpande, A., Taylor, K.: The challenges that challenge: engaging with agile practitioners' concerns. Inf. Sotw. Technol. **77**, 92–104 (2016)
9. Grossman-Kahn, B., Rosensweig, R.: Skip the silver bullet: driving innovation through small bets and diverse practices. Lead. Through Des. **14**, 815–830 (2012)
10. Hoda, R., Noble, J., Marshall, S.: The impact of inadequate customer collaboration on self-organizing agile teams. Inf. Softw. Technol. **53**(5), 521–534 (2011)
11. Julian, B., Noble, J., Anslow, C.: Agile practices in practice: towards a theory of agile adoption and process evolution. In: International Conference on Agile Software Development, Montreal, CA, Montreal, CA, pp. 3–18, May 2019

12. Karvonen, T., Rodriguez, P., Kuvaja, P., Mikkonen, K., Oivo, M.: Adapting the lean enterprise self-assessment tool for the software development domain. In: Euromicro Conference on Software Engineering and Advanced Applications, pp. 266–273. IEEE (2012)
13. Karvonen, T., Sharp, H., Barroca, L.: Enterprise agility: why is transformation so hard? In: Garbajosa, J., Wang, X., Aguiar, A. (eds.) XP 2018. LNBIP, vol. 314, pp. 131–145. Springer, Cham (2018). https://doi.org/10.1007/978-3-319-91602-6_9
14. Krippendorff, K.: Content Analysis: An Introduction to Its Methodology. SAGE, Thousand Oaks (2018)
15. McHugh, O., Conboy, K., Lang, M.: Agile practices: the impact on trust in software project teams. IEEE Softw. **29**(3), 71–76 (2012)
16. Norman, D., Draper, S.: User Centered System Design: New Perspectives on Human-Computer Interaction. CRC Press, Boca Raton (1986)
17. Paasivaara, M., Behm, B., Lassenius, C., Hallikainen, M.: Large-scale agile transformation at Ericsson: a case study. Empirical Softw. Eng. **23**, 2550–2596 (2018)
18. Putta, A., Paasivaara, M., Lassenius, C.: Benefits and challenges of adopting the scaled agile framework (SAFe): preliminary results from a multivocal literature review. In: Kuhrmann, M., et al. (eds.) PROFES 2018. LNCS, vol. 11271, pp. 334–351. Springer, Cham (2018). https://doi.org/10.1007/978-3-030-03673-7_24
19. Ries, E.: The lean startup: how today's entrepreneurs use continuous innovation to create radically successful businesses. Currency (2011)
20. Runeson, P., Höst, M.: Guidelines for conducting and reporting case study research in software engineering. Empirical Softw. Eng. **14**(2), 131 (2008)
21. Signoretti, I., et al.: Boosting agile by using user-centered design and lean startup: a case study of the adoption of the combined approach in software development. In: Proceedings of the Int'l Symposium on Empirical Software Engineering and Measurement, pp. 1–6. IEEE (2019)
22. Signoretti, I., Salerno, L., Marczak, S., Bastos, R.: Combining user-centered design and lean startup with agile software development: a case study of two agile teams. In: Stray, V., Hoda, R., Paasivaara, M., Kruchten, P. (eds.) XP 2020. LNBIP, vol. 383, pp. 39–55. Springer, Cham (2020). https://doi.org/10.1007/978-3-030-49392-9_3
23. Ximenes, B.H., Alves, I.N., Araújo, C.C.: Software project management combining agile, lean startup and design thinking. In: Marcus, A. (ed.) DUXU 2015. LNCS, vol. 9186, pp. 356–367. Springer, Cham (2015). https://doi.org/10.1007/978-3-319-20886-2_34

A Practice-Informed Conceptual Model for a Combined Approach of Agile, User-Centered Design, and Lean Startup

Maximilian Zorzetti[1]([✉]), Ingrid Signoretti[1], Eliana Pereira[2], Larissa Salerno[1],
Cassiano Moralles[1], Cássio Trindade[2], Michele Machado[1], Ricardo Bastos[1],
and Sabrina Marczak[1]

[1] Pontifícia Universidade Católica do Rio Grande do Sul, Porto Alegre, Brazil
{maximilian.zorzetti,ingrid.manfrim,larissa.salerno,
cassiano.mora}@acad.pucrs.br, michele.machado@edu.pucrs.br,
{bastos,sabrina.marczak}@pucrs.br
[2] Instituto Federal do Rio Grande do Sul, Porto Alegre, Brazil
cassio.trindade@pucrs.br, eliana.pereira@restinga.ifrs.edu.br

Abstract. Organizations worldwide have been adopting software development approaches that deviate from common agile methods in order to overcome some of their shortcomings. It has been reported that combining agile methods with Lean Startup and User-Centered Design results in a very powerful development approach, and academic research has developed some high-level process models for it. However, this combined approach is not well-documented, making it hard for inexperienced professionals to start using it. A grounded conceptual model of the combined approach enables the development of further instruments to help in adopting the approach, but such a model does not currently exist yet. We aim to showcase an initial conceptual model based on the empirical study of two software development teams that use the combined approach. We performed a case study where we investigated their day-to-day work using daily observations, semi-structured interviews, and focus group sessions; and built a conceptual model of the activities, techniques, and work products that both teams use daily. We reflect on how the conceptual model was conceived and the next steps in refining it, namely having it augmented with concepts sourced from literature.

Keywords: Agile · Lean Startup · User-Centered Design · Case study · Conceptual model · Software engineering

1 Introduction

There is a rise in the number of organizations that choose to adopt mixed development methods instead of a pure Agile approach, which is not a surprise as it has been suggested that some of its limitations (e.g., lack of user involvement [8]) can be overcome by combining it with other methods [12]. A noteworthy "method

© Springer Nature Switzerland AG 2020
M. Morisio et al. (Eds.): PROFES 2020, LNCS 12562, pp. 142–150, 2020.
https://doi.org/10.1007/978-3-030-64148-1_9

combo" is to add Lean Startup and User-Centered Design (UCD) into the Agile mix, as the former enables software developers to see that user needs are met and the latter introduces experiment-driven development, mitigating risk and guiding the generation of value to business stakeholders [11]. This combined approach (hereinafter referred to as such) has been the subject of research for some time now and its improvements upon regular agile methods have been reported multiple times [3,9] along with studies that propose a workflow for it [1,3].

Motivated by the perceived effectiveness of this development approach, our research group is working on an acceleration model to help organizations who wish to transition to such an approach. To develop this acceleration model, we need a sound basis for what an integration of the aforementioned "pillars" should look like. However, such a foundation is not immediately evident, as the pillars themselves do not have a single, widely accepted theoretical basis, which makes integration efforts difficult. Moreover, the difficulty in conceptualizing such an integration is exacerbated by obstacles such as pillars handling the same issues differently or even untangling a pillar from one another, which is the case for Agile and Lean Startup, as both have their roots in Lean manufacturing.

To fill in this knowledge gap, this paper reports on the ongoing development of a conceptual model through design and creation science [10] to better understand the combined approach. We developed an initial conceptual model using the data of a case study of two software development teams that received training on the approach from a consulting firm and highlight concepts used in their development workflow. Our study reveals the activities, roles, techniques, and work products used by the teams in the combined approach, establishing a groundwork to support further interpretations on how the pillars overlap and supplement one another on the subsequent iterations of the modeling effort.

2   Background

2.1   Agile, Lean Startup, and User-Centered Design

As Agile was extensively used in the past two decades, its shortcomings became more apparent [8], such as it not providing much assurance that the right software is being developed, business-wise. Combining it with other approaches to development has been suggested as a way to fix these issues [12], and combining it specifically with Lean Startup and UCD has shown great promise [9].

Tackling business-related issues is Lean Startup, an entrepreneurship methodology that focuses on developing a business plan iteratively through the use of a "build-measure-learn" loop, where business hypotheses are evaluated through experiments [6]. Although not specifically a software development methodology, studies have reported it as a great driving force when developing software [2]. To ensure that the software not only meets business demands but also the users', the use of UCD enables developers to understand the users' real needs and create improved software with better usability and user satisfaction [7].

One successful example of the combined approach is fashion retailer Nordstrom's Discovery by Design [3]. The creation of this development methodology was undertaken in an iterative and "organic" fashion by a dedicated innovation team by combining Agile with Lean Manufacturing, Lean Startup, and Design Thinking. Its process model, however, is described in high-level brush strokes as to emphasize that the most valuable part of their approach is their mindset. In a much more detailed fashion, Dobrigkeit, de Paula, and Uflacker [1] describe InnoDev, a similar development approach that has Scrum tying it all together.

3   Research Method

We conducted our modeling effort following the five phases of the design science research process model defined by Vaishnavi, Kuechler, and Petter [10]:

1. Awareness: recognize and articulate concepts[1];
2. Suggestion: derive concepts into an organized structure;
3. Development: describe the organized structure using a modeling language;
4. Evaluation: evaluate the modeled artifacts in a real-life context; and
5. Conclusion: consolidate findings and discuss possible loose ends.

Do note that these five phases are not rigidly followed in order, but instead in a fluid and iterative fashion. In this particular iteration of the model that we are reporting on, the awareness phase was fueled by case study data and an evaluation procedure was not yet performed.

3.1   Case Study

We conducted a case study with two software development teams from a multinational company named ORG (name omitted for confidentiality reasons). ORG has development sites in the USA (headquarters), India, and Brazil. With over 7,000 employees and responsible for about 1,200 internal software products, it moved to the combined use of Agile, Lean Startup, and UCD principles in late 2017. Before adopting the combined approach, ORG had a well defined roadmap for software product improvements based on an annual budget negotiated among business departments and organized into software projects. High-level business features were prioritized and decided upon by business personnel to later be turned into requirements by IT project teams with strict project deadlines.

With the introduction of an agile transformation in 2015, project teams used Scrum as the guiding development framework—although some participants of this study reported that the strict quarterly deadlines made it waterfall-like. In 2017 they decide to hire Pivotal Software Inc. consulting to support their transformation to a Pivotal Labs-like approach. Pivotal Labs proposes a "team rhythm" composed of principles and ceremonies based on the three aforementioned pillars. Pivotal Labs' main goal is to help teams to build software products

---

[1] Vaishnavi et al. originally define this phase as recognizing the problem statement, but also as intimately linked to the Suggestion phase, so we adapted it as seen here.

that deliver meaningful value for users and their business. It offers a framework and a starting point for any team to discuss its needs and define its own way towards software development, including roles, practices, work products, etc.

The Teams. We observed *in loco* two software development teams from ORG's financial department located in Brazil. Both teams were built as a catalyst to prove the worth and spread the use of Pivotal Labs throughout the company and have been rated as high-performance and proficient in its use. To achieve this, some members underwent an immersive Pivotal Labs hands-on training at the company headquarters over the supervision of Pivotal Software Inc. consulting personnel before coming back to Brazil to teach the others.

Team A is responsible for a software product that manages, calculates, and generates data about company projects related to equipment and service delivery. The product manages general project information, such as personnel assignment and time spent on tasks. The application also generates profit data for each project, which is consumed (along with the rest of the data) by the accounting department. *Team B* is responsible for a product that consumes and automatically validates data from other ORG applications to calculate the cost of equipment developed in Brazil. The application generates reports for internal accounting, such as inventory reports.

These teams worked for 6 months in a dedicated lab that follows Pivotal Labs' collaborative work environment recommendations (e.g., single large table for pair-wise work, large screen TV for reports and news, large whiteboards for idea development and information sharing, and a meeting room that turns into an entertainment space for leisure time). The lab is located on PUCRS's campus grounds and was specifically built for ORG teams as a learning environment.

3.2   Data Collection

We observed both teams for a 6-months period, executing several data collection procedures throughout it. Initial perceptions of the teams were collected using typical case study instruments. A *questionnaire* was used to identify the participants profile, while *observation sessions* were used to shadow team members and attend team ceremonies to learn about their approach to software development and the responsibilities of each of their roles. Several rounds of *semi-structured interviews* were conducted, and two of them were used specifically to gather the team members' perceptions on the combined approach, on role changes, on interactions between roles, and on the impact of changes on their work routine. Sporadic unstructured interviews were used to follow up on unclear aspects of their day-to-day work unveiled in the observation sessions. All interviews were voice recorded and transcribed for analysis. We used *focus group sessions* to confirm our understandings and to further discuss some topics. Six of these sessions were used to discuss the activities, techniques, roles, and work products of the pillars of the combined approach as perceived by the teams. We conducted two sessions for each pillar that lasted 1.5 h on average.

3.3   Data Analysis

We analyzed data following the content analysis procedure by Krippendorff [5], organized into the following steps: organization and pre-analysis, reading and categorization, and recording the results. Using Atlas. TI[2], we first read the dataset, extracted text excerpts and marked them as codes. These codes were revisited and grouped into larger codes, forming categories—concepts to be included in our modeling efforts.

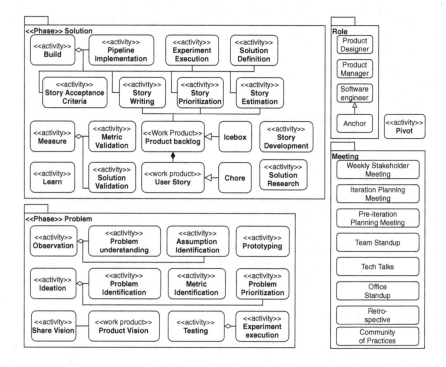

Fig. 1. Conceptual model of the case study, sans toolboxes

We used all acquired data to develop the conceptual model, following Gutzwiller's common elements of method descriptions [4] as our study focused particularly on the teams' workflow. We chose UML as our metamodel as it is a language we are familiar with and is flexible enough for our modeling needs.

4   Empirically-Grounded Conceptual Model

We categorized the concepts into seven packages (see Fig. 1 and Fig. 2): *Problem*, for concepts related to exploring the problem space the teams were assigned

---

[2] atlasti.com.

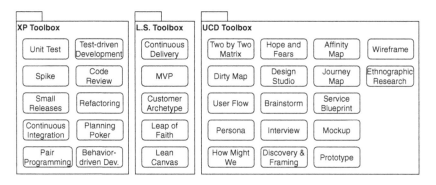

Fig. 2. Techniques used in the combined approach.

to; *Solution*, for concepts related to exploring possible solutions and developing them; *Meetings*, for gatherings in general; *Roles*, for the positions assigned to each team member; and three "toolbox" packages, one for each pillar, that contain the work techniques used by the teams. The *Problem* and *Solution* packages arose from our understanding of their work process at the time: teams would explore stakeholder demands and context in order to fully grasp the problem at hand (*Problem*) and then develop the best solution they came up with as determined by experiment data (*Solution*). The toolboxes (see Fig. 2) originated separately from the *Problem* and *Solution* packages as techniques were not mutually exclusive to each phase. Concepts were categorized according to their affinity to each package. Of note is the *Pivot* activity, which was purposely left out of any package as teams reported it could happen at any given moment.

The teams reported on 3 roles: *Product Designer*, a facilitator that enables the team in communicating with the user, typically by conducting interviews and promoting the use of techniques to understand and foster empathy towards the user; *Product Manager*, provides the business vision of things, helping the team in addressing business needs and establishing assumptions to experiment on; and *Software Engineer*, responsible for implementing solutions and the environment in which they are developed, in addition to participating in decision making and other activities, such as user interviews. A specialization of it, the *Anchor*, is an engineer that resolves technical and non-technical issues by serving as a bridge from the engineers to the user and the business side of things.

4.1   Discussion

The teams' development approach pushes for a "problem solving" perspective instead of a software development one, hence the lack of typical concepts in software development processes (e.g., "source code" and "coding") and the use of more abstract substitutes instead (e.g., "user story" and "story development"). This "view" can really just be an excuse to break free from any established process and rules in place in order to get to the root cause of a given problem, but still highlights a crucial change in the mindset of software development teams when using the combined approach: they no longer look at software as the *de facto* solution for everything. Their work process provides the necessary tools to find the solution to an existing problem by virtue of the heavy focus on experimentation—the build-measure-learn cycle—whether that solution involves writing code or not: a request for a faster spreadsheet generator was once solved by installing new computer parts to improve the host machine's performance instead of developing a new system.

Typically in agile, product validity is achieved when the customer says so. The constant use of the build-measure-learn cycle shifts this responsibility away from the customer and into experiment data itself, as developers set target metrics that their solution must adhere to, which, to be fair, might be decided together with or involve the customer. Nevertheless, the resulting solution is developed with confidence as it is backed by data. This is in line with previous studies that use the combined approach: InnoDev's authors state that "each [of its] phase[s] can be seen and implemented as a build-measure-learn cycle" [1], corroborating with having Lean Startup as a driving force to development in the case of Discovery by Design [3]. This works wonders to convince upper management of the decisions made by the development teams, which to them hopefully results in increased trust and more freedom to work the way they think is best.

As structured as the process is, both teams previously highlighted how it feels "organic" and how their mindset of problem solving is crucial to the combined approach. This suggests that their process is not as structured as it seems, but they might view it as such given their old work process was waterfall-based. Guiding principles or values are not as evident when discussing such things (none were directly addressed by the teams), even though their influences are most definitely important to the teams' development process.

5   Conclusion

As seen in ORG's case, top-level staff are impressed with the combined approach as they specifically requested it to be spread throughout the organization. Understanding what makes the combined approach tick, however, is not a straightforward task, and adoption efforts are specially difficult for an organization as large as ORG: the steps taken for a team to adopt the combined approach might not work for another. The conceptual model as described in this paper is a first step towards a grounded theoretical basis that will enable the development of other tools to support the combined approach.

Regarding any empirical study, our study has limitations. To mitigate construction validity concerns, we used multiple data sources to triangulate findings and had senior researchers accompany each step of the study. For our modeling efforts, we used automated digital tools to validate their syntactic quality, while semantic quality was strengthened by the supervision and revisions by the aforementioned senior researchers.

Given how the development of the conceptual model was based on the day-to-day activities of the ORG teams, as it stands it is too "low-level" and does not describe more abstract concepts such as guiding principles. We will continue with this "bottom-up" approach to modeling, focusing the next modeling cycles on literature-defined lower level concepts while making our way up to higher level ones. To do so, we will choose (or create) a new metamodel that supports the inclusion of more abstract elements adequately. In sum, the next steps in our research include: identify literature-defined concepts; merge aforementioned concepts into the current conceptual model; select or develop an adequate metamodel to represent the model in; and evaluate the model using our established relationship with ORG.

Acknowledgments. We thank the study participants and acknowledge that this research is sponsored by Dell Brazil using incentives of the Brazilian Informatics Law (Law no. 8.2.48, year 1991).

References

1. Dobrigkeit, F., de Paula, D., Uflacker, M.: InnoDev: a software development methodology integrating design thinking, scrum and lean startup. In: Meinel, C., Leifer, L. (eds.) Design Thinking Research. UI, pp. 199–227. Springer, Cham (2019). https://doi.org/10.1007/978-3-319-97082-0_11
2. Fagerholm, F., Guinea, A.S., Mäenpää, H., Münch, J.: The RIGHT model for continuous experimentation. J. Syst. Softw. **123**, 292–305 (2017)
3. Grossman-Kahn, B., Rosensweig, R.: Skip the silver bullet: driving innovation through small bets and diverse practices. Leading Through Design, p. 815 (2012)
4. Gutzwiller, T.A.: Das CC RIM-Referenzmodell für den Entwurf von betrieblichen, transaktionsorientierten Informationssystemen. Springer, Heidelberg (1994). https://doi.org/10.1007/978-3-642-52405-9
5. Krippendorff, K.: Content Analysis - An Introduction to Its Methodology, 3rd edn. SAGE Publications Inc., Thousand Oaks (2013)
6. Ries, E.: The Lean Startup: How Today's Entrepreneurs Use Continuous Innovation to Create Radically Successful Businesses. Crown Business, New York (2011)
7. Salah, D., Paige, R., Cairns, P.: Patterns for integrating agile development processes and user centred design. In: European Conference on Pattern Languages of Programs, Kaufbeuren, Germany, p. 19. ACM (2015)
8. Schön, E.-M., Winter, D., Escalona, M.J., Thomaschewski, J.: Key challenges in agile requirements engineering. In: Baumeister, H., Lichter, H., Riebisch, M. (eds.) XP 2017. LNBIP, vol. 283, pp. 37–51. Springer, Cham (2017). https://doi.org/10.1007/978-3-319-57633-6_3
9. Signoretti, I., Marczak, S., Salerno, L., de Lara, A., Bastos, R.: Boosting agile by using user-centered design and lean startup: a case study of the adoption of the combined approach in software development. In: International Symposium on Empirical Software Engineering and Measurement, Porto de Galinhas, Brazil, pp. 1–6 (2019)
10. Vaishnavi, V.K., Kuechler, W.L.: Design Science Research in Information Systems. AIS, pp. 1–45 (2004)

11. Vargas, B.P., Signoretti, I., Zorzetti, M., Marczak, S., Bastos, R.: On the understanding of experimentation usage in light of lean startup in software development
context. In: International Conference on Evaluation and Assessment in Software
Engineering, Trondheim, Norway, pp. 330–335. ACM (2020)
12. Vilkki, K.: When agile is not enough. In: Abrahamsson, P., Oza, N. (eds.) LESS
2010. LNBIP, vol. 65, pp. 44–47. Springer, Heidelberg (2010). https://doi.org/10.
1007/978-3-642-16416-3_6

Data Science

Demystifying Data Science Projects: A Look on the People and Process of Data Science Today

Timo Aho[1]([✉]), Outi Sievi-Korte[2], Terhi Kilamo[2], Sezin Yaman[3], and Tommi Mikkonen[4]

[1] TietoEVRY, Tampere, Finland
timo.aho@iki.fi
[2] Tampere University, Tampere, Finland
{outi.sievi-korte,terhi.kilamo}@tuni.fi
[3] KPMG Finland, Helsinki, Finland
sezin.yaman@kpmg.fi
[4] University of Helsinki, Helsinki, Finland
tommi.mikkonen@helsinki.fi

Abstract. Processes and practices used in data science projects have been reshaping especially over the last decade. These are different from their software engineering counterparts. However, to a large extent, data science relies on software, and, once taken to use, the results of a data science project are often embedded in software context. Hence, seeking synergy between software engineering and data science might open promising avenues. However, while there are various studies on data science workflows and data science project teams, there have been no attempts to combine these two very interlinked aspects. Furthermore, existing studies usually focus on practices within one company. Our study will fill these gaps with a multi-company case study, concentrating both on the roles found in data science project teams as well as the process. In this paper, we have studied a number of practicing data scientists to understand a typical process flow for a data science project. In addition, we studied the involved roles and the teamwork that would take place in the data context. Our analysis revealed three main elements of data science projects: Experimentation, Development Approach, and Multidisciplinary team(work). These key concepts are further broken down to 13 different sub-themes in total. The found themes pinpoint critical elements and challenges found in data science projects, which are still often done in an ad-hoc fashion. Finally, we compare the results with modern software development to analyse how good a match there is.

Keywords: Data science · Data engineering · Software process · Prototyping · Case study

M. Morisio et al. (Eds.): PROFES 2020, LNCS 12562, pp. 153–167, 2020.
https://doi.org/10.1007/978-3-030-64148-1_10

1   Introduction

The layman's view to a data science project is glorified, to the brink of data scientists being modern-day fortune tellers, seemingly effortlessly creating predictions based on existing data. The reality, however, is somewhat different. While the final outcomes of a data science project can appear miraculous, the actual data science – as well as related activities such as data engineering and data mining – build on well-established ground rules on what the data says and what it does not say.

The terminology in the field of data science is somewhat mixed, with overlapping terms like data analytics, machine learning, data mining and big data. In this study, we use the term data science for extracting knowledge from data sets, which might be large, using multidisciplinary techniques such as statistics and machine learning, in order to understand and analyze the data and to gain insights. However, here we exclude traditional business intelligence and data warehousing from the scope of data science.

Today's data science projects exhibit some problems that could be tackled with more mature project management methodologies [8, 9]. These include minimal focus on identifying result quality and problems in estimating budget and scheduling in advance [18]. In addition, since many of the data science results are applied in the context of software systems, seeking synergy between software development approaches and data science seems to open promising avenues. For instance, Sculley et al. [23] state that for a mature machine learning system, it could be that only at most 5% of the overall code base can be regarded as machine learning, a subset of data science. Rest of the code is about, e.g., data collection and preparation, configuration and management, and serving layer. This raises the question, whether following readily available approaches in software development could help in data science projects [1, 22].

In this paper, our goal is to understand a typical process flow for a data science project, as well as to learn about the role of a data scientist and teamwork that would take place in the context of data-centric projects. Our precise research questions are:

1. What is the typical process flow of a data science project?
2. What kind of people are part of a data science project?

The research was executed as a multiple case study with a series of interviews with experienced data scientists working in the field of data science consultancy.

Our results indicate that data science is experimentation-centric and multidisciplinary team work. The role of a data scientist is identified as distinctively separate from that of a data engineer. Development is mainly iterative in nature. As the work relies heavily on experimentation on data, models, algorithms and technical approaches utilized, knowledge gained during the project can change goals or requirements of the work. However, in the context of larger projects, practices sharing characteristics with modern software development are common, in particular when the team size increases.

The rest of this paper is structured as follows. Sect. 2 gives the background for the paper and presents related work. Section 3 introduces the research approach we have followed, and Sect. 4 presents the results of the study. Section 5 provides an extended discussion regarding the results, including also threats to validity. Finally, Sect. 6 concludes the paper with some final remarks.

2   Background and Related Work

Typically, data science related research concentrates on the technological solutions and their use cases as presented in the survey by Safhi et al. [16]. At the same time, literature on data science project roles and project methodologies is scarce, while there has been some growth in the field [21].

So far, data science projects have been following their own processes and practices, which have been different from those that have been typically used in the context of software development [13,19]. Data science specific project methodologies include KDD [4], CRISP-DM [26] and SEMMA[1]. Of these, CRISP-DM seems to be the one most referred to. It describes an iterative process with six stages: *a*) business understanding, *b*) data understanding, *c*) data preparation, *d*) modeling, *e*) evaluation, and *f*) deployment. The stages follow one other linearly, but the process allows both moving back and forth between the stages. For a comparison of the frameworks, we refer to the work of Shafique and Qaier [24], and Azevedo and Santos [3]. There are also extensions (e.g. [2,7]) on these methodologies that aim at tackling some of the problems the practitioners have identified.

In an older 2015 Internet poll [13], CRISP-DM was shown to be the most popular process methodology in data science. However, according to a more recent 2018 survey by Salz et al. [19], 82% of data science teams did not follow any explicit project management process or practices, even though 85% thought such would be beneficial. According to the survey, teams either were not sure of the used process methodology, or used an ad hoc approach. Moreover, 15% of teams reported the use of some agile methodology and 3% a CRISP-DM based methodology.

Grady et al. [8] note the similarity of data science projects with software development before the adoption of agile methodologies. Such similarities can also be seen in a study revealing difficulties related to processes in data science projects [18]. Issues were found particularly with estimating the budget, schedules and the successfulness of the project in advance. Also quality assurance of results is often insufficient. Moreover, data science projects still rely quite heavily on individual effort instead of team work.

However, it is important to note that there are differing categories of data science projects. For example, in an ethnographic study [20] the authors found two kinds of data science projects: routine data transformation projects and exploratory projects. Especially the latter ones were one-off and did not have

---

[1] Available at https://documentation.sas.com/?docsetId=emref&docsetTarget=n061 bzurmej4j3n1jnj8bbjjm1a2.htm&docsetVersion=15.1.

standard process methodologies in use; for example, the projects lacked milestones and schedules. Moreover, the time used for different stages varied a lot and included a lot of manual work on, e.g., data transformations.

In a further study, Saltz et al. [17] could label data science projects with two dimensions (infrastructure and discovery), based on which they could identify four different types of data science projects depending on where projects could be placed on the axes. The project types were: Hard to Justify, Exploratory, Well-Defined and Small data.

Similarly, Amershi et al. [1] discuss how data science teams at Microsoft have merged their data science workflows into pre-existing agile processes. While data scientists have learned to adapt to the agile workflow, the authors recognize several issues related to data, model creation and handling AI components, that clearly distinguish data science projects from software projects. The authors note, though, that the problems faced by data scientist change significantly based on the maturity of the team, and have created a maturity measure to help identify issues.

The nature of data science teams and member backgrounds have also been studied. Kim et al. [11,12] identify that data scientists could have very different kinds of roles in teams and projects, partially due to their interest, skills and background, and partially due to company principles on how work is divided. Data scientist profiles vary from "Polymath" who has a strong mathematical background and can handle technical implementation, to "Insight actor" whose main job is to act based on findings from the data.

In general, most of the studies concentrate on a single company or are structured surveys with large target groups. There are only few (e.g. [10,17]) data science interview studies over multiple companies. Kandel et al. [10] concentrate on individual analyst skill set and workflow mentioning within team collaboration briefly. Moreover, Saltz et al. [17] give a data science project framework mentioning management and organization as a social context.

To summarize, prior work on data science projects investigates software development approaches and highlights the parallels and differences. However, to the best of our knowledge, no current research across multiple data science companies exists. Further, there are studies on different workflows and types of data science projects, and also studies on what kind of teams are used within data science projects. Nevertheless, to the best of our knowledge, no study yet exists that would combine these to angles together. Our paper attempts to fill this gap.

3   Research Methodology

The goal of this work is to understand a typical process flow for a data science project, and to learn about the role of teamwork that would take place in the context of data science projects, and what is the role of the data scientist there. The study was conducted as a multiple-case study of six companies with a business area in data science consultancy (interview protocol is online[2]). Case study research [15,27] as an approach is suitable when the aim is to gain knowledge on a topic tied to and not clearly separable from its practical context. This is true for industrial data science projects where practitioners can provide a good view on how everyday data science work is done today.

The interview questions were iteratively designed by the authors, taking into consideration existing related work and some baseline assumptions. We identified five assumptions based on prior research and our own observations from industrial experience – authors 1 and 4 are currently working as data scientists where as author 5 has extensive experience in industrial software development. The assumptions driving the focus of the work were the following:

- Data scientists are lone warriors or miracle workers, who come in to do a data science element and then leave after a short time, never seeing the project complete and never being truly part of the development team.
- Broken data presents challenges to data science work.
- Insufficient data presents challenges: clients' needs can not be met because there is no available data to answer the clients' targets.
- Data science projects are vaguely specified and customers do not exactly know what they want in the beginning of the project.
- Data engineering and data science are clearly separated tasks.

Note that the assumptions are not hypotheses, but are included for the sake of openness and validity.

Six data science consultancy companies were selected into the study based on availability and the nature of data science projects they work with. Three of the companies were general ICT consultancy companies with roughly 500–1000 personnel. The other three focus specifically on AI, data analysis and concept design. Two in the latter group were independent companies with less than 50 employees. One was a data science unit of a similar size within a large, global business consultancy company.

Table 1. Data science experience of the interviewees in years.

Experience type	Experience in years					
Data science consultancy	2	4	4	7	7	12
Overall data science	NA	9	NA	13	21	12

An experienced data scientist was interviewed from each company (see Table 1). The interviews concentrated on overall experience of the data scientists over their whole career. Thus, interview questions did not address, e.g., the related project details. The interviews were conducted from November to

---

[2] The interview protocol https://drive.google.com/file/d/1rKvt_10oeINv0hXvQU QHgIgtFyEj9sAf/view?usp=sharing.

December 2019 as a semi-structured interview lasting approximately half an hour. The interview protocol was designed based on the assumptions, and the first interview acted as a pilot interview for the interview protocol. As no changes were needed after the pilot, the pilot interview is included in the analysis. Five of the interviews were done on the companies' premises and one on a university campus. All interviews were done in the native language of the interviewees. Two researchers were present in each of the interviews, one of them taking notes. Each interview was recorded and transcribed.

The used definition of a data science project was given in the beginning of each interview but further specifics were left to each interviewee. In the scope of the study, a data science project must apply programming and not just use graphical tools in the analysis. Furthermore, the project has to include artificial intelligence or data science development, for instance predictive or exploratory analytics. It was also emphasized that traditional business intelligence or data warehousing were not within the scope of the study.

The results were thematically analyzed [5] based on the notes and the transcriptions. One researcher made the thematic analysis based on the notes and the transcripts, arriving at three higher level themes which comprised of 13 lower-level themes in total. Once an initial thematic analysis was made, another researcher validated the analysis by placing 20 quotes (chosen randomly but in such a way that all themes were represented) under themes identified. Once the themes were agreed upon by two researchers, their analysis was further validated by a third researcher in the same way. The coding essentially remained the same after validation, and no changes were made to the lower-level themes. However, two higher-level themes were named more appropriately, and some re-arranging was done in how lower-level themes were grouped under the higher-level themes. The themes are described in the following section.

4   Interviews

Based on our thematic analysis, we created a conceptual model of key elements encountered in a data science project (Fig. 1). The three main concepts are *Experimentation, Development Approach*, and *Multidisciplinary Team(work)*, which we will present in more detail in the following.

4.1   Experimentation

Data science projects revolve around experimentation and dealing with the uncertainty of unpredictable outcomes. Data scientists need to experiment with data, models, algorithms, and technical approaches to find the most satisfying way of meeting their goals. Knowledge gained during the experimentation phase may lead to changes in goals or requirements, to more accurate models, and eventually to a Proof-of-Concept implementation.

Data—Based on our own experiences, we approached the interviews with an assumption that incomplete or broken data would present significant challenges in data science projects. All our interviewees agreed that data is never perfect: it is often flawed and incomplete, and has far less information value than what customers usually believe. It is accepted as status quo that you simply need to invest the necessary time to fix and clean the data. However, contrary to our assumptions, this was not considered to be a particular challenge, as it is something that data scientists come against in virtually every project.

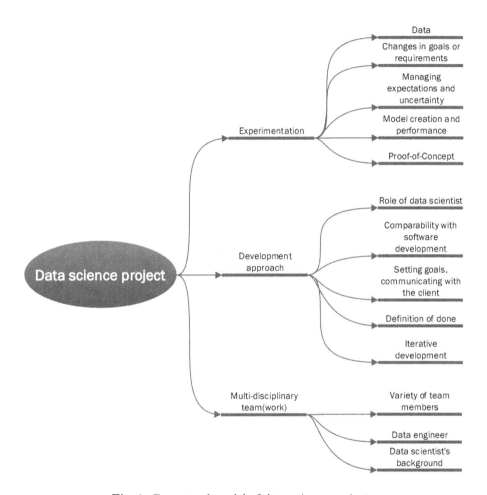

Fig. 1. Conceptual model of data science projects

Changes in Goals or Requirements—Due to the experimental nature of data science projects, goals or requirements often change over time. One reason is the aforementioned incompleteness of data: once the data scientist has done a first look through and created an understanding of the data, it may become apparent that the original goals simply are not feasible with the existing data. Our interviewees had a consensus that on a larger scale the goals and requirements for a data science project stay the same, but on a smaller scale the details may change based on the knowledge gathered through experimentation. Another setup is that new goals are created to complement the original ones. *"It's data science – you don't know in advance what can be achieved, chances may be improved with experience. It's common that goals slightly change."*

Managing Expectations and Uncertainty—The strongest message conveyed by our interviewees was that in data science one never really knows the outcome. This unfolds as significant challenges when communicating with the client and specifying the project. Our interviewees report that the present hype around AI is making things even more difficult. Various companies are reacting to the hype and on stories how data science projects have created value for others. However, the level of maturity for data collection and understanding the boundaries of data science varies significantly. Data scientists feel pressed in keeping expectations realistic and clearly communicating that one simply cannot know what, e.g., a machine learning algorithm will actually learn from the given data: *"Results aren't certain. If you promise too much, you are facing a difficult project. You have to be honest."*

Model Creation and Performance—The core of data science is creating models and utilizing algorithms to generate information value from the data. Our interviewees discussed various ways of conducting data science: doing reinforcement learning, "simple" machine learning, data exploration, predictive modeling, and natural language processing. However, they also raised some issues: 1) exploratory approaches may be problematic, if data is separated from the context, 2) having a model that somehow works with the data is only 5% of the project done, and 3) models are a product of iterative improvement and their performance could be honed forever.

Proof-of-Concept—As described, data science projects have a high level of uncertainty, an experimental and iterative nature of developing models for data, and an increased need to have something tangible to discuss goals with the client. Hence, it appears natural that the projects are heavily reliant on creating Proof-of-Concept (PoC) implementations. Our interviewees unanimously discussed situations where the feasibility of creating a model for the given data and making some sensible results from it were tested by creating a PoC. During the PoC development there may only be one or two data scientists involved and no other team members. The whole PoC would be developed in only a few week's of time. *"We test a little and do PoC versions of what we are planning on developing. We get some certainty that our approach makes sense."*

4.2 Development Approach

The development approach in data science projects seems to incorporate data scientists into larger development teams. The work is also clearly iterative in its nature, as iterative development approach was applied according to five out of the six interviews. Furthermore, a parallel with software development was drawn in four of the six cases. However, there can be significant differences in goal setting based on the maturity of the client.

Role of Data Scientist—Our assumption prior to the interviews was that data scientists' role is solo work, where they only come in to complete the data science element never seeing the project complete and never truly working as a part of a development team. This turned out not to be true. While some data scientists worked on data with a clear cut focus on data science work, there was strong commitment to the overall project. The work effort varied from sharing commitment between jobs to full commitment to one project. This depends on the stage of the project and the need for data scientist in the project. Some data scientists also work on data engineering, but the role of the data engineer is overall recognized separately (see Sect. 4.3). One interviewee also raised the topic of client contact. Data scientists need understanding of the client organization's needs to be able to provide data science solutions to meet those needs.

Comparability with Software Development—A lot of parallels were seen between data science work and general software development. There was a drive to get data science work to follow the process approaches commonplace in software development. Also the data science component was mentioned as just a small piece in a far larger project. One interviewee: *"It comes probably as a surprise to many what I mentioned earlier that you have 5% of machine learning and 95% of something else"*. The ending of the project was seen different from software development in that in data science the project was mentioned to never finish. Instead, only time or budget constraints determined the end of the data science project.

Setting Goals, Communicating with the Client—We assumed that data science projects are vaguely specified and customers do not have a clear goal in mind when the project starts. According to the interviews, the data science experience of the client was seen as a key factor in setting the project's goals. Business goals were mentioned as being at the heart of project goal setting. While having clear goals at the start of the project was considered valuable compared to starting with "what can you find out from the data", how well such goals are defined were seen to depend on the maturity level of the customer. However, the quality of goals set was considered to have begun to go down as data science has become more widely utilized. Communication with the client requires, in addition to having understanding of the clients business, the ability to set the expectations to a suitable level in order to meet the goals set.

Definition of Done—Definition of done in data science projects was twofold. Firstly, the maintenance phase can act as a clear ending to the project. Once the data science component is validated and in production, the work is done. Secondly, there are projects that go on indefinitely. There is always room for improvement, such as model calibration, and the project either goes on with new improvements as long as it is funded or spawns new projects to continue the work in.

Iterative Development—Based on the interviews, there is a clear link between the iterative nature of development and experimentation. Still, when viewed as a theme of its own, the role of the iterative development approach is clearly seen. Data and algorithm selection require iteration to find the most suitable solutions. Also having unclear goals requires iterations to make it possible to see what can be achieved. In some cases a specific approach for development was utilized: Scrum was mentioned as well as the use of sprints. When specified, the length of a sprint was one to two weeks.

4.3 Multi-disciplinary Team(work)

While data science projects can be executed as small PoC efforts, where only one or two data scientists use a week's effort in testing an idea, teamwork is required when the data science modules are used in production. If a PoC is successful in demonstrating the feasibility of an idea, it can be utilized in a larger concept – a software product, automation, or another domain. In this setting a larger team with varied expertise and roles is required with different roles in, e.g., sales, marketing, and software development, to complement the data science and engineering skills.

Variety of Team Members—As the interviews revealed, data science can be a small part of a larger development project. When the data science component needs to be integrated with other components, a variety of team members are required for the project to succeed. Our interviewees stressed the role of software developers, to quote: *"A software developer is really important, and a good developer will save you from the trouble you didn't know you'd get into."* Developers' expertise varies similarly as in any regular software development project. Additionally, the interviewees stressed the importance of having someone who can understand the business side of things and fluently communicate with the customer. As noted, managing expectations, dealing with uncertainty and setting goals requires some special effort in data science projects, and, thus, team members with communication skills and business understanding are highly valued.

Data Engineer—As discussed, data is far from perfect in terms of being usable for data scientists. Also our initial assumption was that engineering the data is a clearly separated task, preceding the actual data *science*. Before a data scientist can begin, a working technical pipeline is required to actually access and gather data. Data may need to be fetched from several big databases, it can be in different formats or encrypted, and it can be as big as millions of rows, which requires partitioning. Performing such tasks requires an understanding of the client's data warehouse, as well as strong skills in database design and programming. After required data is gathered from the clients and put in a system where data science tasks will be performed, the data still requires polishing and fixing before it can be used with a model. Our interviews revealed that engineering the data is definitely considered to be distinctively separate from data *science*, and the role of data engineer was unanimously recognized in the interviews. However, who adopts the role of data engineer varies a great deal. In some cases the data scientists do data engineering as well, in some cases a software developer takes on the role of data engineer, and finally there may be people distinctively assigned the role of data engineer. Assignment of the role depends on multiple aspects: the scope and nature of the project and the data, the policies and practices of the company, and the backgrounds and profiles of data scientists. While having developers do the work of data engineer is quite in line with our initial assumptions, cases where a data scientist does data engineering as well is clearly contradictory, and we would need to probe further into defining the scope of data engineering that a data scientist actually does.

Data Scientist's Background—While our interviewees agree that data scientists can come from various backgrounds, they further agree on a common denominator: the ability to understand mathematics, understand, design and implement algorithms, and quickly learn new methods. Data scientists have a variety of educational backgrounds, such as economics, mathematics and physics. In addition, there are a large number with a technical background and even a tailored doctoral degree in machine learning. Finally, there may be so-called "Full stack data scientists", who are able to engineer the data, create the model, implement the algorithms, and also develop the software surrounding the data science module. While various backgrounds give sufficient skills in working as a data scientist, naturally the background affects how the data scientist approaches a problem. To quote one of our interviewees: *"a mathematician looks at the world completely differently from a statistician".*

5   Discussion

Next, we present our analysis of key findings and list some key lessons learned. Then, we address validity concerns of our study.

5.1   Process and Collaboration in Data Science

The main concepts that define the process and roles of data science projects are *Experimentation*, relying on an iterative *Development Approach* and especially larger projects having *Multidisciplinary Team(work)* at their core.

The exploratory nature of many data science projects is evidenced by the proposed models and methods which have built-in learning mechanisms. Furthermore, some characteristics of prototyping [6] can be considered compatible in the context of data science. Proof-of-Concepts done by one or two data scientists appear to be a common mechanism to test the feasibility of a solution, do some initial testing of a model, and get familiar with the data. However, they are rarely sufficient as such.

Our results also reveal that there is a need for larger data science projects where numerous team members participate in different roles. These larger projects can also involve a considerable amount of software development, where data related features are embedded. This is also reflected in team composition. The interviewees state that *"In many cases there are 1–2 data scientists, then a varying number of people in software development"*. Here data scientists are also involved throughout the project, all the way to the maintenance phase.

Based on our results, the *development approach* of data science projects appears to rely at the heart of iterative work – a process familiar in the context of software development. Five out of six of our interviewees commented on the iterative role of the development, and the final interviewee referred to parallels of software development in general. Nevertheless, even in software development, there are multitude of ways of iterating for different purposes [25]. Thus, this shows that there are similarities between data science projects and software development, but this does not necessarily mean that the two could be aligned easily. Data science projects come with an exceptionally high level of uncertainty on the outcome, as was revealed both by our study and in related work [19]. Within data science, that uncertainty is acknowledged and accepted to a point – data scientists are well aware that one cannot know what can be derived from the data before experimentation. However, that uncertainty stretches from the start of the project (vague specifications) to the end (very varied conceptions of what is the "definition of done"), and may be very difficult to accept when moving to a software development context.

Drawing our findings together indicates that data science projects can benefit from development processes of software development, especially in larger projects. Based on the experimentative nature of data science work one can argue that what is commonly called a Proof-of-Concept implementation in data science could probably be regarded as a prototype in software terminology. Team work is at heart of data science work – both between several data scientists as well as between the data scientist and other, often software, professionals. These elements of working up iteratively from Proof-of-Concepts and prototypes and forming multidisciplinary teams for development are commonplace in agile and lean software development practices.

5.2   Threats to Validity

Several threats to validity [15,27] are recognized. Mitigation factors are also taken into account. For the study, we especially address construct validity, external validity and the reliability of the work.

Construct Validity—Construct validity considers how well research investigates what it means to investigate. In this study, construct validity is threatened by how representative the interviewed cases were of data science and how the interview data was analyzed. Also the case selection was partly based on a convenience sample. To mitigate the threat, what was meant by a data science project was defined in the beginning of each interview. However, the definition given left room for further specifics by each interviewee. Furthermore, the interviewees were selected based on their prior experience in data science projects specific to the scope of the study. All researchers participated in the planning and development of the interview protocol, which was also piloted in a pilot interview.

External Validity—External validity refers to how well the study results can be generalized beyond the scope of the study. This study has been planned as a preliminary to a larger survey study, that is currently being designed. While the sample size of this study is limited, the interviewees were selected to represent a range of experience and from two fields of data science industry (general ICT and artificial intelligence specific external consultancy companies) with small to medium company sizes. Our findings may not be applicable to in-house teams, nor to larger enterprises or smaller companies considering the sample size. However, we believe that the study results give important insights toward understanding data science projects and developing a theory. As future work, we aim at validating these results.

Reliability—The main threats to the reliability of the results is in the thematic analysis. To mitigate the threat, three researchers took part in the interviews and all five participated in the analysis of the results. The main thematic analysis was done by one researcher and was validated by two researchers separately. The conflicts that occurred during the validation were resolved in a separate analysis sessions with the rest of the researchers' participation. This way, researcher bias was also minimized, as three of the authors had prior experience with regard to data science and software engineering in practise. To enable to replication of the study, the interview protocol is available online.

6 Conclusions

In this multiple case study, we interviewed six data scientists with different levels of experience from six small to medium-sized consultancy companies. Our aim was to understand a typical process flow for a data science project, as well as to learn about the role of teamwork and data scientists there.

Three main concepts describing data science project methodology and roles were found. *Experimentation* is a core nature of data science projects. The data science projects commonly have an iterative *Development Approach* that incorporates them into larger teams. In addition, successful Proof-of-Concepts (PoCs) often end up in larger projects having *Multidisciplinary Team(work)*.

Our first research question was: *1. What is the typical process flow of a data science project?* From the project perspective we found that process elements in data science projects were, to some extent, the same as in software development. However, what sets the data science projects clearly apart from software development is the inherent uncertainty of data science work. It must be acknowledged and clearly communicated that there is no guarantee of specific results or achieving the initial goals. At the same time, requirements in software development are also fuzzy even at best. Nevertheless, software development has processes and tools to handle the uncertainty whereas data science, in turn, has to live with the data being inherently broken. Furthermore, the uncertainty cuts through the entire data science project life cycle – from vague specifications to differences in the definition of done. Data science projects are at core about experimentation and exploration, making them somewhat similar to the Lean Startup [14] cycle of Build – Measure – Learn.

To answer our second research question, *2. What kind of people are part of a data science project?*, the assumption of data scientists as lone soldiers was debunked. Firstly, data science is often only a small part of a larger development project. As the projects can be long ranging, there is commitment to the project throughout its life cycle. Especially, when a PoC demonstrates a feasible idea, a larger team with varied expertise and roles is called for.

All in all, data science is emerging into the mainstream software development projects. However, data science entails only a small portion of overall work and the role of a data scientist is often clearly identifiable in the development team. Nevertheless, it is likely that the processes of data science will continue to draw practices from software development. There is a level of uncertainty that is an inherent trait of data science. Hence all processes suitable in the context of software development do not necessarily apply to data science work. Instead the processes themselves should evolve to be able to take data science components with built-in uncertainty into account as part of the process.

There is clearly need for further research on the nature of data science project methodology. First of all, the results found in this paper should be validated with larger source material. In addition, it would be interesting to further test different project methodology approaches in a data science environment. These results already indicate that data science is increasingly using development processes to guide the work and rely on experimentation and multidisciplinary team work.

Acknowledgments. The authors wish to thank the professionals who provided their time and experience for our interviews. This study would not have been possible without them.

References

1. Amershi, S., et al.: Software engineering for machine learning: a case study. In: IEEE/ACM International Conference on Software Engineering: Software Engineering in Practice (2019)
2. Angée, S., Lozano-Argel, S.I., Montoya-Munera, E.N., Ospina-Arango, J.D., Tabares-Betancur, M.S.: Towards an improved ASUM-DM process methodology for cross-disciplinary multi-organization big data & analytics projects. In: International Conference on Knowledge Management in Organizations (2018)
3. Azevedo, A., Santos, M.F.: KDD, SEMMA and CRISP-DM: a parallel overview. In: IADIS European Conference on Data Mining (2008)
4. Brachman, R.J., Anand, T.: The process of knowledge discovery in databases: a first sketch. In: AAAI Workshop on Knowledge Discovery in Databases (1994)
5. Braun, V., Clarke, V.: Using thematic analysis in psychology. Qual. Res. Psychol. **3**(2), 77–101 (2006)
6. Budde, R., Kautz, K., Kuhlenkamp, K., Züllighoven, H.: What is prototyping? Prototyping, pp. 6–9. Springer, Heidelberg (1992). https://doi.org/10.1007/978-3-642-76820-0_2
7. Grady, N.W.: KDD meets big data. In: IEEE International Conference on Big Data (2016)
8. Grady, N.W., Payne, J.A., Parker, H.: Agile big data analytics: AnalyticsOps for data science. In: IEEE International Conference on Big Data (2017)

9. Hill, C., Bellamy, R., Erickson, T., Burnett, M.: Trials and tribulations of developers of intelligent systems: a field study. In: IEEE Symposium on Visual Languages and Human-Centric Computing (2016)
10. Kandel, S., Paepcke, A., Hellerstein, J.M., Heer, J.: Enterprise data analysis and visualization: an interview study. IEEE Trans. Visual Comput. Graphics 18(12), 2917–2926 (2012)
11. Kim, M., Zimmermann, T., DeLine, R., Begel, A.: The emerging role of data scientists on software development teams. In: IEEE/ACM International Conference on Software Engineering (2016)
12. Kim, M., Zimmermann, T., DeLine, R., Begel, A.: Data scientists in software teams: state of the art and challenges. IEEE Trans. Software Eng. 44, 1024–1038 (2018)
13. Piatetsky, G.: CRISP-DM, still the top methodology for analytics, data mining, or data science projects. KDnuggets (2014). https://www.kdnuggets.com/2014/10/crisp-dm-top-methodology-analytics-data-mining-data-science-projects.html. Accessed June 2020
14. Ries, E.: The lean startup: how today's entrepreneurs use continuous innovation to create radically successful businesses. Currency (2011)
15. Runeson, P., Höst, M.: Guidelines for conducting and reporting case study research in software engineering. Empirical Softw. Eng. 14(2), 131 (2008)
16. Safhi, H.M., Frikh, B., Hirchoua, B., Ouhbi, B., Khalil, I.: Data intelligence in the context of big data: a survey. J. Mobile Multimedia 13(1&2) (2017)
17. Saltz, J., Shamshurin, I., Connors, C.: Predicting data science sociotechnical execution challenges by categorizing data science projects. J. Assoc. Inf. Sci. Technol. 68, 2720–2728 (2017)
18. Saltz, J.S.: The need for new processes, methodologies and tools to support big data teams and improve big data project effectiveness. In: IEEE International Conference on Big Data (2015)
19. Saltz, J., Hotz, N., Wild, D., Stirling, K.: Exploring project management methodologies used within data science teams. In: Americas Conference on Information Systems (2018)
20. Saltz, J.S., Shamshurin, I.: Exploring the process of doing data science via an ethnographic study of a media advertising company. In: IEEE International Conference on Big Data (2015)
21. Saltz, J.S., Shamshurin, I.: Big data team process methodologies: A literature review and the identification of key factors for a project's success. In: IEEE International Conference on Big Data (2016)
22. Schmidt, C., Sun, W.N.: Synthesizing agile and knowledge discovery: case study results. J. Comput. Inf. Syst. 58(2), 142–150 (2018)
23. Sculley, D., et al.: Hidden technical debt in machine learning systems. In: Advances in Neural Information Processing Systems (2015)
24. Shafique, U., Qaiser, H.: A comparative study of data mining process models (KDD, CRISP-DM and SEMMA). Int. J. Innov. Sci. Res. 12, 217–222 (2014)
25. Terho, H., Suonsyrjä, S., Systä, K., Mikkonen, T.: Understanding the relations between iterative cycles in software engineering. In: Hawaii International Conference on System Sciences (2017)
26. Wirth, R., Hipp, J.: CRISP-DM: Towards a standard process model for data mining. In: International Conference on the Practical Applications of Knowledge Discovery and Data Mining (2000)
27. Yin, R.K.: Case Study Research: Design and Methods, 5th edn. SAGE Publications, Thousand Oaks (2013)

Data Pipeline Management in Practice: Challenges and Opportunities

Aiswarya Raj Munappy[1(✉)], Jan Bosch[1], and Helena Homström Olsson[2]

[1] Department of Computer Science and Engineering, Chalmers University
of Technology, Hörselgången 11, 412 96 Gothenburg, Sweden
{aiswarya,jan.bosch}@chalmers.se
[2] Department of Computer Science and Media Technology, Malmö University,
Nordenskiöldsgatan, 211 19 Malmö, Sweden
helena.holmstrom.olsson@mau.se

Abstract. Data pipelines involve a complex chain of interconnected activities that starts with a data source and ends in a data sink. Data pipelines are important for data-driven organizations since a data pipeline can process data in multiple formats from distributed data sources with minimal human intervention, accelerate data life cycle activities, and enhance productivity in data-driven enterprises. However, there are challenges and opportunities in implementing data pipelines but practical industry experiences are seldom reported. The findings of this study are derived by conducting a qualitative multiple-case study and interviews with the representatives of three companies. The challenges include data quality issues, infrastructure maintenance problems, and organizational barriers. On the other hand, data pipelines are implemented to enable traceability, fault-tolerance, and reduce human errors through maximizing automation thereby producing high-quality data. Based on multiple-case study research with five use cases from three case companies, this paper identifies the key challenges and benefits associated with the implementation and use of data pipelines.

Keywords: Data pipelines · Challenges · Opportunities · Organizational · Infrastructure · Data quality · Issues

1 Introduction

Data is being increasingly used by industries for decision making, training machine learning (ML)/deep learning (DL) models, creating reports, and generating insights. Most of the organizations have already realized that big data is an essential factor for success and consequently, they use big data for business decisions [9,13]. However, high-quality data is critical for excellent data products [3]. Companies relying on data for making decisions should be able to collect, store, and process high-quality data. Collecting data from multiple assorted sources to producing useful insights is challenging [1]. Moreover, big data is difficult to configure, deploy, and manage due to its volume, velocity, and variety [12].

© Springer Nature Switzerland AG 2020
M. Morisio et al. (Eds.): PROFES 2020, LNCS 12562, pp. 168–184, 2020.
https://doi.org/10.1007/978-3-030-64148-1_11

The complex chain of interconnected activities or processes from data generation through data reception constitutes a data pipeline. In other words, data pipelines are the connected chain of processes where the output of one or more processes becomes an input for another [19]. It is a piece of software that removes many manual steps from the workflow and permits a streamlined, automated flow of data from one node to another. Moreover, it automates the operations involved in the selection, extraction, transformation, aggregation, validation, and loading of data for further analysis and visualization [11]. It offers end to end speed by removing errors and resisting bottlenecks or delay. Data pipelines can process multiple streams of data simultaneously [14].

Data pipelines can handle batch data and intermittent data as streaming data [14]. Therefore, any data source will be compatible with the data pipeline. Furthermore, there is no strict restriction on the data destination. It does not require data storage like a data warehouse or data lake to be the end destination. It can route data through a different application like visualization or machine learning or deep learning model.

Data pipelines in production should run iteratively for a longer duration due to which it has to manage process and performance monitoring, validation, fault detection, and mitigation. Data flow can be precarious, because there are several things that can go wrong during the transportation of data from one node to another: data can become corrupted, it can cause latency, or data sources may overlap and/or generate duplicates [5]. These problems increase in scale and impact as the number of data sources multiplies and complexity of the requirements grows.

Therefore, data pipeline creation, management, and maintenance is a complicated task which demands a considerable amount of time and effort. Most of the companies do this maintenance manually by appointing a dedicated person to guard the data flow through the pipeline. This study aims to investigate the opportunities and challenges practitioners experience after the implementation of the data pipeline at their organization.

The contribution of this paper is three-fold. First, it identifies the key challenges associated with data pipeline management. Second, it describes the opportunities of having a dedicated data pipeline. These challenges and opportunities are validated through a multi-case study with three leading companies in telecommunication and automobile domains. Furthermore, the paper provides a taxonomy of data pipeline challenges including infrastructural, organizational, and technical ones.

The remainder of this paper is organized as follows. In the next section, we present the background of the study. Section 3 discusses the research methodology adopted for conducting the study. Section 4 introduces the use cases and Section 5 describes the opportunities created by the pipelines. Section 6 details the challenges faced by practitioners while managing data pipelines. Section 7 outlines the threats to validity. Section 8 summarizes our study and the conclusions.

2   Background

Several recent studies have recognized the importance of data pipelines. Raman et al. [19] describes Big Data Pipelines as a mechanism to decompose complex analyses of large data sets into a series of simpler tasks, with independently tuned components for each task. Moreover, large scale companies like Google, Amazon, LinkedIn, and Facebook have recognized the importance of pipelines for their daily activities. Data errors and their impact on machine learning models are described in [6] by Caveness et al. They also propose a data validation framework that validates the data flowing through the machine learning pipeline.

Chen et al. describes the real-time data processing pipeline at Facebook [8] that handles hundreds of Gigabytes per second across hundreds of data pipelines. The authors also identify five important design decisions that affect their ease of use, performance, fault tolerance, scalability, and correctness and also demonstrate how these design decisions satisfy multiple use cases on Facebook. LinkedIn also has a similar real-time data processing pipeline described by Goodhope et al. in [10]. Data management challenges of deep learning is discussed by Munappy et al. through a multiple case study conducted with five different companies and classifies the challenges according to the data pipeline phases [16]. Lambda architecture proposed by N. Marz et al. and Kappa architecture [18] solves the challenge of handling real-time data streams [14]. Kappa architecture that considers both online and offline data as online is a simplified version of lambda.

Most of these studies illustrate the significance of data pipelines and the opportunities it can bring to the organizations. However, the challenges encountered in the industrial level during the development and maintenance of the data pipelines in production is still not completely solved.

3   Research Methodology

The objective of this study is to understand the existing data pipeline as well as the challenges experienced at the three case companies and to explore the opportunities of implementing a data pipeline. Specifically, this study aims to answer the following research question:

RQ: What are the practical opportunities and challenges associated with the implementation and maintenance of Data Pipelines at the industry level?

3.1   Exploratory Case Study

A qualitative approach was chosen for the case study as it allows the researchers to explore, study, and understand the real-world cases in its context in more depth [23]. Since the concept of data pipelines is a less explored topic in research, we have adopted a case study approach [21]. Moreover, the case study approach can investigate contemporary real-life situations and can provide a foundation for the application of ideas and extension of methods. Each case in the study pertains to a use case that makes use of data. Table 1 details the selected five use cases from three companies.

Table 1. Outline of use cases and roles of the interviewees

Company	Use cases	Interviewed experts	
		ID	Role
A	Data collection pipeline	R1	Senior data scientist
A	Data governance pipeline	R2	Data scientist
		R3	Analytics system architect
		R4	Software developer
A	Data pipeline for machine learning applications	R5	Data scientist
		R6	Senior data scientist
		R7	Software developer
		R8	Senior data scientist
B	Data collection pipeline	R9	Senior data engineer
		R10	Data engineer
		R11	Data engineer
		R12	Data analyst and superuser
C	Data quality monitoring pipeline	R13	Director of data analytics team
		R14	ETL developer
		R15	Software developer
		R16	Product owner for data analytics team

3.2 Data Collection

Qualitative data was collected by means of interviews and meetings [22]. Based on the objectives of the research, to explore and study the applications consuming data in the companies, an interview guide with 43 questions categorized into nine sections was formulated. The first and second sections focused on the background of the interviewee. The third and fourth sections focused on the data collection and processing in various use-cases and the last section inquired about data testing and monitoring practices and the impediments encountered during the implementation and maintenance of data pipelines. All interviews were conducted virtually via videoconferencing due to the COVID-19 pandemic. Each interview lasted 40 to 60 min. The interviews were recorded with the permission of respondents and were transcribed later for analysis. The first author is an action researcher for the past one year/six months at company A and B respectively who attend weekly meetings with data scientists and data analysts. The data collected through these means are also incorporated.

3.3 Data Analysis

The contact points at the companies helped with analyzing the parts of the pipeline as well as the infrastructure used for building that pipeline. These notes together with the codes from transcripts were further analyzed to obtain an end-to-end view of different use cases. The audio transcripts were investigated for relations, similarities, and dissimilarities. The interview transcripts and meeting notes were open coded following the guidelines by P. Burnard [2]. After careful analysis of collected data and based on the inputs from the other two authors, the first author who is an action researcher at two of the companies developed the findings of the study which were then validated with the interviewees from the companies by conducting a follow-up meeting. For further validation and to collect feedback from a different team, the findings were also presented before another panel including super users, managers, software developers, data engineers, and data scientists at all three companies who were not involved in the interviews. The results were updated according to the comments at each stage of the validation which in turn helped to reduce the researcher bias.

4   Use Cases

In this multi-case study, we explore data pipelines in real-world settings at large-scale software intensive organizations. Company A is within the telecommunication industry with nearly 100,000 employees who distributes easy to use, adoptable, and scalable services that enables connectivity. Further, we investigate Company B from automobile domain with 80,000 employees manufacturing its own cars responsible for collecting data from multiple manufacturing units as well as repair centers. Company C with 2,000 employees focus on automotive engineering and depends on Company B and does modular development, advanced virtual engineering and software development for them. In this section, we present five use cases of data pipelines studied from these three case companies A, B and C.

Case A1: Data Collection Pipeline
The company collects network performance data(every 15 min) as well as configuration management data(every 24 h) in the form of data logs from multiple sources distributed across the globe which is a challenging activity. Data collection from devices located in another country or customer network requires compliance with legal agreement. The collected data can have sensitive information like use details which needs responsible attention. Furthermore, data generated by sources can be of different formats and frequencies. For instance, data generation can be continuous, intermittent or as batches. Consequently, the data collection pipeline should be adaptable with different intensities of data flow.

When data collection pipeline is implemented, these challenges should be carefully addressed. Figure 1 shows the automatic data collection pipeline that collects data from distributed devices. In this scenario, the device is placed inside a piece of equipment owned by customers. However, the device data is extracted by filtering the customer's sensitive information. Base stations have data generation devices called nodes as well as a device for monitoring and managing the nodes. Data collection agents at the customer premise can interact either with nodes directly. However, access service is used for authentication. The data thus collected is transmitted through a secure tunnel to the data collection toolkit located at the company premise which also has access service for authentication. Data collection toolkit received the data and store it in the central data storage from where the teams can access the data using their data user credentials.

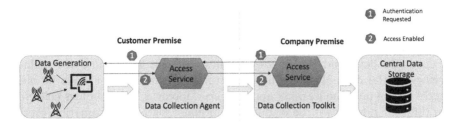

Fig. 1. Data collection pipeline

Case A2: Data Governance Pipeline

Figure 2 illustrates the data pipeline that serves a subset of teams in the company who are working with data whenever they need it (With the term 'data', we mean the link from which the original data can be downloaded). This data pipeline gets two types of data dumps: internal and external which is the performance management data collected in every 15 min from the devices deployed in the network. The internal data dump is the data that is ingested by the teams inside the company and external data dump is the data collected directly from the devices in the fields. The data ingestion method varies according to the data source and the ingested data is stored in the data storage for further use. The data can be encrypted form which needs decryption before storing it. Data archiver module sends encrypted data dump to the third-party services for decryption. Decoded links from the third party are transferred to data storage. Therefore, data from distributed sources are made available in a central location. Teams can request data from any stage of the pipeline. The monitoring mechanism in the pipeline is manually carried out by the 'flow guardian' who is responsible for fixing the issues in the pipeline.

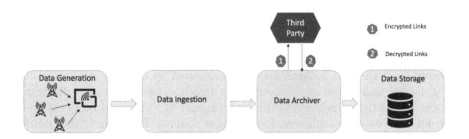

Fig. 2. Data governance pipeline

Case A3: Data Pipeline for Machine Learning Applications

Data for this pipeline is obtained from the devices that are sent to the repair center. Data pipelines for machine learning applications has four main steps namely ingest, store, transform and aggregate. Data generated by the source is gathered at a special zone in the field. The data ingestion module connected to those zones in the field collects data and ingest into the pipeline as batches. When new compressed files are found in the periodic checks, the transaction is logged and downloads it. These new files are then loaded into the archive directory of the data cluster. The data stored in the cluster cannot be used directly by the machine learning applications. Moreover, the data logs collected from different devices will be of different formats. Data transformation checks for the new files in the archive directory of the data cluster and when found, it is fetched, uncompressed and processed to convert it to an appropriate format. The converted data is then given as input to the data aggregation module where the data is aggregated and summarized to form structured data which is further given as input to the machine learning applications. Figure 3 illustrates the data pipeline for machine learning applications.

Fig. 3. Data pipeline for machine learning applications

Case B1: Data Collection Pipeline

The Company B collects and stores three types of data and distributes it for teams as well as co-working organizations distributed around the globe. Plant data, delivery data, warranty data and repair data are the different types of data that are collected from sources such as manufacturing plants, service centers, delivery centers and warranty offices. The company B collects product data from distributed manufacturing plants every 24 h. These manufacturing units will generate data for each product built there. However, not all the data generated by the plants are collected by the data collection agent of company B. Group Quality IT platform in the company demands the data that needs to be collected from the plants. Also, the data requested by the delivery centers are also collected and stored in the company's data warehouse. Figure 4 illustrates the data collection pipeline working in company B. The data collected from different sources are in different formats and volume. Therefore, data transfer mechanism as well as data storage is different for all data sources. The data is ingested from the primary storage and then transformed into a uniform format and stored in a data warehouse which then acts as a supplier for teams as well as other organizations who demand for data. For instance, the delivery centers needs data about the products that are manufactured in the plants.

Fig. 4. Data collection pipeline

Case C1: Data Quality Analysis Pipeline

The company C receives data collected and stored by company B and creates data quality reports which is used by data scientists team for analysing the product quality. For instance, the report can be used to understand the model that is sent to repair centers frequently. When the data quality is not satisfactory, investigation is initiated and actions are taken to fix the data quality issues. Company B sends data through private network to company C, and they store it in a data storage from where data scientists access it for creating reports and training machine learning models. Figure 5 shows the data pipeline for data quality analysis at Company C.

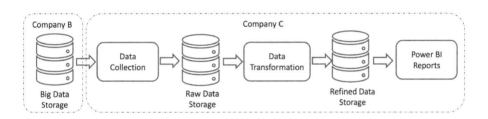

Fig. 5. Data quality analysis pipeline

5 Challenges to Data Pipeline Management

Based on our research, we see that organizations benefit from developing and maintaining data pipelines because of the automation it provides. On the other hand, there are certain challenges faced by practitioners while developing and managing data pipelines. This section describes the challenges of data pipelines derived through the interpretation of interviews based on the use cases described in Sect. 4. After careful analysis of the challenges obtained from the interviews, we formulated a taxonomy for the classification of challenges namely Infrastructure Challenges, Organizational Challenges and Data Quality Challenges which are described in detail below.

5.1 Infrastructure Challenges

Data pipelines are developed to solve complex data infrastructure challenges. However, data pipeline management has to deal with some infrastructural challenges listed below.

Integrating New Data Sources: Data pipelines collect data from multiple distributed devices and make it available in a single access point thus solving data accessibility problem. However, the data sources increase rapidly in most of the business scenarios. Therefore, data pipelines should be able to integrate the new data source and also accommodate the data from that new source which is often difficult due to many reasons. Based on the empirical findings from the case study, three common reasons are listed below.

- The data source can be entirely different from the existing sources.
- Format of the data produced by the source might not be compatible with the data pipeline standards.
- Addition of the new source may introduce overhead on the data handling capability of the pipeline.

All the use cases except case C1 described in Sect. 4 experience the challenge of integrating new data sources.

Data Pipeline Scalability: The ability of a data pipeline to scale with the increased amount of ingested data, while keeping the cost low is a real challenge experienced by the data pipeline developers. When the data produced by the source increases, the data pipeline loses the ability to transfer the data from one node to another leading to the data pipeline breakage and loss of data.

Increased Number of Nodes and Connectors in Upstream: Data pipelines are a chain of nodes performing activities connected through connectors that enable data transportation between the two nodes. Essentially, the nodes can have more than one capability. However, for the easy detection of faults, each of the nodes should be preferably assigned a single capability. Thus, the number of nodes and connectors increases in the upstream in relation to the data product yielded from the pipeline. This in turn increases the complexity of the data pipeline and decreases ease of implementation. The fragility and complexity of the data pipeline lead to inevitable delays in adding new types of activity data, which resulted in sticking new activities into inappropriate existing types to avoid human effort, or worse, not capturing activities at all. Practitioners R9, R10, R11 and R14 working on case B1 and C1 raised this challenge.

> "With the increased number of components in the data pipeline which in turn makes it difficult to understand and maintain. It is difficult to attain the right balance between robustness and complexity" - Senior Data Scientist (R6)

Trade-off Between Data Pipeline Complexity and Robustness: To build a robust data pipeline, we should have two essential components called fault detection and mitigation strategies. Fault detection identifies faults at each of the data pipeline stages and mitigation strategies help to reduce the impact of the fault. Including these two components increases the complexity of data pipelines. Moreover, it requires the data pipeline developers to anticipate the faults that can occur at each stage and define mitigation actions such that the data flow through the pipeline is not hampered. Some of the common faults can be anticipated and mitigated. However, it is not possible to identify all possible faults and define mitigation actions for those. Senior data scientists working on Case B1 and C1 and data scientist, R5 working on case A3 pointed out this as an important challenge.

Repeated Alarms: Sending alarms are the most common and simple mitigation actions automatically taken by the data pipelines. Some faults take time to get fixed and during this time, the person or the team responsible for fixing the issues will get repeated alarms for the same issue. In the worst scenario, this can even lead to new alarms left unnoticed. Sending alarms is a mechanism adopted by all five data pipelines described in Sect. 4. However, data engineers and software developers who participated in the study want to have an alternate mitigation strategy to replace the repeated automatic alarms in the data pipeline such as sending the notification only once and then waiting for a fix for some time.

"Sending notifications is less appreciated by the teams as we get totally submerged in alarms during some days and some notifications are repeatedly sent and it is hard to identify new ones from the huge pile" - Senior Data Engineer (R9)

5.2   Organizational Challenges

This section gives a brief overview of the organization level challenges to data pipeline management.

Dependency on Other Organizations: Data pipelines can be spread between more than one company like case IV and V. Therefore, co-operation and collaboration are required from all the participating companies to maintain a healthy data pipeline. In most cases, external companies will have very minimal knowledge of what is happening in the other part of the pipeline. For instance, to deliver high-quality data product, company C requires support from company B as they are the suppliers of data.

Lack of Communication Between Teams: Data pipelines are meant to share data between various teams in the organization. However, each team builds pipelines for their use case and thus at least some initial activities are repeated in several data pipelines leading to redundant storage of data. Moreover, if any of the steps fails, the responsible person gets a notification from different teams at the same time for the same issue. Cases A1, A2, and A3 are collecting the same data and storing it in their databases. Data pipeline in case A3 can fetch data stored by data pipeline A2 instead of collecting raw data from the data sources. However, practitioners working on these use cases were completely unaware of these repeated activities in their pipelines.

Increased Responsibilities of Data Pipeline Owner: All faults in the data pipeline cannot be fixed automatically. Some faults demand either partial or complete human intervention. Therefore, a flow guardian or data pipeline owner is assigned for each of the pipelines who pays attention to data pipeline activities and takes care of the faults requiring a manual fix. Further, it is hard to assess what code might break due to any given change in data. With the increased use of data pipelines, the responsibilities of the flow guardian or data pipeline owner also increase. Practitioner R11 is assigned responsibilities of a flow guardian, and he has to manually monitor the data pipelines and initiate an investigation and fix whenever a problem is encountered. As Company C is also dependent on Company B, responsibilities are shared between R10 and R11. R10 takes care of request from Company C and R11 attends to the problems with company B.

> "Nobody wants to take up the responsibility of flow guardian. We feel that it consumes a lot of time and effort" - Director of Data Analytics Team (R13)

DataOps-DevOps Collaboration: When seeking to obtain better results from machine learning models require better, more focused data, better labeling, and the use of different attributes. It also means that data scientists and data engineers need to be part of the software development process. DataOps is concerned with a set of practices for the development of software and management of data respectively. Both concepts emphasize communication and collaboration between various teams of the same organization. DataOps combines DevOps with data scientists and data engineers to support development. The challenge of managing and delivering massive volumes of discordant data to those who can use it to generate value is proving extremely hard. Moreover, people working with data are less interested in learning new technologies and tools while it is not a hassle for DevOps users.

5.3   Data Quality Challenges

This section gives a detailed list of the data quality challenges due to improper data pipeline management.

Missing Data Files: Data files can be lost completely or partially during the transmission from one node to another. Fault detection mechanism can identify the exact point of disappearance. However, obtaining the missing files once again is a complicated task. Missing data files are only detected at the end of the data pipeline and in some cases, this results in poor quality data products. All the use cases experience the challenge of missing data files at different stages of data pipelines and one of the practitioners, R4 identified that 38,732 files had gone missing at a particular stage of the data pipeline over five months.

> "Data quality is a challenge that is being discussed over years. But, at industry level we still struggle to achieve desired level of data quality" - Senior Data Scientist (R1)

Operational Errors: Data pipelines encounter operational errors which hampers the overall functioning. Operational errors are very common in non-automated data pipelines. Some parts of the data pipelines cannot be completely automated. Human errors at these steps are the reasons for operational errors. For instance, data labeling in a data pipeline cannot be automated completely due to the unavailability of automated annotation techniques that are compatible with all types of datasets. Practitioner R12, R13, R4, and R3 raised the problem of operational errors and their impact on their respective data pipelines.

Logical Changes: Data drifts and change in data distribution results in the data pipeline failures due to the incompatible logic defined in the data pipeline. Therefore, the data pipeline needs to be monitored continuously for change in data distributions and data shifts. Besides, data pipelines should be updated frequently by changing the business logic according to the changes in data sources. Practitioner R12, R13, and R16 explained the struggles of working with outdated business logic in their data pipelines.

6 Opportunities

The previous section illustrated the challenges of data pipelines when implemented in real-world. However, there are many opportunities the data pipeline offers through automating fault detection and mitigation. In this section, we survey some of the most promising opportunities of data pipelines and how practitioners working on data are benefited by the implementation of it.

6.1 Solve Data Accessibility Challenges

Data generated by assorted multiple devices are collected, aggregated, and stored in central storage by data pipelines without human intervention. As a result, data teams within and outside the organization can access data from that central storage if they have proper data access permissions. Accessing data from devices located on the customer premises is a difficult and tedious task. Most often, the devices will be distributed around the globe and teams has to prepare legal agreements complying with the rules of that specific country where the device is located for accessing data. When the data is stored after aggregation, data loses its granularity, and as a result, teams working with fine-grained data has to collect data separately. With data pipelines, teams can access data from any point of the data pipeline if they have necessary permissions. This eliminates repeated collection and storage of the same data by multiple teams.

6.2 Save Time and Effort of Human Resources

Automation of data-related activities is maximized through the implementation of data pipelines thereby reducing the human intervention. When a data pipeline has inbuilt monitoring capability, faults will be automatically detected and alarms will be raised. This reduces the effort of data pipeline managers and flow guardians. As the data pipeline is completely automated, requests by teams will be answered quickly. For instance, if the data quality is not satisfactory to the data analyst, he can request the data from the desired store in the data pipeline, and he receives it without delay. On the other hand, if the workflow is not automated, the data analyst has to investigate and find out where the error has occurred and then inform the responsible person to send the data again which eventually delays the entire data analysis process. Moreover, the effort of the data analyst is also wasted while investigating the source of data error.

"We spent time cleaning the data to meet the required quality so that it can be used for further processing such as training or analytics. With the data pipeline, it is easy to acquire better quality data." - Analytics System Architect (R3)

6.3 Improves Traceability of Data Workflow

Data workflow consists of several interconnected processes that make it complex. Consequently, it is difficult to detect the exact point that induced error. For instance, if the end-user realizes that part of the data is missing, it might be lost during data transmission, while storing the data in a particular schema or due to unavailability of an intermediate process. The end-user has to guess all the different possibilities of data loss and has to investigate all the possibilities to recover the lost data. This is a time-consuming task especially when the data workflow is long and complex. Company C has reported that they have experienced this problem several times and as they are getting data from company B, it took a lot of time for them to rectify the error, and sometimes they won't be able to recover the data. After implementing data pipelines, the process of detecting faults is automated thereby increasing traceability.

"Everyone in the organization is aware of the steps and with data pipelines, you will have full traceability of when the pipeline slowing down, leaking, or stops working." - Data Scientist (R5)

6.4 Supports Heterogeneous Data Sources

Data pipelines can handle multiple assorted data sources. Data ingestion is a process through which data from multiple sources are made available to the data pipeline in a uniform format. Data Ingestion is the process of streaming-in massive amounts of data in our system, from several external sources, for running analytics and other operations required by the business.

"Data streams in through several sources into the system at different speeds and sizes. Data ingestion unifies this data and decreases our workload. Data ingestion can be performed as batches or real-time." - Data Engineer (R10)

6.5   Accelerates Data Life Cycle Activities

The data pipeline encompasses the data life cycle activities from collection to refining; from storage to analysis. It covers the entire data moving process, from where the data is collected, such as on an edge device, where and how it is moved, such as through data streams or batch-processing, and where the data is moved to, such as a data lake or application. Activities involved in the data pipeline are automatically executed in a predefined order and consequently, human involvement is minimized. As the activities are triggered by themselves, the data pipeline accelerates the data life cycle process. Moreover, most of the data pipeline activities are automated thereby increasing the speed of data life cycle process and productivity.

6.6   Standardize the Data Workflow

The activities in a data workflow and their execution order are defined by a data pipeline which gives the employees in the organization an overall view of the entire data management process. Thus, it enables better communication and collaboration between various teams in the organization. Further, data pipelines reduce the burden on IT teams thereby reducing support and maintenance costs as well. Standardization through data pipelines also enables monitoring for known issues and quick troubleshooting of common problems.

> *"Data pipelines provide a bird's eye view of the end to end data workflow. Besides, it also ensures a short resolution time for frequently occurred problems."* - Product Owner (R16)

6.7   Improved Data Analytics and Machine Learning Models

Organizations can make use of carefully designed data pipelines for the preparation of high quality, well-structured, and reliable datasets for analytics and also for developing machine learning as well as deep learning models. Besides, data pipelines automate the movement, aggregation, transformation, and storage of data from multiple assorted sources. Machine learning models are highly sensitive to the input training data. Therefore, quality of training data is very important. Data pipelines are traceable since the stages are predefined yielding better quality data for the models. Moreover, data pipelines ensure a smooth flow of data unless it fails in one of the steps.

6.8   Data Sharing Between Teams

Data pipelines enable easy data sharing between teams. Practitioners R4, R8, and R9 mentioned that the data collected from devices in the field are undergoing the same processing for different use cases. For instance, data cleaning is an activity performed by all the teams before feeding the data to ML/DL models. Therefore, there is a possibility of the same data going through the same sequence of steps within different teams of the same organization. Further, data storage also is wasted in such cases due to redundant storage. With the implementation of data pipelines, the teams can request data from a particular step in some other data pipeline and can process the subsequent steps in their data pipeline. However, the data pipeline should be able to serve the requests in such cases.

6.9 Critical Element for DataOps

DataOps is a process-oriented approach on data that spans from the origin of ideas to the creation of graphs and charts which creates value. It merges two data pipelines namely value pipeline and innovation pipeline. Value pipeline is a series of stages that produce value or insights and innovation pipeline is the process through which new analytic ideas are introduced into the value pipeline. Therefore, data pipelines are critical elements for DataOps together with Agile data science, continuous integration, and continuous delivery practices.

7   Threats to Validity

External Validity: The presented work is derived from the cases studied with teams in the domains of automobile and telecommunication. Some parts of the work can be seen in parts of the company differently. All the terminologies used in the company are normalized and the implementation details are explained with necessary level of abstraction [15]. We do not claim that the opportunities and challenges will be exactly the same for industries from a different discipline.

Internal Validity: To address internal validity threat, the findings were validated with other teams in the company who were not involved in the study. Further validation can be done by involving more companies, which we see as future work [21].

8   Related Works

This section presents the most related previous studies on data pipeline development and maintenance.

P. O'Donovan et al. describes an information system model that provides a scalable and fault tolerant big data pipeline for integrating, processing and analysing industrial equipment data [17]. The authors explain the challenges such as development of infrastructures to support real-time smart communication, cultivation of multidisciplinary workforces and next-generation IT departments. However, the study is solely based on a smart manufacturing domain. A survey study by C.L.Philip Chen et al. discusses about Big Data, Big Data applications, Big Data opportunities and challenges, as well as the state-of-the-art techniques and technologies to deal with the Big Data problems [7]. A Big Data platform Quarry is proposed by P. Jovanovic et al. [11] manages the complete data integration lifecycle in the context of complex Big Data settings, specifically focusing on the variety of data coming from numerous external data sources. Data quality challenges and standards/frameworks to assess data quality are discussed in many works [4,5,20]. Although there exists significant number of data quality assessment and mitigation platforms, the industrial practitioners experience data quality issues which indicates that the problem is not solved.

9 Conclusions

The multi-case study indicates challenges and opportunities involved in implementing and managing data pipelines. The challenges are categorized into three namely infrastructural, organizational, and data quality challenges. Nevertheless, the benefits data pipeline brings to the data-driven organizations are not frivolous. A data pipeline is a critical element that can also support a DataOps culture in the organizations. The factors inhibiting Data pipeline adoption were mostly concerned with human aspects e.g. lack of communication and resistance to change; and technical aspects e.g. the complexity of development. Suitability of completely automated data pipelines might be questioned for certain domains and industry sectors, at least for now. However, a completely automated data pipeline is beneficial for the domains that can adopt it. Frequent updates are advantageous, but the effects of short release cycles and other data pipeline practices need to be studied in detail. Understanding the effects on a larger scale could help in assessing the real value of data pipelines.

The purpose and contribution of this paper is to explore the real-time challenges of data pipelines and provide a taxonomy of the challenges. Secondly, it discusses the benefits of data pipelines while building data-intensive models. In future work, we intend to further extend the study with potential solutions to overcome the listed data pipeline challenges.

References

1. Batini, C., Rula, A., Scannapieco, M., Viscusi, G.: From data quality to big data quality. In: Big Data: Concepts, Methodologies, Tools, and Applications, pp. 1934–1956. IGI Global (2016)
2. Burnard, P.: A method of analysing interview transcripts in qualitative research. Nurse Educ. Today 11(6), 461–466 (1991)
3. Cai, L., Zhu, Y.: The challenges of data quality and data quality assessment in the big data era. Data Sci. J. 14 (2015)
4. Carlo, B., Daniele, B., Federico, C., Simone, G.: A data quality methodology for heterogeneous data. Int. J. Database Manage. Syst. 3(1), 60–79 (2011)
5. Carretero, A.G., Gualo, F., Caballero, I., Piattini, M.: MAMD 2.0: environment for data quality processes implantation based on ISO 8000–6X and ISO/IEC 33000. Comput. Stand. Interfaces 54, 139–151 (2017)
6. Caveness, E., GC, P.S., Peng, Z., Polyzotis, N., Roy, S., Zinkevich, M.: Tensorflow data validation: Data analysis and validation in continuous ml pipelines. In: Proceedings of the 2020 ACM SIGMOD International Conference on Management of Data, pp. 2793–2796 (2020)

7. Chen, C.P., Zhang, C.Y.: Data-intensive applications, challenges, techniques and technologies: a survey on big data. Inf. Sci. **275**, 314–347 (2014)
8. Chen, G.J., et al.: Realtime data processing at Facebook. In: Proceedings of the 2016 International Conference on Management of Data, pp. 1087–1098 (2016)
9. Davenport, T.H., Dyché, J.: Big data in big companies. Int. Inst. Anal. **3**, 1–31 (2013)
10. Goodhope, K., et al.: Building Linkedin's real-time activity data pipeline. IEEE Data Eng. Bull. **35**(2), 33–45 (2012)
11. Jovanovic, P., Nadal, S., Romero, O., Abelló, A., Bilalli, B.: Quarry: a user-centered big data integration platform. Inf. Syst. Front. 1–25 (2020). https://doi.org/10.1007/s10796-020-10001-y
12. Kaisler, S., Armour, F., Espinosa, J.A., Money, W.: Big data: issues and challenges moving forward. In: 46th Hawaii International Conference on System Sciences, pp. 995–1004. IEEE (2013)
13. Marr, B.: Big Data in Practice: How 45 Successful Companies used Big Data Analytics to Deliver Extraordinary Results. Wiley, New York (2016)
14. Marz, N., Warren, J.: Big Data: Principles and Best Practices of Scalable Real-time Data Systems. Manning Publications Co., New York (2015)
15. Maxwell, J.A.: Designing a qualitative study. In: The SAGE Handbook of Applied Social Research Methods, vol. 2, pp. 214–253 (2008)
16. Munappy, A., Bosch, J., Olsson, H.H., Arpteg, A., Brinne, B.: Data management challenges for deep learning. In: 45th Euromicro Conference on Software Engineering and Advanced Applications (SEAA), pp. 140–147. IEEE (2019)
17. O'Donovan, P., Leahy, K., Bruton, K., O'Sullivan, D.T.J.: An industrial big data pipeline for data-driven analytics maintenance applications in large-scale smart manufacturing facilities. J. Big Data **2**(1), 1–26 (2015). https://doi.org/10.1186/s40537-015-0034-z
18. Pathirage, M.: Kappa architecture - where every thing is a stream. http://milinda.pathirage.org/kappa-architecture.com/. Accessed 28 Sept 2020
19. Raman, K., Swaminathan, A., Gehrke, J., Joachims, T.: Beyond myopic inference in big data pipelines. In: Proceedings of the 19th ACM SIGKDD International Conference on Knowledge Discovery and Data Mining, pp. 86–94 (2013)
20. Redman, T.C.: Data's credibility problem. Harvard Bus. Rev. **91**(12), 84–88 (2013)
21. Runeson, P., Höst, M.: Guidelines for conducting and reporting case study research in software engineering. Empirical Softw. Eng. **14**(2), 131 (2009)
22. Singer, J., Sim, S.E., Lethbridge, T.C.: Software engineering data collection for field studies. In: Shull, F., Singer, J., Sjøberg, D.I.K. (eds) Guide to Advanced Empirical Software Engineering, pp. 9–34. Springer, London (2008). https://doi.org/10.1007/978-1-84800-044-5_1
23. Verner, J.M., Sampson, J., Tosic, V., Bakar, N.A., Kitchenham, B.A.: Guidelines for industrially-based multiple case studies in software engineering. In: 2009 Third International Conference on Research Challenges in Information Science, pp. 313–324. IEEE (2009)

From a Data Science Driven Process to a Continuous Delivery Process for Machine Learning Systems

Lucy Ellen Lwakatare[1]([✉]), Ivica Crnkovic[1], Ellinor Rånge[2], and Jan Bosch[1]

[1] Chalmers University of Technology, Gothenburg University, Gothenburg, Sweden
{llucy,ivica.crnkovic,jan.bosch}@chalmers.se
[2] Ericsson, Gothenburg, Sweden
ellinor.range@ericsson.com

Abstract. Development of machine learning (ML) enabled applications in real-world settings is challenging and requires the consideration of sound software engineering (SE) principles and practices. A large body of knowledge exists on the use of modern approaches to developing traditional software components, but not ML components. Using exploratory case study approach, this study investigates the adoption and use of existing software development approaches, specifically continuous delivery (CD), to development of ML components. Research data was collected using a multivocal literature review (MLR) and focus group technique with ten practitioners involved in developing ML-enabled systems at a large telecommunication company. The results of our MLR show that companies do not outright apply CD to the development of ML components rather as a result of improving their development practices and infrastructure over time. A process improvement conceptual model, that includes the description of CD application to ML components is developed and initially validated in the study.

Keywords: Machine learning system · Software process · Continuous delivery

1 Introduction

Artificial intelligence (AI) techniques are increasingly incorporated in diverse real-world software applications [18]. The development process of AI-enabled applications and systems[1] that employ machine learning (ML) techniques rely on high quality data to build ML models. When built, the ML models are used in production to make inference on new data. A significant large amount of development effort is spent on improving efficiency in data management and feature engineering during ML model development [22].

Few studies report on co-development of traditional software components and AI components in software-intensive systems [18], which in practice employ

---

[1] By AI-enabled systems we mean the software systems that include ML components.

© Springer Nature Switzerland AG 2020
M. Morisio et al. (Eds.): PROFES 2020, LNCS 12562, pp. 185–201, 2020.
https://doi.org/10.1007/978-3-030-64148-1_12

different software development paradigms [3]. And even though ML components are reported to impact existing software development practices, such as software requirements and testing [27], there is a little consideration on the ML development process. This is problematic because ML components are often integrated into a software system containing traditional software components and there is a tendency of wanting to use existing software development practices [25]. At the same time, it is not clear how companies can integrate existing software development practices when developing ML components. Investigating the latter helps in defining an integrated and well-managed development process for an AI-enabled system [21].

Modern software development approaches, such as continuous delivery (CD) are well-established in practice and emphasise frequent delivery of software changes [24]. According to practitioners [9], applying CD to development of ML components can accelerate the delivery of ML artifacts (code, data and ML models) and helps to ensure reproducibility and increased rate of experimentation of ML models. However, there is limited reporting of the use of CD in development of ML-enabled systems.

A disconnection between ML-processes and software development processes can cause problems in the overall process, require additional efforts and result in a lower quality of the final products [18]. The aim of the study is to investigate the potential use of existing software development approaches, in particular CD, to the development process of ML components. The main research question of the study is the following.

Research Question: How to enable modern software development process with continuous delivery for AI-enabled systems?

To investigate the application of CD to development of ML components, we first performed a multivocal literature review (MLR) [7]. From MLR, we analysed development practices and infrastructure of ML-enabled systems and derived a conceptual model. The conceptual model distinguishes five stages for integration of ML and software processes towards CD process for ML enabled systems. We then performed an initial validation of the conceptual model using a focus group discussion [15] with ten practitioners who are actively developing ML-enabled systems, and three case studies, from a large telecommunication company.

The main contributions of the paper is twofold. First, the study presents a conceptual model of process improvement for ML-enabled systems that synthesizes transformation of development practises over time. Second, the study provides an initial empirical validation of the proposed conceptual model.

The rest of the paper is organised as follows. Section 2 gives an overview of basic activities in a ML workflow, and main principles in a modern software development process. Section 3 describes the applied research methods. Section 4 provides findings and their initial validation in Sect. 5. Section 6 briefly discusses the findings and Sect. 7 concludes the paper.

2   Background and Related Work

This section presents an overview of the development process of ML-enabled systems. First, the section presents the ML workflow, which constitutes development stages and activities commonly performed in development of ML systems. Second, a summary of CD and its application to the development process of ML systems is presented.

2.1   Development Process of ML-Enabled Systems

The development of ML-enabled systems is data-centering, as the starting problem for such systems is data collection, understanding and preparation for ML modeling [22,26]. These processes originate from the CRISP-DM model [11,28], which focuses on data-mining process that identifies five stages, namely *business understanding, data understanding, data preparation, modeling, evaluation, and deployment*. An overview of the development process of ML-enabled software system developed at Microsoft is provided by Amershi et al. [1]. The development process consists of nine stages that primarily focus on developing, deploying, and operating ML models. The nine stages include *model requirements, data collection, data cleaning, data labeling, feature engineering, model training, model evaluation, model deployment, and model monitoring* [1].

A short overview of these stages is as follows. In the ML model requirement stage, the designers reason about the relation between system requirements and ML model requirements [1]. The stage involves gaining an understanding of what input data is needed, while clearly specifying the expected output, and experimenting with different ML algorithms [1,27]. Once the model requirements are determined, input data is collected, processed and prepared (data cleaning, data labeling, and feature engineering) for ML algorithms. Data cleaning involves handling data inaccuracies (e.g. missing values or outliers) from the collected raw data. Data labeling involves assigning ground truth 'labels' to each record, which can be done manually or automatically depending on the domain. Data management and feature engineering activities are the most critical and challenging parts of ML system development. Model training and evaluation activities are conducted frequently and, with each iteration, designers perform different optimizations in order to improve the model based on evaluation results. When the final model is selected, it is deployed and monitored in production in order to improve and maintain its quality. For most software applications it remains crucial that deployed models adapt to the changes of the incoming data and that the development practices and infrastructure support timely updates of the models. A commonly used method is to periodically retrain deployed models offline using historical data. This is because as often the size of data collected is large and requires much pre-processing to create training datasets [18].

For most software applications, ML components are developed alongside other traditional software components. However, the development process of ML components neglects existing software development processes and practices

[10]. Wan et al., [27] synthesize the impacts of ML components across various software development practices (e.g. software requirements, design, testing) and work characteristics (e.g. skill variety, problem-solving, and task identity). Their work as well as that of others show that the existing software development practices need to be adapted and extended [14,19,29]. In particular, software requirements practices need to be data-driven while mostly relying on existing data of a particular application domain. Software testing and quality assurance practices for ML systems will not only focus on detecting bugs in code, but also in ML frameworks, the models (learning program) as well as data in order to ensure correctness, model relevance, security, privacy, and fairness [29].

2.2   Continuous Delivery for ML-Enabled Systems

CD is an established software development approach emphasizing on creating a repeatable, reliable process for releasing software changes frequently to production environment [12]. According to the authors [12], a key tenet in CD is to automate almost everything especially software build, testing, and deployment processes while also ensuring that all software artifacts are kept in a version control system. CD is a particular method of agile software development approach influenced by lean principles [17]. DevOps—concept emphasizing collaboration between development and operations—is important in the implementation of CD [17,24]. In CD, the deployment pipeline is an automated manifestation of the entire software development process starting with getting software changes from a version control system until when the changes are visible to end-users [12]. DevOps practices in the deployment pipeline involve automation of the deployment process, including automatic provisioning of the environments aimed at eliminating (or minimizing) manual system hand-overs from the development team to the operations team.

There is limited reporting on the use of CD to development of ML system development in literature. Studies report on applying and adapting agile software approach, including continuous integration (CI) practice, to development of ML systems [13]. According to the authors [13] the use of agile approaches in ML system development is hampered by poor architectural designs and limited maintenance plans of ML systems. Renggli et al. [23], proposed a CI system for ML system, which largely follows traditional CI system by allowing users to define ML-specific test conditions. However, in contrast to traditional CI system, the proposed CI system for ML is *probabilistic* meaning test conditions are evaluated with respect to the probability of valid test and error tolerance measures [23]. One main challenging issue that is driving the adoption of CD to ML system development is ad-hoc processes in the iterative ML model development activities. According to practitioners [9], CD addresses this problem by automating the process of ML model building through version control and dependency management of ML artifacts.

3   Research Method

To explore how CD is applied to the development of ML systems, we used exploratory case study and collected data by first performing a multivocal literature review (MLR) and then conducting a focus group discussion with practitioners.

3.1   Multivocal Literature Review (MLR)

MLR was selected because our systematic literature review (SLR) [18] that focused on peer-reviewed papers showed that the aspect was discussed in only a few papers. We performed MLR by following the guideline for conducting MLR in software engineering provided by [7]. The goal was to review reports that describe the application of CD to the development of ML-enabled systems.

Data Sources and Search Strategy. We used our previous literature review [18] to include formal literature (1 study), while Google search engine was used to identify grey literature (e.g. white papers and blog posts). The search string used to source grey literature was "continuous delivery" AND "machine learning". After an initial review of the records, we observed a common use of the term 'MLOps'. The term was also used in the search process. The search process on the Google search engine was conducted in April 2020. The first author went through the retrieved records page-by-page while applying inclusion and exclusion criteria (below) in order to select relevant records. A total of 17 records were retrieved from the Google search engine and only 8 (Table 1) were selected for further data extraction and analysis.

Table 1. Overview of included documents from MLR. (*Included from SLR*)

Ref.	ML-enabled system - use case/objective
[2]	Spotify's discover weekly – *to improve music discovery*
[9]	Uber self-driving vehicle systems – *object detection, motion planning*
[13]	Healthcare cost analytics product – *estimating healthcare cost*
[16]	Onfido identify verification SaaS – *to verify people's identity*
[20]	Twitter timelines – *to show the best Tweets first*
[25]*	MeetMe application – *Recommender system*
[5,6,8]	General

Inclusion and Exclusion Criteria. Inclusion and exclusion criteria were carefully defined to ensure that relevant records were included and not those which were outside the scope of the study. The inclusion criteria considered sources that (i) described in detail the application of CD to development process of ML system, preferably also referencing an existing application in real-world settings, (ii) authorship and evidence of the described experiences can be established e.g., published on organisation's blog or there is audit trail via multiple sources (videos, links to other posts) and (iii) written in English. For exclusion criteria, records were excluded if they did not meet the inclusion criteria.

Data Extraction and Quality Assessment. All selected records were retrieved as PDF documents and stored in NVivo for data extraction using thematic coding technique [4]. At first, codes were assigned inductively to the 'CD for ML' category and *meaning, rationale, practices and tools* as its sub-categories. The other theme emerging across the sources was also coded in Nvivo as 'practice transformations' category and with *stage1, stage2, stage3, stage4, and stage5* as its sub-categories. This was followed by several iterations of reviewing and improving the coding for clarity and saturation.

3.2 Focus Group

A focus group is a technique that extends an open-ended interview to a group discussion [15]. Data is primarily collected through planned discussions on a topic determined by the researcher [15]. In this study, the researcher moderated a group discussion, and the guideline by Kontio et al. [15] was used in designing the focus group.

Designing and Conducting Focus Group. We formed a focus group with ten participants *(operational product owner, line manager, ML engineer, software developer, and six data scientists)* from a large telecommunication company. The participants were selected based on their experience and active involvement in the development of ML-enabled systems. Specifically, developing ML systems that improve the quality of telecommunication hardware (HW) by using product life cycle data collected from the field. The researcher made initial contact with the line manager of the data analytics R&D organization, who together with one developer selected suitable participants for the focus group. The analytics R&D organization employs roughly 100 persons at three different sites of which half are data scientists or have AI/ML competence.

The researcher was introduced to the selected ten participants and then later sent an invitation containing information about the objective of the group discussion and agenda. The group discussion was conducted virtually and lasted for 1 h and 45 min. Prior to the actual meeting, the researcher first interviewed the developer to get an overview of development context information. The developer also provided additional documents related to development practices and ML uses cases being worked on. Later, the researcher and developer had a meeting to review materials planned for the focus group as well as getting background information of each participant. During the focus group meeting, the researcher moderated the first part of the discussions using open-ended questions. In the second part, the researcher presented the findings of MLR for further discussion. The entire virtual meeting was recorded and the researcher summarized the recording for analysis and reporting.

Data Analysis. From the focus group discussion, a summary of descriptions of past and present development practices and infrastructure of three selected ML use cases were thematically coded. In addition, the additional documents provided by the developer were also coded. The pre-defined themes from previous MLR were used during thematic data analysis.

4   Findings

This section presents the findings of our MLR that investigated the application of CD to the development of ML-enabled systems. Our data analysis revealed that typically companies do not outright apply CD to ML system development but rather tend to achieve it as a result of improving their development practices and infrastructure. This improvement is depicted in five stages, visualized in Fig. 1 and described in Table 2.

We distinguish five different stages of development practices improvement: (i) Manual data science-driven process, (ii) Standardized experimental-operational symmetry process, (iii) Automated ML workflow process, (iv) Integrated software development and ML workflow processes, and (v) Automated and fully integrated CD and ML workflow process. We discuss the characteristic, practices, and challenges of each stage next sections.

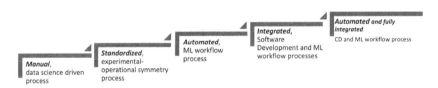

Fig. 1. Development process improvement model for ML-enabled systems

4.1   *Manual*, Data Science-Driven Process

Characteristic. Early development of ML-enabled systems is driven by manual development activities conducted by research data scientists [6,8,9,13,20]. At this stage, data scientists and ML researchers focus on building state-of-the-art ML models, but their process of collecting training datasets and building ML models is entirely manual, i.e. by using basic tools and manually entering instructions for data manipulation [8].

Practices. The development process is driven by experimental code that is interactively written and executed in notebooks until a workable model is achieved.

Table 2. Description of development process improvement model stages

Stage	Characteristics
Manual, data science-driven process	Data scientist's manual execution of ML model development activities and the disconnect of the process with production environment
Standardized, experimental – operational ML process	Systematization of ML model development steps and its alignment with operations processes
Automated, ML workflow process	Increased automation within and across the standardized ML workflow steps
Integrated, software development and ML workflow processes	ML component is versioned and tested w.r.t other system components and redeployed with requirements from software system
Automated and fully integrated, CD and ML workflow process	Orchestration services to automate and coordinate build, test and deployment of ML pipelines, and runtime support for system monitoring and data collection

Data scientists tend to switch back and forth between different ML libraries and frameworks implemented in their preferred programming languages [2]. There is a disconnection between ML model development and its operation in production [6,8]. To deploy trained ML model in production, data scientists handover the trained model to software developers [8,13], e.g. through checked code in repository or ML model registry. In turn, application developers have their own complex setup of integrating and deploying the models in production [2,8]. For deployment, application developers need to make available the features that are required by the models in order to avoid problems, e.g. training-serving skew [8].

Challenges. An inadequately-defined training dataset negatively affects the functioning of all ML workflow steps [13] (described in next stage). While models often break when deployed in a production environment, there is no active monitoring ML models in production [8]. The latter together with the lack of clearly defined and quality training datasets make all future updates to the product unnecessarily challenging [13]. The different manual activities increase the risk for new errors throughout the process making debugging difficult [2,6,20,25].

4.2 *Standardized,* Experimental – Operational Symmetry Process

Characteristic. This stage focuses on implementing synergy between ML model development and the operational processes, including model deployment and maintenance activities.

Practices. Specifying and instituting structured ML workflow process steps that apply to a wide array of scenarios e.g. data organisation methods, model experimentation, and deployment management [2,8,9,20]. This is in addition to building connectors to commonly used ML frameworks and libraries by different teams

[2,6,20]. Common steps of ML workflow include data ingestion, data validation, model training, model evaluation, and model training. Each step in itself touches a variety of different systems and custom scripts or ad-hoc commands are used for extracting, transforming, loading data, training, validating, and serving models [9]. As such, to construct ML workflow, the components need to be reusable, composable, and potentially sharable across ML workloads [8].

Challenges. The process of establishing a standardized ML workflow reveals several problems that need to be addressed. Each full run of the ML model development step requires active monitoring from ML engineers in order to trigger subsequent ML steps and remedy issues with data or custom scripts [20]. Numerous iterations in model development require a capability to perform parallel experimentation quickly for both debugging and model optimization purposes [13,20,25]. A high number of models for complex systems makes it difficult to keep track of different model versions and manage their dependencies [9,13].

4.3   Automated, ML Workflow Process

Characteristics. This stage is characterized by increased automation within and across the standardized ML workflow steps. The entire ML workflow process is productized as a system using in-built or open source technologies used to create, manage, and run end-to-end ML steps. Example of such systems include Google's TensorFlow Extended (TFX) [8], Kubeflow at Spotify [2] and Airflow at Twitter [20].

Practices. This stage allows for the creation and sharing of ML workflow components, which are self-contained sets of code that perform one step in the ML workflow process (e.g. data preprocessing, data transformation, data validation, and model training). The transition between ML workflow steps is automated leading to rapid experimentation and better readiness to move the whole pipelines to production [8]. ML platforms, constituting an integrated set of tools that can tackle all steps of ML workflow, provide consistent development experience for all designers and are well designed for tasks of all sizes. Across the different iterations of model training, importantly there is a capability to automatically track metadata information about each pipeline execution in order to explore, compare and examine pipelines' runs in detail [8,9].

Challenges. Although open source tools such as Kubeflow and TFX provide high-level orchestration to build data sets and train models, they require a significant amount of integration [9]. Furthermore, they stop short at delivering a single workflow and do not fully implement CD [9].

4.4   Integrated, Software Development and ML Workflow Processes

Characteristics. The first three stages are ML workflow-centric in which integration of the ML component into software is the final activity in the process.

In complex software systems, ML components are not necessarily the central part of the entire system, but as components of a system that have to be built, tested, and deployed [9,13]. Different from previous stages, the ML component is under version control, i.e. identified as a component with a version specification, and re-deployed when there is a requirement from the system. Such an ML component is typically managed as a COTS (Commercial of the shelf) component. The prior formalization of model development neglects contemporary SE practices [13].

Practices. This stage is typical for many companies that use ML components as developed in a separate process (like COTS components) and tested and integrated into the system as other components. There is however a specific procedure of managing ML components - tests related to its ML characterizes, such as accuracy, or performance characteristics. For example, once model metrics are exhibiting good results, system metrics (e.g. safety and comfort measurements on the overall vehicle motion) and hardware metrics (e.g. inference serving time on self-driving vehicle hardware) are performed [9]. System metrics give a comprehensive overview of how all the parts of the system perform between component versions e.g., how new models might act other system components [9].

Challenges. Due to poor integration of ML and software development processes (for example, CD). The system employing CD with fast feedback from the system operation requires fast cycles and updates of ML components but the ML workflow process requires too many efforts in collecting new data and re-training the models [5]. Another challenge is difficulty in finding the root cause of errors, which might be a combination of ML component and software failure.

4.5   Automated and Fully Integrated CD and ML Workflow Process

Characteristics. This stage extends the integrated software development and ML workflow processes with an orchestration service for coordinating build, test, and deployment of ML pipelines, and run-time support for system monitoring and collection of data. The deployed models can thus be continuously retrained based on current model parameters and a combination of constantly incoming and existing data with minimum human involvement[5,16].

Practices. At this stage, rather than deploying ML model e.g. as an API for prediction, the ML pipeline that can automate retraining and deployment of new models is deployed [2,5,8,9]. This allows to quickly test the workflows with regularly updating data. An orchestration service is used to initiate the model training scheduler to start executing model training job described in the deployed ML pipeline [2,5,6,8,9]. The orchestration service can be implemented using, for example, Jenkins CI tool [9]. The training job leverages the stored and tracked information of ML artifacts' (training code, evaluation code, data, models) versions, dependency and metadata to automatically build, test, and deploy the new pipeline components to the target environment [9].

Challenges. 'Concept drift', as changes in data over time, have an impact on the performance of deployed models [5]. The challenge is both in detecting concept drift but also being able to alleviate, which may require training fundamentally new and complex models [5]. This aspect is not considered in CD since models are retrained using currently deployed model parameters.

5   Validation of Conceptual Model

In this section, we present the initial validation of the conceptual model based on findings from one company. The focus group with practitioners at the organization looked in-depth at three ML use cases (Table 3) to compare the practice with the conceptual model. Two ML uses cases (A and B) are in operation and the third ML use case C is currently in the exploration phase.

Typically, some telecommunication HW units (of radio networks and base stations) that are produced at the company's factory and shipped to the customer network get sent back when something goes wrong and the customer suspects HW problems. For returned HW units, the company has a screening process that uses an ML-enabled system to determine if something is indeed wrong with the HW or not (use case A), especially since oftentimes the company receives non-faulty HW units. At the screening center, the operator –an end-user of the ML-enabled system – connects the returned HW to the system and gets predictions that identify whether the HW is good or not good. Upon connecting, zipped log files containing information on what has happened in the field are extracted from the returned HW and used by the ML-enabled system to make the predictions. If there is a problem with HW, it is sent to a repair center (use case B). At the repair center, an ML-enabled system is used to classify the category of the fault. The last ML component under exploration (use case C) aims to detect if an HW unit is at risk of being returned if shipped while still at the factory facilitating further analysis of the HW. Altogether, these use cases aim to reduce the number of faulty HW units from being shipped to the customer.

Table 3. Overview of ML use cases.

ID	ML use case	Description
A	Fault screening of returned HW units	Predict no fault found in returned HW units
B	Fault categorization of returned and faulty HW units	Classify the category of faults
C	Supply deviation detection	Detect faulty HW units at factory that are potentially to be returned if shipped

Manual, Data Science-Driven Process. The team of our focus group was initially approached by a stakeholder (end-user organization) with a problem of how to use ML to reduce returns of HW units. This led the team to initially implement an ML-enabled system for predicting No Fault Found (NFF) in returned HW (use case A). Exploration and prototyping development was done iteratively in Jupyter Notebook. Other use cases, including predicting HW fault category (use case B) were also explored and experimented. In the end, demonstrations based on the iterative development were done and discussed together with stakeholders, who collectively agreed on the next steps, including to productify use cases A and B. For these use cases, the team did not implement unit tests for the training code, which was also not version controlled. However, after a period of six months and with at most three data scientists, the team was able to develop ML models for the use cases A and B, as well as implemented a dashboard for comparing manufacturing volumes with the number of returns over each month, factory and product.

At the time of our focus group discussions, the team was in the early phase of experimenting with use case C and facing difficulties with data. Compared to use cases A and B, use case C does not have ground truth data. For each manufactured HW unit, there are several hundreds of tests that are being performed on the HW. The team uses this test data, consisting a feature vector of about over 1500 features, to train ML models. Building ML models by the analysis of HW units test results without having labels turned out to be difficult. Currently, much of the efforts are on collecting and improving the quality of the labeled dataset. An example of an approach being explored is to look at aggregated test results of HW units and return rates of HW units on different days over the past two years. A threshold is set on the return rates, such that a very small number of return HW units e.g. if 2% is returned, it is considered as an acceptable day otherwise it is a problematic day.

Standardized, Experimental – Operational ML Process. After finding the two ML use cases (A and B) to productify, the team started to systematize the process of implementing them. Initially, this included moving Jupyter notebook code into git repositories and spending most of the efforts on data processing and feature engineering. The latter is because the team was not able to extract features from data collected by an external tool and the implementation did not scale well in terms of the number of files the team wanted to process on a daily basis. The team had to create a service for ingesting big zip-files with logs and a service for parsing out features in order to send out predictions. For the dashboard, the ingestion and preprocessing flows were scheduled on a daily basis and the tables were exposed to Tableau. To serve predictions, all ML models were stored in a common database and the predictions were exposed via API on a user-interface (UI) of a software application built by another team. The training code was versioned control but training was not done on a regular basis.

At this step, the team had created technical debt, as they did not implement unit tests to code. Problems emerged as a result of pushing buggy code, which at times gave incorrect data for both dashboard and models. The buggy code was often found in discussions with stakeholders. There was a high demand for the team to deploy the ML model in time which caused the team to cut some corners.

According to data scientists, it was a very stressful period for which the team could have benefited from DevOps thinking. Productifying the use cases A and B took about six months and with altogether four data scientists. During this time period, the team also started to look into creating a model using insights from the dashboard (use case C).

Automated ML Workflow Process. The ML pipeline consisted of a data collection step, a dataset builder (ingestion and parsing) step, and a predictions step. In data collection, all raw data e.g., field logs of returned HW and other from an external tool, are stored in a common database and the collection is outside the control of the team. The external tool provides log analysis results information on whether the HW has passed or failed assessment giving labels for mostly the failed cases. Prior to the dataset builder step, the team has implemented an ingestion service that is used to ingest raw zip files containing logs into a Hadoop Distributed File System (HDFS) cluster. In addition, a parsing service was implemented and used to parse out logs from the zipped files to JSON. In the dataset builder step, the team has written rules for transforming and preparing datasets containing several features. As such, there can be several paths to building the dataset depending on the project. For use cases A and B, the training dataset is collected during model building because it is fast (about 500MB file size) and once completed it is stored in artifactory. Model training and evaluations are done manually, often in local machines.

At the time of focus group discussions, the team considered the environment where the models are trained and deployed as not 'sophisticated or industrialized environment'. There is manual tracking of the model experiments and there is no automated way to compare model results every time new models are trained. A major challenge is that there are still some manual steps in model training. For instance, a data scientist can forget to copy a newly trained model into the repository. As such, currently, the team is exploring different environments particularly Kubeflow and a company's internal platform with the aim of utilizing one of the platforms in the near future.

Integrated, Software Development and ML Workflow Processes. Initially, the high demand from stakeholders to create new models and the lack of a good infrastructure raised many concerns, especially those related to the risk of deploying models that were not automatically tested. After much learning from previous mistakes, the team started to add more unit tests into the development process so as to spot errors earlier and ensure that new changes do not break existing implementations. The team had a unit test hackathon to get started with writing unit tests, which helped to reduce some technical debt. Most of the team members, who are data scientists also joined a study circle of DevOps and were beginning to do smaller commits and more testing.

At present, the team has recently added CI for unit tests and code linting in their screening models. In addition, the team has added version handling of docker images, but are still doing model training manually on local branches. The CI for the dashboard and other models (except for use case A) has been a bit unstable and issues are being fixed together with the organization's CI team. However, the team is missing the feedback loop from the screening center. Once the model is deployed, the team can continuously monitor the performance of the models. Through discussions with the stakeholder and 'if the team feels like the performance is degrading' only then is model retraining performed. The retraining of the models is currently done less frequently.

Automated and Fully Integrated CD and ML Workflow Process. The team has not achieved this stage. Related efforts are on the recent implementation of the capability to store trained models along with metadata information (e.g. name, version, the classifier, expected features). The team is currently working on ensuring versioning of code (label creation code, feature creation, model training configuration, model training code and model serving code) as well as storing information and dependency tracking of other artifacts (e.g., train and test datasets, model image).

6   Discussion

The five stages of practice improvement for ML-enabled software systems identified in our study show that applying CD to the development process of ML components gives the ability to update deployed models continuously. While automation and robust infrastructures achieved by applying CD are essential for the continuous operation of AI-enabled systems, they call for additional resources, that many organizations may not be equipped with [21].

Developing ML-enabled software system is challenging but existing "conventional" software development techniques provide a good starting point to addressing the challenges [21]. The role of a data scientist is critical in development teams but as observed in our study data scientists have limited SE knowledge, particularly of the development practices. As observed also in our study, this can be improved through effective collaboration and communication across different expertise e.g., between data scientists, software engineers, a quality assurance (QA) engineer, and product owner [13,14]. One cause of failures in deploying and maintaining ML-enabled software systems is due to the effects of disjointed development processes among data scientists, software engineers, and operations staff [21]. In our study, the description of the characteristics and practices of the last two stages attempt to integrate the process steps of data science and software engineering. More empirical studies will need to be conducted to further validate and give details of a well-managed development process of AI enabled system [21].

7   Conclusion

This study explored how modern software development approaches, particularly CD, are applied to the development process of ML-enabled systems. The results show that companies do not outright apply CD to ML system development but rather tend to achieve it as a result of improving their development practices and infrastructure over time. A conceptual model that shows the evolution of practice improvement over time is presented. In future work, we will focus on further validation of the model in other companies serving as inputs in our attempt to define an integrated and well-managed development process of AI-enabled systems.

While these findings are based on a case study, in discussions with other industrial partners in Software Center (http://www.software-center.se/) there is a strong indication that similar challenges exist for these companies (which will be a matter of further studies). Our findings may not generalize to companies of much smaller size. As such, multiple case studies at organizations of different sizes will need to be conducted in order to establish more general results.

Acknowledgement. This research was supported by Software Center, Chalmers AI Research Centre (CHAIR), and Vinnova project HoliDev. The authors would also like to thank all the participants of focus group discussions.

References

1. Amershi, S., et al.: Software engineering for machine learning: a case study. In: 41st International Conference on Software Engineering: Software Engineering in Practice (ICSE-SEIP), pp. 291–300. IEEE (2019). https://doi.org/10.1109/ICSE-SEIP.2019.00042
2. Baer, J., Ngahane, S.: The winding road to better machine learning infrastructure through Tensorflow extended and Kubeflow, December 2019. https://labs.spotify.com/2019/12/13/the-winding-road-to-better-machine-learning-infrastructure-through-tensorflow-extended-and-kubeflow/
3. Bosch, J., Olsson, H.H., Crnkovic, I.: It takes three to tango: Requirement, outcome/data, and AI driven development. In: SiBW, pp. 177–192 (2018)
4. Braun, V., Clarke, V.: Using thematic analysis in psychology. Qual. Res. Psychol. **3**(2), 77–101 (2006). https://doi.org/10.1191/1478088706qp063oa
5. Derakhshan, B., Mahdiraji, A.R., Rabl, T., Markl, V.: Continuous deployment of machine learning pipelines. In: EDBT, pp. 397–408 (2019)
6. Fowler, M.: Continuous delivery for machine learning, September 2019, https://martinfowler.com/articles/cd4ml.html
7. Garousi, V., Felderer, M., Mäntylä, M.V.: Guidelines for including grey literature and conducting multivocal literature reviews in software engineering. Inf. Softw. Technol. **106**, 101–121 (2019). https://doi.org/10.1016/j.infsof.2018.09.006
8. Google: MLOps: continuous delivery and automation pipelines in machine learning, April 2020. https://cloud.google.com/solutions/machine-learning/mlops-continuous-delivery-and-automation-pipelines-in-machine-learning
9. Guo, Y., Ashmawy, K., Huang, E., Zeng, W.: Under the hood of Uber ATG's machine learning infrastructure and versioning control platform for self-driving vehicles (2020). https://eng.uber.com/machine-learning-model-life-cycle-version-control/
10. Hill, C., Bellamy, R., Erickson, T., Burnett, M.: Trials and tribulations of developers of intelligent systems: a field study. In: Symposium on Visual Languages and Human-Centric Computing, pp. 162–170. IEEE (2016). https://doi.org/10.1109/VLHCC.2016.7739680

11. Huber, S., Wiemer, H., Schneider, D., Ihlenfeldt, S.: DMME: data mining methodology for engineering applications - a holistic extension to the crisp-DM model. Procedia CIRP **79**, 403–408 (2019). 12th CIRP Conference on Intelligent Computation in Manufacturing Engineering, 18-20 July 2018, Gulf of Naples, Italy. https://doi.org/10.1016/j.procir.2019.02.106

12. Humble, J., Farley, D.: Continuous Delivery: Reliable Software Releases through Build, Test, and Deployment Automation. Addison-Wesley Professional, Boston (2010)

13. Jackson, S., Yaqub, M., Li, C.X.: The agile deployment of machine learning models in healthcare. Front. Big Data **1**, 7 (2019). https://doi.org/10.3389/fdata.2018.00007

14. Kim, M., Zimmermann, T., DeLine, R., Begel, A.: Data scientists in software teams: state of the art and challenges. IEEE Trans. Softw. Eng. **44**(11), 1024–1038 (2018). https://doi.org/10.1109/TSE.2017.2754374

15. Kontio, J., Bragge, J., Lehtola, L.: The focus group method as an empirical tool in software engineering. In: Shull, F., Singer, J., Sjøberg, D.I.K. (eds.) Guide to Advanced Empirical Software Engineering, pp. 93–116. Springer, London (2008). https://doi.org/10.1007/978-1-84800-044-5_4

16. Lara, A.F.: Continuous delivery for ml models (2018). https://medium.com/onfido-tech/continuous-delivery-for-ml-models-c1f9283aa971

17. Lwakatare, L.E., Kuvaja, P., Oivo, M.: Relationship of DevOps to agile, lean and continuous deployment. In: Abrahamsson, P., Jedlitschka, A., Nguyen Duc, A., Felderer, M., Amasaki, S., Mikkonen, T. (eds.) PROFES 2016. LNCS, vol. 10027, pp. 399–415. Springer, Cham (2016). https://doi.org/10.1007/978-3-319-49094-6_27

18. Lwakatare, L.E., Raj, A., Crnkovic, I., Bosch, J., Olsson, H.H.: Large-scale machine learning systems in real-world industrial settings: a review of challenges and solutions. Inf. Softw. Tech. 106368 (2020). https://doi.org/10.1016/j.infsof.2020.106368

19. Murphy, C., Kaiser, G.E., Arias, M.: An approach to software testing of machine learning applications. SEKE **167**, 52–57 (2007)

20. Ngahane, S., Goodsell, D.: Productionizing ML with workows at Twitter, December 2019. https://blog.twitter.com/engineering/en_us/topics/insights/2018/ml-workflows.html

21. Ozkaya, I.: What is really different in engineering AI-enabled systems? IEEE Softw. **37**(4), 3–6 (2020)

22. Polyzotis, N., Roy, S., Whang, S.E., Zinkevich, M.: Data management challenges in production machine learning. In: International Conference on Management of Data, pp. 1723–1726. ACM (2017). https://doi.org/10.1145/3035918.3054782

23. Renggli, C., et al.: Continuous integration of machine learning models with ease. ml/ci: towards a rigorous yet practical treatment. In: 2nd SysML Conference (2019)

24. Rodríguez, P., et al.: Continuous deployment of software intensive products and services: a systematic mapping study. J. Syst. Softw. **123**, 265–291 (2017)

25. Schleier-Smith, J.: An architecture for agile machine learning in real-time applications. In: International Conference on Knowledge Discovery and Data Mining, pp. 2059–2068. ACM (2015)

26. Sculley, D., et al.: Hidden technical debt in machine learning systems. In: Advances in Neural Information Processing Systems (NIPS) vol. 28, pp. 2503–2511. Curran Associates, Inc. (2015)

27. Wan, Z., Xia, X., Lo, D., Murphy, G.C.: How does machine learning change software development practices? IEEE Trans. Softw. Eng. 1–15 (2019). https://doi.org/10.1109/TSE.2019.2937083

28. Wirth, R., Hipp, J.: CRISP-DM: towards a standard process model for data mining. In: Proceedings of the 4th International Conference on the Practical Applications of Knowledge Discovery and Data Mining, January 2000

29. Zhang, J.M., Harman, M., Ma, L., Liu, Y.: Machine learning testing: survey, landscapes and horizons. IEEE Trans. Softw. Eng. 1 (2020). https://doi.org/10.1109/TSE.2019.2962027

Data Labeling: An Empirical Investigation into Industrial Challenges and Mitigation Strategies

Teodor Fredriksson[1]([✉])(iD), David Issa Mattos[1]([✉])(iD), Jan Bosch[1]([✉])(iD), and Helena Holmström Olsson[2](iD)

[1] Chalmers University of Technology, Hörselgången 11, 417 56 Gothenburg, Sweden
{teodorf,davidis,jan.bosch}@chalmers.se
[2] Malmö University, Nordenskiöldsgatan 1, 211 19 Malmö, Sweden
helena.holmstrom.olsson@mau.se

Abstract. Labeling is a cornerstone of supervised machine learning. However, in industrial applications, data is often not labeled, which complicates using this data for machine learning. Although there are well-established labeling techniques such as crowdsourcing, active learning, and semi-supervised learning, these still do not provide accurate and reliable labels for every machine learning use case in the industry. In this context, the industry still relies heavily on manually annotating and labeling their data. This study investigates the challenges that companies experience when annotating and labeling their data. We performed a case study using a semi-structured interview with data scientists at two companies to explore their problems when labeling and annotating their data. This paper provides two contributions. We identify industry challenges in the labeling process, and then we propose mitigation strategies for these challenges.

Keywords: Data labeling · Machine learning · Case study

1 Introduction

Current research estimates that over 80% of engineering tasks in a machine-learning ML project concern data preparation and labeling. The third-party data labeling market is expected to almost triple by 2024 [8,21]. This massive effort spent in data preparation and labeling often happens because, in industry, datasets are often incomplete. After all, some or all instances are missing labels. Also, the available labels are of low quality in some cases, meaning that the label associated with a data entry is incorrect or only partially correct. Labels of sufficient quality are a prerequisite to perform supervised machine learning as the performance of the model in operations is directly influenced by the quality of the training data [2].

Crowdsourcing has been a common strategy for acquiring quality labels with human supervision [6,32], particularly for computer vision and natural language

M. Morisio et al. (Eds.): PROFES 2020, LNCS 12562, pp. 202–216, 2020.
https://doi.org/10.1007/978-3-030-64148-1_13

processing applications. However, crowdsourcing has several limitations for other industrial applications, such as allowing unknown third-party access to company data, lack of people with an in-depth understanding of the problem, or the business to create quality labels. In-house labeling can be half as expensive as crowdsourced labels while providing higher quality [7]. Due to these factors, companies still perform in-house labeling. Despite the large body of research on crowdsourcing and machine learning systems that can overcome different label quality problems, to the best of our knowledge, no research investigates the challenges faced and strategies adopted by data scientists and human labelers in the labeling process of company-specific applications. In particular, we focus on the problems seen in applications where labeling is non-trivial and requires an understanding of the problem domain.

Utilizing case study research based on semi-structured interviews with practitioners in two companies, one of which has extensive labeling experience, we study the challenges and the adopted mitigation strategies in the data labeling process that these companies employ. The contribution of this paper is twofold. First, we identify the key challenges that these companies experience concerning labeling data. Second, we present an overview of the mitigation strategies that companies employ regularly or potential solutions to address these challenges.

The remainder of the paper is organized as follows. In the next section, we provide a more in-depth overview of the background of our research. Subsequently, in Sect. 3, we present the research method that we employed in the paper and an overview of the case companies. Section 4 presents the challenges that we identified during the case study, observations, and interviews at the company, the results from the expert interviews to validate the challenges as well as the mitigation strategies. Finally, the paper is concluded in Sect. 6.

2   Background

Crowdsourcing is defined as a process of acquiring required information or results by request of assistance from a group of many people available through online communities. Thus crowdsourcing is a way of dividing and distributing a large project among people. After each process is completed, the people involved in the process are rewarded [33]. According to [21], crowdsourcing is the primary way of achieving labels. In the context of machine learning, crowdsourcing has its own set of problems. The primary problem is annotators that produce bad labels. An annotator might not be able to label instances correctly. Even if an annotator is an expert, the labels' quality will potentially decrease over time due to the human factor [2]. Examples of crowdsourcing platforms are the *Amazon Mechanical Turk* and the *Lionbridge AI* [12].

Allowing a third-party company to label your data has its benefits, such as not developing your annotation tools and labeling infrastructure. In-house labeling also requires investing time training your annotators, which is not optimal if you don't have enough time and resources. A downside is that sensitive and confidential company data has to be shared with the crowdsourcing platforms.

Before selecting crowdsourcing platforms, there are essential factors, such as how many and what kind of projects has the platform been successful with previously? Does the platform have high-quality labeling technologies so that high-quality labels can be obtained? How does the platform ensure that the annotators can produce labels of sufficient quality? What are the security measures taken to ensure the safety of your data?

A tool to be used in crowdsourcing when noisy labels are cheap to obtain is *repeated-labeling*. According to [15] repeated labeling should be exercised if labeling can be repeated and the labels are noisy. This approach can improve the quality of the labels which leads to improved quality in the machine learning model. This seems to work especially well when the repeated-labeling is done selectively, taking into account label uncertainty and machine learning model uncertainty. However, this approach does not guarantee that the quality is improved. Sheshadri and Lease [27] provides an empirical evaluation study that compares different algorithms that computes the crowd consensus on benchmark crowdsourced data sets using the *Statistical Quality Assurance Robustness Evaluation* (SQUARE) benchmark [27]. The conclusions of [27] is that no matter what algorithm you choose, there is no significant difference in accuracy. These algorithms includes *majority voting* (MV), *ZenCrowd* (ZC), *David and Skene (DS)/Naive Bayes (NB)* [15]. There are also other ways to handle noisy labels. For example, in [29], they improve accuracy when training a deep neural network with noisy labels by incorporating a noise layer. So rather than correcting noisy labels, there are ways to change the machine learning models to handle noisy labels. The downside to this approach is that you need to know which instances are clean and which instances are noisy. This can be difficult with industrial data. Another strategy to detect noisy labels is *confident learning* which can be used to identify noisy labels and learn from noisy labels [18].

3   Research Method

In this paper, we report on case study research. We explored the challenges of labeling data for machine learning and what strategies can be employed to mitigate them. This section will present the data we collected and how we analyzed it to identify the challenges.

A case study is a research method that investigates real-world phenomena through empirical investigations. These studies aim to identify challenges and find mitigation strategies through action, reflection, theory, and practice, [19,22,28].

A case study suits our purpose well because of its exploratory nature, and we are trying to learn more about specific processes at Company A and B. The two main research questions we have are:

- **RQ1:** *What are the key challenges that practitioners face in the process of labeling data?*
- **RQ2:** *What are the mitigation strategies that practitioners use to overcome these challenges?*

3.1 Data Collection

Our case study was conducted in collaboration with two companies. Company A is a worldwide telecommunication provider and one of the leading providers in Information and Communication Technology (ICT). Company B is a company specialized in labeling. They have developed an annotation platform to provide the autonomous vehicles industry with labeled training data of top quality. Their clients include software companies and research institutes.

- **Phase I: Exploration** - The empirical data collected during this phase is based on an internship from November 18 2019 to February 28 2020 in which the first author spent time at Company As office two-three days a week. The data was collected from the data scientist by observing how the they were working with machine learning and how they deal with data where labels are missing as well as having access to data sets. We held discussions with each of the data scientist working with each particular dataset to collect data regarding the origin of the data, what they wish to use it for in the future, and how often it is updated. Using Python we could investigate how skew the label distribution is of the label distribution as well as examine the data to potentially find any clustering structure in the labels. The datasets studied in phase I came from participant I and II.
- **Phase II: Validation** - After the challenges had been identified during phase I, both internal and external confirmation interviews were conducted to validate if the previous phase's challenges were general. Four participants in the interviews where from company A and one participant was from company B. Company A had several data scientists, but we only included scientists that had issues with labeling. Each participant was interviewed separately, and the interviews lasted between 25–55 min. All but one interview was conducted in English. The one interview was conducted in Swedish and then translated to English by the first author. During the interview, we asked questions such as *What is the purpose of your labels?*, *How do you get annotated data?* and *How do you assess the quality of the data/labels?*

Based on meetings and interviews, we managed to evaluate and plan strategies to mitigate the challenges we observed during our study (Table 1).

Table 1. List of the interview participants of phase II

Company	Participant Nr	Title/role	Experience
A	I	Data Scientist	4 years
A	II	Senior Data Scientist	8 years
A	III	Data Scientist	3 years
A	IV	Senior Data Scientist	2 years
B	V	Senior Data Scientist	7 years

3.2   Data Analysis

The interviews were analyzed by taking notes during the interviews and internship. We then performed a *thematic analysis* [5]. Thematic analysis is defined as "a method for identifying, analyzing and reporting patterns" and was used to identify the different themes and patterns in the data we collected. From the analysis, we were able to identify themes and define the industrial challenges based on the notes. For each interview, we identified different themes, such as topics that came up during the interviews. Several of these themes were present in more than one interview, so we combined the data for each of the interviews, and based on that, we could draw conclusions based on the information on the same theme.

3.3   Threats to Validity

According to [22] there are four different concepts of validity to consider, *construct validity*, *internal validity*, *external validity* and *reliability*. To achieve construct validity, we provided every participant of company A with an e-mail containing all the definitions of concepts and some sample questions to be asked during the interview. We also provided a lecture on how to use machine learning to label data before the interviews so that the participant's could reflect and prepare for the interview. We can argue that we achieved internal validity through data triangulation since we interviewed every person at Company A that had experience with labels. Therefore it is implausible that we missed any necessary information when collecting data.

4   Results

In this section, we shall present the results of our study. We begin by listing the fundamental problems found from phase I of the study. Coming up next, we state the problems we encountered from Phase II. The interview we held with participant V was then used as an inspiration for formulating mitigation strategies for the data scientist's problems from Company A.

4.1   Phase I: Exploration

Here we list the problems that we found during Phase I of the case study.

1. **Lack of a systematic approach to labeling data for specific features:** It was clear that automated labeling processes was needed. The data scientists working at Company A had all kinds of needs for automatic labeling. Currently, they have no idea how to approach the problem.
2. **Unclear responsibility for labeling:** Data scientists do not have the time to label instances manually. Their stakeholders can label the data by hand, but they do not want to do it either. Thus the data scientist is expected to come up with a way to do the labeling.

3. **Noisy labels:** Participant I has a small subset of his data labeled. These labels come from experiments conducted in a lab. The label noise seems to be negligible, but that is not the case. There is a difference between the generated data and the true data. The generated data will have features that are continuous, while the generated data will be discrete. Participant II works on a data set that contains tens of thousands of rows and columns. The column of interest includes two class labels, "Yes" and "No". The first problem with the labels is that they are noisy. The "Yes" is dependent on two errors, I and II. Only "Yes" based on error I is of interest. If the "Yes" is based on error II. then it should be relabeled as a "No". Furthermore, the stakeholders do not know if the "Yes" instances are due to error I or error II.

4. **Difficulty to find a correlation between labels and features:** Participant I works with a dataset whose label distribution contains five classes that describe grades from "best" to "worst". Where 1 is "best" and 5 is "worst". Cluster analysis reveals that there is no particular cluster structure for some of the labels. Labels of grade 5 seem to be in one cluster, but the other 1–4 seem to be randomly scattered in one cluster. Analysis of the data from participant II reveals no way of telling whether the "Yes" is based on error I or error II. This means that many of the "Yes" are mislabeled.

5. **Skewed label distributions:** The label distribution from both datasets is highly skewed. The dataset from participant I has fewer instances that has a high grade compared to low grades. For participant II the number of instances labeled "No" is greater than the number of labels set as "Yes". When training a model on this data, it will overfit.

6. **Time dependence:** Due to the nature of participant IIs data, it is possible that some of the "No" can become "Yes" in the future and so the "No" labels are possibly incorrect too.

7. **Difficulty to predict future uses for datasets.** The purpose of the labels in both datasets was to predict new labels for future instances provided by the stakeholder on an irregular basis. For participant I, the labels might be used for other purposes later. There are no current plans to use the label for different machine learning purposes.

4.2   Phase II: Validation

The problems that appeared during the interviews can be categorized as follows:

1. *Label distribution related.* Question regarding the distribution.
2. *Multiple-task related.* Questions regarding the purpose of the labels.
3. *Annotation related.* Questions regarding the oracle and noisy labels.
4. *Model and data reuse related.* Questions regarding reuse of trained model on new data.
   Below we discuss each category in more detail.

1. **Label Distribution:** We found several issues related to the label distribution. Participant Is data has an unknown label distribution. The current

labels are measured in percentages and need to be translated into at least two classes, but if more labels are needed, that can be done. Participant II has a label distribution that contains two classes, "Yes" and "No". Participant IIIs data has a label distribution that includes at least three labels. Participants IV has more than three-thousand labels, so it is hard to get a clear picture of its distribution. Participant I-III all have skewed label distributions. If a dataset has a skew label distribution, then the machine learning model will overfit. This means that if you have a binary classification problem and you have 80% of class A and 20% of class B, the model might predict A most of the time even when an actual case is labeled as B [10].

2. **Multiple tasks:** Participant I, II,and III say that that for now, the only purpose of their labels is to find labels for new data, but the chances are that it will be reused for something else later on. Participant IV does not use its labels for machine learning purposes but other practical reasons. If you do not plan ahead and only train a model concerning one task, then if you need to use the labels for something else later, you will have to relabel the instances for each new task.

3. **Annotation:** Participant I has some labeled data that comes from laboratory experiments. However, these labels are only used to help label new instances to be labeled manually. Participant II has its labels coming from the stakeholders, but these instances need to be relabeled since they are noisy. Participant III has labeled data coming from stakeholders, and these are expected to be 100% correct. Participant IV defines all labels by itself and does not consult the stakeholders at all. The problem here is that the data scientists are often tasked to do labeling on their own. Even if the data scientists get instances from the stakeholders, the amount of labels are often of insufficient quantity and/or quality.

4. **Data Reuse:** Participant III has had problems with reusing a model. First the data was labeled into two classes "Yes" and "No. Later the "Yes" category would be divided into sub-categories "YesA" and "YesB". When running the model on this new data, it would predict the old "Yes" instance as "No" instance. Participant III has no idea as to why this happens.

4.3   Summary from Company B

Participant V of Company B has earlier experience with automatic labeling. Therefore interview V was used to verify some actual labeling issues from the industry. According to participant V, Company B has worked and studied automatic labeling for at least seven years. Company B uses crowdsourcing to label data using 1000 people. Participant V confirms that the labeling task takes 200 times less time thanks to active learning than if active learning was not used. The main problem company B has with the labeling is that it is hard to evaluate the quality labels and access the human annotator's quality. A final remark from Company B is that they have experienced a correlation between automation and quality. The more automation included in the process, the less accurate will the labels be. Three of the authors of this paper performed a systematic literature review on automated labeling using machine learning [11]. Thanks to that paper, we can conclude that active learning and semi-supervised learning can be used to label instances.

4.4 Machine Learning Methods for Data Labeling

Here we present and discuss Active Learning and Semi-supervised learning methods in terms of how they can be used in practice with labeling problems.

Active Learning: Traditionally labels would be chosen randomly to be labeled and used with machine learning. However, choosing instances to be labeled randomly could lead to a model with low predictive accuracy since non-informative instances could be selected for labeling. To mitigate the issue of choosing non-informative instances, active learning (AL) is proposed. Active learning queries instances by informativeness and then labels them. The different methods used to pose queries are known as *query strategies* [24]. According to [11] the most commonly used query strategies are *uncertainty sampling, error/variance reduction, query-by-committee (QBC)* and *query-by-disagreement (QBD)*. After instances are queried and labeled, they are added to the training set. A machine learning algorithm is then trained and evaluated. If the learner is not happy with the results, more instances will be queried, and the model will be retrained and evaluated. This iterative procedure will proceed until the learner decides it is time to stop learning. Active learning has proven to outperform passive learning if the query strategy is properly selected based on the learning algorithm [24]. Most importantly, active learning is a great way to make sure that time is not wasted on labeling non-informative instances, thus saving time and money in crowdsourcing [21].

Semi-supervised Learning: Semi-supervised learning (SSL) is concerned with algorithms used in the scenario where most of the data is unlabeled, but a small subset of it is labeled. Semi-supervised learning is mainly divided into *semi-supervised classification* and *constrained clustering* [34].

Constrained clustering is an extension to unsupervised clustering. Constrained clustering requires unlabeled instances as well as some supervised information about the clusters. The objective of constrained clustering is to improve upon unsupervised clustering[3]. The most popular semi-supervised classification methods are *mixture models using the EM-algorithm, co-training/multi-view learning, graph-based SSL* and *semi-supervised support vector machines (S3VM)* [11].

Below we list eight practical considerations of Active Learning.

1. **Data exploration to determine which algorithm is best.** When starting on a new project involving machine learning, it is hard to know which algorithm will yield the best result. Often there is no way of knowing beforehand what the best choice is. There are empirical studies on which one to

choose, but the results are relatively mixed [17,23,25]. Since the selection of algorithms varies so much, it is essential to understand the problem beforehand. If it is interesting to reduce the error, then expected error or variance reduction is the best query strategies to choose from [24]. If the sample's density is easy to use and there is strong evidence that support correlation between cluster structure to the labels, then use density-weighted methods [24]. If using extensive probabilistic models, uncertainty sampling is the only viable option [24]. If there is no time testing out different query strategies, it is best to use the more simple approaches based on uncertainty [24]. From our investigation, it is clear that company A needs labels in their projects. However, since they have never implemented an automatic labeling process before, it is important to do right from the beginning. The data scientists must carefully examine the distribution of data set, check whether there are any cluster structures and if there are any relationships between the clusters and the labels. If the data exploration is done in a detailed, correct way, then finding the correct machine learning approach is easy, and we don't need to spend time testing different machine learning algorithms.

2. **Alternative query types:** A traditional active learner queries instances to be labeled by an oracle. However, there are other querying ways, e.g. *human domain knowledge*, incorporated into machine learning algorithms. This means the learner builds models based on human advice, such as rules and constraints, and labeled and unlabeled data. An example of domain knowledge with active learning is to use information about the features. This approach is referred to as *tandem learning* and incorporates feature feedback in traditional classification problems. *Active dual supervision* is an area of active learning where features are labeled. Here oracles label features that are judged to be good predictors of one or more classes. The big question is how to query these feature labels actively.

3. **Multi-task active learning:** From our interview we can see that there are cases where labels are needed to predict labels for future instances. In other cases the labels aren't even needed for machine learning. In one case the data scientist thinks that the labels will be used for other prediction task but is unsure. The most basic way in which active learning operates is that a machine learner is trying to solve a single task. From the interviews it is clear the same data needs to annotated in several ways for several future tasks. This means that the data scientist will have to spend even more time annotating at least one time for each task. It would be more economical to label a single instance for all sub-tasks simultaneously. This can be done with the help of multi-task active learning [14].

4. **Data reuse and the unknown model class:** The labeled training set collected after performing active learning always has a bias distribution. The bias is connected to the class of the model used to select the queries. If it is necessary to switch learners to a more improved learner, it might be troublesome to reuse the training data with models of a different class. This is an essential issue in practical use for active learning. If you know the best

model class and feature set beforehand, then active learning can safely be used. Otherwise, active learning will be outperformed by passive learning.

5. **Unreliable oracles:** It is essential to have access to top-quality labeled data. If the labels come from some experiments, there is almost always some noise present. In one of the data sets from company A, a small subset of the data was labeled. The labels of that particular data set come from experiments conducted in a lab. The label noise seems to be negligible, but that is not the case. There is a difference between the generated data and the actual data. The actual data will have continuous features, while the generated data will have discrete features. Another dataset that we studied has labels that came from customer data. The labels were coded "Yes" and "No". However, the "Yes" was due to factors A and B. So the problem here is to find a model that can predict the labels, but we are only interested in the "Yes" that is due to factor A. The "Yes" due to factor B needs to be relabeled to a "No". Since the customer data does not provide whether the "Yes" are due to factor A or B. The second problem was that some of the "No" could develop into a "Yes" over time. It was up to the data scientist to find a way to relabel the data correctly. The data scientist had a solution to the problem but realized that it was faulty and asked us for help. We took a look at the data and the current solution. We saw two large clusters, but no significant relationship existed between the different labels and the features. We found two clusters, but both contained almost equally many "Yes" and "No". Let's say that the first cluster contained about 60% "Yes" and 40% "No" and in the second cluster we had 60% "No" and 40% "Yes". After doing this, all of the first cluster instances were relabeled as "Yes" and all instances in the second cluster were relabeled as "No". We conclude that this is an approach that will yield noisy labels. The same goes if the labels come from a human annotator because some of the instances might be difficult to label. People can easily be distracted and tired over time, so the labels' quality will vary over time. Thanks to crowdsourcing, several people can annotate the same data, and that it is easier to determine which label is the correct one and produce "gold-standard quality training sets". This approach can also be used to evaluate learning algorithms on training sets that are non-gold-standard. The big question is: How do we use noisy oracles in active learning? When should the learner query new unlabeled instances rather than update currently labeled instances if we suspect an error. Studies, where estimates of both oracle and model uncertainty were taken into account, show that data can be improved by selectively repeated labeling. How do we evaluate the annotators? How might the effect of payment influence annotation quality? What to do if some instances are noisy no matter what oracle you use and repeated labeling does not improve the situation?

6. **Skewed label distributions:** In two of the data sets we studied, the distributions of the labels are skewed. That is, there is more of one label than there is of another. In the "Yes" and "No" labeled example, there are way more "No" instances. When the label distribution is skewed, active learning might not give much better results than passive learning. If the labels are not

balanced, active learning might query more of one label than another. The skewed distribution is a problem, but the lack of labeled data is also a problem. In one of the datasets, we have instances labeled from an experiment. Very few labels are labeled from the beginning, and new unlabeled data is coming every fifteen minutes. "Guided learning" is proposed to mitigate the slowness problem. Guided learning allows the human annotator to search for class-representative instances in addition to just querying for labels. Empirical studies indicate that guided learning performs better than active learning as long as it's annotation costs are less than eight times more expensive than labeling queries.

7. **Real labeling costs and cost reduction:** From observing the data scientists at Company A, we would say that they will spend about 80% of the time they spend on data science prepossessing the data. Therefore we recognize that they do not have time to label too many instances, and it is crucial to reduce the time it takes to label things manually. If the possibility exists, avoid manual labeling. Assume that the *cost* of labeling is uniform. The smaller the training set used, the lower will the associated costs be. However, in some applications, the cost might be varying, so simply reducing the labeled instances in the training data does not necessarily reduce the cost. This problem is studied within *cost-sensitive active learning*. To reduce the effort in active learning, *automatic pre-annotation* can help. In automatic pre-annotation the current model predictions helps to query the labels [4,9]. This can often help the laboring efforts of the learner. If the models make many classification mistakes, then there will be extra work for the human annotator to correct them. To mitigate these problems *correlation propagation* can be used. In correlation propagation, the local edits are used to update the prediction interactively. In general automatic pre-annotation and correction propagation do not deal with labeling costs themselves. However, they do try to reduce the costs indirectly by minimizing the number of labeling actions performed by human oracle. Other cost-sensitive active learning methods take varying labeling costs into account. The learner can incorporate both current labeling costs and expected future errors in classification costs [16]. The costs might not even be deterministic but stochastic. In many applications, the costs are not known beforehand. However, they might be able to be described as a function over annotation time [26]. To find such a function, train a regression cost-model that predicts the annotation costs. Studies involving real human annotation cost shows the following results.

   – Annotation costs are not constant across instances [1,20,30,31].
   – Active learners that ignore costs might not perform better than passive learners [24].
   – The annotations costs may vary on the person doing the annotation [1,13].
   – The annotation costs can include stochastic components. *Jitter* and *pause* are two types of noise that affect the annotation speed.
   – Annotation can be predicted after seeing only a few labeled instances [30,31].

8. **Stopping criteria:** Since active learning is an iterative process, it is relevant to know when to stop learning. Based on our empirical findings, the data scientists have no interest in doing any manual labeling, and if they have to, they want to do it as little as possible. So when the cost of gathering more training data is higher than the cost of the current system's errors, then it is time to stop extending the training set and hence stop training the machine learning algorithm. From our experience at company A the data scientist have so little time free from doing other tasks than data prepossessing, so time is the most common stopping factor.

4.5 Challenges and Mitigation Strategies

Many of the problems identified during phase I and phase II overlap to a certain degree, so we took all the problems and summarized them into three challenges (C1–C3) that were later mapped to three mitigation strategies (MS1–MS3). These mitigation strategies are derived from the practical consideration above. Finally, we map MS1 to C1, MS2 to C2, and MS3 to C3.

C1: **Pre-processing:** This challenge represents all that needs to be done during the planning stage of the labeling procedure. This would include creating a systematic approach for labeling (problem 1 of phase I), doing an exploratory data analysis to find the correlation between labels and features (problem 4 of phase I), as well as choosing a model that can be reused on new data (problem 6 of phase I) and label instances concerning multiple tasks (problem 7 of phase I, problem 4 of phase II).

MS1: **Planning**: This strategy contains all the solution frameworks from practical consideration 1, 2, 3, 4, 7 and 8 as they all involve the steps necessary to plan an active learning strategy for labeling.

C2: **Annotation:** This challenge represents the problems concerning choosing an annotator as well as evaluating and reduce the label noise (problems 2, 3 from phase I and problem 3 from phase II).

MS2: **Oracle selection**: This strategy contains only solution frameworks from practical consideration 5. It describes how we can choose oracles to produce top quality labels.

C3: **Label Distribution:** This challenge represents all the problems concerning the symmetry of the label distributions such as learning with a skew label distribution (problem 5 of Phase I and problem 1 o Phase II).

MS3: **Label distribution**: This strategy contains solution frameworks from practical consideration 6. It describes how we can do labeling when the label distribution is skew.

5   Discussion

We learned that active learning is a popular tool for acquiring labels from our verification interview with Company B. Thanks to active learning, the labeling task takes 200 times less than if active learning was not used.

In the background, we presented some current practices that can help with labeling. The most popular practice being crowdsourcing. However, crowdsourcing has its own set of problems. The primary concern is those bad annotators will produce noisy labels due to inexperience or human factors. Secondly, The benefit of allowing third-company to label data is that you don't have to spend time training your employees to do the job, nor do you need to develop your own annotation tools and infrastructure. The big downside is that you have to share confidential company data with the crowdsourcing platform. Repeated labeling can improve the quality of the labels, but there are no guarantees that this will enhance the quality. Rather than correcting noisy labels, there are ways in which you can change the machine learning models to handle noisy labels. The downside to this is that you need to know which instances are bad, and this can be difficult in an industrial setting.

None of the techniques discussed in the background utilizes automated labeling using machine learning. Thanks to our efforts, we formulated three labeling challenges and provided mitigation strategies based on active machine learning. These challenges are related to questions such as, How can labeling processes be structured? Who and how do we label the instances? Can the correlation between labels and features be found, so that labels can be determined from the features? Both manual and automatic labeling involves some noise in the labels. How should these noisy labels be used? What do we do if the distribution of the labels is skewed? How do we consider the fact that some of the labels might change over time, due to the nature of the data? How do we label instances so that the labels can be useful for several future tasks?

Three mitigation strategies that could possibly solve the three challenges were presented.

6   Conclusion

This study aims to provide a detailed overview of the challenges that the industry faces with labeling and outline mitigation strategies for these challenges.

To the best of our knowledge 95% of all the machine learning algorithms deployed in the industry are supervised. Therefore, every dataset must be complete with labeled instances. Otherwise, the data would be insufficient, and supervised learning would not be possible.

It proves to be challenging to find and structure a labeling process. You need to define a systematic approach for labeling and examine the data to choose the optimal model. Finally, you need to select an oracle to produce top-quality labels as well as plan how to handle skewed label distributions.

The contribution of this paper is twofold. First, based on a case study involving two companies, we identified problems that companies experience in relation to labeling data. We validated these problems using interviews at both companies and summarized all problems into challenges. Second, we present an overview of the mitigation strategies that companies employ (or could employ) to address the challenges.

In our future work, we aim to further develop the challenges and mitigation strategies with more companies. In addition, we intend to develop solutions to simplify the use of automated labeling in industrial contexts.

Acknowledgments. This work was partially supported by the Wallenberg AI Autonomous Systems and Software Program (WASP) funded by Knut and Alice Wallenberg Foundation.

References

1. Arora, S., Nyberg, E., Rose, C.: Estimating annotation cost for active learning in a multi-annotator environment. In: Proceedings of the NAACL HLT 2009 Workshop on Active Learning for Natural Language Processing, pp. 18–26 (2009)
2. AzatiSoftware: AzatiSoftware Automated Data Labeling with Machine Learning (2019). https://azati.ai/automated-data-labeling-with-machine-learning
3. Bair, E.: Semi-supervised clustering methods. Wiley Interdiscip. Rev. Comput. Stat. **5**(5), 349–361 (2013)
4. Baldridge, J., Osborne, M.: Active learning and the total cost of annotation. In: Proceedings of the 2004 Conference on Empirical Methods in Natural Language Processing, pp. 9–16 (2004)
5. Braun, V., Clarke, V.: Using thematic analysis in psychology. Qual. Res. Psychol. **3**(2), 77–101 (2006)
6. Chang, J.C., Amershi, S., Kamar, E.: Revolt: collaborative crowdsourcing for labeling machine learning datasets. In: Proceedings of the 2017 CHI Conference on Human Factors in Computing Systems, pp. 2334–2346 (2017)
7. Cloud Factory, H.: Crowd vs. Managed Team: A studo on Quality Data Processing at Scale (2020). https://go.cloudfactory.com/hubfs/02-Contents/3-Reports/Crowd-vs-Managed-Team-Hivemind-Study.pdf
8. Cognilytica Research: Data Preparation & Labeling for AI 2020. Technical report, Cognilytica Research (2020)
9. Culotta, A., McCallum, A.: Reducing labeling effort for structured prediction tasks. In: AAAI, vol. 5, pp. 746–751 (2005)
10. DataScience, T.: What To Do When Your Classification Data is Imbalanced? (2019). https://towardsdatascience.com/what-to-do-when-your-classification-data set-is-imbalanced-6af031b12a36
11. Fredriksson, T., Bosch, J., Holmström-Olsson, H.: Machine learning models for automatic labeling: a systematic literature review (2020)
12. hackernoon.com: Crowdsourcing Data Labeling for Machine Learning Projects (2020). https://hackernoon.com/crowdsourcing-data-labeling-for-machine-learnin g-projects-a-how-to-guide-cp6h32nd
13. Haertel, R.A., Seppi, K.D., Ringger, E.K., Carroll, J.L.: Return on investment for active learning. In: Proceedings of the NIPS Workshop on Cost-Sensitive Learning, vol. 72 (2008)
14. Harpale, A.: Multi-task active learning. Ph.D. thesis, Carnegie Mellon University (2012)
15. Ipeirotis, P.G., Provost, F., Sheng, V.S., Wang, J.: Repeated labeling using multiple noisy labelers. Data Min. Knowl. Discov. **28**(2), 402–441 (2013). https://doi.org/10.1007/s10618-013-0306-1

16. Kapoor, A., Horvitz, E., Basu, S.: Selective supervision: guiding supervised learning with decision-theoretic active learning. IJCAI **7**, 877–882 (2007)
17. Körner, C., Wrobel, S.: Multi-class ensemble-based active learning. In: Fürnkranz, J., Scheffer, T., Spiliopoulou, M. (eds.) ECML 2006. LNCS (LNAI), vol. 4212, pp. 687–694. Springer, Heidelberg (2006). https://doi.org/10.1007/11871842_68
18. Northcutt, C.G., Jiang, L., Chuang, I.L.: Confident learning: estimating uncertainty in dataset labels. arXiv preprint arXiv:1911.00068 (2019)
19. Reason, P., Bradbury, H.: Handbook of Action Research: Participative Inquiry and Practice. Sage, London (2001)
20. Ringger, E.K., et al.: Assessing the costs of machine-assisted corpus annotation through a user study. In: LREC, vol. 8, pp. 3318–3324 (2008)
21. Roh, Y., Heo, G., Whang, S.E.: A survey on data collection for machine learning: a big data-AI integration perspective. IEEE Trans. Knowl. Data Eng. (2019)
22. Runeson, P., Höst, M.: Guidelines for conducting and reporting case study research in software engineering. Empir. Softw. Eng. **14**(2), 131 (2009)
23. Schein, A.I., Ungar, L.H.: Active learning for logistic regression: an evaluation. Mach. Learn. **68**(3), 235–265 (2007)
24. Settles, B.: Active learning. Morgan Claypool. Synthesis Lectures on AI and ML (2012)
25. Settles, B., Craven, M.: An analysis of active learning strategies for sequence labeling tasks. In: Proceedings of the 2008 Conference on Empirical Methods in Natural Language Processing, pp. 1070–1079 (2008)
26. Settles, B., Craven, M., Friedland, L.: Active learning with real annotation costs. In: Proceedings of the NIPS Workshop on Cost-Sensitive Learning, Vancouver, CA, pp. 1–10 (2008)
27. Sheshadri, A., Lease, M.: Square: a benchmark for research on computing crowd consensus. In: First AAAI Conference on Human Computation and Crowdsourcing (2013)
28. Staron, M.: Action Research in Software Engineering: Theory and Applications. Springe, Chamr (2019). https://doi.org/10.1007/978-3-030-32610-4
29. Sukhbaatar, S., Fergus, R.: Learning from noisy labels with deep neural networks. arXiv preprint arXiv:1406.2080 2(3), 4 (2014)
30. Vijayanarasimhan, S., Grauman, K.: What's it going to cost you?: predicting effort vs. informativeness for multi-label image annotations. In: 2009 IEEE Conference on Computer Vision and Pattern Recognition, pp. 2262–2269. IEEE (2009)
31. Wallace, B.C., Small, K., Brodley, C.E., Lau, J., Trikalinos, T.A.: Modeling annotation time to reduce workload in comparative effectiveness reviews. In: Proceedings of the 1st ACM International Health Informatics Symposium, pp. 28–35 (2010)
32. Zhang, J., Sheng, V.S., Li, T., Wu, X.: Improving crowdsourced label quality using noise correction. IEEE Trans. Neural Netw. Learn. Syst. **29**(5), 1675–1688 (2017)
33. Zhang, J., Wu, X., Sheng, V.S.: Learning from crowdsourced labeled data: a survey. Artif. Intell. Rev. **46**(4), 543–576 (2016). https://doi.org/10.1007/s10462-016-9491-9
34. Zhu, X.J.: Semi-supervised learning literature survey. Technical report. University of Wisconsin-Madison Department of Computer Sciences (2005)

An End-to-End Framework for Productive Use of Machine Learning in Software Analytics and Business Intelligence Solutions

Iris Figalist[1(✉)], Christoph Elsner[1], Jan Bosch[2],
and Helena Holmström Olsson[3]

[1] Corporate Technology, Siemens AG, 81739 Munich, Germany
{iris.figalist,christoph.elsner}@siemens.com
[2] Department of Computer Science and Engineering,
Chalmers University of Technology, Hörselgången 11, 412 96 Göteborg, Sweden
jan.bosch@chalmers.se
[3] Department of Computer Science and Media Technology, Malmö University,
Nordenskiöldsgatan, 211 19 Malmö, Sweden
helena.holmstrom.olsson@mau.se

Abstract. Nowadays, machine learning (ML) is an integral component in a wide range of areas, including software analytics (SA) and business intelligence (BI). As a result, the interest in custom ML-based software analytics and business intelligence solutions is rising. In practice, however, such solutions often get stuck in a prototypical stage because setting up an infrastructure for deployment and maintenance is considered complex and time-consuming. For this reason, we aim at structuring the entire process and making it more transparent by deriving an end-to-end framework from existing literature for building and deploying ML-based software analytics and business intelligence solutions. The framework is structured in three iterative cycles representing different stages in a model's lifecycle: prototyping, deployment, update. As a result, the framework specifically supports the transitions between these stages while also covering all important activities from data collection to retraining deployed ML models. To validate the applicability of the framework in practice, we compare it to and apply it in a real-world ML-based SA/BI solution.

Keywords: Machine learning · Software analytics · Business intelligence

1 Introduction

A vast amount of data is produced by software-intensive systems every day. As a result, software providers often try to gain insights from data using software analytics [23] or business intelligence [24] (SA/BI) tools. As existing tools are typically quite generic and can often not provide the desired depth of product-specific

© Springer Nature Switzerland AG 2020
M. Morisio et al. (Eds.): PROFES 2020, LNCS 12562, pp. 217–233, 2020.
https://doi.org/10.1007/978-3-030-64148-1_14

and stakeholder-targeted information, there is often a need for customized software analytics or business intelligence (SA/BI) solutions that leverage the full potential of modern machine learning (ML) techniques.

However, as such solutions are used as internal systems for monitoring or decision-making, these are often not perceived as something of direct customer value by managers. This results in a lack of priority, time and, resources assigned to setup and maintain ML-based SA/BI solutions [15]. In addition to that, the effort of going beyond a prototypical analysis and deploying it to and maintaining it in production is perceived as extremely high [15,30]. Paired with a lack of expertise in this domain, which is often the case if the actual product is not related to ML [6], custom ML-based SA/BI solutions are rarely deployed in production [15]. Nevertheless, this is considered crucial in order to continuously gain valuable insights and use it for actual decision making [21].

To address this, we conduct a literature review of important domains related to ML, specifically data management and processing, model building, and model deployment. The results are then used to derive a framework for building end-to-end ML-based SA/BI solutions consisting of three iterative cycles: a prototyping cycle, a deployment cycle, and an update cycle. To validate the applicability of the framework in practice, we compare it to and apply it in a real-world, customized ML-based SA/BI solutions.

The contribution of this paper is an end-to-end approach that covers all steps from data collection to retraining deployed ML models while at the same time taking the different conceptual stages into consideration (prototypical, deployment, and update). By specifically addressing the transition between these stages, our framework supports practitioners in advancing their prototypical analysis to a deployed and continuously retrained ML model.

The remainder of this paper is structured as follows: First, we outline the background of our study in Sect. 2. In Sect. 3 we provide an overview of the research method and the study design. The results of the literature review are presented in Sect. 4, before introducing the framework in Sect. 5. The framework validation is outlined in Sect. 6, followed by a conclusion in Sect. 7.

2   Background

The term software analytics (SA) describes analytics performed on software data to generate valuable insights for various stakeholders, from managers to software engineers, that ultimately support their decision making [6,23]. Related to this, the field of business intelligence (BI), sometimes also referred to as business analytics, applies data mining techniques to operational data in order to derive high-quality information for managerial decision making [24].

With its increase in popularity, artificial intelligence soon became an integral part of SA and BI solutions [7,11]. As a result, many companies aim at getting the most out of their data by running ML-based analyses on it. While some knowledge can be extracted using out-of-the-box tools, more in-depth analyses often require custom ML solutions.

In many cases, these custom solutions start out as a prototypical analysis or a proof of concept [15,30]. However, in order to make actual use of the results, they need to be provided in a continuous manner by deploying the model to production and retraining the model on a regular basis [21]. Precisely this is the point at which custom ML-based SA/BI solutions often get stuck. In a previous study [15], we identified a vicious circle that frequently prevents an end-to-end implementation of such analyses. One of the key issues is that an ineffective prototypical analysis can often not prove the value that it could deliver in production, leading to a lack of priority, time, and resources assigned to the topic [15].

Moreover, in the context of SA and BI there is often a lack of expertise in data engineering, data analytics, and in building an infrastructure for both [6,15]. For this reason, the framework presented in our study aims at compensating this to some extent by providing a structured approach for the transition between prototypical analysis and productively usable analysis.

3   Research Method and Study Design

As an end-to-end development of ML-based SA/BI solutions requires broad knowledge that is distributed across several, well-researched domains, we selected a deductive research approach for our study. Deductive approaches rely on existing theories for building hypotheses which are then confirmed or rejected using real-world observations [28]. The overall research process is outlined in Fig. 1.

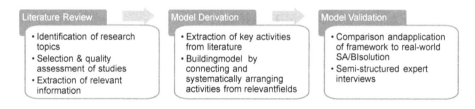

Fig. 1. Research process

As a first step, we conducted a literature review [18] which serves as the foundation for our study. Based on the requirements of our framework, we identified three overarching categories that comprise the results of our review: data management and processing, model building, and model deployment. To achieve our research goal, we queried common scientific libraries (IEEXplore, ACM Digital Library, ScienceDirect, Springer Link) using search terms related to the respective categories: data (quality, cleaning, preprocessing, transformation, management, continuous extraction) and machine learning model (training, evaluation, deployment [pipeline], management, serving).

As inclusion criteria we defined 1) research papers that outline approaches and/or challenges in data management and processing, model building, or model deployment; and 2) case studies and experience reports describing concrete actions and processes for at least one of the categories. We excluded non-scientific contributions (e.g. posters or presentations/talks) and studies that were not written in English.

Next, we extracted all mentioned activities and challenges out of each selected paper and accumulated the results to common activities and challenges based on the frequency of occurrences. In order to derive a framework for productively applying ML in SA/BI solutions, we merged and systematically arranged the key activities of the investigated domains.

To validate the applicability of the framework in practice, we first compare it to the current state of a real-world ML-based SA/BI solution being developed for an industrial platform provider. In a second step, we utilize the framework to strategically plan and direct the upcoming activities. To achieve this, we collaborated with two software architects and two product managers of the platform. The product managers are the future user of the system and, therefore, provided us with a specific use case while the software architects supported us in building the ML-based SA/BI solution. The platform itself is based on Amazon Web Services[1] (AWS). For this reason, we utilize existing AWS services for implementing and deploying our solution. In order to get a comprehensive picture of all the activities, we interviewed the stakeholders in several recap sessions to gain a detailed understanding of individual steps that we could not directly be involved in due to company processes.

4   Literature Review

4.1   Data Management and Processing

The most important prerequisite for training accurate ML models is providing high-quality training data [26,29]. At the same time, assembling high-quality data sets, and engineering and selecting appropriate features based on it, is very time-consuming and requires a vast amount of effort and resources [14].

As a result, we investigate the common activities (see Table 1) in data management and data processing required for a successful application in machine learning systems as well as the challenges (see Table 2) that come with these activities. The identified activities can be grouped into six overarching categories: 1) Data preparation; 2) data cleaning; 3) data validation; 4) data evaluation; 5) data serving; and 6) extract, transform, and load (ETL) tasks.

During the *data preparation*, raw input data is examined for suitable features before being transformed (e.g. aggregations of one or more raw input data fields) into training data [4,5,14,21,26,27]. Next, the data is *cleaned* by filtering out uncorrelated data [10,26], specifying quality rules, detecting errors, inconsistencies and anomalies [4,8,19], and fixing these errors [8,19,26,36].

To guarantee a successful preparation and cleaning of the data, each batch of data needs to be *validated* based on its properties [4,5,26,27,29,36] and potential

---

[1] https://aws.amazon.com/.

dependencies [26], deviations [5, 26], or impact of features on model accuracy or performance [14, 26] need to be identified.

Once a model is trained, the goal of *data evaluation* is to evaluate the choice and encoding of the data based on the results produced by a model trained on the data, for instance by performing sanity checks [14, 26]. After a suitable solution was found, the newly emerging input data needs to be transformed to so-called *serving data* which is processible by the model [4, 26]. This usually involves the same transformation steps as required for the training data. After the serving data was successfully processed by the model, it is channeled back as training data for future iterations [26].

In order to execute the aforementioned steps in an iterative and continuous manner, automated ETL tasks need to be set up. This involves the extraction of data from its source, transporting it to a processing pipeline, transforming it to target values, and finally making it accessible to and loadable by respective machine learning models [13, 34, 35].

Table 1 provides a detailed overview of common activities in data management and data processing grouped into six categories.

Table 1. Common activities in data management and processing for machine learning

Activity	Publications
Data preparation	
Identification of features and their properties based on raw data	[14, 21, 26]
Transformation of input data to training data	[4, 5, 14, 26, 27]
Data cleaning	
Investigating and understanding effect of cleaning data on model accuracy & filtering out uncorrelated data	[10, 26]
Ensure data quality, specification of (quality) rules & actions for rules	[4, 8, 19]
Detection of data errors	[8, 19]
Definition of data fixes & execution of error repairs	[8, 19, 26, 36]
Data validation	
Triggering validation pipeline for each batch of data	[5, 29, 36]
Generation of descriptive statistics of data, checking data properties based on specified schema/patterns & identification of errors or anomalies in training data	[4, 5, 26, 27, 29, 36]
Identification of features with significant impact on model accuracy	[14, 26]
Identification of dependencies to other data sources or infrastructure	[26]
Comparison of training and serving data to identify potential deviations	[5, 26]
Data evaluation	
Performing sanity checks on data	[26]
Evaluation of choice and encoding of data based on model results	[14, 26]

(continued)

Table 1. (continued)

Activity	Publications
Data serving	
Transformation of serving input data to serving data processible by model	[4, 26]
Channeling serving data back as training data	[26]
Extract, transform, load (ETL)	
Extraction of data from sources	[13, 34, 35]
Transportation of data to processing pipeline (e.g. for data cleaning or filtering)	[13, 34, 35]
Transformation of source data to target values	[13, 34, 35]
Loading of cleaned & transformed data	[13, 34, 35]

As a natural consequence, these activities also entail a couple of challenges which are presented in Table 2 and mostly related to 1) data understanding; 2) data preparation; 3) data cleaning; and 4) data validation.

Table 2. Common challenges in data management and processing

Category	Challenge
DU	Set expectations of data; How to know something (e.g. a distribution) is "right"? [26]
DU	Analysis of features in conjunction [26]
DU	Understanding if data reflects reality [26]
DU	Identification of sources of data errors [26]
DC	Dealing with data inconsistency, missing features, unit changes,... [26], [29], [36]
DC & DV	Dealing with dynamic data environments (constantly changing constraints) [10], [29], [36]
DV	Formulation of understandable and actionable alerts [4], [26]
DP	Engineering set of features most predictive of the label [26]
DP	Unused data due to data overload / too much data to be processed [14]
DP	Feature experiments (e.g. different combinations of input features to examine their predictive value) affect multiple stakeholders (e.g. software or site reliability engineers responsible for pipeline) [26]
DP & DC	Merging data from multiple sources & deal with unstructured data [8], [10], [13], [16], [29]
DP, DC & DV	Achieving scalability of data processing and error detection in distributed settings [8], [10], [19]

Data understanding = DU, data cleaning = DC, data validation = DV, data preparation = DP

4.2 Model Building

In the model building phase, one or multiple models are prepared, built, and evaluated based on the previously generated input features. This is typically an iterative process that involves running an analysis, evaluating the results, and adapting or optimizing parameters and input features until an adequate solution is found [14, 22, 33]. Table 3 outlines common activities that are part of this process.

Table 3. Common activities in model preparation, building, and evaluation

Activity	Publications
Model preparation	
Selection of appropriate analysis/model type	[14, 17, 21, 27]
Selection of input features	[4, 12, 14, 21]
Model building	
Splitting input data into training and test set	[14, 21]
Model training on training data	[4, 14, 21, 25, 27, 31, 33]
Application of model to test data	[4, 14, 21, 31, 33]
Model evaluation	
Quality evaluation based on test results (e.g. accuracy, precision, recall, F1-score)	[4, 14, 21, 25, 27, 31, 33]
Decision: accept or rework model (e.g. by adapting input features or model parameters)	[3, 14, 21]

Initially and based on the respective problem to solve, appropriate analysis techniques and model types need to be selected as part of the *model preparation* [14, 17, 21, 27]. For instance, if the input data is labeled and the goal is to classify data according to these labels, a supervised ML technique (e.g. logistic regression, support vector machines etc.) can help to achieve this. On the other side, if the requirement is to group unlabeled objects by their similarity, an unsupervised approach (e.g. k-means clustering, hierarchical clustering etc.) is the better choice.

Oftentimes, it is not advisable to use all available features as input features for the selected model as this can create noise and cause a decrease in model accuracy [14]. This results in the need for feature selection techniques that aim at identifying the most relevant input features for a given model [4, 12, 14, 21].

Once the input data is filtered according to the determined feature relevance, a training and a test data set need to be created as part of the *model building* phase [14, 21]. In a next step, the training set is used to train a model that was selected to solve a specific problem [4, 14, 21, 25, 27, 31, 33]. Before being able to validate the quality of the model, it is applied on the test set to investigate how it performs on previously unseen data [4, 14, 21, 31, 33].

Consequently, the results of this step can be used for the *model evaluation*. There are several metrics that support practitioners in assessing the quality of their models, for instance by calculating the accuracy, precision, recall, or F1-score [4, 14, 21, 25, 27, 31, 33]. Based on the evaluation results, the model can either be accepted as a reasonable solution or it needs to be reworked, for example by adapting the parameters or input features that are used for training the model [3, 14, 21].

This iterative process is often accompanied by several challenges. Table 4 summarizes a few of these challenges that we feel like are most important for our study. The presented challenges are categorized in *model preparation*, *model building*, and *model evaluation*.

Table 4. Common challenges in model preparation, building, and evaluation

Category	Challenge
MP	Selecting appropriate model types for a specific problem [1], [14], [20]
MP	Dealing with too many (irrelevant) input features [14]
MP	Coordination and communication of involved stakeholders (e.g. ML specialists, software engineers,...) [1], [2], [20]
MB	Avoidance of overfitting [14]
MB	Debugging of ML models [1], [2], [32]
ME	Defining quality specifications (e.g. "when is the prediction quality good enough?", "is the model save to serve?" [4]

Model preparation = MP, model building = MB, model evaluation = ME

4.3   Model Deployment and Serving

In order to fully leverage the benefits of ML to gain valuable insights, it is crucial to go beyond prototypical analyses by deploying models in production where they are actually used [21]. It has even been observed that "organizations that make the most of machine learning are those that have in place an infrastructure that makes experimenting with many different learners, data sources, and learning problems easy and efficient" [14].

For that reason, we summarize the common activities in model deployment and model serving in Table 5.

Deployment infrastructures for ML models often consist of multiple *components* each responsible for a specific task and executable as an automated

Table 5. Common activities in model deployment and model serving

Activity	Publications
Components	
Component for model validation (before serving & often coupled with data validation)	[4,9,25]
Component for continuous model evaluation & monitoring (performance, quality,...)	[4,9,25,27]
Component or serving solution to deploy model in production	[4,9,21]
Component for monitoring pipelines (checkpoint after each pipeline)	[27,31]
Setups	
Setup model lifecycle management (to keep overview of deployed models)	[9,33]
Setup workflow manager for job coordination	[9,21]
Process	
Loading new model before unloading old model	[25]
Validation of model and serving infrastructure (incl. reliability checks) before pushing to production environment	[4,9,25]
Continuous application of model to (new) serving data	[9,21,27]
Continuous model evaluation / monitoring	[4,9,25,27]
Rollback in case of errors	[25,27]
Periodically update models	[9,21]

workflow coordinated by a workflow manager. Besides the component that handles the actual deployment of models in production [4,9,21], it is advisable to have additional components for validating the model before deployment [4,9,25], for continuously evaluating and monitoring the model after being deployed in production [4,9,25,27], and for monitoring if all pipelines are up and running as expected [27,31].

In addition to the components, a few *setups* are required for automating the deployments while keeping an overview of the deployed models. For one, a model lifecycle management should be set up that allows the comparison and monitoring of models over time and provides information on the currently deployed models [9,33]. For another, the jobs required to deploy a model can be coordinated an executed using a workflow manager [9,21]. After triggering the workflow, the model is updated in an automated manner and in case of errors a predefined rollback plan is executed.

In general, the *process* of model deployment and model serving requires the following steps which are typically encapsulated in respective components: First, a new model is loaded for deployment before unloading the old model [25]. In a next step, the model as well as the serving infrastructure are validated (e.g. reliability checks) before pushing the new model to the production environment [4,9,25].

Once the model is deployed to production, it can be used and continuously applied to newly emerging serving data [9,21,27]. In order to guarantee that the model works as expected, a continuous evaluation and monitoring of the model is required [4,9,25,27]. In case the model does not behave as expected, a rollback plan is executed and typically the current model is replaced by a previous well-working version of the model [25,27]. Following this process, models can be periodically updated and deployed to production [9,21].

Analogously to data management and model building, model deployment and model serving also entails several challenges. Four of the key challenges are presented in Table 6. The challenges are categorized into *infrastructure* and *model*-specific topics.

Table 6. Common challenges in model deployment and model serving

Category	Challenge
I	Integration of third-party packages or tools [21], [30]
I	Brittle pipelines / "pipeline jungle" [21], [30]
M	Managing and monitoring multiple models [9], [30], [33]
M	Dealing with expected and unexpected variations during model evaluation [4], [30]

Infrastructure = I, model = M

5   Framework Derivation

Based on the insights gained from the literature review, we derive a framework for supporting an end-to-end development and deployment of ML models in the context of software analytics and business intelligence (see Fig. 2).

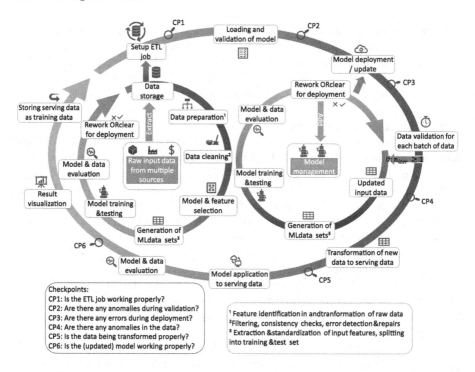

Fig. 2. Framework for productively applying machine learning (Color figure online)

While the literature review examines the topics *data management and processing*, *model building*, and *model deployment and serving* individually, in reality a separation of the three is not that trivial. In fact, for building end-to-end solutions the fields are very much interrelated as the activities depend on each other and sometimes even overlap.

Oftentimes, ML projects start out as a *prototypical* analysis due to a limited amount of time and resources [15,30]. In order to use and actually benefit from the ML model, it needs to be *deployed* to a production environment which can be time and cost-intensive but nonetheless crucial [21,30]. To avoid the deployed models from being outdated, it is important to provide a functionality for dynamically deploying new models or iteratively *retraining and updating* existing models [9,21].

As a result, we identify three iterative cycles which are passed through during an end-to-end development of ML solutions and, therefore, serve as the main dimensions in our framework: 1) Prototyping cycle (blue), 2) deployment cycle (green), and 3) update cycle (orange).

5.1   Prototyping Cycle

In software analytics and business intelligence, relevant input data typically emerges from multiple sources that need to be extracted, set in relation, and stored in a common data storage [15]. As part of the data preparation, potential input features can be identified and extracted based on a snapshot of raw data [14,21,26]. To ensure a sufficient data quality, a couple of data cleaning activities need to be performed (e.g. filtering, consistency checks, or other error detection techniques and repairs) [4,8,19,26,36].

Depending on the overarching goal of the analysis, appropriate ML models have to be selected that are suitable to achieve a specific task [14,17,21,27]. Based on the selected model, it is recommended to apply feature selection techniques to the input data set to identify a subset of the most relevant input features [4,12,14,21]. This subset is then extracted from the overall data set and the values of each input features are standardized. Before training the model, the respective subset should be split into a training and a test data set (usually 70%/30% or 80%/20%) [14,21].

Training the model using training data and testing it on test data, allows an examination of how well the model performs on previously unseen data [4], [14,21,31,33]. Based on the test results, the choice of model parameters and input features should be evaluated [4,14,21,25,27,31,33]. If the evaluation indicates a decent quality of the model (e.g. based on accuracy, precision, recall, and F1-score), it can be cleared for deployment. Otherwise, the cycle is run through again and the model is reworked until its quality reaches a desired level.

5.2 Deployment Cycle

Taking a ML model to production involves much more than only model deployment. For one, a ETL job needs to be set up that continuously extracts, transforms, and loads the latest input and serving data [13,34,35]. Before a new model is deployed, it is loaded and validated to avoid errors of faulty behavior in the production environment [4,9,25].

For each batch of new data a data validation pipeline is triggered that checks the data for anomalies [5,29,36]. After one or more iterations, the update cycle can be entered at this point in case the model needs to be retrained which is evaluated during the model evaluation later on.

Analogous to the training data, the new input data is transformed to serving data [4,26]. This involves data cleaning, feature extraction and standardization. In a next step, the model can be applied to the new and preprocessed data [9,21,27].

Since both data and model behavior evolves over time, it is crucial to continuously evaluate the model performance and its input data [4,9,25,27]. If the model does not perform as expected, a retraining of the model is triggered for the next iteration [9,21].

In addition to this, the results of the analysis need to be visualized. By explaining the results as intuitively as possible, users of SA/BI solution will be able to understand and interpret the results and turn it into actionable insights [15]. In the last step before the cycle is repeated from the beginning, the recently processed serving data is channeled back as training data which will be included in upcoming retrainings of the model [26].

Since these steps are typically automated in one or multiple pipelines, it is important to implement several checkpoints along the way, that continuously monitor and check whether each task is working properly [27,31]. In case of errors or anomalies, an alert should be sent to the respective stakeholder.

5.3   Update Cycle

As a natural consequence of constantly evolving data, the model's accuracy can start to decrease some time after being deployed [21]. As soon as this is detected during the model evaluation in the deployment cycle, a retraining of the model will be triggered after the upcoming data validation.

An updated data set is created that consists of the initial training data as well as the new serving data that was channeled back as training data [26]. Analogous to the initial training only the relevant input features are extracted, standardized and split into a training and a test set. The model is retrained based on the new training set and tested on the test set respectively [4,14,21,31,33].

Based on the results, the model's input features and parameters needs to be evaluated before deciding whether to improve the model's quality in an additional iteration or whether to clear it for deployment and add both the current and the new model to the model management [4,14,21,25,27,31,33]. The latter enables a clear overview of all models and allows an easy rollback in case of erroneous behavior in production.

6   Framework Validation

In order to validate the applicability of our framework in practice, we use a real-world ML-based SA/BI solution that is currently being developed for an industrial platform provider to 1) compare the activities of the framework to the actual activities executed in practice; and 2) to strategically plan and direct upcoming activities to finalize the end-to-end implementation.

6.1   Current Status

At the beginning of our collaboration, the product managers were interested in running customized analyses on their customers' usage data. Specifically, whenever a customer's action triggers a request to the platform or one of its applications, it is tracked in the platform and app usage logs. The platform itself is based on AWS. Therefore, we decided to setup the custom ML-based SA/BI solution using the existing AWS infrastructure and services.

Currently, the platform and app usage logs produce 100 GB of data every day. For this reason, the data is aggregated and stored in a compressed format (26 GB per day) in AWS S3 buckets[2]. The log data is available for the past 1.5 years and, in addition to that, we also have access to the sales data that keeps track of which customer purchased what kind of licenses.

---

[2] https://aws.amazon.com/s3/.

Prototyping Cycle. As the future users of the system, the product managers were interested in analyzing customer churn for the applications hosted on the platform as a first use case.

In the beginning, we focus on one specific application to build a first prototype. Therefore, we identify potential input features based on the information that is available in the logs (e.g. user id, http status code, relative URL path) and pre-filter the data by the selected application. We setup a script that extracts and aggregates the input features on customer level ($n = 174$) while enriching and labeling it with the sales data (binary label for churn/non-churn).

Next, we applied several different supervised ML models (support vector machines, decision trees, logistic regression, neural network) to the data set in an iterative manner. We apply principal component analysis to the standardized input data in order to identify the most relevant subset of features, before splitting the data set into a training and a test set.

Based on this, the models were trained on the training data and tested using the test set. It took us several iterations and experiments with different models, model parameters and input features before ending up with the final model that is being deployed in the upcoming step.

Deployment Cycle. At the current state of our ML-based SA/BI solution, we have not yet completed the deployment cycle. Before being able to deploy the model, we had to come up with an efficient, reliable and robust solution for handling the enormous amounts of data (100 GB per day). It was a complex task to get an overview of the data, to define which fields to keep for long-term storage, and finally to specify the format to store it in.

After coming up with a concept for this, one of the software architects setup pipelines that continuously extract, transform, compress and load the latest log data into a S3 bucket using the specified format. In addition to that, he also setup data validation pipelines that check each batch of new data for anomalies and inconsistencies. It is important to continuously monitor all pipelines. During one of the interviews, the software architect explains that "we have to make sure the pipelines are not failing for whatever reasons and if they're failing we're notified and can restart them". Moreover, they need to ensure that "the pipeline elements that are doing the preprocessing are always up and triggered at appropriate times". The software architect also notes that it "requires a lot of engineering effort to keep the pipeline running in a correct manner."

After the data pipelines are set up, we load and deploy our ML model using Amazon SageMaker[3]. The SageMaker modules for Python offer out-of-the-box functionalities for deploying ML models to an AWS instance that are accessible via an API (see Fig. 3).

---

[3] https://aws.amazon.com/sagemaker/.

Fig. 3. Model deployment in Amazon SageMaker

> **Findings - current status**: The activities identified in literature are consistent with the activities we had to perform for successfully implementing our prototype, setting up continuous data extraction, processing and validation pipelines, and deploying our model; it is important to accept that prototyping is an iterative process; continuous checkpoints after each automated task are crucial

6.2 Planning and Evolution

In order to use the deployed model to make actual predictions, we now plan and execute the remaining steps following the presented framework.

Deployment Cycle. In the upcoming step, the model is applied to new serving data. This constitutes a bit of a challenge as up until now all extracted data is stored in the same S3 bucket. As a result, we now need to create an additional S3 bucket for storing the serving data. In order to preprocess the newly emerged data to serving data, we can reuse the script created during prototyping for transforming and extracting the input features out of the raw data.

In order to continuously evaluate the model in production, we setup Amazon SageMaker's Model Monitor that provides summary statistics, detects concepts drifts and indicates when a model needs to be retrained. In order to perform potential retrainings on the newest data available, we transfer the data from the serving S3 bucket to the training S3 bucket once it was processed by the model. Lastly, we plan to visualize the results in Amazon QuickSight[4].

Update Cycle. For continuous updates of models, AWS offers the Step Functions Data Science SDK[5] for Amazon Sagemaker to automate model retraining and deployment. An ETL job is setup to extract and preprocess the latest data. Following this, a new model is trained and evaluated. If the model accuracy is above a certain threshold (e.g. 90%), a new endpoint is created for deployment and the model is added to the model management.

---

[4] https://aws.amazon.com/quicksight/.

[5] https://docs.aws.amazon.com/step-functions/latest/dg/concepts-python-sdk.html.

> **Findings - planning and evolution**: the framework supported us in keeping an overview of remaining tasks; by following the cycles and activities in the framework the definition of the roadmap and next steps was efficient and easy; we were able to quickly identify errors or missing components in our original approach (storage of training and serving data)

7   Conclusion

Gaining customized insights on product or usage behavior can be a valuable asset for many stakeholders involved in software-intensive businesses which results in a need for ML-based SA/BI solutions. Building and, more importantly, deploying and maintaining such solutions is, however, time-consuming, complex and burdensome as it requires knowledge from several different domains.

For this reason, we scanned existing literature on data management and processing, model building, and model deployment to derive a framework that comprises all key activities from data collection to retraining of deployed models. In addition to that, our framework is structured in three iterative cycles: a prototyping cycle, deployment cycle, and an update cycle. These cycles resemble stages in the lifecycle of a ML model and by outlining the transitions between stages, our framework specifically guides the journey from a prototypical analysis to a productively running ML model.

The results of the validation indicate that the activities of the framework are consistent with the activities performed in practice. Moreover, the framework is a practical tool to keep an overview of all required steps and to efficiently define and plan upcoming activities. Moreover, we observed that the separation of activities across the conceptual phases creates the perception that the overall, potentially overwhelming process now consists of several smaller ones that are easier to handle.

One limitations of our study is the development state of our ML-based SA/BI solution. As we are still in the process of implementing parts of the deployment and update cycle, we are only partially able to compare the framework's activities to the activities executed in practice. Further research could, therefore, be dedicated to a long-term validation of the framework based on already established SA/BI solutions and to identifying remaining challenges and needs for more in-depth guidance by practitioners to adapt the framework to their needs.

References

1. Amershi, S., et al.: Software engineering for machine learning: a case study. In: 2019 IEEE/ACM 41st International Conference on Software Engineering: Software Engineering in Practice (ICSE-SEIP), pp. 291–300. IEEE (2019)
2. Arpteg, A., Brinne, B., Crnkovic-Friis, L., Bosch, J.: Software engineering challenges of deep learning. In: 2018 44th Euromicro Conference on Software Engineering and Advanced Applications (SEAA), pp. 50–59. IEEE (2018)

3. Bauer, E., Kohavi, R.: An empirical comparison of voting classification algorithms: bagging, boosting, and variants. Mach. Learn. **36**(1–2), 105–139 (1999). https://doi.org/10.1023/A:1007515423169
4. Baylor, D., et al.: TFX: a tensorflow-based production-scale machine learning platform. In: Proceedings of the 23rd ACM SIGKDD International Conference on Knowledge Discovery and Data Mining, pp. 1387–1395 (2017)
5. Breck, E., Polyzotis, N., Roy, S., Whang, S.E., Zinkevich, M.: Data validation for machine learning. In: Conference on Systems and Machine Learning (2019)
6. Buse, R.P., Zimmermann, T.: Information needs for software development analytics. In: 34th International Conference on Software Engineering, pp. 987–996. IEEE (2012)
7. Chen, H., Chiang, R.H., Storey, V.C.: Business intelligence and analytics: from big data to big impact. MIS Q. **36**, 1165–1188 (2012)
8. Chu, X., Ilyas, I.F., Krishnan, S., Wang, J.: Data cleaning: overview and emerging challenges. In: Proceedings of the 2016 International Conference on Management of Data, pp. 2201–2206 (2016)
9. Crankshaw, D., et al.: The missing piece in complex analytics: low latency, scalable model management and serving with velox (2015)
10. Cuzzocrea, A., Song, I.Y., Davis, K.C.: Analytics over large-scale multidimensional data: the big data revolution! In: Proceedings of the ACM 14th International Workshop on Data Warehousing and OLAP, pp. 101–104 (2011)
11. Dam, H.K., Tran, T., Ghose, A.: Explainable software analytics. In: Proceedings of the 40th International Conference on Software Engineering: New Ideas and Emerging Results, pp. 53–56 (2018)
12. Dash, M., Liu, H.: Feature selection for classification. Intell. Data Anal. **1**(3), 131–156 (1997)
13. Dayal, U., Castellanos, M., Simitsis, A., Wilkinson, K.: Data integration flows for business intelligence. In: Proceedings of the 12th International Conference on Extending Database Technology: Advances in Database Technology, pp. 1–11 (2009)
14. Domingos, P.: A few useful things to know about machine learning. Commun. ACM **55**(10), 78–87 (2012)
15. Figalist, I., Elsner, C., Bosch, J., Olsson, H.H.: Breaking the vicious circle: Why AI for software analytics and business intelligence does not take off in practice. In: 46th Euromicro Conference on Software Engineering and Advanced Applications. IEEE (2020)
16. Hernández, M.A., Stolfo, S.J.: Real-world data is dirty: data cleansing and the merge/purge problem. Data Min. Knowl. Disc. **2**(1), 9–37 (1998). https://doi.org/10.1023/A:1009761603038
17. Jordan, M.I., Mitchell, T.M.: Machine learning: trends, perspectives, and prospects. Science **349**(6245), 255–260 (2015)
18. Keele, S.: Guidelines for performing systematic literature reviews in software engineering. Technical report, Version 2.3 EBSE Technical Report (2007)
19. Khayyat, Z., et al.: BigDansing: a system for big data cleansing. In: Proceedings of the 2015 ACM SIGMOD International Conference on Management of Data, pp. 1215–1230 (2015)
20. Kim, M., Zimmermann, T., DeLine, R., Begel, A.: Data scientists in software teams: State of the art and challenges. IEEE Trans. Softw. Eng. **44**(11), 1024–1038 (2017)
21. Lin, J., Kolcz, A.: Large-scale machine learning at twitter. In: Proceedings of the 2012 ACM SIGMOD International Conference on Management of Data, pp. 793–804 (2012)

22. Lwakatare, L.E., Raj, A., Crnkovic, I., Bosch, J., Olsson, H.H.: Large-scale machine learning systems in real-world industrial settings a review of challenges and solutions. Inf. Softw. Technol. **127**, 106368 (2020)
23. Menzies, T., Zimmermann, T.: Software analytics: so what? IEEE Softw. **30**(4), 31–37 (2013)
24. Negash, S., Gray, P.: Business Intelligence. In: Handbook on Decision Support Systems 2. International Handbooks Information System. Springer, Heidelberg (2008). https://doi.org/10.1007/978-3-540-48716-6_9
25. Olston, C., et al.: Tensorflow-serving: flexible, high-performance ml serving. In: Workshop on ML Systems at NIPS (2017)
26. Polyzotis, N., Roy, S., Whang, S.E., Zinkevich, M.: Data lifecycle challenges in production machine learning: a survey. ACM SIGMOD Rec. **47**(2), 17–28 (2018)
27. Rajaram, S., Mishra, K., O'mara, M.: Finite state automata that enables continuous delivery of machine learning models, US Patent App. 16/229,020, April 2020
28. Runeson, P., Höst, M., Rainer, A., Regnell, B.: Case study research in software engineering: guidelines and examples. Wiley, Hoboken (2012)
29. Schelter, S., Lange, D., Schmidt, P., Celikel, M., Biessmann, F., Grafberger, A.: Automating large-scale data quality verification. Proc. VLDB Endow. **11**(12), 1781–1794 (2018)
30. Sculley, D.: Hidden technical debt in machine learning systems. In: Advances in neural information processing systems, pp. 2503–2511 (2015)
31. Sparks, E.R., Venkataraman, S., Kaftan, T., Franklin, M.J., Recht, B.: KeystoneML: Optimizing pipelines for large-scale advanced analytics. In: 2017 IEEE 33rd International Conference on Data Engineering (ICDE), pp. 535–546. IEEE (2017)
32. Tata, S., et al.: Quick access: building a smart experience for google drive. In: Proceedings of the 23rd ACM SIGKDD International Conference on Knowledge Discovery and Data Mining, pp. 1643–1651 (2017)
33. Vartak, M., et al.: ModelDB: a system for machine learning model management. In: Proceedings of the Workshop on Human-In-the-Loop Data Analytics (2016)
34. Vassiliadis, P.: A survey of extract-transform-load technology. Int. J. Data Warehous. Min. (IJDWM) **5**(3), 1–27 (2009)
35. Vassiliadis, P., Simitsis, A.: Extraction, transformation, and loading. Encycl. Database Syst. **10**, 1–10 (2009)
36. Volkovs, M., Chiang, F., Szlichta, J., Miller, R.J.: Continuous data cleaning. In: 30th International Conference on Data Engineering, pp. 244–255. IEEE (2014)

Test and Evolution

A Systematic-Oriented Process for Tool Selection: The Case of Green and Technical Debt Tools in Architecture Reconstruction

Daniel Guamán[1,2](✉) ⓘ, Jennifer Pérez[1](✉) ⓘ, Juan Garbajosa[1](✉) ⓘ,
and Germania Rodríguez[2](✉) ⓘ

[1] Universidad Politécnica de Madrid, Madrid, Spain
{jenifer.perez,juan.garbajosa}@upm.es
[2] Universidad Técnica Particular de Loja, Loja, Ecuador
{daguaman,grrodriguez}@utpl.edu.ec

Abstract. Well-established methods in software engineering research, such as Systematic Literature Reviews, Systematic Mappings and Case Studies are effective research methods to explore emerging areas, since they are systematic and replicable, and produce reusable result avoiding bias. Frequently, software engineers have to evaluate and select CASE (Computer Aided Software Engineering) tools that address trending issues with a non-systematic and replicable processes. This work addresses this problem by tailoring the ISO/IEC 14102:2008 to a systematic-oriented process for the evaluation of software engineering CASE tools in order to embrace the advantages of software engineering systematic methods in the exploration of new areas or emerging issues. This tailored ISO/IEC 14102:2008 standard prescribes a process for the preparation, design and conduction of the software engineering CASE tools evaluation and selection. This process is founded in the application of systematic methods and the generation of a pre-established assets to ensure the reusability of knowledge. In this paper, this tailored process has been applied to address two great emerging concerns in architectural reconstruction: technical debt and energy consumption. As result of this adoption, this paper details the reporting analysis and the set of reusable assets that have been generated during the evaluation process. Specifically, this contribution presents a set of tables, statistics and a decision-making tree of the selected tools for technical debt and energy consumption analysis in architecture reconstruction.

Keywords: ISO/IEC14102:2008 · Systematic process · Green software · Architecture reconstruction · Technical debt · Tools

1 Introduction

Last decades, software engineering research has taken a step forward in the study of the new areas and the means of reporting results by using systematic methods. Several

This work is sponsored by Universidad Técnica Particular de Loja (Computer Science Department) and by the project CROWDSAVING (TIN2016-79726-C2-1-R).

© Springer Nature Switzerland AG 2020
M. Morisio et al. (Eds.): PROFES 2020, LNCS 12562, pp. 237–253, 2020.
https://doi.org/10.1007/978-3-030-64148-1_15

methods have been defined, such as Systematic Literature Reviews (SLR) [1, 2], Systematic Mappings (SM) [3] or Case Studies [4], among others. SLR and SM follow a process driven by a set of research questions, a search string, and inclusion and exclusion criteria for analyzing the selecting studies. On the other hand, case studies are reported by defining the research questions and goals, the data collection and analysis of results procedures. These research methods provide clear advantages to study emerging issues or new areas, since they are systematic and replicable avoiding bias and also provide reusable knowledge. Currently, software engineering undergoes a continuous emergence of new areas and technologies, that at the same time, entails the construction of a large amount of new tools to support them. Software engineers from industry and academy must continuously address the evaluation of these new tools. All parties would benefit from the availability of a systematic process that favors reusing results and, therefore, avoids starting from scratch each time a new set of tools have to be evaluated. This work presents a process obtained by tailoring the standard ISO/IEC 14102:2008 Information Technology-Guideline for the Evaluation and Selection of CASE tools [5] by applying its recommendations and systematic-methods.

The Standard ISO/IEC 14102:2008 was designed to discern, based on results, the CASE tool that best suits the needs required for a given context or objective. The goal of this systematic-oriented tailored process of the ISO/IEC 14102:2008 is twofold: to be replicable and avoiding bias, together with providing reusable knowledge for engineers about the tools of a specific emerging field in software engineering. The process prescribes the preparation, design and conduction of tool evaluation in an evidenced research context, and the kind of reusable assets that have to be obtained to ensure the knowledge reusability. To that end, the process includes additional activities such as SLRs or SMS, and analysis techniques based on search strings, hypothesis and RQs.

In this paper, we illustrate the adoption of the systematic-oriented tailored process of the ISO/IEC14102:2008 standard to address two emerging issues in software engineering, the technical debt (TD) and sustainability of software applications when they are continuously evolving. Evolution [6] require the adoption of appropriate measures and practices at design and implementation, because a degradation in application structure and coding may occur, affecting the internal software quality. Currently, this quality is highly-related with technical debt (TD) [7] and software sustainability [8]. The technical dimension of the sustainability manifest is referring to: "longevity of information, systems, and infrastructure and their adequate evolution with changing surrounding conditions. It includes maintenance, innovation, obsolescence, data integrity, etc." This definition clearly states the relevance of sustainability in evolution, especially in reverse engineering processes and its sub-process of architecture reconstruction [9, 21]. In addition, during architecture reconstruction, refactoring techniques are applied to reduce technical debt and improve the internal structure without affecting the system functionality [10, 11]. Specifically, we illustrate the adoption of the process to identify and select tools that semi-automatically support architectural reconstruction activities in reverse engineering to extract energy metrics and analyze technical debt. As a result of the adoption, this work provides a set of tables, statistics and a decision tree, prescribed by the tailored version of the standard, as a reusable knowledge to assist the software engineers in the tool selection decision-making process.

Based on the aforementioned aspects, the structure of this paper is as follows: Sect. 2 provides an overview of related work; Sect. 3 describes the tailoring of the Standard ISO/IEC 14102:2008; Sect. 4 details the description of the conducting phase, the reporting of results and the generation of the reusable assets from the selected tools; and finally, Sect. 5 presents the conclusions and future work.

2 Related Work

There are well-established evaluation methods to evaluate tools as DESMET [19] and standards such as IEEE 1209-1992 [20] and ISO/IEC 14102:2008. DESMET proposes nine evaluation types and a set of criteria, which help the evaluator to choose the most suitable tool for its/her needs. Users, companies, academic institutions interested in experimental software engineering can use this method, where the evaluation context means that we do not expect a specific method/tool to be the best in all circumstances. DESMET has been used in works such as [12] and [13], which evaluate the impact of using a method/tool or the suitability of a tool in terms of the needs and culture of an organization. On the other hand, the standard IEEE 1209-1992 defines a process with a set of inputs to obtain a candidate tool. The inputs of this process is a list of criteria based on the user needs, an initial list of the available tools, the objectives, and the assumptions and constraints about the evaluation. This standard has been used in the evaluation of several frameworks such as [14, 15] and [16]. In addition, some works use the standard ISO/IEC 14102:2008 to provide some recommendations or select tools, take into account some criteria for different domains [17] and [18]. In this paper, we take a step forward in the state-of the-art by providing a process with systematic techniques to the standard in order to provide the replicability and reusability features.

3 A Systematic-Oriented ISO/IEC 14102:2008 Process

The Standard ISO/IEC 14102:2008 is a guide to select a CASE tool that best suits the needs within a context [5]. It consists of four processes (Preparation, Structuring, Evaluation and Selection) defined by the standard and their outputs. To construct the systematic-oriented process the standard has been tailored with a systematic and exploratory purpose by prescribing how performing these processes, the definition of outputs and the kind of assets that should produce these outputs. It aims to assist software engineers in their study and evaluation of tools that meet trending issues determining which tools meet certain needs or requirements and to what extent. For tailoring ISO/IEC 14102:2008, the clauses provided in it on how to address tailoring and annexes A and B were used [5]. The systematic-oriented tailored process of the ISO/IEC14102:2008 is presented in Fig. 1.

The **Preparation process** was tailored as follows: the project plan, high-level goals and criteria outputs of the standard are specialized into the definition of the objectives, expectations, criteria, and hypothesis that are important in an exploratory process. The high-level goals are the *objective/s* that the process that support the tool should deal with. This objective should be complemented by answering a set of *research questions* that help to understand how the objective is supported. The *hypothesis* are proposals to

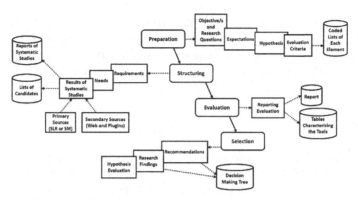

Fig. 1. Systematic-oriented tailored version of the ISO/IEC 14102:2008

meet the objective of the selection process that should be validated after the analysis in order to determine in what extent the objective is fulfilled. *Expectations* must be associated with the objectives proposed, and should allow quantifying and classifying the candidate tools for the study purpose. Finally, the *characterization criteria* have to respond to the objectives and expectations through a set of selection decision (Yes/No) to search the candidate tools that best fit within the specific context of search. From this process is prescribed to elaborate a coded list for each of the elements: research questions, expectations, hypothesis and criteria (see Fig. 1).

The structured requirements of the **Structuring process** have been tailored into the identification of needs and the definition of requirements to search the list of candidates. *Needs* are given by engineers/users or arise from the adoption context; whereas the *requirements* are conditions or capabilities that must be met or provided by the tools. Both, needs and requirements, are used to complement the process of searching candidate tools and determine if these candidates satisfy the established objectives. In addition, the structuring process is tailored by prescribing that the *list of candidates* must be obtained using *systematic research methods*. In particular, the set of primary sources must be obtained conducting a Systematic Mapping (SM) or a Systematic Literature Review (SLR). Then, the list of candidate tools is complemented with a *search in the grey literature* that consist in searches on the web and plugins of the most used frameworks in the field (see Fig. 1). The reports of these reviews are reusable knowledge, but it is also prescribed to elaborate a list of candidates to be extended with its characteristics in the next process.

In the **Evaluation process**, the tools from the list of candidates are reported answering the research questions and analyzing the expectations and the characterization criteria. As the systematic-oriented process establishes, a set of tables should be produced synthesizing the results (see Fig. 1). As a result, these tables, their derived statistics and report are reusable knowledge.

Finally, the **Selection process** has been specialized by presenting the recommendation, as well as the criteria and the guidelines applied to recommend those tools that satisfy the objectives, expectations and requirements defined in the Preparation process within a given research context. As a result, the tailored version adoption, in addition to strictly identify the tool/s, it also provides the decision-making process and the knowledge extracted. The asset that integrates all this information is the decision tree that the tailored version of the standard prescribes (see Fig. 1). The decision tree is ordered by the priority decisions of the researches that conduct the study, however with the information that the tree provides, it is possible to reorder it following another priority order.

4 The Case of the Evaluation of Green and Technical Debt Tools in Architecture Reconstruction

This section presents a case study in order to illustrate engineers about how to use the Systematic-Oriented ISO/IEC 14102:2008 Process. In particular, this case study evaluates tools that allow architectural reconstruction and the measurement of technical debt and software energy consumption metrics.

4.1 Preparation

In the Preparation process, the objective, expectations, characterization criteria and hypothesis are defined (see Fig. 1).

In our evaluation, the **objectives** are: (O1) to recommend a tool or a set of tools that allow the extraction of architectural elements and metrics to evaluate technical debt and estimate energy consumption in software, and (O2) to study how the extraction is supported by the tools. The **research questions** to address both objectives are the following: (RQ1) What are the techniques of architecture reconstruction that are implemented by the tools? (RQ2) What are the purpose and the process that follow the techniques/methods implemented in the tools? and (RQ3) What are the outputs and formats provided by the tools?. In this work, three expectations and five characterization criteria were defined (see Table 1).

Table 1. Expectations and characterization criteria

Expectations	Characterization criteria
EX1: Tools use static and/or dynamic analysis techniques and visualization is supported by views EX2: Tools extract metrics used to estimate technical debt EX3: Tools extract metrics used to estimate software energy consumption	CC1: Tools support at least the activities of architecture reconstruction: extraction, analysis and/or visualization CC2: Tools visualize elaborated outputs: graphics, tables or matrices CC3: Tools support the loading of the applications under analysis locally or from Git repositories CC4: Tools' license is open source, commercial and/or trial CC5: Tools analyze applications coded in C, C++, Java, C#, PHP, among others

Finally, the **hypothesis** are the following: H1. There are tools that in semi-automatic way fully or partially perform software architecture reconstruction by executing its activities (extraction, analysis and/or visualization). H2. There are tools that extract metrics and architectural elements outputs using the source code or other software artefacts as inputs. H3. There are tools with a graphical interface to help configure (activate or inactivate) and customize metrics to be executed during the extraction and analysis. H4. There are tools that include technical debt analysis and energy consumption estimation.

4.2 Structuring

During the Structuring process, the needs and requirements were defined (see Table 2). The objectives and requirements were used to include or exclude the tools for producing the list of candidate tools from the search (see https://bit.ly/39ficiz). Following the systematic-oriented process, we applied the following three activities:

Table 2. Needs and requirements

Needs	Requirements
NI1. The tool meets the objectives regardless its type of license	REQ1. Windows and/or Linux OS operation and installation
NI2.There is supporting source code and/or documentation for using the tool	REQ 2. Local, web and/or cloud services execution
NI3. The tool's inputs are source code, executable, binary and/or UML architectural documentation	REQ 3. Loading applications using as inputs source code or architectural documentation (UML)
NI4.The tool supports the extraction of metrics and/or architectural elements	REQ 4. Extraction, visualization and/or exportation of measurements and metrics
NI5. The tool supports the search and selection of applications from Git open repositories	REQ 5. A single tool for analyzing technical debt and/or energy consumption based on metrics
NI6. The tool allows storing the generated data in a local or a cloud repository	REQ 6. The extracted and analyzed data is stored in local or cloud storages
NI7. The tool generates data for analyzing technical debt and estimating the energy consumption	REQ 7. The metrics are exported in different formats
NI8. The generated data by the tool can be shown using different representations, formats and/or architectural views	
NI9. The tool can be extended or integrated with other tools or plugins	

Primary Sources – Secondary Study with a Systematic Literature Review (SLR). In a previous work [19], we performed an SLR that was conducted following the guidelines proposed by Kitchenham [20] to identify the process, techniques and tools used in architecture reconstruction and reverse engineering. The search string used was the following: *"software architecture" and "pattern*" and "recommend*" and ("reverse* *engineering" or "re-engineering" or "reconstruction"*). The search was performed in the four scientific databases (ACM DL, IEEE Xplore, Science Direct, and Springer). As result of this SLR, 34 tools were identified. 11 tools were discarded because its last version and technical support is outdated (under 2009), and 23 candidate tools were selected after their first analysis. It was evidenced that these 23 tools allow: to extract metrics and evaluate architectural designs; and to identify and analyze architectural styles and architectural patterns using different strategies (top-down and bottom-up) and techniques [19].

Secondary Sources - Complementary Study. Web Search: The primary sources only provided evidence the extraction of source code metrics and architectural elements through architecture reconstruction activities; however, there were no evidences of technical debt and green metrics. Therefore, the complementary study was used to search dedicated tools for technical debt analysis and energy consumption, which in certain scenarios use data generated from architecture reconstruction tools. The search in the Web was performed on Google Scholar using as search string: *"software architecture reconstruction tool" OR "green software tool" OR "technical debt tool"*. From the review of resulting papers, we selected those tools that support (i) the extraction of code and design metrics that can be used for energy consumption estimation and technical debt analysis, (ii) architectural reconstruction, and/or (iii) the identification of smells that affect the quality that increases the energy consumption or the technical debt. As a result, 14 tools were selected, discarding those already identified as a primary source (see Web Search, Table 3).

Table 3. Selection of tools

Source	Number of tools	Tools selected
Systematic literature review (SLR)	34	23
Web search (Web)	17	14
Plugins	11	4
Total	**62**	**41**

Secondary Sources - Complementary Study: Frameworks/Plugins. To extend the primary and secondary sources, plugins that use source code to extract architectural elements and code metrics from applications written in Java were searched in Eclipse. The keywords used in the search string was the following: "reverse engineering", "software reconstruction", "technical debt" and "energy consumption". As a result, 4 tools were selected (see Plugins, Table 3).

4.3 Evaluation

The evaluation consists in reporting the analysis of the selected tools and synthesizing in tables those properties that have been evidenced from the analysis. To that end, each tool/plugin was downloaded, installed and tested with the purpose of identifying if they fulfil the defined objectives and requirements (see the list of 41 candidates in https://bit.ly/39ficiz and Table 4). Next, the 41 selected tools were reported answering the research questions and checking the characterization criteria:

Table 4. Characterization of tools (list of candidates)

Search Mechanism	Tools	Technique	Input	Output	Purpose	Update Year
SLR	Axivion Bauhaus Suite	Static Analysis	Source code	Architectural elements, design metrics	Architecture visualization, architecture validation, interface analysis, clone detection	2020
SLR	Lattix LDM	Static Analysis	Source code, JAR file	Architectural elements, design metrics	Architecture refactory, understand architecture, dependence between software artifacts	2020
SLR	imagixtD	Static Analysis	Source code	Architectural elements, code metrics	Structural Analysis, understand architecture, design quality, collect source code metrics	2020
SLR	Structure101	Static Analysis	Source code	Architectural elements, code metrics	Structural Analysis, understand design, architecture, collect source code metrics	2018
SLR	Structural analysis for Java	Static Analysis	Source code, JAR file	Architectural elements, code and design metrics	Structural Analysis, structural quality, collect design and code metrics	2019
SLR	JavaNCSS	Static Analysis	Source code	Source code metrics	Collect source code metrics	2011
SLR	Classycle	Static Analysis	Source code, Java Project	Architectural elements, code metrics	Collect source code metrics, code smell, package dependencies and cycles	2014
SLR	Designite	Static Analysis	Source code, JAR file	Architectural elements, code and design metrics	Technical Debt, code and design smell, energy smell	2019
SLR	Squale	Static Analysis	Source code	Source code metrics	Code analysis	2011
SLR	Jdeodorant	Static Analysis	Source code, Java Project	Source code metrics	Code analysis, code smell, energy smell	2020
SLR	iPlasma	Static Analysis	Source code	Source code metrics	Code analysis, code smell, energy smell	2010
Web	PhpMetrics	Static Analysis	Source code	Source code metrics	Collect source code metrics	2020
Web	Xradar	Static Analysis	Source code	Source code and design metrics	Collect design and source code metrics, code quality	2009
Web	MoDisco	Static Analysis	Source code, Java Project	Source code and design metrics	Collect design and source code metrics, code quality	2020
Web	Jlint	Static Analysis	Source code	Source code metrics	Collect source code metrics, code smell, energy smell	2014
Web	Sonarqube	Static Analysis	Source code	Architectural elements, code and design metrics	Technical Debt, code smell, collect design and source code metrics	2020
Web	Sonargraph	Static Analysis	Source code	Architectural elements, design metrics	Technical Debt, design smell, collect design metrics	2020
Web	Codacy	Static Analysis	Source code	Source code metrics	Technical Debt, collect source code metrics, code quality	2020
Web	Kiuwan	Static Analysis	Source code	Source code metrics	Code analysis, security analysis	2020
Web	CheckStyle	Static Analysis	Source code	Source code metrics	Code analysis, code smell, energy smell	2020
Web	Ndepend	Static Analysis	Source code, Net assemblies	Source code metrics	Code analysis, code quality	2020
Web	Nitriq	Static Analysis	Source code, Net assemblies	Source code metrics	Code analysis	2012
Plugins	Findbugs	Static Analysis	Source code, JAR file	Source code metrics	Structural Analysis, code quality	2015
Plugins	Jdepend	Static Analysis	Source code, Java Project	Source code and design metrics	Structural Analysis, design quality, collect design and source code metrics	2020
Plugins	Eclipse metrics	Static Analysis	Source code, Java Project	Source code metrics	Collect design and source code metrics	2013
Plugins	PMD	Static Analysis	Source code	Source code metrics	Code analysis, code smell	2020
SLR	Sigar	Dynamic Analysis	Executable file	Hardware and energy consumption metrics	System information gatherer and reporter (IT Resource)	2016
SLR	Joulemeter	Dynamic Analysis	Executable file	Energy consumption metrics	Computational energy measurement (Specific application, Process Id)	2020
SLR	Intel Platform Power Estimation	Dynamic Analysis	Executable file	Energy consumption metrics	Power consumption, power monitoring (Process Id)	2014
SLR	PowerTop	Dynamic Analysis	Executable file	Energy consumption metrics	Power consumption and power management (Process Id)	2019
SLR	jRAPL	Dynamic Analysis	Java Source code, JAR File	Energy and power consumption metrics	Energy and power consumption, profiling Java programs (method level, process Id)	2017
SLR	RAPL	Dynamic Analysis	Java Source code, JAR File	Hardware and energy consumption metrics	Energy and power consumption information (Specific application, method level, process Id)	2014
SLR	PowerAPI	Dynamic Analysis	Executable file, Java Source code	Hardware and energy consumption metrics	Energy and power consumption (Specific application, Process Id)	2020
SLR	Jalen	Dynamic Analysis	Java Source code	Energy consumption metrics	Energy consumption (Specific application, method level, process Id)	2014
SLR	JouleUnit	Dynamic Analysis	Java Source code	Energy consumption metrics	Energy profiling (Specific application)	2014
SLR	pTop	Dynamic Analysis	Executable file	Energy consumption metrics	Energy profiling (Specific application, Process Id)	2009
SLR	Java Interactive Profiler	Dynamic Analysis	Java Source code, JAR file	Energy consumption metrics	Energy profiling (Process Id)	2013
SLR	Oktech Profiler	Dynamic Analysis	Java Source code, JAR File	Energy consumption metrics	Energy profiling (Specific application, Process Id)	2010
Web	Oshi	Dynamic Analysis	Java Source code, JAR File	Hardware and energy consumption metrics	System information, memory and CPU usage (Specific application, method level, process Id)	2020
Web	Powerstat	Dynamic Analysis	Executable file	Hardware and energy consumption metrics	Power consumption (Process Id)	2020
Web	Dstat	Dynamic Analysis	Executable file	Hardware and energy consumption metrics	System resources monitor (Process Id)	2018

RQ1) What are the techniques of architecture reconstruction that are implemented by the tools? The tools/plugins apply top-down and bottom-up strategies for architecture reconstruction and use static and dynamic analysis techniques to evaluate the architectural design. They extract different measurements and metrics, and they visualize the information in a different way. These expectations (see Table 1 and Table 4) are analyzed following:

Static. Tools that use static analysis are widely-extended (academic, research and industrial areas) due to their facilities of installation, configuration and integration with other tools [22]. Lattix, Axivion Bauhaus Suite and MoDisco are an option in this category. Lattix supports visualizing the system's structure organization through class diagrams, component diagrams or composite structure diagrams such as a Design Structure Matrix (DSM) to analyze the software architecture and its dependencies. Axivion Bauhaus Suite is a commercial tool used to understand and analyze architecture conformance, through the extraction of information to determine which parts of the software are connected. This tool supports architecture conformance assure thanks to its mechanisms of dependency analysis, quality metrics analysis and different views of visualization. MoDisco is a reverse engineering tool, which supports the extraction of information from the system to help understand some aspects (structure, behavior, persistence, data flow, and change impact) through the generation of a Knowledge Discovery Metamodel (KDM). In tools, such as MoDisco, the Architecture Design Documentation (classes, packages and components diagrams) is considered an input to analyze the architecture using a bottom-up strategy.

Dynamic. There are some tools used for measuring energy consumption using dynamic analysis. The SIGAR Framework, JouleMeter, Intel Platform Power Estimation, RAPL, jRAPL Framework, Powerstat, PowerAPI, Jalen and Oshi extract and visualize metrics for energy consumption.

RQ2) What are the purpose and the process that follow the techniques/methods implemented in the tools?

Tools to Extract Source Code Metrics and Design Metrics. One of the purposes of the automated static analysis (ASA) tools is the extraction of a set of features and metrics that are quantified or qualified to get the resulting measurements. Tools as JDepend, Structural analysis for Java (STAN), PhpMetrics, Structure 101, Eclipse Metrics, Sonarqube, Sonargraph, and Imagix4D are used to extract metrics that can be the input to mathematical models to later use them with different purposes. JDepend plugin-tool uses computation metrics. This tool analyses Java classes and source file directories and it generates quality metrics for each Java package based on the dependencies among its classes. STAN is an open source tool used to analyze the structure of Java programs. It shows the design classes, packages and their dependencies using a reverse engineering process, which later will allow one to measure the software quality and to identify the errors at the design and implementation levels by using code and design metrics. In addition, it supports the analysis of structural dependencies to measure software stability and complexity, as well as to detect anti-patterns. Structure 101 helps us to understand the system structure and evaluate its complexity. It provides a visual representation of dependencies between modules at a various architectural levels of abstraction, assisting architects in identifying where undesirable dependencies may have occurred. Eclipse metrics is an eclipse plugin used to collect automatically metrics such as lines of code, number of classes, packages and files, instability, abstractness, and distance from the main sequence. Sonargraph uses a Groovy based scripting engine and a Domain-Specific Language for describing the software architecture. PhpMetrics applies static analysis to PHP projects, which run with the help of the composer in the command line. Limitations of the test medium made analysis is done by dividing the source code into their respective folders. PhpMetrics allows extracting metrics associated with complexity, volume, object oriented and maintainability. Finally, Imagix4D is a commercial reverse engineering tool that helps check and systematically study software at any level of abstraction, using views to describe dependencies. It provides a large set of built-in facilities for the automatic documentation-generation from source code. A comparison about the kind of metrics that ASA tools are able to extract are presented in Table 5. Specifically, they are analyzed in terms of size, complexity, CK metrics [23], Rober C. Martin [24], dependency and maintainability.

Tools to Extract Metrics for Technical Debt Analysis. Another objective of ASA tools is to analyse the quality of the source code or design. It is especially relevant, the technical debt caused by the poor quality, the misuse of rules or code writing standards, the code smells, or the anti-patterns. The selected tools with this purpose are PMD, Findbugs, Sonargraph, Sonarqube, Codacy, Kiuwan, Designite, JDeodorant, and iPlasma. PMD is a Java static analysis tool that identifies code smells (God Classes, Feature Envy, and Blob Classes), defects, bugs, and unused code by using a configurable set of rules. Findbugs

Table 5. Metrics

Static Analysis tools						
Tools	Size	Complexity	Chidamber & Kemerer	Roberth C. Martin	Dependency	Maintainability
Axivion Bauhaus Suite				√	√	
LattixLDM	√	√			√	
Imagix4D	√	√	√			√
Structure101	√	√			√	
Structural analysis for Java	√	√	√	√	√	
JavaNCSS	√	√				
Classycle	√					
Designite	√	√		√	√	
Squale	√	√	√		√	
iPlasma	√	√			√	
Jdeodorant	√					
PhpMetrics	√	√		√		√
Xradar	√	√	√			√
MoDisco	√	√				√
Jlint	√					
Sonarqube	√	√			√	√
Sonargraph	√				√	
Codacy	√	√				
Kiuwan	√					√
CheckStyle	√	√				
Ndepend	√	√			√	
Nitriq	√					
Findbugs	√	√			√	
Jdepend	√				√	√
Eclipse metrics	√	√		√	√	
PMD	√					

Dynamic Analysis Tools								
Tools	OS & HW Info	CPU	GPU	Package	Memory/RAM	Filesystems/disk usage	JVM Process	Network Interface
Sigar	√	√			√	√	√	
Joulemeter		√				√		
Intel Platform Power Estimation		√	√	√				
PowerTop		√						
JRAPL		√	√	√	√			
RAPL		√	√	√	√			
PowerAPI		√						√
Jalen		√				√		√
JouleUnit		√						√
pTop		√		√		√		√
Java Interactive Profiler							√	
Oktech Profiler							√	
Oshi	√	√	√	√	√	√		√
Powerstat		√	√	√	√			
Dstat		√				√		

is a static analysis tool used to extract code smells such as the occurrences of bugs and the potential security violations. Findbugs, PMD and CkeckStyle are implemented by Sonarqube to obtain an overview of source code analysis, and classifying the errors and smells according their impact. Sonarqube is an open source tool used to extract metrics, manage the code, and to measure the design quality through seven aspects: architecture and design, duplications, unit test, complexity, potential bugs, coding rules, and comments. Designite is a tool to identify technical debt, architecture smells, design smells on Java and C# applications. Codacy is a static analysis tool used to improve the code quality of software systems by identifying common security problems, code complexity, and code coverage, among others. JDeodorant applies a static source code analysis to examine code smells. This tool automatically checks the syntactic correctness of smell as the clone fragments, and fixes any discrepancies by removing incomplete statements and adding the missing closing brackets from incomplete blocks of code. Finally, Kiuwan supports the certification, quality management and productivity of source code. In addition, Sonarqube, Codacy and Kiuwan provide analysis in the Cloud through their websites, which makes to interact easier with Git repositories (see Table 5).

Tools to Extract Metrics Used in the Software Energy Consumption Estimation. To estimate the energy consumption of a software system at the code and design levels, it is necessary to define and make use of measurements and metrics extracted through an iterative process using tools that implement static and dynamic analyses. The metrics and characteristics of Green software [25, 27] help the monitoring and evaluation processes of software in an ecological context. This evaluation depends on the structure of the application and the hardware infrastructure that is used for its deployment [26]. Tools such as Sigar, JouleMeter, RAPL, jRAPL, Power API, Jalen, Java Interactive Profiler (JIP), Oktech Profiler, Oshi, Powerstat and Dstat, are used to extract metrics to estimate energy consumption. These tools allow one to analyze the algorithms, code structures, patterns or other architectural elements implemented in the code that influence the software energy consumption. From these tools, we only selected those that address the objectives of our evaluation. A comparison about the metrics that Dynamic Analysis tools are able to extract related to energy consumption are presented in Table 5.

(RQ3) What are the output representation formats provided by the tools? An important set of tools or plugins, which implement static and/or dynamic techniques, generate as output, metrics that can be used to evaluate technical debt or estimate energy consumption (see Table 4). Another group of tools are used to identify and to show architectural elements (components and connectors) that allow the data exchange and interoperability. Combining the metrics and architectural elements, an architectural reconstruction process can be carried out, driven by design and implementation decisions that are technical debt and energy consumption-aware. However, as can be seen in Table 4, there is no integral tool that allows analyzing technical debt and energy consumption. Characterization Criteria are described following (see Table 1, Table 6 and https://bit.ly/39doYoQ)

Table 6. Output representation format, operating system and license supported by tools

Tool	Output representation format	Activities	Limited to	Operating System	License
Anvion Bauhaus Suite	Dependency graph	E-A-V	C/C++, Java, .Net	Windows, Linux	Commercial
Lattix LDM	Matrix	E-A-V	C/C++, Java	Windows, Linux	Commercial, Trial
Imagix4D	Dependency graph	E-A-V	C/C++, Java	Windows	Commercial, Trial
Structure101	Dependency graph	E-V	C/C++, Java, .Net	Windows, Linux, MacOS	Commercial
Structural analysis for Java	Graph, dependency graph, matrix, treemaps	E-V	Java	Windows, Linux, MacOS	Commercial, Free for non-commercial use
JavaNCSS	Table	E	Java	Windows, Linux	GNU Lesser General Public License 2.0
Classycle	Table, dependency graph	E	Java	Windows, Linux, MacOS	GNU Lesser General Public License 2.0
Designite	Graph, dependency graph, matrix, treemaps	E-A-V	Java, .Net	Windows	Commercial, Free for non-commercial use
Squale	Table	E-A-V	C/C++, Java, .Net, Php, others	Windows, Linux	GNU Lesser General Public License 2.0
Jdeodorant	Table	E-A-V	Java	Windows, Linux, MacOS	MIT License
iPlasma	Table	E-V	C/C++, Java	Windows	Open Source
Phploletrics	Graph, table	E-V	PHP	Windows, Linux	MIT License
Xradar	Graph, table	E-V	Java	Windows, Linux	BSD License
MoDisco	Table, graph, matrix, treemaps	E-A-V	Java	Windows, Linux	Eclipse Public License 2.0
Jlint	Table	E	Java	Windows, Linux	GNU Lesser General Public License 2.0
Sonarqube	Table, graph, matrix, treemaps	E-A-V	C/C++, Java, .Net, Php, others	Cloud - Windows, Linux	Commercial, GNU Lesser General Public License 2.0, Open Source
Sonargraph	Table, dependency graph	E-A-V	C/C++, Java, .Net	Windows, Linux, MacOS	Commercial, Trial
Codacy	Graph, table	E-A-V	C/C++, Java, .Net, Php, others	Cloud	Commercial
Klocwork	Graph, table	E-A-V	C/C++, Java, .Net, Php, others	Cloud - Windows, Linux, MacOS, Unix	Commercial
CheckStyle	Table	E-V	Java	Windows, Linux, MacOS	GNU Lesser General Public License 2.0
Ndepend	Graph, Treemaps	E	C++, .Net	Windows	Commercial, Trial
Nitriq	Table, graph, matrix, treemaps	E	C++, .Net	Windows	Commercial, Trial
Findbugs	Table	E	C/C++, Java, .Net	Windows, Linux, MacOS	GNU Lesser General Public License 2.0
Jdepend	Table	E-V	Java	Windows, Linux, Centos	MIT License
Eclipse metrics	Table	E	Java	Windows, Linux, MacOS	Eclipse Public License 2.0
PMD	Table	E-V	C/C++, Java, .Net, Php, others	Windows, Linux, MacOS	Apache License 2.0
Sigar	Screen	E	Java and other programming languages	Windows, Linux, MacOS	Apache License 2.0
Joulemeter	Screen, CSV File	E	Java and other programming languages	Windows	Free
Intel Platform Power Estimation	CSV File, log file, text file	E	Java and other programming languages	Windows	Free
PowerTop	Screen, CSV File	E	Java and other programming languages	Linux	GNU Lesser General Public License 2.0
jRAPL	CSV File, log file, text file	E	Java	Linux	Open Source
RAPL	CSV File, log file, text file	E	Java	Linux	Open Source
PowerAPI	CSV File, log file, text file, database	E	Java and other programming languages	Linux	BSD License
Jalen	Table, Graph, CSV file	E-V	Java	Linux	Free, AGPL License
JouleUnit	Table, Graph, CSV file	E-V	Java	Windows, Android	Free
pTop	CSV File, log file, text file	E	Java and other programming languages	Linux	Free
Java Interactive Profiler	Screen, CSV file	E	Java	Linux	BSD License
Oktech Profiler	Screen, CSV file	E	Java	Linux	Apache License 2.0
Oshi	Table, Graph, CSV file	E-V	Java	Windows, Linux, MacOS, Unix	MIT License
Powerstat	CSV File, log file, text file	E	Java and other programming languages	Linux	GNU Lesser General Public License 2.0
Dstat	CSV File, log file, text file	E	Java and other programming languages	Linux	GNU Lesser General Public License 2.0

CC1: Tools that supports at least the activities of reverse engineering such as extraction (E), analysis (A) and/or visualization (V). All tools/plugins implement the extraction activity. This means that a syntactic and semantic analysis is carried out to extract code and design metrics, but not always for an architecture reconstruction purpose. As a result

of the analysis, 44% of the tools perform only the process of extraction, while 29% carry out extraction + visualization, and 27% of tools include the three activities extraction + analysis + visualization.

CC2: Tools that visualize elaborated outputs graphically, through tables or matrices. Some tools that carry out static analysis present the analysis results only using matrices (4%), Tables (38%), dependency graphs (11%), tables + dependency graphs (8%), tables + graphs + matrices + tree maps (12%), graphs + Tables (15%), graphs + dependency graphs + matrices + tree maps (8%), graphs + tree maps (4%). Regarding to dynamic analysis the metrics are visualized only using screens (6%), screens + CSV files (27%), CSV files + log files + text files (40%), CSV files + log files + text files + databases (7%), and tables + graphs + CSV files (20%).

CC3: Tools that support the loading of the applications under analysis locally or from Git repositories. 7% of tools, i.e. Sonarqube, Codacy and Kiuwan, support loading applications from Git repositories. It is remarkable that 93% of the tools only have the option of loading the source code or other input element if they are stored locally. Only Sonarqube supports the loading of applications, both locally and online.

CC4: Tools license is open source, commercial and/or trial. The analysis of the results shows that 7% of the tools can be downloaded and used because they have an open source license and 10% are free. Only 17% of the tools have a trial/commercial license and they can be only used temporarily. They are more specialized and have business functionalities. Tools with a commercial type license correspond to 5%, the tools that belong to the MIT license correspond to 10%, 7% of tools have BSD license, 5% of tools have Eclipse Public License that are part of Eclipse software. The GNU Lesser General Public License 2.0 have 22%, whereas the rest have: 7% Apache license; 5% Commercial, Free for non-commercial use; 3% Commercial, GNU Lesser General Public License, Open Source; and 2% Free, AGPL License.

CC5: Tools analyze applications coded in C, C++, Java, C#, PHP, among others. 42% of the tools provide the reverse engineering process or reconstruction of applications written only in Java, 2% of tools support the identification of applications written only in Php and 20% of the tools support the evaluation of applications written in Java and other programming languages such as C, Python, C#. The rest of tools are distributed as C/C++, Java 7%, tools that support C/C++, Java, .Net 10%, tools that support Java and .Net 2%, C/C++, Java, .Net, php and others programming languages 12%, C/C++ and .Net 5% (see Table 6).

From this analysis report, it is possible to conclude that the four defined expectations of the study (see Table 1) are fulfilled, but their degree of coverage depends on the needs of the researcher and the application context.

4.4 Selection

Decision Tree, Recommendations and Findings. The selection defines a tree-based model that works as a mechanism to help the software engineer during the decision making process of choosing the right tool or set of tools. In this case, the tool that assist in architecture reconstruction while considering metrics to analyse technical debt and energy consumption (see Fig. 2). This tree model also helps to determine a set of findings (F.number coding) and recommendations (R.number coding) as the standard establishes.

The decision tree is composed by three types of nodes and the transitions between them. The decision nodes are represented by squares, transition nodes (no decision) are represented by circles, and leaf nodes with a final decision are represented by a triangle. The transition between nodes is represented by an arrowed labelled with the selected option. The option is an instance of the criterion that represents the column where the arrow is drawn. These criteria are the *objective, license, use, type, input, output, activities, programming languages and decision*. They are delimited by swim lanes, where the nodes of the corresponding criterion are included. It is important to emphasize that those options that are not supported have not been included in the tree, omitting the death leaf nodes; instead of including these death options, we have introduced transition options that maybe changed in the future into decision nodes if new options are implemented.

Based on results of the decision tree study, it reveals through its initial decision that *there are no tools/framework/plugins for both analysing technical debt and energy consumption combining static and dynamic analysis (F.1)*. Therefore, in this case, recommendations of two types have to be made, one for each branch. Browsing throughout the tree, it can be observed that *technical debt is addressed using static analysis and the tools vary in their output metrics (F.2)*, whereas *energy consumption is evaluated using dynamic analysis because it is necessary to analyse the runtime code and the hardware where it is deployed (F.3)*. To evaluate technical debt, Sonarqube, Codacy and Designite are the recommended tools (R.1) since they allow the extraction, visualization and analysis activities in their open source, trial and free for non-commercial use versions, respectively. *Sonarqube and Codacy, which use source code as input, can be applied to extract code metrics whose values can be compared or used in conjunction with tools such as PMD, Findbugs, Kiuwan, iPlasma Jdeodorant to assess technical debt, code smell and bad smell from the point of view of code or design (F.4)*. One of the advantages of *Codacy and Sonarqube is that they support entry elements loading remotely using Git open repositories. Being relatively new tools, both tools provide updates, documentation and technical support for carrying out the identification, extraction and analysis of applications of different types, sizes, domains and programming languages such as Java, C, C++, C#, PHP, among others (F.5)*. However, if we pay attention to metrics (see Table 5), from the set of open source tools, *Sonarqube has wider coverage than Imagix4D, Designite, Lattix and Codacy (F.6)*. On the other hand, if we want *to measure the metrics that are part of Robert C.Martin, CK and other kind of metrics, is suggested to use additional tools such as Structural Analysis and Eclipse metrics to complement the extraction and visualization activities (R.2)*. To estimate energy consumption, every tool extract metrics at runtime such as RAM, CPU, GPU, among others. The values of metrics are different depending of two factors: (i) the hardware where software is deployed and (ii) the size, the type and the complexity of software specially when styles, patterns, and code and design practices are used. *Frameworks such as jRAPL, Sigar, Oshi, tools such as RAPL, Powerstat, Joulemeter, Intel Platform Power Estimation and Middleware as PowerAPI are proposed to extract and calculate metrics associated with energy consumption (F.7)*. *If the researcher needs precision on the results instead of facility in settings, we recommend the four frameworks jRAPL, PowerAPI, Oshi and Powerstat (R.3)*, since they run under Linux and have more accurate measurements

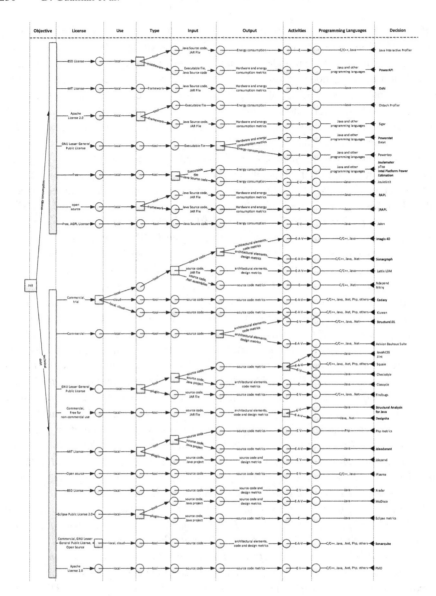

Fig. 2. Decision tree (https://bit.ly/3hmREie)

because they avoid the consumption of additional resources (e.g. peripherals) and measure the effective energy of the application. However, they only support applications written in Java. *Alternatively, if the engineer prefers easy settings or require non-Java applications, he/she has to select the tools Joulemeter, Intel Platform Power Estimation (R.4).* These tools have a simpler configuration than frameworks. Finally, it is important to analyse our final objective to support architecture reconstruction driven by metrics to analyse technical debt and estimate energy consumption (see O1). Since there is no tool that support all three together (see Fig. 1 and Fig. 2). It is required the combination of tools to deal with the objective and the **summary** of the **recommendations R1-R4** is the following: (1) to extract structure + design metrics using the tools Sonargraph, Structure101, Structural Analysis, Lattix or Imagix4D. (2) To extract source code metrics + analyse technical debt using the tools Sonarqube, Designite, Jdeodorant and Codacy.; and (3) To analyse energy consumption applying dynamic analysis in execution time using source code metrics using the frameworks and tools RAPL, jRAPL, PowerAPI, Oshi, Powerstat, Joulemeter, Intel Platform Power Estimation, depending on the requirements, as it has been previously detailed. This integration allows the complete analysis for supporting the architecture reconstruction decision-making driven by technical debt and green metrics.

Hypothesis Evaluation. After finishing the analysis and selection, it is required the evaluation of the defined hypothesis (see Fig. 1). With regard to H1, it is possible to conclude that all the selected tools carry out the extraction of metrics from source code in a semiautomatic way, and later perform the analysis and visualization. In the case of H2, there are tools that use source code to extract metrics and architectural elements. Before using these metrics, they have to be manually collected and normalized. Respect to H3, tools such as Sonarqube and the frameworks that estimate energy consumption can be configured and customized to obtain specific metrics depending of the calculation models, it can make with open source tools. From this analysis, it is also concluded that hypothesis number four (H4) has not been already met, since there are no tools that integrate technical debt analysis and energy consumption evaluation.

5 Conclusions and Future Work

This work presents a tailored ISO/IEC/IEEE 14102:2008 systematic-oriented process for the evaluation and selection of tools that address emerging areas avoiding bias and promoting knowledge reusability. This process combines systematic literature methods and complementary studies to provide not only the resulting selected tools, but also the acquired knowledge from the study through a set of reusable assets. Specifically, the tailored standard has been applied for the selection and recommendation of tools that support architecture reconstruction and the extraction of technical debt and energy consumption metrics. This adoption has obtained the following reusable assets: the report and its synthesized information, i.e. a set of tables and statistics, a decision tree, four recommendations and seven findings. These assets provide valuable synthesized information about the tools that allow the architecture reconstruction and the technical debt and energy consumption measurement. As future work, it will be necessary to formalize the management and extension of the reusable assets; as we plan to consolidate this systematic-oriented process evaluating other types of tools. In addition, the results of the evaluation evidence the need of creating a new tool to fulfil the hypothesis H4, as well as extending the current assets in the future.

References

1. Keele, S.: Guidelines for performing systematic literature reviews in software engineering. Technical report, Ver. 2.3 EBSE Technical report. EBSE (2007)
2. Petersen, K., Feldt, R., Mujtaba, S., Mattsson, M.: Systematic mapping studies in software engineering. EASE **8**, 68–77 (2008)
3. Petersen, K., Vakkalanka, S., Kuzniarz, L.: Guidelines for conducting systematic mapping studies in software engineering: an update. Inf. Softw. Technol. **64**, 1–18 (2015)
4. Runeson, P., Host, M., Rainer, A., Regnell, B.: Case study research in software engineering: Guidelines and examples (2012)
5. ISO/IEC 14102:2008 Information Technology - Guideline for the Evaluation and Selection of CASE Tools. Accessed 2020
6. Lehman, M.M., Belady, L.A.: Program evolution: processes of software change. Academic Press, Cambridge (1985)
7. Cunningham, W.: The WyCash portfolio management system. ACM SIGPLAN OOPS Messenger **4**(2), 29–30 (1993)
8. Y.E. Consortium and others: Overview of ICT energy consumption, Report FP7-2888021, European Network of Excellence in Internet Science (2013)
9. Guo, G.Y., Atlee, Joanne M., Kazman, R.: A software architecture reconstruction method. In: Donohoe, P. (ed.) Software Architecture. ITIFIP, vol. 12, pp. 15–33. Springer, Boston (1999). https://doi.org/10.1007/978-0-387-35563-4_2
10. Tom, E., Aurum, A., Vidgen, R.: An exploration of technical debt. J. Syst. Softw. **86**(6), 1498–1516 (2013)
11. Verdecchia, R., Procaccianti, G., Verdecchia, R.: Empirical evaluation of the energy impact of refactoring code smells, vol. 52, pp. 365–383, February 2018
12. Hedberg, H., Lappalainen, J.: A preliminary evaluation of software inspection tools, with the DESMET method. In: Fifth International Conference on Quality Software (QSIC 2005), pp. 45–52 (2005)
13. Mealy, E., Strooper, P.: Evaluating software refactoring tool support. In: Australian Software Engineering Conference (ASWEC 2006) (2006)
14. Kabbani, N., Tilley, S., Pearson, L.: Towards an evaluation framework for SOA security testing tools. In: IEEE International Systems Conference, pp. 438–443 (2010)
15. Rivas, L., Pérez, M., Mendoza, L.E., Grimán, P., Anna, C.: Tools selection criteria in software-developing Small and Medium Enterprises. J. Comput. Sci. Tech. **10**, 1–5 (2010)
16. Alnafjan, K.A., Alghamdi, A.S., Hossain, M.S., Al Qurishi, M.: Selecting the best CASE tools for DoDAF based C4I applications. International Information Institute (Tokyo). Information **16** (2013)
17. Lundell, B., Lings, B.: Comments on ISO 14102: the standard for CASE-tool evaluation. Comput. Stand. Interfaces **24**(5), 381–388 (2002)
18. Krawatzeck, R., Tetzner, A., Dinter, B.: An evaluation of open source unit testing tools suitable for data warehouse testing. In: PACIS, p. 22 (2015)
19. Guamán, D., Pérez, J., Diaz, J., Cuesta, C.E.: Towards a reference process for software architecture reconstruction. IET Softw. (accepted, publication pending) (2020)
20. Kitchenham, B.:Procedures for performing systematic reviews. Keele, UK, Keele University, vol. 33, no. 2004, pp. 1–26 (2004)
21. Riva, C.: Reverse architecting: an industrial experience report. In: WCRE, p. 42 (2000)
22. Schmerl, B., Aldrich, J., Garlan, D., Kazman, R., Yan, H.: Discovering architectures from running systems. IEEE Trans. Softw. Eng. **32**(7), 454–466 (2006)
23. CK Metrics, Chidamber, S.R., Kemerer, C.F.: A metrics suite for object oriented design. IEEE Trans. Softw. Eng. **20**(6), 476–493 (1994)

24. Martin, R.C., Martin, R.: OO design quality metrics. Anal. Depend. **12**(1), 151–170 (1994)
25. Kumar, M., Li, Y., Shi, W.: Energy consumption in Java: an early experience. In: 8th International Conference on Green and Sustainable Computing (IGSC), pp. 1–8 (2017)
26. Chatzigeorgiou, A., Stephanides, G.: Energy metric for software systems. Softw. Qual. J. **10**(4), 355–371 (2002)
27. Naumann, S., Dick, M., Kern, E., Johann, T.: The GREENSOFT model: a reference model for green and sustainable software and its engineering. Sustain. Comput. Inf. Syst. **1**(4), 294–304 (2011)

Redefining Legacy: A Technical Debt Perspective

Ben D. Monaghan$^{(\boxtimes)}$ and Julian M. Bass

University of Salford, 43 Crescent, Salford M5 4WT, UK
`B.D.Monaghan1@edu.salford.ac.uk`, `J.Bass@salford.ac.uk`

Abstract. Organisations that manage legacy systems at scale, such as those found within large government agencies and commercial enterprises, face a set of unique challenges. They manage complex software landscapes that have evolved over decades. Current conceptual definitions of legacy systems give practitioners limited insights that can inform their daily work. In this research, we compare conceptual definitions of large-scale legacy and technical debt. We hypothesise that large-scale legacy reflects an accumulation of technical debt that has never been through a remediation phase. To pursue this hypothesis, we identified the following question: *How do practitioners describe their experience of managing large-scale legacy landscapes?* We conducted 16 semi-structured open-ended, recorded and transcribed interviews with industry practitioners from 4 government organisations and 9 large enterprises involved with the maintenance and migration of large-scale legacy systems. A snowball sampling technique was used to identify participants. We adopted an approach informed by grounded theory. There was consensus among the practitioners in our study that the landscape is fragmented and inflexible, consisting of many dispersed and fragile applications. Practitioners report challenges with shifting paradigms from batch processing to near real-time customer-focused information systems. Our findings show there is overlap between challenges experienced by participants and symptoms typified by technical debt. We identify a novel type of technical debt, "Ecosystem Debt" which arises from the scale, and age, of many large-scale legacy applications. By positioning Legacy within the context of Technical Debt, practitioners have a more concrete understanding of the state of the systems they maintain.

Keywords: Legacy software · Technical debt · Software evolution · Industry perspectives · Ecosystem debt · Software ecosystems

1 Introduction

Legacy Software [4,5] is everywhere. From local companies to tech giants, it is an issue every industry faces. Despite the issues (and costs) being well known for decades, it's a problem which has persisted. One area where legacy is particularly persistent is within governments and large enterprises. The definition of Legacy

© Springer Nature Switzerland AG 2020
M. Morisio et al. (Eds.): PROFES 2020, LNCS 12562, pp. 254–269, 2020.
https://doi.org/10.1007/978-3-030-64148-1_16

Software varies. It has been defined as software that is outdated and old [4], or, software that is mission critical but brittle, expensive to maintain and resistant to changes [5].

Legacy Systems are typically associated with mainframe-based languages such as COBOL and Fortran [12]. This, however, is not always the case. Modern software developed using new techniques can also satisfy the criteria of legacy [22]. This is especially true in large-scale web development where a product has a long development time before it goes to market and the latest web framework is now outdated. One common thread throughout however is that they are mission critical and therefore maintenance costs must be tolerated.

Challenges to managing and maintaining legacy software are well understood [5,12]. It is difficult to maintain and difficult to port to new technologies. Often legacy software is heavily integrated with the physical hardware it operates in (i.e. mainframes). However, legacy software persists. It has been estimated that there are still billions of lines of legacy code in use [16]. This raises the question of why are companies unwilling, or unable, to modernise their legacy applications? We posit that current conceptual definitions of legacy fail to accurately convey the day to day challenges faced when managing legacy systems. To this end, we propose an alternative way of defining legacy by viewing it from the perspective of technical debt. However, in order to understand how legacy relates to technical debt we first need to capture the experiences of industry practitioners involved in the maintenance and migration of legacy systems. This leads to the question: *How do practitioners describe their experience of managing large-scale legacy landscapes?*

In this paper we adopt a grounded theory approach, analysing 16 open-ended, transcribed interviews from industry practitioners who have been involved in the maintenance or migration of large scale legacy systems. We identify common characteristics of large scale legacy systems. We present a taxonomy mapping these to types of technical debt. We propose a new type of technical debt, which we refer to as "Ecosystem Debt". We also extend existing definitions of technical debt to account for the impact of age on code related debt. Specifically in relation to the cognitive gap which arises from shifts in development paradigms. The rest of this paper is organised as follows: the next section provides the background. Section 3 describes the research methods used. In Sect. 4 we present our findings. In Sect. 5 we discuss those findings any threats to validity. Finally we conclude in Sect. 6.

2   Background

2.1   Legacy Systems

The definition of Legacy Software varies. They are defined as software that is outdated, or old, software that is mission critical but brittle, expensive to maintain and resistant to changes [4]. One definition proposed by [8] is that they simply belong to a previous generation of technology. This, however, isn't always the case. Modern software developed using new techniques can also satisfy the criteria of legacy [17]. This is especially true in modern web development where if a product has a particularly long development time before it goes to market, what's modern has probably evolved and the latest web framework is now old. One common thread throughout however is that they are mission critical and therefore worth the costs associated with maintaining them.

Research into legacy modernisation typically focuses on technical challenges, with little focus on industry perceptions. Research often runs on the assumption that legacy software is obsolete. However there is evidence that this may not always be the case [16]. Practitioners from a spectrum of positions and fields were interviewed about their perception of what their experiences with legacy software. Their results echo existing views regarding the challenges associated with legacy software, however they also reveal that to a number of respondents held a favourable view of legacy software. There is a perception that legacy software is proven technology, reliable and perhaps counter intuitively, performant.

2.2   Technical Debt

The term Technical Debt (TD) was first introduced by Cunningham [7]. TD is used to describe developing poor-quality systems for short term gain (often for expedience), with the view that at some point in the future the work will need to be revisited. TD, much like financial debt, can bring benefits in the short term (on the provision that is paid back promptly).

Although the term debt might be viewed as a bad thing, this is not necessarily the case. Going into TD can be part of a larger strategic decision to bring a product to market quicker, delaying quality and robustness until further into the future [24].

While accruing TD may be a strategic decision, much like conventional debt, it needs to be kept under control and managed. Failure to do so results in brittle, hard to maintain software that becomes costly and difficult to comprehend [26]. In certain cases the build-up of TD may not be a conscious decision [6]. Martin Fowler suggests breaking down reasons for TD into reckless, prudent, inadvertent and deliberate [10]. There are also types of TD, such as code related or architectural debt, Alves et al. present an ontology where they identify 12 different types [1]. Similar types are identified by both Kutchens et al. [19] and Rios et al. [23].

2.3   Relationship Between Technical Debt and Legacy

Legacy software and Technical debt share similarities in that they are both perceived to mean software that is in a poor state or of low quality. Holvitie et al. [15] explore the closeness of technical debt and legacy software. They present conceptual definitions of both, highlighting the similarities and that, depending on the context and interpretation both terms can be used to describe the same symptoms.

Technical debt also offers a potential mechanism for improving the quality and longevity of existing legacy software. Gupta et al. [14] present a case study on managing a legacy application by tackling technical debt issues. They show a decrease in a number of quality defects, such as memory issues, system crashes and performance related issues, suggesting that approaching legacy from a technical debt perspective can alleviate issues commonly associated with ageing software.

2.4   Software Ecosystems

Definitions of Software Ecosystems (SECO) vary [11]. Efforts have been made to create a more concrete definition by [20], they provide the definition of a SECO *'as the interaction of a set of actors on top of a common technological platform that results in a number of software solutions or services'.*

Research into SECOs is a growing area, however we note that there is little research into the impact of technical debt and SECOs, much of existing research focuses on the context and ecosystem health [11]. McGregor et al. [21] present software ecosystems within the context of technical debt, they highlight that the effects of technical debt in one aspect of a software ecosystem can have impacts on other components within the same ecosystem.

3   Method

In this paper we analyse industry practitioner experiences when managing large scale legacy software. The research question we answer is: *How do practitioners describe their experience of managing large-scale legacy landscapes?*

A qualitative method approach was adopted in this study to capture and analyse industry practitioner experiences within the context of large scale legacy software. We adopted a Grounded Theory (GT) approach, analysing data collected from semi-structured open ended interviews. GT was chosen to avoid preconceived assumptions about how legacy is maintained and perceived by practitioners.

3.1   Research Sites

A mix of practitioners from a variety of backgrounds and industries were identified using a snowball sampling technique. Initial participants were identified through the authors professional contact network, subsequent participants were then identified on recommendation by initial participants. The criteria for selection was to be, or have been, involved in managing or maintaining large scale legacy systems. Interviews were conducted both in person through meetings and where that was not possible via Skype. The participants in this study are listed in Table 1. To highlight the scale of the organisations that participants were from, we briefly describe P1, Major City Council and P9, Large Insurance Company.

P1, Major City Council. P1 Is an Enterprise Architect for a Major UK City Council (population >400k), which employs >15,000 staff. P1 is involved in ensuring ICT systems across the City Council are aligned to the overall business strategy.

P9, Large Insurance Company. P9 Is an IT Development manager for a large UK based Insurance company. They have a revenue of >£5 Billion and employ >2000 staff. P9 is involved in managing the legacy estate that the organisation maintains, they operate out of a business unit specifically designed to manage large scale legacy within the organisation.

Table 1. List of research participants

Identifier	Job title	Industry	Experience
P1	Enterprise architect	Major city council	18 Years
P2	CTO	Start-up	15+ Years
P3	IT Director	High street retailer	30 years
P4	CIO	Government agency	15+ Years
P5	Head of project delivery	Government department	15+ Years
P6	CIO	Banking	40+ Years
P7	Senior delivery leader	Government department	40+ Years
P8	CIO	Large enterprise	40+ Years
P9	IT development manager	Large insurance company	40+ Years
P10	CIO	High street retailer	30+ Years
P11	Lead DBA	Regional energy company	17 Years
P12	CIO	Consultancy company	25+ Years
P13	Head of software engineering	Government agency	16 Years
P14	CIO	High street retail & banking	40 Years
P15	Principal architect	Government agency	25+ Years
P16	Digital directory	Government department	30 Years

3.2 Data Collection

A total of 16 semi-structured interviews [3] were conducted for data collection. An open-ended approach was adopted to allow the interviewee a chance to cover any other issues of interest beyond the semi-structured interviews. Interviews were conducted in person where possible, otherwise remotely via Skype and recorded. The interview recordings were then transcribed by hand. Questions were revisited after each interview and refined. Each interview continued for between 45–60 min.

3.3 Data Analysis

3.4 Interviews

For this paper we adopted a classical grounded theory (Glasserian) approach [13]. Grounded Theory aims to develop a theory from data without any pre-conceived perceptions. To enable this approach Interview transcripts were analysed using an industry standard qualitative analysis tool *nVivo*. We first went through the initial transcripts, using a line by line coding. As we began to understand the data we grouped codes into category, this allowed us to identify recurring topics within the interview transcripts. These categories were then further grouped into concepts. Each concept was analysed using memos. Memos were iteratively refined via constant comparison of the concepts with the raw data.

3.5   Classifying Legacy in Terms of Technical Debt

In order to classify legacy in terms of technical debt, we identified the major types of technical debt from literature. We limited our search to 2015–2020, using the keywords *"Technical Debt Types" OR "Technical Debt Dimensions" OR "Technical Debt Categories"*. Digital libraries considered for this search were ACM Digital Library, IEEE Xplore, Science Direct and Springer Link. Selection criteria was defined as papers which define or describe types/dimensions/categories of Technical Debt. We identified three main sources which provided definitions of technical debt types; Alves et al. [1], Krutchen et al. [19] and Rios et al. [23]. For each concept generated as a part of interview data analysis, we compared participants descriptions of symptoms/difficulties that they have to manage with those described in literature to see how much, or if any, overlap there was.

4   Findings

The following section presents our findings and is structured as follows; Subsect. 4.1 presents how respondents viewed and defined legacy systems. Subsect. 4.2 presents the results of our analysis of practitioner experiences as compared with Technical debt types. The remaining Subsects. (4.3 through to 4.8) present the interview responses that formed the concepts highlighted in Table 2. Figure 1 presents an example of how this process was applied to produce the concept *Growing Skills Gaps Impacts on ability to maintain and evolve*, the findings that support this concept are presented in Subsect. 4.7.

4.1   Practitioner Understanding of Legacy

Participants describe legacy as old code on old hardware, *"They tend to be older systems developed with older technology. Typically older programming languages, or even sitting on older hardware"* - P1, Enterprise Architect Major City Council. And potentially no longer supported by vendors, *"Coupled with that, potentially, the vendors no longer support the products as well"* - P1, Enterprise Architect Major City Council.

Interviews reveal that legacy systems are at the end of their useful life, *"The legacy system has been in place 10 or 15 years. It's at the end of its useful life now"* - P5, Head of Project delivery, Government Department. This is echoed by P14, CIO High Street Retailer & Bank, *"Sometimes, when people talk about*

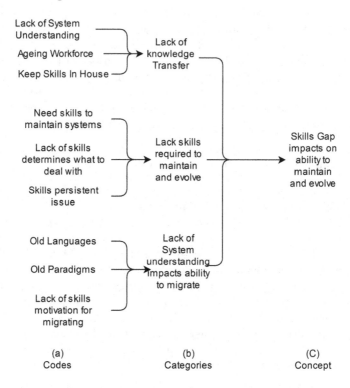

Lack of System Understanding

Ageing Workforce

Keep Skills In House

Lack of knowledge Transfer

Need skills to maintain systems

Lack of skills determines what to deal with

Skills persistent issue

Lack skills required to maintain and evolve

Skills Gap impacts on ability to maintain and evolve

Old Languages

Old Paradigms

Lack of skills motivation for migrating

Lack of System understanding impacts ability to migrate

(a)
Codes

(b)
Categories

(C)
Concept

Fig. 1. Illustration on process of iterating through codes, categories and concepts

legacy they are talking about things that are nearing end of life". However P14 also suggests that legacy is simply something which has been there for a long time, *"sometimes when people talk about legacy they just mean things that have been there a long time, but it still does the job, it still works.".* P14 goes onto provide a more concrete definition within their organisation, *"So, in [Practitioners Organisation], when people talk about legacy systems, they talk about the things that they want to replace, they want to get rid of".*

When discussing the term legacy, P16 suggests *"I sort of try not to use the term heritage and legacy. They have a certain connotation, which is these are old things that we shouldn't have"* P16, Digital Director, Government Department. They go on to then suggest that the driving force should be meeting business needs, *"when you look forward you look at; what is your business looking to achieve?"* - P16, Digital Director Government Department. Respondents describe the importance of these systems to business value, *"We have many systems that deliver over £100b...to the public running on COBOL-based VME"* – Digital Director, Government Department. They need to support large numbers of customers, *"they had about 4,000,000 customers"* CIO, High Street Retail, that represents significant value *"average daily sales was about £2,000,000"* - CIO, High Street Retail.

4.2   Legacy as a Product of Technical Debt

The concepts that were formed from interview analysis were compared with definitions of technical available in literature [1,19,23], we present the results of this analysis in Table 2.

Table 2. Taxonomy Classifying Participants Experience with Legacy to Types of Technical Debt

Legacy Concept	Symptoms	TD type
Legacy Applications support surrounding systems	Difficult to modify due to external dependencies	Ecosystem Debt
Applications are fragmented	Unforeseen consequences when modifying or removing legacy	Ecosystem Debt
Inherited Legacy	Difficult to evolve, maintain and integrate	Ecosystem Debt, Code Debt Architectural Debt Infrastructure Debt Design Debt, Build Debt, Test Debt Documentation Debt
Applications no longer represent the organisation needs	System Architecture no longer supports business needs Code quality has eroded over time impacting maintainability	Code Debt Architectural Debt
Skills Gap impacts ability to maintain or evolve	Challenges understanding system. Developer premiums. Fear of modifying underlying system. Lack of maintainability and difficult to evolve.	Code Debt, Design Debt Architectural Debt Documentation Debt
Complex System Architectures	Difficult to maintain or evolve New functionality is bolted on Architectural Drift	Code Debt, Architectural Debt

4.3   Legacy Applications Support Surrounding Systems

The interviews reveal that large-scale legacy systems are composed of significant numbers of applications, *"in the retail bank you had over 600 applications"* - P12 CIO Consultancy Company. P13 describes a large number of product platforms *"in the Cobol estate there are 29 products platforms"* – P13 Head of SWE Government Department, a similar situation is also confirmed by P2, *"There are quite a lot of applications"* – P2, CTO of Start-up.

Participants describe the size and scale of the legacy systems they are managing, *"One is, we've got a legacy fraud system. It's the system that we use for all of our fraud casework here. Bearing in mind, we're a big organisation – 80,000 people – so fraud is a big deal to us."* – Head of Project Delivery, Government Department. And need to support large numbers of internal operations *"I look after all our contact centre solutions. We have 30,000 contact centre seats here "* – P16, Director of Digital Platforms, Government Department.

Respondents describe how they need to manage many independent applications. These applications support large numbers of internal and external users. They describe how they process significant numbers of transactions, both in number, and in value.

4.4 Applications Are Fragmented

Participants describe highly dispersed and fragmented application landscapes, *"The application landscape is highly fragmented. There are a lot of dispersed systems that aren't necessarily connected together"* – P2, CTO of Start-up.

P2 goes on to describe how individual applications support surrounding systems, *"that system had been there so long it was supported by a number of other surrounding systems as well."* – P2, CTO of Start-up. They describe that this them difficult to replace as they impact the wider functionality of a system, *"Simply replacing the legacy system wouldn't necessarily solve all of our problems. We'd be impacting other parts of the process as well"* – P2, CTO of Start-up. In one example, a single application was interfacing with upwards of 200 other systems.

"For example, one of the legacy systems I've replaced, I think it had interfaces with about 200 other systems. So you've got this real jigsaw of all these different systems that link together" – P5, Head of Project Delivery, Government Department.

Respondents describe a highly fragmented application landscape. These applications can be disconnected and dispersed, or part of a complex jigsaw of dependencies. Migrating or replacing these legacy applications can be a challenge.

4.5 Inherited Legacy

The interviews reveal a number of participants have inherited applications when companies are bought up, *"So at the moment it's a complex collection of legacy systems, some of which even came into the [High Street Retailer] when we acquired the [High Street Retail] a very long time ago"* – P10, CIO, High Street Retail. P9 describes a similar scenario, *"we have really big acquired insurance businesses which all come with their own large large legacy estates"* - P9, IT Development Manager, Large Enterprise. One respondent, when describing acquiring a smaller company highlighted the impact this can have,

"they had to go through all of these scripts, either, switching them off and seeing what happened or trying to put logging into them to try to see if and when they got touched...just monitoring the whole thing to try to gradually unpick this delicate, fragile, kind of landscape of scripts" – P2, CTO of Start-up.

Respondents describe acquiring smaller companies. As part of this acquisition they inherit the pre-existing systems that support the newly acquired company. This expands their existing landscape even further. In some cases, the applications they inherit may be problematic.

4.6 Applications No Longer Represent the Organisation's Needs

Participants describe how a shift in user expectation drives evolution, *"A lot of people expect to interact with us, as an organisation – and many other organisations – in the way that they do with the likes of the Amazon platforms."* - P1, Enterprise Architect, Major City Council. One participant describes *"the organisation is transforming quite significantly, we've got lots of new policy measures coming in, new ways of working"* - P5, Head of Project Delivery, Government Department. The same participant goes on to say

> *"Because the organisation is transforming quite significantly, we've got lots of new policy measures coming in, new ways of working. I think we're also moving towards a more digital organisation. It means that some of our legacy systems just don't work in the new world"*, and that *"In terms of what our users expect, so citizens – but also some of our business processes – the current systems just don't work"* - P5, Head of Project Delivery, Government Department.

Participants from Government departments describe organisation needs are driven by driven by policy change, *"we have policy units that take the government legislation, interpret it into what it is intended to do; that is translated into, "Right. So, we need to change what we actually provide to our customers." So, the systems will change underneath."* – P7, Senior Delivery Leader, Government Department. This is compounded by the frequency in which government policy changes, *"They change all the time, because government policy changes."* - P7, Senior Delivery Leader, Government Department

One participants reveals that attempts to evolve with frequently policy driven needs results in the degradation of the system, *"...we tend to append technology so if we started off with a nice and clean nucleus of an estate 20 or 30 years ago is essentially we've gone right we need to implement this new policy and we will add that on and add that"* – P13, Head of SWE, Government Department.

Participants describe their legacy systems as no longer being able to support organisation needs. Those from government departments describe the need to keep up with frequent shift in government policy causing systems to degrade over time.

4.7 Skills Gap Impacts Ability to Maintain or Evolve

Participants describe how Legacy systems can be many years old *"so the majority of our systems are on VME so some of these VME machines have been around maybe something like 40 years"* – Principal Architect, Government Department. These systems reflect a different world, *"These systems reflect what the world was, maybe, 10 or 20 years ago"* – P1, Enterprise Architect, Major City Council.

Knowledge is lost as developers retire, *"if somebody is approaching retirement and they are one of the only ones that know about that system, we should really start to have some sort of formal handover and transfer of knowledge as well. Otherwise, there is a knowledge gap and a skills gap there"* – P1, Enterprise Architect, Major City Council. This in turn creates risk, *"The big challenge is risk because when you get inside these things you don't always know what you'going to find, and there's a danger that if you do that, you break that"* – P10, CIO, High Street Retailer.

Knowledge loss combined with change in programming paradigms means new developers struggle to understand existing code bases, *"If you've only ever learned, for example, object-orientated languages, and then you're faced with a 20-year-old procedural language, it's completely different"* – P1, Enterprise Architect, Major City Council.

Developers tend to want to work on the latest technology, *"they're all [developers] chasing the next shiny thing the new languages and technology"* – P13, Head of SWE, Government Department. This inevitably leads to high developer turnover, this loss of knowledge makes future development hard, *"If their coding style, if they way they've written the application, is unfamiliar to the next group of people who come in, it's really hard. It takes longer to do development."* – P2, CTO of Start-up.

Finding developers with the correct skill-set and understanding of procedural code is a challenge, *"Typically, it was really difficult to get the programming skills in place to get enough of an understanding of all the nuts and bolts of the procedural code before we could migrate away onto any new solution "* - P1, Enterprise Architect, Major City Council.

However, P12 describes their experience with a skills gap, *"when they get old and retire you're not going to be able to find anybody who codes in that language"* - P12, CIO, Consultancy Company. They follow up with, *"well that's just not the case we found that we started to take in A-level apprenticeship scheme"*. Another participant echoes similar sentiment regarding the value of apprenticeships, *"We've got a number of apprenticeships. We've got a number of apprentices in our department as well. It's having that mix, to be perfectly honest."* - P1, Enterprise Architect, Major City Council.

The interviews reveal that there is a lack of knowledge in the languages that legacy systems were written in and the paradigms that were prominent at the time. Respondents describe how developers want to use the latest technology and that many applications have evolved through significant shifts in technology. Additional, they reflect the world from many years ago, and participants describe how finding the skills to bridge this gap between old and new is difficult, and comes at a premium.

4.8   Complex System Architectures

The interviews reveal that system architectures become complex over time, P2 describes one situation *"Then you just get this layering of stuff that all, kind of, pretty much hangs together"* - P2 CTO of Start-up. This is echoed by P8, who

described *"layers of sort of complexity sitting on the top of the base systems"* -
P8, CIO, Large Enterprise. A lack of long term view causes systems to degrade,
P2 describes how *"Each group that had come in had tried to create good modular
well-structured code and all the rest of it. It was in 10 different languages and 30
different frameworks"* P2, CTO of Start-Up. They believe this is due to *"This
is what happens when you've got project-based budgeting within an organisation,
rather than product-based."*, and that *"If you've got a product that you're continuously evolving, people care about the product and there's a much more long-term
view taken with it."* - P2, CTO Of Start-Up.

Participants describe to degradation over time as the systems as new functionality is added. There is described as being due to short term decisions
being made when evolving legacy systems over time. Participants describe how
this degradation leads to complex architectures, with systems that just "hang
together" and are made up of many "layers".

5 Discussion

In this section discuss our findings. We also introduce a new type of technical
debt, which we refer to as "Ecosystem Debt". We extend existing definitions of
code related debt to include the impact of shifting technological paradigms, such
as that which has occurred over the last few decades.

5.1 Practitioners Experience with Legacy Systems

Participants describe a mixed experience of legacy. They corroborate existing
definitions within literature, including challenges with old code [4], and inflexi-
bility [5]. We find similar responses to Khadka et al. [16], in that participants view
legacy systems as no longer support the organisations future direction. However,
we note that our participants provided a more varied experience. Notably, we find
a more pronounced conflict between participants from a technical background
and those from management.

5.2 Legacy vs Technical Debt

Our participants experiences suggest that many of the challenges they face today
are a consequence of the decisions (or lack of) made in the past. We therefore
draw parallels between legacy systems and that of technical debt [7] i.e. decisions made in the past result in costs that need to be paid for in the future.
It is therefore our view that legacy can be classified in terms of technical debt.
Specifically, legacy software is an accumulation of technical debt that is never
paid off. This can be compared to the stages of technical debt as described by
Kruchten et al. [19]. It is our view that Legacy software is software which has
reached *tipping point* but never gone through any form of *remediation* phase.

Similar overlap between legacy and technical debt is highlighted in [15]. While
we agree with the authors assessment that software practitioners managing technical debt could learn from the many decades of legacy modernisation research,

we also believe the reverse to be true; practitioners managing legacy can borrow from research (including tools and techniques) on managing technical debt. Indeed, some of the benefits of this approach have already been highlighted by [14].

Many organisations are faced with a difficult choice; do they modernise or do they maintain? We believe that presenting legacy in technical debt terms goes some way to helping organisations make that decision. Technical Debt can give insight into the current state of a software system [18, 19], moreover it can provide a shared vocabulary between technical and non-technical practitioners, giving technical practitioners the tools needed to convey the risk and costs associated with maintaining an application [2, 9].

5.3   Ecosystem Debt

The size, scale and age of large scale legacy systems brings a unique set of symptoms that do not map directly to current types of technical debt [1, 19]. We note that practitioners describe a complex application landscape that often work together, typically supporting a number of services and staff. To the authors this is very similar to the definition of a software ecosystem as outlined in [20]. And while there has been some research into ecosystem health [11], as well as technical debt within the context of a software ecosystem [21] we do not believe the ecosystem itself has been described in terms of technical debt. To this end we define ecosystem debt as follows.

"Software systems, and the systems they support, create a software ecosystem. Like any ecosystem, the impact on one aspect can influence others. If dependencies between software systems are not managed, future changes to the individual software systems that make up this ecosystem can be costly, if not impossible"

While current definitions of technical debt capture the state of individual applications, we believe they fail to capture the challenges that arise from the evolution of (or to) a software ecosystem. Ecosystem debt is therefore the consequence of decisions made during an ecosystems evolution (such as inheriting external software, integrating different, independently developed applications) that are done for expediency, but which later cause friction and hinder development.

5.4   The Impact of Older Programming Languages and Paradigms

A common theme from all participants is having to contend with older languages and programming paradigms. Languages such as COBOL are no longer widely taught which makes developer recruitment difficult, indeed, many participants cited lack of available skills as a motivation for wanting to move away from legacy systems. However, the internal quality of legacy systems not necessarily being of low quality they still incur the same penalties of poor quality software (for example, difficulty onboarding new developers, hard to understand code) [16]. We believe this to be due to the cognitive gap [25] which opens up as programming languages become dated. In this instance, new developers have to contend with learning not only COBOL, but also understanding the way COBOL applications were developed (structured, procedural code vs Object Oriented). This cognitive gap makes it harder to onboard new developers. This has a compounding affect as a lack of knowledge can itself cause technical debt as code quality is reduced.

5.5   Threats to Validity

External Validity: The organisations who were part of this study were all located within the United Kingdom, including Government Departments. These organisations have evolved within the UKs political and regulatory environment, as a consequence our findings may not be generalisable outside of the context of the UK. However, to mitigate against this, we interviewed a range of different organisations, including large scale enterprises.

Internal Validity: The target demographic for this study was practitioners involved in large scale legacy systems. This represents a very small, focused demographic within the IT and Software industry, as such a snowball sampling technique was used to identify participants. To limit potential bias from respondents in similar industries, we have included respondents from a varied industry background, including a mix of enterprise and government departments.

Conclusion Validity: For this paper we used semi-structured open ended interviews to collect data. These interviews were refined and revised after initial interviews were conducted. We utilised open ended questions, including allowing practitioners the opportunity discuss anything they felt relevant to limit the impact of the researchers own biases.

6   Conclusions

Organisations that manage legacy systems at scale face a set of unique challenges. They manage complex software landscapes that have evolved over decades. Over this period user expectations have evolved dramatically, as have technical paradigms. Current conceptual definitions of legacy systems gives little insight into the challenges associated with managing them, nor does it give much insight in how to avoid the transition from non-legacy to legacy.

In this paper we identify practitioner experiences while managing large scale legacy systems. We propose an alternative method for defining legacy systems by classifying respondents experiences in terms of types of technical debt. We present a new type of technical debt, which we refer to as "Ecosystem Debt" and extend current definitions of code related debt to include the effects of age, language choice and coding paradigm on code understanding.

We adopted a Grounded Theory approach to analysing 16 semi-structured, open ended interviews. We interviewed industry practitioners who maintain, or have maintained, large scale legacy systems. We used a snow ball sampling technique to identify industry practitioners for this paper. We selected industry practitioners from both large scale enterprises and large government department, including practitioners from both technical and non-technical backgrounds.

Our work in this paper contributes to understanding practitioner perspectives on Large Scale Legacy, to our knowledge there is only one similar study on this topic. Furthermore, we position Legacy in terms of technical debt, identifying similarities between both legacy and technical debt types. We additionally present a new type of technical debt, and expand current understanding of existing types of technical, namely code related debt.

Acknowledgments. We would like to acknowledge and thank the participants who took part in this study. Many of which are in senior positions, as such we appreciate them taking the time to participate in this study.

References

1. Alves, N.S., Mendes, T.S., de Mendonça, M.G., Spínola, R.O., Shull, F., Seaman, C.: Identification and management of technical debt: a systematic mapping study. Inf. Softw. Technol. **70**, 100–121 (2016)
2. Arvanitou, E.M., Ampatzoglou, A., Bibi, S., Chatzigeorgiou, A., Stamelos, I.: Monitoring technical debt in an industrial setting. In: Proceedings of the Evaluation and Assessment on Software Engineering, EASE 2019, pp. 123–132. Association for Computing Machinery, New York (2019)
3. Bass, J., Monaghan, B.: Legacy systems interview guide, July 2020. https://doi.org/10.17866/rd.salford.12662537.v1
4. Bennett, K.: Legacy systems: coping with success. IEEE Softw. **12**(1), 19–23 (1995)
5. Bisbal, J., Lawless, D., Wu, B., Grimson, J.: Legacy information systems: issues and directions. IEEE Softw. **16**(5), 103–111 (1999)
6. Brown, N., et al.: Managing technical debt in software-reliant systems, pp. 47–52 (01 2010)
7. Cunningham, W.: The WyCash portfolio management system. SIGPLAN OOPS Mess. **4**(2), 29–30 (1992)
8. Dedeke, A.: Improving legacy-system sustainability: a systematic approach. IT Prof. **14**(1), 38–43 (2012)
9. Eisenberg, R.J.: A threshold based approach to technical debt. SIGSOFT Softw. Eng. Notes **37**(2), 1–6 (2012)
10. Fowler, M.: bliki: Technicaldebtquadrant (2020). https://martinfowler.com/bliki/TechnicalDebtQuadrant.html
11. García-Holgado, A., García-Peñalvo, F.J.: Mapping the systematic literature studies about software ecosystems. In: Proceedings of the Sixth International Conference on Technological Ecosystems for Enhancing Multiculturality, TEEM 2018, pp. 910–918. Association for Computing Machinery, New York (2018)
12. Gholami, M.F., Daneshgar, F., Beydoun, G., Rabhi, F.: Challenges in migrating legacy software systems to the cloud - an empirical study. Inf. Syst. **67**, 100–113 (2017)
13. Glaser, B.G.: The discovery of grounded theory: strategies for qualitative research (2003)
14. Gupta, R.K., Manikreddy, P., Naik, S., Arya, K.: Pragmatic approach for managing technical debt in legacy software project. In: Proceedings of the 9th India Software Engineering Conference. ISEC 2016, pp. 170–176. Association for Computing Machinery, New York, NY, USA (2016)

15. Holvitie, J., Licorish, S.A., Martini, A., Leppänen, V.: Co-existence of the'technical debt'and'software legacy'concepts. In: QuASoQ/TDA@ APSEC. pp. 80–83 (2016)
16. Khadka, R., Batlajery, B., Saeidi, A., Jansen, S., Hage, J.: How do professionals perceive legacy systems and software modernization?, no. 1, pp. 36–47. IEEE Computer Society (2014)
17. Khadka, R., Saeidi, A., Idu, A., Hage, J., Jansen, S.: Legacy to SOA evolution: a systematic literature review. In: Migrating Legacy Applications: Challenges in Service Oriented Architecture and Cloud Computing Environments, pp. 40–70 (2012)
18. Kontsevoi, B., Soroka, E., Terekhov, S.: Tetra, as a set of techniques and tools for calculating technical debt principal and interest. In: Proceedings of the Second International Conference on Technical Debt, TechDebt 2019, pp. 64–65. IEEE Press (2019)
19. Kruchten, Philippe, A.: Managing technical debt: reducing friction in software development. In: SEI Series in Software Engineering (2019)
20. Manikas, K., Hansen, K.M.: Software ecosystems-a systematic literature review. J. Syst. Softw. **86**(5), 1294–1306 (2013)
21. McGregor, J.D., Monteith, J.Y., Zhang, J.: Technical debt aggregation in ecosystems. In: Proceedings of the Third International Workshop on Managing Technical Debt, MTD 2012, pp. 27–30. IEEE Press (2012)
22. Razavian, M., Lago, P.: A systematic literature review on SOA migration. J. Softw. Evol. Process **27**(5), 337–372 (2015)
23. Rios, N., de Mendonça Neto, M.G., Spínola, R.O.: A tertiary study on technical debt: types, management strategies, research trends, and base information for practitioners. Inf. Softw. Technol. **102**, 117–145 (2018)
24. Wolff, E., Johann, S.: Technical debt. IEEE Software **32**(4), 94–c3 (2015)
25. Zaytsev, V.: Open challenges in incremental coverage of legacy software languages. In: Proceedings of the 3rd ACM SIGPLAN International Workshop on Programming Experience, pp. 1–6. PX/17.2. Association for Computing Machinery, New York (2017)
26. Zazworka, N., Shaw, M., Shull, F., Seaman, C.: Investigating the impact of design debt on software quality, pp. 17–23 (2011)

Improving a Software Modernisation Process by Differencing Migration Logs

Céline Deknop[1,2(✉)], Johan Fabry[2], Kim Mens[1], and Vadim Zaytsev[2,3]

[1] Université catholique de Louvain, Louvain-la-Neuve, Belgium
{celine.deknop,kim.mens}@uclouvain.be
[2] Raincode Labs, Brussels, Belgium
johan@raincode.com
[3] Universiteit Twente, Enschede, The Netherlands
vadim@grammarware.net

Abstract. Software written in legacy programming languages is notoriously ubiquitous and often comprises business-critical portions of codebases and portfolios. Some of these languages, like COBOL, mature, grow, and acquire modern tooling that makes maintenance activities more bearable. Others, like many *fourth generation languages* (4GLs), stagnate and become obsolete and unmaintained, which first urges and eventually forces migrating to other languages, if the software needs to be kept in production. In this paper, we dissect a software modernisation process endorsed by Raincode Labs, utilised in particular to migrate software from a 4GL called PACBASE, to pure COBOL. Having migrated upwards of 500 MLOC of production code to COBOL using this process, the company has ample experience with this process. Nevertheless, we identify some improvement points and explain the technical side of a possible solution, based on migration log differencing, that is currently being put to the test by Raincode migration engineers.

Keywords: Software modernisation · Legacy programming languages · Software migration · Software evolution · Code differencing · COBOL · PACBASE · 4GL

1 Introduction

When COBOL was first introduced and published in 1960 [6], it enabled writing software that replaced the manual labour of thousands of people previously performing pen-and-paper bookkeeping or at best manual data entry and manipulation. When 4GLs (fourth generation languages) started emerging, they allowed developers to write significantly shorter programs, and enabled automated generation of dozens of pages of COBOL code from a single statement [22,29]. Nowadays, in the era of intentionally designed software languages [18] and domain-specific languages [31], conciseness and brevity is appreciated as much as readability, testability, understandability and ultimately, maintainability [9].

© Springer Nature Switzerland AG 2020
M. Morisio et al. (Eds.): PROFES 2020, LNCS 12562, pp. 270–286, 2020.
https://doi.org/10.1007/978-3-030-64148-1_17

Yet, legacy software continues to exist due to the sheer volume of it: just COBOL alone is estimated to have at least 220 billion lines of code worldwide, according to various sources. Business-critical legacy systems still make up a massive fraction of the software market: in 2017, it was reported that 43% of all banking systems in USA were built on COBOL, and that 95% of ATM swipes end up running COBOL code [27]. Migration projects are possible, but extremely challenging [30] and prone to failure due to overconfidence, misunderstanding, and other factors [5].

Over the last 25 years, Raincode Labs [25], a large independent compiler company, has conducted many different legacy modernisation projects. In this paper, we focus on the modernisation process for one specific kind of such projects [26]: removing the dependency on the compiler and the infrastructure of PACBASE [14], a 4GL that will be explained in Sect. 2. The research presented in this paper is a part of the CodeDiffNG [39] research project, an Applied PhD grant of the Brussels Capital Region that funds a collaboration between the UCLouvain university and the Raincode Labs company. The project is aimed at exploring the opportunities to push code differencing further by investigating advanced forms thereof, providing engineers with a structural view of the changes and with an explanation of their intent, especially in the context of realistically large codebases being used over long periods of time. In that context, this collaboration initiative with Raincode engineers aims to identify some of the problems they are still facing in their different software modernisation processes relating to the topic of code differencing, and design use cases based around those.

In Sect. 2 we will explain in detail the problem context and software modernisation process currently adopted by the company to migrate PACBASE-generated COBOL code to a more maintainable and human-readable equivalent. In Sect. 3, we will present the concept of code differencing, which we want to use to improve on the process described in the previous section. We will then detail where exactly our solution would fit, as well as describe the principles that we intend to put in place. Then, we will present the current state of our work in Sect. 4. Finally, in Sect. 5, we provide an overview of other approaches that we have explored to some extent and might explore in the farther future.

2   The Problem Space: PACBASE Migration

PACBASE [14] is a language and a tool created in the 1970s. Its original name was PAC700, for "programmation automatique Corig" (French for "Corig automated programming", where Corig was "conception et réalisation en informatique de gestion", a structured programming methodology popular in the 1970s). Its selling point was offering a DSL to its users that was at a higher level than available alternatives such as COBOL. The end users would program concise PACBASE macros, and COBOL code would be generated for them automatically. PACBASE was widely used since its creation throughout its life cycle [2]. The "Compagnie Générale d'Informatique", which developed it, was absorbed by IBM in 1999. In 2000, PACBASE itself was modernised and rewritten in

Java [28], but this did not suffice to prolong its life. The first attempt to suspend its support was made in 2005, and its definitive retirement was announced in 2015 [11]. Hence in companies that still rely on it, there is a pressing need to migrate software written in PACBASE to plain COBOL.

Since 2002 Raincode Labs has often undertaken such projects of PACBASE-generated COBOL to plain COBOL migration, one example being the case of the insurance broker DVV Verzekeringen reported by Bernardy [4]. Raincode Labs takes PACBASE-generated COBOL code and refactors it into a shorter, more readable equivalent that can be maintained manually [26]. PACBASE is an aged technology that will ultimately disappear, and an extensive discussion of the way PACBASE itself works is out of scope of this paper. Our main focus here is on the migration process of PACBASE-generated COBOL to a more concise, maintainable, and human-readable equivalent, and on how differencing of migration logs can help to improve that process.

The PACBASE migration process is achieved through a set of 140 transformation rules developed and refined by Raincode Labs over many years. Each single transformation rule can be seen as a local automated refactoring designed to be simple enough so that it can be proven not to change the semantics of the code; yet making it just a bit more concise, readable or maintainable. All rules are applied iteratively to the code until no further refactorings can be applied. This entire process and the artefacts involved are summarised in Fig. 1. Apart from summarising the migration process, which is the focus of this section, Fig. 1 also illustrates how, as a side-effect of the migration process, a migration log is produced. We will see in Sect. 4 how differencing of such migration logs could help to further improve the migration process.

A concrete example of a COBOL-to-COBOL program transformation is given in Fig. 2. All GO TO statements are removed and the control flow is turned into a PERFORM, the COBOL equivalent of a for loop. The logic that allows to iterate 10 times, contained in lines 1 to 9, has been translated into a more familiar VARYING UNTIL clause. Additionally, the concrete action of the loop, on lines 10 to 15 and 17 to 22 before, was simplified into a single IF ELSE that performs the same actions. Undeniably, this new COBOL code is more concise, more readable and more maintainable than the original (generated) one.

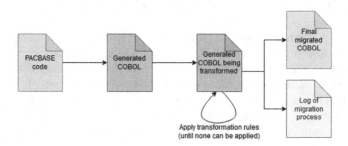

Fig. 1. Summary of the migration process, showing the different artefacts involved and their transformations.

```
 1   F05DC.
 2        MOVE         1        TO ICATR.
 3        GO TO        F05DC-B.
 4   F05DC-1.
 5        ADD          1        TO ICATR.
 6   F05DC-B.
 7        IF           10       < ICATR THEN
 8           GO TO     F05DC-FN
 9        END-IF.
10        IF        CATX(ICATR) = '0' THEN
11           NEXT SENTENCE
12        ELSE
13           GO TO F05DC-C
14        END-IF.
15        MOVE 'X' TO CATM(ICATR).
16   F05DC-C.
17        IF        CATX(ICATR) NOT = '0' THEN
18           NEXT SENTENCE
19        ELSE
20           GO TO F05DC-D
21        END-IF.
22        MOVE 'Y' TO CATM(ICATR).
23   F05DC-D.
24        GO TO F05DC-A.
25   F05DC-FN.
26        EXIT.
```

```
 1   PERFORM
 2        VARYING ICATR    FROM 1
 3                         BY 1
 4        UNTIL 10 < ICATR
 5        IF CATX(ICATR) = '0' THEN
 6           MOVE 'X' TO CATM(ICATR)
 7        ELSE
 8           MOVE 'Y' TO CATM(ICATR)
 9        END-IF.
10   END-PERFORM.
```

Fig. 2. Example of a migration from PACBASE-generated COBOL to equivalent COBOL code that is more concise, readable and maintainable.

Transformation rules are applied iteratively, and it takes 33 intermediary steps to perform the migration from Fig. 2. Let us take a closer look at some of them. The first transformation rule that is triggered is fairly simple as it simplifies the code in "one go", while others may need a few iterations, as we will see later. This first rule is called **NEXT SENTENCE Removal**, and is applied twice. As the name suggests, it removes the two NEXT SENTENCE instructions on lines 11 and 18, replacing them by the instruction CONTINUE. In COBOL, NEXT SENTENCE jumps to the instruction after the next full stop (here, it jumps respectively to lines 15 and 22), whereas the CONTINUE instruction simply does nothing and is used as a placeholder where code is required but nothing needs to be done (here, in the body of an if statement). In this particular example, we can easily see that this transformation preserves behaviour, since the full stop is right after the end of the if statement, where execution naturally continues.

Some transformation rules remove artefacts that are no longer useful. An example of such rule would be **Remove Useless Dots**, that is applied four times to the code a few steps later. Indeed, since we removed our NEXT SENTENCE instructions, we do not need the full stops signalling such sentences anymore. Therefore, the full stops on lines 21 and 14 get removed. At the same time, the ones on lines 2 and 9 are deleted as well, since they never really served a purpose. Another example of such a transformation rule would be to **Remove Labels**, i.e., delete labels when they are no longer needed (in our example all labels ultimately get removed).

Some bigger transformations, such as the creation of the PERFORM loop visible in the resulting code in Fig. 2, may require applying quite a few intermediate transformation rules. To remain relatively concise, we will highlight only a few of

```
1    * Raincode removed Label F05DC.
2        MOVE 1 TO ICATR
3        GO TO F05DC-B.
4
5    F05DC-A.
6        ADD 1 TO ICATR.
7
8    F05DC-B.
9        IF 10 < ICATR
10           GO TO F05DC-FN
11       END-IF
12       IF CATX(ICATR) NOT = '0'
13           GO TO F05DC-C
14       END-IF
15       MOVE 'X' TO CATM(ICATR).
16   F05DC-C.
17       IF CATX(ICATR) = '0'
18           GO TO F05DC-D
19       END-IF
20       MOVE 'Y' TO CATM(ICATR).
21   F05DC-D.
22       GO TO F05DC-A.
23
24   F05DC-FN.
25       EXIT.
26
```

```
1    * Raincode removed Label F05DC.
2        MOVE 1 TO ICATR
3        GO TO F05DC-B.
4
5    F05DC-A.
6        ADD 1 TO ICATR.
7
8    F05DC-B.
9        IF 10 < ICATR
10           GO TO F05DC-FN
11       ELSE
12           IF CATX(ICATR) = '0'
13               MOVE 'X' TO CATM(ICATR)
14           END-IF
15       END-IF
16   * Raincode removed Label F05DC-C.
17       IF CATX(ICATR) NOT = '0'
18           MOVE 'Y' TO CATM(ICATR)
19       END-IF
20   * Raincode removed Label F05DC-D.
21       GO TO F05DC-A.
22
23   F05DC-FN.
24       EXIT.
25
26
```

(a) Flipped conditions without `CONTINUE`   (b) Start of the if/else `GO TO` loop structure

```
1    * Raincode removed Label F05DC.
2        MOVE 1 TO ICATR
3        .
4
5
6    F05DC-B.
7        IF 10 < ICATR
8            GO TO F05DC-FN
9        ELSE
10   * Raincode removed Label F05DC-C.
11           IF CATX(ICATR) = '0'
12               MOVE 'X' TO CATM(ICATR)
13           ELSE
14               MOVE 'Y' TO CATM(ICATR)
15           END-IF
16       END-IF
17   * Raincode removed Label F05DC-D.
18   * Raincode removed Label F05DC-A.
19       ADD 1 TO ICATR.
20       GO TO F05DC-B.
21
22   F05DC-FN.
23       EXIT.
24
25
26
```

```
1    * Raincode removed Label F05DC.
2        MOVE 1 TO ICATR
3        .
4
5
6    F05DC-B.
7        PERFORM UNTIL FALSE
8            IF 10 < ICATR
9                GO TO F05DC-FN
10           ELSE
11   * Raincode removed Label F05DC-C.
12               IF CATX(ICATR) = '0'
13                   MOVE 'X' TO CATM(ICATR)
14               ELSE
15                   MOVE 'Y' TO CATM(ICATR)
16               END-IF
17           END-IF
18   * Raincode removed Label F05DC-D.
19   * Raincode removed Label F05DC-A.
20           ADD 1 TO ICATR
21           END-PERFORM.
22
23   F05DC-FN.
24       EXIT.
25
26
```

(c) Simplified if/else clause doing the `MOVE`s   (d) Creation of the `PERFORM`

Fig. 3. Snapshots of the loop-creation process

them in Fig. 3. First, a transformation rule **Remove Idle Instructions** is triggered, allowing to flip the condition of the if statements and the corresponding line of code, so that we then can get rid of the else condition now containing the `CONTINUE` (Fig. 3a). Then, a transformation rule **Recognise Loop-like Patterns** is triggered twice in a row, and after some clean-up steps, we can start to see an if-else structure containing `GO TO`s that starts to resemble a loop on lines 9, 10 and 21 (Fig. 3b). Quite a few more steps are needed however to bring all the conditions into the simple if-else clause that we get in the end (Fig. 3c); before the **Replace GO TO by Loop Exit** transformation rule can finally create the `PERFORM` loop that we can see in Fig. 3d. The final steps create the `VARYING` and performs some cleanups, resulting in the code on the right-hand side of Fig. 2.

Need for Redelivery. The process of migrating an entire codebase takes on average around two weeks, which includes tweaking the configuration, enabling/disabling/applying the transformation rules, testing the produced result, etc. (Although all transformations were designed to be behaviour

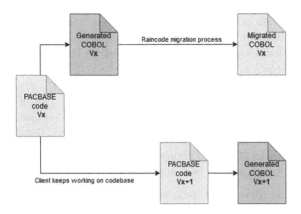

Fig. 4. Migration process, affected by the customer still working on the PACBASE code.

preserving, this testing phase can help convince the customer that the program indeed behaves the same way before and after the transformation.) During those two weeks, the customer's programmers typically continue with active development on the original system, making it diverge from the snapshot Raincode's migration team is working on, as depicted in Fig. 4. The process to integrate these changes to the original code into the already migrated code is called a *redelivery*, and will be explained shortly. The larger the migration project, the more redelivery phases can be required to ensure the customer's complete satisfaction at the end of Raincode's migration process.

The PACBASE migration process is largely automated, yet some manual steps remain. In what follows, we will explain how we believe they could be improved through advanced code differencing. One of our goals is to produce tools that are both academically relevant and concretely useful for the company. In the paragraphs below, we dive deeper into the process that Raincode engineers go through when migrating PACBASE projects, in order to identify manual work that possibly can be facilitated.

Raincode Labs' migration service is as tailored to the customer as possible. Raincode engineers experienced in PACBASE migration collaborate closely with the customer's engineers familiar with customer-specific coding standards. In the first phase, the customer selects from the 140 available transformation rules, the ones they want to apply to their codebase. The available transformation rules include universally appreciated `GO TO` elimination and rearranging control flow for code readability. Other transformations are more cosmetic and concern data alignment, code formatting or layout—they can be switched off when incompatible with the customer's coding standards. Raincode Labs' migration engineers coach the customer in choosing which rules to include, showing the transformation effect and providing suggestions about what would work best.

Once the chosen set of rules is validated, the customer wants to be sure that the original behaviour of their programs is maintained after migration.

Since the PACBASE migration service has been used for over fifteen years and has seen millions of processed lines of code successfully go in production, it is quite exceptional that bugs are introduced by the PACBASE migration. Nonetheless, the customer typically wishes to be convinced that the migrated code (that is often business-critical) will work as intended.

To facilitate this, Raincode engineers perform a test run of the migration, and in collaboration with the customer partition their codebase in three parts:

- 10–30 critical programs to be tested exhaustively;
- 80–100 programs to be tested thoroughly with unit and integration tests;
- the rest of the programs, to be tested for integration or not tested at all.

It is verified that all transformation rules that were triggered in the migration process are applied at least once in the first partition, assuring that all rules get manually tested at least once by the customer. When all lights are green, the customer's entire PACBASE-generated COBOL codebase is sent to Raincode engineers, who perform a cursory analysis of the codebase. Due to the scale of the codebase (typically 10–200 MLOC), the delivery may contain uncompilable code or non-code artefacts. Only when both parties agree on what exactly needs to be migrated, the actual process starts and after a few quality checks, the result is delivered to the customer.

As previously mentioned, it is frequent that in the meantime modifications have been introduced to the PACBASE code on the customer's side, in parallel with the migration process. In that case, a *redelivery* is needed. The customer sends all PACBASE-generated COBOL code that has changed, triggering another phase of manual analysis for Raincode engineers. This time, not only do they have to make sure that all the code is compilable, but also need to determine for each program if it has been migrated previously, or is something completely new. If it is new, they have to reevaluate whether it should indeed be migrated. If it is an update, they need to know if it has actually changed, since come minor readability tweaks on the PACBASE level might not propagate at all to the COBOL code or yield functionally equivalent code.

After this manual verification, the automated migration process is performed again. Before sending the results to the customer, Raincode's engineers now need to do not only some quality-checks, but also make an analysis of what changed since the delivery. This is done mostly manually and is a very subjective process: the engineer that we interviewed described it as *"we send the new migrated files to the customer when they look good enough"*. More concretely, they check if new rules got triggered in the migration process, then look at the output of a `diff` between the migrations of the previously sent version and the new one. If the difference is small enough to be manageable, they analyse it; if it is not and they feel like they can't confidently assure that the behaviour is identical, they ask the customer to perform a new test phase on those files.

Challenges of migration engineers were identified in two key places where nontrivial manual work tends to occur in this migration process: analysis of the initial codebase and redelivery. The codebase analysis is almost completely manual, but fairly quick and painless. There have also been successful attempts to automate it with language identification powered by machine learning [15]. Thus, we have chosen not to focus on this part at the moment.

The remainder of the paper will focus on addressing codebase redelivery instead. Raincode engineers could benefit from a tool that would allow them to say precisely and confidently, what (parts of a) program(s) need(s) to be tested again by the customer after a redelivery. Such a tool would allow the engineers to present the changes in the migrated codebase (that were triggered by changes to the PACBASE-generated COBOL) to the customer in an easy-to-understand way, instead of expecting them to trust their instincts. It would help negotiations if such a tool could provide insights on the reasons of why and how the migrated code was changed. Indeed, sometimes even very small changes to the original PACBASE code can have consequences on the COBOL output so significant that the new migrated version will also drastically change. This effect is not anticipated by most customers.

3   The Solution Space: Code Differencing

Code differencing aims at comparing two pieces of data, typically textual source code. One piece of data is considered as source and one as target. Code differencing produces difference data that specifies what changes or edits are necessary to go from the source to the target. This technique can be used directly, in version control systems such as `git` or the Unix command `diff`. It is also used indirectly, in the context of code merging [23], compression [12], convergence [38] and clone detection [24].

Even today, many differencing tools still rely on the basic algorithm created by Hunt and McIlroy [13] in 1976, or variants thereof. These tools treat their input as simple lines of text or binary data. However, code is more than just a random stream of characters. It conforms to quite specific and strict syntactical structure, ready to be exploited, and it implies a logical flow of control and dependencies among its components. A same code fragment can also reoccur in multiple places within a file or across multiple files. Such subtleties are lost when using the Hunt-McIlroy algorithm. Flat textual comparison does not reflect developer goals and obscures the intent of the changes due to the excess of low level information displayed, which can lead to frustrating and tedious experiences.

Using this algorithm thus often results in outputs that are hard to use or understand by developers, because they are too detailed or miss important relationships between the components involved in the change. They neither communicate nor reflect the intent, and ignore the semantics of the changes—the very thing one tends to seek when looking at a diff. When interacting directly with the output of a diff tool, it is often hard to get a good understanding of what functionalities—if any—changed since the last version, simply because there is just too much information to process at once. For example, if refactorings were applied, the behaviour of the program was expected to remain unchanged. Yet, the actions taken may result in changes that span over multiple files, and a developer would need to put a lot of effort in analysing these changes to understand or verify whether they indeed still respect the original program semantics.

Even interacting with diffs indirectly, like using a version control system with a good visualisation frontend (gitk, gitx, Git Kraken, Git Extensions, etc.), can still be frustrating to users. This is because it occasionally forces them to be confronted with the differences at a fine-grained level and makes them perform the merge manually. Examples of this are when just a few edits and moves caused a file to be flagged as completely different, or when there were simultaneous changes to the same set of lines.

3.1 Improvement Opportunities

As was illustrated in Fig. 1, the migration process takes the initial generated COBOL files and produces new migrated versions of this code, as well as some logs of the process. There is one log file per migrated program, and it contains the order and nature of the transformation rules that were triggered during the migration. This log file describes the exact process to go from the initial to the final version of each program, splitting it in multiple subversions. A snippet of such a log is shown in Fig. 5. Each line represents either a triggered rule along with the number of times (patches) it got triggered, or an intermediary version. Those intermediary versions are stored to disk, to enable analysis of the exact effect of the rule that got applied. Two different types of intermediary versions exist: the main phases denoted with a letter (rea, reb, . . .) and the subversions marked with numbers (here, 0030). Other lines containing warnings or debug information have been removed from the snippet as they will not be studied— we just assume that Raincode engineers will only diff successfully migrated files.

We could apply differencing to any of the above artefacts: we have both versions of the PACBASE-generated COBOL programs, the migrated COBOL programs and migration logs for each migrated program. The idea of using the initial generated COBOL files was quickly discarded: they are known to be hard

```
1:tmp/filename.COB.rea
Rename Level 49 (0 patches done)
Done (0 patches done)
1:tmp/filename.COB.reb

..
1:tmp/filename.COB.rec
Next-Sentence removal (28 patches done)
1:tmp/filename.COB.0030
Remove Useless Dots (51 patches done)
...
Done (0 patches done)
1:Result/filename.COB
```

Fig. 5. A simplified migration log

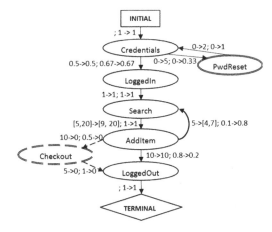

Fig. 6. The result of log differencing for a simple shopping cart example [19].

to understand, can change drastically when regenerated from a slightly adjusted PACBASE source, and can already be `diff`'ed.

Both remaining artefacts (the log files and the migrated programs) are capable of providing valuable information, each addressing some of the challenges of migration engineers. One would give an explanation as to *why* and *how* things changed, the other giving a clearer answer as to *where* things changed in the output code. Thus, we think it would be beneficial to use a combination of differencing both these artefacts to construct a full picture. First, we will look at the log produced by the migration process.

3.2 Log Differencing

In prior work, Goldstein et al. [10] presented a way to use log messages to create Finite State Automata representing the behaviour of a service when it is known to be in a normal and working state. They create a second model from updated logs and compare it to the first model. With that, they manage to identify outliers or behaviour that is different and therefore considered abnormal. This work was used in the context of mobile networks where an abnormal behaviour can translate to network congestion.

An example of the results obtained by them [10] is shown in Fig. 6. Nodes considered different (added or removed) have a specific border, in our example these are the nodes *PwdReset* (added) and *Checkout* (removed). Edges are adorned with two values separated by a semicolon. The first value is the time in seconds that the transition took in the underlying log, which we will not consider in our work since we are not interested in the performance of the migration process. The second value is the transition probability evolution. The probability to go from the first INITIAL node to the *Credentials* node remains unchanged while the probability to go to the new node *PwdReset* evolves from 0 to 0.33.

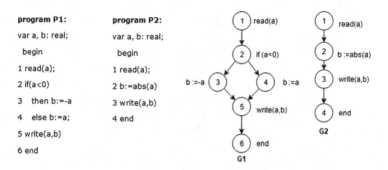

Fig. 7. Two reduced CFGs representing successive program versions [19]

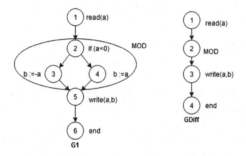

Fig. 8. Getting an isomorphic graph for the program **P1** from Fig. 7 [19]

As we will see shortly in Sect. 4, translating this example to our specific context is fairly simple. Nodes will correspond to log lines (representing either an intermediary version or a rule), and the edges and their probabilities will model the iterative process of the migration.

3.3 Code Differencing

The second approach we consider is to use the migrated COBOL programs directly, and compare them in a way useful for our use case. Laski and Szermer [19] propose a way to make structural diffs using reduced flow graphs (see Fig. 7) in the context of code revalidation, which may suit our purpose quite well.

They create reduced flow graphs for both versions (before and after the transformation) and apply classical modifications (relabelling, collapsing and removal) to their nodes in order to find an isomorphic graph (see Fig. 8). In the resulting graph, all nodes having their initial labels represent code that did not change, whereas all the differences abstracted by *MOD* are nodes that were transformed.

This representation is way more concise than the hundreds of lines given by a *diff* output, and has better chances of being more legible for both the customer's developers and the migration engineers. Places where modifications occurred are clearly identified and can easily be found in the code under consideration for re-test, giving a clear answer as to *where* things changed in the migrated code.

It is important to note that the algorithm aims at giving the most coarse result possible without losing precision. Whenever possible, it would give an output such as the one in Fig. 8 with parts left unchanged that do not need to be tested. However, if the difference in the code is too big, it would output a graph that just consists of a *MOD* node, which is still useful: it gives the migration engineers footing when they tell their customer that the entire code needs to be retested.

4   Differencing Log Files

Of the two approaches we presented, we needed to start with one. We chose to focus on log differencing for now because it was more recent, but we fully intend to explore diffs of the code later on.

In our efforts to improve Raincode Lab's software modernisation process, we started adapting the log differencing method presented by Goldstein et al. [10] to their use case. First, we analysed the data provided by Raincode for the pilot study of a specific migration project. The entire migration process concerned about 3000 artefacts in total, and two redeliveries were performed. The first concerned 47 files, the second only 8.

The log files generated by the migration process were quite substantial with an average of around 1200 lines before cleaning up all unneeded information and around 900 useful log lines. Even if we hope that this amount can be reduced further by translating to graphs, we made some design choices early on to ensure having something small enough that we could analyse.

First, we decided to divide the logs into the main phases that can be observed in Fig. 5: rea, reb, rec, red and ref. These correspond to naturally independent phases (preprocessing, clean up, etc.) which have always been analysed separately by Raincode engineers. For the main migration phase, which still contains upwards of 400 lines, we are abstracting from all intermediate subversions by removing their identification number. Those numbers are too specific to a particular instance of migration, and would prevent the resulting graphs to be anything but linear and a simple offset in the identifying numbers would result in the two graphs being flagged as entirely different, even if the rules were applied in the same order.

With those decisions, we implemented the first prototype of a log file differencing tool. As the main algorithm has already been implemented, but no visualisation support is available yet, the images visible in Fig. 9 were produced manually from our data. The upcoming versions of our prototype will generate these images automatically. Our preliminary conclusions drawn from analysing the three sets of files from both pilot study redeliveries are as follows:

First, we observed that less work-intensive phases (like rea, reb, red and ref) produced no differences between the two sets of files. Although we cannot guarantee that this finding would remain valid when analysing more than just a small sample of files, one might find it somewhat intuitive that phases of preprocessing or cleanup are likely not to change when the changes made to the files are not substantial. We will see whether this hypothesis can be verified for most of our other files.

The second observation on both examples is that the resulting graphs tend to be quite linear. Most often, we find long successions of nodes having a transition probability of 1 to the next one. Then, we find some clusters where something changed between the two versions, creating a less linear path. This can probably be explained by the fact that the migration process is iterative, and could also provide an interesting way to improve our future visualisation. By collapsing such linear parts of the graphs, we could emphasise the parts that are different, enabling a more easy analysis of the differences "at a glance".

The result in Fig. 9a is representative of what we see most: a long, linear graph with changes that are quite localised (for this specific example, the entire rest of the graph is identical between the two logs). The changes are either variations in transition probabilities, indicating that the rules were applied more or less times, or the creation of new path, such as between the nodes **consecutive IFs into IF THEN ELSIF** and **Intermediate version**, meaning that the changes resulted in a new order in which rules got triggered.

The result presented in Fig. 9b is the only occurrence we found so far of a node being added (no removal of node has been found yet). The added node is only an intermediary step and not a new rule, so it does not raise a major red

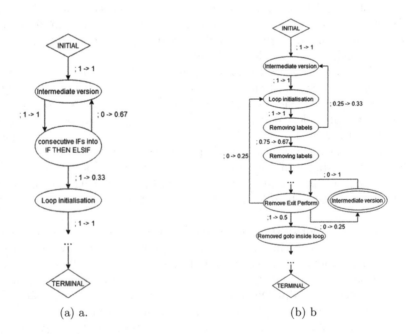

(a) a.   (b) b

Fig. 9. A shortened mock-up of the log differencing of one of Raincode's redelivered file.

flag. It should nonetheless be analysed in more detail by an engineer since it creates an entirely new path moving through a big part of the graph.

5 Related Work

We have presented two approaches directly related to the pilot experiments we are conducting at the time of writing this paper, in the hope of improving Raincode Labs' software modernisation process. Many other options were explored as well, that may or may not prove useful for our future endeavours. We detail some of those here.

Papers presenting ideas or tools that perform differencing in specialised or *advanced* ways, though a rare find, still exist. The one closest to our current interest is be Kim and Notkin's *LSdiff* [16] (Logical Structural DIFFerencing), an approach aiming at representing structural changes in a very concise manner, focusing on allowing the developer to understand the semantics of the changes. However, this approach seems to be more suited for object-oriented code, which does not correspond to our COBOL use case. There are other papers focusing on the object-oriented paradigm, among them the tools cal-cDiff [3] and Diff-CatchUp [35].

The **modelling** community could teach us a few things in this regard as well, so we studied tools that are made to perform clear and efficient differencing on a specific kind of model. Many of those exist for the widely-used models like UML (e.g., UMLDiff [34]), activity diagrams (e.g., ADDiff [21]) or feature models (e.g., in FAMILIAR [1]). Witnessing the abundance of many different tools for each kind of model, an approach to allow for a more generic way to difference models was also proposed by Zhenchang Xing [33].

We also took note of different techniques used when performing **data** differencing. From the starting point of the Hunt-McIlroy algorithm treating said data as simple text, to the extension to binary [32] when the need of differencing more heterogeneous artefacts. Afterwards, many different and modern techniques were developed, including those based on control flow graphs, as described in our second approach to the PACBASE use case and other tools making use of ASTs or at least parse trees as with GumTree [8] or cdiff [37]. We are also exploring the idea of enriching the initial data format with infrastructures as *srcML*, and how it can be applied to differencing [20] as well as about its corresponding tool *srcDiff* [7].

Finally, we are also looking at what ideas could be leveraged from other software engineering disciplines, like software **mining** or code **clone** detection. For instance, in the work of Kim et al. [17], logical rules are mined from the code to help represent the structural changes. Tools using those practices were also developed, for example ROSE [40], that mines the code to be able to suggest which changes should happen together, or CloneDiff [36], that uses differencing in the context of clone detection.

6   Conclusion

In this paper, we have presented a real industrial case study of a process of software modernisation and language/technology retirement by way of iterative code transformation. We identified some of the weakest links of this process, stemming from limitations of contemporary code differencing techniques, and showed how those restrictions can impact industrial processes like our PACBASE migration use case. Finally, we described some of the state of the art in code differencing and presented early results of how our work could build on them to improve the current migration practices within Raincode Labs.

To reiterate, the main limitation of the way code differencing is used today is its disregard for the *nature* of what is being analysed. Some research has been done to try and overcome this, but the way differencing is still taught in classes or used in the industry more or less corresponds to the initial Hunt-McIlroy algorithm in most cases. Moving forward, we should keep those limitations in mind, and try to surpass them, when designing new solutions and tools.

Acknowledgments. We thank the Raincode migration engineers Boris Pereira and Yannick Barthol for their collaboration, as well as the participants of the seminar SATToSE 2020, where an early version of this work was presented in June, for their feedback.

References

1. Acher, M., Heymans, P., Collet, P., Quinton, C., Lahire, P., Merle, P.: Feature model differences. In: Ralyté, J., Franch, X., Brinkkemper, S., Wrycza, S. (eds.) CAiSE 2012. LNCS, vol. 7328, pp. 629–645. Springer, Heidelberg (2012). https://doi.org/10.1007/978-3-642-31095-9_41
2. Alper, A.: Users say Pacbase worth effort. Computerworld **21** (1987)
3. Apiwattanapong, T., Orso, A., Harrold, M.J.: A differencing algorithm for object-oriented programs. In ASE, pp. 2–13. IEEE (2004)
4. Bernardy, J.-P.: Reviving Pacbase COBOL-generated code. In: Proceedings of the 26th Annual International Computer Software and Applications. IEEE (2002)
5. Blasband, D.: The Rise and Fall of Software Recipes. Reality Bites (2016)
6. CODASYL. Initial Specifications for a Common Business Oriented Language (COBOL) for Programming Electronic Digital Computers. Technical report, Department of Defense, April 1960
7. Decker, M., Collard, M., Volkert, L., Maletic, J.: srcDiff: a syntactic differencing approach to improve the understandability of deltas. J. Softw. Evol. Process **32**, 10 (2019)
8. Falleri, J.-R., Morandat, F., Blanc, X., Martinez, M., Monperrus, M.: Fine-grained and accurate source code differencing. In: ASE. ACM (2014)
9. Feathers, M.: Working Effectively with Legacy Code. Prentice-Hall, Upper Saddle River (2004)
10. Goldstein, M., Raz, D., Segall, I.: Experience report: log-based behavioral differencing. In: ISSRE, pp. 282–293 (2017). https://doi.org/10.1109/ISSRE.2017.14
11. Hewlett-Packard. Survival guide to PACBASE^{tm} end-of-life, October 2012. https://www8.hp.com/uk/en/pdf/Survival_guide_tcm_183_1316432.pdf

12. Hunt, J.J., Vo, K.-P., Tichy, W.F.: An empirical study of delta algorithms. In: Sommerville, I. (ed.) SCM 1996. LNCS, vol. 1167, pp. 49–66. Springer, Heidelberg (1996). https://doi.org/10.1007/BFb0023080
13. Hunt, J.W., McIlroy, M.D.: An algorithm for differential file comparison. CSTR #41, Bell Telephone Laboratories (1976)
14. IBM. PACBASE documentation page (2020). https://www.ibm.com/support/pages/documentation-visualage-pacbase
15. Kennedy van Dam, J., Zaytsev, V.: Software language identification with natural language classifiers. In: SANER ERA, pp. 624–628. IEEE (2016)
16. Kim, M., Notkin, D.: Discovering and representing systematic code changes. In: ICSE, pp. 309–319. IEEE (2009)
17. Kim, M., Notkin, D., Grossman, D.: Automatic inference of structural changes for matching across program versions. In: ICSE, pp. 333–343. IEEE (2007)
18. Lämmel, R.: Software Languages: Syntax, Semantics, and Metaprogramming. Springer, Heidelberg (2018)
19. Laski, J.W., Szermer, W.: Identification of program modifications and its applications in software maintenance. In: ICSM, pp. 282–290. IEEE (1992)
20. Maletic, J.I., Collard, M.L.: Supporting source code difference analysis. In: ICSM, pp. 210–219. IEEE (2004)
21. Maoz, S., Ringert, J.O., Rumpe, B.: ADDiff: semantic differencing for activity diagrams. In: FSE, pp. 179–189. ACM (2011)
22. Martin, J.: Applications Development Without Programmers. Prentice-Hall, Upper Saddle River (1981)
23. Mens, T.: A state-of-the-art survey on software merging. IEEE Trans. Softw. Eng. **28**(5), 449–462 (2002)
24. Min, H., Li Ping, Z.: Survey on Software Clone Detection Research. In: ICMSS, pp. 9–16. ACM (2019)
25. Raincode Labs. https://www.raincodelabs.com
26. Raincode Labs. PACBASE Migration: More than 200 Million Lines Migrated (2018). https://www.raincodelabs.com/pacbase
27. Reuters Graphics. COBOL blues, April 2017. http://fingfx.thomsonreuters.com/gfx/rngs/USA-BANKS-COBOL/010040KH18J/
28. Rémy, C.: Un nouveau PacBase, entièrement Java. 01net, July 2000. https://www.01net.com/actualites/un-nouveau-pacbase-entierement-java-114108.html
29. Schlueter, L.: User-Designed Computing: The Next Generation. Lexington, Lanham (1988)
30. Terekhov, A.A., Verhoef, C.: The realities of language conversions. IEEE Softw. **17**(6), 111–124 (2000)
31. Völter, M., et al.: DSL engineering: designing, implementing and using domain-specific languages (2013)
32. Z. Wang, K.P., Mcfarling, S.: BMAT - a binary matching tool for stale profile propagation. J. Instr. Level Parallelism **2**, 1–20 (2000)
33. Xing, Z.: Model Comparison with GenericDiff. In: ASE, pp. 135–138. ACM (2010)
34. Xing, Z., Stroulia, E.: UMLDiff: an algorithm for object-oriented design differencing. In: ASE, pp. 54–65. ACM (2005)
35. Xing, Z., Stroulia, E.: API-evolution support with diff-catchup. IEEE Trans. Softw. Eng. **33**(12), 818–836 (2007)
36. Xue, Y., Xing, Z., Jarzabek, S.: Clonediff: semantic differencing of clones. In: IWSC, pp. 83–84. ACM (2011)
37. Yang, W.: Identifying syntactic differences between two programs. Softw. Pract. Exp. **21**(7), 739–755 (1991)

38. Zaytsev, V.: Language convergence infrastructure. In: Fernandes, J.M., Lämmel, R., Visser, J., Saraiva, J. (eds.) GTTSE 2009. LNCS, vol. 6491, pp. 481–497. Springer, Heidelberg (2011). https://doi.org/10.1007/978-3-642-18023-1_16
39. Zaytsev, V., et al.: CodeDiffNG: Advanced Source Code Diffing (2020). https://grammarware.github.io/codediffng
40. Zimmermann, T., Weisgerber, P., Diehl, S., Zeller, A.: Mining version histories to guide software changes. In: ICSE, pp. 563–572. IEEE (2004)

The Effect of Class Noise on Continuous Test Case Selection: A Controlled Experiment on Industrial Data

Khaled Walid Al-Sabbagh$^{(\boxtimes)}$, Regina Hebig , and Miroslaw Staron

Computer Science and Engineering Department,
Chalmers | University of Gothenburg, Gothenburg, Sweden
{khaled.al-sabbagh,regina.hebig,miroslaw.staron}@gu.se

Abstract. Continuous integration and testing produce a large amount of data about defects in code revisions, which can be utilized for training a predictive learner to effectively select a subset of test suites. One challenge in using predictive learners lies in the noise that comes in the training data, which often leads to a decrease in classification performances. This study examines the impact of one type of noise, called class noise, on a learner's ability for selecting test cases. Understanding the impact of class noise on the performance of a learner for test case selection would assist testers decide on the appropriateness of different noise handling strategies. For this purpose, we design and implement a controlled experiment using an industrial data-set to measure the impact of class noise at six different levels on the predictive performance of a learner. We measure the learning performance using the Precision, Recall, F-score, and Mathew Correlation Coefficient (MCC) metrics. The results show a statistically significant relationship between class noise and the learner's performance for test case selection. Particularly, a significant difference between the three performance measures (Precision, F-score, and MCC) under all the six noise levels and at 0% level was found, whereas a similar relationship between recall and class noise was found at a level above 30%. We conclude that higher class noise ratios lead to missing out more tests in the predicted subset of test suite and increases the rate of false alarms when the class noise ratio exceeds 30%.

Keywords: Controlled experiment · Class noise · Test case selection · Continuous integration

1 Introduction

In testing large systems, regression testing is performed to ensure that recent changes in a software program do not interfere with the functionality of the unchanged parts. Such type of testing is central for achieving continuous integration (CI), since it advocates for frequent testing and faster release of products to the end users' community. In the context of CI, the number of test

© Springer Nature Switzerland AG 2020
M. Morisio et al. (Eds.): PROFES 2020, LNCS 12562, pp. 287–303, 2020.
https://doi.org/10.1007/978-3-030-64148-1_18

cases increases dramatically as commits get integrated and tested several times every hour. A testing system is therefore deployed to reduce the size of suites by selecting a subset of test cases that are relevant to the committed code. Over the recent years, a surge of interest among practitioners has evolved to utilize machine learning (ML) to support continuous test case selection (TCS) and to automate testing activities [2,8,10]. Those interests materialized in approaches that use data-sets of historical defects for training ML models to classify source code as defective or not (i.e. in need for testing) or to predict test case verdicts [2,3,8].

One challenge in using such learning models for TCS lies in the quality of the training data, which often comes with noise. The ML literature categorized noise into two types: attribute and class noise [6,9,20]. Attribute noise refers to corruptions in the feature values of instances in a data-set. Examples include: missing and incomplete feature values [16]. Class noise, on the other hand, occurs as a result of either contradictory examples (the same entry appears more than once and is labeled with a different class value) or misclassification (instances labeled with different classes) [21]. This type of noise is self-evident when, for example, analyzing the impact of code changes on test execution results. It can occur that identical lines are labeled with different test outcomes for the same test. These *identical lines* become noise when fed as input to a learning model.

To deal with the problem of class noise, testers can employ a number of strategies. These can be exemplified by eliminating contradictory entries or re-labeling such entries with one of the binary classes. These strategies have an impact on the performance of a learner and the quality of recommendations of test cases. For example, eliminating contradictory entries results in reducing the amount of training instances, which might lead to a decrease in a learner's ability to capture defective patterns in the feature vectors and therefore decreases the performance of a learner for TCS. Similarly, adopting a relabeling strategy might lead to training a learner that is biased toward one of the classes and therefore either include or exclude more tests from the suite. Excluding more tests in CI implies higher risks that defects remain undetected, whereas including more tests implies higher cost of testing. As a result, it is important for test orchestrators to understand how much noise there is in a training data set and how much impact it has on a learner's performance to choose the right noise handling strategy.

Our research study examines the effect of different levels of class noise on continuous testing. The aim is to provide test orchestrators with actionable insights into choosing the right noise handling strategy for effective TCS. For this purpose, we design and implement a controlled experiment using historical code and test execution results which belong to an industrial software. The specific contributions of this paper are:

- providing a script for creating a free-of-noise data-set which can facilitate the replication of this experiment on different software programs.
- presenting an empirical evaluation of the impact of class noise under different levels on TCS.
- providing a formula for measuring class noise in source code data-sets.

By seeding six variations of class noise levels (independent variable) into the subjects and measuring the learning performance of an ML model (dependent variables), we examine the impact of each level of class noise on the learning performance of a TCS predictor. We address the following research question:

RQ: Is there a statistical difference in predictive performance for a test case selection ML model in the presence and absence of class noise?

2   Definition and Example of Class Noise in Source Code

In this study, we define noise as the ratio of contradictory entries (mislabelled) found in each class to the total number of points in the data-set at hand. The ratio of noise can be calculated using the formula:

$$\text{Noise ratio} = \frac{\text{Number of Contradictory Entries}}{\text{Total Number of Entries}}$$

Since the contradictory entry can only be among two (or more) entries, the number of all entries for which a duplicate entry exists with a different class label. A duplicate entry is an entry that has the same line vector, but can have different labels. For example, a data-set containing ten duplicate vectors with nine that are labeled `true` and one labeled `false` has ten contradictory entries. It is not trivial to define a general rule to identify which class label is correct based on the number of entries. For example, noise sources might systematically tend to introduce false "false" labels. Since we do not know exactly which class should be used in this context, we cannot simply re-label any instance, as suggested by the currently used solutions (e.g. using majority voting [7] or entropy measurements [17]) and therefore we count all such entries as contradictory. As an illustration of the problem, in the domain of TCS, Fig. 1 shows how a program is transformed into a line vector and assigned a class label. It illustrates how a data-set is created for a classification task to predict whether lines of a C++ program trigger a test case failure (class 0) or a test case pass (class 1). The class label for each line vector is determined by the outcome of executing a single test case that was run against the committed code fragment in CI. In this study, a class value of '0' annotates a test failure, whereas a class value of '1' annotates a passed test. The Figure shows the actual code fragment and its equivalent line vector representation achieved via a statistical count approach (bag-of-words). The line vectors in this example correspond to source code tokens found in the code fragment. Note how lines 5 and 11 are included in the vector representations, since brackets are associated with loop blocks and function declarations, which can be important predictors to capture defective patterns. All shaded vectors in the sparse matrix (lines 7 to 10) are class noise since pairs (7,9) and (8,10) have the same line vectors, but different label class – 1 and 0. The green shaded vectors are 'true labeled instances' whereas the gray shaded vectors are 'false labeled instances'. Note that the Table in Fig. 1 shows an excerpt of the entries for this example. Since there are 11 lines of code, the total number of entries is 11. The formula for calculating the noise ratio for this example is thus:

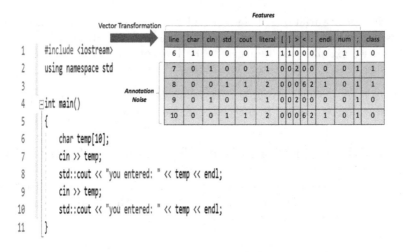

Fig. 1. Class noise in code base. (Color figure online)

$$\text{Noise ratio} = \frac{4}{11} = 0.36$$

If lines 7 to 10 are fed as input into a learning model for training, it is difficult to predict the learner's behavior. It depends on the learner. We also do not know which case is correct – which lines should be re-labelled or whether we should remove these lines. The behavior of the learner, thus, depends on the noise removal strategy, which also impacts the test selection process. If we choose to re-label lines 7 and 8 with class 0 (test case failure), this means that the learner is biased towards suggesting to include the test in the test suite. If we re-label lines 9 and 10 with class 1 (test case pass), then the learner is biased towards predicting that a test case should not be included in a test suite. Finally, if we remove all contradictory entries (7, 8, 9, and 10), then we reduce the learner's ability to capture the patterns in the feature vectors for these lines – we have fewer training cases ($11 - 4 = 7$ cases).

3   Related Work

Several studies have been made to identify the effect of class noise on the learning of ML models in several domains[1,12,19]. To our knowledge, no study addresses the effect of class noise on the performance of ML models in a software engineering context. Therefore, understanding the impact of class noise in a software engineering context, such as testing, is important to utilize its application and improve its reliability. This section presents studies that highlight the impact of class noise on performances of learners in a variety of domains. It also mentions studies that use text mining and ML for TCS and defect prediction.

3.1   The Impact of Noise on Classification Performances

The issue of class noise in large data-sets has gained much attention in the ML community. The most widely reported problem is the negative impact that class noise has on classification performance.

Nettletonet et al. [12] examined the impact of class noise on classification of four types of classifiers: naive Bayes, decision trees, k-Nearest Neighbors, and support vector machines. The mean precision of the four models were compared under two levels of noise: 10% and 50%. The results of the comparison showed a minor impact on precision at 10% noise ratio and a larger impact at 50%. In particular, the precision obtained by the Naive Bayes classifier was 67.59% under 50% noise ratio compared with 17.42% precision for the SVM classifier. Similarly, Zhang and Yang [19] examined the performance of three linear classification methods on text categorization, under 1%, 3%, 5%, 10%, 15%, 20% and 30% class noise ratios. The results showed a dramatic, yet identical, decrease in the classification performances of the three learners after noise ratio exceeded 3%. Specifically the f-score measures for the three models ranged from 60% to 60% under 5% noise ratio and from 40% to 43% under 30% noise ratio. Pechenizkiy et al. [14] experimented on 8 data-sets the effect of class noise on supervised learning in medical domains. The kNN, Naïve Bayes and C4.5 decision tree learning algorithms were trained on the noisy datasets to evaluate the impact of class noise on accuracy. The classification accuracy for each classifier was compared under eleven class noise levels 0%, 2%, 4%, 6%, 8%, 10%, 12%, 14%, 16%, 18%, and 20%. The results showed that when the level of noise increases, all classifiers trained on noisy training sets suffer from decreasing classification accuracy. Abellan and Masegosa [1] conducted an experiment to compare the performance of Bagging Credal decision trees (BCDT) and Bagging C4.5 in the presence of class noise under 0%, 5%, 10%, 20% and 30% ratios. Both bagging approaches were negatively impacted by class noise, although BCDT was more robust to the presence of noise at a ratio above 20%. The accuracy of BCDT model dropped from 86.9% to 78.7% under a noise level of 30% whereas the Bagging C4.5 accuracy dropped from 87.5% to 77.2% under the same level.

3.2   Text Mining for Test Case Selection and Defect Prediction

A multitude of early approaches have used text mining techniques for leveraging early prediction of defects and test verdicts using ML algorithms. However, these studies omit to discuss the effect of class noise on the quality of the learning predictors. In this paper, we highlight the results of some of these work and validate the impact of class noise on the predictive performance of a model for TCS using the method proposed in [2].

A previous work on TCS [2] utilized text mining from source code changes for training various learning classifiers on predicting test case verdicts. The method uses test execution results for labelling code lines in the relevant tested commits. The maximum precision and recall achieved was 73% and 48% using a tree-based ensemble. Hata et al. [8] used text mining and spam filtering algorithms to classify software modules into either fault-prone or non-fault-prone. To identify faulty modules, the authors used bug reports in bug tracking systems. Using the 'id' of each bug in a given report, the authors tracked files that were reported as defective, and consequently performed a 'diff' command on the same files between a fixed revision and a preceding revision. The evaluation of the model on a set of five open source projects reported a maximum precision and recall values of 40% and 80% respectively. Similarly, Mizuno et al. [11] mined text from the ArgoUML and Eclipse BIRT open source systems, and trained spam filtering algorithms for fault-prone detection using an open source spam filtering software. The results reported precision values of 72–75% and recall values of 70–72%. Kim et al. [10] collected source code changes, change metadata, complexity metrics, and log metrics to train an SVM model on predicting defects on file-level software changes. The identification of buggy commits was performed by mining specific keywords in change log messages. The predictor's quality on 12 open source projects reported an average accuracy of 78% and 60% respectively.

4   Experiment Design

To answer the research question, we worked with historical test execution data including results and their respective code changes for a system developed using the C language in a large network infrastructure company. This section describes the data-set and the hypotheses to be answered.

4.1   Data Collection Method

We worked with 82 test execution results (passed or failed) that belonged to 12 test cases and their respective tested code (overall 246,850 lines of code)[1]. First, we used the formula presented in Sect. 2 to measure the level of class noise in the data-set - this would help us understand the actual level of class noise found in real-world data-sets. Applying the formula indicated a class noise level of 80.5%, with 198,778 points identified as contradictory. For the remainder of this paper, we will use the term 'code changes data-set' to refer to this data-set. Our first preparation task for this experiment was to convert the code changes data-set into line vectors. In this study, we utilized a bi-gram BoW model provided in an open source measurement tool [13] to carry out the vector transformation. The resulting output was a sparse matrix with a total of 2251 features and 246,850 vectors. To eliminate as many confounding factors as possible, we used the same vector transformation tool and learning model across all experimental trials, and fixed the hyper-parameter configurations in both the vector transformation tool and the learning model (see Sect. 5.3).

---

[1] Due to non-disclosure agreements with our industrial partner, our data-set can unfortunately not be made public for replication.

4.2   Independent Variable and Experimental Subjects

In this study, class noise is the only independent variable (treatment) examined for an effect on classification performance. Seven variations of class noise (treatment levels) were selected to support the investigation of the research question. Namely, 0%, 10%, 20%, 30%, 40%, 50%, 60%. To apply the treatment, we used 15-fold stratified cross validation on the control group (see Sect. 5.1) to generate fifteen experimental subjects. Each subject is treated as a hold out group for validating a learner which gets trained on the remaining fourteen subjects. A total of 105 trials derived from the 15-folds were conducted. Each fifteen trials was used to evaluate the performances of a learner under one treatment level.

4.3   Dependent Variables

The dependent variables are four evaluation measures used for the performance of an ML classifier – Precision, Recall, F-score, and Matthews Correlation Coefficient (MCC) [4]. The four evaluation measures are defined as follows:

- Precision is the number of correctly predicted tests divided by the total number of predicted tests.
- Recall is the number of correctly predicted tests divided by the total number of tests that should have been positive.
- The F-score is the harmonic mean of precision and recall.
- The MCC takes the four categories of errors and treats both the true and the predicted classes as two variables. In this context, the metric calculates the correlation coefficient of the actual and predicted test cases for both classes.

4.4   Experimental Hypotheses

Four hypotheses are defined according to the goals of this study and tested for statistical significance in Sect. 6. The hypotheses were based on the assumption that data-sets with class noise rate have a significantly negative impact on the classification performance of an ML model for TCS compared to a data-set with no class noise. The hypotheses are as follow:

- *H0p: The mean Precision is the same for a model with and without noise*
- *H0r: The mean Recall is the same for a model with and without noise*
- *H0f: The mean F-score is the same for a model with and without noise*
- *H0mcc: The mean MCC is the same for a model with and without noise*

For example, the first hypothesis can be interpreted as: *a data-set with a higher rate of class noise will result in significantly lower Precision rate, as indicated by the mean Precision score across the experimental subjects.* After evaluating the hypotheses, we compare the evaluation measures under each treatment level with those at 0% level.

4.5   Data Analysis Methods

The experimental data were analyzed using the scikit learn library with Python [15]. To begin, a normality test was carried out using the Shapiro-Wilk test to decide whether to use a parametric or a non-parametric test for analysis. The results showed that the distribution of the four dependent variables did not deviate significantly from a normal distribution (see Sect. 6.2 for details). As such, we decided to use two non-parametric tests, namely: Kruskal-Wallis and Mann-Whitney. To evaluate the hypotheses, the Kruskal-Wallis was selected for comparing the median scores between the four evaluation measures under the treatment levels. The Mann–Whitney U test was selected to carry out a pairwise comparison between the evaluation measures under each treatment level and the same measures at a 0% noise level.

5   Experiment Operations

This section describes the operations that were carried out during this experiment for creating the control group and seeding class noise.

5.1   Creation of the Control Group

To support the investigation of the hypotheses, a control group was needed to establish a baseline for comparing the evaluation measures under the six treatment levels. This control group needs to have a 0% ratio of class noise, i.e. without contradictory entries. To have control over the noise ratio in the treatment groups, these will then be created by seeding noise into copies of the control group data-set (see Sect. 5.2). The classification performance in the treatment groups will then be compared to that in the control group (see Sect. 5.3). In addition, the distribution of data points in the control group is expected to strongly influence the outcome of the experiment. To control for that we aim to create optimal conditions for the algorithm. ML algorithms can most effectively fit decision boundary hyper-planes when the data entries are similar and linearly separable [5]. Therefore, we decided to start from our industrial code changes data-set (See Sect. 4.1) and extract a subset of the data, by detecting similar vectors in the "Bag of Words" sparse matrix. In this study, we decided to identify similarity between vectors based on their relative orientation to each other. What follows is a detailed description of the algorithm used for constructing the control group. The algorithm starts by loading the feature vectors from our industrial code changes data-set and their corresponding label values (passed or failed) into a data frame object. To establish similarity between two vectors we use the cosine similarity function provided in the scikit learn library [15] working with a threshold of 95%. For each of the two classes (passed or failed), one sample feature vector is randomly picked and used as a baseline vector to compare its orientation against the remaining vectors within its class. The selection criterion of the two baseline vectors is that they are not similar. This is important to guarantee that the derived control group has no contradictory entries (noise ratio = 0). Each of the two baseline vectors is then compared with the remaining vectors (non-baseline) for similarity. The only condition for selecting the vectors is based on their similarity ratio. If the baseline and the non-baseline vectors are similar more than the predefined ratio of 95%, then the non-baseline vector is added to a data frame object. Table 1 shows the two baseline entries before being converted into line vectors. Due to non-disclosure agreement with our industrial partner, words that are not language specific such as variable and class names are replaced with other random names.

Table 1. The two baseline entries before conversion

Line of code	Class
measureThreshold(DEFAULT_MEASURE)	1
if (!Session.isAvailable())	0

The script for generating the datasets is found at the link in the footnote[2]. The similarity ratio of 95% was chosen by running the above algorithm a multiple times using five ratios of the predefined similarity ratio. The criterion for selecting the optimal threshold was based on the evaluation measures of a random forest model, trained and tested on the derived control data-set. That is, if the model's Precision and Recall reached 100%, i.e. made neither false positive nor false negative predictions, then we know that control group has reached sufficient similarity for the ML algorithm to work as efficient as possible. The following threshold values of similarity were experimented using the above algorithm: 75%, 80%, 85%, 90%, and 95%. Experimenting on these ratios with a random forest model showed that a ratio of 95% cosine similarity between the baseline vector and the rest yield a 100% of Precision, Recall, f-score, and MCC. As a result, we used a ratio of 95% to generate the control group. The resulting group contained 9,330 line vectors with zero contradictory entries between the two classes. The distribution of these entries per class was as follow:

- Entries that have at least one duplicate within the same class: 3679 entries labeled as failed and 4280 entries as pass.
- Entries with no duplicates in the data-set: 1 entry labeled as failed and 1370 entries as passed.

5.2   Class Noise Generation

To generate class noise into the experimental subjects, we followed the definition of noise introduced in Sect. 2 by carrying out the following two-steps procedure:

1. Given a noise ratio Nr, we randomly pick a portion of Nr from the population of duplicate vectors within each class in the training and validation subjects.

---

[2] https://github.com/khaledwalidsabbagh/noise_free_set.git.

2. We re-label half of the label values of duplicate entries selected in step 1 to the opposite class to generate Nr noise ratio. In situations where the number of duplicate entries in Nr are uneven, we re-label half of the selected Nr portion minus one entry.

In this experiment, a design choice was made to seed each treatment level (10%, 20%, 30%, 40%, 50%, and 60%) into both the training and validation subjects. This is because we wanted to reflect a real-world scenario where the data in both the training and test sets comes with class noise. The above procedure was repeated 15 times for each level, making a total of 90 trials.

A common issue in supervised ML is that the arithmetic classification accuracy becomes biased toward the majority class in the training data-set, which might lead to the extraction of poor conclusions. This effect might be magnified if noise was added without checking the balance of classes after generating noise. In this experiment, due to the large computational cost required to check the distribution of classes across 90 trials, we only checked the distribution under 10% noise ratio. Figure 2 shows how the classes in the training and validation subjects were distributed across 15 trials for a 10% noise ratio. The x-axis corresponds to the binary classes and the y-axis represents the number of entries in the training and validation sets. The Figure shows a fairly balanced distribution in the training subjects with an average of 3421 entries in the passed class and 3993 entries in the failed class.

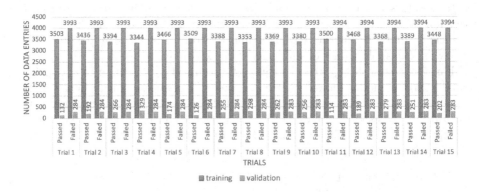

Fig. 2. The Distribution of the binary classes after generating noise at 10% ratio.

5.3   Performance Evaluation Using Random Forest

We evaluate the effect of each noise level on learning by training a random forest model. The choice of using a random forest model was due to its low computational cost compared to deep learning models. The hyper-parameters of the model were kept to their default state as found in the scikit-learn library (version 0.20.4). The only configuration was made on the n_estimator parameters (changed from 10 to 100), which corresponds to the number of trees in the forest. We tuned this parameter to minimize chances of over-fitting the model.

6   Results

This section discusses the results of the statistical tests conducted to evaluate hypotheses *H0p, H0r, H0f, and H0mcc* and to answer the research question.

6.1   Descriptive Statistics

The descriptive statistics are presented in Tables 2, 3, 4, and 5 individually for each dependent variable. The values for Precision (Table 2), Recall (Table 3), F-score (Table 4), and MCC (Table 5) are shown for each of the noise ratio (0%, 10%, 20%, 30%, 40%, 50%, and 60%). A first evident observation from the tables is that there is a statistically significant relationship between the mean values of the four dependent variables and the noise ratio, where a lower value of a given dependent variable indicates higher noise ratio. Three general observations can be made by examining the data shown in the four tables:

- There is an inverse trend between noise ratio and learning precision, f-score, and MCC. That is, when the noise level increases, the classifier trained on noisy instances suffers a small decrease in the four evaluation measures. Figure 3 shows this relationship where the x-axis indicates the noise ratio and the y-axis represents the evaluation measures.
- There exists a higher dispersion in the evaluation scores when the noise level increases (i.e. higher standard deviation [SD]).
- The mean difference between the recall values under each noise ratio is relatively smaller than those with the other three dependent variables.

Table 2. Descriptive stats for precision.

Noise	N	Mean	SD	SE	95% Conf.
0%	15	0.997	0.000	0.000	0.997
10%	15	0.966	0.009	0.002	0.961
20%	15	0.933	0.019	0.005	0.923
30%	15	0.900	0.029	0.007	0.884
40%	15	0.867	0.039	0.010	0.846
50%	15	0.834	0.048	0.012	0.808
60%	15	0.801	0.059	0.015	0.770

Table 3. Descriptive stats for recall.

Noise	N	Mean	SD	SE	95% Conf.
0%	15	1.000	0.000	0.000	1.000
10%	15	0.984	0.032	0.008	0.967
20%	15	0.970	0.061	0.015	0.937
30%	15	0.955	0.086	0.022	0.910
40%	15	0.940	0.109	0.028	0.883
50%	15	0.931	0.134	0.034	0.860
60%	15	0.897	0.144	0.037	0.821

Table 4. Descriptive stats for F-Score.

Noise	N	Mean	SD	SE	95% Conf.
0%	15	0.998	0.000	0.000	0.998
10%	15	0.974	0.013	0.003	0.967
20%	15	0.949	0.025	0.006	0.936
30%	15	0.923	0.034	0.008	0.905
40%	15	0.897	0.044	0.011	0.873
50%	15	0.871	0.055	0.014	0.842
60%	15	0.836	0.059	0.015	0.805

Table 5. Descriptive stats for MCC.

Noise	N	Mean	SD	SE	95% Conf.
0%	15	0.996	0.000	0.000	0.996
10%	15	0.946	0.030	0.007	0.930
20%	15	0.894	0.060	0.015	0.863
30%	15	0.841	0.088	0.022	0.795
40%	15	0.790	0.119	0.030	0.727
50%	15	0.742	0.156	0.040	0.660
60%	15	0.674	0.181	0.046	0.579

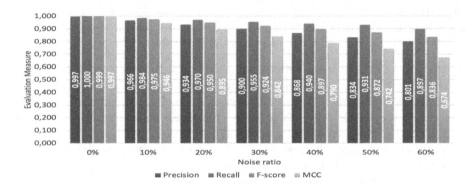

Fig. 3. Mean distribution of the evaluation measures.

6.2 Hypotheses Testing

We begin the evaluation of the hypotheses by checking whether the distribution of the dependent variables deviates from a normal distribution. The Shapiro-Wilk test results were statistically significant for all the evaluation measures in the majority of the noise ratios. Table 6 shows the statistical results of normality for the dependent variables on all noise ratios. These results indicate that the assumption of normality in the majority of the samples can be rejected, as indicated by the p-value ($p < 0.05$) in Table 6. Since we have issues with normality in the majority of samples, we decided to run a non-parametric test for comparing the difference between the performance scores under the six noise ratios.

To examine the impact of class noise on the four dependent variables, the Kruskal-Wallis test was conducted. Table 7 summarizes the statistical comparison results, indicating a significant difference in Precision, F-score, and MCC. Specifically, the results of the comparison for precision showed a test statistics of 56.8 and a p-value below 0.001. Likewise, a significant difference in the comparisons between the evaluation measures of F-score and MCC (F-score Results: Test Statistics $= 54.172$, p-value < 0.005, MCC Results: Test Statistics $= 53.398$, p-value < 0.005) groups was found. In contrast, no significant difference between the Recall measures was identified.

Table 6. Statistical results for normality.

	0%	10%	20%	30%	40%	50%	60%
Precision	Stat=0.59 p<0.005	Stat=0.82 p=0.02	Stat=0.87 p=0.11	Stat=0.91 p=0.28	Stat=0.91 p=0.32	Stat=0.88 p=0.13	Stat=0.92 p=0.40
Recall	Stat=1.00 p=1.00	Stat=0.36 p<0.005	Stat=0.50 p<0.005	Stat=0.50 p<0.005	Stat=0.54 p<0.005	Stat=0.56 p<0.005	Stat=0.53 p<0.005
F-Score	Stat=0.59 p<0.005	Stat=0.78 p=0.009	Stat=0.67 p<0.005	Stat=0.74 p=0.003	Stat=0.83 p=0.037	Stat=0.69 p=0.001	Stat=0.8 p=0.02
MCC	Stat=0.68 p=0.001	Stat=0.77 p=0.01	Stat=0.65 p<0.005	Stat=0.69 p=0.001	Stat=0.77 p=0.01	Stat=0.63 p<0.005	Stat=0.69 p=0.001

Table 7. Statistical comparison between the evaluation measures at all noise levels.

	p-value	statistics
precision	p<0.005	Statistics=56.858
recall	p=0.164	Statistics=9.180
f-score	p<0.005	Statistics=54.172
mcc	p<0.005	Statistics=53.398

The Mann–Whitney U test with Precision, F-score, and MCC as the dependent variables and noise ratio as the independent variable revealed a significant difference (p-value below 0.005) under each of the six levels when compared with the same measures in the no-treatment sample. However, the statistical results for recall only showed a significant difference when the noise level exceeded 30%. Table 8 summarizes the statistical results from the Mann–Whitney test under the six treatment levels. The analysis results from this experiment indicate that *there is a statistical significant difference in predictive performance for a test case selection model in the presence and absence of class noise.* The results from the Kruskal-Wallis test were in line with the expectations for hypotheses *H0p, H0f, H0mcc*, which confirm that *we can reject the null hypotheses for H0p, H0f, H0mcc*, whereas *no similar conclusion can be drawn for hypothesis H0r*. While no significant difference between the recall values was drawn from the Kruskal-Wallis test, the Mann-Whitney test indicates that there is a significant inverse causality between class noise and recall when noise exceeds 30%. In the domain of TCS, the practical implications can be summarized as follow:

- Higher class noise slightly increases the predictor's bias toward the pass class (lower precision rate), and therefore leads to missing out tests that should be included in the test suite.
- A class noise level above 30% has a significant effect on the learner's Recall. Therefore, the rate of false alarms (failed tests) in TCS increases significantly above 30% noise ratio.

Table 8. The comparison results from Mann-Whitney test

	10%	20%	30%	40%	50%	60%
Precision	Stat=7.5, p<0.005	Stat=0.000, p<0.005	Stat=0.000, p<0.005	Stat=0.000, p<0.005	Stat=0.000, p<0.005	Stat=0.000, p<0.005
Recall	Stat=45, p=0.184	Stat=40.000, p=0.084	Stat=40.000, p=0.084	Stat=35.000, p<0.005	Stat=30.000, p=0.017	Stat=25, p=0.007
F-Score	Stat=7.5, p<0.005	Stat=0.000, p<0.005	Stat=0.000, p<0.005	Stat=0.000, p<0.005	Stat=0.000, p<0.005	Stat=0.000, p<0.005
MCC	Stat=7.5, p<0.005	Stat=0.000, p<0.005	Stat=0.000, p<0.005	Stat=0.000, p<0.005	Stat=0.000, p<0.005	Stat=0.000, p<0.005

7   Threats to Validity

When analyzing the validity of our study, we used the framework recommended by Wohlin et al. [18]. We discuss the threats to validity in four categories: external, internal, construct, and conclusion.

External Validity: External validity refers to the degree to which the results can be generalized to applied software engineering practice.

Test Cases. Since our experimental subjects belong to twelve test cases only, it is difficult to decide whether the sample is representative. However, to increase the likelihood of drawing a representative sample and to control as many confounding factors, we randomly selected a small sample of 12 test cases. Also, the random selection of tests has the potential of increasing the probability of drawing a representative sample.

Control Group. The study employed a similarity based mechanism to derive the control group, which resulted in eliminating many entries from the original sample. This might affect the representativeness of the sample. However, our control group contained points that belong to an industrial program, which is arguably more representative than studying points that we construct ourselves. This was a trade-off decision between external and internal validity, since we wanted to study the impact of class noise on TCS in an industrial setting and therefore maximize the external validity.

Nature of Test Failure. There is a probability of mis-labelling code changes if test failures were due to factors external to defects in the source code (e.g., machinery malfunctions or environment upgrades). To minimize this threat, we collected data for multiple test executions that belong to several test cases, thus minimizing the probability of identifying tests that are not representative.

Internal Validity. Internal validity refers to the degree to which conclusions can be drawn about the causal effect of independent on dependent variables.

Instrumentation. A potential internal threat is the presence of undetected defects in the tool used for vector transformation, data-collection, and noise injection. This threat was controlled by carrying out a careful inspection of the scripts and testing them on different subsets of data of varying sizes.

Use of a Single ML Model. This study employed a random forest model to examine the effect of class noise on classification performances. However, the analysis results might differ when other learning models are used. This was a design choice since we wanted to study the effect of a single treatment and to control as many confounding factors as possible.

Construct Validity. Construct validity refers to the degree to which experimental variables accurately measure the concepts they purport to measure.

Noise Ratio Algorithm. Our noise injection algorithm modifies label values without tracking which entries that are being modified. This might lead to relabeling the same duplicate line multiple times during noise generation. Consequently, the injected noise level might be below the desired level. Thus, our study likely underestimates the effects of noise. However, the results still allowed us to identify a significant statistical difference in the predictive performance of TCS model, thereby to answer the research question.

Majority Class Problem. Due to the large computational cost required to check the balance of the binary classes under the six treatment levels, we only checked for the class distributions for one noise level - 10%. Hence, there is a chance that the remaining unchecked trials are imbalanced. Nevertheless, the downward trend in the predictive performances as noise ratio increases indicates that the predictor was not biased toward a majority class.

Conclusion Validity. Conclusion validity focuses on how sure we can be that the treatment we use really is related to the actual outcome we observe.

Differences Among Subjects. The descriptive statistics indicated that we have a few outliers in the sample. Therefore, we ran the analysis twice (with and without outliers) to examine if they had any impact on the results. Based on the analysis, we found that dropping the outliers had no effect on the results, thus we decided to keep them in the analysis.

8   Conclusion and Future Work

This research study examined the effect of different levels of class noise on the predictive performance of a model for TCS using an industrial data-set. A formula for measuring the level of class noise was provided to assist testers gain

actionable insights into the impact of class noise on the quality of recommendations of test cases. Further, quantifying the level of noise in training data enables
testers make informed decisions about which noise handling strategy to use to
improve continuous TCS if necessary. The results from our research provide
empirical evidence for a causal relationship between six levels of class noise and
Precision, F-score, and MCC, whereas a similar causality between class noise
and recall was found at a noise ratio above 30%. In the domain of the investigated problem, this means that higher class noise yields to an increased bias
towards predicting test case passes and therefore including more of those tests
in the suite. This is penalized with an increased hardware cost for executing the
passing tests. Similarly, as class noise exceeds 30%, the prediction of false alarms
with the negative class (failed tests) increases.

There are still several questions that need to be answered before concluding
that class noise handling strategies can be used in an industrial setting. A first
question is about finding the best method to handle class noise with respect to
efficiency and effectiveness. Future research that study the impact of attribute
noise on the learning of a classifier and how that compares with the impact of
class noise are needed. Other directions for future research include evaluating
the level of class noise at which ML can be deemed useful by companies in
predicting test case failures, evaluate the relative drop of performance from a
random sample of industrial code changes and compare the performance of the
learner with the observations drawn from this experiment, study and compare
the effect of different code formatting on capturing noisy instances in the data
and the performance of a classifier for TCS. Finally, we aim at comparatively
exploring the sensitivity of other learning models to class and attribute noise.

References

1. Abellán, J., Masegosa, A.R.: Bagging decision trees on data sets with classification
   noise. In: Link, S., Prade, H. (eds.) FoIKS 2010. LNCS, vol. 5956, pp. 248–265.
   Springer, Heidelberg (2010). https://doi.org/10.1007/978-3-642-11829-6_17
2. Al-Sabbagh, K.W., Staron, M., Hebig, R., Meding, W.: Predicting test case verdicts using textual analysis of committed code churns. In: Joint Proceedings of the
   International Workshop on Software Measurement and the International Conference on Software Process and Product Measurement (IWSM Mensura 2019), vol.
   2476, pp. 138–153 (2019)
3. Aversano, L., Cerulo, L., Del Grosso, C.: Learning from bug-introducing changes
   to prevent fault prone code. In: Ninth International Workshop on Principles of
   Software Evolution: In Conjunction with the 6th ESEC/FSE Joint Meeting, pp.
   19–26. ACM (2007)
4. Boughorbel, S., Jarray, F., El-Anbari, M.: Optimal classifier for imbalanced data
   using Matthews Correlation Coefficient metric. PloS one **12**(6), e0177678 (2017)
5. Frénay, B., Verleysen, M.: Classification in the presence of label noise: a survey.
   IEEE Trans. Neural Netw. Learn. Syst. **25**(5), 845–869 (2013)
6. Gamberger, D., Lavrac, N., Dzeroski, S.: Noise detection and elimination in data
   preprocessing: experiments in medical domains. Appl. Artif. Intell. **14**(2), 205–223
   (2000)

7. Guan, D., Yuan, W., Shen, L.: Class noise detection by multiple voting. In: 2013 Ninth International Conference on Natural Computation (ICNC), pp. 906–911. IEEE (2013)
8. Hata, H., Mizuno, O., Kikuno, T.: Fault-prone module detection using large-scale text features based on spam filtering. Empir. Softw. Eng. **15**(2), 147–165 (2010). https://doi.org/10.1007/s10664-009-9117-9
9. John, G.H.: Robust decision trees: removing outliers from databases. KDD **95**, 174–179 (1995)
10. Kim, S., Whitehead Jr., E.J., Zhang, Y.: Classifying software changes: clean or buggy? IEEE Trans. Softw. Eng. **34**(2), 181–196 (2008)
11. Mizuno, O., Ikami, S., Nakaichi, S., Kikuno, T.: Spam filter based approach for finding fault-prone software modules. In: Proceedings of the Fourth International Workshop on Mining Software Repositories, p. 4. IEEE Computer Society (2007)
12. Nettleton, D.F., Orriols-Puig, A., Fornells, A.: A study of the effect of different types of noise on the precision of supervised learning techniques. Artif. Intell. Rev. **33**(4), 275–306 (2010). https://doi.org/10.1007/s10462-010-9156-z
13. Ochodek, M., Staron, M., Bargowski, D., Meding, W., Hebig, R.: Using machine learning to design a flexible LOC counter. In: 2017 IEEE Workshop on Machine Learning Techniques for Software Quality Evaluation (MaLTeSQuE), pp. 14–20. IEEE (2017)
14. Pechenizkiy, M., Tsymbal, A., Puuronen, S., Pechenizkiy, O.: Class noise and supervised learning in medical domains: The effect of feature extraction. In: 19th IEEE Symposium on Computer-Based Medical Systems (CBMS 2006), pp. 708–713. IEEE (2006)
15. Pedregosa, F., et al.: Scikit-learn: machine learning in Python. J. Mach. Learn. Res. **12**, 2825–2830 (2011)
16. Sáez, J.A., Luengo, J., Herrera, F.: Evaluating the classifier behavior with noisy data considering performance and robustness: the equalized loss of accuracy measure. Neurocomputing **176**, 26–35 (2016)
17. Sluban, B., Lavrač, N.: Relating ensemble diversity and performance: a study in class noise detection. Neurocomputing **160**, 120–131 (2015)
18. Wohlin, C., Runeson, P., Höst, M., Ohlsson, M.C., Regnell, B., Wesslén, A.: Experimentation in Software Engineering. Springer, Heidelberg (2012). https://doi.org/10.1007/978-3-642-29044-2
19. Zhang, J., Yang, Y.: Robustness of regularized linear classification methods in text categorization. In: Proceedings of the 26th Annual International ACM SIGIR Conference on Research and Development in Informaion Retrieval, pp. 190–197 (2003)
20. Zhao, Q., Nishida, T.: Using qualitative hypotheses to identify inaccurate data. J. Artif. Intell. Res. **3**, 119–145 (1995)
21. Zhu, X., Wu, X.: Class noise vs. attribute noise: a quantitative study. Artif. Intell. Rev. **22**(3), 177–210 (2004). https://doi.org/10.1007/s10462-004-0751-8

On Clones and Comments in Production and Test Classes: An Empirical Study

Steve Counsell[(✉)], Steve Swift, Mahir Arzoky, and Giuseppe Destefnas

Department of Computer Science, Brunel University, London, UK
steve.counsell@brunel.ac.uk

Abstract. While many OO class features have been explored in detail, little work in the past has explored the characteristics of *test* classes. In this exploratory paper, we investigate traits of these classes which we believe demonstrate distinct differences between test classes and production classes. We explore differences between the number of clones, the number of comments and the maintainability of each class type. We believe that developers unjustifiably treat test classes as "second-class citizens" and we would therefore expect test classes to contain a) far more clones, b) a far lower (i.e., poorer) comment density and, c) worse maintainability levels. Six open-source systems were used as a basis of the work. Results showed that all three suppositions were indeed supported; this suggests the need to explore test classes in more detail and to remedy this clear problem that contributes to the level of technical debt.

1 Introduction

Many aspects of code have been empirically studied over the past forty or so years, including those of coupling, cohesion, complexity and size [1,7,11]. These have all contributed to a deep understanding of, for example, how systems evolve and the relationship between those factors and faults [2]. One aspect of empirical analysis that has been overlooked however, (for reasons unknown to the authors) is the relationship between production and (unit) test code. In this paper, we explore those differences from three perspectives: firstly, we examine the number of clones in each type of class [9]. Secondly, the number of comments found in each. Finally, we explore the maintainability of each type of class with respect to clones *and* comments. The general hypothesis running through this paper is that test classes are treated differently by developers and, as a result, they will firstly, contain far more clones than production classes because of regular, haphazard and uncontrolled copy and pasting (cloning). Secondly, they will have fewer comments and thirdly, be more difficult to maintain. We adopt this negative stance because we believe that developers unjustifiably treat test classes "like second class citizens" compared to production classes and, as a result, tend to invest less time in housekeeping activities (test classes consequently "smell" more [4]). We feel that their proper upkeep is as important as any component in a system since they work closely with (and for) a system's production classes.

© Springer Nature Switzerland AG 2020
M. Morisio et al. (Eds.): PROFES 2020, LNCS 12562, pp. 304–311, 2020.
https://doi.org/10.1007/978-3-030-64148-1_19

2 Preliminaries

2.1 Metrics Studied

We analysed different types of feature from six open-source systems. The six systems were first used in a different study by Kadar et al., [6] and it is their data, made freely available for download, that we analyse and use in this paper. The first of the two metrics was the number of instances of clones in a class. Four types of clone can be defined [10]; however, the SourceMeter tool[1] which was used to collect the metrics uses just one, namely: *"Identical code fragments except for variations in white space, layout and comments"*. It is this definition that we use in the paper. The second metric was *Comment Density* (CD) calculated by dividing the total number of comments in a class by the number of lines of code (LOC). A CD value of 0.5 tells us that half the lines in the class are comments; equally, a CD value of zero implies that the class contains zero comments. The metric therefore gives us an idea of the extent of class commenting, relative to class size. We note that the data set of Kadar et al., [6] provided all three of these metrics (i.e., number of clones, CD and LOC). The paper itself examined refactoring and values of source code metrics from open-source systems improved by those refactorings. Their results showed that lower class maintainability triggered more code refactorings in practice; those refactorings decrease complexity, code lines, coupling and clone metrics in those systems. To support *our* analysis, we sub-divided their data set into test and production classes.

2.2 Systems Analysed

In [6], multiple releases of Java open-source systems were used. In this study, however, we chose just the latest version of each system to provide us with the most up-to-date and most *decayed* picture of what the system looked like. A brief summary of each of the six systems follows: Antlr4 is a parser generator for reading or translating structured text or binary files; Junit is a system to write and run repeatable tests and Mapdb an embedded database engine. The Mct system is a NASA-based for visualization framework for mission operations, Oryx a web-based editor for modeling business processes and finally, Titan a system for developers to manage their development artefacts. Table 1 summarises the six systems and shows the URL, number of production classes (Prod.) and number of test classes for each.

3 Data Analysis

3.1 Summary Statistics

Table 2 shows summary data for the clone metric. The table shows the mean and maximum (Max.) values of the metric for the six systems for both production

---

[1] www.sourcemeter.com.

Table 1. Six systems studied (summary data)

System	URL	#Production	#Test
Antlr4	https://github.com/antlr/antlr4	397	119
JUnit	https://github.com/junit-team/junit	152	717
Mapdb	https://github.com/jankotek/MapDB	161	170
Mct	https://github.com/nasa/mct	1341	821
Oryx	https://github.com/cloudera/oryx	469	76
Titan	https://github.com/thinkaurelius/titan	1022	464

(Prod.) and test classes. We note that the median clone value was zero in all six systems and are hence excluded from the table. We see that there is clear trend for clones to be more frequent in test classes than production classes. Looking at the data, the mean number of clones in the former exceeds that of the production data by some margin, except for the JUnit system, but even then, it is only marginal: 0.13 versus 0.11. The notable system is Mapdb. One test class in this system had no less than 2188 clones. Inspection of the raw data revealed this class to be `TreeMapExtendTest`. This class had 1525 methods, 13459 lines of code and was coupled to just one other class. Other classes also featured prominently in the data. The Mct system had a test class containing 137 clones. This was `TestPanAndZoomManager` with 10 methods, 852 lines of code and was coupled to 20 other classes. Equally, the Antlr4 system had a high mean number of clones, with one test class containing 158 clones. This class was called `TestTokenStreamRewriter` and comprised just 47 methods, 865 lines of code and was coupled to 10 other classes.

Table 2. Clone summary data

System	Prod.		Test	
	Mean	Max.	Mean	Max.
Antlr4	0.12	2	8.14	158
JUnit	0.13	4	0.11	9
Mapdb	1.27	33	22.39	2188
Mct	1.13	81	1.86	137
Oryx	0.38	21	0.26	4
Titan	0.16	8	0.81	71

Table 3 shows the CD values for each of the six systems. Here, we include the median values, since, in contrast to the clone data, they were mostly non-zero valued. In keeping with our initial surmise, it is clear from the data that test classes tend to have a lower number of comments given by the CD metric than production classes and, in some cases, significantly so; in fact, for every system, the mean CD in production classes exceeds that of test classes. The most striking feature of the data in Table 3 however, is the wide gap between the mean and median values for each of the systems. For example, the mean CD for production classes was 0.19, but for test classes was only 0.05. This was a trend replicated across almost all six systems (the Oryx system had matching means (0.12)). The system with the highest mean in production classes for CD was JUnit (value 0.20), closely followed by Antlr4 (0.19); this last system had the highest median CD (0.13). Approximately half of the production classes in this system therefore had at least one comment line for every 14–15 lines of code compared with one comment line for every 50 lines of code in its test classes (median 0.02).

Table 3. CD summary data

System	Prod.			Test		
	Mean	Median	Max.	Mean	Median	Max.
Antlr4	0.19	0.13	0.86	0.05	0.02	0.51
JUnit	0.20	0.04	0.81	0.03	0.00	0.80
Mapdb	0.13	0.05	0.95	0.10	0.01	0.78
Mct	0.14	0.03	0.82	0.04	0.00	0.77
Oryx	0.12	0.07	0.60	0.12	0.00	0.77
Titan	0.10	0.05	0.95	0.09	0.03	0.96

3.2 Statistical Analysis

Clones Versus CD. One question arising from the analysis of differences between the Clone and CD data is the extent of the relationship *between* the two sets of data. In other words, is it the case that classes with larger numbers of clones have fewer comments or vice versa? Moreover, does that relationship hold across both production and test classes? We suggest that clones in production classes will have significantly more comments than those in test classes, since developers will take more care of production classes when they clone code and actually think about adding comments when they add a clone. Test classes, on the other hand, will have fewer comments associated with their clone code because developers will simply "dump" clones judiciously into test classes without care and attention to basic housekeeping. To test our position, we extracted the CD for all production and test classes and excluded classes containing zero clones. This gave a sample size of 454 production classes and 621 test classes with at least one clone. Figure 1 shows the plot of CD for production classes and test classes in the six systems. It shows the range of CD values on the x-axis and the percentage that lay in that range on the y-axis. The scale on the x-axis is in increments of 0.1, with the leftmost measure for number of zeros. For example, for production classes, 25.60% of those classes had a value greater than zero and less than or equal to 0.1 (the second pair of bars from the left); the corresponding value for test classes was 36.78%. Fig. 1 shows a trend that we suspected. In the low range of CD values from 0.0–0.1, test classes had a higher frequency. However, from 0.1–0.7, the opposite is the case. The trend implies that test classes had a lower CD than production classes across almost the entire range of CD values and are clearly treated differently to production classes in this sense.

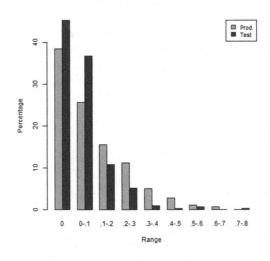

Fig. 1. Plot of CD percentage for classes (Prod. vs. Test)

Maintainability Analysis. We have seen from Table 2 and Table 3 that there were noticeable differences between test and production classes, both in number of clones and in terms of comment lines. To delve a little deeper into the differences between the two types of class, we then explored the relationship between clones and CD in the set of test and production classes through a metric which captures class maintainability. We believe that the presence of clones in a class and a class' number of comments (obtained through the CD metric) have a direct relationship with maintainability. We would expect a class with multiple clones to be less maintainable than one with few clones, since a single change to one clone may require multiple changes to identical clones. Equally, we might reasonably expect a class with relatively few comment lines (and a low CD) to be less maintainable than one with a high CD on the assumption that comments are "useful to have around" for comprehension purposes. To this end, we correlated each set of clone and CD data with the *Relative Maintainability Index* (RMI) metric of Hegedus et al., [5]. The aim of this metric according is to react the level of maintainability of a class compared with the other classes in the system. It is similar to the well-known maintainability index [8], but is calculated using dynamic thresholds from a benchmark database instead of a xed formula. Further technical details of the RMI can be found in [5]. Table 4 shows the results for the six systems and gives three correlation coefficients: Pearson's, Spearman's and Kendall's. Pearson's is a parametric measure and assumes a distribution (i.e., usually normal). Spearman's and Kendall's coefficients are non-parametric, making no assumption about the data distribution (i.e., usually non-normal) [3]. So, for example, for production classes in the Antlr4 system, the three correlation coefficients were all negative and significant (Pearson's value -0.42, Kendall's -0.27 and Spearman's -0.33). In fact, every value in the table shows a negative value; this might be expected from our viewpoint since, in theory, the higher the number of clones in a class, the lower the level of maintainability. If a class has the same snippet of code in multiple places, then any change may also have to be made in multiple places, capturing one reason why cloning is considered danger-ous. What is interesting about Table 4 is the large difference between the values for production and test classes. In every case apart from the Oryx system (and a single value for Mct), the significance values for test classes exceeded those of production classes. This suggests that the effect on maintainability of clones in test classes is far more pronounced than for production classes. In other words, the greater the number of clones, the more difficult it is to make a change(s) to that class. This supports our initial view that test classes get relatively low support and are less well maintained than test classes. The presence of clones makes the job of the developer in maintaining classes more difficult.

Table 4. Correlation data for clones vs. RMI

System	Prod.			Test		
	Pear.	Kend.	Spear.	Pear.	Kend.	Spear.
Antlr4	-0.42	-0.27	-0.33	-0.67	-0.66	-0.79
JUnit	-0.17	-0.23	-0.27	-0.29	-0.24	-0.30
Mapdb	-0.75	-0.44	-0.54	-0.97	-0.51	-0.62
Mct	-0.54	-0.45	-0.56	-0.49	-0.46	-0.57
Oryx	-0.55	-0.43	-0.52	-0.51	-0.39	-0.49
Titan	-0.25	-0.25	-0.30	-0.82	-0.38	-0.46

Table 5 shows the correlation values for CD against RMI. In this table, an '∗' denotes that the value was **not** significant at the 1% level. Most of the values in the table are negative and significant at the 1% level. This is particularly true of the JUnit system, which has the highest correlation values. Many of the value (13 of the 36) however, were not significant at the 1% level. This seemed to be more pronounced in the Mapdb and Oryx systems; many (8 in number) of the '∗' values are in test classes. While the over-riding message is that the higher the CD, the lower the RMI and vice versa, this is not the case as much for test classes in some systems. From the data, maintainability is not influenced as highly by comments in test classes to the extent it is in production classes.

Table 5. Correlation data for CD vs.RMI

System	Prod.			Test		
	Pear.	Kend.	Spear.	Pear.	Kend.	Spear.
Antlr4	−0.07*	−0.14	−0.21	−0.24	−0.42	−0.57
JUnit	−0.24	−0.23	−0.31	−0.17	−0.22	−0.28
Mapdb	−0.07*	−0.27	−0.37	0.02*	−0.09*	−0.14*
Mct	−0.03*	−0.13	−0.18	−0.07*	−0.17	−0.23
Oryx	−0.08*	−0.17	−0.26	0.00*	0.02*	−0.06*
Titan	−0.10*	−0.26	−0.37	−0.02*	−0.17	−0.24

4   Discussion

The preceding analysis raises some interesting discussion points. The first question that naturally arises is why these results were found for test classes? We believe that test classes are seen as a necessary part of any system, but there is an attitude that because they are not the *public face* of a system and are very much in the background, they are treated accordingly. Of course, we have only looked at a few aspects of test classes and it may be the case that other OO aspects might show the relationship in a different light. One interesting avenue for future work would be to explore fault incidence in each class type. This might help pinpoint with more certainty the true influence of clones and comments and how they aid or hinder maintainability. If faults occur less in test classes, then our results becomes academic only. Also, in this paper, we have assumed that comments are a generally beneficial thing to have in code and that a low CD value reflects poor practice. We accept that comments have their darker side; sometimes, inaccurate comments are worse than no comments. However, generally speaking, it is accepted that comments are useful. We have also assumed that clones are bad practice; yet one of the main reasons why cloning takes place is to prevent the rewrite of code that already exists. We think that it is the side effects of this process where the danger lies (poor copying and pasting practice).

We also need to consider the threats to the validity of the study. Firstly, we only used six systems in our study. In this short paper, our intention was to highlight key features of production and test classes and we fully intend to illustrate more issues in a later, wider study. Secondly, we have assumed that maintainability, as measured by the RMI metric properly captures elements of the maintenance process. In defence of the metric, Hegedus et al., [5] showed that it accurately captured many of the intuitive aspects of the process and we feel confident using it on that basis. Thirdly, it may be that other types of clone (apart from that studied) have a more sinister effect on classes of both types on maintainability and class composition. For example, clones that carry out the same computation but use different variable names. Fourthly, this is a short research paper and there are many aspects of the work that we would have liked to, but could not cover (e.g., a full literature review, an analysis of further metrics). The sole intention of the work however, was to explore the ideas and present preliminary findings. Finally, we have only examined open-source systems. It may be that the same traits do not arise in commercial software; we also leave this question for further work.

5   Conclusions and Future Work

In this paper, we explored the characteristics of test classes in six open-source systems. Our aim was to establish traits in test classes compared to that of production classes. Our supposition was that test classes were given less attention by developers and that would firstly, contain far more clones than production classes because of regular, haphazard and uncontrolled copy and pasting (cloning); secondly, would have fewer comments and thirdly, be more difficult to maintain. We adopted this stance because we believed that developers care less about test class upkeep, treat test classes like second class citizens compared to production classes and, as a result, tend to invest less time and effort in basic housekeeping activities on test classes; our results bore out our initial views. Future work will focus on repeating this analysis with more systems and to investigate other OO aspects such as coupling with class type.

References

1. Basili, V., Briand, L., Melo, W.: A validation of OO design metrics as quality indicators. IEEE Trans. Soft. Eng. **22**(10), 751–761 (1996)
2. Cartwright, M., Shepperd, M.: An empirical investigation of an object-oriented software system. IEEE Trans. Softw. Eng. **26**(8), 786–796 (2000)
3. Field, A.: Discovering Statistics Using IBM SPSS Statistics, 4th edn. Sage Publications Ltd., Thousand Oaks (2013)
4. Fowler, M.: Refactoring: Improving the Design of Existing Code. Addison-Wesley Longman Publishing Co., Inc., Boston (1999)
5. Hegedus, P., Bakota, T., Ladányi, G., Faragó, C., Ferenc, R.: A drill-down approach for measuring maintainability at source code element level. Commun. EASST **60** (2013)
6. Kadar, I., Hegedus, P., Ferenc, R., Gyimothy, T.: A manually validated code refactoring dataset and its assessment regarding software maintainability. In: PROMISE 2016, Ciudad Real, pp. 10:1–10:4. ACM (2016)
7. McCabe, T.J.: A complexity measure. IEEE Trans. Softw. Eng. **2**(4), 308–320 (1976)
8. Oman, P., Hagemeister, J.: Metrics for assessing a software system's maintainability. In: Proceedings of the Conference on Software Maintenance, pp. 337–344 (1992)
9. Roy, C., Cordy, J.: Benchmarks for software clone detection: a ten-year retrospective. In: Software Analysis, Evolution and Reengineering, SANER, Campobasso, Italy, pp. 26–37. IEEE Computer Society (2018)
10. Roy, C., Cordy, J., Koschke, R.: Comparison and evaluation of code clone detection techniques and tools: a qualitative approach. Sci. Comput. Program. **74**(7), 470–495 (2009)
11. Stevens, W.P., Myers, G.J., Constantine, L.L.: Structured design. IBM Syst. J. **13**(2), 115–139 (1974)

Social and Human Aspects

Dimensions of Consistency in GSD: Social Factors, Structures and Interactions

Outi Sievi-Korte[1]($\boxtimes$), Fabian Fagerholm[2], Kari Systä[1], and Tommi Mikkonen[3]

[1] Tampere University, Tampere, Finland
outi.sievi-korte@tuni.fi, kari.systa@tuni.fi
[2] Aalto University, Espoo, Finland
fabian.fagerholm@aalto.fi
[3] University of Helsinki, Helsinki, Finland
tommi.mikkonen@helsinki.fi

Abstract. Global software development (GSD) implies a distributed development organization, where coordination is needed to efficiently achieve development objectives. So far, socio-technical congruence has examined coordination needs and activities through software code dependencies. However, GSD requires coordination beyond software artifacts. In this paper, we present an interview-based study of software practitioners from companies engaged in GSD. The study examines how different dimensions of interactions are interrelated, and how they affect software development. Our study suggests that, in addition to the relationship between organizational and technical system structure, GSD performance is affected by consistency in communication, operational procedures, and social structures. These can only partially be impacted through formal procedures, and we suggest that distributing coordination work by empowering developers could lead to increased performance.

Keywords: Global software development · Human factors · Socio-technical system · Coordination · Communication

1 Introduction

Global software development (GSD) can be defined as "software work undertaken at geographically separated locations across national boundaries in a coordinated fashion involving real time (synchronous) and asynchronous interaction" [25]. GSD is said to have several benefits in terms of productivity, cost savings, skill pool access, and customer proximity [1], but it accentuates the need to coordinate work tasks among those involved. With group members being separated geographically, temporally, and culturally, coordination becomes more difficult.

The concept of socio-technical congruence (STC) captures the notion of a relationship between coordination needs and actual coordination activities: if there is a match between the two, congruence is high (and vice versa) [8]. STC can be measured through a family of techniques that are based on extracting task

© Springer Nature Switzerland AG 2020
M. Morisio et al. (Eds.): PROFES 2020, LNCS 12562, pp. 315–330, 2020.
https://doi.org/10.1007/978-3-030-64148-1_20

dependencies from source code repositories [26]. Files that are commonly changed together are assumed to have a technical dependency [8]. It is thus possible to calculate to what extent current coordination activities, as played out through the communication and collaboration tools used by software developers, match the dependencies indicated by previous source code change sets.

Several researchers have identified factors that can hamper coordination in GSD, and ways in which sub-optimal coordination can surface as a worsening in STC metrics [26]. However, STC does not draw a complete picture of coordination challenges in GSD. STC measurements use after-the-fact data that describe some of the most detailed-level tasks operating closest to or directly on the source code. They do not consider the planning and deliberation that precedes these tasks, the coordination judgments that are made while the tasks are carried out, or the human relationships that form the basis of coordination. A study on architectural design in GSD [29] implies that many issues voiced by practitioners concern social interactions and the organization of communication.

Increasing STC requires additional effort in the form of specific coordination activities, which run the risk of decreasing developer productivity [26]. STC techniques do not describe how to avoid such risks. What is often overlooked in GSD is its effect on developers' behavior and habits, and a consideration of the cognitive, affective, motivational, and social processes involved. From that perspective, coordination in GSD is an active human process unfolding in a socio-technical system. Its results can be partially observed by measuring STC – but to understand the process itself, we must look beyond artifact repositories.

In this paper, we aim to uncover more of the social factors, structures, and interactions that are at play when the coordination process unfolds in GSD. We utilize the data collected by Sievi-Korte et al. [29] to find instances of social aspects of coordination in GSD. We describe factors that influence the quality of the coordination process, describe threats to that process, and discuss means by which those threats might be mitigated. Through this knowledge, we aim to assist organizations that wish to utilize GSD to gain more of the potential benefits while avoiding adverse effects on both internal and external stakeholders.

2   Background

When practicing GSD, temporal, geographical, and socio-cultural distance has a direct and immediate effect on developers' socio-technical environment. For example, time-zone differences make communication asynchronous. Emails and even instant messages receive delayed answers, and phone and video calls are difficult to schedule with no overlapping office hours between sites. Product development may be slowed, rather than allowing effective utilization of time zone differences [7]. Increased coordination needs present another challenge, and can arise due to delays, integration issues, and mismatches in required skills. Inspired by Conway's Law [9], researchers have examined STC, formal communication structures, and tool support as vehicles for improved coordination (e.g., [2]). To successfully operate in a GSD setting, developers should thus be able to consider how their own actions influence both the social and technical sides of the software development activity.

Difficulties in distributed software projects can be forecasted by various theories and empirical findings in the organizational, behavioral, and social sciences. For example, when groups bring their behaviors under normative control, those norms begin to regulate team members' behavior [11]. Norms usually develop informally from corporate and national cultures, but may be set collectively or by leaders through rewards and sanctions. Unless their norms are compatible, different groups may expect different behaviors, causing misinterpretation of actions and intentions, and resulting in inefficiency and enmity [6]. This provides an explanation of a social mechanism influencing software projects: norm alignment requires communication, and hinges on the complexity, richness, and speed of the real communication networks connecting developers. In other words, addressing the problem requires entering the social world of developers and agreeing on behavioral changes. It then becomes necessary to trust developers' social skills and adapting formal procedures and structures to support them.

Relying on developers' social skills requires that the management is more informed regarding the mechanisms of social behavior among developers. An understanding of the social aspects of software development and promoting social awareness and constructive social behavior among developers (see [21]) can begin to address the deeper issues involved. Those issues are present at the level of individuals, but they also become built into the processes, working methods, and artifacts involved in software projects – all part of the socio-technical system in which software development happens. Failing to take social behavior into account may lead to accumulating social debt in the organization, which in turn leads to deterioration of the software itself [32].

Through practitioner workshops, Rothman and Hastie [24] found issues related to how the socio-technical environment is set up. For example, enforcing processes does not work if inter-team practices are not considered. Not enabling meetings ends up costing more than arranging meetings between sites as issues accumulate due to lack of trust. Teams struggle with handling inequality and accommodating differences. However, the reasons behind these issues were not studied further. We attempt to address this gap in the present paper.

Solutions to software engineering problems are often sought in technical methods and practices, but many problems in GSD require a different approach. Sievi-Korte et al. [27] used a systematic literature review (SLR) to create a conceptual model of software architecting in GSD. The model encompasses areas such as ways of working, knowledge management, and task allocation – all subject to communication and process challenges that could potentially be mitigated by architecting guidelines and technical solutions. These challenges and potential solutions were further investigated in an empirical study [29]. The empirical study revealed an abundance of issues that stemmed from social interactions between stakeholders and the organization of communication. Mechanisms based on repository measurement or tools were not able to bring adequate solutions. Such social and behavioral issues are further investigated in the present paper.

3   Research Approach

We utilize data from an earlier study by Sievi-Korte et al. [29], that consists of semi-structured interviews with 13 software developers or architects from seven companies engaged in GSD. All participants had several years of experience from globally distributed projects. Five companies had their headquarters in Finland and two in other countries (Europe and North America). The interview questions were based on the results obtained in an SLR [27].

The previous study [29] collected challenges and practices that practitioners faced doing software architecture design in the context of GSD. In this study, we focus only on material that did *not* consider architecting challenges or practices. Instead, we reanalyze the data to examine the social side of software development. An initial extraction of data relevant to this theme gave us a working set of 109 quotes[1]. As Sievi-Korte et al. [29] only concentrated on findings related to architectural design, this paper thus complements their findings.

Research Questions. As mentioned above, current methods based on STC that utilize the structural dependency between technical artifacts and communication seem insufficient to tackle challenges that have been reported in GSD. We should thus expand the picture and assume that more flexible structures are needed in large-scale software development. We should more carefully consider the social mechanisms that underlie the challenges in GSD also from other perspectives than development activities and related artifacts. We pose the following research questions in the context of software product design in GSD:

> RQ1: *How does the coordination process in GSD manifest in terms of social factors, structures, and interactions?*
> RQ2: *What factors influence the quality of the coordination'process?*
> RQ3: *How can the threats to the coordination process be mitigated?*

Research Process. The research process for this study is depicted in Fig. 1 and described below. During the process we used thematic analysis [5]. First, in an *initial analysis* of the interviews, conducted jointly by all authors, there appeared to be repeating patterns in the challenges described by the practitioners. As an experiment, we divided individual quotes from the interviews equally between all authors and attempted to extract anti-patterns from them, if possible. Each found anti-pattern was expected to include context containing a problem, (wrong) solution to the problem, and (negative) consequences.

We then conducted a joint workshop to *validate* the found anti-patterns. During the workshop we examined each anti-pattern on completeness and discussed it in relation to the original quote. At this time we could immediately see that 1) not all quotes had resulted in anti-patterns, and 2) in many cases the anti-pattern was incomplete, i.e., either there was not enough context in the

---

[1] The transcripts were coded in full by the first author. The codes "practice" and "challenge" were predetermined; other codes were freely generated during the coding process. The coding process has been reported elsewhere in detail [28].

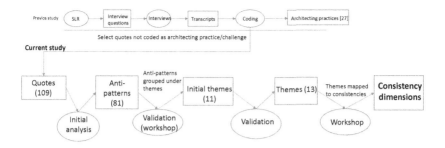

Fig. 1. Research process

quote, or the solution or consequences was unclear. We decided not to pursue with anti-patterns in the sense that they would be presented as a result of this study. However, we did continue using the anti-pattern drafts in our analysis, as they had allowed us to abstract the vast number of often very verbose quotes into a condensed format, easing their further analysis. Reviewing the set of anti-patterns, we could identify a number of recurring *themes* from keywords found in the patterns. Based on the validation workshop notes, one author created a set of 11 initial themes, and coded the anti-patterns according to the themes. Doing so, it appeared that each anti-pattern supported two themes, and thus was coded with a primary and secondary theme.

The themes and coding were *validated* by all other authors. Each of them individually and separately attempted to code the anti-patterns using the initial themes. When we cross-checked our coding, we could find a number of conflicts. Upon solving conflicts in the coding, the set of themes was redesigned to contain 13 different themes, which all authors agreed upon. We then conducted a second joint *workshop* to resolve the remaining conflicts. As a way to resolve the conflicts, we revisited the data in a more holistic manner, going back to the original quotes and the context surrounding them. We shortly noticed that while STC could easily be seen as an underlying phenomenon behind many of the themes, they appeared to touch other dimensions as well that were yet undefined. In the end we could see that the intertwined dimensions of individual developer and organization could complement STC. These dimensions are discussed in the following.

4 Results

Our analysis uncovered two sets of themes that we call *consistency dimensions*. Communication between and within teams and sites, in all forms reported by the participants, were grouped as *communication consistency*. The relationships between technical processes, organizational hierarchy and the social interactions between developers were termed *operational consistency*. We also saw how the dimensions of social interactions, communication, and processes were linked to STC. We see these consistency dimensions as independent of, yet interlinked with, STC. Whereas STC is grounded in detailed code artifacts, our consistency dimensions concern other parts of the socio-technical system where software development happens. They currently lack a numerical operationalization like the STC metrics discussed previously. In this paper, they are instead represented by the themes that specify concrete problems related to each consistency dimension.

Figure 2 presents the themes forming our model of social interactions in GSD organizations. The themes either describe communication (in)consistency or operational (in)consistency. Our two consistency dimensions are linked to STC both as concerns that individual developers may have to address and as aspects of the overall socio-technical system (represented by the outermost gear with its corresponding distances; see, e.g., [1,13]). At the heart of our model is the developer, who must find means to communicate with others, follow processes, and produce technical artifacts – and engage in social interactions during such activities. In the following, we first describe the themes (highlighted in bold) together with quotes from our interviewees, to illuminate the abstract consistency dimensions, and then discuss the model as a whole.

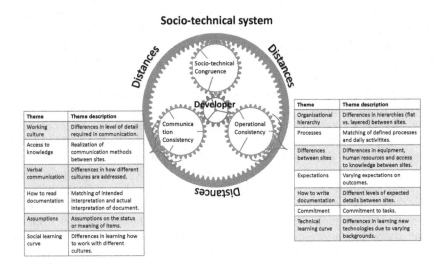

Fig. 2. Social interactions in a GSD organization.

4.1 Communication Consistency

Communication consistency concerns the match between *ways* (technical arrangement of communication), *forms* (presentation of content) and *balance* (amount of interaction) of communication in different parts of the organization and between individuals. Major issues in communication may arise from **differences in working cultures** between sites. Cultural misunderstandings can result in severe difficulties, such as avoidant behavior, as in this example: *"the* *issue is that in some cultures you don't tell the manager something won't be done, you only tell him when you have no choice and that's because it is due now, and it just isn't there. And that can be a big problem."* This is not necessarily a factor of any particular culture but rather reflects the lack of a trustful relationship between people from different cultures. One party may be accustomed to very direct communication and have a long history with colleagues, whereas another party is used to a more subtle form or has just joined the development effort. In general, it is known that developers' views on productivity varies [19] and that they communicate with their managers in different ways, so it is not surprising that issues arise in GSD when the communication bandwidth is limited or trust has not yet been built.

While **verbal communication** is understandably challenging between different sites, a bigger issue is that when live meetings are not feasible, developers are forced to settle for **reading documentation**. Misunderstandings easily arise, like *"when somebody writes [something that] is perfectly clear to the person who wrote it and their nearby colleagues [but that] can be interpreted entirely differently at a remote site, and that sometimes comes true in differences of implementation"*. These challenges are linked to operational consistency through procedures for how documentation is written. The process and practices for writing documentation should consider that documentation may be used to substitute verbal communication, and thus it needs to be self-explanatory and unambiguous.

Above all else, problems arise from actual lack of communication and from communication that parties are not able to understand. A big issue for practitioners is **assumptions** about what people at other sites know or how they view the project's status and goals. Team mental models – representations of key elements in the environment shared across team members [20] – are critical for mutual understanding among individuals. In GSD, mental models must be shared across geographically separated teams [3]. The salience of key elements may differ considerably between teams at different sites, and the environment may even be completely different, with varying understanding of common key elements. Convergence in mental models does not occur by itself over time even within the same geographically collocated team. Rather, as team member roles become more differentiated, interaction can decrease and the shared mental models decline [16]. These conditions can cause wildly different mental models across distributed teams, leading to assumptions that stifle communications.

Conflicting views may even result in using incorrect information to question solutions. As noted in our material, *"people quite easily develop their own notion of what's going on and their own image on what we're doing, and then all of the work is filtered through that notion, and then they wonder why we're doing this, why aren't we doing that, and they might not realize at any point that we're talking about two different things."* Apart from assumptions on the technical aspects, information may be interpreted incorrectly because of assumptions arising from cultural differences. Easing the **social learning curve** would help communication between developers from different cultures. A concrete example from a case company is to arrange multi-cultural parties to celebrate diversity, instead of treating it as an obstacle.

These issues describe the effects of poor *communication consistency*. Communication has already been identified as a part of STC as a structural property of an organization [8] and as a factor that is associated with development speed [13]. We extend the viewpoint from aspects of communication that are measurable on the surface (number of meetings and interactions) to considering ways, forms, and balance of communication, as well as expectations regarding them. These are factors that stem directly from individual developers, and how they are enabled to and actually do communicate with each other.

Our presentation of communication consistency further supports the Media Synchronicity Theory [10], which states that working communication requires working processes both for *conveyance* (i.e., distributing information), and *convergence* (i.e., reaching a common understanding of the information). Communication consistency in ways, forms and balance are required to enable good conveyance and convergence. The issues we have found are often due to insufficient means (or will) for distributing particular information, or inadequate processing of that information between parties, leading to conflicting views.

To increase communication consistency, two core issues must be addressed. The first is to ensure consistency in how communication is technically arranged. All sites and teams must be provided with adequate means to communicate with each other, thus providing consistent **access to knowledge**. The second is ensuring consistency in how content is communicated, which is much more difficult. Teams and individuals should be able to reflect on their communication mechanisms and recognize critical differences and similarities that prohibit working communication. A method to handle issues leading to inconsistent communication should then be constructed. The method should also promote equality – communication should be a dialogue, effectively requiring developers to use and develop their social skills.

4.2 Operational Consistency

With operational consistency, we mean the extent to which social structures in an organization are aligned with operational structures governing how work is performed. When these are inconsistent, the formal, operational structure pulls in a different direction than what employees do, creating tension and problems. Such issues are amplified when there are inconsistencies between sites.

Differences in **organizational hierarchy** between sites easily create disruptions. Developers working with certain assumptions of organizational hierarchy may find it difficult to interact with others operating under different assumptions, as illustrated in our material: *"because in Central Europe [there tends to be] a steeper hierarchy. You cannot dismiss the rules of conversation. Architects only talk to architects and software developers to software developers. In Finland, there's no need for such hierarchy. We can speak freely with anyone."* Furthermore, many operational practices include assumptions of organizational structure, e.g., many agile methods assume cross-disciplinary and self-organized teams. This theme is also linked with communication consistency, particularly working culture – the norms and guidelines developers from different sites and cultures are accustomed to, and how they should be communicated to be understood correctly. Operational consistency focuses on organizational structures; communication consistency is concerned with how developers talk about them.

Processes are the primary means to organize software development activities over time, and they contain many assumptions about social work organization. For instance, how strictly processes are followed, how exactly they are assumed to specify what to do, and what developers can do beyond what processes say. Issues related to processes often escalate due to mismatches in **expectations** about results, progress, and what others do: *"it might be that in some places [...] you are told very specifically what you must do and how you must do it, and initiative is not part of the process. Then again others might think that if you just say something very broadly, like start doing something like this, [...] people expect you to be more active [or] you make more independent choices."*

Differences between sites can lead to differences in available resources (both people and equipment). For example, sites A and C in our material were both working on a hardware-dependent piece of software, but had different versions of the hardware. Tests that passed at Site A would fail at Site C. Developers at Site A would *"think that Site C are in the wrong, and then no one knows where the problem is."* Finding the root cause of a problem in such a situation can take a long time, particularly when the other site feels like they are being blamed for problems they have not created. **Commitment** is closely linked to site differences. Feeling blamed for problems, experiencing a lack of respect and not being involved in decision-making will quickly lead to uncommitted developers, particularly at remote sites. Lack of commitment, in turn, will affect how well work is carried out, how processes are followed, and how communication is handled, and thus commitment issues should be carefully handled.

Participants reported issues arising from assumptions that everyone has understood things the same way. Integrating **documentation instructions** into the operational procedures is one way of combating this problem, as in this example from a case company: *"we aim to say every obvious thing out loud ... and then we also write these so-called self-evident truths down in the design documents. "*. Here, developers had noted how mismatches in assumptions could lead to serious problems, and had created a consensus to help each other via documentation. However, inconsistency may arise if sites differ in how they approach the documentation activity: *"I have seen some examples [where expectations], particularly in Site B, for documentation was to be extremely detailed. It's almost instructions [for] 'how to write code', and that's not how we work here.".* We can see how both parties can quickly become equally frustrated – Site A from feeling the need to document items they feel are self-evident, and Site B from feeling they are not being given all the information they need. Flexibility from developers on both sites is required to find a working process.

Operational inconsistency may appear as differences in **technical learning curve**. Developers working at different sites often have different educational backgrounds. Thus, learning new tools and technologies is easier for some than others. If an organization does not give sufficient support via training to bridge this gap, differences in the skill base may result in conflicts.

The aforementioned issues describe poor *operational consistency*. Development processes, practices, ways of working, and other operational methods may be implemented or understood differently at different organizational sites due to differences in organizational structure, local organizational or national culture and norms, or other social factors. Low operational consistency leads to clashes between planned work practices and people's natural social interactions and dynamics around work organization. Operational consistency can be improved if the organization, operational practices, and social interaction between individuals match. Thus, to enforce operational consistency, managers should allow teams of developers (in effect, the organization structure) to flexibly restructure itself around tasks. An organizational structure or mode of working should not be imposed on teams as a matter of standard policy, but such decisions should be based on situational evidence and followed by attention to the social interactions that emerge, leaving room for individuals to take initiative. A key prerequisite of operational consistency is trust. The less trust people at different sites have, the heavier and less flexible processes need to be used. Thus, establishing trust between developers should be a high priority for GSD managers [22].

4.3   Wheels in Motion

To aid the aforementioned challenges in people management and soft issues, we need to explore the GSD organization beyond STC. Our analysis reveals two dimensions affecting GSD – operational and communication consistency – that complement the existing and widely recognized STC. The new consistency dimensions are distinct from STC as they do not directly concern the software artifacts under development. Rather, they reflect the fit between work imagined on the drawing board and how developers are actually able to carry it out.

The different consistencies in our model are interlinked, and *if one wheel breaks, the whole system comes to a halt*. Problems in one organizational dimension will reflect on and spread to other dimensions (see Fig. 2). Poor operational consistency is often caused, e.g., by processes that do not support daily activities, such as those with hierarchies and actions that do not fit agile development within teams. Lack of support for daily activities will easily lead to developers not knowing what they should be doing and with whom. This will soon be visible as erratic communication between developers – a decrease in communication consistency. Vice versa, developers who are unable to properly communicate (inconsistent communication) will likely be unable to follow desired processes. Thus, inadequate support for operational consistency (poor match between daily work and process) will manifest as poor communication, and poor communication consistency will reflect back on operational consistency. The two will impact STC, as they either disrupt coordination activities or deteriorate the software architecture in such a way that coordination no longer matches what the organization is capable of handling. Improvement and maintenance actions that strive to make GSD work better must focus on the root causes within the consistency dimensions. Similarly – if communication between developers is fluent, hick-ups in processes are easier to solve, and when processes support daily tasks, there is both less need for communication and better grounds for fruitful, two-way conversations.

Finally, distances affect the consistency dimensions. We saw social distance particularly in issues related to organizational hierarchies, inequality, commitment, working culture, assumptions and social learning curve. Temporal and geographical distance were visible particularly in processes and communication mechanisms – how to handle development tasks and communication when face-to-face meetings are not possible. Distances also often create distrust, and unclear reasoning (often due to poor communication) can also easily create fear. Fear and distrust can cause inconsistency, and that inconsistency can feed distrust in a vicious cycle. Similar findings, stressing the need to agree about the norms of work and build discipline toward the process are reported by Piri [22].

5   Discussion

Our empirical material suggests that social factors in GSD can be viewed as a multi-dimensional system, having two consistency dimensions interacting with STC, all affecting one another and being influenced by distances. In the following we will discuss our research questions and the limitations of our study.

5.1   The Socio-technical System

Based on our study, we propose reconsidering how we view GSD. We set out to study social interactions in GSD, starting with RQ1: *How does the coordination process in GSD manifest in terms of social factors, structures, and interactions?*. The coordination process in GSD manifests in terms of social factors, structures, and interactions as a model with two consistency dimensions. With STC, these form a system (as given in Fig. 2) that can explain why coordination works or breaks down in the interactions between individual developers and the overall socio-technical system that is active in GSD.

We wanted to probe deeper in to the coordination process with RQ2: *"What factors influence the quality of the coordination process?"*. The quality of the coordination process is influenced by the degree of consistency in the communication and operational dimensions. Our interview material highlights the difficulties practitioners face when there are inconsistencies between processes and practices. A lack of consistency commonly caused increased dissatisfaction, lack of motivation, and frustration among the practitioners. These co-occur with delays in schedule and with sub-optimal quality of the resulting software.

Finally, our attempt was to elicit a way of correcting found issues in addition to just identifying them, as we posed RQ3: *"How can the threats to the coordination process be mitigated?"*. The first step is to identify how inconsistencies in communication and operations can threaten effective coordination of software development. These threats can then be mitigated by distributing coordination work and empowering developers to coordinate their parts of the socio-technical system. Distributing coordination work requires workforce training and a high degree of trust. It also requires improving ways, forms, and balance in communication and aligning the formal, operational structure in the organization with the natural social interaction structures that exist on an interpersonal level. These activities could be built into the software development process by including distributed coordination activities on all levels of the organization.

Accepting that the development of any large piece of software requires social interaction, the stereotypical image of a programmer as technology-oriented and socially inept is challenged in GSD. A developer should be capable of adapting to different communication styles to increase communication consistency as well as to different ways of coordinating work to increase operational consistency. Several of the comments by participants in our study shows that some developers are already tacitly aware of such issues.

Achieving wide improvement in GSD escapes formal definitions of organization, processes, and procedures, and relies on organizations' ability to foster social developers and their cooperative skills. Furthermore, relying on developers' social skills requires that the management is more informed regarding the mechanisms of social behavior among software developers.

5.2   Related Work

Mariani [17] presents recent advances in coordinating socio-technical systems, and stresses the need to include socio-cognitive aspects in technical solutions from the very beginning of design. While current work in GSD mostly relates to the technical-to-social mindset as defined by Mariani, we could utilize the principles and theories of social-to-technical mindset to improve coordination. Similar relationships between social protocols, coordination mechanisms (operations) and communication, as presented here, have also been given as a framework by Giuffrida and Dittrich [12]. They base the framework on theories of coordination mechanisms and communicative genres, and support the rather abstract framework with ample examples from their empirical study. However, this framework concentrates heavily on communication alone, while we present a more balanced view of the different social aspects in GSD projects.

Furthermore, Jolak et al. [15] discuss communication aspects of GSD in the light of geographical and social distance. They analyzed the categories of collaborative discussions in joint design tasks and noted that collocated and distributed teams differed in the quality of the communication – the amount of creative debate was smaller in distributed cases. This can be seen as lack of communication consistency and is assumed to lead poorer design since creative thinking and constructive criticism are reduced. Robinson [23], in turn, reports findings how team members spread across sites do not feel that they belong into the same team, even though week-long face-to-face meetups are arranged twice a year. This highlights the need for continuously upholding communication consistency. Similar problems in communication consistency, and particularly the *form* and *balance* of communication have been identified by Stray et al. [31], who studied the use of Slack in virtual agile teams. They noted that even when using such direct messaging, there are significant differences in levels of activity, stemming mainly from language skills and knowledge level. Further, using too much personal mode was found a barrier - supporting our identification of social learning curve as an essential theme in communication consistency.

Problems similar to what we found with regard to operational consistency have also been reported by Hussain et al. [14] in the context of requirements management and informal change requests. Informal requirement changes are a direct product of deviating from defined processes, and contain elements of challenges related to organizational hierarchy, varying expectations and inequality between sites – all elements of operational consistency. Furthermore, Björn et al. [4] also report issues around similar themes in their empirical study on how agile methods were adopted in a global setup – severe challenges were discovered as a direct result of inadequate matching of operations (development methodology) and social interactions.

Finally, Sigfridsson [30] reports empirical findings from an organization where consistency was well supported. Teams would actively work on and adjust their practices to allow for better collaboration across sites, and the organization had several actions alleviating, e.g., inequality between sites, such as worldwide seminars to learn new technologies. In the organization in question, teams did not think of distribution as a problem, but just as a mundane thing. This work shows how truly important it is to support and achieve a balance of consistencies.

5.3   Limitations and Validity

There are some limitations to be addressed regarding our study, namely completeness, potential bias and limits to data synthesis. In addition to limitations, as with any study, we must consider the potential threats to the validity of our results. We address threats to validity following Maxwell's categorization [18].

Limitations. We first consider potential bias. While the first author was involved in a previous study utilizing the same interview material as here, none of the other three authors were involved in the previous study in any way. There were thus three researchers, who had a neutral and objective stance to the material, validating all the findings. As all steps in the research process were defined jointly and included validation with all authors involved, we are confident that there are no substantial risks related to bias.

Second, we consider the completeness and coverage of our interview material. While one could always wish for a larger set of interviewees, thirteen interviewees already gives us a credible sample when we consider the variance in companies. Our interview material was gained from seven different companies, covering together almost 20 different sites, with headquarters in three different countries. The companies also varied in sizes and domain.

Finally, we need to consider the limits of our data synthesis. We used a form of thematic analysis [5], which potentially lacks in transparency. To avoid this potential drawback, all steps leading to creation of the consistency model have been validated - anti-patterns derived from the quotes, coding of anti-patterns under themes, and arranging of themes in the consistency model. Thus, we have traceability from our model back to raw data (quotes) as well as validated outcomes. However, the actual creation of our consistency model did not follow a strict procedure, but is a product of joint interpretative synthesis conducted in a workshop setting, and we acknowledge the weakness of its repeatability.

Threats to Validity. Descriptive validity concerns accurate recording and presentation of the data, based on which conclusions are made. All the interviews were recorded, and the recordings were transcribed by an independent professional. Transcriptions were copied verbatim into an analysis tools (NVivo), from which individual quotes have been extracted. In case a single quote was difficult to interpret, using the tool it was easy to find the context surrounding the quote.

Threats related to theoretical validity are ultimately concerned with whether we captured what we intend to in relation to our hypothesis. Our study was exploratory. As we had no hypothesis, but an open research question, there were no risks that interview subjects, questions or the process would be biased towards confirming our hypothesis. However, there are validity threats regarding how well our material is suited to answer our research questions. The interview protocol was not designed to uncover issues or practices related to social interactions. Thus, issues discovered in the interviews may lack sufficient context or details.

Interpretive validity threats concern correct interpretations of the material. As discussed above, we consider researcher bias not to be a real risk in this study, as we did not have a clear hypothesis or a pre-determined vision of how the material would answer our research question. The results were derived purely based on the research process and combined analyses of the researchers. To strengthen the validity of our joint analyses, we always referred back to the original interview quotes and checked that the quotes supported our findings.

Regarding generalizability, we are confident that internal generalizability (within the field of software engineering) is fairly well satisfied due to variance in the represented companies in terms of size, involved sites and domains. There is no reason to believe that the results would not in general apply to companies in the field of software engineering involved in GSD.

6   Conclusion

We explored social factors affecting GSD beyond those defined as a part of STC. We specifically wanted to answer questions related to the coordination process in GSD, it's quality and how can threats to the process be mitigated. Our research has led to a new model of the GSD organization, composed of two consistency dimensions, STC, the developer at the center, and distances affecting all actions.

Solving the problems of GSD requires continuous attention to multiple, complex and interlinked phenomena with organizational, architectural, operational, cultural, and communication factors. Given the complexity of this challenge, it is unlikely that a formal, top-down approach alone will be successful. The role of management shifts towards incentivizing, coaching and mentoring, and providing developers with resources they need to accomplish organizational goals. By identifying threats related to inconsistencies and carefully considering the interlinked nature of organizational dimensions as revealed in our study, GSD organizations can increase consistency in all dimensions and make their software development engine run more smoothly.

References

1. Ågerfalk, P.J., Fitzgerald, B., Holmström Olsson, H., Ó Conchúir, E.: Benefits of global software development: the known and unknown. In: Wang, Q., Pfahl, D., Raffo, D.M. (eds.) ICSP 2008. LNCS, vol. 5007, pp. 1–9. Springer, Heidelberg (2008). https://doi.org/10.1007/978-3-540-79588-9_1
2. Bano, M., Zowghi, D., Sarkissian, N.: Empirical study of communication structures and barriers in geographically distributed teams. IET Softw. **10**(5), 147–153 (2016)
3. Bass, M.: Monitoring GSD projects via shared mental models: a suggested approach. In: Proceedings of the 2006 International Workshop on Global Software Development for the Practitioner, GSD 2006, pp. 34–37. ACM, New York, NY, USA (2006)
4. Bjørn, P., Søderberg, A.M., Krishna, S.: Translocality in global software development: the dark side of global agile. Hum. Comput. Interact. **34**, 174–203 (2019)
5. Braun, V., Clarke, V.: Using thematic analysis in psychology. Qual. Res. Psychol. **3**(2), 77–101 (2006)
6. Carmel, E., Agarwal, R.: Tactical approaches for alleviating distance in global software development. IEEE Softw. **18**(2), 22–29 (2001)
7. Casey, C., Richardson, I.: Implementation of global software development: a structured approach. J. Softw. Evol. Process **14**(5), 247–262 (2009)
8. Cataldo, M., Herbsleb, J.D., Carley, K.M.: Socio-technical congruence: a framework for assessing the impact of technical and work dependencies on software development productivity. In: Proceedings of the Second ACM-IEEE International Symposium on Empirical Software Engineering and Measurement, pp. 2–11. ACM (2008)
9. Conway, M.E.: How do committees invent? Datamation **14**(4), 28–31 (1968)
10. Dennis, A.R., Fuller, R.M., Valacich, J.S.: Media, tasks, and communication processes: a theory of media synchronicity. MIS Q. **32**(3), 575–600 (2008). http://dl.acm.org/citation.cfm?id=2017388.2017395
11. Feldman, D.C.: The development and enforcement of group norms. Acad. Manag. Rev. **9**(1), 47–53 (1984)
12. Giuffrida, R., Dittrich, Y.: A conceptual framework to study the role of communication through social software for coordination in globally-distributed software teams. Inf. Soft. Technol. **63**, 11–30 (2015). https://doi.org/10.1016/j.infsof.2015.02.013. http://www.sciencedirect.com/science/article/pii/S095058491500049X
13. Herbsleb, J.D., Mockus, A.: An empirical study of speed and communication in globally distributed software development. IEEE Trans. Softw. Eng. **29**, 481–494 (2003)
14. Hussain, W., Zowghi, D., Clear, T., MacDonell, S., Blincoe, K.: Managing requirements change the informal way: when saying 'no' is not an option. In: 2016 IEEE 24th International Requirements Engineering Conference (RE), pp. 126–135, September 2016. https://doi.org/10.1109/RE.2016.64

15. Jolak, R., Wortmann, A., Chaudron, M., Rumpe, B.: Does distance still matter? Revisiting collaborative distributed software design. IEEE Softw. **35**, 40–47 (2018)
16. Levesque, L.L., Wilson, J.M., Wholey, D.R.: Cognitive divergence and shared mental models in software development project teams. J. Organ. Behav. **22**(2), 135–144 (2001)
17. Mariani, S.: Coordination in socio-technical systems: where are we now? Where do we go next? Sci. Comput. Program. **184**, 102317 (2019). https://doi.org/10.1016/j.scico.2019.102317. http://www.sciencedirect.com/science/article/pii/S0167642319301157
18. Maxwell, J.A.: Understanding and validity in qualitative research. Harv. Educ. Rev. **62**, 279–301 (1992)
19. Meyer, A., Fritz, T., Murphy, G., Zimmermann, T.: Software developers' perceptions of productivity. In: Proceedings of the 22nd ACM SIGSOFT International Symposium on Foundations of Software Engineering, pp. 19–29. ACM (2014)
20. Mohammed, S., Ferzandi, L., Hamilton, K.: Metaphor no more: a 15-year review of the team mental model construct. J. Manag. **36**(4), 876–910 (2010)
21. Oshri, I., Kotlarsky, J., Willcocks, L.P.: Global software development: exploring socialization and face-to-face meetings in distributed strategic projects. J. Strateg. Inf. Syst. **16**(1), 25–49 (2007)
22. Piri, A., Niinimäki, T., Lassenius, C.: Fear and distrust in global software engineering projects. J. Softw. Evol. Process **24**, 185–205 (2012)
23. Robinson, P.: Communication network in an agile distributed software development team. In: Proceedings of the ACM/IEEE 14th International Conference on Global Software Development (ICGSE), pp. 90–94 (2019)
24. Rothman, J., Hastie, S.: Lessons learned from leading workshops about geographically distributed agile teams. IEEE Softw. **30**, 7–10 (2013)
25. Sahay, S., Nicholson, B., Krishna, S.: Global IT Outsourcing: Software Development Across Borders. Cambridge University Press, Cambridge (2003)
26. Sierra, J.M., Vizcaíno, A., Genero, M., Piattini, M.: A systematic mapping study about socio-technical congruence.Inf. Softw. Technol. **94**, 111–129 (2018)
27. Sievi-Korte, O., Beecham, S., Richardson, I.: Challenges and recommended practices for software architecting in global software development. Inf. Softw. Technol. **106**, 234–253 (2019)
28. Sievi-Korte, O., Richardson, I., Beecham, S.: Protocol for an Empirical Study on Software Architecture Design in Global Software Development, Lero Technical report No. TR_2019_01 (2019). https://www.lero.ie/sites/default/files/TR_2019_01_Protocol_for_GSD_Arch_Design_Framework.pdf
29. Sievi-Korte, O., Richardson, I., Beecham, S.: Software architecture design in global software development: an empirical study. J. Syst. Softw. **158** (2019). https://doi.org/10.1016/j.jss.2019.110400
30. Sigfridsson, A.: A conceptual framework to study the role of communication through social software for coordination in globally distributed software teams. Ph.D. thesis, University of Limerick, Department of Computer Science and Information Systems (2010)
31. Stray, V., Moe, N.B., Noroozi, M.: Slack me if you can! using enterprise social networking tools in virtual agile teams. In: Proceedings of the ACM/IEEE 14th International Conference on Global Software Development (ICGSE), pp. 101–111 (2019)
32. Tamburri, D.A., Kruchten, P., Lago, P., Vliet, H.: Social debt in software engineering: insights from industry. J. Internet Serv. Appl. **6**(1), 1–17 (2015). https://doi.org/10.1186/s13174-015-0024-6

Ethical Guidelines for Solving Ethical Issues and Developing AI Systems

Nagadivya Balasubramaniam[(✉)], Marjo Kauppinen, Sari Kujala, and Kari Hiekkanen

Aalto University, 02150 Espoo, Finland
{nagadivya.balasubramaniam,marjo.kauppinen,sari.kujala,
kari.hiekkanen}@aalto.fi

Abstract. Artificial intelligence (AI) has become a fast-growing trend. Increasingly, organizations are interested in developing AI systems, but many of them have realized that the use of AI technologies can raise ethical questions. The goal of this study was to analyze what kind of ethical guidelines companies have for solving potential ethical issues of AI and developing AI systems. This paper presents the results of the case study conducted in three companies. The ethical guidelines defined by the case companies focused on solving potential ethical issues, such as accountability, explainability, fairness, privacy, and transparency. To analyze different viewpoints on critical ethical issues, two of the companies recommended using multi-disciplinary development teams. The companies also considered defining the purposes of their AI systems and analyzing their impacts to be important practices. Based on the results of the study, we suggest that organizations develop and use ethical guidelines to prioritize critical quality requirements of AI. The results also indicate that transparency, explainability, fairness, and privacy can be critical quality requirements of AI systems.

Keywords: AI system development · AI ethical issues · AI ethical guidelines · Quality requirements

1 Introduction

The utilization of AI technologies has unlocked significant social benefits [29]. However, the black box nature of AI technologies has raised several ethical questions among its stakeholders concerning safety, privacy, security, and transparency of AI systems [27, 33]. Questions about value priorities and minimizing value trade-offs in designing AI systems have led to several studies on AI ethics [13, 17].

Autonomous systems, such as autonomous cars and health robots, extend ethical issues into a domain where making imprecise recommendations could impact human lives [4, 32]. To develop a responsible AI, human and ethical values need to be embodied in the system design, rather than considering them merely part of an obligatory checklist [13].

Ethical issues, such as bias, diversity, and privacy preferences need to be considered during the software engineering (SE) process [3, 23]. Aydemir and Dalpiaz [3]

© Springer Nature Switzerland AG 2020
M. Morisio et al. (Eds.): PROFES 2020, LNCS 12562, pp. 331–346, 2020.
https://doi.org/10.1007/978-3-030-64148-1_21

highlighted the importance of analyzing ethical issues from the very beginning of SE process, that is, right from the requirements definition. To develop ethical AI, there are over 80 ethical AI guidelines documents and standards [22]. However, studies on applying ethical practices when developing AI are lacking.

The goal of this study was to explore what kind of ethical guidelines companies have for solving potential ethical issues and developing AI systems. First, we performed a literature review to identify the potential ethical issues of AI systems and compared the AI ethical guidelines by three expert groups. Next, we conducted the case study in three Finnish companies and analyzed their ethical guidelines for developing AI systems. The participating companies were from the retail, banking, and software consultancy domains. In this paper, we use "AI systems" to refer to intelligent systems, AI solutions, AI applications, AI services, and AI products.

This paper is organized as follows. Section 2 describes the related work focusing on the ethical issues and ethical guidelines of AI systems. In Sect. 3, we present the research method used in this study. Section 4 describes the results of the analysis of the case companies' AI ethical guidelines. In Sect. 5, we discuss how these ethical guidelines can be used during the development of AI systems. Finally, we draw conclusions based on the results of the study and suggest future research directions.

2   Related Work

2.1   Ethical Issues of AI

Organizations are embracing many new digital technologies, such as AI and machine learning. These developments, however, raise new ethical issues that impact their users [33]. The common ethical issues of AI are: autonomy [17, 23, 26, 30], anonymity [14], fairness [23, 26, 30], privacy [17, 23, 30], safety [2, 5, 23, 28, 30], security [23, 26, 28, 30], transparency [16, 23, 30], and trust [16, 23, 28].

Ethical issues related to **autonomy**, **anonymity**, and **privacy** are interrelated. For many AI systems, collecting volumes of personal data from different sources is the cornerstone of their operation. The potential misuse of data could lead to major privacy threats [23]. In some cases, privacy issues of AI are bound to produce both individual- and society-level impacts [17, 30]. Likewise, ethical concerns related to autonomy include 1) the extent to which technologies can influence humans [30], 2) the level of consideration of personal autonomy, such as the surveillance of workers [26], 3) the capacity of individuals to make their own choices [23], and 4) the possibilities of man out-of-the-loop operations and their impact [30].

Data exclusion and discrimination by AI systems lead to the ethical issue of **fairness,** which is also related to public values, such as human dignity and justice [23, 30]. AI technology is expected to cater to everyone without any discrimination with respect to gender, age, accessibility, etc.; it has "the moral obligation to act on fair adjunction between conflicting claims" [23]. One ethical issue AI systems run into, however, is producing unfair outcomes because of data bias, exclusion, or discrimination [30]. For example, profiling users based on their data could lead to unfair outcomes for some user groups [30].

With the influx of new technologies and smart devices, **security** issues are increasingly complex [30]. For instance, hacking a coffee machine in someone's home can help the hackers to open their front door. Similarly, AI **safety** triggers ethical and societal issues. When designing technologies such as autonomous vehicles [11], virtual-reality applications [30], and tracking technologies, such as using GPS to track elderly patients in everyday settings [28, 30], the safety of users is crucial. In the AI system development, compromising users' safety is an ethical issue [28].

The lack of **transparency** in the data used for AI decision-making and the neglect of transparency rights when developing AI systems also create ethical issues [16, 30]. The lack of visibility or simply the black box nature of these AI systems leaves many users confused about certain suggestions made by the AI devices. Transparency represents the significance of the stakeholders' "right to know" [16]. This enables the transparency and **trust** to go hand in hand [16, 23]. Explanations of AI decisions are key to building trustworthy AI systems [16, 28]. Although the lack of explanation does not stop all users from relying on the systems, explanation plays a major role in building trust [28]. Moreover, incorporating adequate measures with respect to ethical issues related to security, privacy, autonomy, and transparency during AI system development helps acquire users' trust [23].

2.2 Ethical Guidelines for Practitioners to Develop AI Systems

More than 80 public and private AI ethical guidelines documents exist [22]. In this literature review, we focus on recently published ethical guidelines by three established expert groups: European Commission's (EU) *Ethical guidelines for trustworthy AI* [18], Institute of Electrical and Electronic Engineers' (IEEE) *Ethically Aligned Design* [19], and Software and Information Industry Association's (SIIA) *Ethical Principles for Artificial Intelligence and Data Analytics* [31]. These high-level guideline documents targeted for all types of organizations, including both the public and private sectors. Table 1 summarizes the ethical guidelines of the three expert groups.

Transparency, autonomy, fairness, safety, and privacy ethical guidelines are related to the ethical issues of AI discussed in the previous section. The ethical guidelines on well-being involve both societal and environmental well-being. Encompassing sustainability and monitoring social impact are key phenomena in the well-being of users [18, 19]. Examining the risks of misuse also protects and prevents AI systems from causing harm. In addition, these expert groups defined explainability, accountability, and responsibility guidelines to consider potential ethical concerns in AI system development. The ethical guidelines on purpose of AI system was defined to clarify the effectiveness and impact of AI systems [19]. Also, the necessity of having teams with diverse skills and competence to operate of AI systems effectively is highlighted in their competence guidelines [18, 19].

Floridi et al. [20] proposed an ethical framework that synthesized the opportunities, risks, recommendations, and principles to develop "Good AI Society". The framework's five ethical principles were beneficence, non-maleficence, autonomy, justice, and explicability [20]. Apart from such AI ethical guidelines documents, other tools are available, such as data ethics canvas [25] and ethics matrix [24], to aid practitioners in identifying ethical issues of AI.

Table 1. Overview of the ethical guidelines of the three expert groups. E – ethical guideline defined explicitly in the document; I – ethical guideline mentioned implicitly in the document.

Ethical guidelines	EU [19]	IEEE [20]	SIIA [32]
Transparency	E	E	E
Well-being	E	E	E
Awareness of misuse and harm	E	E	E
Explainability	E	I	E
Accountability	E	E	
Autonomy	E	E	.
Fairness	E	I	I
Responsibility	I	I	E
Safety	E	I	
Privacy	E	I	
Purpose of AI system	I	E	
Competence	I	E	

3 Research Method

3.1 Research Process

The research question of this study was **what kind of ethical guidelines companies have for solving potential ethical issues and developing AI systems**. We conducted this study using qualitative methods [7] to understand companies' current situations relating on AI ethics and ethical guidelines. As a first step, we defined the objectives and questions of our interviews. Then, the interview questions were validated by senior researchers and improved based on their feedback. Afterward, we conducted two pilot interviews and three actual interviews. Finally, we analyzed the interview data and ethical-guideline documents. The data collection and analysis are described in more detail in the following sections.

The unit of analysis in our empirical research process was a company that had already defined ethical guidelines for developing AI systems. We sought companies that represented different application domains for a multiple cases study, a method that Yin [34] has recommended for exploring a relatively new issue, such as ethical AI. We selected three case companies that were recommended by an AI expert who was knowledgeable about which organizations have already invested in ethical guidelines for AI systems.

3.2 Case Companies

Company A is a software consultancy company. It designs and delivers new digital services and products and has a data science team with around 20 people who are mainly data scientists and coders. Moreover, the company had organized AI ethics coaching for its employees and customers.

Company B is a Finnish retail company involved in the car, food, and building trades. Its AI team comprises of 25 people with different skills and capabilities. At the time of the interviews (2019), it had discussed AI ethics internally for a few years.

Company C is one of the largest financial service providers in Finland with millions of customers. It provides banking and insurance services. It had formed data science teams of 15 persons and started working on ethical AI since 2017. The company has also organized ethics training for its data scientists. Table 2 summarizes each company's number of employees and application domain.

Table 2. Overview of the case companies.

Company	ID for interviewee	Number of employees	Application domain
A	P1	500	Software consultancy
B	P2	~22 500	Retail
C	P3	~12 300	Banking

3.3 Data Collection

This paper's first author designed the interview questions using Boyce and Neale's [6] guidelines, which were then improved based on the feedback received from the three senior researchers, who are the other authors of the paper. We also tested the questions with two practitioners in order to check their feasibility and understandability. We did not make any changes to the interview questions after the pilot testing. However, these two pilot interviews were not included in this study because the first company did not have concrete ethical guidelines for the development of AI systems. The second company of the pilot interviews had recently started to develop a technology platform for helping organizations deliver explainable AI services. A representative at this second company recommended the companies and interviewees for this case study.

We organized our interview questions into two parts: the organizational context of the interviewees, and the ethics and ethical guidelines of their companies. The first two authors of the paper interviewed one person from each case company. The interviewees were deeply knowledgeable about the ethical guidelines of their companies and had closely collaborated with professionals of various backgrounds such as data scientists, designers, and developers.

We conducted the interviews in late 2018 and early 2019. The lengths of the interviews varied from 60 to 80 min. The interviewees agreed to audio recordings of the interviews, and we assured anonymization in results. After the interviews, the interviewees shared the ethical guideline documents of their respective companies.

Company A had designed a data ethics canvas to capture possible ethical issues and the actions needed to mitigate them. The canvas consisted of 40 questions categorized into five sections. The company also shared its AI ethics training document, which contained a set of ethical guidelines. Company B's ethical principles document had five guideline categories and ten guidelines in total. Similarly, Company C had defined five ethical guideline categories in its document.

3.4 Data Analysis

The next step was to analyze the data we collected from the documents and interviews. The audio files from the interviews were transcribed, and the notes taken during the interviews were attached to the transcriptions. We applied the Eisenhardt research method [15] in the data analysis. We performed a within case analysis with the codes categorized based on the ethical issues of AI and created a case description report for each company. Thereafter, based on the case description written for each company, the cross-case analysis method was employed, during which evidence data from one case description was compared to the other cases to report the results [15]. Figure 1 gives an overview of the data analysis process employed in this study.

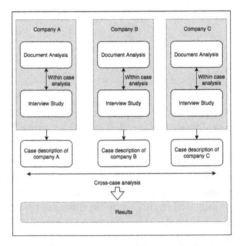

Fig. 1. Overview of data analysis

We used Charmaz's [8] grounded theory method on coding and code-comparison practices to the qualitative interview data for the purpose of analysis only. To elaborate the coding process, the first two authors of this paper first read the documents and transcripts separately. Then, they inductively applied descriptive labels (i.e., "codes") to segments of text in each document and transcript. These high-level categories of codes were formed based on the ethical issues of AI. Next, the first two researchers iteratively compared and discussed the codes and categorizations. Missing codes were added, and ambiguous codes were resolved during the iterations. In addition to the codes related to ethical issues of AI, the authors also identified codes related to ethical practices for solving ethical issues at the case companies.

4 Results

The first subsection below describes what kind of ethical guidelines the case companies have for solving potential ethical issues of AI. The second subsection describes a small set of practices that can support the use of the ethical guidelines during AI system development.

4.1 Ethical Guidelines Focusing on Potential Ethical Issues of AI

Table 3 summarizes the ethical guidelines the case companies defined for developing AI systems, which have been categorized according to potential ethical issues.

Accountability: To ensure accountability, the ethical guidelines of Company A suggest assigning a responsible person to each project to identify any possible unintended consequences of the AI system. Then, the responsible person is in-charge of handling and controlling the harm, ethical issues, and consequences of the AI system.

At Company B, the ethical guidelines for accountability highlighted the importance of responsibility in AI systems. The guideline states that the company is responsible for its AI systems and its decisions. Moreover, the company's data collection and utilization when creating algorithms is driven by acting responsibly. The company is also responsible for AI developed outside the company and used in their systems (P2). At the time of the interview, the data scientists of the company were attempting to open AI black box and trying to understand its underlying decision mechanism, as the company is accountable and responsible for all AI services they provide to customers.

The interviewee at Company B (P2) mentioned that AI ethics is part of the company's sustainable strategy. Therefore, the company and its partners use AI systems to build a better society and a better world. The goal of their corporate responsibility is to improve social welfare, and P2 asserted that the company held itself responsible for creating values for consumers and society.

Company C's ethical guidelines on accountability required defining owners who will be responsible for guiding the company's operations and the algorithms developed by the company. They also aim to keep track of the ethics of AI system throughout its life cycle. The company also focuses on using data and AI responsibly with people-first approach, and its ethical guidelines underscore that the company's choices when applying AI should always be responsible. P3 expressed a high-level viewpoint on corporate responsibility that comprised company responsibility, societal responsibility, and customers' responsibility. Currently, Company C prioritizes societal responsibility, which P3 supported: *"We have to act sustainably in society and take good care of the society.... People expect the bank to do right things."*

The accountability-related ethical guidelines in our case companies associate accountability with developing responsible AI. Companies A and C mentioned defining a person or owner who would be responsible for identifying the unintended consequences and ethical issues of AI. However, Company B portrayed its own responsibility for the decisions of AI systems. In particular, Companies B and C emphasized developing responsible AI as a part of their societal responsibility.

Explainability: The ethical guidelines of Company A comprehended the importance of designing explainability from the beginning of AI system development, which the adoption of the General Data Protection Regulation (GDPR) in the EU pushed them to do (P1). To guide the development teams with respect to explainability, the following basic questions were defined in the data ethics canvas: 1) Is explainability needed? 2) Who needs it? and 3) How much are you able to explain the system? The interviewee also mentioned that considering the explainability from the beginning helps in choosing the right algorithmic model for the AI system.

Table 3. Overview of ethical guidelines and ethical issues of AI

Ethical issue of AI	Ethical guidelines of AI
Accountability (A, B, C)	Decide who will be responsible and contacted if the system is seen causing harm, and decide who in the project resolves ethical issues (A) Use responsibility and security to direct the collection and utilization of the data and the creation of AI solutions and algorithms (B) Be responsible for the AI systems and the decisions they make (B) Define owners for the principles guiding the company's operations and for the algorithms the company has developed. Ensure the ethics of AI throughout its life cycle (C) Use data and AI responsibly for the good of the customers (C)
Explainability (A)	Design and build in explainability from the beginning, where it is paramount to provide justification for the outcomes of the system Do not use manipulative design – instead design for understanding
Fairness (A, B)	Avoid creating or reinforcing bias that can lead to unfair outcomes (A) Use diverse/inclusive training and test data to ensure fairness and inclusivity (A) Respect human rights and the use of AI systems must not lead to discrimination (B)
Privacy (A, B, C)	Collect, store, and use personal data safely and default to high privacy (A) Anonymize data as much as possible (A) Use responsibility and security direct the collection and utilization of the data and the creation of AI solutions and algorithms (B) Protect the data and privacy of the customers (B) Guarantee privacy and personal data protection for the individuals represented in the data used, in accordance with our data protection principles (C)
Transparency (A, B, C)	Prioritize transparency in the system and strive to increase trust in all of them (A) Go for maximum transparency and openness in the system whenever possible (A) Inform transparently to customers of where and how the company utilizes the data they have provided (B) Act openly in relation with customers, partners, and stakeholders, ensuring sufficient transparency for the evaluation of the AI the company has developed (C) Discuss the company's use of AI openly and subject the work to public scrutiny (C)

According to the interviewee P1, explainability is also about understanding. The biggest problem with understandability is that it is difficult to explain an AI system's results, even for the people who built it. Furthermore, P1 said *"It is important to design easy systems to use; that is, whoever is using the system must also know what happens under the hood"*. The problem, however, is that explanations provided by the system are difficult for the users to understand, so they do not add any value (P1).

According to the interviewee at Company B (P2), it is an important, necessary skill for the data scientists to explain the AI systems they create. They should understand what is inside the AI black box, that is, what kind of data there are and how the AI system uses them (P2). Company B highlights explainability as a key part of building responsible AI.

To summarize, the companies represented their ethical guidelines on explainability as a branch of transparency. The interviewees at Companies A and B indicated that explainability was doable by understanding the AI system, and they mentioned a lack of skills in explaining the AI as a hurdle for implementing explainability guidelines.

Fairness: Company A's ethical guidelines on fairness aim to remove bias from its data. Fairness in AI systems is closely related to the inclusion and exclusion of the data, which were described as either overrepresentation or underrepresentation or as bias and gaps in the data. Their ethical guidelines require representation of diverse set of people as possible during AI system design. Likewise, our interviewee (P1) pointed to inclusion as a hot topic in the industry.

One of Company A's ethical guidelines on fairness advocates for avoiding creating or reinforcing bias that produces unfair results. According to P1, *"There is no right way to erase or handle bias, because it is always context sensitive."* The interviewee also mentioned that each team analyzes and decides how to make results less biased, based on their particular project.

The interviewee at Company C pointed to fairness in relation to customers' trust. P3 highlighted it by saying *"To gain the trust of the customer, they have to trust that the bank is doing fair, right and so forth."* P3 added that acting fairly is vital to ethical banking. To elaborate, the key point related to acting fairly is that customers can trust that analysis and decisions that concern them are made correctly by following the correct process (P3). According to the interviewee, fairness concerns not only individuals but also society, so it is ethical to work openly, friendly, and equally to do right things that people expect from the company (P3).

In summary, the companies' fairness ethical guidelines aimed to eliminate bias and discrimination from their data. Company A showcased the need for inclusion in data to achieve fair outcomes. Likewise, Companies B and C described how their AI systems which do not discriminate, helped protecting human rights and contribute to common good to the whole society.

Privacy: The privacy ethical guidelines of Company A focused mainly on personal data protection. The GDPR was a key reason for prioritizing data privacy ethical guidelines. Data anonymization is one way to ensure privacy in AI systems (P1). To handle personal data safely, it is essential to reveal to the users on how their personal data is utilized by the AI system. Their ethical guidelines also emphasized collecting minimal sensitive data from users.

From the Company A interviewee's perspective, privacy and safety are important for any project that deals with data. Furthermore, P1 highlighted that *"AI projects introduce new vulnerabilities, so that we have to be extra careful with data security and privacy.*" Privacy, security and safety were mentioned as tightly coupled concepts by our interviewee. P1 also commented about users' right to check their data privacy in compliance with the GDPR. It is important to make it as easy as possible for users to exercise their rights to data privacy (P1).

The ethical guidelines of Company B on privacy highlighted data protection and the privacy of customers. The interviewee explained that "*it is really important to understand privacy that we are using customer data heavily.*" so, the company needs to ensure what is their rights with respect to customer data (P2). The interviewee also pointed out the influence of the GDPR when creating the data platforms. The GDPR affects how the privacy and security of customer data is handled (P2).

A key concept mentioned by the interviewee was about permission. That is, permission from users to use their data and to combine them with data from other sources. Customers have a right to their data, and they can decline permission to use them (P2). According to P2, the company must be aware of why it is collecting the data, and what kind of permissions it has from its customers.

Company C has ethical guidelines on privacy protection that aim to guarantee privacy and personal data protection to the individuals represented in their data. P3 emphasized that "*banking and financial services are as sensitive as health issues from an ethical point of view and privacy point of view.*" The company also provides data protection and ethics courses which mainly focus on privacy, privacy issues, privacy regulations, data security, and ways to use data in compliance with the GDPR. Because the company complies with privacy laws in the EU (P3), one important question in its training material is about trust and privacy: "*Can customers trust that the information that concerns them stays private?*"

According to the interviewee, the company is trying to protect its rights to utilize the data it collects, especially according to the latest version of privacy regulations. P3 also added that there are many constraints on what the company can do with data, and that the company is cautious about using data. The foremost thing Company C does is to look at it from customers' perspective. This is because, according to the privacy laws, the customers have extensive rights to know and control what is done with their data. In addition, the company has proposed employing data anonymization so that they can observe customers' behavior without pinpointing individuals.

In summary, the case companies' ethical guidelines on privacy illustrated the contribution of the GDPR. Data privacy, personal data protection, data security, and data anonymization are the foundation of defining ethical guidelines in the case companies. In the same way, the companies exhibited their compliance with privacy laws and regulations. In addition, Companies B and C highlighted the importance of privacy ethical guidelines in order to ensure customers' trust.

Transparency: The ethical guidelines of Company A highlighted the importance of transparency, one of its values – in addition to trust, caring, and continuous learning (P1). Therefore, its ethical guidelines recommended that development teams to prioritize maximum transparency and openness in their AI systems whenever possible. However, maximizing transparency is not straightforward. The interviewee mentioned that there can also be several reasons, such as business secrets and privacy, that development teams have to manage with transparency.

According to the interviewee, transparency starts with technical transparency, which means exposing the data and algorithms of AI systems. The interviewee's definition of transparency also included explainability: "It *doesn't need to be lengthy explanation, but it needs to be understandable, otherwise it is not transparency.*" P1 also explained that transparency is doable despite problems such as lack of data (or inclusive data) and data plus algorithm opacity.

The ethical guidelines of Company B feature transparency, along with the responsibility and security ethical guidelines. The guidelines focus on informing the customers on how the company utilizes their data. Being open and transparent is the goal of Company B. The interviewee mentioned privacy as a prerequisite for transparency. That is, if the customer has given permission to use their data, then it is easy for the company to implement transparency (P2).

At the time of our interview, the company was discussing how to be more transparent about the AI behind its recommendations and results. The interviewee mentioned that the company needs to improve transparency and the related technical things. One of the proposals to ensure transparency is to open algorithms (P2).

Company C's ethical guidelines on transparency are associated with openness. The guideline highlights that it is crucial to act openly with customers, partners, and stakeholders. This means discussing the use of AI openly and opening the work of the company to review and public scrutiny.

To summarize, all the case companies aimed to work openly and transparently. They see opening their data and algorithms as a starting point to ensure transparency. It is also critical to ensure that the data and analytics are correct. Being transparent with customers gains their trust, which the companies portray as a key value.

4.2 Practices Supporting the Use of the Ethical Guidelines of AI

This section describes the following three practices that can support the use of ethical guidelines in the development of AI systems:

- Defining the purpose of the AI system
- Analyzing the impacts of the AI system
- Using multi-disciplinary teams

Defining the Purpose of the AI System. All our case companies focused on defining the purpose of the AI system clearly. Company A emphasized that it is important to ensure the system that the company designs and builds have a clear purpose so that the system will be trusted to behave adhering to its purpose. In addition, the key factors like what is the expected result of the system and how it will be measured need to defined.

In their ethical guidelines, Company B highlighted their objective of creating solutions that are useful for customers. The company focused on the practice of placing the needs of the customers first and creating an AI system that is useful to customers. Furthermore, the company only uses their customer data for purposes for which their customers have given permission. Customers should control the data that the company can use (P2). Altogether, the company aims to achieve the best customer experience.

Company C's viewpoint is that, when defining the purpose, the objectives guiding the use of AI need to be determined clearly. This objective can be refined if necessary, based on changed data, technical possibilities, and the work environment. In addition, the company also considers things from customers' perspectives, which is also the focus of Company B.

Analyzing the Impact of the AI System. Company A's analysis of the impact of its AI system is supported by the following two guidelines:

- Respect and be mindful of the impact on people affected by the system
- Consider the impact of the system beyond its users, and consider the positive and negative consequences of the system

Company B mentioned that when analyzing the impact, the data-driven insight enables the company to provide added values to the everyday lives of its customers. This adheres to their guideline of placing customers needs' first. Company C's approach to analyzing its impact is carefully studying the effects of their choices on the company, customers, and the society.

Using Multi-disciplinary Teams. Companies A and B highlighted the importance of multi-disciplinary teams when developing AI systems. According to one interviewee (P1), the key thing for Company A is to make sure that development teams are truly multi-disciplinary. The reason to have designers, social scientists, and domain experts in addition to data scientists is to ensure that all the relevant viewpoints are taken into account and explanations provided by AI systems are understandable to people (P1). The interviewee from Company B (P2) explained that they had *"different kinds of backgrounds in all teams so that they can really give new kind of value to the team"*

5   Discussion

5.1   Ethical Guidelines of AI for the Development of AI Systems

In this section, we first compare the ethical guidelines of the case companies with the ethical issues reported in the existing literature and the ethical guidelines defined by the three expert groups. Then, we discuss how organizations can use their ethical guidelines to convert potential ethical issues into quality requirements for AI systems.

The analysis of the ethical guidelines of the case companies revealed that their guidelines focused on solving the potential ethical issues of AI systems, such as accountability, explainability, fairness, privacy, and transparency. When comparing these results with the ethical issues of AI systems that we identified in the existing literature, we observed several similarities. The ethical guidelines of the case companies covered the following ethical issues reported in the literature: anonymity [14], fairness [23, 26, 30], privacy [17, 23, 30], security [23, 26, 28, 30], transparency [16, 23, 30], and trust [16, 23, 28].

The ethical guidelines of the case companies on accountability, explainability, fairness, privacy, and transparency also corresponded to the ethical guidelines recommended by the three expert groups [18, 19, 31]. Also, the case companies' guidelines on accountability related to the well-being and responsibility guidelines specified by the expert groups. Furthermore, both the ethical guidelines of the expert groups [18, 19] and the interviewees of our study recommend defining the purpose of AI system.

The existing literature already offers many ethical guidelines. However, it can be difficult for companies to know which one of these guidelines they should select to be used in their AI development. In addition, existing guidelines can be too comprehensive and broad for development teams to apply, especially in agile projects. The case companies in this study have defined company-specific guidelines that are compact. These guidelines bring up a set of potential ethical issues that the AI development teams can focus on.

Based on the results of this case study, we propose that organizations define a set of ethical guidelines for handling potential ethical issues during the development of AI. We also recommend that organizations use their ethical guidelines to identify and prioritize the critical quality requirements of the AI systems.

All our case companies had defined guidelines on transparency. The transparency guidelines of the case companies emphasized the need for being open to the use of AI and informing customers what data is used and how it is used in the AI system. The companies also highlighted prioritizing transparency when developing AI systems to gain users' trust. Cysneiros et al. [11, 12] have also proposed transparency as a key quality requirement of AI systems, and Horkoff's [21] study on the quality requirements of machine learning revealed transparency as a key quality.

The findings of our study indicate that the explainability guidelines complement and support the transparency guidelines. The companies' ethical guidelines related to explainability pointed out the importance of justifying the outcomes of AI systems and building in explainability from the beginning. Similarly, Chazette and Schneider [9, 10] highlighted explanation as an option to mitigate the lack of transparency of a system and portrayed explainability as an emerging quality requirement of systems.

The fairness guidelines of our case companies focused on two goals: avoiding bias and respecting human rights. First, it is critical to avoid discrimination, which could lead to unfair results. In addition, one of the solutions to tackle fairness issues is to adopt inclusivity in data used to train AI. The literature [9, 10, 21] indicates that fairness is a quality requirement.

The privacy guidelines of the case companies covered anonymity, security, and data protection aspects. All the interviewees especially pointed out the importance of ensuring the privacy of personal data because of the GDPR. Cysneiros et al. [11, 12] have also highlighted privacy as a potential quality requirement of AI systems.

The accountability guidelines of the case companies recommended assigning owners for the AI algorithms the company has developed. In addition, the guidelines suggested naming responsible persons who will be contacted when the AI system is causing harm and who will resolve ethical issues. Based on these accountability guidelines, we deduce that the companies perceive accountability as a characteristic of professional conduct rather than a system characteristic i.e. quality requirement of the AI system.

In addition to the ethical guidelines of AI systems, the case companies recommended practices that can support the application of these guidelines to development projects. For example, two of the case companies recommended using multi-disciplinary teams when considering different viewpoints on ethical issues. The interviewees also highlighted the importance of defining a clear purpose for AI systems by focusing especially on customer needs. The ethical guidelines of one of the companies even emphasized the necessity of considering the impacts of the system beyond the user, and consider any positive and negative consequences the system might have for society. The analysis of potential negative consequences relates closely to misuse cases, which is a requirements engineering practice to be used for identifying use cases with hostile intent and negative scenarios [1].

5.2 Limitations of This Study

Generalizability. One important question related to case studies is: to what extent can the results of the study be considered representative of a broader range of organizations? We acknowledge that the number of our case companies was rather low. They represent, however, three different application domains. These companies were also recommended by an AI expert who is knowledgeable about which organizations have already invested in ethical guidelines of AI systems. According to that expert, these case companies are forerunners. Therefore, we believe that other organizations can learn from the ethical guidelines described in this paper.

Reliability. The data collection and analysis processes also left room for researcher bias. To avoid misinterpretation and bias in the interview questions, three senior researchers reviewed the interview questions, which we also tested with two practitioners. In addition, two researchers conducted the interviews together. The first author asked the interview questions, and the second author asked follow-up questions based on the interviewees' answers. Likewise, researcher triangulation was used in order to avoid researcher bias in the data analysis.

Construct Validity. The number of interviewees in our case study was also low, as we interviewed only one person from each company. To handle this limitation, the triangulation of data sources was used. In order to gain more knowledge about the ethical guidelines, we were also able to analyze the ethical guideline documents of all the case companies. Furthermore, the study was done at company level. Therefore, we are not able to report how the ethical guidelines are applied in AI projects. We believe that this kind of company-level study provides valuable knowledge about the commitment to and support of companies for the ethical development of AI systems. We also understand that ethical guidelines are valuable when they are used in development projects.

6   Conclusions

The goal of this study was to analyze what kind of ethical guidelines companies have defined for solving potential ethical issues of AI and developing AI systems. The ethical guidelines of the case companies focused on solving ethical issues, such as accountability, explainability, fairness, privacy, and transparency. Based on the results of this study, we suggest that organizations develop and use their ethical guidelines to identify and prioritize critical quality requirements of AI. The results also indicate that transparency, explainability, fairness, and privacy can be critical quality requirements of AI systems. In addition, defining the purposes of their AI systems clearly and analyzing impacts of their AI systems can assist multi-disciplinary development teams in solving ethical issues during the development of AI systems.

One important direction in our future research is to conduct case studies and investigate how ethical guidelines are used in AI projects. Our goal is to compare the ways development teams have applied the ethical guidelines of their organizations, the challenges they have faced, and their positive experiences using those ethical guidelines. Our particular research interest is to understand how critical quality requirements of AI systems are defined and tested in practice.

References

1. Alexander, I.: Misuse cases: use cases with hostile intent. IEEE Softw. **20**, 58–68 (2003)
2. Arnold, T., Scheutz, M.: The "big red-button" is too late: an alternative model for ethical evaluation of AI systems. Ethics Inf. Technol. **20**(1), 59–69 (2018)
3. Aydemir, F.B., Dalpiaz, F.: A roadmap for ethics-aware software engineering. In: ACM/IEEE International Workshop on Software Fairness (FairWare 2018), pp. 15–21 (2018)
4. Bonnemains, V., Claire, S., Tessier, C.: Embedded ethics: some technical and ethical challenges. Ethics Inf. Technol. **20**(1), 41–58 (2018)
5. Bostrom, N., Yudkowsky, E.: The ethics of artificial intelligence. In: Frankish, K., Ramsay, W.M., (eds.) Cambridge Handbook of Artificial Intelligence, pp. 316–334. Cambridge University Press (2011)
6. Boyce, C., Neale, P.: Conducting in-depth interviews: a guide for designing and conducting in-depth interviews. Evaluation **2**(May), 1–16 (2006)
7. Cassell, C., Symon, G.: Essential Guide to Qualitative Methods in Organizational Research. SAGE Publications, London (2012)
8. Charmaz, K.: Constructing Grounded Theory: A Practical Guide Through Qualitative Analysis. SAGE Publications, London (2006)
9. Chazette, L., Karras, O., Schneider, K.: Do end-users want explanations? Analyzing the role of explainability as an emerging aspect of non-functional requirements. In: RE 2019, pp. 223–233 (2018)
10. Chazette, L., Schneider, K.: Explainability as non-functional requirement: challenges and recommendations. Requirements Eng. (2020)
11. Cysneiros, L.M., Raffi, M.A., Leite, J.C.S.P.: Software transparency as a key requirement for self-driving cars. In: RE 2018, pp. 382–387 (2018)
12. Cysneiros, L.M., do Prado Leite, J.C.S.: Non-functional requirements orienting the development of socially responsible software. In: Nurcan, S., Reinhartz-Berger, I., Soffer, P., Zdravkovic, J. (eds.) BPMDS/EMMSAD -2020. LNBIP, vol. 387, pp. 335–342. Springer, Cham (2020). https://doi.org/10.1007/978-3-030-49418-6_23
13. Dignum, V.: Ethics in artificial intelligence: introduction to the special issue. Ethics Inf. Technol. **20**(1), 1–3 (2018)
14. Doyle, T., Veranas, J.: Public anonymity and the connected world. Ethics Inf. Technol. **16**(3), 207–218 (2014). https://doi.org/10.1007/s10676-014-9346-5

15. Eisenhardt, K.M.: Building theories from case study research. Acad. Manage. Rev. **14**(4), 532–550 (1989)
16. Elia, J.: Transparency rights, technology, and trust. Ethics Inf. Technol. **11**, 145–153 (2009)
17. Etzioni, A., Etzioni, O.: AI assisted ethics. Ethics Inf. Technol. **18**(2), 149–156 (2016). https://doi.org/10.1007/s10676-016-9400-6
18. European Commission: Ethics Guidelines for Trustworthy AI. https://ec.europa.eu/futurium/en/ai-alliance-consultation/guidelines. Accessed 24 Jan 2020
19. IEEE: Ethically Aligned Design, First Edition https://ethicsinaction.ieee.org/. Accessed 24 Nov 2019
20. Floridi, L., Cowls, J., Beltramatti, M., et al.: AI4people: an ethical framework for a good AI society: opportunities, risks, principles, and recommendations. Mind. Mach. **28**, 689–707 (2018)
21. Horkoff, J.: Non-functional requirements for machine learning: challenges and new directions. In: International Requirements Engineering Conference, pp. 386–391 (2019)
22. Jobin, A., Lenca, M., Vayena, E.: The global landscape of AI ethics guidelines. Nat. Mach. Intell. **1**, 389–399 (2019)
23. Jones, S., Hara, S., Augusto, J.C.: eFRIEND: an ethical framework for intelligent environment development. Ethics Inf. Technol. **17**, 11–25 (2015)
24. Mepham, B., Kaiser, M., Thorstensen, E., Tomkins, S., Millar, K., et al.: Ethical Matrix Manual (2006)
25. Open Data Institute: Data Ethics Canvas. https://theodi.org/wp-content/uploads/2019/07/ODI-Data-Ethics-Canvas-2019-05.pdf. Accessed 24 Jun 2020
26. Palm, E.: Securing privacy at work: the importance of contextualized consent. Ethics Inf. Technol. **11**, 233–241 (2009)
27. Peslak, A.R.: Improving software quality: an ethics-based approach. In: SIGMS 2004, pp. 144–149 (2004)
28. Pieters, W.: Explanation and trust: what to tell the user in security and AI? Ethics Inf. Technol. **13**, 53–64 (2011)
29. Rahwan, I.: Society-in-the-loop: programming the algorithmic social contract. Ethics Inf. Technol. **20**(1), 5–14 (2018)
30. Royakkers, L., Timmer, J., Kool, L., van Est, R.V.: Societal and ethical issues of digitization. Ethics Inf. Technol. **20**, 1–16 (2018). https://doi.org/10.1007/s10676-018-9452-x
31. SIIA (Software and Information Industry Association): Ethical Principles for Artificial Intelligence and Data Analytics, pp. 1–25 (2017)
32. Stanford University: One hundred year study on artificial intelligence (AI100). In: Artificial Intelligence and Life in 2030. Stanford University. https://ai100.stanford.edu/. Accessed 15 Dec 2019
33. Vampley, P., Dazeley, R., Foale, C., et al.: Human-aligned artificial intelligence in a multi objective problem. Ethics Inf. Technol. **20**(1), 27–40 (2018)
34. Yin, R.K.: Case Study Research Design and Methods. Sage, Thousand Oaks (2013)

Sentiment Polarity and Bug Introduction

Simone Romano[1], Maria Caulo[2]([⊠]), Giuseppe Scanniello[2],
Maria Teresa Baldassarre[1], and Danilo Caivano[1]

[1] University of Bari, Bari, Italy
{simone.romano,mariateresa.baldassarre,danilo.caivano}@uniba.it
[2] University of Basilicata, Potenza, Italy
{maria.caulo,giuseppe.scanniello}@unibas.it

Abstract. Researchers have shown a growing interest in the affective states (*i.e.,* emotions and moods) of developers while performing software engineering tasks. We investigate the association between developers' sentiment polarity—*i.e.,* negativity and positivity—and bug introduction. To pursue our research objective, we executed a case-control study in the Mining Software Repository (MSR) context. Our exposures are developers' negativity and positivity captured, by using sentiment analysis, from commit comments of software repositories; while our "disease" is bug introduction—*i.e.,* if the changes of a commit introduce bugs. We found that developers' negativity is associated to bug introduction, as well as developers' positivity. These findings seem to foster a continuous monitoring of developers' affective states so as to prevent the introduction of bugs or discover bugs as early as possible.

Keywords: Bug · Sentiment analysis · Case-control study

1 Introduction

The Software Engineering (SE) community has displayed a growing interest in the affective states (*i.e.,* emotions and moods) of developers [10,12,16,29,40]. To capture developers' affective states in SE work, researchers have borrowed self-assessment measurement instruments (*e.g.,* based on questionnaires) from the Psychology research community [10]. Such measurement instruments require developers to explicitly share their affective state during and/or after performing SE tasks [11]. Other researchers have leveraged measurement instruments based on biometric sensors to capture how developers feel while performing SE tasks [29]. In both cases, researchers must hand out measurement instruments to developers. Therefore, these instruments are not feasible solutions when mining existing software repositories, which are known to contain valuable information on software projects and developers [14]. In this type of studies, a more appropriate solution is *sentiment analysis*, which allows mining developers' affective states—usually sentiment polarity (*i.e., positivity, negativity,* and *neutrality*)—from SE textual artifacts like commit and issue comments [12,13,30,33].

© Springer Nature Switzerland AG 2020
M. Morisio et al. (Eds.): PROFES 2020, LNCS 12562, pp. 347–363, 2020.
https://doi.org/10.1007/978-3-030-64148-1_22

In this paper, we rely on sentiment analysis to capture developers' sentiment polarity from commit comments of software repositories, and then investigate the association between sentiment polarity and bug introduction. In particular, we study the following main Research Question (RQ):

RQ. Is there an association between developers' sentiment polarity—specifically, developers' negativity and positivity—and bug introduction?

We hypothesize that developers' negativity might cause developers to introduce bugs in source code. This hypothesis is consistent with the findings of a survey, which lists *low code quality* (*e.g.,* buggy code) as a possible consequence of developers' *unhappiness*—an affective state associated to negativity [10]. Moreover, according to the respondents of this survey, being happy leads them to introduce fewer bugs. Therefore, we also hypothesize that developers' positivity might be negatively associated to bug introduction.

To answer our main RQ, we borrowed a kind of observational study, namely the *case-control* one [24], from the medical field, and applied it in the Mining Software Repository (MSR) context. Case-control studies compare two groups— *i.e., cases* and *controls*—differing in an outcome (*e.g.,* having or not a certain disease) to determine whether or not a supposed factor (or multiple supposed factors) can explain that outcome. We identified the cases and controls based on our outcome of interest, namely being *Bug-Introducing-Change* (*BIC*) commit— *i.e.,* commits whose changes introduce bugs—or not. Accordingly, the cases were BIC commits and the controls were non-BIC commits. Afterward, we employed human raters to detect negativity and positivity in both BIC and non-BIC commits. In other words, we exploited human raters, rather than sentiment analysis tools, to determine, and then compare, the proportions of commits containing negativity and positivity in the case and control groups.

Paper Structure. In Sect. 2, we provide background information and summarize related work. Our case-control study is detailed in Sect. 3. We present the results in Sect. 4 and discuss them in Sect. 5. Potential threats to validity are in Sect. 6. Final remarks and future work conclude the paper.

2   Background and Related Work

We provide background information on case-control studies. We then present sentiment analysis tools for use on SE textual artifacts along with their empirical evaluations. Finally, we explore work related to ours.

2.1   Case-Control Studies

In the medical field, case-control studies provide a powerful method for studying rare outcomes of interest (*e.g.,* rare disease) [22]. In particular, they are used to determine whether an association exists between some exposures (*i.e.,* some supposed causal factors) and an outcome of interest [24]. To this end, researchers first identify the cases—a group of people known to have a certain outcome—and then select the controls—a group of people known to not have that outcome. Afterward, researchers look back to find which people in each group had some exposures and which did not. It is easy to grasp that case-control studies are *retrospective*—in contrast to those *prospective* in which researchers record some supposed causal factors and then wait for the outcome to arise. Another characteristic of case-control studies is that the ratio of cases and controls is not the same as in the population—usually, the ratio of the cases in the population is very small as the outcome of interest is rare [22].

Based on the selection of the controls, case-control studies are either *unmatched* or *matched* [22]. In unmatched case-control studies, controls are entirely selected at random or at random but preserving some proportions of certain confounding factors[1] (*e.g.,* by keeping the proportions of males between cases and controls constant). This latter kind of selection is known as *frequency matching*. On the other hand, in matched case-control studies, controls are selected to match individual cases based on some matching factors (*e.g.,* each case and the matched control have the same date of birth).

2.2 Sentiment Analysis Tools and Their Empirical Assessment in SE

Early work in the SE research field has leveraged general-purpose sentiment analysis tools (*e.g.,* SentiStrength [41]) to mine sentiment polarity from SE textual artifacts [12,13,33]. Later, researchers have showed that general-purpose sentiment analysis tools can perform poorly when applied to SE textual artifacts [19]. To improve the performance of such tools on SE textual artifacts, researchers have first tuned general-purpose sentiment analysis tools for use in the SE context—*e.g.,* Islam and Zibran [16] tuned SentiStrength to mine sentiment polarity from commit comments—and then devised SE-specific sentiment analysis tools—*e.g.,* SentiCR [1], Senti4SD [3], SentiSW [7], and SentiStrength-SE [18]). The above-mentioned tools have been also empirically validated by their authors. In particular, these tools have been validated on datasets of *JIRA* issue comments [7,18]; code review comments [1]; questions, answers, and comments extracted from *Stack Overflow* [3]; and *GitHub* issue comments [7].

Novielli *et al.* [31] investigated the extent to which sentiment analysis tools agree with human raters (as well as to which extent they agree with each other). The results suggest that, in general, tools leveraging supervised learning (*i.e.,* SentiCR and Senti4SD) perform slightly better. However, their performance is quite comparable to that of a lexicon-based tool like SentiStrength-SE. Also, the performance of tools based on supervised learning varies when applied on datasets different from those used in the training phase. Finally, the performance of lexicon-based tools like SentiStrength-SE varies from a dataset to another.

---

[1] They are factors associated to an exposure, which cause the outcome of interest [24].

Lin *et al.* [25] also performed a comparison among sentiment analysis tools on different datasets (*i.e.,* Stack Overflow posts, app reviews, and JIRA issue comments). Similarly to Novielli *et al.* [31], they observed variations in tools' performance when applied on different datasets.

Summing up, the results of our study of the literature suggested that: *(i)* researchers should not use general-purpose sentiment analysis tools [19]; *(ii)* no SE-specific tool has been empirically assessed on commit comments; and *(iii)* the performance of sentiment analysis tools varies from a dataset to another [25,31]. Based on these results, we decided not to use sentiment analysis tool in our case-control study; rather, similarly to Murgia *et al.* [30], we exploited human raters to detect sentimental polarity. Although employing human raters to execute a sentiment analysis task requires more effort and time than using sentiment analysis tools, the measures resulting from the use of human raters should be more reliable, and then allowed us to mitigate threats concerned to the reliability of the measures [43].

2.3 Developers' Affective States and Bug Introduction

Graziotin *et al.* [10] investigated the consequences of developers' happiness and unhappiness while developing software through a survey. The authors elicited 42 consequences of unhappiness and 32 consequences of happiness. Low code quality (*e.g.,* buggy code) is listed as a possible consequence of developers' unhappiness, while high code quality is listed as a possible consequence of their happiness. Souza and Silva [40] studied, through an MSR study, if broken continuous-integration builds—*i.e.,* builds that cannot compile or cannot pass all tests because of bugs—are associated to developers' negativity. To capture developers' negativity from commit comments, the authors used SentiStrength. The results suggest that commits containing negativity are slightly more likely to result in broken builds than those that do not contain negativity. Islam and Zibran [17] conducted an MSR study to understand if there are differences in the intensity of developers' negativity and positivity when introducing bugs (*i.e.,* among BIC commits). To this end, they ran SentiStrength-SE on a dataset by Ray *et al.* [34] containing BIC commits, which were identified by applying a heuristic. They found that the intensity of developers' positivity is significantly higher than the intensity of developers' negativity. Also, they compared BIC commits with Bug-Fixing-Change (BFC) commits—*i.e.,* commits involved in bug-fixing operations—in terms of intensity of developers' negativity and positivity. They reported that neither the intensity of positivity nor the one of negativity differs so much between BIC and BFC commits. These studies [10,17,40] differ from our study in a substantial way. First, the kind of empirical investigation is different. Second, only our investigation compares BIC to non-BIC commits so as to demonstrate that an association exists between developers' sentiment polarity and bug introduction. In this respect, it is worth highlighting that, although Islam and Zibran's study [17] focuses on BIC commits, the authors did not compare BIC commits with non-BIC ones and, therefore, that study cannot prove that developers' sentiment polarity is associated to bug introduction.

Huq *et al.* [15] studied whether sentiment polarity of commit comments (and code reviews) of pull requests can indicate bug introduction in the next commits. The authors used `SentiStrength-SE` to extract sentiment polarity from commit comments. The commits of pull requests, of six open-source Java projects (different from those used by Ray *et al.*), were classified as BIC or non-BIC—to identify BIC commits, a heuristic was applied. The authors found that, within pull requests, commit comments preceding BIC commits were more negative than those preceding non-BIC commits. Then, the authors concluded that when developers submit commits containing mostly negativity, then their next commits are prone to introduce bugs. Unlike Huq *et al.*, we do not: *(i)* exclusively focus on the commits of pull requests and *(ii)* compare BIC and non-BIC commits based on the sentiment polarity of the preceding commits (*i.e.,* we are not interested in studying whether sentiment polarity of commit comments can indicate bug introduction in the next commits). Finally, we manually inspected the comments of BIC and non-BIC commits.

3 The Case-Control Study

In our case-control study, we considered commits of software repositories of projects included in the `Defects4J` dataset (v.1.5.0) [21], which contains 438 bugs from 6 open-source Java projects. We conducted such a kind of study because: *(i)* case-control studies are appropriate for the investigation of a rare outcome of interest [22] like BIC commits[2] and *(ii)* case-control studies require fewer data points (*i.e.,* fewer commits) as compared to prospective studies [39].[3]

To conduct our study, we selected commits from `Defects4J` that played the role of either case or control. The cases were BIC commits, while the controls were non-BIC commits. We then applied, for each BIC commit, sentiment analysis on the commit comment to ascertain which was the sentiment polarity of the developer who modified the source code of that commit (so introducing some bugs). Similarly, we ascertained developer's sentiment polarity for each non-BIC commit playing the role of control. It is easy to grasp that we assume, based on empirical evidence [32] and similarly to previous work in SE [16,30], a causal relationship between developers' sentimental polarity and what developers write in their commit comments. Summing up, our outcome of interest is being a BIC commit or not, while the exposures are developers' negativity—*i.e.,* if a commit comment contains negativity or not—and developers' positivity—*i.e.,* if a commit comment contains positivity or not.

---

[2] According to Campos Neto *et al.* [4], the number of BIC commits in `Defects4J` is 284. This number is much smaller than the total number of commits in `Defects4J`, namely 17402, so suggesting that BIC commits are rare—in particular, less than 2% of the commits in `Defects4J` are BIC.

[3] This is, if we had first identified commits containing negativity, or positivity, and then determined the proportions of BIC and non-BIC commits, we would have needed more commits to achieve the same statistical power as our case-control study.

3.1   Selection of Cases and Controls

We used `Defects4J` because the selection of the cases required the identification of BIC commits that, in turn, can be identified only when bugs are documented. This dataset directly archives, for each bug, the corresponding BFC commit; however, it does not directly store information on BIC commits. Such information has been recently provided by Campos Neto et al. [4], who have manually identified, in `Defects4J` (v.1.5.0), BIC commits of 302 bugs, out of a total of 438, so complementing `Defects4J`. Some descriptive statistics of `Defects4J`, complemented with BIC-commit information, are shown in Table 1. A BIC commit can be BFC at the same time. That is, the changes made to fix a bug might cause the introduction of some other bugs. In Table 1, we show in parentheses the number of BIC commits that are BFC and the total number of commits that are BFC.

Table 1. Summary of `Defects4J` complemented with BIC-commit information.

Project	#BIC commits	#Commits
JFreeChart	7 (0 are BFC)	916 (26 are BFC)
Closure compiler	68 (8 are BFC)	2989 (176 are BFC)
Commons lang	47 (4 are BFC)	3598 (65 are BFC)
Commons math	91 (9 are BFC)	4918 (106 are BFC)
Mockito	50 (2 are BFC)	3263 (38 are BFC)
Joda time	21 (4 are BFC)	1718 (27 are BFC)
Sum	284 (27 are BFC)	17402 (438 are BFC)

We selected, as cases, all BIC commits Campos Neto et al. [4] identified in `Defects4J`, in total 284. It is worth noting that the number of (unique) BIC commits is less than the number of bugs (i.e., 302) because a given commit can introduce one or more bugs.

As suggested in the literature [22], we selected the controls from the same "population" at risk as the cases (i.e., `Defects4J`). To have the same distribution of some confounding factors (also known as confounders) between cases and controls, we sampled the controls by applied frequency matching. That is, we selected non-BIC commits at random, but taking into account two constraints. First, the proportions of the software projects had to be constant between the cases and controls (e.g., since the commits of `Commons Math` accounted for 32% of the cases, we randomly selected the controls so that 32% of them belonged to `Commons Math`). We fixed this constraint because we hypothesize that the project might affect the sentiment polarity of its developers. This hypothesis is consistent with the results reported by Guzman et al. [12] (e.g., the proportion of developers' negativity was higher on commit comments from `CraftBukkit` as compared to six other projects). Second, the proportions of BFC commits had to be the same between the cases and controls for each software project (*e.g.*, since the BFC commits of Commons Math account for 3% of the cases, we randomly selected the controls so that 3% of them were BFC commits of Commons Math). We fixed this constraint because we hypothesize that being or not a BFC commit might affect developers' sentiment polarity. In this respect, it has been shown that developers feel rewarded, so raising positivity, when watching a test suite pass (*i.e.*, when the bar of JUnit turns into green) [35]. Furthermore, when selecting the controls, we only took into account commits where developers had modified at least one Java file—*i.e.*, commits that did not concern the modification of Java files were discarded. This is because the cases were BIC commits with at least one Java file modified—*i.e.*, taking into account non-BIC commits with no Java file modified would have implied a selection bias.

To increase statistical power, we applied a well-known technique that consists of selecting more than one control per case [24]. However, selecting more than two controls per case only produce small gains in statistical power [24]. By keeping this in mind, we sampled the controls so that their number was twice the number of the cases (*i.e.*, 568 vs. 284).

3.2   Ascertainment of Exposures

We hypothesized that developers' negativity might be a *risk* factor for BIC commits (*i.e.*, we hypothesized a positive association), while developers' positivity might be a *protective* factor against BIC commits (*i.e.*, we hypothesized a negative association). Therefore, the exposures we took into account are: negativity and positivity. We treated both negativity and positivity as binary factors, each having two levels, namely *yes* or *no*. For example, *yes* for the negativity factor means that a developer felt negative feelings while modifying the source code of a commit, while *no* means that a developer did not feel negative affects. It is worth mentioning that commit comments, being textual artifacts, can contain negativity and positivity at the same time [41].

To capture negativity and positivity of developers who modified source code, we involved human raters, who were asked to execute a sentiment analysis task on the comments of 852 commits, of which 284 were cases and 568 were controls. In total, four SE researchers with knowledge of sentiment analysis (*i.e.*, four out of the authors of this paper) played the role of raters. The workload was equally and randomly divided among the raters so that each commit comment was evaluated by two raters. When evaluating a commit comment, the two raters worked independently from one another. This is to avoid that a rater could influence the evaluation of the other. Moreover, besides the comment of a commit, the two raters were unaware of any other information about that commit. For example, the two raters did not know whether a comment corresponded to a case or a control. This is because we arranged a level of *blinding*[4] to mitigate a threat of

---

[4] It means concealing research design elements (*e.g.*, treatment assignment) from individuals involved in an empirical study (*e.g.*, raters) [27].

experimenter bias [43]. The use of blinding has been encouraged in the Medicine research field [27], as well as in the SE one [9].

Each rater was asked to read one commit comment at a time and provide: *(i)* a polarity label for negativity *(i.e., yes* if the comment contained negativity, *no* otherwise); and *(ii)* a polarity label for positivity *(i.e., yes* if the comment contained positivity, *no* otherwise). To do this, the raters had to keep into account Shaver *et al.*'s emotion framework [36], which organizes emotions according to a hierarchy of three levels: basic emotions, II-level emotions, and III-level emotions. Thanks to this framework, the emotions the raters recognized in commit comments could be mapped to positivity and negativity. In Table 1 of our online appendix,[5] we show the mapping between sentiment polarity and emotions from Shaver *et al.*'s framework—note that *surprise* can be either a positive or negative emotion depending on the context [3,18]. The use of Shaver *et al.*'s framework [36] to manually rate sentiment polarity of texts is not new in SE work [3,30].

Table 2. Sample commit comments with the corresponding emotions, based on Shaver *et al.*'s framework, and polarity labels.

Commit comment	Basic emotion	II-level emotion	III-level emotion	Negativity	Positivity
"Removed those pesky getDateOnlyMillis and getTimeOnlyMillis methods."	Anger	Irritation	Annoyance	Yes	No
"fixed the build:) (compiles fine under eclipse...)"	Joy	Cheerfulness	Happiness	No	Yes

In Table 2, we show two examples of commit comments with the corresponding emotions, according to Shaver *et al.*'s framework, and polarity labels.

The pairs of raters agreed on negativity contained in commit comments 758 times (89%), while on positivity 755 times (88.6%). We also computed Cohen's kappa coefficient (κ) [5] to measure the strength of the agreement between the pair of raters, and thus estimate the reliability of their evaluations. We chose this coefficient because it was conceived for the measurement of the agreement between two raters only [5] and used for purposes similar to ours [6]. κ ranges in $[-1, 1]$, where 1 means perfect agreement. For both negativity and positivity, we observed a fair agreement[6] ($\kappa = 0.37$ for negativity and $\kappa = 0.26$ for positivity) for our initial ratings. Such a level of agreement can be considered acceptable since it concerns initial ratings, not those finals. For the 94 commit comments on which we had disagreements on negativity, as well as the 97 commit comments on which we had disagreements on positivity, we planned a series of meetings in which the other two raters had to determine the final ratings. That is, if a pair of raters disagreed on the negativity contained in a commit comment, or similarly on the positivity, then the other two raters attempted to reach a

---

[5] https://tinyurl.com/y2f62sz9.

[6] The agreement is: *poor* if $\kappa < 0$; *slight* if $0 \leq \kappa \leq 0.2$; *fair* if $0.2 < \kappa \leq 0.4$; *moderate* if $0.4 < \kappa \leq 0.6$; *substantial* if $0.6 < \kappa \leq 0.8$; or *almost perfect* if $0.8 < \kappa < 1$ [23].

consensus by discussing that commit in a meeting. Again, besides the comment of a commit, the two raters involved in the meeting were unaware of any other information about that commit. Our rating protocol based on two levels—*i.e.*, individual and independent ratings of SE artifacts followed by meetings in case of disagreements between raters—is similar to that used by Ahmed *et al.* [1] and Corazza *et al.* [6].

3.3 Data Analysis

As usual in case-control studies [22,24], we computed the *Odds Ratios* (ORs) for developers' negativity and positivity to measure the strength of their association to BIC commits (*i.e.*, bug introduction). The interpretation of the OR for negativity follows:

Table 3. Results on the association between developers' sentiment polarity and bug introduction. In bold, CIs and p-values that suggest significant associations.

Factor	Level	BIC commits	Non-BIC commits	OR	95% CI	p-value
Negativity	No	252 (88.7%)	534 (94%)	-	-	-
	Yes	32 (11.3%)	34 (6%)	1.994	**[1.203 − 3.306]**	**0.009**
Positivity	No	250 (88%)	534 (94%)	-	-	-
	Yes	34 (12%)	34 (6%)	2.136	**[1.297 − 3.516]**	**0.003**

- If the OR is greater than 1, there is a positive association between negativity and BIC commits—*i.e.*, the odds of negativity among BIC commits are greater than the odds of negativity among non-BIC commits. Thus, negativity can be a risk factor for BIC commits.
- If the OR is less than 1, there is a negative association—*i.e.*, the odds of negativity among BIC commits are lower than those of negativity among non-BIC commits. Thus, negativity can be a protective factor against BIC commits.
- If the OR is 1, negativity is not associated with BIC commits.

As for positivity, the OR interpretation is similar to that mentioned above. To determine if the associations of negativity and positivity to BIC commits are *statistically significant* (from here on, simply *significant*), we computed 95% Confidence Intervals (CIs) of the ORs. If a CI does not cross the null value (*i.e.*, 1), the association is considered significant [24]. Also, we ran Fisher's exact test [8] to confirm the significance of the associations. We opted for that test of independence, rather than others (*e.g.*, chi-square test), because it is recommended when the total sample size is less than 1000 [26]—our total sample size is 852. As usual, we fixed the significance level, α, at 0.05. That is, if the *p-value* returned by Fisher's exact test is less than α, the association is considered significant. Both analysis script and raw data can be found in our replication package.[7]

---

[7] https://tinyurl.com/yxgk7vye.

4   Results

We present the results on the association between developers' sentiment polarity and bug introduction. We also report the results of a subgroup analysis on *Java files changed* (*i.e.,* a potential confounder) to study if the number of changed files in BIC and non-BIC commits could affect our outcomes.

4.1   Sentiment Polarity and Bug Introduction

In Table 3, we summarize the results on the association between developers' sentiment polarity and bug introduction.

Negativity. As shown in Table 3, commit comments containing negativity are quite rare as compared to those non-containing negativity. Only 11.3% of comments among BIC commits contain negativity, while only 6% of comments among non-BIC commits contain negativity. In total, the prevalence of commit comments containing negativity is equal to 7.7%. Despite the proportions of commit comments containing negativity are quite small for both BIC and non-BIC commits, we can observe that the proportion of commit comments containing negativity among BIC commits is higher than that among non-BIC commits (11.3% vs. 6%). In particular, the OR (1.994) is greater than one; therefore, negativity can be a risk factor for BIC commits, namely for bug introduction. The question now arises on whether such an association between negativity and BIC commits is significant or not. The CI ([1.203 − 3.306]) suggests a significant association as it does not cross 1. This outcome is confirmed by Fisher's exact test as the p-value (0.009) is less than α. We can thus answer our RQ as follows:

> A positive association exists between developers' negativity and bug introduction. The odds of developers' negativity are 1.994 times greater in those commits whose changes introduce bugs than they are in those commits whose changes do not introduce bugs. Such an association implies that developers' negativity can be a risk factor for bug introduction.

Positivity. Commit comments containing positivity are quite rare as well (see Table 3). Only 12% and 6% of comments among BIC and non-BIC commits, respectively, contain positivity. Overall, 8% of commit comments contain positivity. The proportion of commit comments containing positivity among BIC commits is higher than the same proportion among non-BIC commits (12% vs. 6%) so resulting in an OR of 2.136. That is, unlike our initial hypothesis in which we supposed that positivity might be a protective factor against BIC commits, the OR indicates the opposite, namely positivity can be a risk factor for BIC commits. This outcome is also significant as the CI ([1.297 − 3.516]) does not span 1 and the p-value (0.003) is less than α. We can thus answer our RQ as follows:

A positive association exists between developers' positivity and bug introduction. The odds of developers' positivity are 2.136 times greater in those commits whose changes introduce bugs than they are in the commits whose changes do not introduce bugs. Such an association implies that developers' positivity can be a risk factor for bug introduction.

Neutrality (Further Analysis). We found, unexpectedly, that both negativity and positivity can be risk factors for bug introduction. Accordingly, neutrality could be a protective factor against bug introduction if the (negative) association between neutrality and BIC commits was significant. To ascertain whether such a speculation was true, we performed a further analysis. In particular, we computed the proportions of commit comments containing neutrality for both BIC and non-BIC commits (which are equal to 79.2% and 88.2%, respectively). We then computed the strength (*i.e.*, OR) of the association between neutrality and BIC commits (which was equal to 0.51) and checked the significance of that association. The results indicate that the (negative) association between neutrality and BIC commits is significant as the CI ([0.347 − 0.748]) did not cross 1 and the p-value (0.001) returned by Fisher's exact test was less than α. Therefore, neutrality can be a protective factor against bug introduction.

4.2   Subgroup Analysis About Java Files Changed

Sinha *et al.* [38] found a strong correlation between the number of files changed in commits and the sentiment polarity captured from the comments of those commits. Therefore, we performed a subgroup analysis to understand if the

Table 4. Results on the association between developers' sentiment polarity and bug introduction for the Java-files-changed confounder.

Confounder level	Factor		BIC commits	Non-BIC commits	OR	95% CI	p-value
	Name	Level					
1	Negativity	No	21 (77.8%)	217 (91.9%)	-	-	-
		Yes	6 (22.2%)	19 (8.1%)	3.263	[1.175 − 9.061]	0.03
	Positivity	No	22 (81.5%)	225 (95.3%)	-	-	-
		Yes	5 (18.5%)	11 (4.7%)	4.649	[1.481 − 14.597]	0.015
2	Negativity	No	74 (92.5%)	145 (92.9%)	-	-	-
		Yes	6 (7.5%)	11 (7.1%)	1.069	[0.38 − 3.004]	1
	Positivity	No	75 (93.8%)	141 (90.4%)	-	-	-
		Yes	5 (6.2%)	15 (9.6%)	0.627	[0.219 − 1.791]	0.465
3–4	Negativity	No	55 (88.7%)	83 (97.6%)	-	-	-
		Yes	7 (11.3%)	2 (2.4%)	5.282	[1.058 − 26.371]	0.036
	Positivity	No	52 (83.9%)	3 (96.5%)	-	-	-
		Yes	10 (16.1%)	82 (3.5%)	5.256	[1.382 − 19.998]	0.015
>4	Negativity	No	102 (88.7%)	89 (97.8%)	-	-	-
		Yes	13 (11.3%)	2 (2.2%)	5.672	[1.246 − 25.818]	0.014
	Positivity	No	101 (87.8%)	86 (94.5%)	-	-	-
		Yes	14 (12.2%)	5 (5.5%)	2.384	[0.825 − 6.887]	0.145

number of Java files changed in BIC and non-BIC commits could have influenced the association between developers' sentiment polarity and bug introduction. To this end, for each commit, i, in the case and control groups, we counted the number of Java files changed, x_i, and computed the first (Q_1), second (Q_2), and third (Q_3) quartiles of this distribution. The quartiles resulted to be equal to 1, 2, and 4, respectively. We then categorized each commit into four categories depending on whether: (i) $x_i \leq Q_1$; (ii) $Q_1 < x_i \leq Q_2$; (iii) $Q_2 < x_i \leq Q_3$; or (iv) $x_i > Q_3$. Accordingly, the first category included commits with just one Java file changed, while the second one included commits with just two Java files changed. As for the third category, it comprised commits with either three or four Java files changed. Finally, the fourth category included commits where developers had changed more than four Java files changed. The categorization of factors by using quartiles is a common technique in case-control studies [42].

Table 4 summarizes the results on the association between sentiment polarity and bug introduction for each level of the Java-files-changed confounder.

Negativity. By looking at the results in Table 4, we can notice that there is a positive association—*i.e.,* the ORs are greater than 1—between developers' negativity and bug introduction for any level of the Java-files-changed confounder. These positive associations are also significant—the CIs do not span 1 and the p-values are less than α—for three out of four levels, namely: when the number of Java files changed is equal to one, equal to three or four, and greater than four. For these three levels, the strength of the association between developers' negativity and bug introduction grows up to 3.263, 5.282, and 5.672, respectively.

Positivity. The results in Table 4 also show a positive association—*i.e.,* the ORs are greater than 1—between developers' positivity and bug introduction for three out of four levels of the Java-files-changed confounder—the only exception is when the number of Java files changed is equal to two (the same held for negativity). The results indicate a significant association when the number of Java files changed is equal to one and equal to three or four (see both CIs and p-values). For these two levels, the strength of the association grows up to 4.649 and 5.256, respectively. When the number of Java files changed is equal to two, the OR suggests a negative association since is it less than 1. However, such a negative association could be due to chance as it is not significant—the CI crosses 1 and the p-value is not less than α.

Summary. The positive association between developers' negativity and bug introduction we observed on the whole in Subsect. 4.1 is confirmed when considering different amount of Java files changed. Similarly, we can confirm the positive association between positivity and bug introduction we found on the whole—although we found a negative association when the number of Java files is equal to two, it is not significant.

5   Overall Discussion

We found, in line with our initial hypothesis, that a positive association (OR = 1.994) between developers' negativity and bug introduction exists, namely developers' negativity can be a risk factor for bug introduction. This finding is consistent with that of the survey by Graziotin *et al.* [10]—low code quality (*e.g.*, buggy code) can be a consequence of developers' unhappiness—and Souza *et al.* [40]—commits containing negativity are slightly more likely to result in broken builds than those that do not contain negativity.

We also hypothesized that developers' positivity might be a protective factor against bug introduction. Rather, we found that a positive association (OR = 2.136) exists, namely developers' positivity can be a risk factor for bug introduction. This result seems to contrast with that by Graziotin *et al.* [10], who list high code quality (*e.g.*, bug-free code) as a possible consequence of developers' happiness. However, there is a plausible explanation for this finding: feeling positivity (*e.g.*, being enthusiastic for something) could divert the attention of developers away from their code so leading developers to introduce bugs.

Both extremes of sentiment polarity—*i.e.*, negativity and positivity—can be risk factors to bug introduction; on the other hand, neutrality (which is the complement of negativity and positivity) can be a protective factor against bug introduction. These findings justify a more expensive and time-consuming observational study with a cohort of developers to assess causality between developers' sentiment polarity and bug introduction. Also, our findings and those by Graziotin *et al.* [10] and Souza *et al.* [40] seem to foster a continuous monitoring of developers' affective states so as to prevent the introduction of bugs or discover bugs as early as possible. In particular, software companies could supply their developers with measurement instruments of affective state, like *Affective Slider*[8] (*AR*) [2] or by means of wearable smart bracelets [37], to continuously monitor the affective states of the developers and then suggest countermeasures. Examples of countermeasures are letting developers take a break to wash out developers' negativity, or positivity; or recommending developers who feel negativity, or positivity, to spend more time in testing their code than what they would normally do to discover bugs as early as possible. Furthermore, when looking for commits introducing bugs, those commits containing negativity or positivity should be prioritized.

6   Threats to Validity

We discuss threats to internal, external, construct, and conclusion validity.

Internal Validity. Case-control studies prove associations, they do not demonstrate causation [24]. Therefore, our study can just prove that an association between developers' sentiment polarity—*i.e.*, negativity and positivity—and bug introduction exists.

---

[8] It consists of two sliders to collect in real-time self-reported ratings of pleasure and arousal—two dimensions of emotions.

External Validity. We ran our study within the context of `Defects4J` [21], which comprises six Java projects, because of the need of knowing actual bugs and thus their BIC commits. We did not run our case-control study within the context of the dataset by Ray *et al.* [34] because, unlike Campos Neto *et al.* [4], the authors of that dataset automatically identified BIC commits by applying a heuristic. Although the use of a heuristic might allow identifying more BIC commits, the reliability of the identified BIC commits would be worse as compared to manually-identified BIC commits. That is, if we had run our case-control study with Ray *et al.*'s dataset, we would have had a stronger threat of reliability of measures [43]. Furthermore, since we drew upon the work of external researchers who manually identified BIC commits [4], we should have also mitigated a threat of *experimenter bias* [43].

Although `Defects4J` is widely used in SE experimentation [4,28] and has allowed us to know actual bugs and have more reliable BIC commits as compared to other solutions we cannot guarantee that our results can be generalized to other contexts (*e.g.*, Ray *et al.*'s dataset, industrial projects, non-Java projects, and so on) or the universe of Java projects. When we planned our study, we had to reach a trade-off between generalizability of results and reliability of measures. Since this is the first study investigating on an association between developers' sentiment polarity and bug introduction, we preferred to maximize reliability of measures, rather than generalizability of results. In the future, we plan to triangulate our results through replications in other contexts like Ray *et al.*'s dataset or projects hosted on GitHub (*e.g.*, by using an implementation of the SZZ algorithm [4]).

Construct Validity. We executed sentiment analysis on commit comments to determine the sentiment polarity of developers who modified the source code of those commits. That is, we assume a causal relationship between developers' sentimental polarity and what developers write in their commit comments. Despite such an assumption is based on empirical evidence [32] and shared by SE researchers [16,30], there might be a threat due to this assumption.

Although we controlled and analyzed some confounders, other confounders might affect the studied association.

Conclusion Validity. To increase statistical power, we doubled the number of the controls with respect to that of the cases—such a technique is well-known in the context of case-control studies [24]. Doubling the number of controls allowed us to reach values of statistical power equal to 71.6%, for the association between developers' negativity and bug introduction, and 81%, for the association between developers' positivity and bug introduction. According to Juristo and Moreno [20], 70% of statistical power is acceptable.

Another potential threat concerns the manual sentiment analysis. To limit raters' subjectivity, two raters evaluated each commit comment by taking into account Shaver *et al.*'s framework [36] and, although there were discussions between two other raters in case of disagreements, we still could not prevent eventual unreliable ratings. For instance, one rater could have dominated the discussion and biased the other rater. Nevertheless, the use of human raters should allow having more reliable outcomes as compared to the use of sentiment analysis tools.

The identification of BIC commits might affect the result. It might be happened that the set of cases does not include some BIC commits and then some BIC commits were wrongly selected as controls. Nevertheless, we found that both negativity and positivity are positively associated to bug introduction and such associations are both significant. That is, BIC commits contain both more negativity and positivity as compared to non-BIC commits. If we assumed that *(i)* some BIC commits had been wrongly selected as controls and *(ii)* BIC commits contain both more negativity and positivity, this would have lead us to underestimate the strength of the actual associations of negativity and positivity to bug introduction, but such actual associations would have been still positive and statistically significant. Therefore, wrongly selecting some BIC commits as controls should not represent a big issue since the statistical conclusions of our case-control study would be the same.

7   Conclusion and Future Work

We presented the results of a case-control study to investigate the association between developers' sentiment polarity—negativity and positivity—and bug introduction. We found that there is a positive association between developers' negativity, as well as developers' positivity, and bug introduction. This means that both negativity and positivity could be risk factors for bug introduction. The findings of our study seem to foster a continuous monitoring of developers' affective states so as to prevent the introduction of bugs or discover bugs as early as possible. The obtained results also justify a prospective observational study with a cohort of developers to investigate the effects of their polarity on bug introduction. We also plan to replicate our study in different contexts (*e.g.*, industry) to gather further evidence on the association between developers' sentiment polarity and bug introduction.

References

1. Ahmed, T., Bosu, A., Iqbal, A., Rahimi, S.: SentiCR: a customized sentiment analysis tool for code review interactions. In: Proceedings of ASE, pp. 106–111. IEEE (2017)
2. Betella, A., Verschure, P.F.M.J.: The affective slider: a digital self-assessment scale for the measurement of human emotions. PLoS ONE **11**(2), 1–11 (2016)
3. Calefato, F., Lanubile, F., Maiorano, F., Novielli, N.: Sentiment polarity detection for software development. Empirical Softw. Eng. J. **23**(3), 1352–1382 (2018)
4. Campos Neto, E., da Costa, D.A., Kulesza, U.: Revisiting and improving SZZ implementations. In: Proceedings of ESEM, pp. 1–12. IEEE (2019)
5. Cohen, J.: A coefficient of agreement for nominal scales. Educ. Psychol. Measur. **20**(1), 37–46 (1960)

6. Corazza, A., Maggio, V., Scanniello, G.: Coherence of comments and method implementations: a dataset and an empirical investigation. Software Qual. J. **26**(2), 751–777 (2016). https://doi.org/10.1007/s11219-016-9347-1
7. Ding, J., Sun, H., Wang, X., Liu, X.: Entity-level sentiment analysis of issue comments. In: Proceedings of SEmotion, pp. 7–13. ACM (2018)
8. Fisher, R.A.: Statistical Methods for Research Workers, 5th edn. Oliver and Boyd, Edinburgh (1934)
9. Fucci, D., et al.: An external replication on the effects of test-driven development using a multi-site blind analysis approach. In: Proceedings of ESEM, pp. 3:1–3:10. ACM (2016)
10. Graziotin, D., Fagerholm, F., Wang, X., Abrahamsson, P.: What happens when software developers are (un)happy. J. Syst. Softw. **140**, 32–47 (2018)
11. Graziotin, D., Wang, X., Abrahamsson, P.: Are happy developers more productive? In: Heidrich, J., Oivo, M., Jedlitschka, A., Baldassarre, M.T. (eds.) PROFES 2013. LNCS, vol. 7983, pp. 50–64. Springer, Heidelberg (2013). https://doi.org/10.1007/978-3-642-39259-7_7
12. Guzman, E., Azócar, D., Li, Y.: Sentiment analysis of commit comments in GitHub: an empirical study. In: Proceedings of MSR, pp. 352–355. ACM (2014)
13. Guzman, E., Bruegge, B.: Towards emotional awareness in software development teams. In: Proceedings of ESEC/FSE, pp. 671–674. ACM (2013)
14. Hassan, A.E.: The road ahead for mining software repositories. In: Proceedings of FoSM, pp. 48–57 (2008)
15. Huq, S.F., Sadiq, A.Z., Sakib, K.: Understanding the effect of developer sentiment on fix-inducing changes: an exploratory study on GitHub pull requests. In: Proceedings of Asia-Pacific Software Engineering Conference, pp. 514–521. IEEE (2019)
16. Islam, M.R., Zibran, M.F.: Towards understanding and exploiting developers' emotional variations in software engineering. In: Proceedings of SERA, pp. 185–192 (2016)
17. Islam, M.R., Zibran, M.F.: Sentiment analysis of software bug related commit messages. In: Proceedings of SEDE, pp. 3–8 (2018)
18. Islam, M.R., Zibran, M.F.: SentiStrength-SE: exploiting domain specificity for improved sentiment analysis in software engineering text. J. Syst. Softw. **145**, 125–146 (2018)
19. Jongeling, R., Sarkar, P., Datta, S., Serebrenik, A.: On negative results when using sentiment analysis tools for software engineering research. Empirical Softw. Eng. **22**(5), 2543–2584 (2017). https://doi.org/10.1007/s10664-016-9493-x
20. Juristo, N., Moreno, A.M.: Basics of Software Engineering Experimentation. Kluwer Academic Publishers, Boston (2001)
21. Just, R., Jalali, D., Ernst, M.D.: Defects4J: a database of existing faults to enable controlled testing studies for java programs. In: Proceedings of ISSTA, pp. 437–440. ACM (2014)
22. Keogh, R.H., Cox, D.R.: Case-Control Studies. Institute of Mathematical Statistics Monographs. Cambridge University Press, Cambridge (2014)
23. Landis, J.R., Koch, G.G.: The measurement of observer agreement for categorical data. Biometrics **33**(1), 159–174 (1977)
24. Lewallen, S., Courtright, P.B.: Epidemiology in practice: case-control studies. Commun. Eye Health **11**(28), 57–8 (1998)
25. Lin, B., Zampetti, F., Bavota, G., Di Penta, M., Lanza, M., Oliveto, R.: Sentiment analysis for software engineering: how far can we go? In: Proceedings of ICSE, pp. 94–104. ACM (2018)

26. McDonald, J.H.: Handbook of Biological Statistics. Sparky House Publishing, Baltimore (2009)
27. Miller, L.E., Stewart, M.E.: The blind leading the blind: Use and misuse of blinding in randomized controlled trials. Contemp. Clin. Trials **32**(2), 240–243 (2011)
28. Miranda, B., Cruciani, E., Verdecchia, R., Bertolino, A.: Fast approaches to scalable similarity-based test case prioritization. In: Proceedings of ICSE, pp. 222–232. ACM (2018)
29. Müller, S.C., Fritz, T.: Stuck and frustrated or in flow and happy: sensing developers' emotions and progress. In: Proceedings of ICSE, vol. 1, pp. 688–699 (2015)
30. Murgia, A., Tourani, P., Adams, B., Ortu, M.: Do developers feel emotions? An exploratory analysis of emotions in software artifacts. In: Proceedings of MSR 2014, pp. 262–271. ACM (2014)
31. Novielli, N., Girardi, D., Lanubile, F.: A benchmark study on sentiment analysis for software engineering research. In: Proceedings of MSR, pp. 364–375. ACM (2018)
32. Pang, B., Lee, L.: Opinion mining and sentiment analysis. Found. Trends Inf. Retrieval **2**(1–2), 1–135 (2008)
33. Pletea, D., Vasilescu, B., Serebrenik, A.: Security and emotion: sentiment analysis of security discussions on GitHub. In: Proceedings of Working Conference on Mining Software Repositories, pp. 348–351. ACM (2014)
34. Ray, B., Hellendoorn, V., Godhane, S., Tu, Z., Bacchelli, A., Devanbu, P.: On the "naturalness" of buggy code. In: Proceedings of ICSE, pp. 428–439. ACM (2016)
35. Romano, S., Fucci, D., Scanniello, G., Turhan, B., Juristo, N.: Findings from a multi-method study on test-driven development. Inf. Softw. Technol. **89**, 64–77 (2017)
36. Shaver, P., Schwartz, J., Kirson, D., O'Connor, G.: Emotion knowledge: further exploration of a prototype approach. J. Pers. Soc. Psychol. **52**(6), 1061–86 (1987)
37. Shu, L., et al.: Wearable emotion recognition using heart rate data from a smart bracelet. Sensors **20**(3), 718–736 (2020)
38. Sinha, V., Lazar, A., Sharif, B.: Analyzing developer sentiment in commit logs. In: Proceedings of MSR, pp. 520-523. ACM (2016)
39. Song, J.W., Chung, K.C.: Observational studies: cohort and case-control studies. Plast. Reconstr. Surg. **126**(6), 2234–42 (2010)
40. Souza, R., Silva, B.: Sentiment analysis of travis CI builds. In: Proceedings of MSR, pp. 459–462. IEEE (2017)
41. Thelwall, M., Buckley, K., Paltoglou, G.: Sentiment strength detection for the social web. J. Am. Soc. Inform. Sci. Technol. **63**(1), 163–173 (2012)
42. Turner, E.L., Dobson, J.E., Pocock, S.J.: Categorisation of continuous risk factors in epidemiological publications: a survey of current practice. Epidemiol. Perspect. Innov. **7**(9), 10 (2010)
43. Wohlin, C., Runeson, P., Hst, M., Ohlsson, M.C., Regnell, B., Wessln, A.: Experimentation in Software Engineering. Springer, Heidelberg (2012). https://doi.org/10.1007/978-3-642-29044-2

Software Development

Kuksa*: Self-adaptive Microservices in Automotive Systems

Ahmad Banijamali[1](✉) , Pasi Kuvaja[1] , Markku Oivo[1] ,
and Pooyan Jamshidi[2]

[1] M3S Research Unit, ITEE Faculty, University of Oulu, Oulu, Finland
{ahmad.banijamali,pasi.Kuvaja,markku.oivo}@oulu.fi
[2] Computer Science and Engineering Department, University of South Carolina,
Columbia, USA
pjamshid@cse.sc.edu

Abstract. In pervasive dynamic environments, vehicles connect to other objects to send operational data and receive updates so that vehicular applications can provide services to users on demand. Automotive systems should be self-adaptive, thereby they can make real-time decisions based on changing operating conditions. Emerging modern solutions, such as microservices could improve self-adaptation capabilities and ensure higher levels of quality performance in many domains. We employed a real-world automotive platform called Eclipse Kuksa to propose a framework based on microservices architecture to enhance the self-adaptation capabilities of automotive systems for runtime data analysis. To evaluate the designed solution, we conducted an experiment in an automotive laboratory setting where our solution was implemented as a microservice-based adaptation engine and integrated with other Eclipse Kuksa components. The results of our study indicate the importance of design trade-offs for quality requirements' satisfaction levels of each microservices and the whole system for the optimal performance of an adaptive system at runtime.

Keywords: Microservices · Self-adaptive systems · Automotive · Cloud

1 Introduction

The importance of software in the automotive domain has increased because most of the innovations in new cars originate from software, large computing power, and modern sensors. A vehicle is now a part of a network to collaborate with other vehicles, cloud, edge, and the surrounding infrastructure to deliver value-added services [19]. Cloud and edge platforms have enabled new services based on access to car data and functions from outside the car. Because of the large volume of these data, service management in the domain of connected vehicles is appealing for reliable and efficient solutions [23], allowing for scalable and autonomous processing.

© Springer Nature Switzerland AG 2020
M. Morisio et al. (Eds.): PROFES 2020, LNCS 12562, pp. 367–384, 2020.
https://doi.org/10.1007/978-3-030-64148-1_23

In the highly dynamic environment that automotive systems operate, services should be able to automatically and quickly adapt to changes at runtime to preserve a level of quality under the complex operating conditions, such as scaling workloads and faults [17]. To turn vehicles into self-adaptive systems, we have to combine self-managing capabilities with architectural design patterns that enable self-adaptive functioning under complex working conditions [2].

Microservice architectures are a potential solution for designing and deploying self-adaptive business capabilities [18]. Although there have been many attempts in the development of self-adaptive systems, a small number of microservices solutions, such as Kubernetes, load balancers, and circuit breakers could find their ways to the industry to facilitate autonomic management of microservice systems [17].

There is also an increasing interest in microservices in the automotive domain; however, the research on the microservice architectures that enable self-adaptive automotive systems is still in the early stage. A previous survey [4] highlighted this research gap for architecture-based self-adaptation in automotive systems. To address this need, we empirically investigated how microservices patterns, such as load balancing, resiliency mechanisms, and monitoring systems can improve the self-adaptive quality performance under the dynamic conditions of the automotive domain [3]. In this paper, we extend the study on the microservice architectures in the automotive domain *to suggest a framework called Kuksa* that aims at improving the self-adaptation capabilities of automotive systems by proposing a microservice-based autonomic controller.* We employed the Eclipse Kuksa architecture[1] in the automotive domain to design Kuksa* and evaluated it in an automotive experimental laboratory setting.

The results of this study are valuable for the system architects and academic researchers in the automotive domain. Industrial practitioners can benefit from experimental results on the performance and configurations of self-adaptive microservice systems in a real-world industrial case in the automotive domain. Academics can also gain insights into quality research gaps, service optimisation, and quality trade-off challenges in self-adaptive systems. The key contributions of the study are as follows: (1) the Kuksa* framework to enhance the self-adaptation capabilities of automotive systems by using microservice architectures and (2) the empirical evaluation of the framework in an experimental setting and showing the results of design and runtime trade-offs.

2   Background and Related Work

This section provides a brief overview of previous studies and related work.

2.1   Background

Microservices: Large monolithic systems hardly can scale when different modules have conflicting resource requirements, life cycles, and deployment frameworks [3]. Thus, there has been an increasing interest to migrate systems to

---

[1] https://www.eclipse.org/kuksa/.

more scalable and reliable architectures, such as microservices [5]. Breaking down applications into a set of smaller, interconnected services trades external complexity for microservice simplicity [18].

Microservices are a design alternative that is used to foster further research on self-adaptive systems [17]. They isolate business functions into small services to optimise the autonomy, modifiability, and replaceability of the services. Microservice architectures pertain to challenges that should be carefully addressed. For example, they increase the complexity due to only the fact that they are distributed. Therefore, it is necessary to have inter-process and autonomic communications among different microservices [5]. Although microservices improve the communication with the back-end databases, they apply partitioned database architecture, which means it is often necessary to update multiple databases that are owned by different services [21] and to have an eventual consistency-based approach. Also, a large number of microservices in an application may increase latency and performance issues [5]. Therefore, microservices should work as self-adaptive systems that dynamically learn and adapt their behaviours to preserve specific quality levels under dynamic operating conditions [17].

Cloud Platforms in the Automotive Domain: Cloud platforms in the automotive domain are designed for high scalability and flexibility and offer the continuous delivery of new software applications, such as telematics, infotainment, fleet management, and remote diagnostics and maintenance [13]. The creation of scalable, extensible, and hardware-agnostic platforms has facilitated the deployment of collaborative vehicle applications [25]. With the vehicle movement, it is necessary not only to have access to an infinitely scalable architecture supporting data analytics and application development in the cloud [24] but also to adapt to changes in the operating conditions [26]. For instance, when there is an interruption in the communication network, services in vehicles or the cloud should adopt alternative offline scenarios [26].

2.2 Related Work

Architecture-based adaptation is addressed by (1) the adaptation capability of a system to change with minimal human intervention and (2) the control loop mechanisms in the system that separate core services from adaptation services [27]. Policy-based architecture adaptation is an approach to map a functional situation to relevant action, strategy, or reconfiguration [12]. We used this approach to decouple a system adaptation logic with knowledge about how to react when an adaptation is required. Architecture-based adaptation allows architectural reconfiguration based on predefined rules [27].

Architectural configurations impact the performance of self-adaptive software systems [20]. There exist many techniques, such as Bayesian optimisation [14] and multi-objective optimisation [10] that have been used for moving towards the optimal performance of self-adaptive systems. Furthermore, many approaches, such as planning and constraint-solving algorithms have been used to find a new target configuration that satisfies the given constraints of a system [29].

Control loops are commonly used in policy-based architecture adaptation approaches to collect data about external environments and make autonomic decisions [15]. In this regard, inducing microservices with the primitives of self-adaptivity is a strong candidate for addressing autonomic trade-offs [11]. Pereira et al. [22] presented an adaptive system that designed the control loop components in the form of microservices that are easily deployed in a container-based system, such as Kubernetes. Another study [1] proposed an architecture-based self-adaptation service for cloud-native applications based on the Rainbow self-adaptation framework with support for Docker containers and Kubernetes. Current approaches mainly rely on the quantitative verification of system properties, including techniques to produce formal guarantees about the quantitative aspects of systems, such as performance [8].

There has been considerable work in the area of managing software systems by using service compositions and adaptations [7]. However, they hardly address the problem from the dynamic adaptation perspective by balancing microservices performance at runtime, specifically in the automotive domain. Our study has tackled this issue and investigated how self-adaptive microservices can optimise automotive systems' performance at runtime.

3   Research Method

This section describes the current study's objective, research questions, research methods, and the Eclipse Kuksa framework.

3.1   Objective and Research Questions

The study objective is to design a microservice architecture for enhancing the self-adaptation capabilities of automotive systems. To achieve this objective, we devised the following research questions (RQs):

- RQ1: How can microservices be applied in the design of self-adaptive systems in the automotive domain?
- RQ2: What are the quality trade-offs at runtime when using self-adaptive microservices in the automotive domain?

3.2   Research Methods

To propose the Kuksa* framework, we applied the concept of control loops (MAPE-K) [15] to render a design solution that improves over the system life cycle through accumulating knowledge. In addition, we opted for an experimental method and a laboratory setting (see Sect. 5 for the detailed description of the experimental scenario and setting) that allowed us to investigate performance trade-offs from the Kuksa* framework and the system under evaluation regarding self-adaptation capabilities. We investigated how self-adaptation microservices can adapt the system to changes and how they can register changes into the whole system. The laboratory setting helped us to demonstrate and control the impact of changes on the performance of the designed architecture because real context evaluations are often safety-critical, complex, and costly [28].

We designed multiple microservices to enable the self-adaptation in our designed setting and to evaluate the system performance based on an *"adaptive video streaming scenario"*. We selected this scenario because of its importance in other automotive scenarios, such as the driver assistance, collision-avoidance, safety-critical scenarios, vehicle-to-vehicle communication, autonomous driving, and comfort systems and its significance in security scenarios in the automotive domain. The video streaming presents an example scenario to show the performance of self-adaptive microservices under highly dynamic conditions of automotive systems, although Kuksa* has high flexibility to be adopted and customised for other scenarios in the automotive domain.

We used the results of previous studies [8,16] to create a metric for measuring the performance of the self-adaptive system under evaluation and comparing it with the static system architecture. The performance of software systems denotes its capabilities in its execution [8], in which two important measures include the solution quality and the time taken to achieve the solution [16]. Hence, the total performance in our designed system composed of time performance and solution quality performance [8], as follows:

$$p(sys) = wt.tp(sys) + wq.qp(sys)$$

where $wt + wq = 1$. The parameters of wt and wq, respectively, indicated the weight factors (importance) for time performance $tp(sys)$ and quality performance $qp(sys)$. Normalisation of $tp(sys)$ and $qp(sys)$ in a range of 0 to 1 allowed us to sum them up in our metric.

Time and quality performances were measured based on the average performance from multiple runs. The $tp(sys)$ used the average time required for the reconfiguration of the video streaming microservice which translates into the time involved in finding a new adaptation strategy configuration in a separate run r. The $tp(sys)$ was calculated based on the ratio of the time needed for reconfiguration in a run r, as follows:

$$tp(r) = 1 - \frac{\sum Reconfiguration\ time(r)}{Duration(r)}$$

The quality performance was calculated based on the achieved video stream quality, using two factors of *frame rate* and *frame quality*, that the system was able to apply within a run r, as follows:

$$qp(r) = \frac{\sum Quality(r)}{Quality\ max}$$

The codomain of qp(r) was $[0, 1]$ and a value close to 1 indicated a better-achieved quality as 1 would imply that the maximum quality performance was reached.

3.3   Eclipse Kuksa

Eclipse Kuksa is a project that provides an open and secure cloud platform to connect a wide range of vehicles to the cloud via in-car and Internet connections. It aims at the mass differentiation of vehicles through application systems, software solutions, and services. The project comprises three open-source software platforms for the (1) in-vehicle, (2) cloud, and (3) application integrated development environment, shown in Fig. 1 (adopted from [3]).

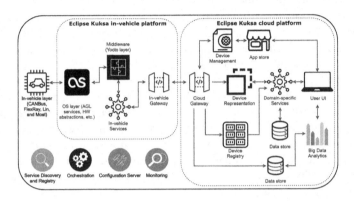

Fig. 1. Software architecture of Eclipse Kuksa.

Gateways (in-vehicle/cloud) enable data communication from vehicles (i.e., car CAN-Bus) or control commands delivery to vehicles. The gateways provide remote service interfaces for connecting vehicles and devices to the cloud back-end using protocols, such as MQTT. The *middleware layer* in the in-vehicle platform includes APIs to abstract the vehicle's electrical/electronic architecture and communication libraries to enable communication services and manage the network access. *OS layer* includes, for example, AGL core services, boot loader, hardware abstractions, and platform update manager.

Device representation provides a digital representation of devices to realise the distinct functionality of domain-specific services. *Device registry* grants access to a distinct functionality for only eligible devices and users. *Domain-specific services* are developed according to various use cases and scenarios in the cloud or vehicles to handle different functions. *Data storage* is necessary for reliable data management systems that can handle the data complexities related to the size, consistency, performance, scalability, and security of different microservices. *Device management* is responsible for tasks, such as the provisioning, configuration, monitoring, and diagnostics of connected devices. *Kuksa app store* is a digital repository for software applications developed by vehicle manufacturers and other third-party providers. *Visualisation and data analytics* efficiently identify, collect, clean, analyse, and visualise that data to enable new services.

The Kuksa architecture [3] relies on more microservices, including *Service discovery and registry*, which automatically registers and deregisters service instances. It provides a source to find out which of the service instances are currently available. *Configuration server* stores service configurations to isolate the configuration properties from codes and to enable autonomous service rebuilding or restarting. *Monitoring* presents the state of microservices-based systems using consolidated logs, reports, and infrastructure-level metrics, for example, for monitoring service usage and finding performance bottlenecks. *Orchestration* collectively provides the mechanisms that deploy, maintain, and scale services and applications based on configuration settings to meet different workloads.

4   Kuksa*: A Self-adaptive Microservice-based Framework for Automotive Systems

Automotive systems, such as driver assistance or safety-critical systems should allow for modifications of services and systems by taking appropriate actions at runtime based on changes in the vehicle operating condition [7]. The actions can include, for example, replacing one microservice instance with another (e.g., upgrading power train and safety electronic services based on the new trailer attached to the vehicle), changing the number of microservice replicas (e.g., increasing load of vehicular data communication with surrounding objects in a crowded area), and dynamically changing the quality requirements of microservices (e.g., adding new safety requirements and constraints in bad weather conditions) [17]. The functions are automated at runtime in a control loop that collects the details from automotive systems and sensors and acts accordingly.

The autonomic controller, shown in Fig. 2, applies the microservice architecture to improve the in-vehicle and cloud systems with self-adaptation capabilities. It continuously monitors and analyses vehicle's working conditions and executes appropriate actions to resolve issues or improve system quality performance in vehicles with minimal human intervention. Kuksa* was constructed on top of the Eclipse Kuksa platforms, in which container-based services are deployed in Kubernetes clusters to provide actuation and operation of vehicular systems (see Sect. 3.3). The service discovery and registry continuously provides a list of available services and registers and deregisters service instances.

The autonomic controller is responsible for the execution of the MAPE-K control loop by using *Monitoring, Analysis, Planning,* and *Execution* services. These are container images that are registered to the device registry mechanism and deployed in orchestration mechanisms, such as Kubernetes to work as the control loop microservices. The monitoring services provide solutions for collecting, filtering, and reporting runtime executions and performance data from the managed resources in vehicles, such as domain-specific services, sensors, CAN-Bus, Lin, and network nodes. To define variables to be monitored at runtime, it is necessary to collect quality requirements for the healthy functioning of an automotive system (e.g., prioritised emergency messaging of a vehicle accident) and translate them to runtime variables (e.g., network speed ≥ 1 MB/s and processing

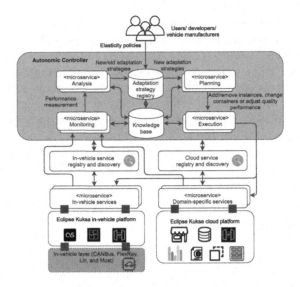

Fig. 2. The Kuksa* framework.

time <1 s). The variables are associated with an automotive scenario (e.g., the emergency braking distance per speed) or the system's behaviour in that scenario (e.g., system reconfiguration time or response time). The monitoring results are affected by sensing issues, such as latency, inaccuracy, or reliability [9].

The values of the monitored variables are sent for runtime analysis services to model the system's operating conditions and provide a perception of the current scenario surrounding the managed system of the vehicle. Many techniques and solutions (i.e., machine learning or fuzzy logic) can be used here to learn about the performing environment, such as traffic states in different urban areas and provide more efficient and reliable models that facilitate the prediction of future conditions (e.g., analysing data loads and driver's profiles to optimise services' data consumption). Using the microservice architecture assures that the analysis services are highly available to model operating conditions at complex runtime situations of vehicles, although the distribution of microservice may require extra monitoring data to decrease the possibility of wrong perceptions of the current environment scenario and the likelihood of triggering faulty adaptation decisions. For example, the adaptive cruise control can receive more data from the vehicle's radar to confirm that it provides reliable results (e.g. no distortion is present). The results of the analysis services are presented as the adaptation strategies, including creating new strategies or keeping existing ones based on the comparison of the optimum and actual working conditions. Adaptation strategies are collected and stored in databases called the adaptation strategy registry.

The adaptation planning services are responsible for making decisions about triggering a new adaptation strategy and sending a set of actions needed to reach the optimum state. The decisions can include, for example, adding or removing microservice replicas, triggering a new service while stopping a running one (e.g., disabling the cruise control service while alarming the user), replacing a container image with a newly downloaded service, optimising quality attributes in a list of multiple running automotive services, updating the service deployment processes (e.g., deploy new applications only when there is a high-speed network connection or the vehicle is parked), or a combination of these actions. The independency among different microservices makes them a secure alternative for runtime planning of new updates and reconfigurations in vehicular systems. The solution space could include inputs from, for example, drivers, application providers, or vehicle manufacturers or be created at runtime by using, for example, artificial intelligence models. The analysis and planning services may confront challenges concerning latency or model uncertainty [9].

The adaptation execution services control the implementation of a strategy and are able to deploy runtime updates. Comparing to monolithic architectures, microservices allow simplifying the solution space as we need to test and execute a smaller set of services. The strategy could be directly updated in services at runtime, e.g., infotainment systems, or it may require extra privileges from vehicle manufacturers before deployment, e.g., cruise control systems. The knowledge from this phase is stored in the knowledge base to be used in more informed decision making over the lifetime of the system. Uncertainties related to execution latency or executor reliability are expected at this stage [9].

The final part of the Kuksa* framework is the knowledge base that contains multiple repositories, which provide access to the knowledge and data from microservices according to the interfaces prescribed by the architecture. The knowledge base maintains data of the managed automotive system (i.e., configuration data, adaptation models, service data consumption, service configurations) and the environment (i.e., traffic modelling data, network data, connected objects profiles), adaptation goals, and the states shared by other four services in the autonomic controller. The challenge with using historical data in future scenarios is the effort to capture the delta in knowledge from prior and posterior states, quality requirements, and quality satisfaction levels.

5   Experimental Evaluation

5.1   Experimental Scenario

To show how we can implement the Kuksa* framework, we used a laboratory setting and deployed a container-based control loop on the in-vehicle platform of the Eclipse Kuksa to demonstrate self-adaptation microservices in the automotive domain. The experiment was implemented on a mobile robotic device called rover. The control loop enabled adaptive services for video streaming from a camera on the rover to the cloud back-end. The video received in the cloud was encoded and forwarded to a cloud-native streaming service. The streaming service was attached to a storage service running on the cloud back-end that was responsible for archiving the received video packages. The evaluation has been done by comparing the system performance under evaluation when we had static and adaptive configurations (see Sect. 5.2 for more detail on the configuration settings). The null hypothesis of this experiment indicates that there is no significant difference between the performance of the static and adaptive systems under evaluation.

We planned that the self-adaptive video streaming scenario uses three microservices in the control loop to monitor, analyse, plan, and execute new configurations based on the changes in the performing conditions and adjust its performance by adapting the video frame rate and scale according to network speed conditions. During the experiment, the rover was constantly moving in a circular path in the lab with a speed of 3 km/h. The *connection speed test service* was responsible for the monitoring of the network connection speed in the rover. The *user's config. service* enabled the registration of new user's configurations over-the-air using a Wi-Fi network. The *video adaptation service* took the responsibility of the planning and generating new adaptation strategies according to the network connection speed and the configuration setup received from users. The list of adaptation strategies was defined as the microservice's input in the adaptation space (see Table 2). The *video-streaming services* dynamically executed new adaptation strategies from the adaptation strategy registry repository in case of changing configurations or network load conditions. We designed multiple data stores (representing the knowledge-base in MAPE-K loop) to be connected to the microservices, in which it allowed us to minimise failures and the overhead load in our system because microservices could access the historical data in case there were service interruptions, service failures, or no new configurations. All services were container-based and were running in a Kubernetes cluster that was responsible for creating managing service replicas. In the designed scenario, the frame rate and scale of the video were automatically and dynamically reduced if the load of the network increased and passed a specific threshold. The threshold was calculated based on the average upload speed in a period of three hours before the experiment.

5.2   Experimental Setting

The In-vehicle Platform: We used an open-source mobile robotic car, which has a RoverSense layer designed for in-vehicle communication demonstrations and a motor driver layer (Arduino) on top of a Raspberry Pi 3 Model B (RPi3). The rover hardware was simulating an electronic control unit (ECU) in vehicles. It runs based on the in-vehicle Kuksa platform, which included AGL as the operating system and an API for handling rover communications. The in-vehicle Kuksa platform also runs customised software called roverapp[2] designed for a Linux-based, embedded single board computer (i.e., RPi3). The RoverSense layer enables control of the rover and sends telemetry data from rover sensors and camera data, such as video streaming, infrared proximity, and ultrasound.

---

[2] https://app4mc-rover.github.io/rover-app/.

In our experiment, the rover sent the video streams using the real-time messaging protocol (RTMP), which was enabled by the FFMPEG project. The list of microservices that were running on the Kuksa in-vehicle platform is as Table 1.

Table 1. Microservices configuration

Microservice	Technology	Configuration
Service discovery	Hashicorp	Consul discovery
Video adaptation	Python	–
Speed test	Speedtest-cli	Dynamic IP (DHCP)
Video streaming	FFMPEG	Maxrate:3M, bufsize:6M, t:30 s

Also, we had three configuration settings of 'low rate' (LR), 'high rate' (HR), and 'adaptive' in the adaptation space, as shown in Table 2.

Table 2. Adaptation space

Configuration setting		Frame rate	Video scale
Static	LR	30	320:240
	HR	60	720:480
Adaptive		30	320:240
		60	720:480

The Cloud Back-End: In the designed experiment, the cloud back-end was running on the Microsoft Azure. We had a message encoder that was connected to a live streaming service on the back-end. The live streaming service was created in "Media service" on Microsoft Azure and allowed transforming, analysing, and streaming media on a single platform. The videos received in the cloud were archived in a database. All communications between the rover and Azure cloud platform were done through an open Wi-Fi connection on the RPi3. Figure 3 shows the automotive setting in our experiment.

5.3 Results

There were three rounds of video streaming from the rover to the cloud back-end. The first two rounds were static with fixed parameters for 'frame rate' and 'video scale', and the third round used the adaptive configuration based on the network load. Each experiment round included 100 runs of video streaming with a length of 30 s each, meaning 3000 s of video streaming in each round.

The adaptive system dynamically changed the video streaming configuration according to the latest adaptation strategies. The video adaptation service

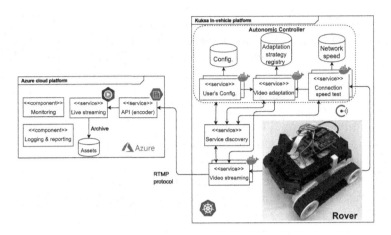

Fig. 3. The experimental setting.

continuously provided new adaptation strategies based on the results from the monitoring and user config. services. In the adaptive configuration setting, the video adaptation service generated the LR configuration in 31% of the total runs, and the rest was done with the HR configuration. Figure 4 shows the outcome of our experiment using different configuration settings. It shows how the video streaming configuration was changing according to network connection loads. It indicates that the adaptive system configuration attempted to reach an optimum for the video frame rate and quality (low values in video frame quality graph means better image quality).

Table 3 provides the aggregated results of our experiment. In this table, $XrYq$ shows quality trade-offs for the video streaming sent to the cloud. For example, $5r5q$ declares equal weight for the video frame rate per second (fps) and the video frame quality. $9r1q$ shows that the importance of having double fps is nine times more than the frame quality, where $1r9q$ shows the opposite.

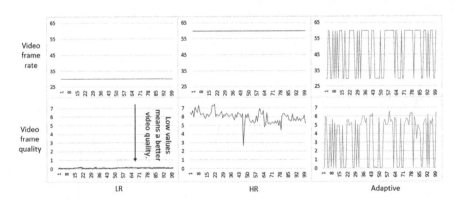

Fig. 4. The system behaviour in three configuration settings.

On the other side, $p1(sys)$ shows equal weight factors for the time and quality performances ($wt = wq = 0.5$), and $p2(sys)$ shows more importance given to the time performance rather than quality performance ($wt = 9 * wq$), where $p3(sys)$ shows the opposite weight factors and more stress on the quality performance ($wq = 9 * wt$).

Table 3. Evaluation results for two architecture designs

Metric	Static system						Adaptive system		
	LR			HR					
	5r5q	9r1q	1r9q	5r5q	9r1q	1r9q	5r5q	9r1q	1r9q
tp	1			1			0.91		
qp	0.74	0.55	0.94	0.6	0.92	0.28	0.68	0.78	0.58
$p1(sys)$	0.87	0.78	0.97	0.8	0.96	0.64	0.8	0.85	0.75
$p2(sys)$	0.97	0.96	0.99	0.96	0.99	0.93	0.89	0.9	0.88
$p3(sys)$	0.77	0.6	0.95	0.64	0.93	0.35	0.7	0.79	0.61

* **Remark:** tp: time perf., qp: quality perf., $pN(sys)$: three weight settings for time and quality perf., $XrYq$: three weight settings for video frame rate and video frame quality.

It was necessary to provide multiple sets of trade-off in the evaluation setting because various scenarios in vehicles require customised, adaptive settings according to the system quality requirements; for example, safety-critical scenarios may need higher frame rates or lower configuration times comparing to the vehicular comfort systems.

The results show a better time performance when we had static system, $p2(sys)$, configurations. The reason for this is that the configuration time was shorter because the video streaming microservice did not require checking external configuration strategies. However, in an adaptive configuration scenario, the video streaming service had to continuously check the new adaptation strategies from video adaptation strategies, in which it reduced the time performance.

The quality performance of the adaptive system stood between the quality performances from the HR and LR configuration settings. This means that depending on the importance of the fps or frame quality in our requirements, the adaptive system configuration can be adjusted to deliver the required outcome. We could see similar results in the total system performance, $p(sys)$, measurements. For example, when we required a higher frame rate with an emphasis on qp, the adaptive system showed better results than the static LR configuration setting, but when we needed higher frame quality and higher qp, we had better results from the adaptive system compared with the static HR setting.

Summary. To have optimal performance from a self-adaptive automotive system, design trade-offs are necessary at runtime for balancing the expected quality requirements' satisfaction levels of each microservice and the whole system.

6 Discussion

6.1 Overview of Findings and Their Implications

RQ1. How can microservices be applied in the design of self-adaptive systems in the automotive domain? The vehicular systems should be able to adjust their behaviours according to uncertainties in operating conditions, such as changes in the list of running services, quality requirements satisfaction levels, accessibility to data, adaptability of resources, and working contexts. Importing several microservices in the control loop of a self-adaptive system architecture can increase the complexity of the whole system, for example, because of the long reconfiguration time of multiple service replicas or a wrong perception of the vehicle's environment as the reason of conflicting data from different services. Although presenting control components in a form of separate microservices to optimise the behaviour of other services increased the modifiability, configurability, and availability of the system when there was a need for reconfigurations. System adaptations were isolated to limited services, while other services were not affected. This provides higher flexibility in proposing new complex adaptation strategies and models into safety-critical systems of a vehicle.

In vehicular systems, it is necessary to prioritise safety-critical quality requirements over other quality requirements when we make quality trade-off decisions. Microservices make it easier to design the safety-critical trade-offs when making adaptation decisions as they minimise the posterior conflicts among services. Microservice design allowed us to keep all services lightweight, which reduced the time and effort necessary for reconfiguration.

RQ2. What are the quality trade-offs at runtime when using self-adaptive microservices in the automotive domain? We evaluated the runtime performance of a self-adaptive architecture based on microservices in a laboratory setting. Our results indicate that the total performance of the system widely depends on the performance of the individual service instances. Increasing communication among the multiple service instances increased the total time of reaching the final optimum state after registering a new adaptation strategy, resulting in reduced configuration time performance in the system.

The designed architecture resulted in better fault-tolerance of the system because different service instances could fetch the historical data from the knowledge base in case there was no updated information available. This kept the whole system running if the control services could not register adaptation strategies; although multiple data stores may raise challenges, such as data inconsistency.

Using service management mechanisms, such as Kubernetes improved resiliency and healthy function of all services.

To guarantee performance levels, we designed multiple sets of configuration settings (see Table 3) that may be considered in various operating situations of vehicles. The preliminary set of quality attributes and their satisfaction levels for each service and the whole system can be negotiated and designed in vehicular systems; although new configurations may be fetched at runtime from analysis services that use machine learning.

6.2   Threats to Validity

There are threats to the validity [28] of our results. Improving the construct validity required using the right measures in the experiment. The measures in this study were composed based on the relevant approaches and metrics for measuring software system performance in peer-reviewed studies. Internal validity is addressed through the relationship between the constructs and the proposed explanation. We applied an experimental approach in a laboratory setting with defined objectives. Also, the study planning and implementation, the experimental setting, and study results were reviewed and discussed among the authors.

External validity is related to the generalisability of the study. We decided to use a real-world platform and a mobile robotic device (simulating the vehicular ECUs) to address the adaptive performance of a video streaming service based on time and quality measures. Even though the system under evaluation does not represent all scenarios in the automotive domain, such as safety-critical situations, the findings show how self-adaption microservices can be used to adapt to dynamic real-time requirements of vehicular systems. In addition, Kuksa* was designed to be flexibly applied in other automotive scenarios. However, the findings of this study should not be generalised beyond its original scope. We have provided all the details about the experimental setting and all publicly available materials on GitHub[3].

6.3   Recommendations for Future Research

The measures used in this study were extracted from the prior software engineering studies. We propose future studies to investigate the performance of self-adaptive automotive microservices using domain-specific measures from automotive software engineering. In addition, future studies could strengthen our results by evaluating our services and experimental setting in a real automotive environment where there exist safety-critical scenarios, such as the service unreliability due to communication network interruptions. To improve the understanding of the self-adaptive microservices in automotive systems, we propose more studies on the learning configuration algorithms, domain-specific testing approaches, and quality measurements of self-adaptive microservices.

---

[3] https://github.com/ahmadbanijamali/Adaptive-video-streaming.

Adaptive video-streaming services are used as an example to introduce the self-adaption microservice into automotive systems. We propose future studies to investigate the application of self-adaptation microservices in other automotive scenarios and review the set decisions about how decentralised each of the MAPE-K services must be made.

7 Conclusions

Microservices have gained increasing popularity in the automotive domain. Considering the dynamic working conditions in vehicles and beyond them, software systems should adapt their behaviours based on changes in the operating and surrounding environments. We aimed to investigate self-adaptation microservices in the automotive domain. To achieve that aim, we proposed the Kuksa* framework by updating the architecture of a real-world automotive platform and investigated the framework applicability in an automotive laboratory setting.

Our proposed design could adapt the system behaviour according to the changes in the performing conditions. Our study showed that system performance requires design trade-offs for balancing the expected quality requirements' satisfaction levels. Our findings show the potential of using microservices for self-adaptive automotive systems at runtime.

References

1. Aderaldo, C.M., Mendonça, N.C., Schmerl, B., Garlan, D., Kubow: an architecture-based self-adaptation service for cloud-native applications. In: Proceedings of the 13th European Conference on Software Architecture, pp. 42–45 (2019)
2. Banijamali, A., Heisig, P., Kristan, J., Kuvaja, P., Oivo, M.: Software architecture design of cloud platforms in automotive domain: an online survey. In: 12th IEEE International Conference on Service-Oriented Computing and Applications, pp. 168–175. IEEE (2019)
3. Banijamali, A., Jamshidi, P., Kuvaja, P., Oivo, M.: Kuksa: a cloud-native architecture for enabling continuous delivery in the automotive domain. In: Franch, X., Männistö, T., Martínez-Fernández, S. (eds.) PROFES 2019. LNCS, vol. 11915, pp. 455–472. Springer, Cham (2019). https://doi.org/10.1007/978-3-030-35333-9_32
4. Banijamali, A., Pakanen, O., Kuvaja, P., Oivo, M.: Software architectures of the convergence of cloud computing and the internet of things: a systematic literature review. Info. Soft. Tech. 122, 106271 (2020)
5. Bass, L., Weber, I., Zhu, L.: DevOps: A Software Architect's Perspective. Addison-Wesley, Boston (2015)
6. Baylov, K., Dimov, A.: Reference architecture for self-adaptive microservice systems. In: Ivanović, M., Bădică, C., Dix, J., Jovanović, Z., Malgeri, M., Savić, M. (eds.) IDC 2017. SCI, vol. 737, pp. 297–303. Springer, Cham (2018). https://doi.org/10.1007/978-3-319-66379-1_26
7. de Lemos, R., et al.: Software engineering for self-adaptive systems: research challenges in the provision of assurances. In: de Lemos, R., Garlan, D., Ghezzi, C., Giese, H. (eds.) Software Engineering for Self-Adaptive Systems III. Assurances. LNCS, vol. 9640, pp. 3–30. Springer, Cham (2017). https://doi.org/10.1007/978-3-319-74183-3_1

8. Eberhardinger, B., Ponsar, H., Klumpp, D., Reif, W.: Measuring and evaluating the performance of self-organization mechanisms within collective adaptive systems. In: Margaria, T., Steffen, B. (eds.) ISoLA 2018. LNCS, vol. 11246, pp. 202–220. Springer, Cham (2018). https://doi.org/10.1007/978-3-030-03424-5_14

9. Esfahani, N., Malek, S.: Uncertainty in self-adaptive software systems. In: de Lemos, R., Giese, H., Müller, H.A., Shaw, M. (eds.) Software Engineering for Self-Adaptive Systems II. LNCS, vol. 7475, pp. 214–238. Springer, Heidelberg (2013). https://doi.org/10.1007/978-3-642-35813-5_9

10. Filieri, A., Hoffmann, H., Maggio, M.: Automated multi-objective control for self-adaptive software design. In: Proceedings of the 2015 10th Joint Meeting on Foundations of Software Engineering, pp. 13–24 (2015)

11. Hassan, S., Bahsoon, R.: Microservices and their design trade-offs: a self-adaptive roadmap. In: International Conference on Services Computing (SCC), pp. 813–818. IEEE (2016)

12. Ho, H.N., Lee, E.: Model-based reinforcement learning approach for planning in self-adaptive software system. In: Proceedings of the 9th International Conference on Ubiquitous Information, Management and Communication, pp. 1–8 (2015)

13. Jain, P.: Automotive Cloud Technology to Drive Industry's New Business Models, 7 May 2019. http://shiftmobility.com/2017/06/automotive-cloud-technology-drive-automotive-industrys-new-business-models

14. Jamshidi P., Casale G.: An uncertainty-aware approach to optimal configuration of stream processing systems. In: 2016 IEEE 24th International Symposium on Modeling, Analysis and Simulation of Computer and Telecommunication Systems, pp. 39–48. IEEE (2016)

15. Kephart, J.O., Chess, D.M.: The vision of autonomic computing. Computer 36(1), 41–50 (2003)

16. McGeoch, C.: A Guide to Experimental Algorithmics. Cambridge University Press, Cambridge (2012)

17. Mendonça, N.C., Jamshidi, P., Garlan, D., Pahl, C.: Developing self-adaptive microservice systems: challenges and directions. IEEE Softw. (2019)

18. Newman, S.: Building Microservices: Designing Fine-Grained Systems. O'Reilly Media Inc., Sebastopol (2015)

19. Nobre, J.C., et al.: Vehicular software-defined networking and fog computing: integration and design principles. Ad Hoc Netw. 82, 172–181 (2019)

20. Pahl, C., Jamshidi, P., Weyns, D.: Cloud architecture continuity: change models and change rules for sustainable cloud software architectures. J. Softw. Evol. Process 29(2), e1849 (2017)

21. Pahl, C., Jamshidi, P., Zimmermann, O.: Architectural principles for cloud software. ACM Trans. Internet Tech. (TOIT) 18(2), 1–23 (2018)

22. Pereira, J.A., et al.: A platform to enable self-adaptive cloud applications using trustworthiness properties. In: 15th International Symposium on Software Engineering for Adaptive and Self-Managing Systems (SEAMS). IEEE (2020)

23. Shukla, R.M., Sengupta, S., Chatterjee, M.: Software-defined network and cloud-edge collaboration for smart and connected vehicles. In: Proceedings of the Workshop Program of the 19th International Conference on Distributed Computing and Networking, pp. 1–6 (2018)

24. Siegel, J.E., Erb, D.C., Sarma, S.E.: A survey of the connected vehicle landscape-architectures, enabling technologies, applications, and development areas. IEEE Trans. Intell. Transp. Syst. 19, 2391–2406 (2017)

25. Staron, M.: Automotive Software Architectures. Springer, Cham (2017). https://doi.org/10.1007/978-3-319-58610-6

26. Sun, J., Yang, C., Tanjo, T., Sage, K., Aida, K.: Implementation of Self-adaptive Middleware for Mobile Vehicle Tracking Applications on Edge Computing. In: Xiang, Y., Sun, J., Fortino, G., Guerrieri, A., Jung, J.J. (eds.) IDCS 2018. LNCS, vol. 11226, pp. 1–15. Springer, Cham (2018). https://doi.org/10.1007/978-3-030-02738-4_1

27. Weyns, D., Iftikhar, M.U., Hughes, D., Matthys, N.: Applying Architecture-Based Adaptation to Automate the Management of Internet-of-Things. In: Cuesta, C.E., Garlan, D., Pérez, J. (eds.) ECSA 2018. LNCS, vol. 11048, pp. 49–67. Springer, Cham (2018). https://doi.org/10.1007/978-3-030-00761-4_4

28. Wohlin, C., Runeson, P., Höst, M., Ohlsson, M.C., Regnell, B., Wesslén, A.: Experimentation in Software Engineering. Springer, Heidelberg (2012). https://doi.org/10.1007/978-3-642-29044-2

29. Zeller M., Prehofer C.: Timing constraints for runtime adaptation in real-time, networked embedded systems. In: 7th International Symposium on Software Engineering for Adaptive and Self-Managing Systems (SEAMS), pp. 73–82. IEEE (2012)

Compliance Requirements in Large-Scale Software Development: An Industrial Case Study

Muhammad Usman[1($\boxtimes$)], Michael Felderer[1,2], Michael Unterkalmsteiner[1], Eriks Klotins[1], Daniel Mendez[1,3], and Emil Alégroth[1]

[1] Blekinge Institute of Technology, Karlskrona, Sweden
{Muhammad.Usman,Michael.Felderer,Michael.Unterkalmsteiner,
Eriks.Klotins,Daniel.Mendez,Emil.Alegroth}@bth.se
[2] University of Innsbruck, Innsbruck, Austria
[3] fortiss GmbH, Munich, Germany

Abstract. Regulatory compliance is a well-studied area, including research on how to *model, check, analyse, enact, and verify* compliance of software. However, while the theoretical body of knowledge is vast, empirical evidence on challenges with regulatory compliance, as faced by industrial practitioners particularly in the Software Engineering domain, is still lacking. In this paper, we report on an industrial case study which aims at providing insights into common practices and challenges with checking and analysing regulatory compliance, and we discuss our insights in direct relation to the state of reported evidence. Our study is performed at Ericsson AB, a large telecommunications company, which must comply to both locally and internationally governing regulatory entities and standards such as GDPR. The main contributions of this work are empirical evidence on challenges experienced by Ericsson that complement the existing body of knowledge on regulatory compliance.

Keywords: Regulatory compliance · Empirical study

1 Introduction

Modern software development is driven by the problems and needs of various stakeholder groups, formulated as requirements that guide software product development. While a majority of these requirements are typically distilled from business stakeholders, e.g. customers or users, a group of growing importance is community stakeholders [3,23]. Community stakeholders, such as governments and other organizations, issue laws, regulations and policies, and best practices, commonly referred to as compliance requirements [2].

Compliance requirements typically aim at a broad range of stakeholders and use cases, and they are, thus, purposefully expressed in general terms, omitting implementation-specific details. Elicitation and interpretation of implementation-specific details are thereby left to the expertise of affected parties, e.g. individual companies or organisations. However, while the requirements

© Springer Nature Switzerland AG 2020
M. Morisio et al. (Eds.): PROFES 2020, LNCS 12562, pp. 385–401, 2020.
https://doi.org/10.1007/978-3-030-64148-1_24

aim at providing guidance, they also pose challenges, especially in the analysis phase as stakeholders with different objectives may interpret the requirements differently [6,11,19,27].

Inconsistent interpretations may have severe consequences. For example, varying interpretations between development organization and regulating bodies may lead to rework, delays, financial and legal repercussions. This risk is exacerbated by the fact that verification of compliance is often performed late in the software development process. Consequently, any issues discovered in the compliance verification are costly to repair.

In this study, we investigate how compliance requirements are handled at Ericsson AB[1], a large telecommunications organization. This study is carried out as part of a long-term research collaboration with the aim of jointly developing and improving software engineering practices in a research-centric environment. In our study at hands, we focus on understanding challenges and potential improvements in interpreting organization-wide compliance requirements for the implementation in specific use cases.

The rest of this paper is structured as follows: Section 2 presents background in regulatory compliance concepts and terms. Section 3 provides an overview of related studies in the area. Section 4 describes the research questions, the studied case, and outlines the research methods. Section 5 presents our findings. Section 6 discusses the findings, Section 7 concludes the paper.

2   Background and Terminology

Regulatory compliance is the act of ensuring adherence of an organization, process, and/or (software) product to regulations like standards, laws, guidelines, or specifications [2]. Regulatory compliance addresses goals and mitigates risks. These goals and risks are typically linked to dependability properties [5] like privacy, security or safety and result in regulatory artifacts like standards, laws, guidelines, or specifications.

Compliance tasks are common activities that are carried out in order to achieve compliance with regulations. These tasks include compliance modeling, checking, analysis and enactment [2].

Compliance modeling tasks address activities involved in the discovery and formalization of text extracted from regulations needing compliance. *Compliance checking* tasks are activities that ensure that the formalized representations of regulations (the models) capture correctly compliance requirements. Often, activities for compliance modelling and checking are intertwined and used iteratively. *Compliance analysis* tasks involve activities that provide insight into the state of compliance of an organization, a process, a (software) product, etc., as a result of the fulfilment or violation of the compliance requirements, possibly measured via models. *Compliance enactment* tasks involve activities for making changes to an organization, a process, or a (software) product in order to establish or re-establish compliance with a regulation.

---

[1] www.ericsson.com.

The study presented in this paper covers compliance checking and analysis tasks that are performed within software and system development, which covers the core activities of software development including analysis, design, construction, and testing.

3 Related Work

In order to collect related approaches we analyzed available secondary studies on the topic of regulatory compliance and extracted relevant primary studies on checking and analysis of regulatory requirements from them. The list of secondary studies is shown in Table 1.

Table 1. Investigated secondary studies on regulatory compliance

Title	Venue	Year	Ref.
A systematic literature mapping of goal and non-goal modelling methods for legal and regulatory compliance	Requirements engineering journal	2018	[2]
Are we done with business process compliance: state of the art and challenges ahead	Knowledge and Information systems journal	2018	[15]
Using business process compliance approaches for compliance management with regard to digitization: evidence from a systematic literature review	International conference on business process management	2018	[33]
An extended systematic literature review on provision of evidence for safety certification	Information and software technology journal	2014	[28]
A systematic review of compliance measurement based on goals and indicators	Advanced information systems engineering workshops	2011	[34]
A systematic review of goal-oriented requirements management frameworks for business process compliance	Workshop on requirements engineering and aw	2011	[10]

From the secondary studies, we extracted overall 22 primary studies related to checking and analysis of regulatory and legal compliance requirements. As regulations like laws or standards are often region or even country specific, most primary studies explicitly refer to regulations from a specific region or country, i.e., USA or Canada [7,16,17,21], Latin America [35], Australia [1], and Europe [19,36]. Only laws or regulations specific to Asian countries are not covered.

The studies also cover classical regulated domains including finance [17,36], medical [7,19–21,25], law [11,27], public administration [35], automotive [30], and avionics [4,8].

A prominent topic in the studies on regulatory requirements is the extraction or definition of models [7,17,25,36] for compliance checking or monitoring. However, formal checking of compliance is resource-intensive and therefore its complexity is investigated [12,38]. As regulatory requirements intentionally or unintentionally differ in scope, their interpretation is an important topic covered in several publications [6,11,19,27].

Core regulated properties covered are related to security [20], privacy [16,20] and safety [4,18,30].

Most papers are either validated by examples or evaluated based on case studies. Only a few surveys on regulatory compliance are available. Abdullah et al. [1] present a survey on emerging challenges in managing regulatory compliance. The report [31] presents a survey on the state of regulatory compliance in practice.

50% of the 22 papers directly address software development and its artifacts. Most papers cover compliance modelling followed by compliance checking, analysis and enactment. Challenges explicitly mentioned are the complexity and ambiguity of regulations by nature [20], documentation and modeling of the relevant regulatory constraints and their derivations, establishing and keeping traceability of artifacts as well as change management and evolution for keeping the documents, history, and references up to date [30,36], and simple, easy-to-use and aligned modeling and reasoning approaches [18,36].

Via snowball sampling from the related primary studies, we found another very closely related paper to our work by Nekvi et al. [29]. In that paper, the authors present impediments to regulatory compliance of requirements in contractual systems engineering projects based on a case study from the railway domain.

In addition, several other papers, not covered by the secondary studies, discuss software engineering aspects of regulatory compliance. Hamou-Lhadj [14] discusses regulatory compliance and its impact on software development in general. Furthermore, a compliance support framework for global software companies is provided in [13]. Several authors discuss the relationship between agile software development and regulatory compliance. Mishra and Weistroffer [26] discuss issues with incorporating regulatory compliance into agile development.

In the medical domain, McHugh et al. [22] discusses barriers to adopting agile practices when developing medical device software. Soltana et al. [36] refine their UML-based compliance checking approach to enable checking against the GDPR [37]. Fitzgerald and Stol [9] shape the term "continuous compliance" expressing that software development seeks to satisfy regulatory compliance standards on a continuous basis, rather than operating a "big-bang" approach to ensuring compliance just prior to release of the overall product. Finally, Hashmi et al. [15] discuss the potential of blockchain to compliance adherence in distributed software delivery.

Synthesis of this body of work shows that regulatory compliance is a well studied area. However, whilst the theoretical foundation is well established, the amount of empirical industrial case studies [29] and surveys [1,31] on compliance checking and analysis is limited rendering our understanding of what challenges industry faces still weak. This understanding, however, is imperative to steer research activities in a problem-driven manner. This leads us to conclude that there is a gap of knowledge about the regulatory compliance challenges experienced by industrial practitioners. Thereby providing motivation for this study and support for the value of its contribution.

4 Research Methodology

Our goal was to develop support for understanding the current processes and challenges associated with checking and analysis of compliance requirements in a large-scale software development context. To do so, we conducted an exploratory case study [32]. In this section, we describe the research questions, the case, and also the data collection and analysis methods.

4.1 Guiding Research Question

We framed the following guiding research question to steer our study:

What are the challenges and potential improvements for checking and analysis of the compliance requirements?

The research question aims at identifying the challenges faced along the process of checking and analysing the compliance requirements and also the potential improvements to address the challenges.

4.2 Case Description

The case company is Ericsson AB, a large multinational company developing software-intensive products related to Information and Communication Technology (ICT) for service providers. Besides the business requirements of the individual products, there are some generic requirements that are applicable to the entire Ericsson portfolio including over 100 products. The compliance with these generic requirements is mandatory for all products. In this study, we refer to these requirements as compliance requirements. Compliance requirements are specified and maintained by a central unit at the organization level. The central unit also proposes and maintains the design rules and guidelines for supporting the development teams in implementing the compliance requirements.

The case under investigation is a large software product in the telecommunication domain that consists of several sub-systems. Multiple teams, which are geographically distributed, are involved in the development of each sub-system. In the studied case product, the following organisational units work together to handle the compliance requirements:

- Product management: The product management unit selects the compliance requirements that apply to the release under consideration.
- System management: System management, together with the product management, performs the initial analysis to identify the impacted sub-systems. In this initial analysis step, the system management tries to clarify the compliance requirements by reducing assumptions with additional information.
- Sub-systems' development unit: The development unit of each impacted sub-system is responsible for ensuring compliance with the selected compliance requirements, for example, by using the recommended design rules during implementation.

- Verification unit: In the end, the verification unit performs the verification of compliance requirements. The verification process results in a compliance report identifying the sub-systems that are compliant (fully or partially) and non-compliant with the compliance requirements.

The unit of analysis in this study is the compliance process used by multiple units and roles in the case company who specify, analyse, plan, implement and verify compliance requirements.

4.3 Data Collection and Analysis

To maximize the validity of our results, we used a combination of different research methods to collect the data.

- Group discussions - We performed two open-ended group discussions involving multiple researchers and practitioners. The first one was performed at the very beginning of the study to define the scope of the study and agree on a plan. The group discussion involved two researchers (first and third author), unit manager (our main contact for the study) and a member of the verification unit of the case product. The second group discussion was performed towards the end of the study, wherein the researchers (first, second and the fourth author) presented the results and together with the practitioners, representing different units related to the compliance work, identified the future course of actions
- Workshop - To understand the current state-of-the-practice on the verification of the compliance requirements, we conducted a three-hour workshop involving the following roles from the case product: one product manager, one system manager, two architects from two different sub-systems, one product owner and one deployment lead. The verification unit was not represented in the workshop, instead we interviewed them separately to ensure that all the participants feel free to express their opinions. The first author lead the workshop with the support of the third and fourth author. The third and fourth author independently took notes to capture the discussions. During the workshop, we used an instrument (see Sect. 4.4 and Fig. 1 for more details about the instrument) to collect data.
  We conducted the workshop according to the following plan:
  - Introduction (15 min): To introduce the participants to each other and to describe the purpose of the workshop
  - Description of the data collection instrument and the remaining workshop activities (15 min)
  - Data collection using the workshop instrument (30 min)
  - Break (15 min)
  - Open discussion and presentations of the collected data (60 min)
  - Prioritize the ideas to work in the future (30 min)
  - Summary (15 min)

- Interviews - The workshop did not have the representation from the central unit that specifies the compliance requirements nor the verification unit that performs the testing. To cover these two units, we performed two semi-structured interviews that lasted for about an hour each: one with the information owner who is responsible for writing and maintaining the compliance requirements, and second with a test manager of the unit responsible for verifying the compliance requirements.
- Process documentation - We also received and reviewed the official description of the processes related to the compliance work in the case product.

We analyzed the qualitative data about challenges collected during the workshop and the interviews by applying coding [24]. We used the knowledge obtained from the related works and during the initial group discussions to assign interpretative codes [24] to group the challenges into different categories (e.g., process related challenge). The first author assigned these interpretive codes to categorize the challenges. The proposed categories were presented to the other authors and also to the workshop participants.

4.4   Workshop Instrument

In the product under investigation, the compliance work includes various interdependent activities connected through their inputs and outputs. The practitioners involved in the initial group discussion highlighted the importance of alignment between different activities. To systematically collect the data about different compliance activities involving multiple units, we designed a workshop instrument (see Fig. 1). We shared the workshop instrument with the unit manager of the verification team one week before the workshop. We requested the unit manager to review the instrument and provide us their feedback. The unit manager did not suggest any changes in the instrument. The workshop instrument consists of the following parts:

- Activity: Each role relevant to the compliance work is responsible for one or more activities. In this part of the instrument, the workshop participants were asked to describe one compliance work-related activity in which they are involved. The instrument also captures the challenges that the participants face while performing the activity. The activity may involve other resources (e.g., other roles or tools). Therefore, the instrument also has a question about other resources used during the activity, if any. Lastly, some categories of compliance requirements (e.g., security related compliance requirements) are more challenging to handle. The instrument covers the categories of the compliance requirements as well to identify the one that are more challenging to handle.
- Inputs and their owners: Compliance activities depend on certain inputs that are owned or produced by other roles. For example, compliance requirements are described and maintained by a central unit. To understand the alignment and expectations of different roles from each other, it is important to capture

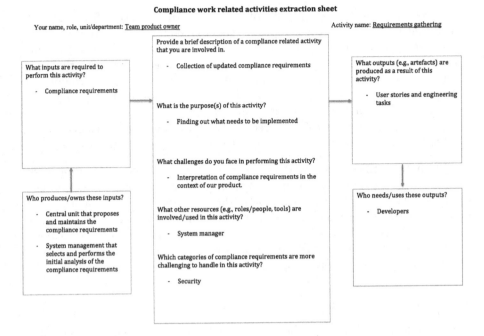

Fig. 1. Instrument used in the case study (one instance filled out by one of our workshop participant).

    if different roles have a shared understanding with regards to inputs and their ownership.

– Outputs and their users: Like inputs, the instrument also captures the outputs produced by the described activity and roles that need that output.

5   Results

In the following, we report on the study results. Note that our discussion of those results in relation to the existing body of knowledge is provided in subsequent sections.

5.1   Overview

In total, seven practitioners from the case product and one from the central unit participated in the study: six in the workshop and two during the interviews. During the workshop and the interviews, the participants highlighted several challenges related to the compliance requirements. The identified challenges are related to the compliance analysis and checking tasks (see Sect. 2 for details on the four types of compliance tasks). The modeling task only came under discussion during the interview with the participant from the central unit that specifies and maintains the compliance requirements. Since the workshop participants do not specify compliance requirements, the focus during the workshop was on interpretation of the requirements, rather than their modeling. Furthermore, the enactment task did not come under any discussion during the interviews or the workshop. The findings of the current study may result in the initiation of some enactment related tasks. Besides challenges, the participants also provided several ideas to further improve the compliance work.

We analyzed the identified challenges and grouped them into three categories: requirements specification related challenges, process related challenges and resource related challenges. We now discuss these challenges and associated improvements suggested by the study participants.

5.2 Requirements Specification Related Challenges

In this category, we included the challenges related to the way the compliance requirements are specified. Compliance requirements are not written for a specific product; instead, they are specified at an abstract level as general requirements that are applicable for all products in the case organization. All participants highlighted the challenge of interpreting the compliance requirements in the context of their product. They view the interpretation of the compliance requirements as the most challenging aspect of the compliance work. Furthermore, at times different units interpret the same compliance requirement differently, which results in disagreements about the expectations. System management is already complimenting the compliance requirements with some additional information to explain them better. The workshop participants suggested to take the additional explanation idea forward and develop a shared interpretation of the compliance requirements in the context of the product.

Some compliance requirements conflict with other requirements (e.g., security and usability), and it becomes challenging to perform the trade-off analysis. In the case product, the business requirements are handled as use cases, while compliance requirements are handled separately. The development teams find it challenging to focus on both business and compliance requirements. Lastly, the central unit that specifies and maintains the compliance requirements, also proposes the design rules to help in the implementation of the compliance requirements. However, in some cases, the link between compliance requirements and the corresponding design rules is not easy to follow. Table 2 lists the requirements specification related challenges.

Challenges: '...Interpreting the compliance requirements, how the general high-level requirements apply to the environment that the product exists within...' Product Owner Challenges: '...Interpretation of the compliance requirements into our product's context...' System Manager Challenges: '...Understanding the intent of the requirements...' Architect

Table 2. Requirements specification related challenges

Challenge description
- Interpretation of compliance requirements in the context of a specific product
- Differences in the understanding of the compliance requirements
- Abstractness of the compliance requirements
- Trade-offs and conflicts between different compliance requirements
- Missing linkage with the business use cases
- Linkage between the compliance requirements and design rules

5.3 Process Related Challenges

In this category, we included the challenges related to the compliance process. The participants highlighted the need to further improve the alignment between different compliance activities. The participants also suggested to improve the coordination between different roles and units involved in the compliance process. In particular, the coordination between the verification unit and the development unit in each sub-system needs to further improve. The case product has several sub-systems, which do not have a consistent process of handling the compliance work.

Furthermore, at times different categories of compliance requirements (e.g., security) are handled differently. The participants highlighted the need to have a consistent process for all compliance requirements. They suggested to further improve the documentation of the entire compliance process with the aim to improve the alignment between different units and to clarify the involved roles and their responsibilities. The participants also shared the view to introduce better requirements management tools to effectively manage and communicate the compliance requirements. Additionally, since compliance requirements and business requirements are managed separately, the participants identified the need to establish a balance between the two types of requirements. Lastly, compliance tasks are not fully automated yet, which makes it a time-consuming and effort-intensive work. Table 3 lists the process related challenges.

Challenges: '...*Different processes used in different organizations resulting in bumpy compliance project requiring extra alignment and project management...*'

Deployment Lead

Challenges: '...*Balance between functional and compliance requirements development...*'

Product Manager

5.4 Resource Related Challenges

In this category, we included challenges that are related to the resources (people, tools) required for handling the compliance requirements. All participants

Table 3. Process related challenges

Challenge description
- Coordination and alignment of the compliance tasks between sub-systems' teams
- Compliance requirements not communicated properly
- Different compliance requirements (e.g., security) managed differently
- Missing dedicated process at the sub-system level
- Lack of coordination between verification and development teams
- Change management of compliance requirements
- Establishing a balance between compliance and business requirements
- Prioritising the right compliance requirements
- Lack of automation

highlighted the lack of available resources and time for handling the compliance requirements. Business requirements that are handled separately consume most of the capacity of the development teams. The teams find it hard to allocate enough resources to handle the compliance requirements. Furthermore, compliance work requires much coordination with other units, which means additional time and resources. The participants also highlighted that the developers are relatively less aware of the compliance requirements and associated design rules as compared to the business requirements. The participants suggested to increase and expand the existing training programs and initiatives to improve the awareness and knowledge about compliance requirements and design rules. Lastly, participants also pointed out that there is a need to introduce better tools to manage the compliance requirements. Table 4 lists the resource related challenges.

Table 4. Resource related challenges

Challenge description
- Lack of dedicated resources and time to handle compliance requirements
- Lack of awareness among developers about compliance requirements
- Lack of awareness among developers about design rules
- Tools used to manage compliance requirements are not appropriate

6   Discussion

While research on supporting modelling, checking, analysing and enacting compliance tasks is abound, as witnessed by the secondary studies discussed in Sect. 3, studies that investigate compliance challenges in practice are rare [29]. Furthermore, most of those studies base their findings on educated opinion or experience [29]. In this paper, we contribute to the body of knowledge of regulatory compliance challenges, initially compiled by Nekvi and Madhavji [29], by adding the case study reported in Sect. 5 and the studies listed in Table 5, which are discussed next. We further provide a brief discussion on fruitful experiences when using this rather unconventional instrumentation before concluding with a discussion of the threats to validity and the mitigation measures.

6.1   Results in Relation to Existing Evidence

Table 5. Studies on challenges in compliance requirements

Paper	Context	Type of study
Abdullah et al. [1]	Compliance management	Case study
Conmy and Paige [8]	Safety standards (avionics)	Educated opinion
Boella et al. [6]	Business processes	Educated opinion
Ghanavati et al. [11]	Business processes	Experience
Nekvi and Madhavji [29]	Railway regulations	Case study

Abdullah et al. [1] grouped compliance management challenges into customer, regulation and solution related factors. Common challenges to our study are the lack of connecting compliance to business objectives, the lack of communicating a common understanding of compliance continuously to employees, inconsistencies in applying regulations, the lack of compliance practices applied throughout an organization, and the lack of tool support for compliance management and monitoring.

Conmy and Paige [8] found that the reuse of models in model-driven architecture (MDA) development processes is challenging when there is a need to certify artefacts. With simple and reusable models, the certification process becomes more burdensome as information is spread between artefacts. On the other hand, if information is duplicated and/or organized such that certification becomes easier, the model artefacts become harder to maintain and reuse, reducing the benefits of MDA.

Both Boella et al. [6] and Ghanavati et al. [11] report on the difficulty of interpreting regulations. The common identified challenges are (1) the need to interpret generic regulations such that they are implementable in specific situations; (2) the communication between stakeholders with different background and viewing compliance issues from their perspective and language; and (3) compliance dynamics, referring to changes in regulations or products that are regulated, and the need to adapt efficiently and effectively to such changes.

Finally, Nekvi and Madhavji [29] found the following common challenges: (1) identifying and accessing relevant set of regulatory documents; (2) the number, size and complexity (in terms of cross-references) of regulations; and (3) cross-cutting concerns of regulations that span different subsystems and require communication between development groups.

Looking at the studies that investigate regulatory requirements, we observe that few developed a dedicated data collection instrument for systematically identifying challenges. Only Nekvi and Madhavji [29] and Abdullah et al. [1] conducted case studies and reported detailed data collection and analysis procedures while the majority of the research relies on experience and educated opinion reports.

Looking at the results of our case study, we find support for all the challenges reported at Ericsson AB. Hence, we conclude that, while the business domains and contexts may differ, there exists a core of common challenges to regulatory requirements that are in need for more solution-oriented research.

6.2 Discussion of Research Methodology

In our workshops, we used a specifically designed instrument to connect different compliance activities using their inputs, outputs and owners/users and to identify the state of compliance practice through which the compliance requirements are analyzed, implemented, and verified. Furthermore, it also aims at capturing the challenges involved in the entire compliance work. The workshop participants were asked to fill one instrument per activity. In total, six company participants filled 11 such instruments (hand-written on A3 paper, see one transcribed example in Fig. 1). Next, the participants were asked to present their instruments during one hour open discussion session.

Overall, we noticed that this discussion facilitated the participants to understand the perspectives of other roles, and also to develop a shared understanding of the compliance work. In particular, the discussion on the challenges faced by each role helped the other roles to realize the importance of better coordination and alignment.

The workshop instrument therefore helped us to not only collect the relevant data efficiently, but it also supported us in structuring the discussion session around the main themes involving compliance activities and their purpose, challenges, categories of the compliance requirements that are more difficult to handle, and the inputs and outputs of the activities. The participants themselves explicitly appreciated the idea of using such a structured instrument during the workshop which is also the reason why we cordially invite interested researchers and practitioners to employ it (or variants of it) themselves report in their respective environments. In our personal view and experience from using it, the workshop instrument provides a good support in understanding the state of compliance practice in large-scale software projects wherein multiple units need to work together to handle the compliance requirements.

6.3 Threats to Validity

As any other empirical study, ours has faced several threats to validity. Here, we report on the most prominent ones related the sampling strategy, subjectivity, and to generalisation.

(Convenience) Sampling. Our choice of industry partner emerges from the pre-existing relationship with them and can be seen as opportunistic. However, we argue that the company is well established and a representative candidate for the research area under investigation. Further, we were able to draw from the insights and experiences of a broad spectrum of stakeholders and, thus, are confident about the completeness in the views and expressed opinions of the involved parties to be able to draw the conclusions we have drawn.

Subjectivity. Subjectivity always plays a vital role in qualitative studies and ranges from several forms of bias of the participants over (mis-)interpreting others' opinions and statements to potential inaccuracies in the coding. While we were particularly interested in gathering subjective experiences and opinions, we were able to mitigate threats emerging from bias and mis-interpretations potentially distorting our results such as by the trustful long-enduring relationship with the partner, by re-assuring the participants transparently about the scope of the study and how we handle the data over them always having the possibility of re-evaluating our results along the final presentation. Especially the latter strengthens our confidence in the accuracy of our coding and in the correctness of how we have captured and interpreted the results.

7   Conclusion

In this paper, we investigated the state of practice in regulatory compliance with an industrial case study. Our primary contribution are the insights gathered on the challenges and a mapping towards existing literature, of what challenges with regulatory compliance can be observed in industrial practice in Ericsson.

To this end, we have further developed a particular workshop instrument. This instrument was effective to identify both the regulatory compliance process used by Ericsson but also gaps and challenges within this process. As such, we perceive this instrument as valuable both for researchers studying the area of regulatory compliance as well as practitioners that wish to evaluate their own compliance process and practices.

Acknowledgments. We would like to acknowledge that this work was supported by the Knowledge Foundation through the projects SERT – Software Engineering ReThought and OSIR (reference number 20190081) at Blekinge Institute of Technology, Sweden.

References

1. Syed Abdullah, N., Sadiq, S., Indulska, M.: Emerging challenges in information systems research for regulatory compliance management. In: Pernici, B. (ed.) CAiSE 2010. LNCS, vol. 6051, pp. 251–265. Springer, Heidelberg (2010). https://doi.org/10.1007/978-3-642-13094-6_21
2. Akhigbe, O., Amyot, D., Richards, G.: A systematic literature mapping of goal and non-goal modelling methods for legal and regulatory compliance. Requirements Eng. **24**(4), 459–481 (2018). https://doi.org/10.1007/s00766-018-0294-1

3. Alexander, I.F.: A taxonomy of stakeholders: human roles in system development. Int. J. Technol. Hum. Inter. (IJTHI) **1**(1), 23–59 (2005)
4. Arthasartsri, S., Ren, H.: Validation and verification methodologies in a380 aircraft reliability program. In: 2009 8th International Conference on Reliability, Maintainability and Safety, pp. 1356–1363. IEEE (2009)
5. Avizienis, A., Laprie, J.C., Randell, B., et al.: Fundamental concepts of dependability. University of Newcastle upon Tyne, Computing Science (2001)
6. Boella, G., Janssen, M., Hulstijn, J., Humphreys, L., Van Der Torre, L.: Managing legal interpretation in regulatory compliance. In: Proceedings of the 14th International Conference on Artificial Intelligence and Law, pp. 23–32 (2013)
7. Breaux, T.D., Anton, A.I.: An algorithm to generate compliance monitors from regulations. Technical report, North Carolina State University, Department of Computer Science (2006)
8. Conmy, P., Paige, R.F.: Challenges when using model driven architecture in the development of safety critical software. In: 4th International Workshop on Model-Based Methodologies for Pervasive and Embedded Software, MOMPES 2007, pp. 127–136. IEEE (2007)
9. Fitzgerald, B., Stol, K.J.: Continuous software engineering: a roadmap and agenda. J. Syst. Softw. **123**, 176–189 (2017)
10. Ghanavati, S., Amyot, D., Peyton, L.: A systematic review of goal-oriented requirements management frameworks for business process compliance. In: 2011 4th International Workshop on Requirements Engineering and Law, pp. 25–34. IEEE (2011)
11. Ghanavati, S., Hulstijn, J.: Impact of legal interpretation in business process compliance. In: 2015 IEEE/ACM 1st International Workshop on TEchnical and LEgal aspects of data pRivacy and SEcurity, pp. 26–31. IEEE (2015)
12. Governatori, G., Hoffmann, J., Sadiq, S., Weber, I.: Detecting regulatory compliance for business process models through semantic annotations. In: Ardagna, D., Mecella, M., Yang, J. (eds.) BPM 2008. LNBIP, vol. 17, pp. 5–17. Springer, Heidelberg (2009). https://doi.org/10.1007/978-3-642-00328-8_2
13. Hamou-Lhadj, A., Hamou-Lhadj, A.: Towards a compliance support framework for global software companies. In: Proceedings of the Software Engineering Conference, p. 2 (2007)
14. Hamou-Lhadj, A.: Regulatory compliance and its impact on software development. Software Compliance Research Group, Department of Electrical and Computer Engineering (2015)
15. Hashmi, M., Governatori, G., Lam, H.-P., Wynn, M.T.: Are we done with business process compliance: state of the art and challenges ahead. Knowl. Inf. Syst. **57**(1), 79–133 (2018). https://doi.org/10.1007/s10115-017-1142-1
16. Hassan, W., Logrippo, L.: Validating compliance with privacy legislation (2008, submitted)
17. Hassan, W., Logrippo, L.: Governance requirements extraction model for legal compliance validation. In: 2009 2nd International Workshop on Requirements Engineering and Law, pp. 7–12. IEEE (2009)
18. Hu, Z., Bilich, C.G.: Experience with establishment of reusable and certifiable safety lifecycle model within ABB. In: Buth, B., Rabe, G., Seyfarth, T. (eds.) SAFECOMP 2009. LNCS, vol. 5775, pp. 132–144. Springer, Heidelberg (2009). https://doi.org/10.1007/978-3-642-04468-7_12
19. Ingolfo, S., Siena, A., Mylopoulos, J., Susi, A., Perini, A.: Arguing regulatory compliance of software requirements. Data Knowl. Eng. **87**, 279–296 (2013)

20. Massey, A.K., Otto, P.N., Hayward, L.J., Antón, A.I.: Evaluating existing security and privacy requirements for legal compliance. Requirements Eng. **15**(1), 119–137 (2010)
21. Maxwell, J.C., Antón, A.I.: Checking existing requirements for compliance with law using a production rule model. In: 2009 2nd International Workshop on Requirements Engineering and Law, pp. 1–6. IEEE (2009)
22. McHugh, M., McCaffery, F., Casey, V.: Barriers to adopting agile practices when developing medical device software. In: Mas, A., Mesquida, A., Rout, T., O'Connor, R.V., Dorling, A. (eds.) SPICE 2012. CCIS, vol. 290, pp. 141–147. Springer, Heidelberg (2012). https://doi.org/10.1007/978-3-642-30439-2_13
23. Midgley, G.: The sacred and profane in critical systems thinking. Syst. Pract. **5**(1), 5–16 (1992)
24. Miles, M.B., Huberman, A.M., Huberman, M.A., Huberman, M.: Qualitative Data Analysis: An Expanded Sourcebook. Sage, Thousand Oaks (1994)
25. Miseldine, P.L., Flegel, U., Schaad, A.: Supporting evidence-based compliance evaluation for partial business process outsourcing scenarios. In: 2008 Requirements Engineering and Law, pp. 31–34. IEEE (2008)
26. Mishra, S., Weistroffer, H.R.: Issues with incorporating regulatory compliance into agile development: a critical analysis. Southern Association for Information Systems (SAIS) (2008)
27. Muthuri, R., Boella, G., Hulstijn, J., Humphreys, L.: Argumentation-based legal requirements engineering: the role of legal interpretation in requirements acquisition. In: 2016 IEEE 24th International Requirements Engineering Conference Workshops (REW), pp. 249–258. IEEE (2016)
28. Nair, S., De La Vara, J.L., Sabetzadeh, M., Briand, L.: An extended systematic literature review on provision of evidence for safety certification. Inf. Softw. Technol. **56**(7), 689–717 (2014)
29. Nekvi, M.R.I., Madhavji, N.H.: Impediments to regulatory compliance of requirements in contractual systems engineering projects: a case study. ACM Trans. Manage. Inf. Syst. (TMIS) **5**(3), 1–35 (2014)
30. Penzenstadler, B., Leuser, J.: Complying with law for RE in the automotive domain. In: 2008 Requirements Engineering and Law, pp. 11–15. IEEE (2008)
31. PWC: Moving Beyond the Baseline: Leveraging the Compliance Function to Gain a Competitive Edge (2015)
32. Runeson, P., Höst, M.: Guidelines for conducting and reporting case study research in software engineering. Empir. Softw. Eng. **14**(2), 131 (2009)
33. Sackmann, S., Kuehnel, S., Seyffarth, T.: Using business process compliance approaches for compliance management with regard to digitization: evidence from a systematic literature review. In: Weske, M., Montali, M., Weber, I., vom Brocke, J. (eds.) BPM 2018. LNCS, vol. 11080, pp. 409–425. Springer, Cham (2018). https://doi.org/10.1007/978-3-319-98648-7_24
34. Shamsaei, A., Amyot, D., Pourshahid, A.: A systematic review of compliance measurement based on goals and indicators. In: Salinesi, C., Pastor, O. (eds.) CAiSE 2011. LNBIP, vol. 83, pp. 228–237. Springer, Heidelberg (2011). https://doi.org/10.1007/978-3-642-22056-2_25
35. da Silva Barboza, L., Gilberto Filho, A.A., de Souza, R.A.: Towards a legal compliance verification approach on the procurement process of it solutions for the Brazilian federal public administration. In: 2014 IEEE 7th International Workshop on Requirements Engineering and Law (RELAW), pp. 39–40. IEEE (2014)

36. Soltana, G., Sabetzadeh, M., Briand, L.C.: Model-based simulation of legal require-
    ments: experience from tax policy simulation. In: 2016 IEEE 24th International
    Requirements Engineering Conference (RE), pp. 303–312. IEEE (2016)
37. Torre, D., Soltana, G., Sabetzadeh, M., Briand, L.C., Auffinger, Y., Goes, P.: Using
    models to enable compliance checking against the GDPR: an experience report.
    In: 2019 ACM/IEEE 22nd International Conference on Model Driven Engineering
    Languages and Systems (MODELS), pp. 1–11. IEEE (2019)
38. Tosatto, S.C., Governatori, G., Kelsen, P.: Business process regulatory compliance
    is hard. IEEE Trans. Serv. Comput. 8(6), 958–970 (2014)

Software Startup Practices – Software Development in Startups Through the Lens of the Essence Theory of Software Engineering

Kai-Kristian Kemell[1]([⊠]) ⓘ, Ville Ravaska[1], Anh Nguyen-Duc[2] ⓘ,
and Pekka Abrahamsson[1] ⓘ

[1] University of Jyväskylä, Jyväskylä 40014, Finland
kai-kristian.o.kemell@jyu.fi
[2] University of Southeast Norway, Notodden, Norway

Abstract. Software startups continue to be important drivers of economy globally. As the initial investment required to found a new software company becomes smaller and smaller resulting from technological advances such as cloud technology, increasing numbers of new software startups are born. Startups are considered to differ from other types of software organizations in various ways, including software development. In this paper, we study software development in startups from the point of view of practices to better understand how startups develop software. Using extant literature and case study data, we devise a list of practices which we categorize using the Essence Theory of Software Engineering (Essence). Based on the data, we propose a list of common practices utilized by software startups. Additionally, we propose potential changes to Essence to make it better suited for the software startup context.

Keywords: Software startup · Essence Theory of Software Engineering · Software development · Software development practice · Case study

1 Introduction

Software startups continue to be important drivers of economy globally. As the initial investment required to found a new software company becomes smaller and smaller as a result of technological progress, more and more startups are founded. While most startups fail [4], just like most new companies [13], some go on to become mature, established software organizations, or even multinational technology giants.

Typically, the main argument for studying software startups is that they differ from mature software organizations in various ways, thus making the findings of many existing studies not directly applicable to them. This is a result of there still being no accurate definition for what a startup is [21, 23]. Various characteristics such as time pressure or resource scarcity are attributed to startups to differentiate them from mature companies [21], but academically drawing an exact line has been a challenge in the area [13]. The way software startups develop software has been one area of study.

© Springer Nature Switzerland AG 2020
M. Morisio et al. (Eds.): PROFES 2020, LNCS 12562, pp. 402–418, 2020.
https://doi.org/10.1007/978-3-030-64148-1_25

For example, Paternoster et al. [21] conducted a more general, large-scale study aiming to understand how software startups develop software. They noted that software startups operate mostly using various Agile practices or ad hoc methods. Specific facets of software development (SWD) in software startups, such as prototyping [19] have also been studied. However, studies focusing on Software Engineering (SE) practices in software startups are still scarce, and studies into SWD in software startups in general are still needed [23]. Some startup practices such as the Five Whys are commonly discussed in e.g. startup education, but systematic studies are lacking.

Thus, to better understand how software startups develop software, we study practices in this paper. Specifically, we seek to understand what practices are commonly used by software startups. In addition, we approach this topic through the lens of the Essence Theory of Software Engineering and seek to understand how this theory fits into the context of software startups. To this end, we study how the seven alphas of the theory (Sect. 2.3) fit the context of software startups, and whether other alphas would be needed to make the theory better suited for this context.

2   Background – Software Startups, Software Development Practices, and the Essence Theory of Software Engineering

This section is split into three subsections. First, we discuss SWD in software startups. Then, we define SWD practices in this context. Finally, we discuss Essence.

2.1   Software Development in Software Startups

Typically, software startups do not strictly follow any formal software development method [21]. Instead, they combine practices from different methods that suit their needs at the moment or simply use ad hoc practices [18].

As the aim of this study is to uncover software development practices universal to (most) software startups, a notable paper is that of Dande et al. [6]. Dande et al. [6] studied software startups in Finland and Switzerland and devised a list of 63 practices commonly utilized by software startups. However, these practices are not solely software development ones but also include practices related to customers and business. Kamulegeya et al. [11] studied these practices and reported that they seemed to apply in the Ugandan startup context as well, further validating this list of practices. They do add, however, that culture and location might influence commonly used practices.

Other studies focusing on practices have not aimed to create such extensive lists of practices but have nonetheless studied software startup practices in different contexts. Klotins, Unterkalmsteiner, and Gorschek [15], for example, created a framework for categorizing software startup practices that differs from the one proposed by Dande et al. [6]. Giardino et al. [9] propose the Greenfield Startup Model to explain software development in early-stage software startups. In the process, they uncovered various practices that supplement and confirm the findings of Dande et al. [6]. Paternoster et al. [21] in their study on how software startups develop software discuss having found 213 practices, which, however, were not listed in their paper. Nonetheless, their findings to lend support to those of Dande et al. [6].

2.2 Software Development Practice as a Construct

Jacobson et al. [10] suggest that a set of practices is what forms a method in the context of SE. Methods, according them, describe ways-of-working, i.e. how work should be carried out. A way-of-working exists in an organization even if a formal SE method is not utilized [10]. A practice, then, describes a more atomic unit of work.

Historically in academic literature, and particularly in Information Systems, the construct *technique* has been used for the same purpose in the context of method engineering [22]. Tolvanen [22] defines a technique to be a set of steps and rules that define how a representation of information system is derived and handled using conceptual structure and related notation. A tool, in this context, refers to a computer-based application supporting the use of a technique.

2.3 The Essence Theory of Software Engineering

The Essence Theory of Software Engineering [10] provides a way of describing methods and practices. It consists of a notational language and a so-called kernel, which includes building blocks that can be used as a basis for constructing methods. The kernel, its authors argue [10], contains elements that are found in any SE project.

The Essence kernel contains three types of objects: alphas (i.e. things to work with), activities (i.e. things to do), and competencies (skills required to carry out the work). In this study, we focus on the alphas in the context of software startups. The seven Essence alphas are as follows: (1) Stakeholders, (2) Opportunity, (3) Requirements, (4) Software System, (5) Team, (6) Way of Working, and (7) Work. These alphas are split into three areas of concern. The first two belong in the customer area of concern, numbers three and four in the solution area of concern, and the last three in the endeavor area of concern. Furthermore, each alpha has alpha states used to track progress on the alpha [10].

The authors of Essence posit [10] that these are the essential elements that are present in every SE project. Every project, then, has its own unique context, which most likely contains more things to work with, but those are not universal to every project. In order to reap the most benefits out of Essence, its users would then extend this basic kernel with the Essence language to include these unique features of their particular project or company to describe their method(s) with it.

In this paper, the role of Essence is two-fold. First, it serves as a framework for analyzing our data. We utilize the alphas to sort the software startup practices we discover into categories. Secondly, in the process of doing so, we study whether all the uncovered practices fit into these seven alphas. I.e., do the alphas also present all the essential elements of software development in software startups?

We chose to utilize Essence as the framework for this study for two reasons. First, Essence is an OMG standard. Standards can shape the industry and should be studied. In this case, we are particularly interested in seeing whether Essence suits startups as well. Secondly, Essence provides one framework for categorizing work in SE projects through its kernel and alphas. In studying practices, we considered it important that we have a framework for categorizing them in some fashion.

3   Study Design

The goal of this study is outlined at the end of the introduction. We approached this topic using a qualitative multiple case study approach. Aside from this empirical data, we utilized the list of 63 startup practices presented by Dande et al. [6].

3.1   Data Collection

The empirical data for this study was collected by means of a multiple case study (n = 13) (Table 1). The interviews were conducted F2F. The audio was recorded, and the recordings were transcribed for analysis. All the respondents were CEOs or founders, as we wanted respondents with extensive case company knowledge.

Table 1. Cases.

Case	Employees	Company domain	Respondents	Age (in years, at the time of interview)
1	6	Software/Hardware	1	<1
2	5	Software	3	1–3
3	3	Software/Hardware	2	<1
4	5	Software	1	1–3
5	7	Software/Consulting	1	<1
6	3	Software/Hardware	1	1–3
7	8	Software	1	>3
8	12	Software	1	>3
9	6	Software	1	1–3
10	5	Software	1	>3
11	85	Software/Hardware	1	1–3
12	5	Software/Hardware	1	>3
13	6	Software	1	>3

We utilized a qualitative, thematic interview approach. We chose a thematic approach because most software startups develop software ad hoc [18, 21]. Data were then collected with one of two interview instruments depending on how technical the respondent(s) were. With technical respondents, we utilized an interview instrument (found on Figshare[1]) more focused on the technical aspects of software development (interviews 6 to 13 in Table 1). With less technical respondents and in group interviews, we utilized an interview instrument built around the Essence alphas (same Figshare link below).

In utilizing two interview instruments, we wanted to gain a deeper understanding of the practices used through triangulation in terms of data collection methods, as suggested

---

[1] https://doi.org/10.6084/m9.figshare.13017227.v1.

by Langley [16] in the context of process data. Using different types of data can provide a more comprehensive understanding of the phenomenon. In this case, we felt that focusing solely on the technical practices might omit less technical ones.

3.2 Data Analysis

The analysis of the empirical material in this paper was conducted following the thematic synthesis guidelines of Cruzes and Dyba [5]. The material was first transcribed for analysis. The material was then read thoroughly for an initial overview of the data. After this, the coding process was started, and each interview was coded. These codes were then arranged into themes. The coding process was done inductively, with codes and themes arising from the data (as opposed to e.g. using Essence as the framework at this stage). E.g., codes included such codes 'team', 'funding', and 'prototype'. Using this approach, we analyzed the data to find practices, either ones already discussed by Dande et al. [6] or novel ones, with the novel ones made into a list.

Practices that were discussed by two or more of the case startups were considered prevalent enough to be included into the list of practices. Once the empirical data had been analyzed and new practices had been formulated, we took the list of 63 software startup practices of Dande et al. [6] and these new practices and inserted them into the framework of the Essence Theory of Software Engineering [10] and its alphas. I.e., we categorized each practice, if possible, under one of these alphas (see Sect. 5.2 for critical discussion about this approach). The categorized practices were then reviewed by three other authors to form a consensus.

4   Results

This section is divided into 9 subsections. In the first one, we present the new practices we uncovered through the case study. In the next seven, we go over the results in relation to each Essence alpha, discussing the practices found in each category. In the ninth and final one, we discuss practices that did not fit under any of these alphas.

Given the space limitations of this paper, the clarifying descriptions for the 63 practices of Dande et al. [6] have not been included in the tables in this section. Such descriptions have, on the other hand, been added for any novel practices proposed by us. Each practice has an identified (Pn), where practices P64 and up are practices based on the empirical data and practices P63 and below are from Dande et al. [6].

4.1   New Practices

Based on the data, we propose 13 new practices (Table 2) that were not present in the list of Dande et al. [6]. These practices were mentioned by at least two case startups. Other new practices were also uncovered but discussed by only one case startup. These practices were not considered common based on this set of data.

Table 2. New practices based on our data.

ID	Practice	Description
P64	Study subjects that support the startup	Studying while working on a startup gains competence in the team without growing in personnel
P65	Attend startup events	Startup events provide opportunity for feedback from experts and allows you to meet potential investors
P66	Create an MVP early on	MVP helps you to focus on the most important features in the beginning
P67	Test features with customers	Testing features with real customers gets you the best feedback
P68	Get advisors	Experienced professionals or investors can help startup to grow in advisor or mentor role
P69	Use efficient tools to plan your business model	Business model canvas, pitch deck etc. help you to focus your business idea and are easy to change if needed
P70	Test different tools	Start with tools team is familiar with and test different ones to find those that work the best for you
P71	Conduct market research	Research the markets and competitors to focus your idea and to find your unique value proposition
P72	Have frequent meetings with the whole team	Use meetings to organize and plan your work at least once a week
P73	Avoid strict roles	Let the team co-operate in all of the tasks
P74	Create a prototype	Create prototype to validate your product or features
P75	Use efficient communication tools	Use tools that allow natural communication inside the team when not working in the same space
P76	Prioritize features	Choose which features are needed now and plan others for future releases

4.2 Opportunity

The opportunity alpha is related to understanding the needs the system is to fulfill and is within the customer area of concern. Practices for this alpha are presented in Table 3 below. No new practices for this category were found in the data.

The case startups were highly focused on understanding their customers and fulfilling the needs of the customer (segments). This is in line with the idea of software startups being product-oriented and customer-focused. On the other hand, the lack of support for

Table 3. Practices for the Opportunity alpha.

ID	Practice	Cases supporting
P1	Focus your product	1, 2, 6, 7, 8, 9, 11, 12, 13
P2	Find your value proposition and stick to it on all levels	9, 13
P4	Focus on goals, whys	9
P18	Validate that your product sells	1, 2, 4, 5, 7, 8, 11
P20	Form deep relations with the first customers to really understand their needs	1, 6, 9, 11, 13
P33	In the development of customer solutions, find a unique value proposition in your way of acting	1, 2, 3, 5, 6, 8, 9
P34	Follow communities	1, 2

P4 makes it seem that these startups were more focused on fulfilling the needs they had uncovered rather than understanding why these needs were important.

Focusing on the system and the needs it was intended to fulfill was considered important from the point of view of competition as well. Focusing on one's unique value proposition is conventionally considered an important strategy for differentiating from one's competitors.

4.3 Stakeholders

Four practices were categorized under the stakeholder alpha (Table 4), which is another alpha in the customer area of concern in Essence. For startups, most notable stakeholders are typically investors and customers or users. In addition, nearly half of the case startups discussed the importance of their advisors as stakeholders (P68).

Table 4. Practices for the Stakeholders alpha.

ID	Practice	Cases supporting
P24	Keep customer communications simple and natural	6
P32	Showing alternatives is the highest proof of expertise	–
P35	Share ideas and get more back	1, 2
P68	Get advisors	1, 4, 5, 6, 8, 9

Especially early-stage startups tend to rely on advisors. For example, startup ecosystems tend to foster advisor relationships in various ways. Startups working in incubators are likely to receive guidance from various experts. Advisors can provide startups with capabilities they are lacking and help them expand their contact networks.

The practice of sharing ideas to hone them and to get feedback was also discussed by some case startups. While in some cases companies may be reluctant to share their ideas in fears of having them stolen, none of the case startups indicated this type of concerns. To this end, advisors can also provide feedback if a startup is afraid of revealing their ideas to potential investors due to such concerns.

4.4 Requirements

Requirements help provide scope for the work being done on the system. Four new practices were uncovered in this category and most existing practices in this category were well-supported by the cases (Table 5).

Table 5. Practices for the Requirements alpha.

ID	Practice	Cases supporting	Cases conflicting
P3	Present the product as facilitating rather than competing to the competitors	–	1, 2, 6
P5	Use proven UX methods	12	–
P10	Design and conduct experiments to find out about user preferences	1, 2, 4, 6, 9, 12, 13	–
P21	Use planning tools that really show value provided to customers	2	–
P51	Anything goes in product planning	1, 2, 11	–
P52	To minimize problems with changes and variations develop a very focused concept	1, 2, 3, 4, 5, 6, 7, 12, 13	–
P53	Develop only what is needed now	1, 2, 3, 12	–
P66	Create an MVP in the beginning	1, 2, 4, 13	–
P67	Test features with customers	1, 3, 4, 5, 6, 7, 8, 9, 11	–
P74	Create prototype	1, 2, 3, 4, 5, 6, 9, 12	–
P76	Prioritize features	1, 2, 3, 9, 11	–

However, P3 was in conflict of what some of the case startups stated. P3 posits that a startup should present its product as facilitating rather than competing. While this is one valid approach, startups do also seek to compete in some cases.

The requirements alpha, in the data, was closely related to the stakeholders alpha: uncovering customer needs was the main focus in requirements (P10). In the case startups, prototypes were typically used to do carry out validation (P67, P74). While a startup should be open to new features and needs (P51), they should be prioritized (P76) to create a clear core product (P52, P53).

4.5 Software System

The software system alpha is focused on the product itself, i.e. the system; software or hardware. The software system alpha is in the solution area of concern of the Essence kernel. Some of the previously proposed practices were largely prevalent in the cases while some received little support from our data. More technical practices (P23, P54, P57) would have required a more technical focus from the interviews. No new practices were proposed for this category. The practices for this category are in Table 6.

Table 6. Practices for the Software System alpha.

ID	Practice	Cases supporting	Cases conflicting
P7	Have a single product, no per customer variants	1, 2, 3, 5, 7, 8, 11, 12	6, 13
P8	Restrict the number of platforms that your product works on	1, 2, 3, 4, 7, 12	–
P14	Anyone can release and stop release	2	–
P23	Adapt your release cycles to the culture of your users	–	–
P54	Make features easy to remove	–	–
P55	Use extendable product architecture	1, 2, 3, 9, 11	–
P57	Bughunt	–	–
P58	Test APIs automatically, UIs manually	2, 13	–
P59	Use generic, non-proprietary technologies	2, 7	–
P60	Create a solid platform	3, 8, 9, 11	–

Out of the practices of this category, only P7 had some conflicts in the data. This practice is largely B2C focused, whereas a B2B startup might understandably focus on tailoring its system especially for larger customers. However, it is perhaps worth aiming for a modular product where such manual tailoring is not needed.

Overall, these practices further underlined that startups should have a clear focus in their development. For example, they should focus on a limited number of platforms, possibly only one initially (P8). Additionally, startups are conventionally seen as agile and their systems as prone to changes based on feedback. Indeed, these practices support the idea that the system should be developed with modifications in mind (P60). Features should be easily added (P55) or removed (P54) when necessary.

4.6 Work

Work in the context of Essence refers to the work tasks required to produce the system. It is under the endeavor area of concern in the Essence kernel. For software startups, this also involves business model development. How the work is carried out from the point of view of e.g. methods, belongs into the way of working category, on the other hand. Few existing practices were considered to belong into this category and no new practices for this category were found (Table 7).

Table 7. Practices for the Work alpha.

ID	Practice	Cases supporting
P44	Tailored gates and done criteria	8
P48	Fail fast, stop and fix	1
P62	Use the most efficient programming languages and platforms	2, 3, 7

While P48 is arguably closely related to prototyping and validation activities which were extensively discussed by the respondents, it was seldom discussed directly. On the other hand, P62 was discussed in relation to system architecture. Efficiency in this case was considered subjectively: the developers focused on languages and platforms they had prior experience with and could thus start working the fastest with.

4.7 Team

The team comprises the individuals working on the startup, the founders or owners and the employees or unpaid ones. It is under the endeavor area of concern in the Essence kernel. The team sizes for the case startups are in Table 1 in Sect. 3. One new practice (P64) was added into this category based on the data (Table 8).

Table 8. Practices for the Team alpha.

ID	Practice	Cases supporting	Cases conflicting
P26	Flat organization	1, 2, 3, 5, 9	–
P27	Consider career expectations of good people	4, 9	–
P28	Don't grow in personnel	1, 2, 3, 12	–
P29	Bind key people	2, 3, 6, 7	–
P36	Small co-located teams	1, 2, 3, 4, 5, 6	12
P37	Have multi-skilled developers	1, 2, 3, 12	–
P38	Keep teams stable in growth mode	1, 2, 3, 4, 6, 7, 13	9
P40	Sharing competence in team	4, 5	–
P41	Start with competence focus and expand as needed	1, 2, 3, 4, 6, 8, 9, 13	–
P42	Start with small experienced team and expand as needed	1, 2, 3, 4, 7, 8, 12, 13	1, 2, 3
P64	Study skills and topics that support your startup	1, 2, 3, 4, 8, 9	–

The most mentioned practices were P41 and P42. The initial team is important as it needs to have the required competencies (P41). To this end, an experienced team may be required (P42). Some of the cases conflicted with P42, although not because the teams did not want an experienced team but simply because they could not find one.

However, this did not mean that the startups did not want and experienced team. Rather, they simply did not have one due to being founded by a group of students with little prior experience.

If the team is lacking competencies and expanding the team is not possible or feasible in a given situation, the existing team members may be have to learn new skills instead (P64). This also ties to P37, as the small team sizes often result in a single employee having to take on various different tasks. A developer is often involved in business decisions as well, especially in early-stage startups.

Flat organization structures (P26) are associated with startups and this was also the case in our data. Involving employees in decision-making may also serve to better bind them (P29). With a small, focused team, staff turnover can be damaging (P38).

4.8 Way of Working

Way of Working refers to how the work is carried out, including practices, tools, processes, and methods [10]. It is under the endeavor area of concern in the Essence kernel. Most previously proposed practices were supported by our data in this category. Four new practices were proposed for this category (Table 9).

Most case startups discussed having taken some existing agile practices and tailoring them rather than using them by the book (P47). While this ties to P72 in that frequent team meetings are common in agile development, it gained enough emphasis to be its own separate practice. On the other hand, the use of by-the-book methods (P46) was not discussed by any respondent, with the startups using various mixed practices.

Communication in general is an important part of agile development, and arguably development in general. The case startups frequently discussed the importance of tools in facilitating communication (P75). While shared physical workspaces can reduce the need for tools, their importance is highlighted when working remotely. An early-stage startup may not have a physical workspace, or its members may have erratic work hours due to day jobs, making communication tools important.

Self-organizing teams are recommended in agile development and this is also arguably common for startups (P39, P73).

4.9 Other Practices Unsuited for Existing Essence Alphas

Not all of the practices we propose, or the ones proposed by Dande et al. [6], fit under any of the existing Essence alphas. These were practices related to the business aspect of software startups, such as marketing, business model development, or funding. Whereas Essence focuses on SE in mature software organizations, the business aspect in software startups is closely intertwined with software development. For example, the needs of the customers or the customers in general, may not be clear to a software startup, which results in the requirements evolving over time.

Table 9. Practices for the Way of Working alpha.

ID	Practice	Cases supporting	Cases conflicting
P9	Use enabling specifications	1, 2, 3	–
P15	Create the development culture before processes	1, 8, 11	–
P39	Let teams self-select	1, 2, 3, 5, 8	–
P43	Have different processes for different goals	–	–
P45	Time process improvements right	3	–
P46	Find the overall development approach that fits your company and its business	–	–
P47	Tailor common agile practices for your culture and needs	1, 2, 3, 4, 6, 7, 8, 13	–
P49	Move fast and break things	4, 7	–
P50	Forget Software Engineering	1	–
P61	Choose scalable technologies	2, 3, 9, 11	–
P63	Start with familiar technologies and processes	1, 2, 3, 7	–
P70	Test different tools	1, 3	–
P72	Have frequent meetings with the whole team	1, 2, 3, 4, 5, 8, 12	–
P73	Don't have strict roles	1, 2, 3	9
P75	Use efficient communication tools	2, 3, 5	–

Practices P6, P11, P25, P31, and P71 concern marketing activities. For example, P25 is about getting a few initial customers who are particularly interested in the system and who can then be used as reference customers in marketing, or who themselves can market the product. P6 and P31 are more general marketing practices. These types of activities are difficult to incorporate into any existing Essence alpha. While marketing is a customer related activity and thus could be linked to stakeholders, the existing stakeholder alpha focuses on clearly identified and involved stakeholders such as the organization commissioning a project, as opposed to obtaining new customers (stakeholders).

P16 and P17 are related to funding. Funding or simply available cash to burn is something that is constantly tracked in a startup, much like the alphas are tracked in Essence. No existing alpha supports funding with clear emphasis. Some of the alpha states of the Work alpha include mentions of securing sufficient funding, but this process is seldom so straightforward in a startup.

The remaining practices in this category are related to overall business model development and business planning. For example, P13 suggests that outsourcing some part of the business can help the startup focus on the core product, and P22 suggests a strategy for rapid and high growth. P30, on the other hand, could be filed under the Stakeholders alpha, but doing so might not place sufficient emphasis on the strategic importance of such decisions from a business point of view.

As we do not formally develop new alphas in this paper, we leave the proposals related to these observations for the following discussion section (Table 10).

Table 10. Practices not applicable to any existing Essence alpha.

ID	Practice	Case supporting	Case conflicting
P6	Do something spectacular	–	–
P11	Use tools to collect data about user behavior	1, 2, 7	–
P12	Make your idea into a product	1, 2, 3, 4, 5, 6, 7, 8, 12, 13	11
P13	Outsource your growth	5, 9, 11, 12, 13	3
P16	Get venture capital and push your product	1, 2, 4, 5, 8, 9	3
P17	Fund it yourself	1, 2, 3, 7, 9	–
P19	Focus early on those people who will give you income in the long run	5, 6, 7, 8, 11, 13	–
P22	Start locally grow globally	1, 2, 3, 6, 7, 8, 9, 13	–
P25	Help customers create a great showcase for you with support	1, 6, 8, 9	–
P30	Form partnerships and bonds with other startups	1, 3, 4, 5, 13	–
P31	Make your own strength as a "brand"	8	–
P56	Only use reliable metrics	5, 6, 7	–
P65	Attend startup events	1, 2, 3, 4, 8	–
P69	Use efficient tools to plan your business model	1, 2, 3	–
P71	Conduct market research	1, 2, 6, 12	–

5 Discussion

The primary contributions of this study are (1) this list of practices 76 and its implications we discuss here, and (2) the implications these practices have for utilizing Essence in the startup context. First, In terms of the practices and the data overall, our findings seem to support existing literature. Paternoster et al. [21] argued that startups develop software using various agile practices or ad hoc. The case startups of this study did discuss the utilization of methods either, only occasionally mentioning singular practices that could be seen as Agile. Many of the practices, such as focusing on a set of functionalities or utilizing MVPs, are also discussed in the Greenfield Startup Model of Giardino et al. [9].

It is common for larger software organizations, too, to take a method such as SCRUM and then omit some practices to create yet another "scrumbut," with quality practices often the first ones to go [8]. Startups, on the other hand, seem to seldom even use tailored methods, pointing to an even higher degree of unsystematic approaches to SE – based on both our data and existing studies (e.g. [18, 21]).

In terms of how startups differ from mature organizations, aside from the aforementioned use of ad hoc methods and singular agile practices, technical debt is one element typically associated with startups [1, 9]. Some of the practices were ones that would arguably generate technical debt (e.g. "move fast, break things"), but the case startups did not explicitly discuss technical debt as an issue.

The list of practices in this paper presents a closer look at the way software startups develop software. These existing studies have focused on method use and specific issues faced by startups such as technical debt accumulation, or MVPs. By better understanding what practices startups use we can further our understanding of how they differ from larger software organizations. This is arguably important as it possible that one factor contributing to the lack of method use in startups may be that they feel that existing methods are not well-suited for the startup context. The practices listed in this paper support existing literature. For example, P66 posits that an MVP should built early on, which is in line with Klotins et al. [14] who argue that one common issue for software startups is taking too long with an initial version of the product.

The other contribution of this paper is related to Essence, which we have used as a theoretical framework for categorizing the practices in this paper. Essence is intended to be used in any SE endeavor. Its so-called kernel, its authors argue [10], contains the elements present in every SE endeavor. This kernel acts as a set of building blocks that can then be extended using the Essence language to describe methods.

In this paper, we looked at Essence from the point of view of software startups. Based on our data and extant literature (e.g. [14, 15]), the business aspect is deeply intertwined with software development in the startup context. In fact, Klotins et al. [14] argue that software startups largely fail due to business issues that originate from SE processes. This supports the idea that SE and business aspects are difficult to separate in software startups. If the goal of Essence is to contain the elements present in every SE endeavor, for the startup context this would thus seem to include business elements.

For example, a conventional software project that is commissioned has clear requirements which have been agreed upon with the customer(s). On the other hand, software startups spend significant effort trying to ascertain whether their idea addresses a real need of a real customer (segment) at all. These idea or business validation activities to hand-in-hand with development activities. Moreover, whereas a developer in a large organization simply develops, in startups roles are seldom so clear-cut, especially early on. In an early-stage startup, a developer may be involved in business activities as well.

Some of the practices in this paper, namely the business-related ones, were not well-suited for any existing Essence alpha. To better incorporate the business aspect into Essence in order to make it more suitable for the startup context, we propose the following: (1) a fourth area of concern for business aspects should be added, and (2) new alphas for this business area of concern should be added. We suggest that funding, business model, and marketing could be new alphas for this area of concern.

Alphas are things to work with and while using Essence one tracks progress on the alphas, each of which is split into alpha states to aid in this process. Therefore, each of these three new alphas should be in some way measurable. First, funding pivotal for any startup [3], and can be quantitatively measured with various metrics, making it a straightforward alpha. Progress on this alpha is likely to fluctuate as cash is burned and new funding is obtained. Secondly, business model development is at the core of a startup [17]. Indeed, one widely used definition for what is a startup posits that a startup is a "temporary organization designed to look for a business model that is repeatable and scalable" [2]. Startups constantly invest resources into validating that they are trying to address a real need. Progress on business model development could be tracked by evaluating how well the current business model is functioning and to what extent it is already operational. Thirdly and finally, marketing may warrant its own alpha. Marketing is as important to startups as it is to any other company [4]. Startups generally have less capital to use on marketing, forcing them to get creative.

Alternatively, one other option would be to look at other theories and frameworks commonly utilized by startups for business model development. Potential business-related alphas could be derived e.g. from the Business Model Canvas [20].

5.1 Practical Implications

The primary practical contribution of this study are the practices listed in the tables in the results section. These practices can help guide work in software startups. Moreover, they can be used to construct methods in conjunction with other practices. Additionally, based on these practices and the data, we suggest the following implications:

- Flat organization and self-organizing teams seem to be an effective way for constructing the initial team. Self-organizing teams have been noted to be beneficial in Agile [12]. It may also be beneficial to avoid strict roles.
- You should have a clear idea of what is the core product and what features are the key features at any given moment. Having a scope too large for the product or an MVP is a frequent reason for failure in software startups [14].
- Forming close relationships with initial customers and users is beneficial. They can help you develop your product and participate in development. They can also aid in marketing. For example, user communities on social media platforms built around your (future) product can be very beneficial.

5.2 Limitations of the Study

There are several limitations in this study. First, defining practices is a challenge in various ways. The level of abstraction in defining a practice can be subjective, and a single practice, when trying to describe how work should be carried out, can be described with varying levels of detail. Thus, some practices could be combined under a single practice of a higher level of abstraction rather than being split into multiple, more detailed practices. This is something that should be taken into account when looking at the practices discussed in this paper.

Secondly, practices in Essence can belong under multiple alphas. For the clarity of presentation, we chose to separate them into categories by alpha. However, some practices under one alpha could also justifiably be assigned under another alpha. Thus, the categorization in this paper is not conclusive and was used to 1) structure the analysis section, and 2) to evaluate whether each practice would fit under *any* existing alpha. Some of the business-focused practices could not clearly fit under any existing alpha, which was one of the main contributions of this study.

Thirdly, eliciting practices is also a challenge. Aside from practices explicitly considered practices by the respondents (e.g. pair programming), practices need to be defined based on what the respondents tell about their startup and its team and their work. This, too, is not a fully process if the practices are defined by an external party (researchers). We present but one way of categorizing work in startups into practices. Indeed, though they never listed them, Paternoster et al. [21] report to have found 213 practices, indicating that many more practices could be found based on different data.

Finally, qualitative studies can suffer from generalizability issues due to the nature of the approach. We, however, argue that 13 cases is sufficient for some generalizability. E.g., Eisenhardt [7] suggests five cases to be sufficient for novel research areas.

6 Conclusions

In this paper, we have studied Software Engineering (SE) in software startups from the point of view of practices, by means of a case study of 13 startups. Data were collected through semi-structured interviews. This set of data was used to complement and expand upon the results of an existing study that produced a list of 63 practices [6]. Based on our empirical data and this list, we propose 76 software startup practices that can be used in method engineering in the startup context.

We then took these practices and inserted them into the framework of the Essence Theory of Software Engineering to understand whether Essence also covers the aspects of SE in software startups and not just conventional SE projects. Our results suggest that the business aspect of startups is so intertwined with SE that the more business-oriented practices could not fit into the framework of Essene. We propose that Essence either be extended to include these business aspects for the startup context, or that other theories and tools are used in conjunction with it to cover the business aspect. We propose potential new alphas that could be used to extend Essence.

References

1. Besker, T., Martini, A., Lokuge, R.E., Blincoe, K., Bosch, J.: Embracing technical debt, from a startup company perspective. In: Proceedings of the 2018 IEEE International Conference on Software Maintenance and Evolution (ICSME). IEEE (2018)
2. Blank, S.: The four steps to the epiphany: successful strategies for products that win. BookBaby (2007)
3. Chang, S.J.: Venture capital financing, strategic alliances, and the initial public offerings of Internet startups. J. Bus. Ventur. **19**(5), 721–741 (2004)

4. Crowne, M.: Why software product startups fail and what to do about it. Evolution of software product development in startup companies. In: Proceedings of the 2002 Engineering Management Conference IEMC 2002, pp. 338–343. IEEE (2002)

5. Cruzes, D.S., Dyba, T.: Recommended steps for thematic synthesis in software engineering. In: Proceedings of the 2011 Symposium on Empirical Software Engineering and Measurement (ESEM), pp. 275–284. IEEE (2011)

6. Dande, A., et al.: Software startup patterns - an empirical study. Tampereen teknillinen yliopisto. Tietotekniikan laitos. Raportti-Tampere University of Technology. Department of Pervasive Computing. Report; 4 (2014)

7. Eisenhardt, K.M.: Building theories from case study research. Acad. Manag. Rev. 14(4), 532–550 (1989)

8. Ghanbari, H., Vartiainen, T., Siponen, M.: Omission of quality software development practices: a systematic literature review. ACM Comput. Surv. 51(2) (2018)

9. Giardino, C., Paternoster, N., Unterkalmsteiner, M., Gorschek, T., Abrahamsson, P.: Software development in startup companies: the greenfield startup model. IEEE Trans. Softw. Eng. 42(6), 585–604 (2016)

10. Jacobson, I., Ng, P.W., McMahon, P., Spence, I., Lidman, S.: The essence of software engineering: the SEMAT kernel. ACM Queue 10(10), 40 (2012)

11. Kamulegeya, G., Hebig, R., Hammouda, I., Chaudron, M., Mugwanya, R.: Exploring the applicability of software startup patterns in the ugandan context. In: Proceedings of the 43rd Euromicro Conference on Software Engineering and Advanced Applications (SEAA), pp. 116–124. IEEE (2017)

12. Karhatsu, H., Ikonen, M., Kettunen, P., Fagerholm, F., Abrahamsson, P.: Building blocks for self-organizing software development teams a framework model and empirical pilot study. In: Proceedings of the 2nd International Conference on Software Technology and Engineering (ICSTE) (2010)

13. Klotins, E.: Software start-ups through an empirical lens: are start-ups snowflakes? In: Proceedings of the International Workshop on Software-intensive Business: Start-ups, Ecosystems and Platforms (SiBW) (2018)

14. Klotins, E., Unterkalmsteiner, M., Gorschek, T.: Software engineering antipatterns in start-ups. IEEE Softw. 36(2), 118–126 (2018)

15. Klotins, E., Unterkalmsteiner, M., Gorschek, T.: Software engineering in start-up companies: an analysis of 88 experience reports. Empir. Softw. Eng. 24(1), 68–102 (2018)

16. Langley, A.: Strategies for theorizing from process data. Acad. Manag. Rev. 24(4) (1999)

17. Lueg, R., Malinauskaite, L., Marinova, I.: The vital role of business processes for a business model: the case of a startup company. Probl. Perspect. Manag. 12(4(contin.)), 213–220 (2014)

18. Melegati, J., Goldman, A., Paulo, S.: Requirements engineering in software startups: a grounded theory approach. In: 2nd International Workshop on Software Startups, Trondheim, Norway (2016)

19. Nguyen-Duc, A., Wang, X., Abrahamsson, P.: What Influences the Speed of prototyping? An empirical investigation of twenty software startups. In: Baumeister, H., Lichter, H., Riebisch, M. (eds.) XP 2017. LNBIP, vol. 283, pp. 20–36. Springer, Cham (2017). https://doi.org/10.1007/978-3-319-57633-6_2

20. Osterwalder, A., Pigneur, Y., Clark, T.: Business Model Generation: A Handbook for Visionaries, Game Changers, and Challengers. Wiley, Hoboken (2010)

21. Paternoster, N., Giardino, C., Unterkalmsteiner, M., Gorschek, T., Abrahamsson, P.: Software development in startup companies: a systematic mapping study. Inf. Softw. Technol. 56(10), 1200–1218 (2014)

22. Tolvanen, J.P.: Incremental method engineering with modeling tools: theoretical principles and empirical evidence. Ph.D. thesis, University of Jyvaskyla (1998)

23. Unterkalmsteiner, M., et al.: Software startups - a research agenda. E-Informatica Softw. Eng. J. 1, 89–124 (2016)

An Empirical Investigation into Industrial Use of Software Metrics Programs

Prabhat Ram[1(✉)], Pilar Rodríguez[2], Markku Oivo[1], Alessandra Bagnato[3], Antonin Abherve[3], Michał Choraś[4], and Rafał Kozik[4]

[1] M3S, Faculty of ITEE, University of Oulu, Oulu 90014, Finland
{prabhat.ram,markku.oivo}@oulu.fi
[2] Faculty of Computer Sciences, Universidad Politécnica de Madrid, 28040 Madrid, Spain
pilar.rodriguez@upms.es
[3] Softeam, 75016 Paris, France
{alessandra.bagnato,antonin.abherve}@softeam.fr
[4] ITTI Sp. z o.o, Poznań and UTP, Bydgoszcz, Poland
chorasm@utp.edu.pl, rafal.kozik@itti.com.pl

Abstract. Practitioners adopt software metrics programs to support their software development from the perspective of either overall quality, performance, or both. Current literature details and justifies the role of a metrics program in a software organization's software development, but empirical evidence to demonstrate its actual use and concomitant benefits remains scarce. In the context of an EU H2020 Project, we conducted a multiple case study to investigate how two software-intensive Agile companies utilized a metrics program in their software development. We invited practitioners from the two case companies to report on the actual use of the metrics program, the underlying rationale, and any benefits they may have witnessed. We also collected and analyzed metrics data from multiple use cases to explain the reported use of the metrics. The analysis revealed improvements like better code review practices and formalization of quality requirements management, either as a direct consequence or as a byproduct of the use of the metrics. The contrasting contexts like company size, project characteristics, and general perspective towards metrics programs could explain why one company viewed the metrics as a trigger for their reported improvements, while the other company saw metrics as the main driver for their improvements. Empirical evidence from our study should help practitioners adopt a more favorable view towards metrics programs, who were otherwise reluctant due to lack of evidence of their utility and benefits in industrial context.

Keywords: Metrics program · Process metrics · Decision-making

1 Introduction

With modern software development methods like Agile, the emphasis is on short feedback cycles and quick decision-making, where it is imperative that facts and not mere impressions drive actions [1]. Software practitioners are interested in both mining data for

© Springer Nature Switzerland AG 2020
M. Morisio et al. (Eds.): PROFES 2020, LNCS 12562, pp. 419–433, 2020.
https://doi.org/10.1007/978-3-030-64148-1_26

insights and using those insights for decision-making [2, 3], thereby facilitating successful software systems development [4]. Software metrics programs (MPs) can empower practitioners to accomplish the above objectives [5, 6]. Metrics can help generate actionable information to help fulfill an MP's purpose of facilitating decision-making [7, 8]. MPs also enable objective evaluation of software development processes, contributing to continuous improvement and learning in industrial software development context [9]. Current literature reports on successful adoption of MPs [10–13] and characteristics that make metrics actionable [14–16] in Agile software development (ASD). However, empirical investigation into actual MP use for software development in industrial context, and the resulting benefits, remains scarce.

In their literature review, Kupiainen et al. [7] highlighted the lack of empirical evidence demonstrating the use and rationale of MPs in ASD in large industrial context. Some studies provide empirical evidence of success factors for adopting an MP [11–13]. However, the limited study scope prevents discussion of successful MP adoption translating into successful use, especially in ASD. Similarly, studies like [16] and [17] provide evidence of MPs influencing actions in organizations using ASD, but do not detail the motivation of such a use and consequent benefits, if any. Studies like [11–13, 16] and [17] provide a curtailed view of MPs in practice, falling short of discussing MP's use in industrial context and how practitioners benefit from them. We argue that providing such details, supported by clear empirical evidence, can act as a strong motivator for practitioners to adopt a favorable view towards MPs. Moreover, such studies can also provide insights that interested practitioners can follow to replicate successful adoption and use of MPs.

We undertook our research in the context of an EU H2020 Project called Q-Rapids (Project), where the goal was to develop an agile-based, data-driven, and quality-aware rapid software development framework [18]. The Project comprised four software-intensive companies as industrial partners, and we focused our research efforts on the two case companies (CCs) that had progressed to use the Project Solution in their daily work, of which the MP is an integral component. We build upon the findings from our previous studies, where we presented software metrics definition [19] and their successful operationalization [20] at these CCs. The practitioners reported positive outcomes from the use of the MP for software development. These developments motivate the following research question:

RQ: *How do software-intensive companies using Agile software development utilize software metrics in their software development?*

On the back of our collaborations with the CCs, we claim following research contributions. These contributions are enriched by the rationale and validation provided by the CC practitioners invited to contribute to this study.

1. Empirical account of MP use at two contextually different software-intensive companies using ASD.
2. Empirical evidence of MP use for software development and decision-making in software-intensive companies using ASD.

In the remainder of the paper, we discuss background and related work in Sect. 2, describe the research method in Sect. 3, and our study's findings in Sect. 4. We discuss the results in Sect. 5, threats to our research's validity in Sect. 6, and conclusion and future research directions in Sect. 7.

2 Background and Related Work

We first provide a brief background on the Project to aid in comprehension of the study, as we reference different elements and features from the Project throughout the paper. Next, we present the state of the art relevant to our study. Literature documenting use of data to inform an organization's software development process would be relevant for our study. However, since our primary focus is on MPs, we discuss only those literature that center on MPs.

2.1 Q-Rapids Project

The goal of the Project is to develop an agile-based, data-driven, quality-aware rapid software development framework [18]. The objective of this framework (Solution) is to help practitioners make data-driven decisions in rapid cycles. The Solution comprises tools and methods for quality requirements elicitation and management. It also includes a dashboard to monitor indicators concerning product quality, process performance, among others [21].

Our collaboration on the Project centers on definition and operationalization of process metrics. Process metrics measure software development processes. Different process metrics are aggregated into process factors, which are further aggregated into strategic indicators (SIs), collectively constituting the MP. Developers are likely to prefer the lowest level of process metrics, which gives them access to process measurements at ground level. Process factors allow stakeholders like Product Owners (POs) and Project Managers (PMs) to get a refined view of the development process at project and team level. SIs are suitable for upper management, interested in high-level representation of the software development process at their organization.

We focus on the *process performance* SI and the process metrics constituting it. The *process performance* SI measures the performance of an organization's software development process. Among the Solution features, the '*quality alert*' feature [22] carries significance in this study, as we discuss in Sect. 4.1. Here, once a metric crosses a user-defined threshold, indicating violation of quality goals defined by the use-case Quality Engineers, this feature triggers a quality alert. The alert includes a recommendation, in the form of an abstract quality issue (e.g. quality requirement), to resolve the said violation.

2.2 Related Work

Staron and Meding [13] recommend success factors for MP implementation based on their study of a five-year old MP at Ericsson AB, where they also report that designers and quality managers believe that the MP provides benefits to the management process. Studies by Hall and Fenton [11] and Iversen and Mathiassen [12] focus on success factors for implementing MPs. Similarly, case studies included in the literature review on measurement programs [23] discuss mainly the experience of implementing an MP, and how use of MP facilitated an organization's transition to ASD. In our previous study [20], we focus on presenting the factors for successful operationalization of a metrics program, and a special emphasis is laid on metrics trustworthiness. One common objective missing from these studies is the discussion of actual MP use in an industrial context. Our research addresses this gap by providing empirical evidence demonstrating how practitioners use MPs towards software development, especially in their decision-making.

In their literature review, Kupiainen et al. [7] call for more empirical studies to explore the rationale and use of MPs, especially in large industrial context. Although most existing studies present initial emerging results of using an MP, lacking empirical evaluation in industrial context, there are few exceptions. A study by Dubinsky et al. [24] report on the use of an MP at an extreme programming (XP) development team of the Israeli Air Force. The authors conclude that use of metrics could lead to more accurate and professional decision-making. Díaz-Ley et al. [25] studied a measurement program (synonymous with metrics programs) targeted towards small-and-medium-size enterprises (SMEs), and found that use of metrics can help practitioners define measurement goals that are well aligned with their organization's maturity. Port and Taber [16] provide empirical evidence of MP use and their actionability in a large industrial context. With the help of metrics and analytics programs, the authors illustrate the supporting role an MP played in strategic maintenance of a critical system at NASA's Jet Propulsion Laboratory. Similarly, Vacanti and Vallet [17] conducted a case study at Siemens Health Services (SHS), and presented results of an MP's actionability, helping SHS increase productivity and improve process performance. These studies highlight MP use and its potential for influencing actions in software development in industrial context, but empirical evidence for the same is limited to only one case company. Furthermore, the rationale that underlie the reported use of the metrics and their alleged benefits lack explicit validation by the practitioners involved. Our research targets the common objective of providing empirical evidence of MP use in large industrial context. However, our research also includes multiple CCs and use cases (UCs) to argue the said objective. Furthermore, we support our claims by inviting the involved practitioners to validate them and to provide additional insights, especially the rationale that drive their MP utilization.

3   Research Method

Following the guidelines recommended by Runeson and Höst [26], we conducted a multiple case study to answer the RQ. In addition, we invited practitioners from each CC to validate our findings and provide supporting rationales.

3.1   Research Context

In order to understand better the MP use and the underlying rationale, we describe both the software development context and the Solution context at the two CCs.

Software Development Context. The following table characterizes the two CCs' software development context (Table 1):

Table 1. Case company characteristics

Parameters	Case Company 1	Case Company 2
ID	CC1	CC2
Size	Large	SME
Domain	Commercial services and solutions	Multi-industry
Development method	Customized Agile	*ScrumBan & ScrumBut*
Use case(s)	Software modeling tool	Warehouse Mgmt. System
Length of solution use	~2.5 years	~2 years
Use case team size	9	15

Case Company 1 (CC1) is a large-size company (>900 employees), with the goal of using the MP to improve the quality of its ASD process through early detection of anomalies in their development. CC1 uses various software development methods that adhere to Agile principles. Among other solutions, CC1 develops modeling tool for model-driven development. Part of a 25-year-old product line, the company has multiple releases of this tool in the market. CC1 has used the Solution in the course of development of the past four releases of the tool. In our study, we utilize data from three product releases (UC1.1–UC1.3) that were developed during the course of the Project.

Case Company 2 (CC2) is an SME type consulting company (around 100 employees), developing solutions for multiple industrial and application domains (e.g. administration, utilities, e-Health, etc.). The company has its own process for acquiring functional and quality requirements, and the initial mockups and user stories collected during this process forms the basis for their development process. Due to these exceptions, the company reports its development method as *ScrumBut*. Similarly, *ScrumBan* refers to the company's iterative software development, and its use of Kanban board to monitor backlogs. Currently, the company is in the process of going agile on a large-scale, and uses the abovementioned customized Agile approach for project management. The company aims to use the MP to allow its developers to anticipate design issues, security issues, and platform limitations. After piloting the Solution on mostly finished projects, the company used it in a project to develop an enterprise class integrated software system for managing warehouses. We focus on this project (UC2.1) for our study.

Solution Context. On the back of their experience of using generic metrics (e.g. Sonar-Qube[1] code quality metrics), CC1 were convinced that an MP could be useful only if it was adapted to their specific context, with respect to their processes and the data available. The MP allowed CC1 practitioners to capitalize and analyze the historical data, and identify problems and obstacles to their processes. This is evident in their choice of process metrics, available in *Appendix*[2]. CC1 found that involvement of MP target users played a significant role in their successful operationalization of the MP. Their involvement and feedback helped CC1 get the results that they deemed reliable.

---

[1] https://docs.sonarqube.org/latest/user-guide/metric-definitions/.
[2] https://zenodo.org/record/3953067#.X2DSo3kzZaQ.

This was accomplished only after adapting the MP to their context, leading to growth in target users' confidence in the MP. As a result, the CC1 UC development team utilizes the metrics in their regular meetings to discuss new releases, and plan steps for the next product releases.

Informed by their positive and formative experience from the pilot UC, CC2 continued to use the Solution in their next UC, albeit with customizations that are exclusive to this company. Influenced by their use of SonarQube code quality metrics, CC2 had reservations about the MP's potential to induce process improvements. They viewed it as a tool that can help monitor the process, and can be of value if and only if it were tailored to CC2's projects. This perspective largely dictated their choice of metrics. For CC2, MP operationalization was a success because of three major factors, (i) some process metrics provided additional value (unavailable elsewhere) in understanding the development process, (ii) the MP was first tested and introduced gradually to complement existing processes, and (iii) the MP facilitated and enhanced CC2's culture of transparency. With respect to the second factor, CC2 evaluated the MP's usefulness by conducting a retrospective session. The objectives were to explore the relevant process metrics used in the first six months of UC2.1, get feedback on the reasons of the impacts of the process metrics, and document the results of these impacts in a template. Consequently, CC2 arrived at a list of process metrics considered most valuable by its practitioners. These metrics were related to estimation efforts, bug density, issues velocity, and bug correction performance. In terms of transparency, the MP helped anchor PO's opinions and decisions in actual data, which the developers could verify and validate by using the Solution dashboard.

3.2 Data Collection

The CCs had been sharing process metrics data with the Project researchers on a monthly basis, along with a short report on their use of the Solution. In the course of several follow-up interactions with the CCs, we also learned that they had been utilizing MP to undertake process improvements. The following table provides context for the data we collected for this study (Table 2):

Table 2. Data collection context

Parameters	CC1	CC2
Data period	Oct. 2018–Sep. 2019	Nov. 2018–Aug. 2019
Use case	UC1.1–UC1.3	UC2.1
Type of data	Process metrics	
Focus	*Process performance* (SI)	

Our decision to focus on process metrics data was based on the objective of evaluating the use of MP, as reported by the CCs, and because we were responsible for implementing only process metrics. Both CCs reported an overall improvement in the *process performance* SI, which is automatically computed and collected on a daily basis. For example, the *process performance* SI in CC1 is the average of the three process factors of *tasks' velocity, testing performance, and testing performance.* These individual process factors are, in turn, the average of the process metrics that constitute them. The same logic applies for SI computation for CC2. These data provide the evidence necessary to support the reported MP use by the two CCs. In addition, the data also provide a quantitative underpinning to the rationale provided by the CC practitioners invited to contribute to this study.

3.3 Data Analysis

The following table presents the analysis approach we adopted for this study. The focus is on analyzing the *process performance* SI data in order to explain CCs' metrics utilization in their software development, especially towards decisions for process improvements. SI data are the only quantitative evidence available to draw any legitimate conclusion towards the reported use of the Solution, and to anchor the subsequent discussion by the invited practitioners (Table 3).

Table 3. Data analysis approach

Parameters	CC1	CC2
Analysis	*Kruskal-Wallis Test*, and *Pairwise Mann-Whitney U Test*	Trend analysis

In CC1, the extent of MP use across the three UCs evolved, as the practitioners customized and refined the process metrics to reflect their way of working. The SI data does not follow normal distribution, so we use *Kruskal-Wallis Test*, also known as one-way ANOVA by rank. It is a non-parametric test that can help us assess whether the difference in the *process performance* SI measured across the three UCs is statistically significant. In the event that it is, we use *Pairwise Mann-Whitney U-Test* as a post-hoc analysis to determine the specific UC that is statistically significant from others. We did not use *Kruskal-Wallis Test* in case of CC2, because the data comes from just one UC. Instead, we perform trend analysis on the UC2.1 SI data. Post analysis, we invited practitioners from each CC to review our findings, and provide rationale to support our claims and their reported MP use.

4 Findings

We first present the empirical evidence of the MP use for software development at each CC, based on the reported use of metrics for specific interventions and improvements. Here, the invited practitioners provide the necessary background, the actual use of the metrics for the above-stated purpose, and the rationale for such use, especially with respect to their decision-making. Next, we analyze the process metrics data to strengthen the above claims, providing a quantitative background to the reported use and the reported benefits, if any.

4.1 CC1

The MP helped CC1 identify the blocking points that could cause potential delays in their release. For example, CC1 used the '*non-blocking files*' metric to identify problems blocking their development tasks, critical for development features for their upcoming release, and prioritized the said development activities. In addition to bottleneck identification, the MP also facilitated process improvements, apparent from the results of using the '*critical issues ratio*' process metric. Here, however, the metric's influence was supplemented by the '*quality alert*' feature. The above metric triggered an alert, which recommended a *quality requirement*. The PM accepted the said quality requirement, and proposed it as a development task to address the problem both the metric and the alert indicated. This formalized quality requirements management is an improvement over CC1's past ad-hoc resource mobilization to address quality-related issues. Based on the above two instances of MP use, CC1 managed to improve their development process by improving their product quality, and optimized their effort to manage that quality.

Overall, and reflecting the improvements described above, CC1 reported an improvement of 10%–20% in their *process performance* SI since they started using the Solution, which includes the MP. UC1.1 data available is from the period when its release was due by around two months. For consistency, we used UC1.2 and UC1.3 data from similar periods. We also excluded data from the process factor '*tasks velocity*' due to reliability issues. The process metrics, and their interrelationships with process factors and the SI specific to CC1, is available in *Appendix*. The following table gives a snapshot of the data we used to support the reported MP use and improvements (Table 4).

Table 4. CC1 data context

Use case	Data	Period	Total data points	Solution use
UC1.1	*Process performance* SI	Two months before the release date	186	Low
UC1.2				Medium
UC1.3				Medium

The extent of *Solution Use* was determined by the Solution's maturity and availability of its different features. This also includes the perceived reliability of the MP data. CC1 Champion confirmed the above labelling of the extent of *Solution Use*. The following table provides descriptive statistics of *the process performance* SI from the three UC datasets, followed by their boxplot visualization in Fig. 1. Each UC dataset comprises the SI data computed and collected on a daily basis, and is from a period of two months prior to the release date (Table 5).

Table 5. Descriptive statistics of CC1 dataset

Solution use	N	Mean	Standard deviation	Median
UC1.1	61	0.829	0.0429	0.845
UC1.2	63	0.854	0.0258	0.855
UC1.3	62	0.907	0.0291	0.920

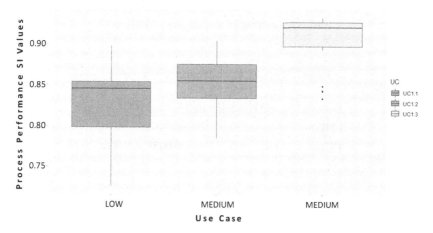

Fig. 1. Box-plot for the CC1 *process performance* SI

In the above box-plot, the Y-axis represents the SI values. The X-axis corresponds to the extent of *Solution Use* for the three respective UCs. The chart demonstrates that the median SI across the three UCs increased as the use of the Solution increased at CC1. Despite the extent of *Solution Use* for both UC1.2 and UC1.3 being the same (*Medium*), the chart suggests performance difference between the two UC samples. We analyzed the SI data using *Kruskal-Wallis Test* with the null hypothesis (H_0): the samples come from the same population, and alternative hypothesis (H_a): the samples do not come from the same population. The results from the test are shown in Table 6:

With the *critical chi-square value* (5.99) less than the *observed chi-square value* (85.27), and with the computed p value less than the significance level alpha = 0.05, we reject H_0 and accept H_a. This suggests that the SI values in three UCs have statistically significant performance difference from each other for at least one UC sample, corresponding to a strong effect size (epsilon squared, $e^2 = .0.46$). In order to determine which UC sample is significantly different, we performed pairwise comparison using *Pairwise Mann-Whitney U Test*. The result of this post-hoc analysis test is shown in Table 7:

Table 7 lists p values as the result from the comparison among UCs. All the computed p values for these comparisons are less than the significance level alpha = 0.05. This suggests that there is a statistically significant difference among UCs. More specifically,

Table 6. Kruskal-Wallis test

Kruskal-Wallis test for CC1 *Process performance* SI	
K (*observed chi-square value*)	85.27
K (*critical chi-square value*)	5.99
df	2
p value	<0.0001
alpha	0.05
epsilon squared (*effect size measure*)	0.46

Table 7. Pairwise Mann-Whitney U test results

Pairwise Mann-Whitney U test	UC1.1	UC1.2
UC1.2	0.011	
UC1.3	<0.0001	<0.0001

UC1.2 is significantly different from UC1.1, and UC1.3 is significantly different from both UC1.1 and UC1.2. This significant difference coincides with the increased use of the Solution across these UCs.

In view of CC1's MP use, informed by their approach to the MP and experience with it so far, CC1 practitioners maintain that the MP was one of the contributors to influence their software development, resulting in benefits like identification of blocking points and formalization of their quality requirements management process. Maturation effect could be one of the reasons why despite the medium *Solution Use* in both UC1.2 and UC1.3, the difference in the *process performance* SI for the latter was statistically significant from the other two UCs. CC1 finds that the MP gives the practitioners a *'behind the scene'* of their development process, broadening their overall perspective. As a result, CC1 views MP more as a decision-support tool, rather than a control tool, which aligns well with the perspective they harbored for MPs in general from the start of the Project.

4.2 CC2

The MP helped improve CC2's code review process, by allowing medium-experienced developers address *merge requests*, a task earlier reserved only for experienced developers. The MP also allowed the PO and Senior Managers (SMs) to identify that four days is the optimal reported effort spent on a task, which in turn improved their developers' efficiency. CC2 was interested in POs and SMs making quick team-oriented decisions without involving too many stakeholders like the CEO or the company board. The MP made this possible, as now the CC2 practitioners had the means to verify and validate PO and SM's actions. The trust CC2 managed to build for the MP is evident in its use in the weekly Scrum meetings, to learn to improve their way of working, motivate the team, and identify problems and find solutions for them.

Similar to the results from the pilot UC, CC2 reported an overall improvement even for their UC2.1 *process performance* SI. The data corresponds to the MP use throughout UC2.1, but we excluded the data for the *'resolved issues throughput'* process metrics due to reliability concerns. The following table (Table 8) provides an overview of the data we used to conduct the trend analysis illustrated in Fig. 2:

Table 8. CC2 data context

Use Case	Data	Period	Total data points
UC2.1	*Process performance* SI	Throughout UC2.1	225

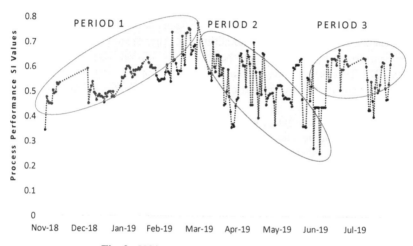

Fig. 2. UC2.1 *process performance* SI trend

CC2 Champion demarcated the three *Periods* in the chart to highlight the exceptional *Period 2*. Certain eventualities at the company impacted CC2's software development performance for a short period, which is reflected in the downward trend of *Period 2*. Otherwise, the chart indicates an upward trend, suggesting improvement in UC2.1's *process performance* SI as the Solution use increased, relative to the use in the pilot UC.

Process metrics from the MP made possible the important changes in CC2, like enabling a suitable team management culture. In addition to other in-house metrics CC2 developed, the process metrics from the MP facilitated PO's understanding of the process dynamics. Based on the MP, CC2's decisions like increasing the number of developers to perform merge requests and improving effort estimation, reveals the practitioners were relying completely and only on the MP for the above improvement decisions. This claim is further supported by the improvement seen in UC2.1 SI, as depicted in the upward trends in Period 1 and Period 3 in Fig. 2.

5   Discussion

Based on the two CCs' reported MP use, their underlying rationales, and the alleged role of the metrics in their decision-making, we argue that the CC practitioners used the MP as either a trigger or the main driver for their software development. We discuss the results from these two perspectives and answer the RQ.

5.1   Metrics Program as a Trigger

Based on the reported MP use by CC1, informed by their experience and their general approach to MPs, the practitioners viewed metrics as a trigger that directed them towards taking certain actions. CC1 practitioners believe a standalone MP is not enough to influence actions and drive development. Other contributing factors play an equally important role. They subscribe to the idea that MPs, and the underlying metrics, are not '*magic*' that can lay out clear and concise action to be taken [14]. The MP can only guide them, provided its data are corroborated using different means like the original data source or an authority at the organization. The need for corroboration is an implicit requirement for evaluating MP data reliability [2]. Any meaningful improvements and development driven by MPs can only be a result of several other factors working in harmony [27]. This principle is visible in CC1's use of '*critical issues ratio*' metric and the '*quality alert*' feature, as part of their new and formalized quality requirement management process.

CC1 is a large-size company, which may explain their reluctance at relying solely on the MP for making development decisions. With respect to project characteristics, it is difficult to draw any conclusion, as every single CC1 UCs involved development of different versions of the same modeling tool. However, based on [7], we argue that at least company size, if not project characteristics, moderated the MP's potential to influence software development at CC1. Furthermore, CC1's perspective towards the MP remained, largely, unchanged throughout the Project, which further dictated their utilization of the MP as only a tool to inform their decision-making. Their original perspective of the MP being only a decision-support tool is also in line with the claim of CC1 using the MP only as a trigger.

5.2   Metrics Program as a Main Driver

The retrospective sessions helped CC2 establish an organization-wide trust in the MP. The resulting transparency compelled the PO and SM to use the MP for improving '*merge requests*' and effort estimation processes, which led to positive outcomes. Therefore, we argue that CC2 are proponents of using MP as a main driver in their software development. This stance is predicated on conditions like adapting the MP to their context, target user feedback, and transparency.

On the back of better visibility and overall transparency, CC2 now completely relies on the MP to carry out improvements. This is compatible with the findings in [17], where specific interventions inferred from the *flow*[3] metrics led to an increase in productivity and process performance at SHS. Furthermore, CC2 also achieved the goal

---

[3] Workflow metrics such as Work in Progress, Cycle Time, and Throughput.

of equipping its POs and SMs with the responsibility to take decisions independent of other stakeholders. The retrospective sessions were instrumental in convincing the CC2 of the MP's resourcefulness for achieving the said goal. With the MP now adapted to CC2's context, its practitioners are confident in using the MP as their main driver towards everyday software development, and even undertaking decisions for improvements. This clearly highlights a diametric shift in CC2's earlier view of MP being useful mainly as a monitoring tool.

6   Threats to Validity

We report on the threats to our study's validity based on the guidelines recommended by Runeson and Höst [26].

The study is designed based on the MP and its constituents of process metrics, process factors, and SIs, which have been verified in theory and in practice in our previous studies [19, 20]. However, there is potential for misrepresentation of the results of the quantitative analysis, which threatens the study's construct validity. To mitigate this threat, we discussed and verified these results with the CC practitioners, particularly the Project/UC champion. Furthermore, we invited them to contribute to this study, and validate the results and the claims derived from them.

Other confounding factors could have influenced our results, affecting the internal validity of our claim regarding how each CC used the MP. For example, improvement in UC1.3 SI values could be due to maturation effect. We have tried to mitigate this threat by allowing the practitioners from the corresponding CC to validate these claims by providing the underlying rationale. Furthermore, we excluded the data that could interfere with the legitimacy of the results, and kept the CC practitioners in the loop of every decision concerning data collection and processing.

The study involves only two software-intensive companies, each with their distinct context, which affects the external validity of our study. However, we have provided a detailed context for each CC, and used that to shape our discussion on their specific MP use for software development and improvement decisions. Therefore, our findings may be applicable to organizations that are similar in context to any of the two CCs. Moreover, rather than a rulebook, our study can serve as a starting point for interested organizations. Additionally, our overarching goal is to trigger further investigations on the research topic and gaps we have attempted to address here.

Multiple researchers and practitioners have helped elaborate and validate the findings from the study. However, only one researcher was involved in metrics data collection, which may affect the reliability of our study.

7   Conclusion

The state of the art provides limited empirical evidence for metrics programs use in ASD in industrial contexts, especially for decision-making. However, studies that provide empirical evidence of metrics programs use in large industrial settings, supported by their usage rationale and consequent benefits, remains scarce. In the context of the EU H2020 Q-Rapids Project, we have tried to address this research gap.

We collaborated with two software-intensive companies, and reported on their metrics programs use for software development, including decisions made towards process improvements. Analyzing process metrics data from the two case companies, we reinforced the empirical evidence to support the rationale provided by the practitioners for their reported use of metrics programs for software development and decision-making. Company size and perspective towards MP's potential for software development are the two probable distinguishing criteria explaining their use at the two case companies. For a large-size company with a cautionary perspective, a metrics program can only act as a trigger for software development and decision-making. In contrast, for SMEs, it can act as the main driver, provided company-specific conditions like adapting to their context, target user feedback and transparency are met.

Future work could include evaluation of several use cases across multiple large-size companies and SMEs to improve generalizability of our findings.

Acknowledgments. This work is a result of the Q-Rapids Project, funded by the European Union's Horizon 2020 research and innovation program, under grant agreement No. 732253.

References

1. Liechti, O., Pasquier, J., Reis, R.: Beyond dashboards: On the many facets of metrics and feedback in agile organizations. In: Proceedings - 2017 IEEE/ACM 10th International Workshop on Cooperative and Human Aspects of Software Engineering, CHASE 2017, pp. 16–22 (2017)
2. Staron, M., Meding, W.: Ensuring reliability of information provided by measurement systems. In: Abran, A., Braungarten, R., Dumke, R.R., Cuadrado-Gallego, J.J., Brunekreef, J. (eds.) IWSM 2009. LNCS, vol. 5891, pp. 1–16. Springer, Heidelberg (2009). https://doi.org/10.1007/978-3-642-05415-0_1
3. Yang, Y., Falessi, D., Menzies, T., Hihn, J.: Actionable analytics for you. IEEE Softw. **35**, 51–53 (2018)
4. Bird, C., Murphy, B., Nagappan, N., Zimmermann, T.: Empirical software engineering at Microsoft Research. In: Proceedings of the ACM Conference on Computer Supported Cooperative Work. CSCW, pp. 143–150 (2011)
5. Menzies, T., Zimmermann, T.: Software analytics: so what? IEEE Softw. **30**, 31–37 (2013)
6. Zhang, D., Han, S., Dang, Y., Lou, J.G., Zhang, H., Xie, T.: Software analytics in practice. IEEE Softw. **30**, 30–37 (2013)
7. Kupiainen, E., Mäntylä, M.V., Itkonen, J.: Using metrics in Agile and lean software development - A systematic literature review of industrial studies. Inf. Softw. Technol. **62**, 143–163 (2015)
8. Staron, M., Meding, W.: Transparent measures: Cost-efficient measurement processes in SE. In: Software Technology Transfer Workshop, pp. 1–4, Kista, Sweden (2015)
9. Van Solingen, R., Berghout, E.: Integrating goal-oriented measurement in industrial software engineering: Industrial experiences with and additions to the Goal/Question/Metric method (GQM). In: Proceedings of Seventh International Software and Metrics Symposium, pp. 246–258 (2001)
10. Mendonça, M.G., Basili, V.R.: Validation of an approach for improving existing measurement frameworks. IEEE Trans. Softw. Eng. **26**, 484–499 (2000)

11. Hall, T., Fenton, N.: Implementing effective software metrics programs. IEEE Softw. **14**, 55–64 (1997)
12. Iversen, J., Mathiassen, L.: Cultivation and engineering of a software metrics program. Inf. Syst. J. **13**, 3–19 (2003)
13. Staron, M., Meding, W.: Factors determining long-term success of a measurement program: An industrial case study. e-Informatica Softw. Eng. J. **1**, 7–23 (2012)
14. Croll, A., Yoskovitz, B.: Lean Analytics: Use Data to Build a Better Startup Faster (2013)
15. Buse, R.P.L., Zimmermann, T.: Information needs for software development analytics - Microsoft research. MSR Technical report 2011-8, pp. 1–16 (2011)
16. Port, D., Taber, B.: Actionable analytics for strategic maintenance of critical software: An industry experience report. IEEE Softw. **35**, 58–63 (2017)
17. Vacanti, D., Vallet, B.: Actionable Metrics at Siemens Health Services (2014)
18. Franch, X., et al.: Data-driven requirements engineering in agile projects: The Q-Rapids approach. In: Proceedings - 2017 IEEE 25th International Requirements Engineering Conference Workshops, REW 2017, pp. 411–414 (2017)
19. Ram, P., Rodriguez, P., Oivo, M.: Software process measurement and related challenges in agile software development: A multiple case study. In: Kuhrmann, M., et al. (eds.) PROFES 2018. LNCS, vol. 11271, pp. 272–287. Springer, Cham (2018). https://doi.org/10.1007/978-3-030-03673-7_20
20. Ram, P., Rodriguez, P., Oivo, M.: Success factors for effective process metrics operationalization in agile software development: A multiple case study. In: Proceedings of the 2019 International Conference on Software and System Process (2019)
21. López, L., et al.: Q-rapids tool prototype: supporting decision-makers in managing quality in rapid software development. In: Mendling, J., Mouratidis, H. (eds.) CAiSE 2018. LNBIP, vol. 317, pp. 200–208. Springer, Cham (2018). https://doi.org/10.1007/978-3-319-92901-9_17
22. Oriol, M., et al.: Data-driven elicitation of quality requirements in agile companies. In: Piattini, M., Rupino da Cunha, P., García Rodríguez de Guzmán, I., Pérez-Castillo, R. (eds.) QUATIC 2019. CCIS, vol. 1010, pp. 49–63. Springer, Cham (2019). https://doi.org/10.1007/978-3-030-29238-6_4
23. Tahir, T., Rasool, G., Gencel, C.: A systematic literature review on software measurement programs. Inf. Softw. Technol. **73**, 101–121 (2016)
24. Dubinsky, Y., Talby, D., Hazzan, O., Keren, A.: Agile metrics at the Israeli Air Force. In: Agile Development Conference (ADC 2005), pp. 12–19. IEEE Computer Society (2005)
25. Díaz-Ley, M., García, F., Piattini, M.: Implementing software measurement programs in non mature small settings. In: Cuadrado-Gallego, J.J., Braungarten, R., Dumke, R.R., Abran, A. (eds.) IWSM/Mensura -2007. LNCS, vol. 4895, pp. 154–167. Springer, Heidelberg (2008). https://doi.org/10.1007/978-3-540-85553-8_13
26. Runeson, P., Höst, M.: Guidelines for conducting and reporting case study research in software engineering. Empir. Softw. Eng. **14**, 131–164 (2009)
27. Meneely, A.: Actionable metrics are better metrics. In: Perspectives on Data Science for Software Engineering, pp. 283–287. Elsevier (2016)

Integration of Security Standards in DevOps Pipelines: An Industry Case Study

Fabiola Moyón[1]([⊠]) [ID], Rafael Soares[2], Maria Pinto-Albuquerque[2] [ID],
Daniel Mendez[3,4] [ID], and Kristian Beckers[5]

[1] Siemens CT and Technical University of Munich, Munich, Germany
fabiola.moyon@siemens.com
[2] Instituto Universitário de Lisboa (ISCTE-IUL), ISTAR-IUL, Lisbon, Portugal
{rafael_soares,maria.albuquerque}@iscte-iul.pt
[3] Blekinge Institute of Technology, Karlskrona, Sweden
daniel.mendez@bth.se
[4] fortiss GmbH, Munich, Germany
[5] Social Engineering Academy, Munich, Germany
kristian.beckers@social-engineering.academy

Abstract. In the last decade, companies adopted DevOps as a fast path to deliver software products according to customer expectations, with well aligned teams and in continuous cycles. As a basic practice, DevOps relies on pipelines that simulate factory swim-lanes. The more automation in the pipeline, the shorter a lead time is supposed to be. However, applying DevOps is challenging, particularly for industrial control systems (ICS) that support critical infrastructures and that must obey to rigorous requirements from security regulations and standards. Current research on security compliant DevOps presents open gaps for this particular domain and in general for systematic application of security standards. In this paper, we present a systematic approach to integrate standard-based security activities into DevOps pipelines and highlight their automation potential. Our intention is to share our experiences and help practitioners to overcome the trade-off between adding security activities into the development process and keeping a short lead time. We conducted an evaluation of our approach at a large industrial company considering the IEC 62443-4-1 security standard that regulates ICS. The results strengthen our confidence in the usefulness of our approach and artefacts, and in that they can support practitioners to achieve security compliance while preserving agility including short lead times.

Keywords: Secure software engineering · Security standards · Agile software engineering · DevOps pipeline · DevSecOps · Industrial control systems

© Springer Nature Switzerland AG 2020
M. Morisio et al. (Eds.): PROFES 2020, LNCS 12562, pp. 434–452, 2020.
https://doi.org/10.1007/978-3-030-64148-1_27

1 Introduction

Agile methodologies aim to deliver software products that satisfy customer needs while enabling collaboration among stakeholders [2]. Lean techniques apply manufacturing flows to deliver software products with waste reduction, increased visibility of the manufacturing pipeline, and better team collaboration [23] DevOps relies on both agile and lean practices to break the barriers between development (Dev) and operation (Ops) teams [13]. This extends the benefits beyond delivery to the operation of software products. By applying DevOps, organizations attempt to deliver and operate software products according to customer expectations, with well aligned teams and with focus on continuous improvement of the process flows. The indicator of improvement is reducing the time-frame to transform a customer need into a usable software functionality at the production environment – so-called lead time [15].

To shorten the lead time, DevOps relies on automation practices [17], where Continuous Integration/Continuous Delivery (CI/CD) pipelines are essential. The term *pipeline* refers to so-called factory swim-lanes and describes a systematic alignment of processes and tools to release software products in a seamless manner, often characterised with the metaphor of "pushing a button". This "button" triggers a set of automated checks and tests aimed at software quality assurance [8].

While DevOps was originally conceptualized for IT companies, industrial companies have started as well to embrace DevOps practices [1,5]. However, there are yet several challenges to overcome before DevOps can be largely applied in highly regulated domains with high demand for quality attributes, in particular security [30].

Especially the domain of industrial control systems (ICS), where software products are vital to support critical infrastructure, is characterised by the need of compliance with security standards. The ICS domain is regulated by the security standards family IEC-62443, where the IEC-62443-4-1 standard (the 4-1 standard) states process requirements for secure product development lifecycle [10].

Nowadays, the software engineering (SE) field lacks methods to demonstrate compliance with security standards when applying DevOps [30]. There are initial contributions on security in agile methods, as well as on DevOps (e.g. [12,19, 28,31]); however, publications which address the compliance of security are very scarce and do not yet cover completely the ICS domain [16,21].

In addition, a challenge for the SE field is the trade-off between adding security activities during development and keeping a short lead time [14].

To achieve security compliance for DevOps, we argue that we first need to understand how to systematically integrate security standard requirements into DevOps pipelines. In this paper, we address this problem for the representative standard in the ICS domain: the IEC 62443-4-1 standard for secure product development. Through a case study, we analyze its application in a large industrial company.

Integration is possible since both the security standard and the DevOps pipeline are based on activity flows. The 4-1 standard requirements are a set of processes to ensure security in the product development lifecycle. The DevOps pipeline is a process chain to deliver software products [8]. Hence, we mapped the 4-1 process requirements into the applicable DevOps pipeline stages, namely: concept, code, build, test, release, deploy, operate and monitor [13].

In addition, given that DevOps relies on automation to keep short lead times, we determine to what extent the 4-1 standard requirements can be automated. Ideally, the more *automatable* the standard security requirement, the less impact on the lead time.

In summary, to improve the product development process in security regulated environments, this work presents two contributions:

1. an approach to systematically describe security compliant DevOps pipelines, together with a first instance for the IEC 62443-4-1 standard, and
2. a description of automation capabilities of the 4-1 standard security requirements, together with details of available security tools, if one exists to date.

Our contributions may support companies driving DevOps for ICS to satisfy not only customer needs but also regulatory demands, without losing the benefits of agile and DevOps. With a description of *non-automatable* standard requirements, we raise awareness of where in the product life-cycle to emphasize collaboration between security and DevOps teams. Also, by describing automation capabilities, we provide paths to implement security with less impact on the lead time. Moreover, for the research field of security compliance, our work reduces the gaps with relation to security compliant DevOps.

To evaluate the applicability and usefulness of our contributions, we conducted a qualitative study consisting of interviews with expert practitioners in a large industrial company. Results show that the integration approach may be applied to describe DevOps compliance with other security standards or in other regulated domains, e.g. finance, telecommunications. Moreover, the study revealed that the 4-1 standard automation capabilities motivate practitioners to implement compliance programs based on automation. Nowadays, this work's artefacts are applied in the company to introduce Dev and Ops teams to security compliance with the 4-1 standard and to perform DevSecOps assessments.

The rest of this paper is structured as follows. In Sect. 2, we discuss fundamentals and related work. Section 3 presents the steps we propose to integrate security standards into DevOps pipelines, through systematic identification of activities and automation capabilities, while pointing out at which stages of the pipeline each security requirement fits. Section 4 presents how the integration approach delivers, for the 4-1 standard, a description of automation capabilities as well as a specification of Security Standard Compliant (S^2C) DevOps Pipeline Specification. Section 5 reports on the evaluation. In Sect. 6, we discuss the main findings, impact and limitations of our work. Finally in Sect. 7, we summarize current and further work.

2 Fundamentals and Related Work

In this section, we describe the DevOps concepts including the automation practice. Later, we present a summary of the relevant work in the field of security compliant DevOps.

2.1 DevOps and Pipelines

DevOps combines working philosophies and practices to remove the barrier between the development (Dev) and operation (Ops) teams. Key elements include collaboration, automation, measurement, and monitoring [18]. An essential aspect for automation is the concept of the Continuous Integration/Continuous Delivery (CI/CD) pipeline. This pipeline describes the alignment of processes and tools to automate steps in the Software Development Life Cycle (SDLC) process, which includes initiating code builds, running acceptance tests, and deploying to staging and production environments. Pipelines produce artefacts that may serve as evidence for compliance [8].

Debates on DevOps concepts, definitions, and practices are active with yet no clear consensus [17]. In the contribution at hands, we concentrate on the so-called *automation practice* [13] and we recognize pipelines as the concrete manifestation of this practice in industrial environments. When using the term DevOps pipeline, we refer to the sequence of processes that transform needs of a customer into valuable product increments and deployed them to production site.

For this work, we chose as main reference the original DevOps Pipeline (the well-known infinite symbol), as it represents the sequence from customer needs to deployed functionalities. For specific details, we analyzed also the pipeline proposals from: Bird, Humbley and Gartner [4,6,8].

2.2 DevSecOps and Security Standards

The term "DevSecOps" has emerged as organisations, that started to apply DevOps techniques, were concerned about security aspects. It refers to the incorporation of security practices in a DevOps environment through the collaboration between development, operation, and security teams [20]. Reports correlated security automation with DevOps success and recommended the integration of security earlier in the development life cycle, moving from operational to development stages [5,27]. To achieve this, CI/CD pipelines were adapted to include security practices [4].

In general, publications, that refer to DevOps and regulations-based security, are scarce. Authors explore security in regulated environments [19,30] and where to introduce security activities in DevOps [12,31]. However DevSecOps compliant with a particular standard or domain is still missing. In our experience in industrial environments, a major gap for security compliance is identifying which DevOps artefacts can serve as compliance evidence.

The ICS domain is regulated by the IEC 62443 standard family, whose sibling the IEC 62443-4-1 (the 4-1) provides process requirements (activities, artefacts, and flows) to achieve a secure product development life-cycle [10]. It contains eight practices, which are: **security management** (SM), to ensure that security activities are adequately executed through the product's life cycle; **specification of security requirements** (SR), to accurately elicit product's security capabilities; **secure design** (SD), to ensure that security is involved from overall architecture to individual components; **secure implementation** (SI), to ensure applicability of secure coding and implementation practices; **security verification and validation testing** (SVV), to ensure that security design was implemented; **management of security-related issues** (DM), to handle product's security-related issues; **security update management** (SUM), to ensure timely delivery of security updates; and finally **security guidelines** (SG) to provide sufficient documentation for secure product deployment.

This work extends the field by specifying which practices of the 4-1 standard apply for each DevOps phase. Although previous work refers to security involvement into pipelines [4], our contribution fills the gap of applying security from the point of view of security standards: involving more than technology, the people and process aspects. In addition, at a granular level, we determine which security standard activities can be automated in a pipeline.

3   Integration of Security Standards into DevOps Pipelines

In industrial environments adopting DevOps, we aim to improve the product development process by achieving security compliance with less impact on the leadtime. Therefore it is our intention to determine to what extent security standard requirements can be automated and how a DevOps pipeline will look like when orchestrating such requirements.

Security compliance requirements are stated in security standards and to integrate them into DevOps, we propose a systematic approach that consists of three steps (see Fig. 1). First, we list the standard activities in a precise way. Second, for each standard activity, we determine the automation capabilities and finally, we map activities into the DevOps Pipeline stages. The approach is applied for the 4-1 security standard for secure product development in ICS. The artefacts presented in this paper are instances for this particular standard; however, the structure can serve as template for the analysis of other standards describing secure development life-cycles and applicable in other domains like the ISO 27034 for secure software development. A complete set of artefacts is part of our contribution and can be accessed in our online material at https://doi.org/10.6084/m9.figshare.11294534.

In the following sub-sections, we describe the steps in detail and present the artefacts.

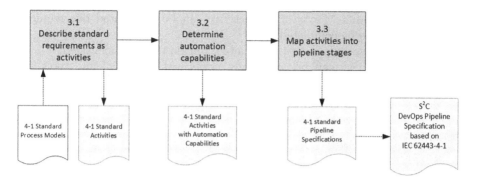

Fig. 1. Approach to integrate security standards into DevOps Pipelines. For illustration purposes, artefacts are shown as particular instances of the 4-1 standard. Artefact in white was adopted from previous work [22]. The final output of this approach is the Security Standard Compliant (S²C) DevOps Pipeline presented in Sect. 4

3.1 Describe Standard Requirements as Activities

This step focuses on a detailed analysis of the standard and its requirements. As result, we obtain a precise description of the standard requirements to the level of activities with inputs and outputs. Each requirement may contain several *activities* to be orchestrated in a pipeline. Inputs and outputs serve to build up the orchestration flow, meaning: the output of one activity is the input of the next.

For this case study, we based this analysis on existent process models of the 4-1 standard [22]. Such models represent the 4-1 standard requirements with the Business Process Model and Notation (BPMN). From the 4-1 process models, we extracted tasks, events, and gateways of the standard requirements. All of them where considered as *activities* to be orchestrated. Further, we also made explicit the input and output based on the artefacts, also depicted in the 4-1 process models. This analysis resulted into 160 activities.

Figure 2 (steps 1 and 2) presents an example of how activities are extracted from a requirement of the 4-1 standard. The example shows an excerpt of how the 4-1 process models depict the requirement *SI-1 Secure implementation review* belonging to the practice Secure Implementation.

3.2 Determine Automation Capabilities for the Standard

This step analyzes if the standard activities can be automated. The term *automation capability* is based in two criteria:

Automation Level. Describes to what extent the security standard activities can be automated. The following are the *automation categories*:

- Human Task: Automation is not possible. A human must perform the activity.
- Transparency: A human can perform the activity based on tool results e.g. visualization.

- Partial Automation: Parts of the activity can be automated but required manual input to be completed.
- Tool Possible: Activity can be automated, but no tool was identified.
- Complete: Activity can be completely performed by a tool and tools are available.

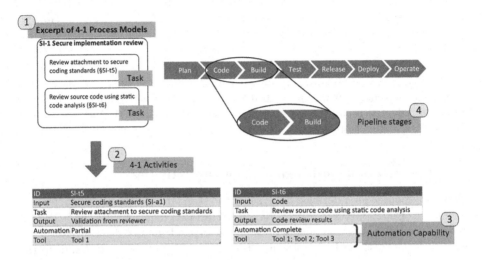

Fig. 2. Description on how IEC 62443-4-1 requirements extracted from process models (1) can be refined as activities (2) with input, output and automation capabilities (3). Finally, the activities are mapped into pipeline stages (4)

Tool Support. For activities that can be automated, we searched available tools in several sources and investigate if the tools fit the automation level [7, 24,25]. Finally, a tool list is compiled including first open source tools as well as those that can be integrated into Continuous Integration tools (e.g.,*Jenkins, Gitlab CI*).

The automation level and tool support are dependent criteria, e.g. an activity may seem to be fully automated, however there may not be a tool that fulfills the activity completely. Figure 2 (step 3) shows an example of how automation capabilities are described for the activities extracted after step 3.1. These activities refer two tasks that implement the requirement SI-1 Secure implementation review. The 4-1 process models notate them as SI-t5 and SI-t6.

3.3   Map Activities into Pipeline Stages

In this step, we identify in which stages of the DevOps pipeline the security standard activities should take place. To this aim, we find characteristics in common in both DevOps pipeline and the 4-1 standard. Afterwards, we determine for each activity of the 4-1 standard the corresponding stage(s) of the DevOps pipeline.

Security standard activities are included as early as possible in the pipeline, prioritizing stages where the product is not yet in the production environment. Figure 2 (step 4) shows an example of the mapping of 4-1 activities into pipeline stages. To have an overview of every 4-1 practice, the individual activities with their automation capabilities are aggregated into per 4-1 practice. These models are called *Pipeline Specifications of the Standard Practice* and are available in the online material.

Finally, this step aggregates the individual activities in a high-level overview, a Security Standard Compliant (S^2C) DevOps Pipeline. In this section, we presented an example for the SI practice of the 4-1 standard. In the following section, we point out key points related to the rest of the standard practices.

4 DevOps Compliant with the 4-1 Security Standard

Applying the integration steps for the 4-1 security standard resulted into: a description of automation capabilities for the 4-1 standard practices and a instance of a (S^2C) DevOps Pipeline for this specific standard. In this section, we describe them.

4.1 Automation Capabilities of the 4-1 Standard

Ideally, to support the DevOps aim of reducing the lead time, security activities require to be completely automated. Summarizing the 4-1 security activities per automation level, this occurs for 31% of the 4-1 security activities. It means that a tool is available and can completely implement the security activity when orchestrated into a pipeline. The opposite occurs for 38% of the standard activities,

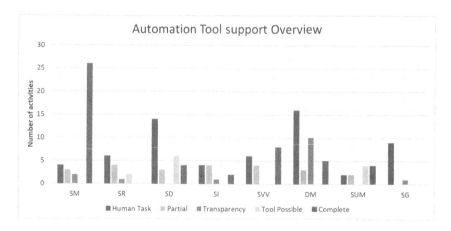

Fig. 3. Summary of Automation capabilities per practice of the IEC 62443-4-1. For the whole standard, this corresponds to: Human Task 38%; Transparency 9%; Partial Automation 14%; Tool Possible 8%; Complete Automation 31%

which cannot be automated at all and where a human must do the task. Hence, these security activities require comprehensive collaboration among stakeholders, either including a security expert into the iterations or providing security knowledge to DevOps team members.

Some 4-1 activities (9%) can be supported from tools to achieve transparency, meaning that a human can take decisions based on automation e.g. dashboard tools that aggregate security findings. Other 14% of security activities can be partially implemented by an existent security tool. Finally, 8% of standard security activities could be automated but, to the best of our understanding, there is not yet documentation in our sources that such a tool is implemented and used, e.g. tool for automatic aggregation of security findings and prioritization into the backlog based on threat models. Figure 3 shows the automation capabilities of the 4-1 activities grouped per practice. The 4-1 standard practices with high automation capabilities are: security management (SM), secure verification and validations testing (SVV), and security update management (SUM). For SM such automation level may not be clear at first sight, but the 4-1 standard includes in this practice security activities for environment verification, encryption/key management and vulnerability checking of third-party components. Several security tools implement these use cases. The SVV practice reflects a common use case, security testing activities like vulnerability checking or port scanning are well automated and supported by tools. For the SUM practice, tools fully automate security activities for updates delivery and installation.

In contrast, we observe practices where no automation is possible: security requirements (SR) and security guidelines (SG). For SR, most security activities rely on human effort (see human and partial automation in Fig. 3). DevOps Teams should find suitable requirements engineering techniques to support DevOps objectives. In our experience, compliance of security requirements practices is challenging for industrial environments applying agile and DevOps practices. For SG, security activities are manual since they refer to documentation of secure configuration guidelines. In addition, we observe some practices largely depending on human tasks, such as secure design (SD) and management of security-related issues (DM). In SD, humans have to generate security architecture diagrams or define measures. Tools can help for drawing or to autogenerate architecture models but humans need to approve them. In DM, security tools aggregate issues but experts decide what to do with findings.

4.2   Security Standard Compliant DevOps Pipeline

Besides automation capabilities, we contribute with a specification of how security standard activities should be involved into DevOps stages. Figure 4 shows the (S^2C) DevOps Pipeline for the 4-1 standard and a brief description of key points is the following:

Plan: Based on the customer need, during this stage, requirements are represented as user stories. Security requirements (SR) should be included in the elicitation flow. The activities of the SR practice are rather manual and no automation is possible (see Fig. 3).

The 4-1 Standard demands to perform *threat modeling* and describe the *product security context*. The latter refers to describing required security measures for the environment where the product will be deployed, e.g. networks or operating systems.

To perform these activities, teams need to involve security specialists who recommend modeling tools. Such tools do not automate the activities but provide transparency and support documentation. Some threat modeling tools provide lists of common threats which consider partial automation as the experts do not need to list the threats.

A key part for compliance is to ensure that these activities are performed, therefore the backlog management tool should include them. Here, we identified potential for automation. User stories referring to critical components (as based on threat models) could be automatically labeled by the backlog management tool as security relevant. Automatic labeling can be based on natural language analysis. This will facilitate collaboration between DevOps teams and security experts, since security experts are included by default in the process.

In addition, in this stage, the 4-1 Practice Secure Design (SD) demands to define *secure design best practices* and *secure design principles*. These are later transformed into security measures for each *interface* of the product. Although most activities are manual, automation may help to add preset lists of security measures that can be included into the design. Repositories that provide compliance evidence are the Backlog and Documentation repository.

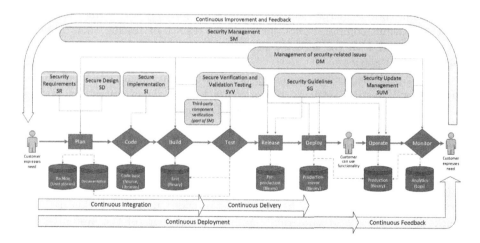

Fig. 4. Security Standard Compliant DevOps Pipeline for the IEC 62443-4-1 Standard: Diagram shows the 4-1 standard practices (in yellow), the DevOps stages (in green). Solid vertical arrows depict in which DevOps stage a 4-1 practice security activity can take place. Standard security activities impact several repositories (in brown) like backlog, code based and test, pre-production and production environments. In addition, security standard demands an explicit repository for documentation and logs maintenance. Continuous practices (gray arrows) describe the flows to which the security activities also apply. (Color figure online)

Finally, the practice Management of Security-related issues (DM) demands that if *security issues* are detected at any stage of the pipeline, the solution should include updates in requirements and design. Although automation exists to detect, track and manage security issues, the manual effort is high specially for disclosure procedures and issues validation and investigation.

Code: At this stage, teams code functionalities based on the concept. DevOps establishes that not only functionalities can be coded, but also infrastructure and environment configurations (the shifting left concept where Operation Teams start working at the Code phase [15]. At this point, the 4-1 security standard demands secure implementation (SI). Automation is possible for static code analysis. Other standard activities are rather manual like definition of coding standards and review of attachment to coding standards e.g. through peer-review.

DevOps recommends that functionalities and configurations should be stored in the same repository and integrated into the version control tool. This allows developers to pull not only code but also an environment that is very similar or mirror to production. From the 4-1 standard point of view, this is relevant since it allows to maintain evidence of all security measures including environment hardening. In addition, it enables compliance with the standard requirements of development environment protection part of the Security Management practice (SM).

Build: During this stage, the teams (not only developers) commit their code. The continuous integration tool triggers different security testing tools. If testing is successful, code is merged and the application is ready for testing. If testing is not successful, commit is not merged and results of testing tools need to be synchronized with the security issues tracking tool to comply with the 4-1 standard DM Practice.

The 4-1 practice Secure Validation and Verification testing (SVV) describes four groups of testing: *security requirements testing, threat mitigation testing, vulnerability testing* and *penetration testing.* During Build, security requirements testing can be done with development frameworks for behaviour-driven development and unit testing. Threat mitigation testing requires manual tasks. Vulnerability testing can be completely automated with specific tools depending on the programming language.

The 4-1 practice Security Management (SM) contains the requirement: *third party component verification.* Several tools provide support for this activity. Checks avoid the use of vulnerable components as part of the system architecture. This process is known as Continuous Integration.

Test: In the test environment, automated and user acceptance tests can occur. The activities of the 4-1 practice SVV as well as third party component verification apply and are highly automated. To achieve compliance, testing documentation should exist and located in the documentation repository.

Release and Deploy: During these phases, the functionalities that implement the customer's need are made available for customers. The release stage refers to Alfa/Beta releases and stored into a pre-production repository and during the Deploy stage to the production environment. Releases allow to gather early feedback about the implemented security measures.

During these stages, penetration testing is performed with tools that partially automate the activities. Tools run tests, identify vulnerabilities, and a team member manually analyzes and tries to exploit them. The 4-1 Practice Security Guidelines (SG) demands documentation which is inherent a manual task. Guidelines describes how to securely integrate, configure and maintain the product. For large systems, such documents are of extreme value.

Note that continuous delivery represent automation until the release stage, while continuous deployment until Production.

Operate and Monitor: The product is available for Customer use. Security monitoring, security testing and compliance checks are highly automated. Monitoring activities are part of Maintenance and artifacts belong to the Analytics repository.

Security-related issues are tracked and redirected to the Concept stage where the countermeasure is packed into an Update. This is known as "Continuous Improvement and Feedback". The 4-1 standard practice Security Update Management (SUM) demands synchronization of updates and roll-out tracking.

5   Evaluation

We performed a qualitative study at Siemens AG, a large company that contributes to the IEC 62443-4-1, and where DevOps practices are applied to develop industrial systems. Based on current practices for empirical studies [26,29], we interviewed practitioners who are part of projects related to security compliance and DevOps. The objective of the study is to answer the following research questions:

- **RQ1.** How do practitioners perceive the precision of the automation classification criteria and automation capabilities of the 4-1 standard?
- **RQ2.** How do practitioners perceive the usefulness of our approach artefacts, specifically the (S^2C) DevOps Pipeline for the 4-1 security standard?

5.1   Study Design

Subjects. In this study, we target practitioners that are knowledgeable of security compliance issues in DevOps projects, and whose products must be compliant with the 4-1 standard. As DevOps is recently being adopted for ICS, we conducted the study in a large industrial company. The subject group involves 7 participants developing products for industries like digital manufacturing, smart infrastructure, or healthcare. The number of subjects reflects the growing status of security compliance DevOps for ICS. In addition, this number is aligned with the current state-of-practice for comparable empirical studies on the field of security with restricted environments (containing similar sampling sizes between 5 and 11 practitioners (c.f. [3])).

Participants are experienced professionals, with different levels of knowledge and expertise in the IEC 62443-4-1 standard and DevOps. For anonymity reasons, we excluded company roles since the number of experts in the field is limited. Table 1 shows how the interviewees' perceived their level of expertise. None of the participants has classified himself as an expert in the given topic. One participant described himself as beginner in security tools, considering, their concentration is processes and people aspects, rather than the technology aspect of security.

Table 1. Interviewees perception of their knowledge level in study related topics

–	Beginner	Medium	Advanced	Expert
4-1 Standard	2	3	2	0
DevOps	2	2	3	0
DevSecOps	2	2	3	0
Security tools	1	3	3	0

Interviews. The interviews involved one participant and two interviewers. A interview protocol was prepared and is available in the online material. As preparation, specific parts of the 4-1 standard are selected to keep the time of the interviews short. Subjects received handouts of the selected parts that correspond to the artefacts presented in Fig. 1. The interviews took an average of one hour, the flow is the following:

Introduction (5 to 10 min) Subjects are informed about the goal and the flow of the interview. We introduce the integration approach, the protocol rigor and measures to avoid bias.

Part 1: Automation Criteria (10 to 15 min) Aided by handouts, subjects provide opinions on the clarity of the categories in the automation criteria, namely: human task, transparency, partial automation, tools possible and complete automation.

Part 2: 4-1 Automation Capabilities in detail (20 to 30 min) Subjects are introduced to parts of the 4-1 pipeline specifications for specific selected 4-1 practices. Handouts have sets of activities that are highlighted. Interviewees provide opinions on the precision of the automation level for the activities and (when applicable) selected tools. They are asked to improve the list of tools.

Part 3: 4-1 Automation Capabilities global and compliant pipeline (10 to 20 min) Subjects take a brief introduction on the global and per practice automation statistics of the 4-1 standard (see Fig. 3). They provide opinions of the expectations of automation capabilities. Later, they visualize the S^2C DevOps Pipeline for the 4-1 standard (Fig. 4) and discuss the usability, benefits, and drawbacks.

5.2 Results

Automation Criteria. The majority of the interviewees (6 of 7) found the automation criteria to be precise, however, some participants argued about the meaning of *"Complete"* automation. They argue that any tool would require some human effort to configure it. Some quotes that resulted from the interviews are listed in Table 2.

Table 2. Interview quotes regarding automation criteria

Interview no.	Participant quote
2	You might come into discussion with technical practitioners about the meaning of automation
5	For me "Partial" and "Transparency" are the same classification; You will always have visualization and it's not relevant for automation
6	What is the meaning of complete automation?
7	The automation criteria would be sufficient to capture the needed information

Automation Capabilities in Detail. The 4-1 standard pipeline specifications seem to be applicable as the participants generally agreed on the automation level, as well as some the selected tools. This is influenced by subjects' levels of awareness of the selected tools to fulfil the 4-1 standard activities. All subjects were aware about the mentioned security tools and their applicability for continuous integration and delivery pipelines. We collected very few extra tools, but received feedback on the applicability of same tools for other use cases, and reference to security tools expert to validate the tools list.

An advanced practitioner suggested to provide catalogs that enable easy discovering of new or alternative tools per activity.

Automation Capabilities Global and Compliant Pipeline. Our interviewees would have expected less activities in the category *Tool possible* and more in *Complete* automation. However, they pointed out that the results seem realistic. Nevertheless, all subjects showed surprise with the automation capabilities for the SM practice. Management is more a human-related practice. Later, after a hint, interviewees with medium and advanced 4-1 knowledge remembered that the 4-1 SM Practice contains third party components security verification which is highly automatable and several tools are available. About the (S^{2}C DevOps Pipeline, they are asked if it would be helpful for building compliant pipelines. Our interviewees were divided between its suitability for building or evaluating pipelines. Selected quotes are listed in Table 3.

5.3   Threats to Validity

To support the representativeness, we confirmed the participants' background and suitability to answer our suggestions at the beginning of the interviews. The sampling size of 5 to 11 practitioners is further in tune with current security research and comparable studies that have a restricted environment [3].

Table 3. Interview quotes regarding the S^2C DevOps pipeline

Interview no.	Quote
3	You could see where you can use a tool for automation
5	A practitioner could discover new tools and easily spot a replacement for the same task
6	You'd have to try it out when you build a task
6	Ignoring the 4-1 standard, it would be a good source of tools to fulfil the tasks; Finding the right tool for the right task
7	Could be helpful to evaluate a pipeline

To further mitigate that participants alter their answers, we informed them about how the anonymity of their answers was preserved. Additionally, the interviewers explained the protocol and took measures to not influence answers like remaining neutral and in silence.

Finally, to avoid false interpretations and overlook information, two interviewers participated, one applying the protocol and other one controlling rigor. Later, the results were validated by two different reviewers.

6   Discussion

6.1   Summary of Conclusions

Security standards are described as linear processes, thus, are not prepared for DevOps iterative processes like continuous integration, delivery, or deployment. Our work translates security standard requirements into a pipeline-ready language describing: activity, input, output, automation capability, and when available, the list of security tools (see examples SI-t5 and SI-t6 in Fig. 2).

Security compliance activities are perceived as overload for DevOps teams, mostly including documentation tasks that are not perceived as customer value and that increase the lead time. Indeed, in industrial environments adopting agile and DevOps practices, practitioners constantly argue that security compliance reduces agility. Our work reveals that 31% of the 4-1 standard security activities can be automated into a pipeline. In continuous software engineering, achieving compliance for this third can be an initial objective to improve the product development process.

We also identified 38% activities that can not be automated. Including them in DevOps implies better collaboration between security experts and DevOps teams. We recommend to improve security skills in the teams in order to avoid bottlenecks due to lacks of security experts. These human tasks may be heavy for the backlog and include documentation, e.g. writing security guidelines or drawing security architecture diagrams. Although, they are not typical for agile approaches, they are still highly demanded by standards.

6.2   Limitations

Limitations to our approach arise from our focus on a ICS specific standard. However, since the 4-1 is derived from the ISO27034 - the main standard for secure software development - our approach applies to other domains as well. Also, it can be used to introduce security standards that demand process requirements for product delivery. Main limitations of using the 4-1 standard are: (a) it does not cover all aspects of secure operations e.g. secure hardening, (b) the 4-1 was released in 2018, therefore knowledgeable practitioners are very rare and belong to industrial companies who can be certified but not necessarily based on DevOps practices. This also forces evaluation endeavours to be performed in restricted environments and to remain qualitative of nature.

6.3   Impact

For Industry Professionals. DevOps practitioners can use our artefacts to establish continuous security improvement roadmaps, e.g. the first iteration could be to introduce in their DevOps pipelines the *complete* automated security activities, subsequently, the *partial automation* activities, and so on. Currently, in the industrial company, S^2C DevOps Pipeline is applied as common language to bridge communication between security experts, dev and ops teams. We forsee the applicability of this pipeline specification as a pre-set documentation template for their pipelines. Further, compliance auditors can evolve our artefacts as templates to perform compliance assessments of DevOps pipelines with regard to the 4-1 standard.

Security experts can use the artefacts to provide certain recommendations on how to apply security activities in a more automated way, while avoiding security tasks not fitting with DevOps engineering practices.

Moreover, safety practitioners may replicate the approach for functional safety standards like the ISO/IEC 26262 or 61508 [9,11].

For Researchers. We extend the work on DevOps security for regulated environments with a systematic method and automation criteria to evaluate how compliance activities can influence DevOps lead time and team collaboration. Using our artefacts, researchers can discover directions for the field like: (a) applying machine learning to build up tools in the category "Tool possible", e.g. to recommend treatments to security issues, or (b) verifying if activities are clear enough to design and build tools.

For Standardization Organizations. Artefacts serve as recommended templates to document compliance and achieve the same level of understanding among practitioners of different fields. Our approach is one way to map and obtain evidence for ambiguous statements in standards. Besides, the industrial scenario may serve as a shareable case study to start discussions on how to achieve the same level of security for several ICS. At the end, this is the aim of standards: to pursue large application of security best practices so that ICS in global critical infrastructures remain resilient to attacks.

7   Conclusion

The present work demonstrates the potential of systematic integration of standard requirements into DevOps pipelines. Considering that pipelines are based on automation, our work analyzes also automation capabilities of security standard requirements as a key element to support DevOps aims. The analysis describes which requirements of the standard can be automated, either fully or partially. We provide an overview of the results and identified gaps. These gaps are requirements that can not be automated and have to be performed manually.

The qualitative evaluation in a large industrial company shows evidence that a S^2C DevOps pipeline specification is useful to assess security compliance of DevOps pipelines. Moreover, the automation capabilities of the standard requirements serves to build security compliant pipelines with a potential of at least partially automating over 60% activities arising from standard requirements.

Our contributions to the field of security compliant DevOps are as follows:

1. We developed an approach to integrate security standards into pipelines and we validated it through an instance for the IEC 62443-4-1 standard that regulates the ICS domain. The main artefact of this approach is the Security Standard Compliant S^2C DevOps Pipeline Specification. It describes how the practices of the security standard fit into the DevOps Pipeline.
2. We analysed and documented the automation capabilities of the 4-1 standard, in the context of a large industrial company that operates in the ICS market. We found that the automation extent of this standard is 31% *Complete*, it means that 31% of the 4-1 requirements can be fully automated. 38% of the 4-1 requirements are manual tasks that have to be executed by a human expert. The remainder has the potential to be at least partially automated with future tools and techniques.

Currently, we use the S^2C DevOps pipeline specification (Fig. 4) to raise awareness for the compliance flow in DevOps as well as possibilities to achieve compliance automation. Also, we experiment with building up automation pipelines for security compliance aided by the 4-1 standard pipeline specifications. Moreover, we look into building tools to increase the percentage of 4-1 requirements that can be fully automated Finally, given our positive experience with the case at hands, we cordially invite researchers and practitioners in joining our endeavour to further scaling up our work to other standards and domains.

Acknowledgements. This work is partially funded by Portuguese national funds through FCT - Fundação para a Ciência e Tecnologia, I.P., under the project FCT UIDB/04466/2020. Furthermore, the third author thanks the Instituto Universitário de Lisboa and ISTAR-IUL, for their support.

References

1. Allspaw, J., Hammond, P.: 10+ deploys per day: dev and ops cooperation at Flickr. In: Velocity: Web Performance and Operations Conference. O'Reilly (2009)
2. Beck, K., et al.: Manifesto for agile software development (2001)
3. Ben Othmane, L., Jaatun, M.G., Weippl, E.: Empirical Research for Software Security: Foundations and Experience. CRC Press, Boca Raton (2017)
4. Bird, J.: Security as code: security tools and practices in continuous delivery, Chap. 4, pp. 32–36. O'Reilly Media, Incorporated (2016)
5. DORA: Accelerate: State of DevOps (2019). https://services.google.com/fh/files/misc/state-of-devops-2019.pdf
6. Gartner: 10 things to get right for successful DevSecOps (2017). https://www.gartner.com/en/documents/3811369/10-things-to-get-right-for-successful-devsecops
7. Hsu, T.H.C.: Hands-On Security in DevOps: Ensure Continuous Security, Deployment, and Delivery with DevSecOps. Packt Publishing Ltd., Birmingham (2018)
8. Humble, J., Farley, D.: Continuous Delivery: Reliable Software Releases through Build, Test, and Deployment Automation. Pearson Education, London (2010)
9. IEC: 61508 - functional safety. International Electrotechnical Commission (2010)
10. (IEC): IEC 62443-4-1. Security for industrial automation and control systems Part 4-1 Product security development life-cycle requirements (2018)
11. ISO: 26262 - road vehicles – functional safety. International Standards Organization (2011)
12. Jaatun, M.G., Cruzes, D.S., Luna, J.: DevOps for better software security in the cloud invited paper. In: Proceedings of the 12th ARES. ACM, New York (2017)
13. Jabbari, R., bin Ali, N., Petersen, K., Tanveer, B.: What is DevOps?: a systematic mapping study on definitions and practices. In: Proceedings of Workshop XP. ACM, USA (2016)
14. Kim, G., Behr, K., Spafford, G.: The Phoenix Project: A Novel About IT, DevOps, and Helping Your Business Win. IT Revolution Press, Portland (2018)
15. Kim, G., Humble, J., Debois, P., Willis, J.: The DevOps Handbook: How to Create World-Class Agility, Reliability, and Security in Technology Organizations. IT Revolution Press, Portland (2016)
16. Laukkarinen, T., Kuusinen, K., Mikkonen, T.: Regulated software meets DevOps. Inf. Softw. Technol. **97**, 176–178 (2018)
17. Leite, L., Rocha, C., Kon, F., Milojicic, D., Meirelles, P.: A survey of DevOps concepts and challenges, vol. 52. Association for Computing Machinery, New York (2019)
18. Lwakatare, L.E., Kuvaja, P., Oivo, M.: Dimensions of DevOps. In: Lassenius, C., Dingsøyr, T., Paasivaara, M. (eds.) XP 2015. LNBIP, vol. 212, pp. 212–217. Springer, Cham (2015). https://doi.org/10.1007/978-3-319-18612-2_19
19. Michener, J.R., Clager, A.T.: Mitigating an oxymoron: compliance in a DevOps environments. In: 2016 IEEE 40th COMPSAC, vol. 1, pp. 396–398 (2016)
20. Mohan, V., Othmane, L.B.: SecDevOps: is it a marketing buzzword?-mapping research on security in DevOps. In: 11th ARES, pp. 542–547. IEEE (2016)

21. Morales, J., Turner, R., Miller, S., Capell, P., Place, P., Shepard, D.: Guide to implementing DevSecOps for a system of systems in highly regulated environments. Technical report, CMU/SEI-2020-TR-002. SEI, Carnegie Mellon University, Pittsburgh, PA (2020)
22. Moyón, F., Beckers, K., Klepper, S., Lachberger, P., Bruegge, B.: Towards continuous security compliance in agile software development at scale. In: Proceedings of RCoSE. ACM (2018)
23. Poppendieck, M., Poppendieck, T.: Lean Software Development: An Agile Toolkit. Agile Software Development Series. Pearson Education, London (2003)
24. SANS: SANS secure DevOps toolchain and securing web application technologies checklist (2018)
25. Shahin, M., Babar, M.A., Zhu, L.: Continuous integration, delivery and deployment: a systematic review on approaches, tools, challenges and practices. IEEE (2017)
26. Shull, F., Singer, J., Sjøberg, D.I.: Guide to Advanced Empirical Software Engineering. Springer, London (2007). https://doi.org/10.1007/978-1-84800-044-5
27. Sonatype: DevSecOps community survey 2019 (2019)
28. Ur Rahman, A.A., Williams, L.: Software security in DevOps: synthesizing practitioners' perceptions and practices. In: Proceedings of International Workshop CSED. ACM, USA (2016)
29. Wagner, S., Fernández, D.M., Felderer, M., Graziotin, D., Kalinowski, M.: Challenges in survey research. ArXiv abs/1908.05899 (2019)
30. Yasar, H.: Implementing secure DevOps assessment for highly regulated environments. In: Proceedings of the 12th ARES. ACM, USA (2017)
31. Yasar, H., Kontostathis, K.: Where to integrate security practices on DevOps platform. Int. J. Secur. Softw. Eng. **7**(4), 39–50 (2016)

Exploring the Microservice Development Process in Small and Medium-Sized Organizations

Jonas Sorgalla[1]([✉])[ID], Sabine Sachweh[1], and Albert Zündorf[2]

[1] IDiAL Institute, University of Applied Sciences and Arts Dortmund,
Otto-Hahn-Str. 27, 44227 Dortmund, Germany
{jonas.sorgalla,sabine.sachweh}@fh-dortmund.de
[2] Department of Computer Science and Electrical Engineering, University of Kassel,
Wilhelmshöher Allee 73, 34121 Kassel, Germany
zuendorf@uni-kassel.de

Abstract. Microservice Architecture (MSA) describes an increasingly popular architectural style in which business capabilities are wrapped into autonomously developable and deployable software units known as microservices. Following Conway's Law, the corresponding microservice development process (MDP) requires a distinct accountable team for each microservice to facilitate service autonomy. Although there are best practices for larger enterprises to take this organizational requirement into account, there is currently a lack of empirically founded understanding, how the adaptation of MSA in smaller organizations that have more constraint resources can be successful. Therefore, we have conducted an interview study comprising six cases of such small to medium-sized development organizations (SMDOs) in which we explore their applied MDP using the Grounded Theory methodology. Among others, we examined team composition, collaboration formats, technology, and central challenges. Our results show that in most of the studied cases, shifts of service ownership occur and most use a code-first approach neglecting documentation. Based on our observations, we assume that SMDOs in particular are threatened to contradict service independence. Overall, our exploratory results provide starting points for further research in the field of microservice development.

Keywords: Microservice architecture · Qualitative research · Empirical software engineering · Exploratory case study

1 Introduction

Microservice Architecture (MSA) [12] describes a novel architectural style for the development of service-based software systems. Hereby, a system comprises multiple microservices, each of which embodies a business capability. Each microservice runs as a dedicated autonomous process and uses stateless communication methods, e.g., RESTful HTTP [7], to communicate with other services in

© Springer Nature Switzerland AG 2020
M. Morisio et al. (Eds.): PROFES 2020, LNCS 12562, pp. 453–460, 2020.
https://doi.org/10.1007/978-3-030-64148-1_28

the system. Following Conway's Law [4], which describes the close relationship between the structure of a system and the structure of the developing organization, the use of several development teams in a microservice development process (MDP) is generally considered reasonable [2]. Hereby, each team *owns* one or more services, i.e., it is solely responsible for the owned services' lifecycle comprising design, development, deployment, and maintenance. This focus on service-specific independence ensures that microservices are well combinable with principles such as DevOps and containerization [2]. Thus, MSA is attributed the advantages of maintainability, scalability, and robustness [12]. Despite all the advantages, applying MSA also comes at a certain cost [15]. The architectural complexity increases significantly. This is exemplified by the fact that microservices require a profound set of additional infrastructure services, e.g. service discovery or service configuration [2], which is particularly demanding in the early development phases [15]. Additionally, software engineers need to familiarize themselves with a broad range of different technologies and practices, which is conceived more challenging than with monolithic system architecture [3].

Overall, the characteristics of MSA have made it a popular architectural style not only with large organizations such as Netflix[1] or Spotify[2], but increasingly also with small and medium-sized development organizations (SMDOs) [10]. Large organizations are able to utilize existing large-scale process models, e.g., the Scaled Agile Framework (SAFe) [1], Scrum at Scale [17], or the Spotify Model [16], to organize the agile development of a microservice system across multiple teams. These models inherently address Conway's Law and provide means to deal with the MSA-related efforts such as new required knowledge or infrastructure development. However, as SMDOs do not have the necessary resources to introduce large-scale models in a feasible way [6], they are not able to overcome these hurdles in the same way as larger organizations do. Therefore, we assume that SMDOs, in particular, could benefit from the adoption of new methods and techniques which address MSA's complexity. Although modern software engineering has already produced promising approaches [13], we still lack knowledge about how such approaches can be successfully integrated into existing MDPs.

In this regard, we present an exploratory multi-case study [20] comprising six cases of SMDOs that apply MSA. Our study's major goal is to get insights into this unique environment and explore how SMDOs organize their collaboration process to develop a microservice system. Based on that we aim to derive hypotheses for future research which contributes to make MSA more applicable for SMDOs.

The remainder of this paper is structured as follows. In Sect. 2 we present related work to our study. Section 3 describes the applied methodology and Sect. 4 introduces the cases. We discuss results and derived hypotheses in Sect. 5. Finally, we state threats to validity of our study in Sect. 6 and conclude the paper in Sect. 7.

---

[1] https://www.netflix.com/.

[2] https://www.spotify.com/.

2   Related Work

Regarding empirical research in the domain of microservices, there are several related contributions to our study. For example, Taibi et al. [18] contribute a survey-based case study and present a process framework focusing on the migration from a monolithic to a microservice architecture. Bogner et al. [3] conducted a study comprising the analysis of 14 systems using interviews. They focused on technologies, architectural characteristics, and the impact on software quality. Haselböck et al. [9] also interviewed ten experts from the industry to gather insights in the design process of microservices. Also, there are mapping studies, e.g., [5], focusing on publication trends, technology, or industrial adoption.

Although mentioned studies provide a deeper understanding of the technical aspects of MSA-based systems and their adaptation in industry, the unique features of the MDP itself remain largely unexplored. With our study, we want to make a first contribution to this field from the perspective of SMDOs.

3   Methodology

Our study can be categorized as an exploratory comparative multi-case study [20] which is especially suitable to inductively build hypotheses. As valid cases for our study, we define SMDOs that have fewer than 100 people involved in the MDP. With this definition, we are also able to include larger companies that have only a small development team. Additionally, the organizations must be in the process of applying MSA either to migrate or to build a new software product. We select the participants based on existing contacts, i.e. on availability [20].

We gather and analyze data by utilizing the Grounded Theory methodology (GTM) [8] and follow the guideline provided by Urquhart [19]. Therefore, we prepared and pre-tested a semi-structured interview guideline[3] relying on open questions centered around the following areas: (i) Structure of the MDP; (ii) MSA system which is built by the MDP; (iii) Challenges and solutions faced when applying MSA; and (iv) Used auxiliary means such as tools and methods.

Our data gathering procedure comprises the audio recording as well as taking notes during the interviews. We then transcribe each interview and align the audio recording with the transcription in our analysis software. We analyze the data by first paraphrasing the statements in each interview and inductively derive an initial set of coding categories. Lastly, we refine the codes through case comparison.

4   Case Description

We conducted a total of five in-depth interviews with leading software architects, each lasting approximately 1.5 h, as shown in Table 1. Our participants (IP1 to 5) reported to us about six cases (CS1 to 6) each from a different SMDO. In

---

[3] Detailed guideline: https://github.com/SeelabFhdo/PROFES2020/.

the following, we briefly describe each case. We categorize them by whether the MDP involves a new development (*greenfield*), a new development based on an existing system as a template (*templated greenfield*), or a *migration* in which parts of a monolithic system are step-wise replaced by microservices.

Table 1. Case overview of explored SMDO cases.

CS	IP	Type	Domain	#Services	#Ppl	#Teams
CS1	IP1	Templated Greenfield	Public Administration	60	≈30	5
CS2	IP2	Migration	B2B E-Commerce	8	10	3
CS3	IP3	Greenfield	IoT	18	28	2
CS4	IP4	Migration	B2B E-Commerce	34	≈10	2
CS5		Migration	B2C E-Commerce	8	≈10	2
CS6	IP5	Templated Greenfield	Logistics	15-20	75	≈10

CS1 describes an SMDO that develops and offers a software product in the domain of public administration. Approximately 30 people work in five teams building the microservice system which comprises 60 services. IP1 is employed as a leading software architect in the company. Although the software is created from scratch, the tailoring of the services is heavily influenced by a previous software solution. Hence, we categorized it as a templated greenfield MDP.

CS2 entails a consulting company and its contractor as a developing organization. IP2 is the leading technical consultant. The organization is responsible for migrating a business-to-business (b2b) e-commerce platform for chemical components from a monolith to a microservice system. It comprises ten people in three teams. They maintain the existing monolith and have migrated functionality into eight microservices.

CS3 involves an SMDO which develops a system for managing IoT assets as its main product in a greenfield MDP. Business customers either purchase the software directly or use it as an as-a-service solution. For each customer, the software is customized to their specific IoT assets and corporate identity. The system consists of 18 microservices. The SMDO comprises 28 people of which 12 work in the core team, which is responsible for the core system, and the rest in the solution team, which customizes the core for customers. Hence, the solution team gets flexibly split depending on the number of ongoing customization processes. IP3 is the leading architect of the core team.

CS4 describes an SMDO consisting of ten people of which four come from a large company and six from a consulting firm. The ten people are organized in two equally-sized teams. The SMDO is migrating a b2b e-commerce platform for electronic products from a monolith to a microservice system currently comprising 34 microservices. IP4 is the accountable principle consultant.

CS5 comprises another SMDO in which IP4 is also the accountable consultant but contracted by a different company. The SMDO's product is a business-to-customer e-commerce platform in the domain of package delivery. Overall, ten people work in two teams to migrate the existing solution to a microservice system currently consisting of eight services.

CS6 entails a microservice system with 15 to 20 microservices in the logistic domain loosely based upon an existing system as a template. The reporting IP5 is a team leader in the SMDO which comprises 75 people in approx. ten teams.

5 Results and Discussion

In the following, we present and discuss our results by categories based on the GTM coding procedure. For each category, we draw hypotheses (**H1** to **6**) based on the cases which could be investigated in future research.

Technology. All of the explored cases are relying on Java whereby the Spring framework with five out of six cases is the prevailing microservice foundation. Asked for reasons, the interview partners state the availability of Java developers on the labor market most prominently, e.g., IP2 elaborates *"You simply don't find any Ruby developers on the market [...]. We had to switch to Java."* Regarding Spring, respondents say that they particularly appreciate the good availability of tutorials and simplicity. A similar picture is shown regarding the communication mechanism. Except for CS6 which uses Kafka[4], RESTful HTTP is the predominant means of inter-service communication. While all the SMDOs state to use Kubernetes[5], the Ops-related aspects generally seem to be a major area of concern. CS2, CS4, and CS6 are hosting their system using a Cloud provider while the remainder currently applies self-hosting but strive to also shift hosting into the cloud. Asked for the complexity of self-hosting a containerization infrastructure such as Kubernetes, IP3 comments *"Have fun installing Kubernetes on your own server, I'm not keen on that. [...] I'll stick to AWS."* Interestingly, the possibility to use heterogeneous technologies across microservices in the same system is not taken up by the SMDOs. This agrees with the findings of Bogner et al. [3].

(**H1**). Overall, the decisions seem to be driven by the need to simplify the learning process and avoid technical complexity. Criteria like performance or maintainability seem secondary. This tradeoff might lead to a tendency for SMDOs to develop higher technical debt [18] in the long run.

Collaboration. Regarding the collaboration during the MDP, we distinguish between two levels: team-internal and cross-team collaboration. On the internal level, all SMDOs state to apply the Scrum methodology [14]. When asked about the existence of specialist roles, all IPs deny, e.g., IP3 states that they *"are generally full stack developers and don't distinguish between special roles except the typical Scrum roles."*

On the cross-team level, CS1 has structured its collaboration inspired by the Spotify Model including, e.g., an architecture and a UI/UX guild. However, at the same time, there is a higher-level technical architecture team to

---

[4] https://kafka.apache.org/.
[5] https://kubernetes.io/.

ensure coordination and alignment between the teams. The SMDO of CS2 is formally embedded in a larger organizational model called Holacracy[6] of the overall enterprise. However, its implementation is not perceived useful as IP2 comments: *"so it feels no different, it is a piece of hierarchy, [...] you still have the same drudgery."* CS3 to 6 each apply a custom approach without stating formal models as inspiration. Overall, we notice that all SMDOs have tried to establish formats for knowledge sharing across teams once a week. However, there are no formats in which the teams exchange information about what they have achieved or what they are working on with each other. In this regard, IP5 clarifies *"we got rid of these lengthy meetings which just burn time and money."*

(**H2**). As a result, individual teams tend to have no overview of the bigger picture of the system and its functionality. This may be harmful to establish a common goal in the organization, thus, drive teams to make decisions not based on what is the best for the overall system but only for their respective services.

(**H3**). There is a trend in all SMDOs to establish specialized units. In particular, there is always a dedicated team for the Ops aspects, such as managing Kubernetes, and a team accountable for the interface structure of the overall team. We identify this as a common strategy applied by SMDOs to deal with MSA's inherent complexity.

Microservice Ownership. One of MSA's core principles is *service ownership*, i.e., one team is accountable for a distinct microservice during its entire software lifecycle [12] (cf. Sect. 1). Although establishing special units, e.g., for service operations or interface design, contradicts the ownership principle, it is not perceived as a concern by the IPs. However, we argue that there is an evident potential conflict between Conway's Law [4] and the SMDOs with two or three teams. The fewer teams are involved in the application of MSA, the greater the risk that all services are implemented by the same organizational unit. This could lead to unwanted dependencies of the services during deployment, which is, e.g., the case with CS2.

(**H4**). Due to the low number of people involved and the trend to establish specialized units, SMDOs in particular are likely to repeatedly shift the responsibility for microservices. We assume this as a major factor that gives rise to an excessive coupling of services.

(**H5**). In addition, especially the migration cases tend to implement one functionality after the other and neglect the maintenance of previous services, i.e., previously migrated functionality. In the long run, such migration MDPs with few involved people suffer a growing decrease in development velocity due to people being bound by the required maintenance of previous services.

Development Infrastructure. Each of the SMDOs explored relies on various auxiliary means during the MDP such as GitLab[7] or Jenkins[8]. However, except

---

[6] https://www.holacracy.org/.

[7] https://gitlab.com/.

[8] https://www.jenkins.io/.

for CS6, no special computer-aided software engineering tools were used. Especially UML modeling was rejected by all IPs as too inefficient, e.g., IP2 states that he rather relies on actual source code to look at service dependencies because it *"shows the reality and not how it was planned."* Instead, textual modeling approaches for interface descriptions such as Swagger[9] are predominant.

(**H6**). Textual approaches are particularly popular because of the perceived quick returns and the derivation from source code. Similar to H2, this focus on means which address only individual services could also be harmful to a common understanding and thus impair the process of collaboration.

6 Threats to Validity

Following the prevailing category system for threats to validity in qualitative research by Maxwell [11], there are five major categories: descriptive validity, interpretive validity, theoretical validity, generalizability, and evaluative validity.

To ensure *descriptive validity* we audio-recorded each interview and transcribed it. We linked the audio to the text sections in our analytic software and used the combined media as a source for our analysis (cf. Sect. 3). This also helped us to ensure *interpretive validity*, as we had emotions such as laughter or irony available during the analysis. Regarding the *theoretical validity*, we checked that the resulting hypotheses (cf. Sect. 5) do not contradict each other and fostered the validity by rigorously applying the GTM coding procedure (cf. Sect. 3). We assume good internal *generalizability*, because the explored SMDOs each generated similar non contradicting insights, i.e., the study felt *saturated*. However, due to the small sample size and case selection by availability, it is mandatory to further test the hypotheses (cf. Sect. 5) with other empirical means to ensure abstract *generalizability*. To facilitate *evaluative validity* we discussed our drawn assumptions in a workshop with our research group.

7 Conclusion and Future Work

In this paper, we presented an exploratory case study among six organizations in the process of adapting MSA. We particularly focused on SMDOs because existing reports from industry and formal process models of MSA adaptation mostly focus on larger organizations (cf. Sect. 1). We transcribed each interview and applied GTM as analysis means (cf. Sect. 3). Based on the interview data we were able to derive six hypotheses (cf. Sect. 5) regarding threats and challenges for a successful application of MSA by SMDOs. We consider these hypotheses interesting starting points for further research. In this regard, in the future, we plan to conduct a prototype study addressing H2 and H6 by implementing an automatic collaboration solution that generates an architectural overview based on existing swagger descriptions.

---

[9] https://www.swagger.io/.

References

1. Achieving business agility with safe® 5.0. Technical report, Scaled Agile Inc.
2. Balalaie, A., Heydarnoori, A., Jamshidi, P.: Microservices architecture enables DevOps: migration to a cloud-native architecture. IEEE Softw. **33**(3), 42–52 (2016)
3. Bogner, J., Fritzsch, J., Wagner, S., Zimmermann, A.: Microservices in industry: insights into technologies, characteristics, and software quality. In: 2019 IEEE International Conference on Software Architecture Companion (ICSA-C), pp. 187–195 (2019)
4. Conway, M.E.: How do committees invent. Datamation **14**(4), 28–31 (1968)
5. Di Francesco, P., Lago, P., Malavolta, I.: Architecting with microservices: a systematic mapping study. J. Syst. Softw. **150**, 77–97 (2019)
6. Dikert, K., Paasivaara, M., Lassenius, C.: Challenges and success factors for large-scale agile transformations: a systematic literature review. J. Syst. Softw. **119**, 87–108 (2016)
7. Fielding, R.: Representational state transfer. In: Architectural Styles and the Design of Network-based Software Architecture, pp. 76–85 (2000)
8. Glaser, B.G., Strauss, A.L.: Discovery of Grounded Theory: Strategies for Qualitative Research. Routledge, Abingdon (2017)
9. Haselböck, S., Weinreich, R., Buchgeher, G.: An expert interview study on areas of microservice design. In: 2018 IEEE 11th Conference on Service-Oriented Computing and Applications (SOCA), pp. 137–144 (2018)
10. Knoche, H., Hasselbring, W.: Drivers and barriers for microservice adoption - a survey among professionals in Germany. Enterp. Model. Inf. Syst. Archit. (EMISAJ) – Int. J. Concept. Model. **14**(1), 1–35 (2019)
11. Maxwell, J.: Understanding and validity in qualitative research. Harv. Educ. Rev. **62**(3), 279–301 (1992)
12. Newman, S.: Building Microservices. O'Reilly Media, Newton (2015)
13. Rademacher, F., Sorgalla, J., Wizenty, P., Sachweh, S., Zündorf, A.: Graphical and textual model-driven microservice development. In: Bucchiarone, A., et al. (eds.) Microservices, pp. 147–179. Springer, Cham (2020). https://doi.org/10.1007/978-3-030-31646-4_7
14. Schwaber, K., Beedle, M.: Agile Software Development with Scrum, vol. 1. Prentice Hall, Upper Saddle River (2002)
15. Singleton, A.: The economics of microservices. IEEE Cloud Comput. **3**(5), 16–20 (2016)
16. Smite, D., Moe, N.B., Levinta, G., Floryan, M.: Spotify guilds: how to succeed with knowledge sharing in large-scale agile organizations. IEEE Softw. **36**(2), 51–57 (2019)
17. Sutherland, J.: The scrum@scale guide version 2.0. Technical report, Scrum Inc.
18. Taibi, D., Lenarduzzi, V., Pahl, C.: Processes, motivations, and issues for migrating to microservices architectures: an empirical investigation. IEEE Cloud Comput. **4**(5), 22–32 (2017)
19. Urquhart, C.: Grounded Theory for Qualitative Research: A Practical Guide. SAGE Publications, Ltd., Thousand Oaks (2013)
20. Yin, R.K.: Case Study Research and Applications: Design and Methods, 6th edn. SAGE Publications, Thousand Oaks (2017)

Author Index

Printed in the United States
By Bookmasters